Writing Theology Well

Writing Theology Well

A Rhetoric for Theological and Biblical Writers

Second edition

Lucretia B. Yaghjian

Bloomsbury T&T Clark
An imprint of Bloomsbury Publishing Plc

B L O O M S B U R Y
LONDON • OXFORD • NEW YORK • NEW DELHI • SYDNEY

Bloomsbury T&T Clark
An imprint of Bloomsbury Publishing Plc

Imprint previously known as T&T Clark

50 Bedford Square	1385 Broadway
London	New York
WC1B 3DP	NY 10018
UK	USA

www.bloomsbury.com

BLOOMSBURY, T&T CLARK and the Diana logo are trademarks of Bloomsbury Publishing Plc

First edition published 2006. This edition published 2015
Reprinted 2016, 2017 (twice)

British Library Cataloguing-in-Publication Data
A catalogue record for this book is available from the British Library.

ISBN: HB: 978-0-567-02219-6
PB: 978-0-567-49917-2
ePDF: 978-0-567-43370-1
ePub: 978-0-567-29621-4

Library of Congress Cataloging-in-Publication Data
Yaghjian, Lucretia B.
Writing theology well : a rhetoric for theological and biblical writers /
Lucretia B. Yaghjian. – 2nd Edition.
pages cm
Includes bibliographical references and index.
ISBN 978-0-567-02219-6 (hardback : alk. paper) –
ISBN 978-0-567-49917-2 (pbk. : alk. paper)
1. Christian literature–Authorship. 2. Theology. I. Title.
BR44.Y34 2015
808.06'623–dc23
2015018444

Typeset by Integra Software Services Pvt. Ltd.
Printed and bound in Great Britain

In Memory of my Parents

Eleanor Welch Bailey
(1912–1994)

Joseph W. Bailey
(1910–1972)

and my Student

Pontiano Victor Okumu, OSB
(1962–2005)

CONTENTS

PREFACE TO AND ACKNOWLEDGEMENTS FOR THE SECOND EDITION

To write anything is ultimately an act of faith. Faith in yourself as a writer; faith in the importance of what you are writing; faith that there will be an audience for what you write; faith that your writing will contribute ultimately to the flourishing of those who read it; and finally, faith in the source of your desire to write, which I name here the Spirit of God. If this is true of writing in general, how much more is it true of writing theology well?

—Conclusion to Chapter 1, "Writing Theology Well in Its Own Context"

When I concluded the first chapter of *Writing Theology Well: A Rhetoric for Theological and Biblical Writers* with the words quoted above, I was addressing all who would read the book with a desire to write theology well. Yet as I reread these words on the cusp of sending the second edition to the publisher, they also seem to describe perfectly both my original process of writing the book and my more recent task of preparing a second edition for publication.

The first edition of *Writing Theology Well* was published in 2006 to provide a discipline-specific writing textbook for use in theological schools and seminaries where writing courses were appearing in increasing numbers to meet the needs of students who had discovered with Thomas Merton that "It is extremely difficult to write theology well." My goal was to integrate the teaching of writing with an introduction to the written discipline of theology, and to provide students with a working guide for the theological writing and research required of them in their theological and biblical courses. The intended audience included students of theology, biblical studies, and religion enrolled in theological schools, seminaries, and related graduate programs; writing teachers and tutors of these students; and theological and biblical professors seeking a relevant writing text to recommend to their students.

The second edition of *Writing Theology Well* has the same purpose: to invite students to "write theology well" in whatever contexts they are engaging theological and/or biblical studies, and to provide a discipline-specific guide for writing the theological and biblical genres encountered in their theological courses. The original twelve chapters and epilogue of the book remain substantially the same, except for updating of bibliographical sources and selective incorporation of materials that I have integrated into my own teaching since the book's first publication. Endnotes in this edition have been placed at the end of each chapter, rather than at the end of the volume, at readers' recommendation, and for their convenience.

Most importantly, the newly added Part Four, "Writing Theology Well in New Contexts," expands the audience of the book to include international student writers from non-native English and multilingual contexts, and online students writing from a distance as well as closer to home. Chapter 13, "Writing Theology Well in a New Language: Rhetorics for International Student Writers and Their Tutors," focuses on the cultural and linguistic issues involved in learning to write theology well in a non-native language, while inviting students to claim theology as a common language that undergirds and empowers writing in a new language. Chapter 14, "Writing Theology Well in a Digital Environment: Rhetorics for Online Writers and Learners," addresses online students and all students utilizing electronic resources and technologies to write theology well, with an emphasis upon writing the digital genres of email, discussion board posts, blogs, and theological research in a digital context. Finally, widening its context to embrace the World Wide Web, an accompanying web site for *Writing Theology Well* expands the book's coverage with bibliographical updates, supplementary materials, and links to other web resources.

I gratefully acknowledge the support I have been given in bringing this second edition to fruition. Arthur D. Yaghjian companioned me throughout as a fellow researcher, writing partner, and supportive spouse. Peter J. Bailey, Roger Haight, Julie A. Lytle, Katherine Mapes, and Linda Williams read drafts of the new chapters from the vantage points of their own expertise, and the finished chapters reflect their insightful responses. Linda Williams painstakingly and patiently checked all of my bibliographical references for accuracy and correctness; any mistakes that remain are my own. Aura A. Fluet, Senior Assistant Librarian at Episcopal Divinity School and Lesley University, provided consultation on theological and biblical research in a digital context, supplying technical support where mine was lacking. She also wrote in support of publication of the second edition at the inception of the project, along with Head Librarian and Professor Mitzi Budde, with whom I taught for a semester at the Virginia Theological Seminary. My "Writing in Faith" companions at St. Elizabeth of Hungary Parish, Acton, Massachusetts, prayed for me and for the successful completion of the book. My deepest debt is to my editor extraordinaire, Anna Turton, who invited me to write a second edition of *Writing Theology Well*, and has guided the project and its author through every vicissitude of the process with consummate grace, expertise, and encouragement. Thanks also to Miriam Cantwell and Balaji Kasirajan, both of whom accompanied me throughout the book production process. This second edition is dedicated to all of my students who have written theology well at the Episcopal Divinity School, the Boston College School of Theology and Ministry, and the Virginia Theological Seminary, and who have deepened my faith that there will also be an audience for this edition of the book.

Lucretia B. Yaghjian
Concord, Massachusetts
Feast of the Ascension,
May 14, 2015

PREFACE TO THE FIRST EDITION

It is extremely difficult to write theology well. The main reason I can't write it is that . . . I don't know precisely what I want to say, and therefore when I start to write I find that I am working out a theology as I go.
—THOMAS MERTON, *Sign of Jonas*

Prior to his novitiate, Merton was completing a Ph.D. in English Literature at Columbia University, teaching English composition and literature courses, and writing for *The New York Times Book Review*. Yet Merton's experience as a student, teacher and reviewer of literature did not spare him the struggle of learning how to "write theology well."

However tempted you might be to think, "If Thomas Merton finds writing theology difficult, what hope is there for me," *Writing Theology Well: A Rhetoric for Theological and Biblical Writers* has been written to invite you to "write theology well" and to help you along the way. This book is for theological students who need a working guide for the writing that they do in theological courses, and for their writing instructors and tutors. Its original audience comprised my students at Episcopal Divinity School, Weston Jesuit School of Theology, and the Boston College Institute for Religious Education and Pastoral Ministry, who have patiently and persistently taught me what they need to learn as writers in a theological context. Its intended audience includes all who desire to write theology well, or better than they do at the moment, whether they are theological novices, as Merton was, or seasoned theological writers.

Writing Theology Well embraces both theological and biblical genres and imagines writing, research, and the theological questions that engender them as integrated parts of an ongoing process of inquiry, reflection and practice. It invites students into that process through the questions arising from their own theological study. It provides practical and conceptual tools for successful writing and research in a theological context. And it offers a methodological, task-oriented framework that can be adapted to students' theological writing assignments in a variety of disciplinary contexts, including systematic theology, pastoral theology, biblical studies, church history, and ethics, among others. Toward that end, each chapter includes a pedagogical sequence of "Theological Memos" that students can use in conjunction with their own writing assignments or as independent exercises in tandem with the material presented in the book.

The book is written in three parts. Part One, "Writing Theological Rhetorics Well," introduces students to the genres of theological writing that they will encounter in their own theological study. Chapter 1, "Writing Theology Well in its own Context," situates the writing of theology in a socio-rhetorical context, provides a brief but suggestive history of theological writing as a discipline in its own right, and surveys the theological audiences for whom students will be writing. Chapter 2, "Writing Theological Reflection Well: Rhetorics of Process, Problem-Solving, and Proclamation," introduces the writing of theological reflection, and identifies two generic styles of theological reflection papers: the pastoral reflection paper, exemplified in this chapter, and the systematic reflection paper, exemplified in the next chapter. Chapter 3, "Writing Theological Argument Well: Rhetorics of Inquiry, Reading, Reflection, and Persuasion," defines theological argument broadly as persuasive argument, focuses on deductive and inductive reasoning as the basic building blocks of theological argument, and applies these tools to the writing of a systematic reflection paper. Chapter 4, "Writing the Theological Essay Well: Rhetorics of Identification, Correlation, Suspicion and Construction," follows the essay from its literary genre to its theological species, and identifies the rhetorics of both the critical and the constructive theological essay.

Part Two, "Writing Theological and Biblical Research Well," introduces students to the process of writing theological research and provides exegetical and hermeneutical tools for writing biblical research well. Chapters 5 and 6, "Writing Theological Research Well (I): Rhetorics of Research and Investigation," and Writing Theological Research Well (II): Rhetorics of Organization and Documentation," engage students in an integrated sequence of tasks that track the writing of a theological research paper from start to finish. Chapter 7, "Writing the Biblical Essay Well (I): Rhetorics of Exegesis and Interpretation," probes the writing of biblical exegesis, with its focus on what the text meant; and Chapter 8, "Writing the Biblical Essay Well (II): A Critical-Hermeneutical Rhetoric," provides hermeneutical resources for the writing of a biblical essay that moves from what the text meant to what the text means today.

Part Three, "Toward a Theological Voice of One's Own," encourages students to discover and develop their own theological style and voice through writing and rewriting in the company of classic and contemporary theologians. Chapter 9, "Writing with Theological Imagination Well," identifies analogy, metaphor and symbol as constituents of the theological imagination and offers "writer-based" approaches for writing with each of these rhetorical elements. Chapter 10, "Rewriting Theology Well (I): Rhetorics of Style and Voice," situates style and voice in relation to writing and rewriting theological papers; exemplifies "pastoral," "systematic," and "constructive" theological styles; and proposes the elements of theological "plain" style as touchstones for rewriting theology well. Chapter 11, "Rewriting Theology Well (II): Rhetorics of Words, Sentences, and Paragraphs," provides the rubrics of a theological grammar by probing the writing of theological words, sentences, and paragraphs well. Chapter 12, "Rewriting Theology Well (III): A Rhetoric of Revision," develops an individualized rhetoric of revision that integrates rewriting, revision and becoming one's own editor, while further defining and refining a theological style and voice. An Epilogue, "Writing Theology Well in Your Next Context: From Writing for Professors to Writing with a Professional Voice," concludes the book.

Four rhetorical presuppositions inform the writing pedagogy of this book. First, writing theology well can be taught as well as learned. Second, the writing of theology is an integral mode of theological learning in which students "work out a theology as they go," or as they write. Third, writing in a theological context is both a rhetorical and a theological practice. Fourth, and finally, all theological writers, while writing "from below," witness to transcendence by enlarging the community of discourse from what is spoken and heard to what is written and read for "generations yet to come" (Psalm 102:18), and, ultimately, by witnessing to the One who inspires and authorizes our theology. In that confidence, I hope that those reading this book will name themselves "writers" and claim the writing that they do as an empowering and grace-filled theological practice that will follow them fruitfully into other personal, professional, and vocational contexts.

It has been difficult and humbling to write a book about "writing theology well." In the process of bringing this book to publication, I have not always followed my own advice and I have had to acknowledge my own limitations as a theological writer. Had I not, however, like Thomas Merton, found it difficult to write theology well as a theological student, I would not have written this book for my own students and others who will read it. If theological faculty were to read this book over their students' shoulders and find it useful in the preparation of their own writing projects, the book will have reached all the audiences for whom it has been intended.

ACKNOWLEDGMENTS FOR THE FIRST EDITION

The Wabash Center for Teaching and Learning in Theology and Religion provided funding for this work, and I thank Lucinda A. Huffaker and William C. Placher for their ongoing encouragement. Episcopal Divinity School and Weston Jesuit School of Theology granted me a sabbatical leave in conjunction with the Wabash grant, and I gratefully acknowledge their support. Western Theological Seminary in Holland, Michigan welcomed me as a visiting scholar for some of that time, and I remember their hospitality with gratitude.

This book is also beholden to those who have read all or parts of it with different eyes than its author. Roger Haight, S.J., read with a theologian's eye and kept me focused on the book's theological purpose. Peter J. Bailey read with an English professor's eye and kept me faithful to my foundations in the teaching of writing and literature. John Spradley read with a rhetorician's eye, and kept me attentive to a wider audience. Aura Fluet, Stephen Kuehler, and Paul Smith read with bibliographic eyes that helped me to refine the theological research chapters. Victor Okumu, O.S.B., read with a multicultural eye that informs and invigorates the "Appendix for Multilingual Writers." Molly Frederick read with a poet's eye, and kept the poet in me alive during long days of writing and revision. Frank Oveis read with an editor's eye and supervised the book's publication with patience, care and professional expertise. From beginning to end, Arthur D. Yaghjian read with a scientist's and a spouse's eye, and companioned me in its final preparation as if the book were his own.

I am indebted as well to each of the theological and biblical writers who exemplify "writing theology well" in this book. I am also indebted to the writing teachers, rhetoricians, and theological writing consultants who have helped me to integrate the disciplines of writing, rhetoric and theology, including Ann E. Berthoff, Kenneth Burke, Richard Coe, Barbara Coogan, Deborah Core, Anne L. Deneen, William Fitzgerald, Jane McAvoy, Katherine Mapes, Jennifer McWhorter, John L. Murphy, Donald Murray, and Robert Worley. I received personal encouragement when I most needed it from Frances Weller Bailey, Carmela D'Elia, Kate Duffy, Christiana Holmes, Sheryl Huebinger, Brigitte Lowe, Katy Rydell, Linda Williams, and Lilly Yaghjian. Finally, my students at Episcopal Divinity School, Weston Jesuit School of Theology, the Boston College Institute of Religious Education and Pastoral Ministry, and Harvard Divinity School read early drafts of these chapters and encouraged me to keep writing them. Without them this book would not have been written.

Lucretia B. Yaghjian
Concord, Massachusetts
July 2006

PART ONE

Writing Theological Rhetorics Well

1
Writing Theology Well in Its Own Context

Theology is a language used by a specific group of people to make sense of their world.
—ROWAN WILLIAMS, *On Christian Theology*

Theology ... is a particular type of rhetorical art.
—MARK WALLACE, *Fragments of the Spirit*

Across the broad spectrum of different academic settings and different cultures, across the even broader spectrum of different paradigms for theology's disciplinary status, most theologians do recognize their responsibility to produce theological discourse which meets the highest standards of the contemporary academy.
—DAVID TRACY, *The Analogical Imagination*

Starting points

At the start of every fall semester, I offer a one-day workshop entitled "Writing Theology in Its Own Context." If you were one of the students in the workshop, I would first invite you to reflect on your strengths and limitations as a writer by describing your own process of writing an academic paper. Then, I would ask you to reflect on what distinguishes "theological writing" from writing you have done in previous academic or professional contexts. As the day continued, we would consider what constitutes good theological writing; we would examine two models for writing a theological essay; and students would contribute papers they had written for constructive feedback with a writing partner or group. At the end of the day, we would look together at excerpts of theological writing from the work of classical and contemporary theologians, and you would choose one excerpt to rewrite in your own words. Finally, you would identify one skill to continue to work on in your own theological writing.

I wish that each of you reading this book could join me for that workshop on a warm September Saturday, bringing with you the writing skills you have and those you need, your fears and frustrations over the next theological writing assignment, and your desire to write theology well that has prompted you to open the pages of this book. Since that is not possible, I must be content to bring the workshop to you in this introductory chapter and throughout this book, and to invite you to read it with a pen in your hand, a notebook (or notebook computer) at your side, and a theological writing project on your mind. Just as Flannery O'Connor advised aspiring writers that "the only way... to learn to write short stories is to write them, and then to try and discover what you have done,"[1] so I am convinced that the only way to learn to write theology well is to write it, and through your own reflection or in conversation with others, to "try to discover what you have done." Toward that end, you will find "Theological Memos" interspersed throughout the text, inviting you to reflect as you read and to write as you reflect. For example:

> *THEOLOGICAL MEMO 1: I invite you to write in response to one of the following suggestions: (1) Reflect on your strengths and limitations as a writer, and what skills you need to develop in order to write theology well. (2) Recall a recent paper that you have written, and narrate your process of writing from its inception to its conclusion. Or (3) consider the context in which you are presently writing theology, and one characteristic of writing in that context that distinguishes it from other kinds of writing.*

In the chapters that follow, you will also find the tools that you need to write particular kinds of theological papers, to develop theological arguments, to do theological research, to document that research accurately, and to develop a more effective theological style. But, first, we shall look more closely at the process of writing theology in its own context by addressing three questions. What is writing and why do people write? What is theology and why do theologians write it? What is theological writing, and what distinguishes it from other kinds of writing? To answer the first question, we will examine the sociorhetorical context of writing in general, and of writing theology in particular. In answer to the second question, we will look at the sociohistorical context of writing theology and its development as a written discipline. To answer the third question, we will focus specifically on writing theology in its contemporary context, including that theological context in which you are reading this book.

The sociorhetorical context of writing theology

What is writing and why do people write? At its most fundamental level, writing is a means of communication through which we convey information to others across time and space. This function of writing was noted by the ancient Psalmist who wrote, "Let this be written for a generation yet to come, so that a people unborn may praise the Lord" (Psalm 102:18). Inasmuch as writers use writing to communicate, writing is a sociorhetorical activity; that is to say, writing happens because a writer has something to say, and both the writer and what s/he writes are situated in a particular social context. We are using the term *rhetoric* broadly here to denote the art of purposeful communication. In later chapters, we use the term *rhetoric* also to denote specific elements of the art of purposeful communication. Within this social context, there are four rhetorical components of writing: (a) the writer, (b) the writer's subject, (c) the writer's audience, and (d) the writer's purpose. A sociorhetorical approach to writing, therefore, asks four questions:

Who Writes?	*What?*	*To Whom?*	*For What Purpose?*
[Writer]	[Subject]	[Audience]	[Purpose]

We will be dealing with the questions Who writes?, What?, and To whom? presently, but let us linger for a moment with the question of Why, or For What Purpose. There are many possible answers to this question, some of which would make us appropriately cautious of our theological use of the written word. The anthropologist Claude Levi-Strauss, for example, has argued that the primary purpose of writing is "to facilitate the enslavement of other human beings"[2] or to exercise control over them. For Brazilian educator Paulo Friere, on the other hand, the purpose of writing and literacy skills is "conscientization" of the oppressed, or liberation from "enslavement."[3] Decrying "the tyranny of writing" fostered by literacy, however, linguist Ferdinand de Saussure claims that writing is a speech-dependent medium whose sole purpose is to inscribe spoken discourse.[4] Philosopher Paul Ricoeur responds that writing is a mode of discourse "parallel and comparable to speech" whose purpose is hermeneutical or directed toward "understanding in and through distance."[5] For those writing theology, as we shall see, it matters what the purpose of writing is imagined to be.

> *THEOLOGICAL MEMO 2: Why, or for what purpose or purposes do you write? Which of the fundamental "purposes" of writing, or of the written word, quoted above best describes your own understanding of the fundamental purpose of writing? Which of the purposes described make sense to you? Which do not? Can you imagine contexts in which each of the above claims might be true?*

I have invited you to reflect in a general way on the purposes of writing described above, because before we write purposefully as theological students or as theologians, we write as persons, even though I have stressed, and will continue to stress, the sociorhetorical location of theological writing. Perhaps this will sound like a paradox. However, it is not. Because we who write are persons, all writing is inherently personal or grounded in our unique personhood. Yet, because we are persons embedded in wider contexts, communities, histories, and ideologies, writing that is personal is also contextual, social, historical, and political. Moreover, because we are persons who "don't know what we think until we see what we write," writing that is personal is also cognitive or constituted by acts of knowing and thinking. Finally, because we are persons who think by writing and write by thinking in time and history, we experience writing as a process. Thus, the writing we do encompasses a variety of processes and purposes, but in order to explore the process and purpose of writing theology well, we are now ready to ask what theology is and why theologians write it.

The sociohistorical context of writing theology

What is theology and why do theologians write it?

The word "theology" literally means "God-talk," language or reasoning about *theos*, or more colloquially, thinking, speaking, and writing about God. Some theologians emphasize the rational and methodical element of theology, as Paul Tillich does when he defines theology as "the methodical explanation of the contents of Christian faith," comprising biblical studies and homiletics as well as systematic theology.[6] Others emphasize its sociorhetorical character, as Rebecca Chopp does when she calls theology "discourse about God in the Christian community."[7] Still others emphasize the symbolic character of theology, as Roger Haight does when he defines theology as "a discipline that interprets all reality—human existence, society, history, the world, and God—in terms of the symbols of Christian faith."[8] Rowan Williams provides a definition that, for our purposes, is inclusive of all of these perspectives when he writes, "Theology is a language used by a specific group of people to make sense of their world."[9]

From its inception, however, theology has been practiced both as a spoken and a written language, and the God whom our theology inscribes has been imagined as its prototypical speaker and writer. For example, we hear God's voice at the beginning of creation, saying, "Let there be light" (Genesis 1:3). But, if someone had not written those words down around the sixth century B.C.E., we would not hear God's *fiat* today as it is recorded in Genesis. As theological writers, we need to be keenly aware that during the first and much of the second millennium of the Christian era, theologians embraced speech and writing as mutually interactive modes of communication. In contrast, however, the writing of theology in our own context often becomes a kind of surrogate speech that tends to disappear like invisible ink into the subject matter about which it "speaks." In order, then, to render the writing of theology more visible in this historical overview, let us leave speaking aside and focus more sharply upon writing.

According to the exodus traditions, the original version of the Mosaic covenant was "written with the finger of God" on stone tablets (Exodus 31:18), and with God's authorization, a second version was written down by Moses (Exodus 34:27). In the prophetic writings of the Hebrew Scriptures, God is portrayed as writing a new covenant on people's hearts (Jeremiah 31:33), and God commands prophets like Habakkuk to "write the vision" of God's justice and "make it plain on tablets" so that even one running by might read it (Habakkuk 2:2).

Turning to the New Testament and writings of the first two centuries of the Christian era, we see that the early Christian communities turned to the written word not only to preserve the Jesus traditions and communicate them to succeeding generations, but also to establish themselves within the emerging literate culture. One of the earliest images of a gospel author provided by Matthew (c. 80–100 C.E.) is that of a "scribe" (Hebrew *sopher*; Greek *grammaticus*), "secretary," or, by extension, "writer," "apprenticed to the kingdom of heaven," who, in the writing of his own gospel, brings forth from the "Writings" (Hebrew *Ketubim*) of Israel's Torah, Psalms, and Prophets "the new and the old" (Matthew 13:52).[10] Shortly thereafter,

Luke the Evangelist declared his intention "to *write* an orderly account ['of the events that have been fulfilled among us'] for you, Theophilus, so that you may know the truth concerning the things about which you have been instructed" (Luke 1:1–4). A century later (second century C.E.), Clement of Alexandria commends Christian authors who "speak through books" and therefore through writing above those who speak to "those who are present" (*Stromata* 1.1.301), and the writer of *The Martyrdom of Saints Perpetua and Felicitas* appeals to the precedent of the New Testament writings as a model for the *Martyrdom*, asserting that "the deeds recounted about the faith in ancient times ... were set forth in writing precisely that honour might be rendered to God and comfort to men by the recollection of the past through the written word."[11]

Writing theology as a rhetorical art with Augustine of Hippo

The first theologian to reflect on the theological uses of writing as a medium of Christian communication was St. Augustine, Bishop of Hippo (354–430 C.E.), who had been a teacher of rhetoric, or the art of "eloquence" in speaking and writing, before his conversion to Christianity. But, if Augustine the theologian left the teaching of classical rhetoric behind, he was soon preparing a "Christian" rhetoric for teachers and preachers of the Christian scriptures. Writing in the fifth century C.E. in *On Christian Doctrine*, Augustine commends students who practice eloquence by reading eloquent Christian writers and "writing, dictating and speaking what [they have] learned."[12] Moreover, just as Aristotelian philosophy would provide Thomas Aquinas with a conceptual logic for his *Summa Theologica*, Augustine appropriated the rhetoric of Cicero as a model of Christian persuasion for Christian teachers, preachers, writers, and theologians. Within this model, theology—both written and spoken—was acknowledged as a rhetorical no less than a "sacred" art; it was written in different styles for different audiences and purposes, and its ultimate end was persuasion that inspired readers or hearers to action.[13] While Augustine's retrieval of Ciceronian rhetoric for Christian speakers and writers was soon to be overshadowed by Aquinas's retrieval of Aristotle, which we turn to next, his rhetorical model continues to flourish in pastoral and praxis-based theological writing today.[14]

Writing theology as a Scholastic science with Thomas Aquinas

The written academic discipline of "theology" had its inception in the eleventh century "Father of Scholasticism," Anselm, who first defined theology as "faith seeking understanding." It came to maturity in such twelfth- and thirteenth-century Scholastics as Abelard and Aquinas, whose writings sought to reconcile faith and reason, the Bible and Aristotle, and science and theology. To do this, Scholastic theologians elevated dialectic, or the art of logical, philosophical argument, as the operative theological "rhetoric," while relegating Augustine's art of Christian persuasion to an inferior status.

To be sure, Aquinas's conviction that all knowledge of God was subject to the reception of the knower, and had to be communicated in a form that the knower could apprehend, is inherently rhetorical.[15] Moreover, his monumental *Summa Theologica* was addressed to a specific audience: the theological students of his day. Nonetheless, the Scholastic shift from a rhetoric of persuasion to a dialectic of logical argument has had enormous consequences for the subsequent writing of theology. While the Scholastic model is one of many rhetorics used by theologians writing today, it persists in contemporary Roman Catholic theology in more reader-friendly versions and provides theologians of all persuasions with classic genres of theological writing that continue to be used in adapted formats: the *summa*, the *quaestio*, and the *article*.[16]

In the *summa* (from the Latin for "summary," or "synthesis"), scholastic theologians like Thomas Aquinas introduced a genre that was both precisely ordered and exhaustive, which consisted of a systematic exposition of a comprehensive field of theological inquiry. While contemporary theologians no longer write "summas" in classical form any more than modern playwrights write Shakespearian tragedies, they do write systematic theologies whose form and content are indebted to this exacting rhetorical structure.

Intrinsic to the structure of the *summa* were the *quaestio*, or "question," and the *article* in which it was expatiated, consisting of a theological question that is posed, followed by the citation of authorities' pro and con, culminating in the theologian's resolution of the question, and concluding with a systematic rebuttal of objections posed by the dissenting authorities. While this structure might appear contrived and conservative to modern readers, it orchestrated a creative synthesis of philosophy and Christian faith revolutionary enough to warrant the posthumous condemnation of Thomas Aquinas's writings in 1278 that would not be revoked until 1325, four years after Thomas was canonized. And, if contemporary theological writing is more committed to asking the questions than to answering them within the a priori conditions of a closed system, questions continue to engender theological writing for beginners and for experts, and the contemporary form of the theological article has a similar argumentative structure, as we shall see more specifically in Chapter 3, "Writing Theological Argument Well."

Is the writing of theology an art or a science, however? For Augustine, theology and the liberal arts were still complementary modes of knowledge, and the writing of theology itself was considered a rhetorical "art." For Scholastic theologians, however, *scientia* meant "knowledge," and theology was "the queen of the sciences," or of all knowledge, including the liberal arts. While our own definition of "science" has changed, the classification of theology as a "science" is a legacy that continues to predispose styles and formats of theological writing, as we shall see as we proceed.

Writing theology as a communal language with Teresa of Avila

We may not learn how to write theology well, however, if we confine our understanding of theology to that of either an "art" or a "science." If, as Rowan Williams suggests, theology is fundamentally a "language used by a group of people to make sense of their world," the writing of theology throughout its history has been done by different groups of people in different communal "languages." For St. Teresa of Avila, writing *Interior Castle* in 1577, theology was preeminently a language of mystical prayer. Our tendency today is to separate prayer and spirituality from the practice of theology; for Teresa, they were inseparable, although not in the mode of the scholastic model. Teresa herself tells us that St. Augustine's *Confessions*, with its more personal and pastoral language, was crucial to her own conversion: "When I began to read the *Confessions*, I thought I saw myself there described."[17]

I have chosen Teresa to introduce us to the discourse of women's theological writing because she is among the first to write theology in her own hand,[18] in her own Spanish vernacular, and in what was deemed to be a language that other women (her own Carmelite sisters) would understand: "I was told by the person who commanded me to write," she explained, [that] "women best understand each other's language."[19]

For a book of mystical theology, that language was deceptively simple and direct, even as it elaborated its central metaphor of the soul as a castle with "many mansions." While she instructed her sisters not to use their "reasoning powers" in the practice of contemplation, "but to be intent upon discovering what the Lord is working in the soul" (4.3.87), she used her own mind consummately as she described the mystical experience and defended its authenticity against its detractors.[20] We are told that Teresa wrote as she spoke, without editing or revising her work, partly because of the press of other responsibilities, and partly to preserve the Holy Spirit's inspiration. Few theological writers give their readers as many intimate glimpses into their own process of writing as she does when she writes, "Truly my daughters, I am so fearful as I write this that, when it comes to my mind.... I hardly know how to get the words down." (3.1.57) She knew the struggle to render the essentially wordless into words, just as she knew that there were potentially "heretical" words concerning her own spiritual experience that she could not write. Writing, then, in the shadow of the Inquisition and in an alternative discourse to the still-dominant scholastic paradigm, she was among the first to write as a woman in a theological context, but by no means the last.[21]

Writing theology with Gutenberg's printing press and the Protestant reformers

In this brief historical overview, we have looked so far at the writing of theology as a rhetorical art, as a Scholastic science, and as a communal language. Yet, there are some glaring omissions in this history of theological writing that readers cannot help but notice. We have not paid proper homage to Johannes Gutenberg and his printing press, which printed the first published version of the Bible in 1454 and would make written theology accessible, at least potentially, to all who could read it. We have not stopped to watch Martin Luther write his ninety-five Theses and post them on the church door in Wittenburg on the Eve of the Feast of All Saints in 1518. Nor have we followed the trail of William Tyndale that led to his being burned at the stake in October 1536 for translating the Bible into the English vernacular for common people as well as clerics. Yet, each of these events and their authors is written between the lines of the writing that we call theology today. When, in 1652, the poet John Milton began to write his own *Christian Doctrine* in the Christian liberty "not only of winnowing and sifting every doctrine, but also of thinking and *even writing* respecting it, according to our individual faith and persuasion,"[22] he wrote on the shoulders of these early Protestant reformers, just as we do today.

Rewriting theology as speech with Friedrich Schleiermacher

With the invention of the printing press and the increase in biblical literacy fostered by the Protestant Reformation, the writing of theology was no longer the sole province of an official religious elite. In this brave new world, John Bunyan, the son of an English tinsmith, could write the narrative theology of his *Pilgrim's Progress* from Bedford Gaol in 1675, while his Oxford-educated contemporary, the Rev. Barnabas Oley, was introducing the word "christology" to other Anglican divines in his writings.[23] Yet, with the Enlightenment of the seventeenth and eighteenth centuries that subjected Christian revelation to the scrutiny of human reason, the concomitant rise of the historical-critical method to apply that scrutiny to biblical and theological writings, and the nineteenth-century Romantic response to this rationalistic program through the poet writing as "a man *speaking* to men,"[24] the writing of theology suffered a curious fate.

At a time when the written genre of theology and its authors were proliferating, writing, or more specifically, the language of writing as an act of communication in its own right, disappeared from the vocabulary of most theologians, and the language of speech replaced it. Friedrich Schleiermacher set the tone for this linguistic shift in his classic work *The Christian Faith* in 1821, when he described Christian doctrines as "accounts of the Christian religious affections set forth in *speech*."[25] We will not probe the full implications of Schleiermacher's theology here but simply stress his relegation of "speech" itself to a secondary medium through which the religious experience that evokes it is expressed.

Yet, Schleiermacher used the language of "speech" to underscore the origin of the Christian faith in the "preached" experience of the apostolic church, not to deliberately displace the act of writing that experience. Moreover, Schleiermacher, like many theologians to this day, typically gave lectures first and then "wrote up" what he had spoken for publication. In fact, when the King of Germany responded to Schleiermacher's *Brief Outline of Theology* (1830) with the comment that "learned people at the university ought to write more intelligibly," Schleiermacher promptly responded that the written "handbook" was intended merely as an "outline" for those listening to his lectures, and thus he did not "view this supposed reproach as one at all." While Schleiermacher would ultimately revise the second edition of his *Outline* (1830) to "make things easier for the reader," those who heard his lectures were his primary audience.[26] Thus, it would be natural for Schleiermacher to emphasize theological "speech" as opposed to writing in his own work.

Yet, this shift to the language of speech, or "phonocentric" language, in theological writing has influenced the way that we teach theology and learn it today. Just as the first train coming into a station hides the one behind it, metaphors of speech in theological prose tend to suppress the act of writing that engenders it, as theologians typically submerge those acts of writing into metaphors of speaking and conversation, preferring to "speak through books," as Clement exhorted in the second century, than to "write" them. Thus, the writing of theology disappears into what is written like invisible ink. However, when the practice of writing becomes invisible, the process of writing disappears as well, to say nothing of the process of learning to write theology well![27] While one of the purposes of this historical sketch is to retrieve the art, science, language, and ongoing practice of writing theology as integral components of the theological enterprise, this retrieval was already in process at the turn of the twentieth century in the writings of Albert Schweitzer, to whom we turn next.

Writing theology as a theological author with Albert Schweitzer

In *The Quest of the Historical Jesus*, published in 1906 when he was a Lecturer in Theology at the University of Strasbourg, Schweitzer opens a new window into the writing of theology that enables its readers to see the theological writer at work. Describing the setting in which David Friedrich Strauss produced the first edition of his *Life of Jesus*, Schweitzer writes, "He wrote it while sitting at the window of the Repetents' [Assistant Lecturers'] room" at Tubingen, "which looks out upon the gateway-arch."[28]

While such a portrait would not be unusual if one were writing about John Keats or Emily Bronte, to draw attention to the theological writer in the act of writing was—in its way—revolutionary. In doing so, Schweitzer was one of the first theologians to treat theological writing as "writing" and to imagine theological writers as authors. His purpose was not to glorify theological authors but to "give a systematic historical account of the critical study of the life of Jesus," which Schweitzer approached as historical theology.[29] By doing this, however, he deconstructed the written "quest of the historical Jesus" and demoted it from "sacred text" to "a kind of writing" among others.[30]

Yet, Schweitzer's relentless attention to the rhetoric of the writers he interrogated has proved constructive for the subsequent writing of theology. Just as he opened a window into the theological writer's study, he also elucidated the characteristics of an effective theological style, which, at its best, integrated form and content in a manner suited to the author's purpose. An exemplary work was Strauss' first *Life of Jesus*, which Schweitzer called "one of the most perfect things in the whole range of learned literature" and pointed out these characteristics of a "learned" style to corroborate his judgment: "In over fourteen hundred pages he has not a superfluous phrase; his analysis descends to the minutest details, but he does not lose his way among them; the style is simple and picturesque, sometimes ironical, but always dignified and distinguished."[31]

To write theology well, then, was to write concisely, precisely, simply, but in a voice appropriate to the subject matter and audience. While the "academic" theological style described here does not exhaust the plurality of theological styles available to those writing theology today,[32] we could do worse than to follow this example as we move on to the writing of theology in our own context, beginning with that of Martin Luther King.

Writing theology as nonviolent resistance with Martin Luther King, Jr.

While Martin Luther King, Jr. identified himself first as "a preacher of the Gospel," others have called him America's greatest public theologian.[33] Yet, with the writing of "Letter from a Birmingham Jail" in April 1963, King also distinguished himself as a theological writer and provided a self-portrait:

> Never before have I written a letter this long (or should I say a book?)....I can assure you that it would have been much shorter if I had been writing from a comfortable desk, but what else is there to do when you are alone for days in the dull monotony of a narrow jail cell other than write long letters, think strange thoughts, and pray long prayers?[34]

Responding to a letter from prominent "liberal" clergy in Birmingham who censured him for participating in "unwise and untimely" civil rights demonstrations, King used writing both to reason with his detractors and to resist their accusations. His letter is a masterpiece of Rogerian rhetoric, so-called because it employs the psychology of Carl Rogers to construct an argument whose starting point is a genuine understanding of the other's point of view, and whose goal is a similar understanding of one's own point of view by the other. To accomplish this, the writer (a) establishes common ground with the audience, (b) removes threatening blocks that hinder communication, and (c) invites the audience to a new perception in a spirit of friendly persuasion.[35]

In "Letter from a Birmingham Jail," King established common ground with the Birmingham clergy by appealing to them as "a fellow clergyman and Christian brother" and enlisting their own theologians—Augustine, Aquinas, Martin Buber, Martin Luther, and Paul Tillich—in defense of his civil disobedience. Against the perceived threat of his extremism, King presented himself as a moderate, standing between the opposing forces of complacency and militancy in the Negro community[36] and advocating the "more excellent way of love and nonviolent protest." In conclusion, King invites the recipients of his letter into a new understanding engendering a common hope "that the dark clouds of racial prejudice will soon pass away and the deep fog of misunderstanding will be lifted...."[37]

We see, then, that Martin Luther King wrote theology both as an extension of his nonviolent protest and also as an appeal to "fellow men" for understanding leading to conversion and social change. Five years after writing this letter he was assassinated, but his writings remain. That is one reason that we write theology: so that the words can be there and stand for us when we are not there. Yet, few words of women appear in King's letter, and fewer are directly addressed to women. However, in a "Foreword" to the collection of King's writings from which I quote, Coretta Scott King writes in her husband's stead, reminding us that "all of the words in these pages were forged in action."[38] Because women writing theology have only recently claimed a more public "piece of the action," we return to them as we continue to examine the writing of theology in our own context.

Writing theology as a feminist practice with Rebecca Chopp

The emergence of feminist theology in our own context began with a woman writing. In *Saving Work: Feminist Practices of Theological Education*, Rebecca Chopp suggests that it began "officially" with the publication in 1960 of an article by Valerie Saiving, "The Human Situation: A Feminine View." In that article, Saiving challenged the predominant theological view that identified sin with self-assertion and love with selflessness and argued that this understanding of sin was based on male experience, not on human experience inclusive of women.[39] Rebecca Chopp also suggests that the act of writing is intimately connected with "writing our own lives in new ways" no less than with writing words on paper,[40] and Saiving's article underscores this connection. In writing an article critiquing a male-dominated theology of sin that excluded the experience of women, Saiving was "writing her own life" in a theological genre ("the article") that originated, as we know, with Thomas Aquinas himself. At the same time, she was claiming the writing of theology as a feminist practice.

With the publication of that article and others like it, women began to write theology out of the same authority of experience that Teresa of Avila had expressed subversively five centuries before, and which Schleiermacher appealed to when he called Christian doctrines "religious affections set forth in speech." Yet, when experience becomes a legitimate source of theology, more modes of expression become available to the theological writer, especially if she is convinced that writing theology is also "writing her life." At the beginning of the third millennium, women continue to claim writing as a feminist practice in ever-increasing numbers and to expand and diversify the forms of theological writing.

We will look more closely at some examples of feminist theological styles in subsequent chapters of this book, but for the moment, let us keep the woman writing in our minds as we proceed. For this historical overview of writing, theology is not the end of the story, and if it were, it would be painfully inadequate. We will be writing theology with many other theologians throughout this book, but we still will leave many gaps in this history. Think of this overview rather as an eclectic but strategic survey of theological writing and writers who have left their mark on the way that we write theology today. Better yet, think of it as a work in progress that invites you into its narrative as you begin or continue to write theology well in your own context.

THEOLOGICAL MEMO 3: (1) Choose one of the theological writers we have encountered in this historical sketch, and imagine him or her writing. Sit with your chosen writer and look over his or her shoulder as they write. Finally, imagine yourself sitting in their place, and write whatever comes from that experience. Or (2) Reflect on the historical backgrounds of theological writing that we have briefly surveyed. Which writers or historical periods have most strongly influenced the kinds of theology you write today? Which writers and historical styles have provided exemplars for your own theological writing?

Writing theology in our own context and its audiences

Writing theology in our own context poses its own challenges and opportunities. While postmodernity has divested theology of its privileged "scientific" status and rendered it merely "a kind of writing" among other kinds of writing, the writing of theology has also become more egalitarian. It does not belong to academic theologians alone but is open potentially to all who seek to join its conversation, as a trip to the corner bookstore will quickly corroborate. But, our trip to the corner bookstore will also reveal that there are as many kinds of theological writing as there are writers and audiences. What kind of writing, then, is theology today, and to whom and for whom is it being written? We can begin to answer this question by asking another one: what distinguishes contemporary theological writing from other kinds of writing?

What distinguishes contemporary theological writing from other writing?

First, its subject matter, or "discourse about God in the Christian community,"[41] identifies it as theological writing. The term *theological discourse* is often used to denote both the spoken and written communication of theology. Second, the languages and styles used by and for those communities distinguish it as theological writing, in all its diversity of argumentative language, analytic language, symbolic language, liturgical language, narrative language, and poetic language. Yet, theology, like all writing, is written for human beings by human beings sitting at computers and kitchen tables, not by the finger of God on Mt. Sinai. It is written "from below," whether its authors are dealing with the transcendence of God, the tragedy of human sin, or their own religious experience of both of these. Finally, theological writing takes its character from the communities to whom it is addressed, whether that audience is the society at large, the theological academy, the church, the transcendent God, or ourselves. We therefore need to look more closely at those to whom and for whom contemporary theology is being written.

To whom and for whom is contemporary theology being written?

There is really no such thing as "contemporary theology," but only "contemporary theologies." Because contemporary theology is pluralistic, the audience for whom it is written is one of its distinguishing factors. Whether one is a beginning theology student or a published theologian, theological writing is written for the audience, not primarily for the writer. "You may write for the joy of it," Flannery O'Connor says, "but the act of writing is not complete in itself. It has its end in its audience."[42] Thus, the audience for whom we write will determine what kind of theology we write, and how we write it. Just as Thomas Aquinas advised his readers centuries ago that discourse about God must be accommodated to the audiences for whom it is spoken or written, contemporary theologians frequently identify particular audiences with particular types of theology.

For example, David Tracy, a Roman Catholic theologian at the University of Chicago Divinity School, suggests that contemporary theology is comprised of three distinct but overlapping theologies: (1) fundamental theology, (2) systematic theology, and (3) practical theology. Their respective audiences, or "publics," are (1) the theological school or academy, (2) the church, and (3) the wider society.[43] Roman Catholic liberation theologian Leonardo Boff, writing from a Latin American context, identifies three analogous levels of liberation theology as (1) professional, (2) pastoral, and (3) popular. He correlates them, respectively, with (1) an academic theological audience, (2) an audience of pastoral ministers and workers, and (3) popular audiences in base communities and bible study groups.[44]

Closer to home, however, you are writing for a very strategic audience of your own: the professor. While students writing theological papers do not always think beyond the immediate audience of the professor who assigned the paper, at least one of the audiences described by Tracy or Boff will be implied in each paper that you write. We will be looking more specifically at these audiences in connection with the theological rhetorics that will be discussed in subsequent chapters. Nonetheless, writing theology well involves writing both for the professor who assigned the paper and for the wider theological audience implicit in the paper. Before we conclude this chapter, you might wish to reflect on the context in which you are presently writing theology, and to identify the theological audiences for whom you are writing:

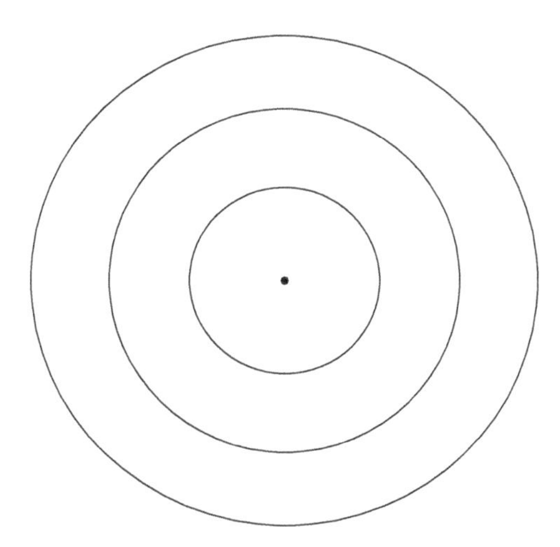

THEOLOGICAL MEMO 4: (1) Draw a small circle that represents your academic community, degree program and discipline, and put yourself in that circle: that is your immediate theological location, and the audience for whom you are writing

your academic papers. (2) Now draw a larger circle around that circle, and label that circle as your particular church community, or ecclesial context. In what way will this context influence your stance as a theological writer? What will this audience require of you?

(3) Next, draw a circle enclosing both of the other two, and identify your societal context, or social location, in this circle. How does this context influence your writing now? How will it influence your writing in your chosen ministry or profession? (4) Finally, look at these three concentric circles and imagine the papers you are writing this semester as tiny pebbles that you throw, one by one, into a pond. How far will the circles in the water that each pebble makes take you? Will they go no further than this immediate academic context? Might some of them—or one of them—contribute to your church, your ministerial setting, or to your society?

Beginning a theological writing assignment: Questions to ask

At this point you may well be saying, "This is all very interesting, but I have a theological reflection paper due on Friday, and I don't even know what theological reflection is, or how to write it. I am not Augustine or Aquinas or Teresa of Avila or Martin Luther King, and I don't really know what my professor wants, let alone a wider audience! How should I begin?" Chapter 2, "Writing Theological Reflection Well," will address each of these questions and invite you into the process of writing your first theological reflection paper. To get you started, here is a checklist of "Questions to ask" when beginning a theological writing assignment:

- From what *SOCIAL LOCATION, PERSPECTIVE, OR CONTEXT* will you approach this writing task? Do you need to specify it for your readers?
- What is the *SUBJECT* of the writing task? (Systematic theology? Church history? Biblical exegesis? How narrowly can you delineate the topic?)
- Who is the *AUDIENCE* for whom you are writing? (The professor assigning the paper? The congregation for whom your sermon is intended? Theological journals and pastoral magazines that might consider your work for publication?)
- What is the *THEOLOGICAL GENRE* of the writing task? (A pastoral reflection paper written from your own experience? A systematic reflection paper introduced by a thesis paragraph that is supported and summarized in subsequent paragraphs? A biblical exegesis, prepared according to specific instructions?)
- What is the *THEOLOGICAL PURPOSE* of the writing task? (Why are you writing it? For example, the purpose of an exegesis might be that of pastoral preparation for preaching a homily, or scholarly exposition for a journal article.)
- What *ORGANIZATIONAL PATTERN* is appropriate for this writing task? (Deductive style—from general to particular? Inductive style—from particular to general? A predefined pattern provided by the professor?)

- What *THEOLOGICAL LANGUAGE* is appropriate to this writing task? (What "technical" theological terms can readers can be assumed to understand? What words should you define for greater clarity?)
- What *THEOLOGICAL VOICE* is appropriate to the writing task? (An impersonal academic voice? A pastoral voice? A more transparent, personal voice? A voice that speaks for a wider academic or pastoral community?)

Concluding reflections: Writing theology well as an act of faith

"To make an end," writes T.S. Eliot, "is to make a beginning."[45] Appropriately, then, we must conclude this introduction to "Writing Theology in its Own Context" where all good writing begins: in the active, inquiring, and engaged faith of the writer who is struggling to put words on paper.

To write anything is ultimately an act of faith. Faith in yourself as a writer; faith in the importance of what you are writing; faith that there will be an audience for what you write; faith that your writing will contribute ultimately to the flourishing of those who read it; and finally, faith in the source of your desire to write, which I name here the Spirit of God. If this is true of writing in general, how much more is it true of writing theology, which from its inception has been concerned no less with "faith seeking understanding" than with "faith seeking *praxis*"?

I invite you to begin writing theology well not merely as an academic exercise, but as an act of faith. Writing from this place will not save you from writer's block the night before a paper is due or solve all your writing problems. Kathleen Norris cautions that such writing can be dangerous, for words written in faith "will take us places we don't want to go."[46] Yet, such writing is a way of inquiry that invites you to find out what you want to know. It is a way of clarity that invites you to communicate effectively what you do know. It is a way of truth that invites you to claim that truth without dismissing other truth claims. It is a way of practice that invites you to write every day, even when you do not feel like it. And finally, it is a way of doing theology—indeed, a theological practice in which you write faithfully for the love of God and for the hope of a transformed human community. But, the rest, as the venerable Hillel said to his disciple, "is commentary." It is now time for us to "go and write."

Notes

1 Flannery O'Connor, *Mystery and Manners: Occasional Prose*, selected and ed. Sally and Robert Fitzgerald (New York: Farrar, Strauss and Giroux, 1969), 102.

2 Claude Levi-Strauss, *Tristes Tropiques* (New York: Atheneum, 1961), 291–92, quoted in David R. Olsen, *The World on Paper: The Conceptual and Cognitive Implications of Writing and Reading* (Cambridge: Cambridge University Press, 1994), 9.

3 Paulo Friere, *Pedagogy of Freedom: Ethics, Democracy and Civic Courage*, trans. Patrick Clarke (Lanham, MD: Rowman & Littlefield, 1998), 79.

4 Ferdinand de Saussure, *Course in General Linguistics* (London: Duckworth, 1983; orig. 1916), 23–24, quoted in Olsen, *The World on Paper*, 8.

5 Paul Ricoeur, "The Hermeneutical Function of Distanciation," in *Hermeneutics and the Human Sciences*, ed. and trans. John B. Thompson (Cambridge: Cambridge University Press, 1981), 131.

6 Paul Tillich, *Systematic Theology*, 3 vols. (Chicago: University of Chicago Press, 1951), 1:28.

7 Rebecca S. Chopp, *Saving Work: Feminist Practices of Theological Education* (Louisville: Westminster John Knox Press, 1995), 73–74.

8 Roger Haight, *Dynamics of Theology* (New York/Mahwah, NJ: Paulist Press, 1990; reprint, Maryknoll, NY: Orbis Books, 1970, 216 (page references are to reprint edition).

9 Rowan Williams, quoted in Todd Breyfoyfogle, "Time and Transformation: A Conversation with Rowan Williams," *Cross Currents* 45 (Fall 1995): 313.

10 The Hebrew *sopher* (scribe) comes from the root *spr*, which referred variously to a written message, a writing, and the one writing it (hence "writer"). The Greek *grammaticus* (scribe) denotes one who "knows letters." In its New Testament context, the word "scribe" embraced diverse technical, administrative, and social roles for which the skills of reading and writing were prerequisite. For the purposes of this book, I focus on "writing" and imagine Matthew as a prototype of "writing theology well." For a more detailed survey, see Anthony J. Saldarini, "Scribes," *The Anchor Bible Dictionary*, 6 vols. ed. David Noel Freedman (New York: Doubleday, 1992), 5:1112–16; Dennis Duling, "Matthew as a Marginal Scribe in an Advanced Agrarian Society," *Hervormde Teologiese Studies* 58, no. 2 (2002): 520–75. For a description of Gospel writers as "scribaliterate," see Lucretia B. Yaghjian, "Ancient Reading," in *The Social Sciences and New Testament Interpretation*, ed. Richard L. Rohrbaugh (Peabody, MA: Hendrickson, 1996), 206–30.

11 *Passio Sanctarum Perpetuae et Felicitas*, in *The Acts of the Christian Martyrs*, ed. and trans. Herbert Musurillo (Oxford: Clarendon Press, 1972; repr. 1979), 107–31.

12 St. Augustine, *On Christian Doctrine*, trans. D.W. Robertson, Jr. (Indianapolis: Bobbs-Merrill [Liberal Arts Press], 1958), 4.3.4 (p. 119). All subsequent references are to this edition.

13 Augustine, *On Christian Doctrine*, 4.17–28 (pp. 142–66). For more on Augustine's "christianization" of Ciceronian rhetoric, see Don H. Compier, *What Is Rhetorical Theology? Textual Practice and Public Discourse* (Harrisburg, PA: Trinity International, 1999), 11–13.

14 For a more sustained discussion, see Lucretia B. Yaghjian, "Writing Cultures, Enculturating Writing at Two Theological Schools: Mapping Rhetorics of Correlation and Liberation," *Teaching Theology and Religion* 5, no. 3 (2002): 135–37.

15 See Thomas Aquinas, *Summa Theologica: Complete English Edition in Five Volumes* (Westminster, MD: Christian Classics, 1961), q. 1, a. 2.

16 This brief sketch of Scholastic writing and rhetoric is indebted to Yves M.J. Congar, O.P., *A History of Theology* (Garden City, NY: Doubleday, 1958), 85–114; Edward J. Gratch, *Aquinas' Summa: An Introduction and Interpretation* (New York: Alba House, 1985), ix–xxxix; John W. O'Malley, *Four Cultures of the West* (Cambridge,

MA: Harvard University Press, 2004), 97–103; Erwin Panofsky, *Gothic Architecture and Scholasticism* (Latrobe, PA: Archabbey Press, 1951), 27–60; Anders Piltz, *The World of Medieval Learning*, trans. David Jones (Totowa, NJ: Barnes & Noble, 1981), 145–86; Frank Whaling, "The Development of the Word 'Theology,'" *Scottish Journal of Theology* 34 (1981): 289–312.

17 Saint Teresa of Avila, *The Life of Saint Teresa of Avila by Herself*, trans. David Lewis, With additional Notes and an Introduction by Rev. Fr. Benedict Zimmerman, O.C.D. (Digireads.com Publishing, 2009), 61.

18 See also Stephanie Paulsell's description of Marguerite D'Oingt, a Carthusian nun in southern France who died in 1310 and predated Teresa of Avila as a cloistered religious writer, in "Writing as a Spiritual Discipline," in *The Scope of Our Art: The Vocation of the Theological Teacher*, ed. Gregory L. Jones and Stephanie Paulsell (Grand Rapids: William B. Eerdmanns, 2002), 17–20.

19 St. Teresa of Avila, Autograph to *Interior Castle*, ed. and trans. E. Allison Peers from the Critical Edition of P. Silverio de Santa Teresa, C.D. (Garden City, NY: Doubleday [Image Books], 1961), 24. All subsequent references are to this edition.

20 For a cogent exposition of this argument, see Terrance G. Walsh, "Writing Anxiety in Teresa's *Interior Castle*," *Theological Studies* 56 (1995): 251–75.

21 See, e.g., Emily A. Holmes and Wendy Farley, eds., *Women, Writing, Theology: Transforming a Tradition of Exclusion* (Waco: Baylor University Press, 201l), esp. Holmes' "Introduction: Mending a Broken Lineage," 1–10.

22 John Milton, Preface to *On Christian Doctrine (De Doctrina Christiana)*, in *John Milton: Complete Poems and Major Prose*, ed. Merritt Y. Hughes (New York: Odyssey Press, 1957), 902.

23 *Oxford English Dictionary of the English Language*, s.v., "Christology."

24 William Wordsworth, "Preface to the Second Edition of *Lyrical Ballads* (1800)," in *Selected Poems and Prefaces by William Wordsworth*, ed. Jack Stillinger (Boston: Riverside/Houghton Mifflin, 1965), 453.

25 Friedrich Schleiermacher, *The Christian Faith* (New York: Harper Torchbooks, 1963), 76.

26 Friedrich Schleiermacher, Preface to the Second Edition of *Brief Outline of Theology as a Field of Study*, ed. and trans. Terence N. Tice (Lewiston/Queenston: Edwin Mellon Press, 1988), xiv. For Schleiermacher's reference to the King of Germany, see Tice's ed. note 1, quoting Heinrich Meisner, *Schleiermacher als Mensch: Swin Wirken—Familien und Freundesbriefe 1784 bis 1834* (Stuttgart:/Gotha: Perthes, 1923), 138.

27 I have described the phonocentric character of contemporary theological writing in Lucretia B. Yaghjian, "Writing Practice and Pedagogy across the Theological Curriculum: Teaching Writing in a Theological Context," *Theological Education* 33 (1997): 39–68, and am drawing upon that material in this chapter. See also David Tracy, "Writing," in *Critical Terms for Religious Studies*, ed. Mark C. Taylor (Chicago: University of Chicago Press, 1998), 383–93.

28 Albert Schweitzer, *The Quest of the Historical Jesus: A Critical Study of Its Progress from Reimarus to Wrede* (Baltimore: Johns Hopkins University Press, 1998 [original 1906]), 71.

29 Ibid., 12.

30 The phrase, "a kind of writing," was coined by Richard Rorty, in his essay "Philosophy as a Kind of Writing," in ed. Richard Rorty, *Consequences of Pragmatism* (Minneapolis, MN: University of Minnesota Press, 1982), 90–109.

31 Schweitzer, *Quest of the Historical Jesus*, 78. For an insightful discussion of authorship as "a peculiarly modern construct," see Andrea Lunsford and Lisa Ede, "Rhetoric in a New Key: Women and Collaboration," *Rhetoric Review* 8, no. 2 (1990): 234–341.

32 As Rowan Williams cautions, "One of the temptations of theology has been—at least in the modern era—to suppose not so much that there is a normative content for theological utterance, but that there is a normative 'style.'" See Rowan Williams, *On Christian Theology* (Oxford: Blackwell, 2000), 9.

33 See Stanley M. Hauerwas, "Remembering Martin Luther King, Jr. Remembering," in *Wilderness Wanderings: Probing Twentieth-Century Theology and Philosophy* (Boulder, CO: Westview Press, 1997), 228.

34 Martin Luther King Jr., "Letter from a Birmingham Jail," in *I Have a Dream: Writings and Speeches That Changed the World*, ed. James Melvin Washington (San Francisco: HarperSanFrancisco, 1992), 100.

35 For an excellent presentation of Rogerian rhetoric, see Richard E. Young, Alton L. Becker, and Kenneth L. Pike, *Rhetoric: Discovery and Change* (New York: Harcourt Brace Jovanovich, 1970). See also Carl Rogers, "Communication: Its Blocking and Its Facilitation," in *Critical Thinking, Reading and Writing: A Brief Guide to Argument*, ed. Sylvan Barnet and Hugo Bedau (Boston: Bedford Books/St.Martin's Press, 1995), 326–33; Douglas Brent, "Rogerian Rhetoric: An Alternative to Traditional Rhetoric," in *Argument Revisited, Argument Redefined: Negotiating Meaning in the Composition Classroom*. ed. Barbara A. Emmel, Paula Resch, and Deborah Tenney (Thousand Oaks, CA: Sage, 1996), 73–96.

36 I am following King's nomenclature here ("the Negro community"), rather than using the more current terminology of "black" or "African-American." See, e.g., King, "Letter from a Birmingham Jail," 93.

37 King, "Letter from a Birmingham Jail," 100.

38 Coretta Scott King, "Foreword" to "*I Have a Dream*," vii.

39 Chopp, *Saving Work*, 35. See also Valerie Saiving, "The Human Situation: A Feminine View," in *Womanspirit Rising: A Feminist Reader in Religion*, ed. Carol P. Christ and Judith Plaskow (San Francisco: Harper & Row, 1970), 25–42.

40 Ibid., 32.

41 Chopp, *Saving Work*, 74.

42 Flannery O'Connor, *The Habit of Being: Letters of Flannery O'Connor*, ed. Sally Fitzgerald (New York: Farrar, Strauss & Giroux, 1979), 458.

43 David Tracy, *The Anagogical Imagination: Christian Theology and the Culture of Pluralism* (New York: Crossroad, 1987), 31.

44 Leonardo Boff, *Introducing Liberation Theology* (Maryknoll, NY: Orbis Books, 1987), 12–14.

45 T.S. Eliot, "Little Gidding," in *Four Quartets*, ed. T.S. Eliot (New York: Harcourt Brace and World, 1943, Copyright T.S. Eliot. repr. 1971, Copyright Esme Valerie Eliot), 58. Page reference is to the 1971 edition.

46 Kathleen Norris, *Amazing Grace: A Vocabulary of Faith* (New York: Riverhead Books, 1998), 273.

2
Writing Theological Reflection Well: Rhetorics of Process, Problem-Solving, and Proclamation

Genuine theology is the fruit of a dynamic process of reflection.
—PATRICIA O'CONNELL KILLEN and JOHN DE BEER, *The Art of Theological Reflection*

Theological reflection frequently transpires as some form of problem-solving.
—ROGER HAIGHT, "Women and the Church: A Theological Reflection"

"You're a writer, you can preach," my friend Alice said ....
—KATHLEEN NORRIS, *Amazing Grace: A Vocabulary of Faith*

Starting points

THEOLOGICAL MEMO 1: Let us imagine that you have been asked to write a "theological reflection paper" for one of your classes, but the professor has not given you explicit instructions for the writing of the paper. How would you approach this writing task? On the basis of your own understanding of "theological reflection," please (1) define this term in one or two sentences and (2) briefly describe the kind of paper you would write in response to the assignment.

The theological memo that begins this chapter is not a mere academic exercise. It is the necessary starting point for the process of writing theological reflection well. If you have not yet responded to this memo, please do so before we proceed. Once again, you are invited to define the term *theological reflection* as succinctly as possible and to describe how you would go about writing a "theological reflection paper" for the assignment you have been given.

The reason that this chapter begins the way that it does is that there is no one model for a "theological reflection paper." There are only "theological reflection papers," written by authors from a variety of theological and pastoral contexts for specific audiences and purposes. "Theological reflection" is what Lewis Carroll's Humpty Dumpty would call a "portmanteau" word. Just as a "portmanteau" word packs more than one meaning into its briefcase, the term "theological reflection" embraces a diversity of forms, contexts, and methodological starting points. Some take "experience" as a starting point for a "mutually critical correlation" with the Christian tradition[1] or engage in "critical incident" reflection for field education and clinical pastoral education programs.[2] Others name the biblical story and our response to it as the genesis of theological reflection.[3] Still others embrace contextual theological reflection from standpoints of culture, gender, race, and class.[4]

Our use of the term *theological reflection* has its roots in the praxis-based reflection of Latin American base communities; in analogous North American liberation-based models of reflection embraced by African Americans, women, and other oppressed groups; and in the Clinical Pastoral Education (CPE) model of on-site reflection that has been adapted to other areas of theological education.[5] Thus, even within your own theological school or seminary, you will encounter this genre in different guises or disguises, depending on whether it is being used by a systematic theologian,[6] a religious educator,[7] a social ethics professor,[8] or a field education supervisor.[9] In whatever form it is encountered, however, the oral and written practice of theological reflection has become a standard genre of the theological curriculum, even if no "standard" rhetorical model exists for writing it.[10] The first thing, then, that you must do in writing a theological reflection paper is to determine what is meant by "theological reflection" and why it is being written in a particular context. The second thing you must do is to determine the type of paper that is required by the assignment. Finally, you must write the paper! We will consider each of these tasks in turn.

What is theological reflection and why do theologians write it?

We have already defined theology as "a language used by a specific group of people to make sense of their world,"[11] and theological reflection is one of its written and spoken dialects. In this book, I shall make a preliminary distinction between "theological reflection," which begins with the experience of the writer who is "reflecting," and "theological research," which begins with someone else's article, or book, or other media that is relevant to the writer's project. Leaving theological research aside for the moment, I cannot define theological reflection without recourse to the theological imagination at the heart of this process of reflection.

By the theological imagination, I understand our active minds thinking, questioning, dreaming, creating, construing, constructing, critiquing, speaking, and writing in the conceptual language of theology.[12] Theological reflection is the disciplined and creative exercise of this theological imagination in dialogue with our individual or communal experience. As it is defined in this book, however, theological reflection embraces a broad rhetorical spectrum of voice and genre. What distinguishes the writing of theological reflection from other kinds of theological writing is its appeal to experience, or to the particular issue, question, problem, or text that "we are trying to make sense of," as a starting point for reflection.

The experience engendering the reflection may be personal or public; it may arise from reading a text or from working in a homeless shelter; it may inspire the telling of stories; or it may require a more rigorously academic mode of argument. Yet, the primary goal of every theological reflection paper is to "make sense" of something that may not initially seem to make sense by thinking about that experience theologically or by viewing it through the lens of a theological imagination. Where is God, or where is the "God-Word" (*theos/logos*) in this experience, or in this text? What images and symbols of the transcendent are evoked? What biblical stories illuminate the experience positively or provide a prophetic critique? Where am I, my faith community and/or my culture in relation to this "God-Word"? What can I/we do in response? To write theological reflection, then, is to engage in a creative *process* characterized by cognitive *problem-solving* whose rhetorical end is *proclamation*, or more simply, having something to say, and hence to write, and writing it for a particular "public"[13] or audience. Before proceeding to the task of writing, we look briefly at each of these characteristic rhetorical elements, or "rhetorics" of theological reflection.

A rhetoric of process

"Genuine theology is the fruit of a dynamic process of reflection," write Patricia O'Connell Killen and John de Beer.[14] Yet, theological reflection that is written is also the result of a disciplined process of writing, and these integrated processes conspire in the writing of theological reflection. What is the "dynamic process of reflection" that energizes this theological genre? Killen and de Beer describe it simply in four movements that I have adapted for theological writers as a "Reflecting on Paper Process." [15] This process entails: (1) identifying a question for reflection arising from an experience; (2) describing that experience in writing to identify the crux of the question; (3) correlating the experience and the question with the Christian tradition, story, and symbols; and (4) constructing a new imagination of the experience that emerges from this writing process. This process of reflection has its roots in the theological method of correlation, which we will examine more closely in Chapter 4, "Writing the Theological Essay Well." At the heart of this model is an interactive process of correlation between experience and Christian tradition that inspires the process of reflection unfolded here. The pastoral reflection paper that you will be invited to write in this chapter will be informed by this "Reflecting on Paper Process."[16]

A rhetoric of problem-solving

If theological reflection unfolds as a process, that process is frequently engendered by the problematic, which theologians call more formally the experience of negativity. The problems addressed may be severe enough to be identified with the seemingly insoluble mystery of evil, or simple enough to yield to a more straightforward resolution. They may arise from human life, or Christian faith, or an apparent conflict between both of these. As Roger Haight explains, "What the phrase 'theological reflection' seems to add to the notion of theology as such is an explicit intention to bring actual current experience to bear on an understanding of Christian symbols so that they may in turn illumine actual experience and practice. For this reason theological reflection frequently transpires as some form of problem-solving."[17]

At its best, the problem-solving encountered in theological reflection is neither facile nor formulaic. However, to write theological reflection from this vantage point is to follow a rhetorical path from problem to solution, which might entail these four movements: (1) explanation and analysis of the problem in the light of current experience; (2) reflection on the problem in (positive and negative) conversation with Christian tradition; (3) proposals for a solution of the problem, which may involve retrieval or reinterpretation of the tradition toward the end of a "re-formed" and reinvigorated praxis; and (4) concluding appeal to the reader that reasserts the gravity of the problem and the urgency of providing a solution, such as the one proposed in the reflection.

Haight's article, "Women in the Church: A Theological Reflection," follows this structure as it (1) identifies the present Vatican position on the ordination of women as a "theological problem" best addressed through the experience-driven genre of "theological reflection"; (2) analyzes the problem more specifically by placing the Vatican position prohibiting women's ordination because of their gender "difference" in conversation with contemporary women's experience of oppression and liberation, using the theological method of correlation; (3) proposes a theological solution to the problem through the assertion of "a new and gratuitous ontological equality that transcends differences" conferred by the limitless love of God, revealed in Jesus Christ; and (4) reasserts the significance of the problem, its far-reaching consequences for the credibility of the universal church, against the backdrop of its mission to be "a sacrament to the world of the boundless love of God revealed to us in Christ Jesus."[18]

THEOLOGICAL MEMO 2: Select a theological article that you are currently reading for one of your classes, and analyze its "process of theological reflection," using either the "Reflecting on Paper" process model or the "Problem-Solving" model described above. What similarities do you see in these "rhetorics of theological reflection"? How do they differ? (If you need a model for your own analysis, see the outline of Haight's "problem-solving" process of reflection, above.)

A rhetoric of proclamation

Informed as it is by the rhetorics of process and problem-solving, the genre of theological reflection is hospitable to preaching and other modes of proclamation, depending upon its intended audience. While we will not focus here upon the writing of sermons—your homiletics professor is your best resource for the mastery of that exacting art—every Sunday homily or sermon is a form of theological reflection that, at its best, invites the congregation into its process. If you are already preaching to a congregation, you know with Kathleen Norris that "[w]riting a sermon is like any other form of writing, because I have to settle for doing the best I can, and then let it go."[19] However, even if you are not preaching to a congregation, and if you are a writer, you not only "can preach," as Norris claims, but you "do" preach, and you do proclaim the truth that transpires from the words you find to evoke it.

In an address to Catholic writers, Flannery O'Connor addressed anyone addressing their own religious audience when she proclaimed, "If the [Catholic] writer hopes to reveal mysteries, he will have to do it by describing truthfully what he sees from where he [or she] is."[20] What is invoked here is the powerful proclamation of a writer's voice, but we are also listening for another voice that might, if we stay respectfully out of the way, inspire and authenticate what we are given to say in the face of the mystery that invokes us. Call this voice God, or the Holy Spirit, or Sophia, or your own inner wisdom: to write theological reflection is ultimately to give voice to that voice by writing in your own voice, in the hope that it will reflect the mystery that inspires it, and in the confidence that there will be an audience who will want to hear or read it. For the moment, however, the goal is more modest: to write a theological reflection paper that will satisfy you and the professor for whom it is written.

Writing theological reflection papers: Purpose, style, and voice

Every theological writing assignment, from a one-page paper to a twenty-page research essay, includes theological reflection. Yet, the form the reflection takes will be shaped by the *purpose*, *style*, and *voice* of the paper, as each of these is determined by the course for which the paper is assigned. The *purpose* of a paper addresses the question, Why is this paper being written? The *style* of a paper addresses the question, What kind of paper is it, and how shall I write it? The *voice* of a paper addresses the question, Who is speaking and in what context?[21]

We have already seen that theological reflection papers come in many shapes and sizes. I focus here, however, on two common styles of theological reflection papers: the pastoral reflection paper and the systematic reflection paper, which are written in the personal voice and the academic voice, respectively. The purpose of the *pastoral reflection paper* is to invite the writer to reflect upon a pastoral issue or situation with which he or she is personally engaged, or upon a text that illuminates the situation under scrutiny. The purpose of the *systematic reflection paper* is to engage students in the analysis and interpretation of a biblical, theological, or historical text, datum, or tradition, by taking a position that they develop into a coherent theological argument.

Writing the one-page theological reflection paper in two voices

Each of the papers described above is written in one of two voices, depending upon their context: the *personal voice* or the *academic voice*. If you can write a one-page theological reflection paper in both a personal and an academic voice, you will be able to write any paper requiring theological reflection, simply adapting the style, focus, and length to the particular needs of the assignment. We look briefly, then, at each of these "voices."

A *personal voice* invokes your own personal experience and engages the subject matter directly from the vantage point of that experience. A paper written in a personal voice will have its own form and logic, because all good theological writing integrates the head and the heart through the play of theological imagination. Writing in a personal voice is encouraged in courses that invite reflection and engagement with course content from the writer's own social location or pastoral perspective.

An *academic voice* is a more formal, scholarly voice that also begins with your own experience, but which generalizes that experience through a more public process of argument and analysis that is common to theological writing for the "academy." If the personal voice is at times content to defer with Pascal to the heart's reasons "that reason does not know," the academic voice struggles to identify the heart's reasons and to bring them coherently to expression according to a particular logic or argumentative structure. While its disciplinary accents may vary across the theological curriculum, the academic voice still prevails in published theological writing, and its mastery remains a prerequisite for all theological writers.

Let us look at two types of papers exemplifying these two voices and then proceed to try our hand at writing in each voice. In this chapter, we begin with the pastoral reflection paper, which is written in the personal voice, because it provides a writer-centered entrée into theological reflection. In the next chapter, we look at the systematic reflection paper, which is written in the academic voice, because it requires a reader, text, and argument-centered approach to theological reflection. Before we look at each type of paper separately, we look at what they have in common: the writing process.

Writing the one-page reflection paper: An overview

What happens when you sit down to write a paper? You might have written a brief description of your own process in response to the theological memo in Chapter 1, but there is much about the process of putting words on paper that is common to everyone who sits down to write. Every writer begins with a writing project that impels him or her to face the blank page in the first place. Every writer engages in various prewriting processes—reading, reflecting, meditating, planning, and even procrastinating—in order to prepare for that writing project. Every writer eventually moves from those preliminary processes to putting words on paper, first by freewriting or outlining and then by more focused composing, often through multiple drafts of the project, until it is completed. And unless one is receiving dictation from on high, every writer practices the process of revision or rewriting, both in the midst of writing and upon its completion. Finally, every writer participates in the process of "publishing" the writing for a particular audience, even if only from one's own desktop.

Simply stated, then, what we call "the writing process" is actually a series of interrelated processes, each of which is integral to the composite activity of writing. Initiated by a particular writing project, they include: (1) prewriting processes (to induce the labor of writing); (2) freewriting processes (to reduce the fear of writing and foster its flow); (3) composing processes (to deduce the evolving form of writing and bring it to completion); (4) rewriting processes (to produce a readable piece of writing); and (5) publication processes (to reproduce writing for its intended audience). Keeping in mind that your own writing process need not follow this generic one slavishly or in the same order, let us begin with the pastoral reflection paper as our writing project and follow its progress through the writing process, focusing on what I call the "Write Three Times" method. According to this method, which Yaroslav Pelikan introduced to his graduate students at Yale Divinity School, a good writer writes everything three times.[22] First, we write to find out what we want to say. Second, we write in order to say that and only that. Third, and finally, we write what we want to say so that others will want to read it. We begin with a brief writing project for a pastoral theology class: "Why do you follow Jesus?"

Writing the one-page pastoral reflection paper: "Why Do You Follow Jesus?"

> *THEOLOGICAL MEMO 3: Please read the following assignment for a Pastoral Theology class, and clarify for yourself (a) the writing task described in the assignment; (b) the required length of the assignment; (c) any supplemental suggestions or instructions that will help you to focus the paper and fulfill the requirements of the assignment. When you are ready to proceed with writing, please write a first, "free-writing" draft of the paper "to find out what you want to say":*
> ***From the perspective of your own ministry or ministerial vocation, please write a one-page reflection in response to one or more of these questions: "Why do you follow Jesus? Who is the Jesus whom you follow? What difference does following Jesus make to your conception of pastoral ministry, and/or to your own ministerial goals?"***

Prewriting the pastoral reflection paper: Reading, reflecting, and preparing

Reading the assignment

Every successfully completed writing assignment begins by reading the instructions for the assignment carefully and by following those instructions appropriately. Needless to say, theological writing assignments are no exception. Nine times out of ten, the student's plaintive response to a mediocre grade on a paper, "I thought that was what you wanted," can be avoided altogether by reading the assignment three times: first, for its explicit written directions; second, for its implicit but unwritten expectations; and finally, to underline, highlight with a marking pen, or make your own notes of the specific guidelines for writing the paper that indicate "what the professor wants." In the assignment above, for example, you are explicitly directed to write (a) a *one-page* (b) *reflection paper* in a (c) *personal voice* and in a (d) *pastoral context* in answer to (e) *one or more* of the questions given. In order to follow these explicit instructions, you are also expected to (f) *limit and narrow your response to the question(s) you choose to answer*, since that task is implicit in the choices given.

Reflecting on the task

Once you have read the assignment and identified its explicit and implicit directives, you will begin to reflect upon what the assignment asks you to do. Do you want to respond to one question or, more succinctly, to all three? Which of the questions leaps out at you? Which is the most difficult to answer for you? Does a personal experience come to mind? How does your own pastoral context shape your response to the questions? Does a passage from Scripture present itself to your reflection? How can you most effectively deal with this critical pastoral question within the limits of a one-page reflection?

This kind of prewriting reflection rewards the writer who begins the process some days before sitting down to write the paper and lets the questions percolate in the shower, on the subway, while making dinner or doing dishes, in prayer, in conversation with other students, while taking a walk, or before falling asleep at night. You may do all of this reflecting "in your head," or you may "write before writing," as Donald Murray suggests,[23] in a small notebook or journal. Whatever style of reflection suits you best, its goal is to induce the labor of writing by engaging your theological imagination in the task at hand. Often this reflection will flow naturally into a "freewriting" draft, especially with papers written in the personal voice that do not require preliminary reading or research. A time will come, however, when you must begin writing, whether you feel ready or not. One way to move positively from "pre-writing" to putting words on paper is to prepare your schedule and your physical space for the activity of writing.

Preparing

While reading the assignment and reflecting on what you want to write are all part of preparing for writing, when you prepare your daily schedule and your personal space for a period of sustained writing, you participate in rituals common to all successful writers. Let's begin with preparing your daily schedule, since that is frequently the more challenging task for theological students.

Preparing a writing schedule

Writing does not get done unless you write, and you will not write unless you make time to write. This will not be so difficult if you are a full-time student with no other responsibilities, but most theological students on the seminary level are already involved in ministry, are raising families, are working part-time or full-time to pay for their seminary education, or are doing all of the above! For such students, writing under pressure becomes the path of least resistance. However, while the pressure of an assignment due the next day will provide a powerful incentive for writing when all else fails, it will not guarantee a well-written paper. Thus, a consistent writing schedule that coordinates regular blocks of writing time with paper due dates will be much more conducive to successful writing.

> *THEOLOGICAL MEMO 4: Make a weekly schedule that indicates your class times, other regular commitments, and blocks of "study time." Then make a list of all your writing assignments for the semester in the order of their due*

dates. Keeping in mind your own best writing times, draft a realistic writing schedule that will accommodate those due dates and provide ample reading time prior to the writing of the paper. Allow more time rather than less for writing until you know how long it will take for you to write various kinds of papers, and always schedule proofreading time before the paper is due. Experiment with this schedule for a week or two, and make any necessary adjustments as you proceed.

Preparing a writing space

Preparing a writing space, furnishing it with all of the materials that you need for writing, and keeping it cleared and ready for writing are similarly conducive to good writing. Thomas Carlyle could only write in a soundproof room; Jane Austen could only write in the family drawing room. Agatha Christie had to have a bowl of brightly polished apples at her desk; William Faulkner had to have a bottle of whiskey (although this is not generally recommended!). Whatever your living arrangements and personal proclivities, finding a comfortable, habitual writing space that is equipped with all the materials you need before you begin writing will both organize and center you, especially if, like Linda Pastan, you cultivate the habit of "clearing your desk" before and after a writing session:

I clear my desk,
it is the only ordering I know:
friends to the one side
the messages
they sent maybe weeks ago
traveling steadily like light from a star;
and on the other side bills
reminding me
I owe. I owe.
In the middle now this small, cleared space.
It is the same each morning,
The day opening
Like the study window,
me leaning on the sill
Eve again:
the whole wide world
to choose from
(poet ... cartographer)
where to go?[24]

THEOLOGICAL MEMO 5: At the beginning of any writing task is "getting down to the work of writing." However assiduously we have reflected on the assignment and perhaps even "written up" our notes, a point comes when we must face the blank page and begin to write a first draft.

What happens when you "get down to work?" What clutter must you push away in order to be free to write, and what is your "small, cleared space?" What do you do to avoid the task at hand, and what do you do to "induce the labor of writing?" Are there specific "rituals" you must perform before feeling free to write? Do you have one procedure that "works" every time, or is every writing task different? For a few moments, reflect on your process of "getting down to the work of writing," and describe in prose, poetry or drawing, how you "get down to work."

Freewriting or outlining draft #1: Finding out what you want to say

Freewriting, so-called because it frees the writer to write whatever comes to consciousness in relation to a given topic, and *outlining*, a more linear process of "pre-writing" a paper, might seem like an unlikely pair of writing strategies to put in tandem. Yet, there are as many ways to begin writing a paper as there are papers to write, and "left-brained" and "right-brained" writers will favor different strategies for beginning the writing process.

Freewriting

The purpose of a freewriting draft is to help you find out what you want to write by writing.[25] Let's imagine that you have read the assignment and reflected on the question, "Why do you follow Jesus?" You have blocked out time to write, and you have a "small, cleared space" that beckons you to write. The computer is on; you have opened a new file; you even have a few notes from your prewriting reflections, but you are still not sure what you want to say in this paper, or how to say it. By freewriting, or writing in response to your question for a stated period of time without stopping to correct, delete or revise your writing, you begin to discover what you want to say and what you do not want to say. For example:

Why do I follow Jesus? I follow Jesus because Jesus called me, somewhere along the way. I follow Jesus because at a certain point in my life, I recognized Jesus Christ as my way to God. I follow Jesus because I am lured by his life and by his death to live my life differently—or at least to try—because of a cross that both scandalizes me and puts my self-centered life to shame.

I follow Jesus like the women in Luke who accompanied him on his journey. Yet I also know the response of Jesus to the man who said, "I will follow you wherever you go," to whom Jesus said, "The foxes have holes; the birds have nests; but the son of man has nowhere to lay his head."

The difference it makes in my ministerial vocation is that I left other nets to follow Jesus to theological school, and I am now pursuing a D.Min. while working as a hospital chaplain. Yet one could also say that I don't follow Jesus—how I am haunted by the rich young man who turned away sorrowful because he had many possessions. I too have many possessions that keep me from following Jesus with abandon: a job, a house, a marriage, a mother-in-law, even a ministry, all of whom from one perspective keep me from following Jesus, but from another, are the only context in which I can. The women in Luke simply accompanied Jesus on the road. Perhaps "accompanying" is a more empowering metaphor than "following," at least for me. What would it mean, then, for me to accompany Jesus on his journey? Would it not mean to accompany those whom I serve in my ministry, and to provide for their needs out of my own resources? Paradoxically, the Jesus whom I follow invites me to accompany him, and this image provides me with a more sustaining model for my life and for my ministry.

This freewriting draft needs work. It is rough, rather trite in places, and turned in upon the writer's internal dialogue with herself rather than actively directed toward an audience. However, this draft reveals a gradual shift of gravity from the predictable and passive imagery of "following Jesus" to the proactive image of "accompanying Jesus." As we will see in later drafts of this paper, this is a very significant shift that provides the writer a way of connecting the original question posed by the assignment with her own conception of ministry. Notice, however, that it takes an entire draft of less inspired writing to elicit this creative reconfiguration of the question. Even if few of the words in this draft will accompany their author to the next one, in that they provide a bridge from what she began to write to what she really wanted to say, none of the words are wasted.

Outlining

The purpose of an outline draft is to clear a preliminary path for writing by walking yourself through the progression of your ideas in a brief but sequential form. In order to clear a path, however, you need to know where you are going; thus, this method works best when you have a rough idea of what you want to write but need to "flesh it out" more coherently before writing a first draft. While outlining may seem more appropriate for writing a paper in an academic voice, it can be used fruitfully for papers in the personal voice as well. While the process is more left-brained than right-brained, it provides the writer with a tentative, exploratory way of proceeding because it is still "just an outline." Moreover, it is a preliminary outline that can be adjusted, changed, or abandoned altogether, without engendering the internal pressure of "writing in progress."

Some writers habitually use outlining as an alternative to freewriting, but let us imagine here that the writer of the freewriting draft, who now has a clearer idea of what she wants to say, has chosen to make a rough outline of her freewriting before proceeding to the next draft. Her outline might look something like this:

Why do I follow Jesus?

- *I. The Predictable Answers*
  - *A. "Jesus called me"*
  - *B. "Jesus is my way to God"*
  - *C. Jesus' life and death challenge me to live differently*
- *II. Scriptural Analogues and Counterpoints*
  - *A. The women who accompanied Jesus on his journey (Luke 8:1–3)*
  - *B. "They left their nets and followed him" (Matt 4:20)*

C. *The potential followers discouraged by Jesus (Luke 9:57–62)*
D. *The young man who had "many possessions" (Matt 19:16–22)*

III. *"Following Jesus" or "accompanying Jesus" in pastoral ministry?*
A. *How I have followed Jesus into pastoral ministry: "leaving my nets"*
1. *To attend theological school*
2. *To serve as a hospital chaplain*
B. *How I have not followed Jesus in total discipleship*
1. *Prior commitments and relationships*
2. *"Too many possessions"*
C. *"Accompanying Jesus" with the women as a more empowering image*
D. *The Jesus I "follow" invites this "accompaniment"*
1. *He was not "patriarchal" but egalitarian*
2. *He invited women to join his "basileia"*
3. *He ministered to women and was ministered to by women*

IV. *"The Final Answer": The image of "accompaniment" provides me with a more sustaining model for my life, no less than for my ministry.*

While the outline generally follows the flow of the narrative, notice that by rendering the freewriting in outline form, the writer is encouraged to generalize her own experience and thus to give it a shape and structure more accessible to readers. At the same time, the outline invites her to extend and elaborate those points of the outline only touched upon in the freewriting exercise. In particular, she skillfully weaves in the "who is the Jesus whom you follow" question into her concluding sentence and includes it in the outline as a potential category, to be developed in more detail in succeeding drafts. Thus, constructing an outline from her freewriting allows her to tease out the potential of that initial draft at the same time that she is structuring it more coherently by means of the outline. So, knowing now more clearly what she wants to write, she should be ready to proceed with "writing that and only that":

> *THEOLOGICAL MEMO 6: To help you sift the wheat from the chaff in your freewriting draft, reread it and outline it, highlighting the "that and only that" which you want to focus on in your essay. When you are ready, rewrite your essay accordingly.*

Draft #2: "Writing That and Only That"

In this draft of the paper, the writer's task is to refocus the freewriting draft in terms of the outline that she has constructed and to provide a structuring frame for the essay with a beginning, a middle, and an end. For example:

> *Why do I follow Jesus? How do I follow Jesus? Who is the Jesus whom I follow? To answer the first question, I must answer each of these in turn.*
>
> *Why do I follow Jesus? I follow Jesus because I was born into a Christian, churchgoing family, through whom I came to experience Jesus Christ as my way to God. I follow Jesus because I have been lured by his life and his death to live*

my life differently. Flowing from that necessity, I follow Jesus in the conviction that he called me first to be a disciple, and now to leave my nets of surgical nursing and prepare for ministry as a hospital chaplain.

How do I follow Jesus? Although the verb "to follow" (Greek "akoloutheo") made radical claims on Jesus' original disciples, the verb "to accompany" provides me with a more radical, empowering image of discipleship today. This image came alive for me during my first CPE experience, when the chaplain supervising me noticed me following her diffidently into the oncology ward, looking more like an anxious relative than a chaplain-in-training. With an encouraging smile and a beckoning gesture, she invited me to walk with her, not behind her, to meet the patients as a co-chaplain sharing equally in ministry, not as an inferior member of the team.

Who is the Jesus whom I follow? Just as the women in Luke's gospel accompanied Jesus on the road, and provided for his needs out of their own resources (Luke 8:1–3), the Jesus whom I follow from hospital bed to hospital bed invites me to accompany him and to practice a ministry of accompaniment with those whom I serve. As I meet this Jesus in the gospels, he was not "patriarchal," but egalitarian. He invited all, including halt, lame, sinners, and women into his "basileia"; and he not only ministered to women but was ministered to by them. Thus the image of accompaniment is a more sustaining model than that of "following" for my life, no less than for my ministry. Prompted by my CPE supervisor's vibrant example, I cannot follow this Jesus without watching him beckon me to join him on the road, however joyful or difficult the journey.

Although this draft is still "in-progress," the writer has made some significant moves toward crafting a coherent essay by (1) defining, or more properly, "re-defining" the question, or topic; (2) discarding unnecessary material; (3) discerning a "form," or structure, for the remaining content; and (4) developing the essay in accordance with that structure into a coherent narrative with a beginning, a middle, and an end. Each of these operations comes vibrantly into play as she seeks in this draft of the essay "to write that and only that."

First, she has "followed" her own reflection on the original question to the image of "accompanying," which more clearly defines her own response to the question. In so doing, she has not merely "repeated" the assignment but has creatively engaged it from her own perspective. Second, she has discarded peripheral material in order to sharpen the contrast between "following" and "accompanying" Jesus. To do this, she has cut both unrelated personal reflections and extraneous biblical references in order to narrow and circumscribe her focus. Concomitantly, she has discerned three leading questions (Why do I follow Jesus? How do I follow Jesus? Who is the Jesus whom I follow?) implicit in the original question and has used them to introduce the essay, delineate a structure, and provide readers with an organizational "map" that they can follow from the beginning to the conclusion of the essay. While the reader might think this was the first move in her revision, this further refinement of the question came much later in the process.

Finally, she has developed each section of the essay more specifically in response to those three questions, in order to "say that and only that" which her response to the questions requires. Notice that she has added the story of her CPE experience that effectively evokes her own journey from a discipleship of "following" to one of "accompanying." No less effectively, her concluding paragraph now reconciles the Jesus whom she "follows" and the Jesus whom she "accompanies" through a retrieval of the egalitarian, non-patriarchal, "feminist" Jesus of the synoptic gospels, in juxtaposition with the exemplary ministerial model of her CPE supervisor.

Whether or not our writer of this pastoral reflection paper is aware of it, in this draft, she has not only written well, she has also begun to write theology well. When the novelist Flannery O'Connor wearied of critics asking her questions about her writing process, she imagined herself replying, "Ah jus writes."[26] In the same way, you may think that what has been described is "just" a writer's process of revision. But, if we look carefully at the paper that has resulted from the process of revision followed here, it is obvious that the author of this paper is doing more than "just writing." Like Thomas Merton, whose struggle to "write theology well" introduced this book,[27] she is "working out a theology as she goes," or more literally, as she writes.

First of all, in writing this pastoral reflection paper, she is engaging in that "dynamic process of reflection" which drives the writing of theological reflection and renders writing a theological act. Recalling the four movements of this process that we considered earlier,[28] we can see that she has (1) reflected on the question, "Why do you follow Jesus"; (2) related an answering experience with her CPE supervisor that illuminates the question; (3) correlated the experience and the emerging question with the synoptic gospels' portrait of the historical Jesus and the women who accompanied him; and (4) written her new theological insight, or "answer," that is engendered from this correlation: to follow Jesus is to accompany him as she too has been accompanied and to accompany those with whom she ministers empowered by that constructive theological model.

Second, and concomitantly, we have also been watching the writer's theological imagination at work in her engagement of the writing process. Before she wrote this pastoral reflection paper, she had not concretely imagined herself as one of the "women journeying with Jesus on the way," nor had she imagined that the Jesus she followed also accompanied her. Before she wrote this draft of the paper, she had not consciously imagined her CPE supervisor as a Jesus figure who mediated God's egalitarian grace to her. If she had not written this paper, she might never have correlated these images in such a way that her own model of doing theology and being a pastoral minister were given what Shakespeare called in *Midsummer Night's Dream* "a local habitation and a name." In short, in constructing this paper, she has also constructed an incipient theology of "accompaniment"[29] and has given it articulation in the personal voice of her own experience. If, in so doing, she has learned that to write theology well is both a writing process and a theological practice, this writing assignment will have served one of its intended purposes, even before she has written the final draft.

However admirably our writer has "worked out her theology as she goes," we are not yet finished with this paper! While the end result of this draft is a substantive pastoral reflection paper with a beginning, a middle, and an end, consider what still remains to be done "so that others will want to read it."

Draft #3: "Writing So That Others Will Want To Read It"

Although the writer now has a presentable essay that could be submitted to her professor without further ado, a final, polished, reader-centered draft frequently makes the difference between a B and an A paper. By "reader-centered" writing, I simply mean writing that effectively communicates with its audience without the author there to "fill in the gaps." As Plato's Socrates cautioned Phaedrus centuries ago, the written word is vulnerable to misreading and misunderstanding without its "parent," the author, physically there to "defend it." No matter how good the writing is, there will always be cognitive gaps between what the author has written and what the reader has understood. The writer's goal in this final draft is to fill in those gaps as conscientiously as possible by anticipating the audience's knowledge of the subject, conventional expectations, and response to the essay.

The gap in question might be preliminary information that the reader needs to understand the author's perspective; an incomplete introduction or conclusion; a missing transition between paragraphs; an undeveloped idea *in medias res* that one has not noticed before; a grammatically incorrect sentence that obscures the writer's thought; and a misspelled word, a missing punctuation mark, or a missing capital letter. For an audience of professors, a paper that is not proofread carefully may create a gap between an A and a B grade, just as a paper that is too short or too long creates a gap between what is required and what is delivered. Finally, a student's failure to observe the conventions of a particular style manual when citing footnotes or bibliography will also reveal a gap between the writer's credibility and his or her scholarly competence.[30] What is ultimately envisioned in this draft is a finely wrought, well-crafted essay that has something to say and says it as best that the writer can, for this assignment, for this particular audience, with this amount of time to work on it. Let us see how the writer of our pastoral reflection paper revised her draft "so that others would want to read it":

> *Why do I follow Jesus? How do I follow Jesus? Who is the Jesus whom I follow? To answer the first question, I must answer each of these. When I do, I discover that I follow Jesus in order to accompany him on the journey to which he has called me.*
>
> *Why do I follow Jesus? I initially followed Jesus because I was born into a Christian, churchgoing family, through whom I came to experience Jesus Christ as my way to God. I continue to follow Jesus because I have been lured by his life and his death to live my life differently. Flowing from that necessity, I follow Jesus in the conviction that he called me, like Simon Peter and Andrew, to be a disciple, and then to leave my "nets" of surgical nursing to prepare for ministry as a hospital chaplain.*
>
> *How do I follow Jesus? Although the verb "to follow" made radical claims on Jesus' original disciples, the verb "to accompany" provides me with a more radical image of discipleship today. This image empowered me during my first CPE experience, when the chaplain supervising me noticed me following timidly at her heels into the oncology ward. With one compelling, beckoning gesture, she invited me to walk with her, not behind her, to meet the patients confidently as a co-chaplain in ministry.*

Who is the Jesus whom I follow? Just as the women in Luke's gospel were "with" Jesus on the road (Luke 8:1–3), the Jesus whom I follow from hospital bed to hospital bed invites me to accompany him and to practice a ministry of accompaniment with those whom I serve. As I meet this Jesus in the gospels, he was not "patriarchal," but egalitarian. He invited all, including women into his "basileia," and he not only ministered to women but was ministered to by them. However, while the image of "accompanying" is more empowering for my life and for my ministry than that of "following," there is no ultimate contradiction between them. Mentored by my CPE supervisor's inspired pastoral example, I cannot follow this Jesus without watching him beckon me to join him on the road, however challenging or consoling the journey.

In her introduction to this draft, the writer has succinctly but suggestively answered the questions she poses in an informal thesis sentence. She has made strategic clarifications in each paragraph, including a penultimate concluding sentence that reinforces the rapprochement between "following" and "accompanying." Because the assignment requires a "one-page paper," she has done considerable cutting to get the essay down to size. She has revised word choices to strengthen essay coherence (e.g., "journey" vs. "mission"), and she may continue to fine-tune these until the essay is out of her hands. If she puts it away, "sleeps on it," and rereads it one more time, a still better paper may emerge. But, in writing three times, she has produced a thoughtful, readable, and presentable one-page pastoral reflection paper. Now it is your turn:

THEOLOGICAL MEMO 7: Please choose one of the following options: (a) reread the second draft of your pastoral reflection paper and when you have completed the draft, share it with an appropriate reader for final feedback before handing in the paper to your professor; (b) reread the second draft of the pastoral reflection paper ("Why do I follow Jesus") included here and write your version of a final draft "so that others would want to read it," noting what revisions you made and why you made them.

If you have accompanied our pastoral student on her writing journey and followed some of the suggestions that were useful to you, you have by now also written a thoughtful, readable, and presentable pastoral reflection paper. If you have time to put it away, sleep on it, and reread it one more time, I recommend the "Checklist for Reviewing, Revising and Refining Papers" below as a final step on your journey before presenting the paper to your professor. In the meantime, congratulate yourself on writing your first (or yet another) theological reflection paper in a personal voice.

Reviewing, revising, and refining papers: A theological writer's checklist

- ***Is it clear?*** *Or, according to Webster, "without clouds; free from mist, haze or dust." If you clear away the dust from your own understanding, your writing will be clear to your readers.*

- ***Is it concise?*** *If you have cut away all extraneous material, your writing will be both concise and more precise for your readers.*
- ***Is it coherent?*** *If your writing has a plan that is explained at the beginning and executed just as you have explained it, your writing will be coherent to your readers.*
- ***Is it considerate?*** *If you are considerate of your audience—remembering to whom you are writing; adapting your writing to the requirements of the assignment—your writing will more effectively communicate with your audience.*
- ***Is it correct?*** *If your writing has been carefully corrected for grammatical accuracy and flawless mechanics—e.g., spelling, punctuation, capitalization, paragraph indentation—your written work will have more credibility and authority.*

Concluding reflections: Writing theological reflection well

In this chapter, we have introduced the writing of theological reflection as a rhetorical process and a theological practice. First, we situated theological reflection broadly within a "correlation" model and proposed a "Reflecting on Paper" process and a "Problem-Solving" model for writing theological reflection well. Second, we identified two "generic" styles of theological reflection papers: the pastoral reflection paper, written in a personal voice and the systematic reflection paper, written in an academic voice. Third, we followed a student writer's progress from the first to final draft of a one-page pastoral reflection paper as she struggled to write theological reflection well and constructed a working theology as she wrote it. In conclusion, we revisited the completed pastoral reflection paper as a strategic example of the dynamic interplay between learning to write theology and writing to learn theology. However, writing pastoral reflection in a personal voice will not provide you with all the tools you need to write theological reflection well. What if you must reflect on a theological question, formulate a thesis statement, or claim, in response, and write a paper that substantiates your claim? In Chapter 3, we explore the writing of the systematic reflection paper in an academic voice, or "Writing Theological Argument Well."

Notes

1 See David Tracy, *Blessed Rage for Order: The New Pluralism in Theology* (New York: Seabury Press, 1975); Patricia O'Connell Killen and John deBeer, *The Art of Theological Reflection* (New York: Crossroad, 1994); James D. Whitehead and Evelyn E. Whitehead, *Method in Ministry: Theological Reflection and Christian Ministry*, rev. ed. (Kansas City, MO: Sheed & Ward, 1995).

2 See, e.g., Jeffrey H. Mahan, B. Troxell and C. Allen, *Shared Wisdom: A Guide to Case Study Reflection in Ministry* (Nashville, TN: Abingdon Press, 1993); Robert L.

Kinast, *Let Ministry Teach: A Guide to Theological Reflection* (Collegeville, MN: Liturgical Press, 1996), 23–41.

3 See, e.g., George Lindbeck, *The Nature of Doctrine: Religion and Theology in a Postliberal Age* (Philadelphia, PA: Westminster Press, 1984); William C. Placher, *Unapologetic Theology: A Christian Voice in a Pluralistic Conversation* (Louisville, KY: Westminster/John Knox Press, 1989), 123–37.

4 4 See, e.g., Susan Brooks Thistlethwaite and M.P. Engel, *Lift Every Voice: Constructing Christian Theologies from the Underside* (Maryknoll, NY: Orbis, 2000); Sheryl A. Kujawa-Holbrook, "Beyond Diversity: Cultural Competence, White Racism Awareness and European-American Theology Students," *Teaching Theology and Religion* 5 (2002): 141–48.

5 See Kinast, *Let Ministry Teach*, xi–xii.

6 See, e.g., Roger Haight, "Women in the Church: A Theological Reflection," *Toronto Journal of Theology* 2/1 (1986): 105–17.

7 See, e.g., Thomas H. Groome, *Sharing Faith: A Comprehensive Approach to Religious Education and Pastoral Ministry* (San Francisco: Harper and Row, 1991).

8 See, e.g., Joe Holland, "Linking Social Analysis and Theological Reflection: The Place of Root Metaphors in Social and Religious Experience," in *Tracing the Spirit: Communities, Social Action, and Theological Reflection*, ed. James E. Hug, (New York: Paulist Press, 1983): 170–91.

9 See, e.g., Joe Gross, "A Model for Theological Reflection in Clinical Pastoral Education," *The Journal of Pastoral Care* 48 (1994): 131–34.

10 Two books have appeared since publication of the first edition of *Writing Theology Well* that extend the methodological conversation and provide useful typologies for the writing of theological reflection in a postmodern theological context. See Elaine Graham, Heather Walton, and Frances Ward, *Theological Reflection: Methods* (London: SCM Press, 2005), esp. pp. 13–14; Heather Walton, *Writing Methods in Theological Reflection* (London, SCM Press, 2014).

11 See Chapter 1, "What Is Theology and Why Do Theologians Write It?"

12 For a more comprehensive introduction to "Writing with Theological Imagination Well," see Chapter 9, which explores the relationship of the theological imagination to the writing of theology.

13 See David Tracy's analysis of the three "publics" of the theologian discussed in Chapter 1, "To Whom and for Whom Is Contemporary Theology Being Written?"

14 Killen and deBeer, *Art of Theological Reflection*, 9.

15 Ibid, 68–69. I have introduced this process and subsequent examples of writing theological reflection in Lucretia B. Yaghjian, "Teaching Theological Reflection Well, Reflecting on Writing as a Theological Practice," *Teaching Theology and Religion* 7/2 (2004): 83–94. Some of the material in that article will inevitably be repeated in this chapter.

16 See also Robert L. Kinast, "A Process Model of Theological Reflection," *The Journal of Pastoral Care* 37, no. 2 (1983): 144.

17 Haight, "Women in the Church," 106.

18 Ibid, 106, 112–13, 115.

19 Kathleen Norris, *Amazing Grace: A Vocabulary of Faith* (New York: Riverhead Books, 1998), 181.

20 Flannery O'Connor, *Mystery and Manners: Occasional Prose*, ed. Sally Fitzgerald (New York: Farrar, Strauss and Giroux, 1969), 150.

21 For a more comprehensive treatment of style and voice in theological writing, see Chapter 10, "Rewriting Theology Well (I): Rhetorics of Style and Voice."

22 To my knowledge, this dictum remains unwritten but has been handed down through the oral tradition of Pelikan's students. I am indebted to retired Professor Jerome H. Neyrey, S.J., University of Notre Dame, for introducing me to Pelikan's method.

23 Donald Murray, "Write Before Writing," in *The Essential Don Murray: Lessons from America's Greatest Writing Teacher*, ed. Thomas Newkirk and Lisa C. Miller (Portsmouth, NH: Boynton/Cook Publishers, 2009), 28–38.

24 Linda Pastan, "Getting Down to Work," in *The Five Stages of Grief* (New York: W.W. Norton, 1976), 56.

25 See Natalie Goldberg, *Writing Down the Bones: Freeing the Writer Within* (Boston: Shambala, 1986), for an introduction to freewriting as a "writing practice." See also Peter Elbow, "Freewriting and the Problem of Wheat and Tares," in Peter Elbow, *Everyone Can Write: Essays Toward a Hopeful Theory of Writing and Teaching Writing* (New York: Oxford University Press, 2000), 85–92.

26 Flannery O'Connor, Letter to Maryat Lee, February 24, 1987, in O'Connor, *The Habit of Being: Letters of Flannery O'Connor*, ed. Sally Fitzgerald (New York: Farrar, Strauss & Giroux, 1979), 205.

27 See "Preface to the First Edition," above.

28 See "A Rhetoric of Process," above.

29 See, e.g., Roberto Goizueta, *Caminemos con Jesus: Toward a Hispanic/Latino Theology of Accompaniment* (Maryknoll, NY: Orbis Books, 2003).

30 See Chapter 6, "Writing Theological Research Well (II): Rhetorics of Organization and Documentation."

3

Writing Theological Argument Well: Rhetorics of Inquiry, Reading, Reflection, and Persuasion

The art of writing well is the art of making up one's mind. It is the art of establishing clarity where there was confusion, of working out one's conclusions and commitments.
—HANS GUTH, *Words and Ideas*

Christian theology is best understood as "persuasive argument."
—DAVID CUNNINGHAM, *Faithful Persuasion*

The most basic requirement for an academic paper is that it make one claim and argue for it.
—NANCEY C. MURPHY, *Reasoning and Rhetoric in Religion*

Starting points

When theologian Nancey C. Murphy writes, "The most basic requirement for an academic paper is that it make one claim and argue for it," she provides a link between writing a pastoral reflection paper in a personal voice and writing a systematic reflection paper in an academic voice.[1] To write in an academic voice, you must "make a claim and argue for it." The act of theological reflection, however, is integral to the articulation of a theological claim. Thus, writing theological reflection in an academic voice entails writing theological argument well, and the term systematic *reflection paper* describes a paper that integrates that reflective process with the rhetorics of argument, which we explore in this chapter as inquiry, reading, reflection, and persuasion. Yet, the basic tools of theological argument—making a claim, supporting the claim with evidence, and showing that the connection between the claim and the evidence is warranted—are already at work in the pastoral reflection paper that concluded the last chapter.

If you take another look at that paper, you will see that its writer also "made a claim and argued for it" in response to a generating question, although in a personal voice. In answer to the question, "Why do you follow Jesus," she wrote, "I follow Jesus in order to accompany him on the journey to which he has called me." That is her *claim*. The rest of the essay explains, elaborates upon, and exemplifies that initial "claim," as it weaves the three threads that she follows from the original question through the correlative looms of her own experience and of the Christian tradition. All of these threads coalesce in her concluding portrait of the historical Jesus, his women followers from the synoptic gospels, and her CPE supervisor's corroborating model of pastoral ministry. Even though the essay is written in a personal, narrative style, it presents a *claim*; it supports that claim with relevant *grounds* or evidence; it is backed by *warrants* or assumptions that are taken for granted by her readers regarding the authority of the writer's experience and the authority of the Christian tradition; and it makes inferences from the evidence that draw the threads of the essay into a clear and credible conclusion.[2] The theological memo that follows invites you to look for a similar argumentative structure in one of your own pastoral reflection papers:

> *THEOLOGICAL MEMO 1: Look again at the pastoral reflection you wrote in response to the invitation in* Chapter 2, *or choose a "personal" reflection paper you have written for another course. Can you discern an argumentative structure in the paper? If so, please identify (1) your claim; (2) the evidence for your claim; and (3) the warrants implicit in your argument (e.g., the unstated but presupposed premises connecting the claim and its evidence). How does the argumentative style of your paper differ from that of a more "academic" theological article?*

We will return to this basic argumentative structure at the conclusion of this chapter in the writing of a one-page systematic reflection paper. Yet, in order to "make a claim and argue for it" in a cogently written paper, one must first "make up one's mind" about what is to be claimed, and this entails a process, no less than writing the pastoral reflection paper did. Thus, in this chapter, we approach writing theological argument well as an invitation to: (1) make up your mind in regard to a presenting question; (2) write what is on your mind, employing the academic voice of theological argument; and (3) keep your audience in mind as you rewrite and revise in conversation with their questions, counterclaims, and clarifications. We will elucidate the steps of this process as we proceed. First, I invite you to imagine theological argument not merely as the logical conclusion of a coherently argued essay, but as the ongoing process of inquiry, reading, reflection, and persuasion that gets you there, and to approach "theological argument" as a rhetorical genre answerable to your subject, purpose, and audience.[3]

We proceed by considering three questions: (1) What is the genre of argument and why do people write it? (2) What is theological argument and how do theologians write it? (3) What are the *rhetorics*, or elements of writing theological argument in an academic voice, that will enable us to write a systematic reflection paper?[4]

What is the genre of argument and why do people write it?

When Humpty Dumpty, our wordsmith-in-residence, says to Alice, "There's a nice knock-down *argument* for you,"[5] he is using the word *argument* to describe a quarrel or conflict. Yet, as a rhetorical genre, argument denotes a rational discourse intended to avert or mediate conflicts, not to incite them. What connects these two understandings in our contemporary understanding of argument?

As defined in this book, argument is a means of persuasion that people use when addressing an audience that may or may not accept their claims at face value. Your freshman composition textbook might have distinguished the writing of "argument" from that of "persuasion," identifying the first with "logic" and the second with "rhetoric." On the other hand, a contemporary freshman English text proposes that "everything's an argument," suggesting that "an argument can be any text—whether written, spoken, or visual that expresses a point of view."[6] We will concentrate on written argument in this chapter, construing argument rhetorically, as one of the "available means of persuasion" cited by Aristotle in his *Rhetoric*, not as a separate genre.[7] Some audiences, including many theological professors for whom you are writing, will be more readily persuaded through a logical process of deduction that proceeds systematically from premises to conclusions. Other audiences, including the parishioners you preach to on Sunday, may be more persuaded by an inductive argument from experience that integrates logic and rhetoric. In practice, much argumentative writing requires a practical integration of both of these, even if one mode of persuasion predominates in a particular assignment. We will examine these different styles of persuasive argument as we proceed, but first, we consider what they have in common.

The word *argument* comes from the Latin *arguo*, whose first meaning is "to make clear." When you argue a claim in speech or in writing, you have to make clear what you are arguing, why you are arguing, what evidence there is for your claim, and what inferences can legitimately be made from that evidence. To paraphrase Aristotle, a good argument must first "state" its claim and then "demonstrate" or prove it.[8] In classical rhetoric, the genre of argument provided the rhetor/speaker with a clear and well-defined path that connected the thesis statement, or "claim," of the speech with its "proof," and it was this same path that he or she cleared for the auditor/reader in the course of the speech or essay. When the path "led away" (*de-ducere*) from the main point of the speech to the evidence or "proof," it was called "deductive." When the path "led into" (*in-ducere*) or through the evidence to the main point of the speech, it was called "inductive." Because these paths continue to describe the predominant forms of spoken and written argument today, we will look at each of them more closely before proceeding to write a theological argument ourselves.[9]

The deductive path

The starting point of the deductive path is a general statement, or premise, whose truth would be accepted by "all rational persons." Those who travel this path proceed from the assumption of "common ground" and are guided by a logical map that ensures that if each of a series of related premises derived from logical inferences is true, their conclusions will also be true. In its categorical form, consisting of a major premise, a minor premise, and a conclusion, this map is called a *syllogism*. In its rhetorical form, in which one premise of the syllogism is considered obvious enough to the audience to be unstated, it is called an *enthymeme*.[10] In both forms, the path follows a "deductive" logical progression in which the operative formula is "statement plus proof." For example:

	SYLLOGISM	ENTHYMEME
Major premise:	*All teachers have students.*	[premise is presupposed]
Minor premise:	*Miss Brooks is a teacher.*	*Miss Brooks is a teacher.*
Conclusion:	*Therefore, Miss Brooks has students.*	*Miss Brooks has students.*

Syllogistic reasoning provides a common language of argument for those trained in formal logic and the mathematical sciences, and it is a useful tool for evaluating the soundness of any deductive argument that you are reading or writing. For example, the argument proposed by Martin Luther King in "Letter from a Birmingham Jail" justifying disobedience of segregation laws can be written as a syllogism:

Major premise: *All unjust laws are laws that one has no moral responsibility to obey.*
Minor premise: *All segregation laws are unjust laws.*
Conclusion: *All segregation laws are laws that one has no moral responsibility to obey.*[11]

However, in disciplines like theology in which basic premises are presupposed because they cannot be proven, enthymematic reasoning, or deductive reasoning in which a knowledgeable audience is expected to supply the missing premise, is much more common. Because the Toulmin "claim/grounds/warrant" model follows the basic structure of deductive argument and provides for those missing premises in the form of "warrants" that are taken for granted by particular audiences, we can correlate its terminology and structure with that of traditional deductive argument:[12]

Toulmin Model		*Traditional Deductive Argument*
CLAIM	the main point or *thesis* of the essay	CONCLUSION
GROUNDS	evidence or support for the *thesis*	MINOR PREMISE
WARRANTS	written or unwritten premises connecting *claim* and *grounds*	MAJOR PREMISE

Notice first of all that the "claim" of the Toulmin model corresponds to the "conclusion" of the deductive syllogism; the "grounds" are analogous to the "minor premise"; and the "warrants" can be correlated with the "major premise." Thus, the structure of formal deduction is reversed in the Toulmin model, and the written argument begins with its "claim." Since academic argument typically follows this "state the thesis and then prove it" structure, this model provides a helpful starting point for "writing in an academic voice," and we will use it for that purpose presently.[13]

The inductive path

To paraphrase Aristotle, "All [speakers and writers] produce logical persuasion by means of paradigms [examples] or enthymemes and by nothing other than these."[14]

The starting point of the inductive path is a particular question, fact, experience, or observation from which one arrives at a general conclusion by means of credible examples, plausible generalizations on the basis of those examples, and, to a greater or lesser degree, an "inductive leap." Although the final draft of the pastoral reflection paper that we wrote in the last chapter was patterned deductively, it was generated inductively, with the telling pastoral "example" of the supervising chaplain's accompaniment at the center of the argument. Because those on this path begin with individual observation and particular "examples," they cannot presume common ground. The goal, however, is to establish it by means of initially unrelated "examples" that are related plausibly by the observer.

For example:
Is the woman sitting next to me on the train a teacher?
She is wearing horn-rimmed glasses.
She has a stack of papers on her lap.
She is reading them.
She is marking them with a red pencil.
Teachers often wear glasses because they read so much.
Teachers have to read and grade their students' papers.
Teachers typically mark their students' papers with a red pencil.
I conclude that the woman sitting next to me on the train is a teacher.

While you might have made the same assumptions if a woman wearing horn-rimmed glasses and marking papers were sitting next to you on the train, you probably also recognize that the inductively derived conclusion that the woman is a teacher cannot be proved valid in the way that a deductive argument can be proved valid. Just as beads remain individual beads until they are strung into a necklace, there is no necessary connection between the individual observations and the observer's conclusion beyond the particular way he or she strings the evidence into a plausible but not infallible hypothesis. The woman may be a proofreader or an editor; she may be a writer correcting her own work; she may be a teacher's assistant grading papers for a teacher. The only way we can know for sure is to start a conversation and ask her, "I notice that you are wearing horn-rimmed glasses and marking papers with a red pencil. Are you a teacher, by any chance?" Even then, she might not tell the truth!

Nonetheless, we live, as we write, inductively, from thought, observation, and experience to generalization and back again. Even a written argument that proceeds deductively has its inception in a process of induction, since that process is essentially the process of generalizing from particulars, and producing new premises that we may choose to organize deductively or inductively into a constructive argument, depending on the writing task, the requirements of the audience, and the purpose of the argument. For example, while we have sampled the deductive logic implicit in Martin Luther King's "Letter from a Birmingham Jail," its essay structure is strategically inductive, in that it leads his audience of critical Birmingham clergy gently but firmly toward his justification for civil disobedience by responding to a series of questions, rather than beginning with an incontrovertible answer that might alienate readers instead of leading them toward an acknowledgment of common ground.

In summary, the deductive path proceeds from common ground, or shared assumptions, and argues from general premises to conclusions that can be proved valid by means of generally accepted rules of argument. Its classic idiom is that of formal logic. The inductive path argues from empirical particulars to plausible conclusions through a process of generalization that, ideally, arrives at common ground with the conclusion of the argument. Its classic idiom is the scientific method. Without induction, we would have no generalizations on which to base deductive reasoning, and hence no way of generating new knowledge. Without deduction, we would have no process for applying those generalizations to particular issues, cases, or problems. While contemporary forms of deduction and induction are more various and less mutually exclusive of each other, both are used in writing theology, as we shall see as we proceed to the next question, "What is theological argument and why do theologians write it?"

What is theological argument and why do theologians write it?

If "theology is a language used by a specific group of people to make sense of their world," as Rowan Williams again reminds us, theological argument is another, more formal dialect of theological conversation used by that group of people. When I speak informally with my friends, most of the time I can converse colloquially without proving every assertion or qualifying every statement that I make. My friends and I share a common understanding of the way the world works, and when our conversation is grounded in that understanding, much can be taken for granted. But, when my friends have different perspectives on particular issues that diverge from our common understanding of how the world works, then my informal and colloquial language is inadequate to the conversation. At this point, I must more formally rehearse all of the dance steps of my argument, step by step by step, in hopes that my conversation partners will recognize the dance, begin to dance with me, and perhaps teach me a few new steps of their own.

Writing theological argument, then, is nothing more than writing theological reflection in a more formal language that obliges me to show my readers all my dance steps, from the opening "do-se-do" to the concluding bow. Just as the steps of the dance will be different for a square dance than from a tango, the steps of a theological argument will differ, depending upon the logical path that is chosen. But, whether one chooses the inductive or deductive path, as Owen Thomas writes, "Theology does not consist simply of assertions or propositions. It involves the giving of reasons, evidence, grounds, or proof for statements. Theology involves argument for its assertions by offering some kind of basis for accepting them over against alternative assertions."[15] This "giving of reasons" is necessary because, as Dorothea Soelle writes, faith must "struggle for the clarity of its cause."[16] This is another way of saying with Roger Haight that "All theology today must be apologetic" or committed to rendering Christian faith coherent and credible for particular audiences.[17]

Examining the different kinds of arguments theologians employ for different audiences, David Tracy distinguishes "formal arguments," or deductive arguments, from "rhetorical arguments," or "topical," contextual, and typically inductive arguments. Noting that systematic theologians more frequently employ formal arguments, while theologians writing from standpoints of "resistance" favor rhetorical arguments, he concludes that contemporary theologians need both of these to write theology well.[18]

Feminist theologian Rebecca Chopp and other theologians writing from standpoints of "resistance" prefer the term "rhetoric" to that of "argument," however, because traditional deductive argument, directed toward "all rational persons," does not take diversity or ideological difference sufficiently into account. As Chopp suggests, "When pluralism is acknowledged and sure foundations cease to be sought after, rhetoric emerges as the way of deliberation."[19] Don Compier also points out that a theology of resistance inevitably "takes sides, so a polemical stance cannot be avoided"[20] by the writer. While some theologians continue to identify "argument" with dispassionate reason and "persuasion" or "rhetoric" with impassioned polemic, most theological writing, including that of the theologians quoted above, necessarily employs both. As David Cunningham asserts, this is as it should be, since "audiences judge not on the basis of deduction alone, nor even on the basis of deduction accompanied by induction, but, rather, according to their ability to synthesize diverse information and to infer a conclusion from a wide range of argumentative premises."[21] For our purposes, then, Cunningham's definition of Christian theology as "persuasive argument" that embraces both "formal" and "rhetorical" styles in its task of "faithful persuasion"[22] provides a more inclusive standpoint for learning to write theological argument well. From that standpoint, we proceed to examine the "rhetorics" of theological argument: inquiry, reading, reflection, and persuasion.

The rhetorics of theological argument: Inquiry, reading, reflection, and persuasion

We defined rhetoric in Chapter 1 as "the art of purposeful communication." When I speak of "rhetorics" here, I refer to constitutive elements of that "purposeful communication" which energize a particular rhetorical genre. Look, for example, at the way in which inquiry, reading, reflection, and persuasion energize the writing of theological argument.

Inquiry

"In any inquiry, argument is often needed," David Tracy writes.[23] Yet, in any argument, inquiry is always needed! Even when the question that engenders a theological argument is not visible to the naked eye of the reader, all argumentation begins with inquiry or questioning. The basic requirement for an academic paper "that makes one claim and argues for it" is that it unfolds from a question that requires an answer. Was Jesus a feminist? Should the church recognize same-sex marriages? Can euthanasia be morally justified? To write a paper that makes a claim in response to these issues, I must first ask the question, for "only a person who has questions can have knowledge."[24] Without questions that challenge me to search for answers, there is nothing about which to "make up my mind." "Argumentation," concludes James Crosswhite, "is a good way to inquire, to move into new selves, new modes of selfhood, new ways of being in and understanding the world,"[25] and this kind of inquiry naturally leads us to the next "rhetoric" of theological argument, that of "Reading."

Reading

Writing theological argument well does not happen in a vacuum. At its best, it flows from a context of inquiry that is pursued in conversation with other texts. In the initial stages of an inquiry, the theological writer might consult relevant texts for information regarding a particular issue or question introduced in a written assignment. More often, perhaps, the texts to be consulted are assigned by the professor. In either case, those texts become the "documents in the case" that propel the inquiry and provide support, qualification, or disconfirmation for a claim. However, theology is not "easy reading," and it does not yield its treasures readily to the casual or careless reader. In order, then, to write theological argument well, it is necessary to read theological argument well.[26] To read theological argument well, I recommend the "Read Three Times" method, which is outlined in "Theological Memo 2," below:

THEOLOGICAL MEMO 2: Among your reading assignments for the next week, choose one biblical or theological article or book chapter to read according to the "Read Three Times" method. You will need a marking or highlighting pen, a yellow-lined pad, notebook, or computer (for taking notes on the reading) and a package of 3 × 5 cards.

(1) ***Reading the first time to summarize:*** *The goal of reading the first time is to read for a general sense of what the author says, by (a) reading the introduction and conclusion first to identify the main thesis of the article, and (b) proceeding to read the rest of the article in the light of that thesis. Do not hesitate to make your own annotations of the article as you read, paying attention to unfamiliar terms, questions to be pursued later, passages you wish to return to. The thrust of this reading, however, is to get a holistic view of the author's argument, and to be able to accurately report to someone else what the thesis of the essay is in a summary statement of two or three sentences that will fit on one side of a 3 × 5 card. When you have written your own summary statement, you are ready to read the article a second time.*

(2) ***Reading the second time to categorize:*** *The goal of reading the second time is to read the text more specifically in terms of your own inquiry or paper topic. In the first reading, you concentrated on the author's agenda. In this reading, you bring your own agenda to the author's text and ask what you need to know to make a claim, to gather evidence for your claim, or to answer a substantive essay question. Depending upon the nature of the assignment for which you are reading, you may or may not take extended notes at this point. However, if you*

can "categorize" the answers you find in the text in terms of the questions you are asking, or according to the points in your essay outline, or in some other logical format that includes passages and page references as well, you will find it much easier to utilize the material when you are ready to write. When you have categorized your "answers" on separate 3 × 5 cards or according to your own system, you are ready to read a third time.

(3) ***Reading the third time to criticize:*** *The goal of reading the third time is to read your author critically from the vantage point of your own project, so that you can respond critically in your own writing. This will entail bringing all of the information you now have from the two previous readings to bear upon your judgment of the text, in the light of your own developing "claim" or "thesis." Some questions to ask are: (a) Does the author's thesis stand after multiple readings? (b) How does the author's theological method (or method of biblical interpretation) inform or otherwise influence his or her argument? (c) Can you identify and follow the steps of the argument? (d) Are there biases or gaps in the argument that weaken its credibility? (e) Has the author provided plausible evidence and/or examples to support the argument? (f) If the author's thesis opposes your own, how would you answer its objections? If you can write a concluding critical response to the article on the opposite side of your first 3 × 5 card, you have already engaged in the rhetoric of "reflection," to which we now turn.*

Reflection

A good theological argument, like the theology that engenders it, is "the fruit of a dynamic process of reflection."[27] We have already seen how variously "reflection" is interpreted across the theological curriculum, and this diversity of usage can be confusing. As an active element in the writing of theological argument, however, reflection is the process of thinking theologically in dialogue with experience. As Schubert Ogden explains, "Reflection is, or should be, present to the highest degree in theological understanding," by which he means that "theology ought to exhibit at least some of the formal marks of any 'science,' including *the methodical pursuit of its questions and the formulation of its answers in a precise conceptuality*."[28] Might we not call this process more simply the practice of theological argument?

However, just as theological reflection is distinguished from other kinds of theological discourse by its attention to experience, the writing of theological argument does not spring from theologians' heads in pure, disembodied syllogisms (or if it does, most of us would rather not read it). "Insofar as the conclusion of any theological argument ... is itself theological," Roger Haight explains, "it cannot be decided on the basis of objective reason alone. Theology always unfolds within the context of ... engaged participatory experience and knowledge."[29] For example, if I am asked to write a one-page systematic reflection paper in answer to the question, Was Jesus a feminist?, to what extent will my gender, my faith experience of Jesus, my interpretation of the synoptic gospels' portrait of him, my construal of what it means to be a "feminist," and my own experience of feminism or feminists influence my response to the question? If "theology always unfolds within the context of engaged participatory experience and knowledge," then my argument that Jesus is or is not a feminist will be informed by that experiential context, whether or not I choose to make that experience explicit in my argument.

To "reflect" theologically is to consider the questions; to sift through the data and evidence that move one toward "answers"; to weigh alternatives and imagine outcomes; to apply tools of intuition and critical reason, imagination and experience, analysis and synthesis, and clarity of thinking and writing to the task of constructing a theological argument. Whether your argument is deductive or inductive or a combination of both, the goal of the reflection process is a "claim" or thesis statement that clearly and cogently expresses "what is on your mind."

To facilitate this process, you may "reflect on paper" in a personal or analytical journal; you may engage in group reflection with classmates or interested friends; or you may find that "...the truth depends upon a walk around the lake," and follow your train of thought to the nearest one "to watch a definition growing certain and [to] wait within that certainty."[30] However you engage it, this process of reflection is integral to the process of making up our minds and organizing our thoughts so that we can write what is on our minds in a coherent and compelling theological argument.

Persuasion

A good written argument is persuasive and is intended to be so. While the notion of "persuasion" has negative connotations for some writers and theologians, most would not make an argument if they were not persuaded of its truth, validity, or significance. Indeed, if I am not "persuaded" by the argument I am proposing, it is doubtful that my readers will be. Understood in this way, persuasion might be defined as the logic and the lure of an argument, which unfold as the writer "lures" the reader to accompany her through the "logic" of the argument, step by step, from introduction to conclusion.

As every good fisherman knows, there are different "lures" for different fish. Aristotle defined three of these "lures" in the rhetorician's bait box as *ethos*, or the speaker/writer's character; *pathos*, or the speech/essay's appeal to the emotions of the hearer/readers; and *logos*, or the logic of the arguments deployed in the spoken or written "word." When you are preaching a sermon, there will appropriately be an equal reliance on all three of these "lures." When you are writing a theological argument, the emphasis will be upon logos, or logic, as a persuasive tool. If we understand logic simply as "patterns for ordering the statements of your message clearly and persuasively,"[31] we will discover that for most audiences, the "logic" of the argument is its "lure," whether one follows the deductive path, the inductive path, or a combination of both. When Martin Luther King wrote his "Letter from a Birmingham Jail" to the pastors of Birmingham, Alabama, he used logic as strategically in that essay as the academic theologians whom he quoted did. Even if it is not your goal in life to be an academic theologian, if you clear a logical path in every paper that you write, and make clear which path you are on, your writing will be that much more persuasive to your audience.

To summarize, an argument that develops from genuine inquiry is not an a priori assertion of a given position, but a process of (1) discovering what you really think through research, reading, and reflection that is logically coherent and congruent with experience; (2) deducing an arguable claim, or thesis, from that thinking; and (3) reproducing the steps that you followed in this process so that your readers can also follow the logic and lure of your argument, which I have defined here as persuasion. Written argument includes all of these strategies. But, how are these strategies specifically employed in writing a theological argument in an academic voice? To write theological argument is to assert a theological claim to which you are committed. To write in an academic voice is to make a claim that you argue formally (using the conventions of deductive or inductive argument) for an academic audience. In the final section of this chapter, we shall write theological argument in an academic voice by writing a one-page systematic reflection paper in answer to another question: Was Jesus a Feminist? Before we do that, we look at four prerequisites of writing theological argument in an academic voice: (1) taking a position, (2) defining premises and vocabulary, (3) mapping the argument, and (4) entering the conversation.

Prerequisites of writing theological argument in an academic voice

Taking a position

We have seen that the scholarly convention of argument—that is, "making a claim" and arguing for it in a reasonable, informed manner by stating the claim clearly, qualifying it appropriately, defending it with supporting evidence, and countering opposing claims reasonably and with respect for one's conversation partners—informs all academic writing, and the academic discipline of theology is no exception. To write in this voice, however, you must become comfortable with developing a claim or "thesis statement" that translates "what is on your mind" into a theological position that you can propose, explain, elucidate, or defend in a sustained and systematic argument. One of the most useful means of developing this skill is writing the theological position paper or, as I call it in this book, the systematic reflection paper. Because theological reflection is integral to the articulation of a theological position, I find the term, "systematic reflection paper," more evocative of the reflective process inherent in writing theological argument well.[32] If, upon your perusal, the style of this paper should bear a suspicious resemblance to the classic five-paragraph essay that was the weekly torture of your worst high school English teacher, Miss Grundy, I urge you to give it another chance. We will begin by developing a thesis statement:[33]

THEOLOGICAL MEMO 3: Developing a Theological Thesis Statement: This step-by-step process will not replace the hard work of thinking through the questions you want to ask and the answer that your claim/thesis seeks to argue; what it will do is invite you to WRITE as you do that work. Choose a paper assignment that requires you to make a claim that you develop into a thesis statement. I suggest that you do the exercise after you have completed the reading for your paper, as outlined in Theological Memo 2, and roughly formulated your question (if the assignment has not already given you the question). At the very least, you will get something on paper as you do this, and at best, you will have a working thesis statement or paragraph to build upon as you continue writing the paper.

1. *Write the general topic of your thesis/claim in no more than ten words.*
2. *Write a minimum of three sentences, each one a possible thesis sentence stating the basic point you would like to make in developing your topic into a thesis/claim.*
3. *Choose the <u>one</u> sentence of the three that says what you want to say the most clearly and effectively. Write that sentence again and then write (for yourself) a brief explanation of why it has more potential as a "thesis sentence" than the other two.*
4. *Write a minimum of five connected statements that develop, tie in with, and support the thesis sentence you have chosen.*
5. *Choose three of those sentences, the three with the "strongest" potential, and determine the most effective sequence in which they could appear in the thesis statement, following the thesis sentence.*
6. *Write out the completed thesis statement, and let it sit overnight.*
7. *When you read it again in the morning, notice what has happened to it. Does it still sound good to you? Does it need to be "punched down," like dough, and revised? Is anything missing that needs to be explicitly stated? Does every word work for you, or do some seem inert, imprecise, or extraneous?*
8. *Make any necessary revisions and reread it. If your thesis statement provides a clearly developed claim in response to the question that generated it, you have begun to write a systematic reflection paper!*

Stating premises and defining vocabulary

However compelling the thesis or "claim" of an essay is, it will lose credibility if necessary premises and vocabulary are not stated and defined, respectively, at the outset. In a critique of a scholarly article sent to her by a friend who had asked for her feedback, Flannery O'Connor wrote, "You probably wrote this four page paper in half an hour. But it is going to take a lot longer to get it right." To get it right, she continued, "…you got to be specific; one thing following from another, and every detail down there; also everything has to be defined."[34] While O'Connor was harder on her friend's writing than most of your professors will be on your first theological paper, her prerequisites for scholarly writing, if taken seriously, will make your theological writing tasks easier. In particular, by defining the terms and premises of your argument briefly but clearly at the beginning of your paper, you will both narrow the gaze of your essay and provide common lenses through which readers can decipher your theological vocabulary. Leaving the definition of premises aside until we tackle the one-page paper, let us turn our attention to formulating meaningful definitions.

Should the task of defining theological terms seem daunting, remember, first, that your goal is not to produce the "definitive" definition of Christology, feminism, or spiritual direction, but to clarify your own use of those terms in your paper. To achieve that goal, you may choose to use a definition from your course readings that you are following in your own argument, or you may begin with an established definition of a term that you then render more simply in your own words. Whichever choice you make, a good definition typically places the term you are defining in a larger class and then sums up its defining features. For example, "Christology is a subdiscipline of theology; it is the study and discussion of Jesus Christ, or Jesus as the Christ."[35] If the definition is too complicated, it will not be useful. If it simply repeats the term that it is supposed to be defining, it will be irrelevant. If it violates the conventional usage of the term without explaining why, it will not be credible. However, if the definition clearly and succinctly tells readers what you mean when you are using the term in question, it will lay the groundwork for your ensuing argument.

> *THEOLOGICAL MEMO 4: Defining Premises and Vocabulary: Take another look at the thesis statement/paragraph that you wrote for Theological Memo 3. Have you used any theological language that should be defined for this paper and this audience? Using the thesis paragraph that follows as a rough model for your own, revise your thesis paragraph as needed to provide necessary definitions of premises and vocabulary.*
>
> Some have called Martin Luther King America's greatest public theologian. Others have called him America's most eloquent preacher. Still others have called him America's greatest civil rights leader. In this essay, I argue that the vocation that most adequately embraces each of these as they culminated in King's leadership of the Southern Christian Leadership Conference is that of "prophet." Although the word "prophet" can be defined in various ways, I use it here, as I believe King did, to refer to one who has a dream that impels that person to listen, to pray, to speak, to write, to act, and—if necessary—to die on behalf of that dream.

Mapping the argument

Just as one swallow does not make a summer, a thesis statement by itself, however carefully defined, does not make a systematic reflection paper. When you write in an academic voice, the term *argument* refers not only to the "what" of your argument but also to the "how," or the means by which you make your case. In other words, argument implies not merely the claim with which you begin your paper, or the subsequent assertions that you make in the course of the paper, but it is constituted by the unfolding rhetorical structure through which the argument is *developed* from the first sentence of the paper to its conclusion. Considered in this way, the paper itself is the "argument" proposed within it, and to write an argument is to propose that argument, paragraph by paragraph, in a coherent paper, whether you are writing a one-page systematic reflection paper or a fifty-page master's thesis. We look below at deductive and inductive patterns for writing a theological argument in five paragraphs:

WRITING A DEDUCTIVE ARGUMENT

I. "Thesis" paragraph:
States thesis and "tells readers what you are going to tell them":
  A. Introduces general topic in a brief but compelling sentence
  B. Narrows to "claim" or "thesis statement" that is outlined in a
  C. Three-pronged topic sentence supported by paragraphs below.

II. Supporting paragraphs:
"Tells them":
  A. ***Paragraph 2***: explicates and gives evidence for point #1 in topic sentence
  B. ***Paragraph 3***: explicates and gives evidence for point # 2 in topic sentence
  C. ***Paragraph 4***: explicates and gives evidence for point #3 in topic sentence.

III. Concluding paragraph:
"Tells them what you've told them":
Paragraph 5: Restates claim or thesis statement in the light of explication and evidence presented in paragraphs 2, 3 and 4.
  A. In summary, I have ...
  B. Concluding implications

WRITING AN INDUCTIVE ARGUMENT

I. "Problem" paragraph:
Leads readers into the question, problem, or issue interrogated in the essay by
  A. Asking a question?
  B. Stating a problem/matic
  C. Introducing a pro/con argument
  D. Concluding with a "map" of the essay/argument (First, I will ... then I will ... Finally, I will ...)

II. Background paragraph:
What the reader needs to know re:
  A. The author and/or
  B. The subject
  C. The context of the argument

III. "Contra" paragraph:
  A. Statement of contrary position
  B. Advantages of this position
  C. Problems of this position

IV. "Pro" paragraph:
  A. Statement of "pro" position
  B. Problems of position (refuted)
  C. Advantages of this position

V. Concluding paragraph:
  A. Assertion of author's position (in the light of preceding discussion)
  B. How readers would benefit if they adopted this position
  C. Concluding appeal to readers (may include brief recapitulation of the discussion)

AN EXAMPLE OF A DEDUCTIVE "THESIS" PARAGRAPH:

Some have called Martin Luther King America's greatest public theologian. Others have called him

AN EXAMPLE OF AN INDUCTIVE "PROBLEM" PARAGRAPH:

Martin Luther King's role in American religious history is difficult to describe. Was he the greatest public theologian?

America's most eloquent preacher. Still others have called him America's greatest civil rights leader. The title that embraces each of these is that of "prophet." In this paper I argue that King was preeminently a latter-day prophet who exercised that calling as (1) theologian (2) preacher (3) civil rights leader.

Was he the greatest preacher of our time? Or was his leadership of the civil rights movement his most significant role? In this essay I first probe these questions in order to discover the vocation that incorporated all of these "callings" in King's life, ministry and vision.

Entering the conversation

Which of the two opening essay paragraphs did you find more informative? Which did you find more inviting? Which argumentative style is more congenial to your own logical path? Which pattern would you choose for writing a homily? Which pattern would you choose for writing a systematic reflection paper? However you answer those questions, if you can write competently in both inductive and deductive patterns of argument, you will have two adaptable "templates" for organizing theological arguments of one page or twenty pages, depending upon the complexity of the assignment. By choosing to converse in one of these academic dialects, you are telling your readers (and most importantly your professor) that you are ready to enter the particular conversation of which your paper is a part. Whether formulated inductively, deductively, or in the more hybrid modes of "faithful persuasion," David Tracy reminds us that "arguments, at their best, are moments within the wider conversation,"[36] not rhetorical ends in themselves. In that spirit, then, we are ready to join that wider conversation and write a one-page systematic reflection paper[37] in the deductive style of argument, using the Toulmin "claim/grounds/warrants" model.

Writing the one-page systematic reflection paper: "Was Jesus a feminist?"

THEOLOGICAL MEMO 5: For a Systematic Theology assignment, you must write a one-page systematic reflection paper of no more than 300 words in answer to the question, "Was Jesus a feminist?" Using course readings as a touchstone for your own reflection, you must begin the paper with a one-sentence thesis statement that you support in a coherent argument as the paper unfolds. How would you begin this task? How would you go about formulating a thesis statement and outlining your argument? Please respond briefly to these questions. If a thesis statement and/ or outline for the paper begin to emerge in the process, write them down as well.

Engaging the question

The first step in writing a systematic reflection paper in response to a "pre-assigned" question is to engage the question. To engage the question is to take the pulse of the assignment until you locate what engages your own theological imagination by calling forth, challenging, disturbing, confirming, or disconfirming your own experience. This starting point is no less personal than that of the pastoral reflection paper we considered in Chapter 14. However, while the theological argument unfolds through the writer's experience in the pastoral reflection paper, the writer's experience is subsumed into the theological argument in the systematic reflection paper, often without leaving a trace of its original fire, except through a clarity and compression of language that still shimmers with the passion that engendered it. If such writing seems beyond your capability, keep engaging the question until you find an answering pulse. The writing you produce may surprise you.

Reengaging the readings

Once you have engaged the question in a way that engages you, the second step in writing a systematic reflection paper is to reengage the assigned readings in the light of your question, as described in Theological Memo 2.[38] Let us assume you have read selections from Elisabeth Schüssler Fiorenza's *In Memory of Her*[39] for this assignment. This text provides a historical reconstruction of the first-century Jesus movement that might warrant an interpretation of Jesus as a feminist. However, feminism is a contemporary phenomenon; Jesus would not have recognized the word! So, you must find some way of bridging the gap between Jesus' world, for which feminism was not a cultural category, and our world, in which it is. As you continue to reengage *In Memory of Her*, you find that bridge in Schüssler-Fiorenza's locus of revelation: "not the androcentric text but the life and ministry of Jesus *and* the movement of women and men called forth by him,"[40] which include those following Jesus today. As you negotiate that bridge between Jesus' world and your own, you focus on the experience of oppression and liberation of contemporary women.

Will this bridge hold in the construction of your argument? You will have to wait and see. But before you proceed, you ask yourself, What do I mean by feminism? What does Schüssler-Fiorenza mean? Thus, your question now raises another question, which you try to answer from the assigned readings, but you do not find a relevant quote. You could fall back on a dictionary definition, but you locate Schüssler-Fiorenza's definition in *Bread Not Stone*, where feminism is defined as "not just a theoretical world view or perspective but a women's liberation movement for social and ecclesiastical change."[41]

Before you complete the task of "re-engaging the readings," you must also engage the original context reflected in the readings. You know that Schüssler-Fiorenza is a feminist and you know what she means by that term. But, what might feminism look like in the first-century world of the Jesus movement? The way that your question is unfolding, you will need New Testament evidence to support the answer that you now claim: "Jesus can be interpreted as a feminist." To make this task less daunting, I suggest working with one or more of the gospels and noting relevant passages that place Jesus in relationship to women in his ministry, along with the references for each citation. You will have to distil and compress this material for a one-page paper, but it will provide useful New Testament documentation for your claim.

Developing a thesis/claim/"answer"

Having engaged the question and reengaged the readings in the light of it, the third step in writing a systematic reflection paper is to answer the question that the assignment poses. This is done by developing a thesis or "claim" that you will defend in the ensuing paragraphs of the paper. Recalling the step-by-step process for developing a thesis paragraph outlined in Theological Memo 3, our goal here is more stringent: to produce a thesis sentence of no more than twenty words that effectively states your "claim."

At this point, you have written, "Jesus can be interpreted as a feminist." However, this claim does not tell us "because," "why," or "in what way" Jesus may be interpreted as a feminist. Nor does it limit or qualify the assertion being made. What you need is an elucidating or qualifying clause to complete the claim. For example, "Jesus can be interpreted as a feminist because ... [please elucidate your thesis here]"; "Although .... [please qualify your thesis here], Jesus can be interpreted as a feminist." To elucidate or qualify the claim, it will be helpful to ask these three questions in the light of your reading and reflection: (1) What do the sources (assigned readings, Scripture) say? (2) What does your experience witness? (3) What theological "norm," or primary hermeneutical principle (e.g., Schüssler-Fiorenza's norm is a feminist critical hermeneutics of liberation) guides your response to the question?

Elucidating and/or qualifying the claim

The fourth step in this process is elucidating and qualifying your claim. When you elucidate a claim, you broaden its focus by placing the claim in a context that extends its relevance to your paper. When you qualify a claim, you narrow its focus by restricting its relevance to your paper. Here are two claims that have been (1) elucidated and (2) qualified:

(1) Because "feminism" is an anachronism in the world of the New Testament, Jesus cannot be considered a feminist, however "liberated" his relationships with women might have been.

(2) When interrogated by contemporary women's experience of liberation and oppression, the earliest Jesus traditions provide warrants for interpreting Jesus as a feminist.

Structuring the argument (grounds and warrants)

The fifth step in writing the systematic reflection paper is structuring your argument. Let us assume, for example, that you wrote claim #2: *When interrogated by contemporary womens' experience of liberation and oppression, the earliest Jesus traditions provide warrants for interpreting Jesus as a feminist.* To structure your argument deductively, you must (1) define your terms; (2) provide your grounds or evidence; and (3) connect claim and evidence with the warrants that authorize them. Since the reader needs to know what you mean when you use the term *feminist* in your claim, you include the definition we discovered previously in the first paragraph:

> When interrogated by contemporary women's experience of liberation and oppression, the earliest Jesus traditions provide warrants for interpreting Jesus as a feminist. In interpreting Jesus as a feminist, I follow Elisabeth Schüssler-Fiorenza's definition of feminism as "not just a theoretical world view or perspective but a women's liberation movement for social and ecclesiastical change" (*Bread Not Stone*: 5).

Having stated your *claim* and having defined your terms, you need evidence for the connection you are making between "contemporary women's experience of liberation and oppression" and "interpreting Jesus as a feminist." You therefore conclude the first paragraph of your paper by stating the *warrants* of your argument for your readers, rather than leaving them unstated:

> Thus for Schüssler-Fiorenza's feminist-critical hermeneutic, these warrants include: (1) Jesus and the praxis of the earliest church as a biblical root model, prototype [36] and locus of revelation [34]; (2) the contemporary experience of women struggling for liberation as a correlative locus of revelation [34] and (3) the *basileia*, or kingdom of God, as the inextricable connection between both of these [153].[42]

The three warrants that you identify also provide you with a path through the essay that will categorize your *grounds* or evidence. You are, in other words, killing two birds with one stone in this brief essay by using your warrants as "topic sentences" to introduce your evidence in a logical progression. First, you detail your New Testament evidence on "Jesus and the praxis of the earliest church" in the next paragraph:

> According to the earliest Christian traditions, Jesus ate with poor women (Matt 14:15–21) and prostitutes (Matt 9:9–13; 21:31–32); engaged (John 4:4–26) and was engaged in conversations with non-Israelite and Gentile women (Mark 7:24–30); touched (Mark 5:41) and was touched (Mark 5:27; Luke 7:38) by ritually "unclean" women; traveled in the company of women patrons (Luke 8:2–3); healed crippled women on the Sabbath (Luke 13:10–17); advocated for widows (Luke 7:12–15; 21:1–4); and appeared first to women after his resurrection (Matt 28:1–10; John 20:11–18). These traditions suggest that Jesus did not restrict women's roles to reproduction, child rearing (Luke 11:27), and the domestic sphere (Luke 10:38–42). Rather, he challenged patriarchal family structures oppressive to women (Mark 10:2–9; 12:18–27), and invited women and men to share his egalitarian *basileia* (Matt 20:24–28).

Second, you proceed to "the contemporary experience of women struggling for liberation," positing a hermeneutics of fused horizons:

> When interrogated by contemporary women's experience of liberation and oppression, these traditions provide warrants for interpreting Jesus as a feminist. If the answers we receive from a text depend upon (a) the questions we ask and (b) the hermeneutic we bring to the text, then the question, "Was Jesus a feminist?"

> must first be asked before it can be answered, and the answer will be predisposed by the hermeneutic that frames the question. Whether or not the question of Jesus and feminism was asked by first century Palestinian women, it is asked by women today, for whom Jesus' advocacy on behalf of the women of his culture becomes both a source of, and a norm for, their own experience of liberation from patriarchy...

Third, you name the *basileia*, or vision of the kingdom of God, as the decisive warrant of your argument, connecting the earliest Jesus traditions and those who followed him then with those women and men who continue to claim his *basileia* vision as their own:

> ...and their continuing struggle to make the "*basileia* vision of Jesus" a reality for all women and men.

Concluding the draft, counting the words, revising to size

Now you must conclude the paper, and, if necessary, revise it to satisfy the required word count (300 words). First, you draw the threads of your argument together in a concluding sentence that not merely restates your thesis, but recapitulates the grounds for its assertion:

> Therefore, through this fusion of hermeneutical horizons that coalesce in the egalitarian vision of the *basileia*, Jesus may be interpreted as a feminist.

Next, you check the word count of your completed draft. At 403 words, you are 103 words above the 300-word limit for the paper. In order to meet the specifications of the assignment, you will have to cut an already concise paper. You do not tear your hair (or your paper) in despair; you reread the paper slowly and with care, looking (a) for words or phrases that can be cut without sacrificing grammatical sense; (b) sentences that can be deleted without compromising the argument of the paper; and (c) quoted material that is not integral to the development of the thesis. When you are ready, you make the necessary deletions and revisions, as prompted in the following Theological Memo:

> *THEOLOGICAL MEMO 6: A completed draft of the one-page paper, "Was Jesus a Feminist?" is printed below. Please revise it from its present 403 words to 300 words (or less) specified by the assignment, and explain briefly why you deleted what you did.*
>
> *"Was Jesus a Feminist"? (Draft A)*
>
> ***THESIS: When interrogated by contemporary women's experience of liberation and oppression, the earliest Jesus traditions provide warrants for interpreting Jesus as a feminist.*** *In interpreting Jesus as a feminist, I follow Elisabeth Schüssler-Fiorenza's definition of feminism as "not just a theoretical world view or perspective but a women's liberation movement for social and ecclesiastical change" (*Bread Not Stone*: 5). Thus for Schüssler-Fiorenza's feminist-critical*

hermeneutic, these warrants include: (1) Jesus and the praxis of the earliest church as a biblical root model, prototype [36] and locus of revelation [34]; (2) the contemporary experience of women struggling for liberation as a correlative locus of revelation [34] and (3) the basileia, *or kingdom of God, as the inextricable connection between both of these [153].*

According to the earliest Christian traditions, Jesus ate with poor women (Matt 14:15–21) and prostitutes (Matt 9:9–13; 21:31–32); engaged (John 4:4–26) and was engaged in conversations with non-Israelite and Gentile women (Mark 7:24–30); touched (Mark 5:41) and was touched (Mark 5:27; Luke 7:38) by ritually "unclean" women; traveled in the company of women patrons (Luke 8:2–3); healed crippled women on the Sabbath (Luke 13:10–17); advocated for widows (Luke 7:12–15; 21:1–4); and appeared first to women after his resurrection (Matt 28:1–10; John 20:11–18). These traditions suggest that Jesus did not restrict women's roles to reproduction, child rearing (Luke 11:27), and the domestic sphere (Luke 10:38–42). Rather, he challenged patriarchal family structures oppressive to women (Mark 10:2–9; 12:18–27), and invited women and men to share his egalitarian basileia *(Matt 20:24–28).*

*When interrogated by contemporary women's experience of liberation and oppression, these traditions provide warrants for interpreting Jesus as a feminist. If the answers we receive from a text depend upon (a) the questions we ask and (b) the hermeneutic we bring to the text, then the question, "Was Jesus a feminist?" must first be asked before it can be answered, and the answer will be predisposed by the hermeneutic that frames the question. Whether or not the question of Jesus and feminism was asked by first century Palestinian women, it is asked by women today, for whom Jesus' advocacy on behalf of the women of his culture becomes both a source of, and a norm for, their own experience of liberation from patriarchy, and their continuing struggle to make the "*basileia *vision of Jesus" a reality for all women and men [153]. Therefore, through this fusion of hermeneutical horizons that coalesce in the egalitarian vision of the* basileia, *Jesus may be interpreted as a feminist.*

Editing other people's writing is always easier than editing your own, but being able to edit your own work and cut it to size is one of the most valuable skills you can learn as a theological writer. More tools for editing and revising can be found in Chapter 12 of this book.[43] Until we get there, do not be daunted by page constraints but approach them creatively, as a challenge to say what you need to say within the limitations assigned. Here is a final version of "Was Jesus a Feminist," revised to under 300 words. How does it compare to your own edited version? After you have read it, I invite you to use this model in a theological assignment of your own or in "Writing the Theological Essay Question Well," for which you will find a "Blueprint" in the next section.

"Was Jesus a Feminist"? (Revised Draft, 290 words)

THESIS: Interrogated by women's experience of oppression, the earliest Jesus traditions provide warrants for interpreting Jesus as a feminist.

I follow Elisabeth Schüssler-Fiorenza's definition of feminism as "not just a theoretical world view or perspective but a women's liberation movement for social and ecclesiastical change" (Bread Not Stone*: 5). Her feminist hermeneutic includes these warrants: (1) Jesus and the praxis of the earliest church as a biblical root model, prototype [36] and locus of revelation [34]; (2) the contemporary experience of women struggling for liberation as a correlative locus of revelation [34] and (3) the* basileia *as the inextricable connection between both of these [153].*

According to the earliest Christian traditions, Jesus ate with poor women and prostitutes; engaged and was engaged in conversations with non-Israelite and Gentile women; touched and was touched by ritually "unclean" women; traveled in the company of women patrons; healed crippled women on the Sabbath; advocated for widows; and appeared first to women after his resurrection. These traditions suggest that Jesus did not restrict women's roles to reproduction, child rearing, and the domestic sphere. Rather, he challenged patriarchal family structures oppressive to women, and invited women and men to share his egalitarian basileia.

*The answers we receive from a text depend upon the questions we ask and the hermeneutic we bring to it. Whether or not the question of Jesus and feminism was asked by first century Palestinian women, women ask it today. Jesus' advocacy for women of his culture becomes a norm for women's experience of liberation from patriarchy and their struggle to make the "*basileia *vision of Jesus" a reality today [153]. Therefore, this fusion of hermeneutical horizons coalesces in the egalitarian vision of the* basileia, *and Jesus may be interpreted as a feminist.*

Writing the theological essay examination well: A "blueprint"

One of the most daunting forms of academic writing is the "blue book" essay examination, in which you must respond to assigned questions in a brief but coherent essay in a limited amount of time. If you can write the one-page systematic reflection paper well, you can write theological essay examination well, using the same basic format, but adapting it to the exigencies of writing within a specified time frame. Here are some guidelines for writing the theological essay examination well.

Preparing for the examination

Prepare by reviewing the material strategically, allowing yourself enough time to take notes and organize them in a way that enhances your own learning. What names, dates, concepts, and definitions do you need to remember? What theological themes or positions should you be able to summarize? What lends itself to analysis, comparison and contrast, or debate? If you were the professor, what questions would you ask?

Reading the questions

Read the essay questions in their entirety before beginning to write; select the questions you wish to answer; determine the order in which you will write them (if there is a choice); and estimate how much time you can spend on each question. Attend carefully to directions embedded in the question, such as "analyze," "argue," "compare and contrast," "describe," "discuss," "interpret," or "outline." If the question includes multiple parts, use them to structure your answer. If you do not understand a question, ask for clarification from the professor before attempting to answer it.

Rehearsing your response

Briefly rehearse your response to a question in an answering "claim" before proceeding to write. Then outline your arguments and evidence for the claim, and use the outline as a guide to writing the question. An outline will keep you focused on elaborating your claim, thus helping you to fulfill the expectations implicit in the question.

Writing the examination

The goal is to successfully *answer the question* in a limited time and space by (1) stating your claim succinctly; (2) elaborating it coherently in three to five points, as the material warrants and time permits; (3) substantiating each point with requisite evidence; (4) reasserting the answer in a concluding sentence; and (5) rereading for corrections and editing accordingly.

Some final suggestions

If the examination process permits, begin with the question for which you are the most prepared, and take the time to write it well. One well-written question may predispose your professor to read the rest more favorably. If you get stuck on a question for which you are not as prepared, refocus it in terms of what you *can* answer rather than what you cannot. Your resourcefulness in responding to the refocused question will demonstrate your mastery of the material and of writing theological essay questions well.

Concluding reflections: Writing theological argument well

"The art of writing well," Hans Guth writes at the beginning of this chapter, "is the art of making up one's mind. It is the art of establishing clarity where there was confusion, of working out one's conclusions and commitments."[44] This description of the art of writing well describes aptly the process of writing theological argument well, which we have engaged here through the rhetorics of inquiry, reading, reflection, and persuasion. By the time you have written a systematic reflection paper, you have made up your mind about something and, in the process of writing what is on your mind, moved from "confusion to clarity." In the formulating of a claim, you have worked out new conclusions and new commitments that you must now acknowledge, defend, review, and continue to clarify as your writing joins a wider theological conversation. Whether that conversation happens across a seminar table, in consultation with your professor, at supper with classmates, or in your own mind, theological argument at its best *is* conversation. As Hans-Georg Gadamer acknowledges, "To reach an understanding with one's partner in a dialogue is not merely a matter of total self-expression and the successful assertion of one's point of view, but a transformation into a communion, in which we do not remain what we were."[45]

To the extent that the claims you make, make claims upon you, and the ensuing conversation opens you to reaffirmation, refinement, and revision, writing theological argument will change you. Like the poor whom Jesus speaks of in John's gospel, papers written merely to fulfill an assignment you will always have with you. More often, however, the inextricable connections between writing theology and doing theology will transform the writing of a routine theological position paper when you least expect it into "personal knowledge" that might even impel you to live differently. To paraphrase words from the liturgy, as you continue to write theological argument well, you may be challenged to become what you write and to write what you become.

In this chapter, we introduced writing theological argument well as an alternative mode of theological reflection, written in an academic voice for an academic audience. First, we reviewed the basic building blocks of theological argument, inductive and deductive reasoning, and provided schematic outlines for writing in each mode. Second, we defined theological argument as "persuasive argument" employing complementary styles of logic and rhetoric to assert a theological position. Third, we identified inquiry, reading, reflection, and persuasion as integral rhetorics of theological argument. Finally, we recommended the Toulmin claims/grounds/warrants model as an adaptable format for writing theological argument well and rehearsed a student's progress in writing a one-page systematic reflection paper in that format. However, writing a one-page systematic reflection paper well will not provide you with all the tools you need to write theological argument well. What if you must write a five-page book review and argue for your own evaluation of the book? What if you must write a ten-page critical essay and assert the relevance of a theologian of your choice? What if you must write a twenty-page constructive theological essay and propose a contemporary theology that flows from your denominational tradition? Without leaving the writing of theological argument behind, we will integrate this "systematic reflection" model into the writing of longer papers in Chapter 4, "Writing the Theological Essay Well."

Notes

1 Nancey C. Murphy, *Reasoning and Rhetoric in Religion* (Valley Forge, PA: Trinity Press International, 1994), 71.

2 The "Claim/Grounds/Warrants" model of argument introduced here is adapted from Stephen Toulmin's *The Uses of Argument* (Cambridge: Cambridge University Press, 1958). For a more detailed exposition of this argumentative model for theologians, see Murphy, *Reasoning and Rhetoric in Religion*, 6–42.

3 See Kenneth Burke, *The Philosophy of Literary Form: Studies in Symbolic Action*, 3rd ed. (Berkeley, CA: University of California Press, 1973), 296, 302–3, who describes the genre of argument, among others, as a rhetorical "strategy" for a particular "situation."

4 See below, pp. 51–57.

5 Lewis Carroll, *Alice in Wonderland* (New York: Washington Square Press, 1951), 190.

6 See Andrea A. Lunsford and John J. Ruszkiewicz, *Everything's an Argument*, 4th ed. (Boston, MA: Bedford/St. Martin's Press, 2007), 4.

7 Aristotle distinguished "dialectic", or logical argument proceeding rigorously from question to answer, from "rhetoric," or persuasive argument unfolding more deliberately as expository prose. Yet, he includes logical argument as one of the "available means of persuasion." See Aristotle, *On Rhetoric: A Theory of Public Discourse*, ed. George A. Kennedy (New York: Oxford University Press, 1991), book 1, ch. 1, 28–36.

8 Ibid., book 3, ch. 13, 1, 258.

9 My brief summary of deduction and induction is indebted to: Sheridan Baker, *The Complete Stylist and Handbook* (New York: Thomas W. Crowell, 1976), 216–22; Richard A. Coe, *Form and Substance: An Advanced Rhetoric* (New York: John Wiley, 1981), 325–31; Hans P. Guth, *Words and Ideas: A Handbook for College Writing*, 5th ed. (Belmont, CA: Wadsworth, 1980), 125–35; Annette T. Rottenberg, *The Elements of Argument: A Text and Reader* (Boston, MA: Bedford Books, 1997), 248–63; and Richard E. Young, Alton L. Becker and Kenneth L. Pike, *Rhetoric: Discovery and Change* (New York: Harcourt Brace Jovanovich, 1970), 230–35.

10 Aristotle, *On Rhetoric*, book 1, ch. 2, 8–12, 40.

11 This syllogism is quoted from Young et al., *Rhetoric: Discovery and Change*, 231.

12 My rough correlation of the Toulmin model of argument with traditional deductive argument is adapted from Rottenberg, *Elements of Argument*, 261–63.

13 Remember, however, that the Toulmin model of argument makes no claims for formal deductive validity but seeks rather to provide criteria for constructing arguments that are "warranted" by the evidence.

14 Aristotle, *On Rhetoric*, book I, chapter 2, 8, 40.

15 Owen Thomas, *Theological Questions: Analysis and Argument* (New York: Morehouse-Barlow, 1983), 14.

16 Dorothea Soelle, *Thinking About God: An Introduction to Theology*, trans. John Bowden (Philadelphia, PA: Trinity International, 1990), 4.

17 Roger Haight, *Dynamics of Theology* (New York: Paulist Press, 1990; repr., Maryknoll, New York: Orbis Books, 2001), 2–3.

18 David Tracy, *Plurality and Ambiguity: Hermeneutics, Religion, Hope* (Chicago, IL: University of Chicago Press, 1987), 27.

19 Rebecca S. Chopp, *Saving Work: Feminist Practices of Theological Education* (Louisville, KY: Westminster John Knox Press, 1995), 92.

20 Don H. Compier, *What is Rhetorical Theology? Textual Practice and Public Discourse* (Harrisburg, PA: Trinity Press International, 1999), 17.

21 David S. Cunningham, *Faithful Persuasion: In Aid of a Rhetoric of Christian Theology* (Notre Dame: University of Notre Dame Press, 1991), 175.

22 Ibid., 5, 164–65.

23 Tracy, *Plurality and Ambiguity*, 24.

24 Hans-Georg Gadamer, *Truth and Method*, 2nd, Rev. ed. and trans. J. Weinsheimer and D.C. Marshall (New York: Continuum, 1997), 365.

25 James Crosswhite, *The Rhetoric of Reason: Writing and the Attractions of Argument* (Madison, WI: University of Wisconsin Press, 1996), 267.

26 See also Kwok Pui Lan, "How to Read a Theological Book," ***kwokpuilan**.blogspot.com/2011/02/how-to-**read-theological-book**.htm* (accessed September 14, 2014).

27 Patricia O'Connell Killlen and John de Beer, *The Art of Theological Reflection* (New York: Crossroad, 1994), 9.

28 Schubert M. Ogden, *On Theology* (San Francisco, CA: Harper and Row, 1986; reprint, Dallas, TX: Southern Methodist University Press, 1992), 2 (emphasis added; page citation is to the reprint edition).

29 Haight, *Dynamics of Theology*, 221.

30 Wallace Stevens, *Notes Toward a Supreme Fiction*, in *Selected Poems* (London: Faber & Faber, 1978), 105.

31 Young et al., *Rhetoric: Discovery and Change*, 232.

32 See Lucretia B. Yaghjian, "Teaching Theological Reflection Well, Reflecting on Writing as a Theological Practice," *Teaching Theology and Religion* 7, no. 2 (2004): 83–94.

33 I am indebted to my former Metropolitan State University (Denver, Colorado) colleague, Professor Margaret Purchatzke, for the use of this handout, which I have adapted for theological writers in this book.

34 Flannery O'Connor, *The Habit of Being: Letters of Flannery O'Connor*, ed. Sally Fitzgerald (New York: Farrar, Strauss, and Giroux, 1979), 290–91.

35 Roger Haight, *Jesus Symbol of God* (Maryknoll, NY: Orbis Books, 1999), 15.

36 Tracy, *Plurality and Ambiguity*, 25.

37 This model of a systematic reflection paper is adapted from that introduced to Weston Jesuit School of Theology students as a one-page "theological position paper" by Roger Haight, S. J. I gratefully acknowledge his editing of the final version of the paper included here to under 300 words.

38 See above, 44–45.

39 Elisabeth Schüssler Fiorenza, *In Memory of Her: A Feminist Theological Reconstruction of Christian Origins* (New York: Crossroad, 1986), 41.

40 Ibid.

41 Elisabeth Schüssler Fiorenza, *Bread Not Stone: The Challenge of Feminist Interpretation* (Boston, MA: Beacon Press, 1984), 5.

42 Bracketed page numbers refer to Schüssler Fiorenza, *In Memory of Her*.

43 See Chapter 12, "Rewriting Theology Well (III): A Rhetoric of Revision."

44 Hans P. Guth, quoted in Coe, *Form and Substance*, 323.

45 Gadamer, *Truth and Method*, 379.

4

Writing the Theological Essay Well: Rhetorics of Identification, Correlation, Suspicion, and Construction

The word is late, but the thing is ancient.

—FRANCIS BACON, Preface to *Essays, 1597*

... the essay is the simplest, most basic format for discursive writing—writing intended to inform, to explain, and to persuade.

—V.A. HOWARD and J.H. BARTON, *Thinking on Paper*

What is it that makes an essay ... theological?

—GORDON KAUFMAN, *Essay on Theological Method*

Starting points

What makes an essay theological? How shall we write a theological essay? These are the questions that we address in this chapter, and they flow from the presupposition that constructing a theological argument and writing a theological essay are integrated, not isolated processes. According to Howard and Barton's definition of the essay in the epigraph above, it could be argued that any piece of theological prose "intended to inform, explain and to persuade" is a theological essay. Without denying this broader definition, our aim is to determine more precisely what distinguishes the theological essay from other types of essays and thus to discover how to write it more effectively. To do this, we begin with four questions: (1) What is an essay, and why do people write it? (2) What is a theological essay, and why do theologians write it? (3) What kinds of theological essays are there, and how shall we write them? (4) What are the rhetorics, or elements of the (a) critical and (b) constructive theological essays? Before we proceed, I invite you to reflect on what an essay is and how it is written in the following Theological Memo:

THEOLOGICAL MEMO 1: When you hear the word essay, what kind of writing comes to mind? When you are asked to write a "theological essay," what is your understanding of what is required? Please define either the "essay" or the "theological essay" in your own words, identify one key characteristic of the genre, and describe how you typically write it.

What is an essay and why do people write it?

The essay has been described as "*the* basic structure for making sense to others on paper," and the common denominator of that structure is the introduction, body, and conclusion that comprise every essay.[1] Defining the essay in terms of its structure will prove useful presently when we adopt the same strategy to identify the "structure of correlation" as "*the* basic theological essay structure." But, without a purposeful author composing a logically connected and coherent piece of writing on a particular subject in an appropriate style and voice for a real or imagined audience, we would have neither a structure nor an essay, so we must begin with a more comprehensive definition of this genre.

Let us define the essay, then, as a purposeful prose composition on a particular subject, with a structure that is divisible into an introduction, body, and conclusion, written in an appropriate style and authorial voice for a specific audience. Accordingly, the six characteristics that define an essay are: (1) purpose, (2) subject, (3) structure, (4) style, (5) voice, and (6) audience.[2] Since each of these characteristics is given varying emphasis in different essays, they are also used to classify different kinds of essays by purpose (to inform; to persuade); subject (literary; scientific); structure (inductive; deductive); style (narrative; argumentative); voice (personal; academic); and audience (popular; professional). However, an essay is more than the sum of these characteristics. Just as the tennis player's racquet becomes the natural extension of the player's arm as it volleys the ball successfully across the net, so the writer's essay becomes a strategic vehicle of her own thinking that conveys her argument effectively to her readers. Yet, just as tennis players must master the requisite form in order to hit a successful serve over the net, essay writers must become familiar with the classic forms of the essay and why people write them.

From its inception as a literary genre, the essay was written for personal, formal, and academic purposes. The sixteenth-century French writer, Michael de Montaigne, coined the word "essay" (from the French *essayer*, "to try") to distinguish his *Essais* (1580), written as personal, informal, "attempts," from the formal, authoritative ecclesiastical writing of his day, and described by a recent biographer as "writing about oneself to create a mirror in which other people recognize their own humanity."[3] In so doing, he invented the "personal" or "informal" essay. Sir Francis Bacon, on the other hand, introduced the "formal essay" to English audiences in his *Essays* (1597), which were brief, impersonal moral and political reflections in the classical tradition of Cicero, Seneca, and Plutarch.[4] As a subspecies of the formal essay, the "philosophical essay" of Enlightenment philosophers like John Locke and David Hume[5] provided the prototype for the academic essay and further reinforced the distinction between "informal" essays, written in a personal voice for a popular audience, and "formal" essays, written for a more specialized audience. As we shall see, the contemporary theological essay embraces both of these.

What is a theological essay and why do theologians write them?

To answer the question, What is a theological essay?, we must ask, What makes an essay theological? Our answer to this question leads to two definitions of the theological essay. The first provides us with a broad definition, encompassing all kinds of theological essays. The second, provided by Paul Tillich, defines the essay more narrowly in terms of its "structure of correlation," which he calls the "backbone" of the theological essay.

We have previously defined the generic essay in terms of its purpose, subject, structure, style, voice, and audience. If the category of the generic essay is analogous to a biological genus, then the theological essay is a species of the genus, "essay," whose general characteristics will be adapted to the specifications of the theological writing tasks that they support. For example, the pastoral reflection paper described in Chapter 2 is a pastoral (*subject*) essay. Its *purpose* is to reflect on experience from a pastoral perspective. Its *structure* is inductive. Its *style* is narrative. Its *voice* is personal, and its *audience*, broadly conceived, is the church. The systematic reflection paper described in Chapter 3 is a theological (*subject*) essay. Its *purpose* is to present a credible and coherent theological argument. Its *structure* is deductive. Its *style* is argumentative. Its *voice* is academic, and its *audience* is the theological "academy." Although most essays require more elaboration than the one-page paper allows, you have already written a theological essay if you have completed either of these papers.

When described broadly, then, what makes an essay theological is simply its theological subject, purpose, structure, style, voice, and audience. However, Paul Tillich has provided a more precise definition of the theological essay that will help us to write it more effectively. For Tillich, the essay is one of the theologian's primary tools for correlating present-day questions with the traditional "answers" of Christian faith. Toward that end, he first defines the *essay* as a form of public theological discourse that "deals explicitly with one actual problem."[6] He then proposes an explicitly "theological" essay structure based upon this method of correlation, which we will use in this chapter to write the constructive theological essay.

More will be said about the structure of correlation and the constructive theological essay later on, but what Tillich adds here to our generic definition of the theological essay is twofold. First, the essay deals with one "question" or "problem" in a methodical and systematic way. Second, it places that "problem" in conversation with the resources of the Christian tradition, in order to provide a constructive theological response to the problem. Gathering these threads together, the theological essay as described in this book is a structured theological reflection, argument, or conversation focusing systematically on one subject, question, or problem through the lens of a particular theological method, or rhetoric, written for a public audience[7] in a style and voice appropriate for that audience.

Contemporary theologians find the essay format conducive to the writing of theology for many reasons. First of all, the essay is a genre that requires its author to actively imagine an audience, engage readers strategically, and write appropriately for that audience. Second, the essay format is traditionally conversational (even when it is structured more formally), and contemporary theologians are more often committed to conversation and dialogue with their audiences than to delivering a monologue or "lecture" to passive listeners.[8] Third, the essay format follows an argumentative structure, just as the conversation of a theological essay typically follows one argument from its inception to its conclusion. Fourth, this conversation always unfolds as an "attempt," not a *fait accompli*, because "we are all in this mystery together; and we need to question one another, criticize one another, make suggestions to one another, help one another."[9] All of these qualities of the theological essay converge in the critical theological essay and the constructive theological essay, the two essay formats used most widely to write theology well. We proceed to look briefly at both of these essay formats.

What kinds of theological essays are there and how shall we write them?

We have described the theological essay broadly in terms of its defining characteristics, and more narrowly in terms of its structure of "correlation," to help you to identify a theological essay assignment. However, these definitions by themselves will not help you to write the essay you have due tomorrow. What is also needed is a familiarity with some typical subspecies of the theological essay that you will encounter most frequently and an ability to recognize the basic elements from which these essays are constructed. We focus on two of the most common subspecies here: (1) the *critical theological essay*, whose purpose is to critique the subject matter of the essay; and (2) the *constructive theological essay*, whose purpose is to construct a theological position within the framework of the essay. We look first at the critical theological essay.

What is a critical theological essay and how shall we write it?

The *critical theological essay* is a theological essay defined by its purpose to assess, evaluate, or mount a critique of a theological author, position, topic, or issue. This essay is also used to critique nontheological material (a current film; a cultural issue) from a theological standpoint, or according to theological criteria. If you have ever written a critical essay for another academic discipline, you can write a critical theological essay. It typically follows the format and elements of the academic "review" or "critique" and adapts them to the theological subject matter under consideration. Even if you have not written a critical essay of any kind, however, we will begin by identifying the elements of the critical theological essay. In the process, you will be invited to write (a) a theological summary; (b) a theological book review; and (c) a theological critique, or critical analysis, as we put the pieces of this essay format together.

What are the rhetorics of the critical theological essay?

Every critical theological essay you write should include one or more of the following four elements: *a problematic*, *an exposition*, *a criticism*, and *an interpretation*. The *problematic* includes the presenting question or issue that inspires the writer to write the essay and the thesis that is formulated in response to the question. The element of *exposition* informs, explains, and develops the question/thesis according to a particular rhetorical pattern (e.g., cause-effect, comparison-contrast, definition). The element of *criticism* analyzes, evaluates, and mounts a critique of what has been expounded on the basis of that analysis and evaluation. The element of *interpretation* draws out the implications of all that precedes it to construct an answering interpretation, imaginative construal, or practical application of the presenting question. Keeping in mind that the focal point of the critical theological essay is the element of *criticism*, let us examine each of these elements more closely.

Problematic

Behind every theological essay is a reason why it was written, and behind that reason is a problem to be solved or a question to be answered, as we have already seen in the pastoral reflection paper and the systematic reflection paper. Whether the problem is posed by a particular assignment or by the specific issues you bring to it, the typical theological essay is problem-centered. But, if all we had were a problem, we would not have an essay. The problem must elicit an answering thesis, or claim, to warrant its development as an essay.

If, then, a theological essay begins with a problematic, we might expect the order of problem to solution to be used frequently by theological authors in constructing their essays.[10] However, there are as many variations on the basic pattern as there are theological writers following the threads of their own thinking from the beginning of the essay to its conclusion. We will look further at some of those organizational paths as we proceed, but once the writer has framed the problematic of the essay as a presenting question and an answering thesis, the next logical step is to explain, elaborate, and develop it, employing the rhetorical element of exposition.

Exposition

The body of a theological essay typically begins with "exposition," which literally means to put things in their proper order, one after another. The theological essay is not a random collection of thoughts or facts that are thrown "a tisket, a tasket" into the writer's basket. Like an artfully composed flower arrangement, it is a prose composition that moves purposefully from an initial statement of thesis to an exposition or development of the problem being addressed in the essay to an inevitable conclusion. Writing that is composed in this way is called expository writing or exposition. While all prose writing is broadly expository, the term has been used more narrowly in theological writing to distinguish writing that informs and explains from writing that takes a critical position,[11] and we will follow that more narrow usage here.

Whatever form it takes, however, the goal of expository writing is to compose the subject matter of the essay clearly, coherently, and in an orderly manner, in keeping with the rhetorical constraints of the essay. For theological writers, this exposition might include a summary of a book to be reviewed, narration of a theologian's biography, a description of a particular theological position, and a step-by-step exegesis of a biblical text. As we shall see below, the theological act of correlation, whereby a present question or problem and the imagination of Christian faith are "co-related" by the theological writer, proceeds in an expository fashion to expound the correlation. However, a formal theological essay typically moves beyond exposition, narrowly or broadly defined, to an answering critique of the theological position, the theologian's contribution, the book under review, the biblical text featured in the exegesis, or the act of correlation.

One cannot critique or evaluate material that has not been carefully read and understood as its author intended. Thus, before critiquing a book's thesis or a writer's theological viewpoint, theological essay writers frequently summarize the book or the writer's position, not only for the convenience of readers, but also to demonstrate that they have understood the premises of what they are critiquing. For this reason, the art of writing a good theological summary is fundamental to the art of writing a good theological essay. Before we move on, then, I invite you to try your hand at that most basic of expository assignments, the theological summary.[12]

THEOLOGICAL MEMO 2: Choose a biblical or theological book that you have chosen to read for a book review assignment. After you have read it carefully, write a brief summary of the book (150 words max.), following the instructions below.

Writing the theological summary well: An outline

I. **Definition and Purpose**

   A. The **summary** is a form of expository writing that digests and condenses a source text in your own words in order to shorten and simplify it.

   B. In theological papers, **summaries** are used to write brief reading reports, to present relevant research, to describe a theological position or interpretation of a biblical passage, and to provide a précis of a book in critical book reviews.

II. **General Characteristics of a Theological Summary**

   A. Its coverage of the source text should be complete (even if abbreviated).

   B. Its coverage of the material should be objective (not evaluative or critical).

   C. Its coverage of the material should be condensed and concise.

   D. Its coverage of the material should be in your own words.

III. **Preparing to Write the Theological Summary**

   A. Read the source text carefully.

   B. Note any headings or subdivisions in the text and outline accordingly.

   C. Distinguish between main points and supporting details; write the summary from the main points; save supporting details for a more extensive project.

   D. Prewrite the summary in outline form, using the main points you have selected from the material; check for completeness, logical order of presentation, and writing in your own words.

   E. Now you are ready to write the summary!

IV. Specific Writing Protocols for a Theological Summary

A. An introductory sentence identifying the source text of the summary;
B. A subsequent sentence describing the controlling thesis of the source text;
C. A logical and sequential organization of the material that follows the source text in succeeding sentences, rendered in:
D. Your own paraphrase of the source text (retain technical terms in quotes where needed for clarity);
E. Smooth connections between the sentences to keep the summary coherent;
F. A concluding sentence that "summarizes the summary" for the reader.

Criticism

The theological essay is not only an expository exercise, but also a finely tuned instrument of critical thinking, reading, and writing, reflected in the writer's mastery of the element of criticism. Thus, the body of a critical theological essay begins with exposition but moves inexorably toward critical assessment of the subject matter. From the moment that Anselm first defined theology as "faith seeking understanding," the discipline of theology embraced critical thinking as a constructive intellectual tool. It should come as no surprise, then, that the theological essay characteristically takes a critical stance toward the problem that it addresses in order to "seek understanding." To take a critical stance begins by taking a questioning stance, and one engages in the activity of "criticism" when one writes from that stance.

Depending upon one's theological perspective, taking a questioning stance may arise either from "a hermeneutic of generosity" or from "a hermeneutic of suspicion."[13] A hermeneutic of generosity walks with the theological tradition, accepts it on its own terms, but asks it to account for itself in terms of an accepted theological norm.[14] A hermeneutic of suspicion questions the theological tradition, does not accept it on its own terms, and provides its own norms for critique of the tradition.[15] From either vantage point, this questioning posture comes naturally to many theological students. If, on the other hand, the prospect of writing a "critical essay" prompts you to ask—"What does 'critical' mean, anyway?"—in asking the question, you have already begun to think (and potentially, to write) critically.

In order to understand what it means to think, write, and reflect critically as theologians, "the key," David Tracy acknowledges, "is [understanding] the word, 'critical.'"[16] This word derives from the Greek word, *krinein* (to separate; to choose; to decide; to judge; to interpret). When applied to a theological essay, the term "critical" implies an interrogative, consciously reflective process that engages the writer and the reader in *analysis*, *evaluation*, and *critique* of the problem, text, or other subject matter addressed in the essay. Let us look briefly at each of these operations.

Analysis

To analyze anything—a situation, a person's motives, a biblical text, a theological position—is first of all to ask what it means. The process of analysis provides a particular way of getting at that meaning, which includes (1) dividing the subject into its constituent parts and (2) considering how those parts are related to the whole phenomenon. Yet, the purpose of a good critical analysis is neither to "murder to dissect," as the poet Wordsworth feared, nor to leave the pieces in disarray after dissecting them. With or without the help of "all the king's men (and women)," the goal is to "put Humpty Dumpty together again," with a fuller understanding of how the parts work together to create a text, or a theology, or, for that matter, a book about "Writing Theology Well." In this chapter, for example, I have divided the theological essay into four elements with the goal of making it easier for students to write.[17]

Evaluation

To evaluate a book, an article, or a critical position is simply to appraise its strengths and weaknesses according to a particular set of criteria. Evaluation is not unsubstantiated opinion or negative criticism for its own sake. The goal of evaluation is a reasoned, reflective assessment of the material that is able to sift the wheat from the chaff and harvest the usable "grain" for one's own constructive argument. In a critical book review, for example, one does not simply summarize the book or tell "what it is about"; one also evaluates the book by asking relevant questions that provide a credible basis for critique and assessment, as we shall see in Theological Memo 3 below. Closely related is the word *criticism*, which is used more technically by theologians and biblical scholars "for the entire process of analyzing how the text does what it does and then judging the quality of the operation."[18] When the term *critical* is applied to a hermeneutic of suspicion, however, it also construes criticism as "strictly empirical *analyses* of our actual economic, political, cultural and social situations."[19] To the dismay of students trying to understand what is meant by an "analytical," "evaluative" or "critical" essay, these terms are often used interchangeably and without precision, but the process of critical thinking is fundamental to all of them.

Critique

When used as a noun, the word *critique* is used to name and characterize the genre of critical writing. When used as a verb, *to critique* refers to the entire process of critical thinking—analysis, evaluation, and critique—that generates critical writing. It also refers to the final stage of that process, in which the writer presents a concluding "critique" on the basis of the preceding analysis and evaluation. In this section, a good writer will weave the elements of the analysis and the evaluation together with his or her own critical conclusions to produce a cogent "critique in a nutshell."

In some theological essays, the element of criticism will predominate. In others, it may be limited to a concluding section. However, whenever the words *critical*, *critical analysis*, or *critique* appear in the title of an assigned essay or in the instructions for writing it, you will be expected to write a critical theological essay. When this critical element is the driving force of a theological methodology, it may also be characterized as a rhetoric of suspicion, as we shall see below. Whether we call this operation "criticism" or "suspicion," writing a theological essay well will always involve some measure of criticism in response to the subject, text, or problem that has engendered it. Since book reviews routinely require the honing of these critical skills, we conclude this section by "essaying" to write a theological book review:

> *THEOLOGICAL MEMO 3: Using the outline that follows, please prepare a* ***critical essay/review*** *of a book assigned for one of your classes. If you have completed Theological Memo 2 you have already written a summary of the book (II, below).*

Writing the theological book review well: An outline

I. **Introduction**
   A. Provide title, author, and publication data at the beginning of your book review.
   B. In an opening summary/thesis sentence, tell what the book is about and why it is theologically significant (hence worthy of review).
   C. Proceed with a "map" of your review, e.g., "In this review I will briefly **summarize** the main argument of the book and describe its parts (or organization of material). I will then offer my own **critique** of the book and evaluate it as a theological resource (or in terms of some criteria that will provide a basis for critique). I will **conclude** with a personal assessment and recommendation of the book for (theological or other audiences designated by the writer)."

II. **Summary**
   A. What specific field of theology (or other discipline) is treated, and how does it fit into the present "literature" of that discipline?
   B. What is the author's intention in writing the book (see preface)?
   C. From what perspective, or "slant," does the author write?
   D. What is the controlling idea or thesis of the book?
   E. What are the main facts or concepts developing the thesis?
   F. How is the book organized, and how does its argument unfold?
   G. Who is the audience for whom the book has been written?

III. **Critique**
   A. Critique of the book as a whole:
      1. Is the treatment of subject matter thorough or superficial?
      2. Is the organization of the book logical and coherent?
      3. Does it unfold in narrative or linear progression?
      4. What scholarly apparatus is provided? Is it reader-friendly?
      5. Is the language clear, readable, appropriate for the intended audience?
   B. Critique of the book's specific content and contribution:
      1. Is the subject matter significant, timely, fresh, and innovative?
      2. Is the material presented objectively or with a discernible bias?

3. Is the author's evidence credible and persuasive?
4. Does the author do what s/he sets out to do (II B, above)?
5. Is the book a useful addition to the present literature?

IV. Conclusion

A. What is your critical assessment of the book, in a nutshell?

B. How did the book teach, move, inspire, change, or disappoint you?

C. To whom and for what audiences would you recommend this book, and why?

Conversely, why would you not recommend it?

D. If you cannot recommend the book, what suggestions do you have for revision?

Interpretation

A final element of the critical theological essay is interpretation.

While the term "interpretation" can refer to the operations of biblical and theological hermeneutics,[20] I use it here to describe the end "product" of that process,[21] the writer's construal and explication of a text's meaning. While many essays, such as the critical book review that we have just outlined, conclude with the writer's critique of the material presented in the essay, other critical theological essays draw the critique forward into a reinterpretation of the problematic posed in the essay. Whether the writer proposes a creative interpretation of a biblical text, a traditional doctrine, or a theologian's work, this element transcends exposition and criticism to present the writer's own constructive theological proposal in response to the problematic.

Because the act of interpretation is integrally connected to that of constructing a theological position, the element of interpretation will also provide us with a bridge from the critical theological essay to the constructive theological essay. Before we traverse that bridge, however, I invite you to "attempt" a theological critique, which employs all the elements of the critical theological essay—the problematic, exposition, criticism, and interpretation—in its interpretive analysis of a theologian/ author and their work:

THEOLOGICAL MEMO 4: Using the outline below, please prepare a theological critique, or interpretive analysis of a theologian and his or her work.[22]

Writing the theological critique well: An interpretive analysis of a theologian and their work

A. Introducing the Theologian/Author, Their Work, and Your Own Thesis/Purpose

1. Age-Period when particular work was written (or begin with #5, below, if you prefer)

2. Different "schools of thought" to which the theologian/author belongs
3. Major events that may have influenced the author's life and philosophy (e.g., war, poverty, the Holocaust)
4. Major and/or general themes of the theological work addressed in the Critique
5. *For example*: My goal in this critical analysis is to.... In order to do that, I will focus on the following.... First I will...; then I will...; in conclusion, I will....

B. Identifying the Main Theme/s for the Focus of Critique

1. Identify the central problematic addressed by the theologian/author (e.g., what is s/he discussing and why?)
2. State the major theoretical position/s (e.g., liberation theology, feminism, racism)
3. State the major thematic position/s (the concrete ways in which the theory or subjects of the theory *experience* the theory or problematic; e.g., African-American women's racial and religious oppression and liberation)

C. Correlating the Methodology and Data Used to Construct a Theological Position

1. *Methodology*: How the theologian/author *names* and *organizes* his/her thoughts and experiences
   (e.g., critical correlation [Tracy]; feminist/critical evaluation [E. Schüssler-Fiorenza]; hermeneutic of the black historical experience [Cone]).
2. *Data*: The nature of the sources used, pro and con

   (e.g., biblical sources; church documents; other theologians; historical/cultural materials; current philosophical, psychological, educational, political, sociological theories)
3. How do *methodology* and *data* correlate with each other in the work addressed?

D. Analyzing the Theologian/Author's Assumptions

1. Classical and/or current thinkers drawn upon
2. Interesting or critical issues raised in footnotes
3. Current interpretations included in the theologian/author's thinking (e.g., race, gender, class)
4. Current interpretations excluded in the theologian/author's thinking (e.g., feminism, multiculturalism, postcolonialism)

E. Summarizing and Critiquing the Theologian/Author's Conclusions, Concluding with Your Own Interpretive Analysis of the Theologian/Author's Work

1. Summary statement of the theologian/author's conclusions
2. Do they follow logically from the writing, the evidence and the data?

3. Your agreement/disagreement with the theologian/author's *theory*
4. Your agreement/disagreement with the theologian/author's *method*
5. Your agreement/disagreement with the theologian/author's *evidence*
6. Your concluding critical interpretation of the theologian/author's *contribution*

What is the constructive theological essay and how shall we write it?

At the beginning of this chapter, we asked what distinguished the theological essay from other kinds of essays. Looking first at a general definition of the essay, we saw that while the generic essay format provided a basic but adaptable structure for the process of thinking on paper in any discipline, the theological essay's distinctiveness lay in its theological subject, purpose, structure, style, voice, and audience. However, in our discussion of the critical theological essay, we also noted that the critical essay format was common to other disciplines as well.

The constructive theological essay, on the other hand, is not common to other academic disciplines. Its distinctiveness lies in its integration of rhetorical and theological processes. Just as writing theology well is a theological practice, so the practice of writing a constructive theological essay integrates the process of writing with that of constructing a theological position, hence "working out a theology as we go." In other words, while the critical theological essay engaged us in the critique and interpretation of theological authors, concepts, positions, and practices, the constructive theological essay invites those who engage it not only to critique and interpret the theology of others, but also to "do theology on paper."

However, in order to "do theology on paper" in the form of a constructive theological essay, writers must not only know the rudiments of writing a coherent essay with a beginning, middle, and end in an inductive or deductive format; they must also know the rhetorical elements, or rhetorics, of the theological essay, which build upon induction and deduction, but are also informed by the theological material being presented and the theological method employed. At the hands of theologians as diverse as Karl Rahner, Nicholas Lash, Gordon Kaufman, and Stanley Hauerwas, the constructive theological essay has become a paradigmatic form of contemporary theological writing.[23] Before we try our hand at writing it, we ask: (1) What is a constructive theological essay and why do theologians write it? (2) What are the rhetorics of the constructive theological essay, and how do these rhetorics inform the writing of the essay? (3) How shall we write a constructive theological essay?

What is a constructive theological essay?

The constructive theological essay is a subspecies of the theological essay, in which theologians construct a theological position in writing. As Gordon Kaufman writes,

"... theology [is] primarily an activity of construction—construction of a conception or picture of God, of human life, and of the world,"[24] and the constructive theological essay is the fruit of that activity. Whether it takes the shape of a critical analysis, a research paper, a lengthier thesis project, or a published book, this genre flourishes across the theological curriculum. It is not always recognized as a distinctive mode of theological writing, however, because a good constructive theological essay is like a chameleon. It changes its coloring to adapt to the theological location from which it is written, and its rhetorical "skin," the essay genre that frames it, is similarly adaptable to the needs of its audience.

Since the uses of this genre are as diverse as the theologians writing it, it is easier to describe what a constructive theological essay does than to define it precisely. If you have written a paper that required you not only to reflect upon, critique, analyze, or interpret the theology of others, but also to formulate your own theology in conversation with them, you have written a constructive theological essay. While professors will describe this essay in different ways, their goal will be to lure you from merely "reading" theology into the active process of "doing" theology. This genre can be described more specifically in terms of the *constructive method* that it employs, the *theological rhetorics* that inform the method, and the *essay structures* characterizing both of these.

What is a constructive method?

The constructive theological essay has developed from the subdiscipline of constructive theology, which is a contemporary form of systematic theology. However, while classical systematic theology has been more concerned with a methodical exposition of the traditional elements of Christian faith within a particular doctrinal tradition, constructive theology engages that tradition in a contemporary conversation that moves beyond "what the tradition says" to "what it means today," in our present situation.

In order to make that move from "then" to "now," however, the theological writer must also move beyond mere description or exposition of a theological position and enter the realm of the constructive imagination. Tillich recognized this activity as integral to the systematic theologian's work when he observed, "In each [theological] system an experienced fragment of life and vision is drawn out constructively even to cover areas where life and vision are missing."[25] Thus, while Tillich identified the writing of systematic theology as "a constructive task" in his *Systematic Theology*[26] over fifty years ago, more recently, Gordon Kaufman has argued that all theology is human imaginative construction conceived in the face of the mystery that we call God, with the goal of critiquing (or deconstructing) inadequate conceptions of God and creating (or reconstructing) theologies that provide more adequate orientation for contemporary life.[27] While not all would arrogate such an exclusive role to the imagination in the writing of theology, all theologians who draw upon resources from the theological tradition to formulate theologies that are conversant with the present situation employ the constructive method in both its critical and constructive (or deconstructive and reconstructive) moments, as we shall see as we proceed.

What are the rhetorics of a constructive theological essay, and how do they inform its writing?

For the writer, to choose a rhetorical structure is also to employ a method (*meta+hodos:* a way, or process of doing something), just as for the theologian, "method reaches into the content of theology to shape the very understanding of the subject matter."[28] For example, the method employed in writing the pastoral reflection paper, which affirmed the writer's own experience as a starting point for reflection, predisposed the paper to an "inductive rhetoric." On the other hand, we identified the method used to write the systematic reflection paper as "deductive rhetoric" from the general thesis statement that introduced the writer's "position" and the particularizing arguments that followed. Thus, it should not surprise us that different theological methods and the theologies they inform have different rhetorical structures, or rhetorics, that "shape the very understanding of the subject matter." We proceed, then, to examine the integration of method and structure in the theological method of correlation, looking both at the method and at the rhetoric undergirding the method.

The method of correlation

"As a method, it is as old as theology," Tillich writes of the method of correlation.[29] The goal of this method is a constructive interpretation of the Christian message in the light of contemporary reality. Toward this end, David Tracy engages the religious tradition in a "mutually critical conversation" with a question or problem arising from the present situation.[30] As Roger Haight explains, this "involves both criticism of present-day experience by the tradition and criticism of traditional symbols by present-day knowledge."[31] Elizabeth Johnson imagines this process as "braiding a footbridge" to describe the theological task of "connecting Christian tradition with the contemporary religious experience of women."[32] Rosemary Radford Ruether observes that "...the correlation of original and authentic human nature (*imago dei*/Christ) over against diminished, fallen humanity has traditionally provided the basic structure of classical Christian theology."[33] Finally, Haight asserts the centrality of this method when he writes, "... a method of correlation is not *a* method of theology, but *the* method of a discipline that seeks to preserve the meaning of the past but understand it in a distinctly present-day manner."[34]

In this book, I am interpreting the method of "correlation" broadly and I invite you to do the same. When Tillich first formulated this "structure of correlation," he imagined the Christian message as the "answer" to all contemporary questions that might be addressed to it, and he deemed it the theologian's task as providing that answer for contemporary audiences through the method of correlation. In order to counter the implication that the religious tradition possesses all the "answers" to the complexity of our "ever-shifting cultural, political, ethical, and religious situation,"[35] contemporary theologians emphasize the "mutually critical" dialogue between tradition and contemporary situation inherent in the method. When interpreted as a dialogical process, this method provides theological writers with a rhetoric of correlation that will support the writing of a constructive theological essay from a variety of theological starting points.[36]

Charting the rhetorics of the constructive theological essay: Identification, correlation, suspicion, and construction

If you have written the pastoral reflection paper in Chapter 2 or the systematic reflection paper in Chapter 3, you have already used the method of correlation. However, you might not have noticed that a pattern of essay organization is built into the method of correlation that can be used to guide your own writing of a theological essay. As it unfolds in a constructive theological essay, the structure or "rhetoric of correlation" is comprised of four parts: (1) *identification*, which introduces the question or problem that engenders the essay and proposes a thesis in response to the question; (2) *correlation*, which places the question in conversation with the relevant resources of the Christian tradition, hence "correlating" present questioning and traditional religious "answers"; (3) *suspicion*, which critiques the negative, problematic, or oppressive elements of the tradition in the light of the pressing question; and (4) *construction*, which fashions a constructive, or "answering" theology from the theological and cultural resources arising from the "mutually critical conversation" between question and tradition that is imagined, conceptualized, reformulated, and synthesized by the writer/theologian.[37]

While I have enumerated these parts in the order in which they typically appear in a constructive theological essay, they should not be considered merely as static building blocks piled one upon another by rote to form a finished structure. On the contrary, each constituent integrates dynamic theological and rhetorical processes that will interact variously according to the argument of the essay and the constructive imagination of its writer/theologian. We might better think of them as ingredients in a delicious stew that you have added in the particular order specified by the recipe, but to which you have added a distinctive "bouquet garni" from your own herb garden. As the pot simmers slowly on the stove, a savory but subtle mingling of flavors is produced that another cook might not have achieved, even if she had followed the recipe to the letter and added the meat, carrots, and potatoes to the pot in the same order.

Or to change the metaphor slightly, we might think of "correlation" as the dynamic platform that is both the foundation and the fulcrum that draws the argument forward into different stages of emphasis (from *question* to *correlation* to *critique* to *construction*). Thus, each of these parts can be imagined as layers in the density of an argument[38] that do not supercede each other, but "gather to a greatness," as Gerard Manley Hopkins's images of "God's Grandeur" do in that poem. And, if we are indeed "working out a theology as we go" in the process of moving from question to correlation to critique to construction, we should expect all of these processes to be at work throughout the writing of the essay. Nevertheless, the following "map" presents each part sequentially to help us focus on them discretely and correlates this structure in turn with the elements of the essay that we have already examined.

Writing the constructive theological essay well: A map of "correlation"

IDENTIFICATION (The Problematic)	**Identifying the Theological Question/Thesis:** *The writer/theologian identifies a theological question or problem and proposes a thesis that will focus and direct the theological process of correlation.*
CORRELATION (Exposition)	**Establishing the Theological Correlation:** *The writer/theologian establishes the grounds of the correlation through an analysis of the question in conversation with the Christian tradition.*
SUSPICION (Criticism)	**Engaging a Dialogue of Critical Suspicion:** *The writer/theologian engages the tradition in a dialogue of critical suspicion regarding its negative or oppressive elements to demonstrate the need for a constructive interpretation.*
CONSTRUCTION (Interpretation)	**Completing the Theological Construction:** *The writer constructs an answering theology through a synthetic integration of (1) his or her own theological imagination and experience; (2) the sources of Christian faith (the Bible, church documents, "tradition"); (3) the theological norm[39] deemed authoritative for the theologian and the community for whom he or she is writing.*[40]

How, then, might this structure be useful in your own writing of a constructive theological essay? Any time that you write an essay that begins with a theological question that you proceed to "answer" using the resources of the Christian tradition in dialogue with your own experience, you will be using the rhetoric of correlation to structure your argument. If, for example, we take another look at the "Was Jesus a Feminist" essay in Chapter 3 through the lens of a rhetoric of correlation, we will easily find (a) an opening question ("Was Jesus a Feminist?") and thesis in response to the question; (b) an explanatory section that limits the parameters of the argument, defines necessary terms and provides relevant textual information; (c) and an "answer" that is asserted in concert with the theological norm being proposed ("contemporary women's experience of oppression"), substantiated with evidence from "earliest Christian traditions" related in New Testament sources, and correlated in terms of a "fusion of hermeneutical horizons that coalesce in the egalitarian vision of the *basileia*," through which vision "Jesus may be interpreted as a feminist."[41] The concluding "answer" correlates "Jesus" and "feminist" and, in so doing, constructs a theological position that was not implicit before the author conceived and completed the essay.

Writing the constructive theological essay well: A structural map

IDENTIFICATION **Identifying the Theological Question/Thesis:**

Question: "Was Jesus a feminist?"

Thesis: "Interrogated by women's experience of oppression, the earliest Jesus traditions provide warrants for interpreting Jesus as a feminist."

CORRELATION **Establishing the Theological Correlation:**

A. *FRAMING THE CORRELATION*

I follow Elisabeth Schüssler-Fiorenza's definition of feminism as "not just a theoretical world view or perspective but a women's liberation movement for social and ecclesiastical change" (*Bread Not Stone*: 5). Her feminist hermeneutic includes these warrants: (1) Jesus and the praxis of the earliest church as a biblical root model, prototype [36] and locus of revelation [34]; (2) the contemporary experience of women struggling for liberation as a correlative locus of revelation [34] and (3) the *basileia* as the inextricable connection between both of these [153].[42]

B. *DRAWING THE CORRELATION*

According to the earliest Christian traditions, Jesus ate with poor women and prostitutes; engaged and was engaged in conversations with non-Israelite and Gentile women; touched and was touched by ritually "unclean" women; traveled in the company of women patrons; healed crippled women on the Sabbath; advocated for widows; and appeared first to women after his resurrection. These traditions suggest that Jesus did not restrict women's roles to reproduction, child rearing, and the domestic sphere. Rather, he challenged patriarchal family structures oppressive to women, and invited women and men to share his egalitarian *basileia*.

SUSPICION **Engaging a Dialogue of Critical Suspicion:**

The answers we receive from a text depend upon the questions we ask and the hermeneutic we bring to the question. Thus the question, Was Jesus a feminist?, must first be asked before it can be answered, and the answer will be predisposed by the hermeneutic that frames the question.

CONSTRUCTION **Completing the Theological Construction:**

Whether or not the question of Jesus and feminism was asked by first century Palestinian women, women ask it today. Jesus' advocacy for women of his culture becomes a norm for women's experience of liberation from patriarchy, and their struggle to make the "*basileia* vision of Jesus" a reality today. Therefore, this fusion of hermeneutical horizons coalesces in the egalitarian vision of the *basileia*, and Jesus may be interpreted as a feminist.

Writing a constructive theological essay of your own: A progressive model

A constructive theological essay assignment will not always provide an opening question like Why do you follow Jesus? or Was Jesus a Feminist? More often, you will be invited to follow the fault lines of your own theological questions and concerns, as they are exposed in the course of your own reading, writing, and reflection for a particular class. Moreover, most constructive theological essays also invite an active integration of "pastoral" and "systematic" styles. For example, in his "Introduction to Theology" class at Episcopal Divinity School, Christopher Duraisingh provides a "progressive model" for writing a constructive theological essay comprised of three assignments that build upon each other strategically during the course of the semester. These assignments enable students to (1) generate their own questions from reflection on a particular theological or pastoral question, (2) correlate those questions with three theological sources that address the issue, and (3) critically analyze and reformulate the issue in a constructive theological proposal that is oriented toward their own context.[43]

Duraisingh's "progressive model" outlines a simple but cumulative process for writing a constructive theological essay of your own. For example, if you were a theological student from Rwanda, you might have searching questions about the horrific genocide in which Christian churches and pastoral leaders were complicit. Those questions might lead you to biblical analogues and theological responses to the conflict; to the current literature on genocide; and to the literature of conflict resolution, models of reconciliation, and so forth. In the process of your own analysis, synthesis, and imaginative appropriation of these sources, illuminated and critiqued by your own experience, you might craft a constructive theology of reconciliation for the Christian churches of Rwanda. Even if your particular theological questions and faith issues are closer to home, they will provide your own starting point for writing a constructive theological essay. In the following Theological Memo, I have adapted Duraisingh's three written assignments to outline a more flexible "three-draft process" that you are invited to adapt in turn to the requirements of your own constructive theological essay.

This "three-draft model" and Duraisingh's assignments on which it is based follow the structure of the "Rhetoric of Correlation" but move purposefully beyond a "mere" correlation model in their constructive method. For example, the movements of "correlation" and "suspicion" are not distinguished by different drafts but coincide in Drafts #2 and #3 of the model. This is as it should be. At times "correlation" will be the dominant motif, and the tradition will be critiqued but not deconstructed. At other times, "suspicion" will require radical deconstruction before the constructive synthesis can be performed. But, just as the piano scales that one practices in individual crescendos as a child disappear into the accomplished pianist's performance of a concerto, so at the hands of a gifted theologian, the discrete theological rhetorics of identification, correlation, suspicion, and construction conspire to create a constructive theological proposal that is faithfully rendered in the constructive theological essay that inscribes it. With this goal in mind, it is time to try your hand at writing the constructive theological essay well:

> *THEOLOGICAL MEMO 5: Writing a Constructive Theological Essay in Three Drafts:*
>
> *(1)* ***Reflecting:*** *In a freewriting exercise or journal entry, reflect on two or three theological questions or faith issues that you struggle with, and describe the shape that your struggle takes. After you have completed the reflection, re-read what you have written. Is any one of the questions more pressing for you? Is there any logical or intuitive relationship between the issues you have raised? Can you formulate the questions/issues into one broad but compelling theological motif? Please identify that question, issue or theme in a concise statement.*
>
> *(2)* ***Correlating/Critiquing:*** *Choose three theologians who have addressed your theological issue in their writings, and write a 7–8 page "Correlation Paper" that (a) summarizes each theologian's contribution and (b) compares and contrasts each theological articulation of the issue. In a concluding section, weave your own theological reflection through the loom of these theological perspectives. What constructive elements have you found in each position? What elements have elicited your critique and/or theological suspicion? Which element remains dominant for you?*
>
> *(3)* ***Constructing:*** *Using the materials in the first two drafts, in concert with your own theological imagination, prepare a 20 page "Constructive Theological Essay" that (a) articulates your pressing theological question; (b) presents the theological formulations of three authors in relation to this question; (c) compares, contrasts and critically analyzes them from your own theological perspective; and (d) constructively reformulates the issue in dialogue with your own context.*

Concluding reflections: Writing the constructive theological essay well

> A novel has a story, a poem rhyme; but what art can the essayist use in these short lengths of prose to sting us wide awake and fix us in a trance which is not sleep but rather an intensification of life....? He [or she] must know—that is the first essential—how to write.[44]

Although Virginia Woolf's reflections on "The Modern Essay," quoted above, were originally addressed to writers of literary essays, they challenge writers of theological essays as well. How long has it been since you have read a constructive theological essay, or a theological essay of any kind, that was written so well that it "stung you wide awake" and "fixed you in a trance which [was] not sleep but rather an intensification of life?" How long has it been since you have written such an essay yourself? If this is a rarer occurrence than you would like to admit, it may be due to the fact that writing a theological essay is more often a means of conveying theological information than a stylistic end in itself. But, think for a moment of the last time you read a theological essay that moved, inspired, challenged, or simply communicated with you clearly and forcefully. The author of that essay undoubtedly knew how to write!

We have already seen that the prerequisite of writing a good essay in any discipline is knowing "how to write" in a style that is in perfect accord with its subject matter, purpose, structure, voice, and audience, and theological writing is no exception to this rule. But, what is that elusive quality that makes an essay "leap off the page" as we read it? While few since Augustine have identified it as a virtue of theological writing,[45] that quality is "pleasure."[46] Although not all theological authors may consider their readers' pleasure a priority, are not being moved, inspired, and challenged by an essay forms of pleasure?

You may protest that the goal of giving the reader pleasure is a luxury reserved for experienced and gifted writers, and certainly not for theological students. Yet, the kind of pleasure that an essay gives is not only due to an author's distinctive gifts of creativity and expression, or even to the author's theological competence alone. As every one of your professors will attest, the pleasure that an essay provides its reader also depends upon its author's mastery of language and style, whether that author is a distinguished theologian or a theological student. If you are still with me as we conclude the fourth chapter of this book, and if you have been writing the Theological Memos along the way, I suspect that your professors have already found your own theological essays more pleasurable to read. Nonetheless, prompted by Augustine and Virginia Woolf, I conclude with nine ways to make a constructive theological essay even more pleasurable to your readers.

First, write about what matters to you, invoking all the resources of your own theological imagination. In order to leave room for your own theological imagination, the topic for a constructive theological essay is typically broad and unspecified. To narrow its focus, begin with "some fierce attachment to an idea," which Woolf describes as the backbone of a well-written essay.[47] If the original essay topic does not attract you, keep reading and reflecting until you find your own path into the subject. This does not mean abandoning the assigned topic but rerouting it through your own center of gravity. What theological questions, ethical debates, justice issues, or pastoral commitments are currently engaging you? What courses have captured your imagination? What did you preach on last Sunday? The most pedestrian essay topic can be transformed into a passionate inquiry if you follow the compass of your theological imagination until it fixates unwaveringly upon a question and rewrite the topic in the light of that question.

Second, capitalize on your own strengths of style and voice. "To write like oneself and call it not writing is a much harder exercise in style than to write like [a writer you admire] and call it writing well," Woolf suggests.[48] While there is both precedent and pretext for imitating the style of accomplished theological writers,[49] it takes courage to "write like oneself" when writing academically. Yet, the essay form is rooted in this kind of self-reflection, and the constructive theological essay allows its author a wide range of expression. Moreover, just as you speak in a different register to your professor than you do to an intimate friend, a constructive theological essay can be written in a formal academic voice or in the more conversational voice of the literary essayist, and still be written in "your own voice."[50]

Third, provide a preliminary "map" of your essay for the reader in the introduction (or introductory section). If your readers are to travel with you for the length of an essay, whether it is five, ten, or twenty pages long, they will not go far without a map. In her introduction to "The Modern Essay," for example, Woolf moves deftly from the seeming "chaos" of the English essay genre to her assertion that one can find "principles" implicit in a well-written essay that will also chart its "progress through history."[51] While she does not tell her readers what those principles are at the outset, she has intimated a trail map by telling them what to look for ("principles") and in what order (a historical survey). Whether your essay is written in an inductive style that saves its full disclosure for the conclusion of the essay, or in a deductive style that begins with a straightforward statement of your thesis, readers will thank you for providing them with a brief but suggestive outline of your essay at the outset. In so doing, you will also have provided yourself with a "short form" of your longer outline.

Fourth, write simply. Choose simple words whenever possible, however tempted you are to emulate your favorite theologian's technical vocabulary. "Of all forms of literature," Woolf declares, "the essay is the one which least calls for the use of long words."[52] To write simply, the weight of your sentences should fall upon concrete nouns and active verbs, with adjectives and adverbs used to clarify and intensify the words they modify, not merely to decorate your essay. Moreover, simple sentences should follow a straightforward "subject/verb/object" word order, and compound or complex sentences should employ parallel sentence structure. Then, when you vary word order and sentence structure for accent and emphasis, it will be all the more effective.

Fifth, write precisely. To write precisely, according to Woolf, is to use language that is "exact," "imaginative," and "truthful."[53] Perhaps you would not put these words together so readily to describe writing that is precise. However, as an equally accomplished writer of fiction and prose, she understood that to write precisely, it was necessary to be imaginative as well and to be imaginative required truthfulness. What else impels writers to select words that truthfully reflect their intended meaning and evoke more than they intend, rather than settling for the first word that comes to mind? The theological language of image, metaphor, and symbol requires this integration of precision and imagination, no less than technical theological terms, which you should use accurately and define clearly when necessary.

Sixth, write truthfully. To write truthfully transcends the precision of individual words, images, or definitions, to embrace the larger truth that you seek to communicate in your essay. "Truth will give it authority," Woolf concludes.[54] The truth of an essay inheres in its sentences because the writer makes statements by constructing assertions in sentences that ring with the writer's "truth." At times you will write what you know is true. At other times you will not know what is true until you write it. You will know that a sentence is "true," as Virginia Woolf uses the term here, when you no longer have to revise it. If you must revise, keep doing so until what you want to say rings true, word by word and sentence by sentence.

Seventh, write constructively. An essay is constructed with words, sentences, and paragraphs that form a beginning, middle, and end. Within this structure, Woolf cautions, "the bounds are strict and facts have to be used in their nakedness."[55] Yet, this does not entail weighing the reader down with pages of quoted "facts," but rather digesting that material for the reader into a cogent narrative that is written in the writer's own words.[56] Toward that end, each essay paragraph should present its material coherently, and each paragraph should build upon the previous one. Think of building each paragraph as if it were an essay in miniature, with (a) an opening sentence, (b) supporting and exemplifying sentences, and (c) a concluding and/or connecting sentence that moves toward the next paragraph. If the essay order seems inevitable when you have finished, you have written constructively. If gaps or incongruities remain, go back to the drawing board!

Eighth, connect the parts of the essay. Just as a well-wrought essay needs an introductory "map," the best-written essay that does not provide transitions between sections of the essay will lose readers along the way. Readers need to be reminded where they are going, where they have been, and what to expect around the next bend, whether you are moving between paragraphs, sections, or chapters. Imagine these transitions as strips of Velcro fastening what you have just said to what you are about to say, whether they are as short as a word ("First;" "Next"; "Finally") or as long as a sentence or paragraph ("In this section we have seen ... (a) ... (b) ... and (c). In the light of this discussion, however, it is still not clear how (d) and (e) are related to this discussion. In the next section we will explore each of these elements before proposing a constructive theology of (f).").

Finally, revise until you get it right, but reserve the right to keep revising. As Montaigne first defined it and Kathleen Norris corroborates, "The essay ... is merely an attempt."[57] In other words, it is a work in progress. It does not have to be perfect. However, few people can write an essay well without revising it. Your final draft should reflect as much revision as is required to allow you to send it on its way confidently to its reader. If your professor, classmate, or writing tutor is willing to read a penultimate draft of your essay before you turn in your final draft, so much the better. While it is not always possible to receive feedback while the paper is in progress, it is also helpful to think of a completed theological essay as a work in progress, open to further conversation and continuing revision in the light of that conversation. If your professor's comments on your completed essay continue the theological conversation the essay began, whether by questioning, critiquing, commending, or referring you to other pertinent sources, that is a good sign. Your essay has succeeded—at least enough to evoke a theological response—in giving that reader pleasure, and you have demonstrated that you know how to write the constructive theological essay well.

In this chapter, we have asked, "What is it that makes an essay theological?" "How shall we write a theological essay?" In response to these questions, we have followed the essay from its literary genre to its theological species. We have identified the elements of the critical theological essay and the rhetorics of the constructive theological essay. Finally, you have been invited to write a constructive theological essay that integrates both pastoral and systematic styles, using all of these resources. Whether your courses involve the writing of critical or constructive essays, your mastery of the essay form, with its carefully crafted beginning, middle, and end, will bode well for you in any paper you are assigned to write. But most essays require some form of research, whether the sources are included in your class readings or invite your own investigation. Without leaving the theological essay behind, in the next two chapters, we quarry theological research as a resource for writing theology and probe the process of writing theological research well, employing rhetorics of *research* and *investigation* (Chapter 5) and *organization* and *documentation* (Chapter 6).

Notes

1 See "The Essay: A Framework for Thinking in Writing" in V.A. Howard and J. H. Barton, *Thinking on Paper* (New York: Quill/William Morrow, 1986), 42.

2 Subject, purpose, and audience are introduced in the discussion of the sociorhetorical context of theological writing in Chapter 1. See also previous discussion and definitions of "purpose, style and voice" in Chapter 2.

3 See Sarah Bakewell, *How to Live: Or a Life of Montaigne in One Question and Twenty Attempts at an Answer* (London: Chatto & Windus, 2010; New York: Other Press, 2010).

4 See Robert P. Ellis, "Michel Eyquem de Montaigne," in *Encyclopedia of Literary Critics and Criticism*, vol. 2, ed. Chris Murray (London: Fitzroy Dearborn, 1999), 784; Cristina Kirklighter, "The Personal, the Political, and the Rhetorical: Montaigne and Bacon's Use of the Essay Form," in *Traversing the Democratic Borders of the Essay*, ed. Kirklighter (Albany, NY: SUNY Press, 2002), 15–38; and Carl H. Claus and Ned Stuckey-French, eds., *Essayists on the Essay: Montaigne to Our Time* (Iowa City, IA: University of Iowa Press, 2012).

5 See, e.g., John Locke, *An Essay Concerning Human Understanding*, ed. P.H. Nidditch (Oxford: Clarendon Press, 1975); David Hume, *Essays: Moral, Political and Literary*, ed. E.F. Miller (Indianapolis, IN: Liberty Classics, 1987).

6 By limiting the scope of the theological essay to the treatment of one problem, or subject, Tillich distinguishes it from the medieval *summa*, which embraced "all actual and potential problems" in its encyclopedic breadth, and from the *system* (the genre employed by systematic theologians, including Tillich himself), which "deals with a group of actual problems which demand a solution in a special situation." See Paul Tillich, *Systematic Theology*, 3 vols. (Chicago: University of Chicago Press, 1951–1963), 1: 58–59.

7 E.g., one of David Tracy's three "publics" of theology (the academy; the church; the wider society) discussed in Chapter 1, or simply the theological "public" represented by the professor assigning an essay and requiring that it be written according to specific conventions.

8 For David Tracy, for example, conversation is the exemplary model of theological interpretation and communication. See Tracy, *The Analogical Imagination: Christian Theology and the Culture of Pluralism* (New York: Crossroad, 1987), 446–55; and Tracy, *Plurality and Ambiguity: Hermeneutics, Religion, Hope* (Chicago: University of Chicago Press, 1987), 16–23. See also Gordon Kaufman, *In the Face of Mystery: A Constructive Theology* (Cambridge, MA: Harvard University Press, 1993), who argues for "conversation" rather than the "text" or the "lecture" as "the proper model for conceiving theology" (64).

9 Kaufman, *In the Face of Mystery*, 64.

10 Roger Haight's article, "Women in the Church: A Theological Reflection," *Toronto Journal of Theology* 2, no. 1 (1986): 105–17, exemplifies a "problem to solution" structure, which coincides with a "structure of correlation." See Chapter 2.

11 See Gordon Kaufman, *An Essay on Theological Method*, 3rd ed. (Atlanta, GA: Scholars Press, 1995), 38.

12 For more detailed treatments of writing the summary, see Sharon Friedman and Stephen Steinberg, *Writing and Thinking in the Social Sciences* (Englewood Cliffs, NJ: Prentice-Hall, 1989, 139–45); and John M. Swales and Charlene B. Feak, *Academic Writing for Graduate Students: Essential Tasks and Skills,* 3rd ed. (Ann Arbor: University of Michigan Press, 2012), 188–226.

13 See Margaret Miles, "Hermeneutics of Generosity and Suspicion: Pluralism and Theological Education," *Theological Education* 23, Supplement (1987): 34–52.

14 A theological norm is a criterion for judging the adequacy of a theological position. For example, Roger Haight's, *Jesus Symbol of God* (Maryknoll, NY: Orbis, 1999), 46–47, asserts faithfulness to the Christian tradition as one of the norms, or "criteria" of the Christology proposed in that book.

15 For example, Elisabeth Schüssler Fiorenza's feminist hermeneutic of critical evaluation claims "women's experience of oppression and liberation" as the norm by which scriptural texts should be evaluated for their "feminist liberating content." See Elisabeth Schüssler Fiorenza, "The Will to Choose or Reject: Continuing Our Critical Work," in *Feminist Interpretation of the Bible*, ed. Letty M. Russell (Philadelphia, PA: Westminster Press, 1985), 130–31.

16 David Tracy, *Blessed Rage for Order: The New Pluralism in Theology* (New York: Seabury, 1975; reprint, Chicago: University of Chicago Press, 1996), 246 (cited from the reprint edition).

17 For a more detailed treatment of analytical writing, see David Rosenwasser and Jill Stephen, *Writing Analytically* (Fort Worth, TX: Harcourt Brace College Publishers, 1997). For a "critique" of analytical writing, see Helen Fox, *Listening to the World: Cultural Issues in Academic Writing* (Urbana, IL: NCTE Press, 1994), 125.

18 Sandra M. Schneiders, *The Revelatory Text: Interpreting the New Testament as Sacred Scripture*, 2nd ed. (Collegeville, MN: Liturgical Press, Michael Glazier, 1999), 124.

19 Tracy, *Blessed Rage for Order*, 246 (italics mine).

20 See, for example, the chapter entitled "Interpretation" in Bernard J.F. Lonergan, *Method in Theology* (London: Darton, Longman & Todd, 1971; repr. Toronto: University of Toronto Press, 1994), 153–73 (page citations are to the reprint edition).

21 See Sandra Schneiders' useful distinction between interpretation as "process" and as "product," which I follow here (Schneiders, *Revelatory Text*, 157–64).

22 This outline is adapted with permission from a class handout by Professor Joan Martin, of Episcopal Divinity School, Cambridge, Massachusetts.

23 See Karl Rahner, *Theological Investigations*, 23 vols., trans. Cornelius Ernst (New York: Crossroad, 1974–1992), a collection of essays that communicate a coherent theology, volume by volume; Nicholas Lash, *Theology on the Way to Emmaus* (London: SCM Press, 1986), and an exemplary essay in his collection, "Criticism or Construction? The Task of the Theologian" (1–17); Kaufman, *Essay on Theological Method*, who employs the essay form intentionally to outline his "constructive" theological method. See Stanley M. Hauerwas, *Wilderness Wanderings: Probing Twentieth-Century Theology*

and Philosophy (Boulder, CO: Westview Press, 1997), in which Hauerwas constructs a "wilderness theology", employing the essay form, as he explains in his Preface (xi–xiv).

24 Kaufman, *Essay on Theological Method*, xviii.

25 Tillich, *Systematic Theology*, I: 58.

26 See Ibid., 53: "... systematic theology is not a historical discipline ...; it is a constructive task. It does not tell us what people have thought the Christian message to be in the past; rather it tries to give us an interpretation of the Christian message which is relevant to the present situation."

27 Kaufman, *In the Face of Mystery*, 58. See also his *Essay on Theological Method*, for his first systematic presentation of this position.

28 Roger Haight, *Dynamics of Theology* (New York: Paulist Press, 1990; repr., Maryknoll, NY: Orbis, 2001), 189.

29 Tillich, *Systematic Theology*, 1: 16.

30 See David Tracy's critique of Tillich and revised theory of "mutually critical correlation" in *Blessed Rage for Order*, 34–35.

31 Roger Haight, "Jesus and Salvation," *Theological Studies* 55 (1994): 225–51, here 234.

32 See Elizabeth A. Johnson, *She Who Is: The Mystery of God in Feminist Theological Discourse* (New York: Crossroad, 1992), 13, paraphrased in her *Friends of God and Prophets: A Feminist Theological Reading of the Communion of Saints* (New York: Continuum, 1998), 3–4.

33 Rosemary Radford Reuther, "Feminist Interpretation: A Method of Correlation," in *Feminist Interpretation of the Bible*, ed. Letty M. Russell (Philadelphia, PA: Westminster Press, 1985), 115.

34 Haight, *Dynamics of Theology*, 192.

35 David Tracy, "Practical Theology in the Situation of Global Pluralism," in *Formation and Reflection: the Promise of Practical Theology*, ed. Lewis B. Mudge and James M. Poling (Philadelphia, PA: Fortress Press, 1987), 141. For example, Elizabeth Johnson's *Friends of God and Prophets: A Feminist Theological Reading of the Communion of Saints* renders the "structure of correlation" in that book as dialogical, exemplified by the three parts of her essay: (1) "Framing the Question" (2) "Dialogue with a Living Tradition" (3) "Theology of the Friends of God and Prophets (ii–ix)."

36 See, e.g., Chapter 8, "Writing the Biblical Essay Well (II): A Critical-Hermeneutical Rhetoric," which engages the dialogical hermeneutic of Mikhail Bakhtin in "Building Dialogical Bridges through a Hermeneutics of Diversity."

37 See Haight, *Dynamics of Theology*, 207–10, for an excellent analysis of the process of constructing a theological position, which includes (1) imagination, (2) conceptualization, (3) mutual critique of positions, and (4) drawing out the consequences for "empowerment of human life" (p. 209).

38 In a personal conversation, Roger Haight offered this lucid metaphor of the structure of theological correlation in describing his own process of theological construction in "Jesus and Salvation," 225–51.

39 That is, "the criterion to which the sources and the mediating experience must be subjected": Tillich, *Systematic Theology*, 1: 47.

40 Examples of a theological norm might include the preferential option for the poor; the historical Jesus of the synoptic gospels; women's experience of oppression and liberation.

41 See Chapter 3.

42 Numbers in square brackets refer to page numbers in Elisabeth Schüssler Fiorenza, *In Memory of Her: A Feminist Theological Reconstruction of Christian Origins* (New York: Crossroad, 1986).

43 Christopher Duraisingh, Syllabus, "Introduction to Theology," Episcopal Divinity School, Fall 2006. I am indebted as well to conversations with Professor Duraisingh in which he elucidated the theological pedagogy that informs this constructive essay assignment.

44 Virginia Woolf, "The Modern Essay," in *The Common Reader*, First Series Annotated Edition, ed. Andrew McNeille (New York: Harcourt Brace, 1925; repr. 1953, 1984), 211–12 (page references are to the 1984 annotated edition).

45 See Augustine, *On Christian Doctrine*, trans. D.W. Robertson, Jr. (Indianapolis, IN: Bobbs-Merrill [Liberal Arts Press], 1958), who validated "pleasure" as an appropriate response to the writings of Scripture (book 2, 6, 7–8) and "delighting" the audience a worthy goal for the pastoral preacher/writer (book 4, 12, 27).

46 Virginia Woolf names "pleasure" the controlling "principle" of the literary essay "Modern Essay," 211).

47 Ibid.

48 Ibid., 215.

49 In *On Christian Doctrine*, book 4, 3, 4, Augustine advised his students that one could learn more about eloquence by imitating classical and theological writers than by following the rules of rhetoric. Nonetheless, he provided his own rules, and I follow his precedent.

50 For more on writing "voice," see Chapter 10, "Rewriting Theology Well: Rhetorics of Style and Voice."

51 Woolf, "Modern Essay," 211.

52 Ibid.

53 Ibid., 221.

54 Ibid., 213.

55 Ibid.

56 For more on the use of quotations in a research essay, see Chapter 6, "Writing Theological Research Well II): Rhetorics of Organization and Documentation."

57 Kathleen Norris, Introduction to *The Best American Essays 2001*, ed. Katherine Norris (Boston, MA: Houghton Mifflin, 2001), xv.

PART TWO

Writing Theological and Biblical Research Well

5

Writing Theological Research Well (I): Rhetorics of Research and Investigation

It is virtually impossible to do theology as if it had never been done before. There is always an element of looking over one's shoulder to see how things were done in the past, and what answers were then given.

—ALISTER E. MCGRATH, *Christian Theology*

I began this research ... with the idea that the communion of saints would provide an untapped resource for developing a contemporary theology of Mary of Nazareth.

—ELIZABETH A. JOHNSON, *Friends of God and Prophets*

Research makes available the data relevant to theological investigation.

—BERNARD J.F. LONERGAN, *Method in Theology*

Starting points

As the quotations that begin this chapter exemplify, *research* is a fundamental resource of theological study, and *investigation* is its primary way of proceeding. In his introduction to Christian theology, Alister McGrath underscores the need for students of theology to investigate past theological questions in order to illuminate current questions.[1] In her investigation of the historical questions concerning the doctrine of the communion of saints, Elizabeth Johnson seeks resources for a contemporary understanding of Mary in Roman Catholic theology.[2] Identifying "research" as one of eight subdisciplines of theological studies, Bernard Lonergan links the data of theological research, or "what was written,"[3] to the ongoing activity of theological investigation. Even if your purpose for doing theological research is more modest than that of these professional theologians, you will need to engage the rhetorics of research and investigation in order to "write theological research well," just as you will need to master the rhetorics of organization and documentation, which are covered in Chapter 6.

In this chapter, we address these questions: (1) What is research and what makes people do it? (2) What is theological research and how do theologians do it? (3) How does writing theological research differ from other kinds of theological writing? (4) What kinds of theological research essays are most frequently encountered across the theological curriculum, and how shall we write them? First, however, we introduce the approach to theological writing and research that informs this chapter and offer a preliminary map of the process.

Approaching the theological writing and research process

Many writing texts strive to provide students with a "one size fits all" research-writing model that is adaptable to various purposes and disciplines.[4] The approach to writing theological research in this chapter, on the other hand, is discipline-specific. Because our concern is with "writing theology well," we approach theological writing and research as integrally related processes that conjoin as a "craft"[5] requiring personal engagement, critical reflection, and the exercise of the theological imagination. Inevitably, this chapter builds upon the theological writing strategies introduced in the preceding chapters, for a theological research paper incorporates theological reflection, theological argument, and both critical and constructive theological essays in its varied disciplinary versions across the theological curriculum.

If you have not yet read Chapter 3, "Writing Theological Argument Well," you are advised to do so before proceeding with this chapter, for the processes of developing a thesis statement and structuring an argument in deductive or inductive style are presupposed here. However, in this chapter and in Chapter 6, we focus on the specific skills required for doing and writing theological research well, whether you are writing a twenty-page research essay for a theology or church history class or a lengthier thesis project. Because these skills are not learned in isolation but unfold as a complex and often challenging array of tasks, we proceed to a preliminary map of the process.

Writing theological research well: A preliminary map

- Writing theological research begins with *inquiry or investigation.*
- Writing theological research presupposes a *methodology or research perspective.*
- Writing theological research engenders a *search for sources.*
- Writing theological research builds upon an ongoing scholarly *conversation.*
- Writing theological research creates and claims *a research space.*
- Writing theological research proceeds by *hypothesis, assertion, and argument.*
- Writing theological research requires *reading and reviewing the literature.*
- Writing theological research involves *writing, rewriting, and revision.*
- Writing theological research demands *documentation.*
- Writing theological research presumes some form of *publication.*

THEOLOGICAL MEMO 1: Please choose a research assignment from one of your classes to complete in connection with this chapter and select a potential research topic in response to the assignment. Please describe the assignment as specifically as you can, and respond briefly to the following questions: What is your topic? Why does it interest you? From what disciplinary (e.g., theological; pastoral; biblical) perspective will you approach the topic? What questions emerge as you reflect on the topic? Where would you begin searching for relevant sources (e.g., the bibliography included on the course syllabus; the library catalog; an electronic database)?

What is research and what makes people do it?

People do research for many reasons, but the best researchers do research because there is something that they do not know that they want to know. What they do not know poses a question that will not let them rest until they have answered it, and in order to answer the question, they undertake a search that culminates in *research*—literally, to "search again." The best researchers "search again and again," until they have answered the question driving them. As Wayne Booth corroborates, "We do research whenever we gather information to answer a question that solves a problem."[6]

For some, the questions arise intuitively from their personal and intellectual history. As cultural anthropologist Carol Delaney suggests, "Each person's work is, to some extent, an excavation of his or her own history. The intellectual problems one chooses to dig into, the tools one employs, and the perspective one takes up are rooted in that history."[7] For others, the questions emerge more directly from the material they are researching. "How many people could read, how many people could write in the Graeco-Roman world?" asks classical historian William V. Harris in the introduction of his monograph, *Ancient Literacy*, and confesses, "These simple-seeming questions are the origin of this book."[8] For still others, they arise from imaginations playful enough to answer questions that no one else has asked. For example, in a poem about the "Three Blind Mice," Billy Collins wonders "how they came to be blind":

And I start wondering how they came to be blind.
If it was congenital, they could be brothers and sisters,
and I think of the poor mother
brooding over her sightless young triplets.

Or was it a common accident, all three caught
In a searing explosion, a firework perhaps?
If not,
if each came to his or her blindness separately,

how did they ever manage to find one another?
Would it not be difficult for a blind mouse

to locate even one fellow mouse with vision
let alone two other blind ones?

And how, in their tiny darkness,
could they possibly have run after a farmer's wife
or anyone else's wife for that matter?
Not to mention why.

Just so she would cut off their tails
with a carving knife, is the cynic's answer,
but the thought of them without eyes
and now without tails to trail through the moist grass

or slip around the corner of a baseboard
has the cynic who always lounges within me
up off his couch and at the window
trying to hide the rising softness that he feels.

By now I am on to dicing an onion
which might account for the wet stinging
in my own eyes, though Freddie Hubbard's
mournful trumpet on "Blue Moon,"

which happens to be the next cut,
cannot be said to making matters any better.[9]

"Without questions," writes Hans Georg Gadamer, "there is no knowledge."[10] Yet, every question begins as an affirmative statement ("Three blind mice! See how they run!") that someone's curiosity turns into a question ("Three blind mice? How could they run?") that engenders other questions, as the imaginative but relentlessly logical string of questions that follow each other in Billy Collins' poem. Whether or not questions about "Three Blind Mice" are keeping you up at night or inspiring you to write poetry, questions like these that no one else has thought of asking are at the heart of every good research project. To write theological research well, therefore, you need to cultivate a habit of inquiry that is not afraid to turn periods (.) into question marks (?), and to follow the trail of the resulting question wherever it leads you. For example:

THEOLOGICAL MEMO 2: Please read another familiar children's nursery rhyme, "Sing a Song of Sixpence":

Sing a song of sixpence! A pocket full of rye!
Four and twenty blackbirds baked in a pie!
When the pie was opened, the birds began to sing!
Wasn't that a dainty dish to set before the king!

The king was in his counting-house, counting out his money;
The queen was in the parlor, eating bread and honey;

The maid was in the garden hanging out the clothes,
When along came a blackbird and bit off her nose!

For a church history course, you are writing a research paper on the ecclesiology of "Mother Goose," a collection of English Nursery Rhymes that appeared around the time of the English Reformation.[11] *Using Billy Collins' questions about "Three Blind Mice" as a springboard, (1) Compose your own questions about this nursery rhyme; (2) Choose* ***three*** *questions that are fundamental to your inquiry, and explain why each is important; (3) Select* ***one*** *question of these three that you would use to launch your own "ecclesiological" investigation, and explain why you have chosen it.*

What is theological research and why do theologians do it?

Just as research in any field implies searching and searching again for answers to something one does not know, theological research is simply research undertaken within the disciplinary context of theology. Yet, however "dogmatic" the shape a fully researched theological argument may ultimately take, the discipline of theology as we know it today began with questions, not with answers. To be sure, some of the questions have erred on the side of the arcane and speculative, such as "How many angels can dance on the head of a pin?" Yet, even this question had meaning and relevance to those medieval theologians who first posed it and has inspired contemporary poets to ask further questions.[12] What medieval, modern, and postmodern theologians have in common, however, is that they do theological research to uncover resources that will help them to reflect on the theological task, to trace its historical development, and to construct theologies that respond adequately to the questions posed by their own situations.

How does writing theological research differ from other kinds of theological writing?

Appropriately, then, theological research expresses itself through (1) the form of the question; (2) an operative methodology or research perspective; (3) a return to sources to "research" the question, using all the bibliographical and technical resources available; (4) an ensuing conversation not only with the past, but also with the present; and (5) a development of the question into a theological research "claim" and argument that is initiated by "claiming a research space." We will look at each of these steps in turn.

The form of the question

As we have already seen in Chapter 1 of this book, Scholastic theology has bequeathed the image of "faith seeking understanding" to succeeding generations of theologians, and that seeking is expressed through questions. "Why did God become man?" asked Anselm of Canterbury and answered his own question in *Cur Deus Homo (Why God Became Man)*, a classic of atonement theology.[13] "Is there an ultimate end of human life?" Aquinas asks[14] and places his "Quaestio" at the center of his scholastic rhetoric of *summa*, *quaestio*, and *article*.[15] However, the form of the question is not limited to classic historical works; theologians also employ it today, as we can see from the titles of their works. Questions can define and clarify, as in Shubert Ogden's *Is There Only One True Religion or Are There Many?* They can challenge, as in Hans Kung's *Infallible?* They can probe the current conversation on a theological issue, as in Robert Kinast, *What Are They Saying about Theological Reflection*? They can pose ecclesiological questions by inquiring into the uses of history, as in Rowan Williams's *Why Study the Past? The Quest for the Historical Church*.[16]

Yet, for theologians, questions provide more than titles of theological books. They inspire and motivate the discipline of theology itself. "The basic theological question," writes Paul Tillich, is "the question of God." "What is the right way to speak about God?" asks Elizabeth Johnson. Jon Sobrino asks, "Is it possible to write a christology? And ... is it a useful thing to do?"[17] As you reflect on these and other questions posed by the theologians that you read, it is fitting that your own theological research projects should begin with a carefully formulated research question. The next theological memo invites you to identify and articulate that question:

> *THEOLOGICAL MEMO 3: Please choose a research project from one of your classes for this assignment, and follow these steps to formulate a preliminary research question: (1) Identify your topic (e.g., Luther's understanding of grace); (2) Rephrase it in the form of a pointed question (e.g., "Was Luther's concept of grace a distinctly 'Protestant' doctrine?"); (3) Extend the relevance of the question into a final clause that further refines and clarifies it (e.g., "... or was it inherent in the Augustinian tradition that grounded his study of the New Testament?"). (4) Motivate the question in a final sentence by explaining briefly why this question interests you, and why it might matter to a wider theological audience.*[18]

A methodology or research perspective

Whoever its author and whatever its subject, theological research is always written from some methodological perspective or methodology. If theological research takes the form of a question, theological method, as Rudolf Bultmann suggests, can be understood as "a kind of questioning, a way of putting questions."[19] However, when one asks questions in a particular way, one is consciously or unconsciously operating out of a methodology or research perspective. "Method is *how* you do something; methodology is *why you do it that way*, rather than some other way," John Dominic Crossan explains.[20]

For example, the questions driving Latin American liberation theologian Jon Sobrino's *Jesus the Liberator* are different from the questions posed by European theologian Paul Tillich's *Systematic Theology*, or by North American feminist theologian Elizabeth Johnson's *She Who Is: The Mystery of God in Feminist*

Theological Discourse. Acknowledging the fact that no theological research is ideologically neutral or value-free, each of these authors prefaces their work with a description of their respective methodologies of liberation, correlation, and a feminist hermeneutical method embracing both of them.[21] Moreover, as theologian Roger Haight explains, "Once one grasps what a given theologian is up to methodologically, one can have a fairly accurate appreciation by anticipation of what his or her conclusions will be. For method reaches into the content of theology to shape the very understanding of the subject matter."[22] As feminist biblical scholar Gale Yee concludes, "By choosing a particular method with which to study a biblical text, a reader automatically sets limits on the kinds of questions that can be asked and on the results of her or his investigation. It therefore behooves a reader to be conscious of what these methodological limitations really are."[23] To write theological research well, then, it is necessary to identify the methodology you will be using in your own study of biblical and theological sources.

> *THEOLOGICAL MEMO 4: Based upon the discussion above and from your own understanding of the term(s), what is a "theological/research methodology"? Please define this term in your own words, and identify the methodology you are using in the research project you have chosen to work on in connection with this chapter.*

Sources

In order to answer the questions posed by present theological problems, a theological researcher must return to the sources, for as Alister McGrath reminds us in the epigraph that begins this chapter, theological discourse is written in conversation with previous texts that provide resources for present theologizing.[24] In order to write theological research well, therefore, you will need to become familiar with the standard theological and biblical sources, as well as the specific sources particular to your own research projects. While one can conceivably write a theological reflection paper without recourse to a library catalog or the Internet, one cannot write a theological research paper well without mastering the basics of theological research—finding both print and electronic sources, incorporating sources into your paper responsibly and without plagiarizing other authors' material, documenting sources accurately, and so on. As will be explored more fully in Chapter 14, a mastery of electronic research skills is imperative for accessing the rapidly growing collection of online sources that are now available for biblical and theological study. Toward that end, a working knowledge of your own university or seminary library and the offline and online research tools it provides will be essential to your own resourcefulness as a theological researcher.[25] The Theological Memo below invites you to familiarize yourself with your library's resources as you work on a theological research project:

> *THEOLOGICAL MEMO 5: Please choose a research project from one of your classes to work on at your school library. Taking a scheduled tour of the library should be your first priority, if you have not yet done that. Then take the time*

to familiarize yourself further with its resources by completing the following research tasks:

- *Find one general or introductory source pertinent to your project—e.g., a dictionary or an encyclopedia–one book, one journal article, and one electronic source in the Library online catalogue.*
- *For each of the materials that you find, please indicate (a) their precise location in the library (so that someone else could find the materials from your directions) and (b) your procedure in locating the materials.*
- *Write a bibliographic citation for each of the sources, using the citation style required by your school or professor.*
- *Write a brief annotation of each source. (An annotation is simply a brief description of the source that indicates enough about it to tell another reader whether or not it would be useful for their own research on the topic.)*

Conversation with the present and the past

We have already described the theological essay as a conversation between the theologian and her or his audience.[26] Extending this metaphor to embrace the writing of research as well, Kenneth Burke suggests that doing research is like entering a room where a heated conversation is already in process, listening to the conversation until you are ready to "put [your own] oar in," and, having done so, exiting that room and its conversation before it has been concluded in order to join the conversation in the next room, which has also begun before you arrived and will continue after you leave.[27] Gerald Graff and Cathy Birkenstein describe this conversation more specifically as listening carefully to what "they say," summarizing their argument accurately, and generating a counterargument of what "I say" in response to it.[28]

Similarly, whether theologians appeal to their sources as normative documents for present faith communities or as less-binding testimonies to what the tradition has said in the past, theological research initiates a conversation between the theologian, the sources he or she consults (and what they say), the current problem being addressed, and the theologian's creative synthesis of all of these resources into a constructive (what he or she says) response. Our focus here is upon entering this conversation as theological researchers and directing the conversation strategically in terms of a particular research goal. As all theologians are, we will be guided by (1) the research question we have formulated, (2) the methodology that drives the question, and (3) the sources we choose to converse with in our response to the question.

We return for a moment to the question formulated in Theological Memo 3 concerning Luther's doctrine of grace: "Was Luther's doctrine of grace a distinctly 'Protestant' doctrine, or was it inherent in the Augustinian tradition that grounded his study of the New Testament?" Let us imagine that you proceed to your online library catalog and undertake a "subject" search for sources on "Luther's concept of grace." However, the resulting list of materials is more than you can read in a year, let alone for a research paper due in six weeks, so you will have to narrow your search in some way. The research librarian assisting you will have some helpful suggestions for refining your search, but the first question you need to ask at this point is "With whom do I want to have a conversation with about Luther's doctrine of grace?"[29] The answer to that question will in turn be determined by the research question you have formulated and the methodology that you bring to the project.

For example, to answer the question, "Was Luther's doctrine of grace a distinctly 'Protestant' doctrine, or was it inherent in the Augustinian tradition that grounded his study of the New Testament?," you will need to converse both with theologians studying Luther's work from a Protestant point of view and with others who are investigating his roots in the Roman Catholic/Augustinian tradition. You will also want to converse with scholars concerned with the historical development of the doctrine of grace. However, the sources you choose will also be influenced by the methodological approach that your paper takes. If you are writing the paper for an ecclesiology course requiring you to evaluate Luther's doctrine of grace from a historical perspective, your conversation partners will be different than if you are writing a paper for a feminist theology course that requires you to critique Luther's theology of grace from a feminist point of view. This does not mean, however, that you will ignore contrasting viewpoints or perspectives that challenge your own. On the contrary, it is often those "opposing" authors (and "what they say") who will help you to identify a counterargument and reframe your original research question into a substantive research claim ("what I [e.g., you] say").

Developing the question into a theological research claim

Just as every question mark (?) is formed by the conjunction of an interrogative "squiggle" and a period, every good research question, however "squiggly" its path of inquiry might be, should culminate in a declarative sentence that asserts a research claim or hypothesis. We have already developed a thesis statement in response to the question, Was Jesus a Feminist?, in Chapter 3. Constructing a substantive research claim also draws upon that initial process of theological reflection in which one or two required readings provide data and evidence for developing a thesis statement.[30] In developing a research claim, however, the path from question to assertion should be paved by research sources in tandem with your own narrowing of the topic. For many students, this simultaneous process of expanding the bibliography while narrowing the topic is the most difficult part of the research process, but it is also the most critical. Therefore, before looking more specifically at the process of constructing a research hypothesis and developing it into a substantive argument, we will first look at how to narrow a topic and then turn to two paths for writing theological research, (1) the "Research-Already-in-Place" path and (2) the "Create a Research Space" path.

Narrowing your topic

In order to narrow a topic, you must first allow it room to grow and develop and then narrow the scope of the question that you are asking. This may sound like a paradox, but it is not. If you have already decided what authors writing on your topic you want to have a conversation with, you have already narrowed the topic strategically. But, in order to find the narrow path into your own research, you need what writing guru Natalie Goldberg calls "a large field to wander in."[31] That is what a "literature search," or "review of the literature," provides, which is typically undertaken at the beginning of a research project. Most often you will enter that "broad field" through your library's online catalog and with the help of other online resources, such as the *Religion Index*, *New Testament Abstracts*, and so on. However, once you have located the library call number of books dealing with your topic, do not rule out wandering through the narrower paths of the library stacks to see what other resources are available there. A book that might otherwise be overlooked might just be waiting there to help you further narrow your topic!

However you choose to begin this process, narrowing a topic proceeds by its own logic. It is not as if I wake up one morning and say, "Today I will narrow my topic." What in fact happens is that as I continue to converse with my sources and my questions about the topic develop and take shape, the topic is refocused and reframed by the questions that I am asking. What Paul Tillich writes about the decision-making process can be applied to the process of narrowing a topic: "The word 'decision,' like the word 'incision,' involves the image of cutting. A decision cuts off possibilities, and these were real possibilities; otherwise no cutting would have been necessary."[32] In the same way, to narrow a topic, I have to ask this question and not that one, and to pursue this line of inquiry and not that one. In so doing, I will have to cut away the extraneous matter that is not relevant to my question. But, my hands will always guide the scissors, just as my head and heart will conspire with them to craft the topic along the bias of my own question.

Let us imagine that after having a conversation with Serene Jones[33] about Luther's understanding of grace, you write this preliminary draft of a thesis paragraph:

> While Luther's concept of grace reflects Augustine's earlier view of grace as a gratuitous act of God on behalf of sinful humanity, its passive and pessimistic view of the human person bears feminist theological scrutiny. Serene Jones introduces a feminist reading of Luther in *Feminist Theory and Christian Theology: Cartographies of Grace*, but her feminist remapping of Calvin's doctrine of sanctification leaves Luther and his sterner preoccupation with justification behind. In this paper I will filter Jones' feminist methodology through the lens of my own pastoral experience to probe Luther's doctrine of grace, epitomized as *simul justus et peccator*, in order to seek some constructive resources for a feminist theology of justification.

This thesis paragraph does not yet contain a fully developed research claim, but it does reflect a significant shift in the direction of your research question. By narrowing your focus strategically, your question has shifted from "Was Luther's doctrine of grace a distinctly 'Protestant' doctrine, or was it inherent in the Augustinian tradition that grounded his study of the New Testament?" to "Does Luther's doctrine of grace, notwithstanding its passivity and pessimism regarding the human person, provide any constructive theological resources for contemporary feminist reflection?" By asking this question, you have relegated the question of Luther's indebtedness to Augustine to the background (if, indeed, you choose to pursue it at all). You have also sidestepped the "Protestant vs. Catholic" question and have chosen instead to enter Luther's doctrine of grace from the "narrower gate" of a feminist point of view. You do not yet have a working hypothesis to structure your research claim, but you have a pressing question that will lead you there, if you persevere. As you do so, you must choose one of two research paths, depending upon the type of paper you are writing. In answer, finally, to the question, "What kinds of theological research essays are most frequently encountered across the theological curriculum," we proceed to examine (1) the "research-in-place" essay and (2) the "create-a-research-space" essay. First, the next theological memo invites you to develop your own research question into a preliminary research claim:

> *THEOLOGICAL MEMO 6: Please return to the theological research question that you framed in Theological Memo 3. Guided by the research you have done thus far, the discussion above concerning narrowing a topic, and the "sample" draft of a preliminary thesis paragraph, please recast your "question" into a preliminary "answer," "claim," or description of your intended research. If you find this process difficult, you might find it helpful to review the material in* Chapter 3 *on "Developing a Theological Thesis Statement." The goal is not to craft a final research claim at this point, but to move your initial question into a tentative assertion, or claim, that will be revised and refined as your work proceeds.*

Is your research in place or must you create a research space?

A master bricklayer was once asked how to lay the brick for a particularly challenging path that wound in and out and around a network of elaborate formal gardens. After giving the novice bricklayer more technical information, he concluded by saying, "One brick at a time, my friend, one brick at a time!" Any time that you consult texts, articles, internet sources, and other required materials to write a paper, you pave your way toward writing "one brick at a time" with the bricks of theological research. For some assignments, the bricks are already "in place" in the form of designated course readings from which you will select the appropriate building blocks to write a "research-in-place" essay. For other assignments, the bricks must be selected and configured from a wider variety of sources according to the more rigorous specifications of a "create-a-research-space" essay. The first mode of research writing follows the "research-in-place" path; the second, more substantive research essay begins by "creating a research space."[34]

The research-in-place path

The "research-in-place" path is one in which you do not have to scour the library for materials; they are already "in place." This path would be used, for example, to research a one-page systematic reflection paper in which you answer a question that is based upon course readings, or a five-page synthesis paper in which you are asked to integrate assigned readings from two or three theological authors into your own coherent reflection. You will readily identify the "Was Jesus a Feminist" systematic reflection paper discussed in Chapter 3 as a "research-in-place" paper. Church history papers that ask you to read and reflect upon various historical sources and then provide your own contemporary integration and application also pursue this path.[35] "Research-in-place" papers require the same research skills on a small scale that more complex research assignments entail, so they provide strategic training in writing theological research well. We move on, however, to the "create-a-research-space" path.

The create-a-research-space path

Although you may not have ever heard of the "create-a-research-space" path, you have probably used its pattern of organization in previous writing assignments without calling it by that name. While the rhetorical conventions of this path are generic to scientific writing,[36] they are used in a variety of academic contexts, including biblical and theological studies. Whenever you attempt to carve a space for your own research within a broader theological conversation, you will find yourself on this path. What makes the "create-a-research-space" path particularly useful, however, is that it provides an answer to a research writer's perennial question: "How should I begin my paper?"

How should I begin?

We have already imagined research as an ongoing conversation between past and present that we enter from the vantage point of our own questions. How do we insert ourselves within this conversation in a way that seamlessly connects our work to what has preceded it while at the same time introducing "new" knowledge? The image of "creating a research space" provides a suggestive metaphor for this process. Following the "create-a-research-space" path, introductions to research articles typically (1) identify a particular *research territory* to be investigated by placing it in a relevant context and citing related research on the topic; (2) establish a *niche* within that territory where "x marks the spot" of a research gap in the previous work; and (3) occupy the *niche*, by stating a *claim* or *thesis* that indicates the potential of the current research to fill that gap and providing a brief outline of the paper to follow.[37]

There are variations on this pattern when it is used in theological research. For example, some writers move swiftly from identifying a research territory to establishing and occupying their niche by stating their research claim explicitly at the beginning of the paper. In the following selection, Roger Haight (1) identifies a research territory, "Spirit Christology"; provides a succinct "review of the literature" of Spirit Christology in his first footnote [1]; (2) carves a research niche by declaring his purpose "to summarize the ground that has been gained" in this conversation, while implying that more work remains to be done; and (3) moves to a research claim in his proposal to "make the case for Spirit language in Christology," all in the first two sentences of his essay:

> Over the past twenty years or so various essays have appeared which deal with Spirit Christology. [1] The purpose of this study is to summarize the ground that has been gained, and at the same time to make the case for Spirit language in Christology.[38]

Other writers, like Elizabeth Johnson, below, introduce their claim indirectly as a *question* whose investigation will confirm their claim, or thesis, in due course (a rhetorical strategy that is more tentative and deliberate when one is dealing with a controversial issue, as Sophia/wisdom Christology was when this article was written):

> *The question probed here*[39] is *whether it is possible* to move from the liberating image of [the historical] Jesus to a christology which does not support patriarchy; in other words, *whether it is possible* with the help of the imagery, concepts and vocabulary of the wisdom tradition to think through a full christology which is faithful to the hard won insights of the tradition's faith proclamation at the same time that it breaks out of the usual androcentric pattern.... Starting, then, with the Jewish figure of Sophia, *this study probes* back to the cult of the goddess which shaped her personification and back to Jesus whom Christians identified with her, *asking about the significance* of the fluidity of the gender symbolism inherent in the tradition for a truly inclusive christology....[40]

Still other writers have employed the metaphor of "creating a research space" to describe their own biblical or theological projects, as Elisabeth Schüssler Fiorenza does at the beginning of *Jesus: Miriam's Child, Sophia's Prophet*:

> By naming Jesus as the child of Miriam and the prophet of Divine Sophia, *I seek to create a "women" defined theoretical space*[41] that makes it possible to dislodge christological discourses from their malestream frame of reference. *The hermeneutical-rhetorical creation of such a space* intends to decenter hegemonic malestream christological discourses and to reframe them in terms of a critical feminist theology of liberation.[42]

Taking our cue, then, from these exemplars to follow this path purposefully but not slavishly, we can describe the process in five steps: (1) framing the conversation, (2) reviewing the literature, (3) carving a research niche, (4) making a research claim, and (5) previewing the paper.

Framing the territory

Imagine that you are writing a ten-to-twenty-page theological research essay in which you, like Elisabeth Schüssler-Fiorenza, seek to "create a research space" for the research claim that your paper presents. Because your own work has taken shape in conversation with the authors and sources you have consulted, your first task is to "frame the territory" for your readers. To do this, the introduction to your paper will identify a *research territory*, or topic, and assert its scholarly significance and relevance to current issues or problems. For example:

> An important conversation is going on among New Testament scholars regarding reading theory, reader-response criticism, and the social environment of biblical texts. As the conversation has developed, however, the difference between ancient and modern understandings of the phenomenon of reading itself has not always been sufficiently recognized. What is needed is a cognizance of the way reading actually worked in the original culture of the biblical documents.[43]

Notice that this introductory paragraph both introduces the research territory to be explored (ancient reading) and identifies the research gap (how reading worked in the ancient world) that this bibliographical article seeks to fill.

Reviewing the literature

After you have framed the conversation for your readers, the next step is to survey the literature that goes with the [research] territory. This can be done in a number of different ways, depending on the nature of your research project. The most complete "reviews of the literature" are to be found in bibliographical essays devoted entirely to surveying relevant research in a given field.[44] Detailed reviews of the literature also frequently comprise a chapter in a longer thesis project, where writers must demonstrate a wide-ranging knowledge of the "research territory" they are exploring before proceeding to carve their own research niche. You might also be asked to "review the literature" for a research paper or thesis proposal. We focus here on more succinct "reviews of the literature" that authors use to "create a research space" and weave into the introduction of a research essay.

It is difficult to "review the literature" adequately but strategically at the beginning of a ten- or twenty-page research essay. However, the goal is not to be exhaustive, but to survey relevant resources while also revealing the gaps in the literature that your work seeks to fill. This is usually accomplished in one of two ways. When a research claim builds upon or refutes the work of another scholar, its author may cite that person's work directly in their introduction, as Eunjoo Mary Kim does in her article, "Conversational Learning: A Feminist Pedagogy for Teaching Preaching":

> The book *Learning Preaching: Understanding and Participating in the Process* (Wardlow 1989) was published by the American Homiletics Task Force more than ten years ago. Although this book is still tremendously helpful for teaching preaching because it incorporates contemporary theories of pedagogy, it does not give particular attention to the learning styles and needs of female students. Moreover, while feminists and female homileticians, such as Christine Smith, Lucy Rose, [and others] have greatly contributed to the development of homiletical theories from feminist perspectives, there are few pedagogical resources to help preaching teachers reflect on the special needs and demands of female students....[45]

More commonly, however, authors of biblical and theological articles encode reviews of the literature into footnotes that support and amplify their thesis paragraph. We will have more to say about writing footnotes presently, but we consider them briefly here because the bibliographical footnote is used much more widely in theological research than more comprehensive reviews of the literature are included in the text itself. For example, having made reference in his article to essays on Spirit Christology published "in the last twenty years or so," Roger Haight provides a representative bibliographical survey in a footnote that begins, "Some essays that may serve as an introduction to Spirit Christology are the following: . . . ."[46]

Another way that authors review the literature is to provide a brief overview of their topic by breaking it into representative parts, each of which is then flagged with a corresponding bibliographical footnote. In the opening paragraph of Jerome H. Neyrey's article below, five interpretations of Jesus in John's gospel are succinctly surveyed, with each bracketed footnote providing supporting bibliographical citations, followed by a concluding sentence in which Neyrey adroitly carves his own Johannine research niche, "the death of the noble shepherd":

> Interpretation of Jesus in the Fourth Gospel has proved fragmentary and elusive. Some interpreters contrast it with the interpretation of Paul [1], while others focus on different motifs, such as glorification [2], sacrificial references [3], ascent and lifting up [4], or cosmic war [5]. This article adds still another study of a select cultural motif, namely, the death of the "noble" shepherd in John 10:11–18.[47]

Before we proceed to carve our own research niche, let us look a bit more carefully at how "seamlessly" Neyrey accomplishes this task. First, Neyrey contends that previous interpretations of Jesus in John's gospel have been "fragmentary and elusive," thereby intimating that there are research gaps in the current conversation. Second, his brief but focused literature review orders the fragments coherently and enables him to insert himself authoritatively into one of the "gaps," culminating in his own proposal of "the noble shepherd." Finally, having carved his research niche, Neyrey hastens to advance his own research claim in continuity with previous work in the field, at the same time promising a new and valuable contribution to the conversation.[48] In the theological memo below, you are invited to "review a review of the literature" in one of your research sources. From there we will proceed to "carving a research niche":

> *THEOLOGICAL MEMO 7: A good research project must (1) respect, acknowledge, and converse with the "literature" that has preceded it; and (2) add something "new" to the conversation that was not there before. Using these requirements as a touchstone, please select one of your research sources that includes a "review of the literature." After you have identified it within the context of the paper (Is it included in the introduction? In a footnote? In a more extensive literature review?), please evaluate the review in a brief paragraph, as I have evaluated Neyrey's review/footnote above. Is the survey balanced, or biased? Would you have included any sources that your author does not? Does your author successfully "create a research space" for the thesis that s/he proposes? (If the thesis proceeds logically from the gaps evidenced by the review of the literature, the author has probably been successful.)*

Carving a research niche, crafting a paper topic

"Carving a research niche" and "reviewing the literature" are interdependent processes, and they may follow or precede each other in theological and biblical articles, depending upon the author's prerogative.[49] To carve a research niche is simply to identify a gap in the current literature on a subject; but to identify the gap, one must be familiar with the literature! If you are a beginning theological student, you may need to review the literature before noticing any scholarly gaps. If you are a more advanced student, you may have discovered a research gap first that has then prompted you to review the literature.

Whether you are a novice or a more seasoned theological researcher, the actual process of establishing a niche for your own research may not be as straightforward as the examples of theological and biblical research writing that we have surveyed might imply. However, carving a research niche is not an arbitrary process, but an inevitable one that flows naturally from what precedes it. In order to fill a research gap, you need not discover a stray Dead Sea Scroll in your backyard or invent an exotic theology. All you have to do is to find your own niche in the scholarly conversation, which you will carve with the paper that you write. In practical terms, "carving the niche" proceeds from the initial "narrowing" of a topic that we considered earlier in this chapter and instigates the process of crafting a paper topic. By crafting a paper topic, you will be filling a scholarly gap and carving a research niche, so we will concentrate here on the process of crafting a paper topic.

Crafting a well-honed paper topic is like trying to find your own pulse in the stream of ideas coursing through the veins of your research, and the process is different for each person. Just as it is easier to locate your pulse after you have been exercising, it is easier to choose a paper topic when you are already exercised about the research topic that you are writing about. But, what if you are assigned a generic research essay for which you must find your own niche in the conversation and come up with a topic that the professor will approve? How would you proceed?

In classical rhetoric, the process of discovering a topic was called "invention," or "heuristics," both of which emphasize the element of "discovery" inherent in that process. A good research paper topic is like treasure hidden in a field; sometimes you have to scour every inch of the field and really dig for it, but at other times, you seem to stumble over it when you were chasing butterflies and looking for four-leaf clovers. Either way, you have to be in the field where the treasure is, or you will not find it, and once you have found it, you have to know what to name it. Until you find your own, I am going to name four treasures that have helped my students craft strong and stimulating theological research topics: (1) context, (2) commitment, (3) correlation, and (4) critique. We shall proceed to see how each of these can help us to carve a research niche and craft a paper topic for the following theological research assignment:

THEOLOGICAL MEMO 8: For an Introduction to Theology Course, you have been assigned a research essay on one of the major themes covered in the course (e.g., God; christology; the church…), using both classic and contemporary sources to present your own theological synthesis of this theme. How would you proceed to (a) choose a theological theme; (b) focus the theme into a paper topic; (c) select a title for the paper?

Context

Crafting a theological research topic with the cutting edge of your own context, or social location, flows naturally from the premise that "the context in which one does theology significantly shapes the method, content, and structure of theology."[50] If you are a student from a culture other than the United States, you have probably been encouraged to use the treasure of your own cultural context as a matter of course when selecting a theological research topic. But, "context" can yield its own treasures to any student who allows his or her own social location to be a starting point for their theological work. For example, in a paper exploring what it means to love God, one student wrote from her contemporary perspective as a suburban wife and mother of four children to challenge Augustine's affirmation of celibacy as "the more excellent way" of loving God and to reformulate a theology of loving God in conversation with Sallie McFague's *The Body of God*. Another student from Zambia, with his feet firmly planted on that African soil, mined classical and contemporary resources of creation theology to construct an ecological theology for the church of Zambia. What treasures of context and social location are waiting for you to use them as a starting point of theological research?

Commitment

The particular commitments that you have brought to your study of theology can provide another catalyst for a theological research topic. Such contemporary issues as peace, nonviolence, racism, ecological awareness, feminism, euthanasia, and human rights have provided thematic lenses by which students have examined the works of theological authors and engaged them in conversation. To read a theological text through the lenses of your own commitments does not presume a license to make the text say what you want it to say on a given issue. On the contrary, it will require a close, attentive reading to what your authors have said that will enable you to infer what they would have said about a particular issue, on the basis of what they have already written. To "infer" means literally "to carry or bring into"; hence when we infer, we draw conclusions from the facts and premises available to us. Making textual "inferences" is a process not only of reading and assimilating a text well enough to know clearly what your author *has said* about a particular issue, but also of internalizing the material so completely that you can imagine what an author *would say* about something else not in the text.

For example, a student deeply committed to peace issues wrote against the grain of Augustine's "just war" theory to find an inherent but unrealized stand for peace in some of his other writings. Another student concerned about violations of human rights around the world traced the theory of the common good from Plato to Augustine to Aquinas to contemporary moral theologians in order to evaluate its role in current discussions of human rights. The gift of this treasure, then, is that it encourages you as a theological researcher to bring your own questions to the theological texts that you are reading, rather than merely digesting someone else's answers. What commitments do you bring to the work of theology and ministry that could be fruitfully explored in a research essay?

Correlation

We have previously discussed the method, or rhetoric of correlation, but my use of the term here refers broadly to the act of comparison and contrast. When this treasure is discovered in the field of your research, it enables you to probe a theological issue by comparing and contrasting different theologians' understandings of that issue. For example, how do Anselm, Martin Luther, Karl Barth, and Gustavo Gutierrez understand the doctrine of salvation? What common threads run through their various construals of that doctrine? What is distinctive about each theologian's perspective? What theological resources would you retrieve from each of them to construct a contemporary definition of salvation? This treasure will be particularly valuable when you have no strong position concerning a topic at the beginning of your research. By placing three or four authors in conversation with each other, you will eventually be drawn into the discussion as well, and your own position on the issues will begin to take shape as you reflect on those of your conversation partners.

For some students, this process of textual correlation follows the bent of their own synthetic thinking, and bringing the essay to a meaningful conclusion comes easily. For example, for a course on "Women and the Church," one of my students in search of an adequate feminist spirituality for Roman Catholic women deftly correlated the work of Joan Chittister, Sandra Schneiders, and Miriam Therese Winter. For others, it is sometimes difficult to draw conclusions that move beyond "a is like b, but b is different from c." If you still have not been able to synthesize the various viewpoints into a constructive thesis at the conclusion of your research, return to your sources; choose one point of convergence or divergence that they share; assess its significance for the theological development of that particular theme or doctrine; and consider what resources these authors have given you and what resources you still need to make sense of this issue in a contemporary context. In the course work you are doing as you read this book, what gifts of correlation are waiting for your reflection, research, and critical synthesis?

Critique

I have left the treasure of "critique" for last, but it is often the one we stumble upon first when doing theological research. As we have already seen in Chapter 4, some element of critique is inherent in most theological assignments, but I use the term here in the sense of a sustained analysis of a topic or issue about which you have questions. Whenever you find yourself questioning a theological doctrine, an ethical position, a biblical interpretation, and so on, a critique of the doctrine, position, or interpretation in question could inspire a thoughtful and engaged research essay. The title of your paper should ultimately move from the general statement, "a critique of," to specify the nature of your critique in a carefully honed subtitle. In fact, finding a title for an essay is the final step in carving a research niche, whether you do it at the beginning or end of the research process. Until you get there, "a critique of" is a respectable starting point for a research inquiry that will yield its own particulars as you pursue the analysis. Following the cue of another one of my students, you might ask Stanley Hauerwas some pointed questions about his distinction between "American" and "Christian" Ethics.[51] Or you might critique David Tracy's method of theological correlation from the postliberal perspective of Hans Frei or George

Lindbeck.[52] Whatever critique you choose to pursue, the gift of this treasure is the intellectual stake that you have in the question, which, in concert with disciplined and well-documented research, will bring clarity and conviction to the writing. What theological questions have you encountered in your theological study that might inspire such a critique?

Making a research claim

In our exploration of the "create a research space" path, we have explored (1) framing the conversation, (2) reviewing the literature, and (3) carving a research niche/crafting a paper topic. Each of these steps on the journey is motivated by the next and crucial step, (4) making a research claim.[53] What distinguishes a research claim from a thesis statement is the medium of research that grounds it. Thus, a research claim is a thesis statement that is accountable to the research that engenders it. The "claim" must be substantiated by the research that you have done. Moreover, as in all argumentative writing, its substantiation should unfold as an extended research argument that skillfully weaves together evidence, interpretation of the data, and logical inference based on the interpretation of the evidence.

As we have seen, a research claim can be as succinct and straightforward as Roger Haight's proposal to "make the case for ... Spirit Christology"[54] or can be propounded more expansively as a question, as Elizabeth Johnson does when she asks "whether it is possible with the help of the imagery, concepts and vocabulary of the wisdom tradition to think through a full christology which is faithful to ... the tradition's faith proclamation at the same time that it breaks out of the usual androcentric pattern."[55] Whichever approach suits your theological writing style, the initial claims are not complete without the supporting arguments that proceed from them to build a composite research essay, as we have already seen in our discussion of "mapping the argument" in Chapter 3. Therefore, the last step in the process of creating a research space is that of "pre-viewing the paper" by outlining the sequence of the argument that will follow.

Previewing the paper

The final challenge of creating a research space is that of inviting readers to enter it. Like the poet William Stafford's creative writing students, most readers entering your research territory will "want a wilderness with a map."[56] That is, they want to learn something new, but they do not want to lose their way amid the vagaries of your paper. Because theological research essays are frequently lengthier and more complex in their structure than other writing assignments, a preliminary "pre-view" of the essay's structure is an essential aid for your readers. Some writers choose not to compose the preview until the essay is completed, and they are assured that everything is in place. However, if you draft a provisional preview at the beginning of your own writing process, it will help to keep you on track as you write the essay.

The simplest way to "pre-view" your essay is to divide it into sections and briefly describe the contents of each section to your readers, as Roger Haight does for the readers of his "Spirit Christology" article:

> I will treat these elements [of a Spirit Christology] in the following order. First, I outline the requirements of Christology. Second, I will provide an outline of the theological framework within which this discussion unfolds. Third, I will try to synopsize the resources for a Spirit Christology in terms of the symbols, categories and principles with which it works. And finally I will discuss the areas of interpretation or reinterpretation to which Spirit Christology gives rise.[57]

In a more conversational but no less competent style, Francine Cardman's introduction to her essay, "The Praxis of Ecclesiology," provides a salient example of writing that uses metaphor effectively without sacrificing clarity:

> In exploring what we might learn from Augustine's handling of the Donatist controversy…I will take soundings at five points along the way: (1) I begin by recalling some key features of the history and theology of Donatism; then (2) look at Augustine's early encounters with the Donatists and their dialogue over the authority of Cyprian; (3) chart the compass shifts that led to Augustine's endorsement of a policy of religious coercion; (4) examine some critical tensions in Augustine's praxis that result from these shifts; and (5) conclude by marking out some directions suggested by this case study for our own developing praxis of ecclesiology.[58]

In a longer essay, a "preface" often previews the shape of the work to come. Because a preface typically combines a personal statement by the author with an outline of the essay, it encourages a lively integration of personal and academic voices. Anne Deneen effects this integration gracefully and with lucidity in the preface below:

> Every piece of academic writing usually has a story behind it, and like all writing, academic writing often integrates many streams of feeling and thought which arise from sometimes obscure origins in the heart. This thesis is no exception, and I found to my surprise, as I wrote it, that the ideas had been swirling around for some years. The theme of communion in action has been a preoccupation of mine in both personal and professional life. Three critical streams of thought and experience are fundamental to the shape of this thesis….[59]

Creating a research space for the historical Jesus with Albert Schweitzer

If you are fortunate, every theological research essay that you write will also "have a story behind it" that arises from those regions where your mind and heart converge upon a question that will not let them go. While Albert Schweitzer has been critiqued for his colonial, patriarchal, and Eurocentric writing and research on the historical Jesus,[60] his original work as a young theological student represented just such a convergence of mind and heart. Before we proceed to create a theological research space ourselves, Albert Schweitzer will provide an exemplary model of the process.

Schweitzer's landmark *Quest of the Historical Jesus* not only used the "create-a-research-space" path in its introductory chapter, but it also "created a research space" for the study of the historical Jesus within the theological landscape of his time. This process of theological exploration and innovation continues today as theologians, biblical scholars, church historians, and others break new ground in their research. Whether or not your own theological research is as groundbreaking, you will produce new knowledge when you write theological research well. To recapitulate this process before playing our own theme and variations on it, we see how this rhetorical pattern unfolds in Schweitzer's introductory chapter, "The Problem."

Framing the historical Jesus research territory

First, he shows that his research is *significant*:

The greatest achievement of German theology is the critical investigation of the life of Jesus....In the history of doctrine its work has been negative; it has cleared the site for a new edifice of religious thought.[61]

Second, he attempts to show that his research is *relevant:*

The critical study of the life of Jesus [is] the most vital thing in the world's history.

Third, he indicates that his research constitutes a *problematic*:

For the problem of the life of Jesus has no analogue in the field of history ... [and] every ordinary method of historical investigation proves inadequate to the complexity of the conditions.

Finally, he introduces and reviews *the theological state of the question*:

The historical investigation of the life of Jesus did not take its rise from a purely historical interest; it turned to the Jesus of history as an ally in the struggle against the tyranny of dogma.

Carving a research niche for the historical Jesus

First, he indicates *a gap in the previous research*:

The history of the study of the life of Jesus has hitherto received surprisingly little attention.

Reviewing the literature

Second, he *reviews the literature* re "the critical study of the life of Jesus":

Hase, in his Life of Jesus of 1829, briefly records the previous attempts to deal with the subject. Friedrich von Ammon...gives some information regarding "the most notable biographies of Jesus of the last fifty years...Otto Schmiedel's lecture...merely sketches the history of the subject"; Hase made ingenious comparisons between [the "Lives" of Jesus], but he was unable to group them according to inner principles.

Making a research claim

Next, he describes the *research claim* that he will advance by providing "a systematic historical account of the critical study of the life of Jesus":

> There is room for an attempt to bring order into the chaos of the lives of Jesus.... Now, when the literary and eschatological methods of solution have led to complementary results ... the time seems ripe for the attempt to trace genetically in the successive works the shaping of the problem as it now confronts us, and to give a systematic historical account of the critical study of the life of Jesus.

Previewing the research plan

Finally, he provides a general *preview* of the plan of his research:

> Our endeavor will be to furnish a graphic description of all the attempts to deal with the subject; and not to dismiss them with stock phrases or traditional labels, but to show clearly what they really did to advance the formulation of the problem, whether their contemporaries recognized it or not.

THEOLOGICAL MEMO 9: Please choose a theological article, or book chapter from your assigned class readings, and examine the introduction of the article or chapter. Does it "create a research space" in the way that is outlined above? What variations do you notice in your author's format? How does this model compare or contrast with your own way of writing and structuring a research project? Please give examples, and reflect on the model's usefulness for your own theological writing.

From creating a theological research space to writing a research proposal

The create-a-research-space path provides a standard academic format that has been adapted by theologians and biblical scholars for their own disciplinary writing. Not only does it offer an adaptable framework for organizing a theological research project, but the create-a-research-space path also provides a structure for writing a research proposal for a course paper or thesis project.

A research proposal is a preliminary map of your writing/research project that serves as an informal "contract" between you and the professor assigning the paper. It also provides an apologia, or rationale, for the topic you have chosen. A research proposal should inform readers of the significance of your project, and the contribution it will make to the discipline in which you are writing. If done with care and attention, it should provide you with a writing/research goal and a concrete, sequential, and time-specific plan to meet that goal. While your professors will have different protocols for their proposals, the generic research proposal outlined below utilizes the create-a-research-space format and can be adapted to the requirements of the course for which you are writing the proposal. You are invited to prepare your own research proposal in Theological Memo 10 below.

THEOLOGICAL MEMO 10: Writing a Theological Research Proposal:
Please choose a research project from one of your classes, for which you have been asked to prepare a preliminary research proposal of no more than five pages. The theological research proposal is—at its best—a preliminary map

of your writing/research project. It is usually assigned early in the semester, to encourage you to begin your research well in advance of the paper due date. It should include:

- *A specific, carefully focused research question*
- *A thesis statement/paragraph that "creates a research space" for your claim*
- *A description of your research methodology*
- *A brief outline of your project*
- *A bibliography of at least five sources, prepared in Turabian style*[62]
- *A projected timeline for completion of the project*

The introduction to a research proposal below follows the "create-a-research-space" path. You may find it helpful in preparing your own research paper proposal:

Dancing before the Lord: A Parish Invitation to Liturgical Dance: A Research Project Proposal

The Research Question: *Why has there been so little progress in introducing liturgical dance to the worship of the local parish?*

The Research Claim: *While liturgical dance is not a new phenomenon in Roman Catholic liturgy, there has been little progress in introducing it to the worship of the local parish. Liturgical theologian Thomas Kane has vibrantly documented "the dancing church" in Africa,*[63] *but few resources are available to assist clergy and lay liturgists closer to home.*[64] *For all of its potential for renewing the worship of the local church, liturgical dance remains a largely untapped resource.*

My research project, tentatively entitled "Dancing before the Lord: A Parish Invitation to Liturgical Dance," seeks to fill that gap by preparing a brief guide for parish clergy, lay liturgists and worship committees that will provide: (a) a brief history of liturgical dance in Scripture and church history; (b) a theological rationale for the use of liturgical dance to deepen, renew and revitalize parish worship; and (c) a pastoral plan for introducing a local parish to liturgical dance as part of their ongoing community prayer and worship.

The Research Methodology: *My methodology in this project is historical, ecclesial, and pastoral. First, I will draw from biblical and historical sources to prepare a brief history of liturgical dance in scripture and church history. Second, I will reflect on Avery Dulles' Models of the Church*[65] *in relation to their support or suppression of dance in the liturgy of the church. Finally, I will employ Thomas Groome's pastoral methodology of "shared praxis"*[66] *in my own pastoral plan for introducing liturgical dance into the worship of my local parish.*

As the sample research proposal above exemplifies, writing theological research is a multidisciplinary enterprise, and more than one methodological approach may be included in your paper. Here is a synopsis/outline for "Writing Church History Well"[67] that employs the "create-a-research space" model. How might you adapt this outline to your next theological research paper assignment?

Writing church history well: A theological writer's outline

How do I write acceptable, responsible essays in church history? With more agony than ecstasy ... over a longer period of time than I might like ... with piles of "sources" to check with ... with lots of editing and self-critique ... with intellectual honesty ... with the Anne Lamott prayer: "Help me! Help me! Help me!"

I. **AN APPROACH TO CHURCH HISTORY WRITING**

A. BEGIN WITH QUESTIONS: What do you want to know? What HUNCHES or questions do you bring to the topic at hand? [These hunches and questions will form the basis for your thesis/argument.]

B. CHECK OUT THE "COMMUNITY OF HISTORIANS": preliminary bibliography, survey of databases, historiography [Who's done what, when, and how on this topic?]

C. READ AND TAKE NOTES: Pay attention to converging/conflicting ideas, views. [Here one builds up an EVIDENCE base for the thesis.]

D. DRAFT AN OUTLINE ... MAKE IT MANAGEABLE ... DETERMINE THE LIMITS OF YOUR TOPIC [Don't lose the forest for the trees!]

II. **A STRUCTURE FOR HISTORICAL ESSAYS/RESEARCH PAPERS**

A. INTRODUCTION: [You tell them what you are going to tell them.]

1. The "Hook"—to motivate reader to get into the paper.
2. Statement of Problem/Question—Significance of this work.
3. Historiography: What have others written? What is missing?
4. Your own thesis ... what's new? Your method ... Narrative? Comparative?

[Give your readers a taste of what is to come.]

B. BODY: [You tell them, with evidence and argument.]

1. Use factual evidence, taken from written sources [primary/secondary] or interviews [oral sources] or other media [websites, video, etc.]
2. Avoid plagiarism and "presentism" [judging texts from OUR context rather than respecting the period from which they come]
3. Be rigorous and honest in your arguments
4. Test your "hunch" against your sources; build your case

C. CONCLUSION: [You tell them what you told them.]

1. Synthesize your thesis and argument into a summary/conclusion
2. Give broader implications, suggestions for further research

D. SCHOLARLY APPARATUS: Footnotes, Bibliography and Appendices

Concluding reflections: Writing theological research well (I): Rhetorics of research and investigation

In this chapter, we have introduced "writing theological research well" through the rhetorics, or elements, of *research* and *investigation*. First, we identified research as a fundamental resource of theological study, and investigation, motivated by theological questions, as its way of proceeding. Next, we outlined the process of investigation in a series of sequential but flexible steps: (1) formulating a research question, (2) identifying one's research methodology, (3) investigating library sources, (4) reviewing the literature, and (5) developing a research claim. We then explored the "create-a-research-space" path as a model for structuring a theological research essay and followed its adaptations at the hands of classic and contemporary theological researchers. Finally, you were invited to write a research proposal for a theological research essay of your own, using the "create a research space" model, which is also employed in the "Writing Church History Well" synopsis that closes this chapter.

Yet, in order to write theological research well, it is not enough to create a space for your theological research, or to make a convincing research claim that you present in a coherent research proposal. It is also necessary to organize your research into a sustained, coherent essay that substantiates your claim and to provide the necessary documentation for your sources. In the next chapter, "Writing Theological Research II: Rhetorics of Organization and Documentation," we tackle the tasks of organizing reading and research; writing a first draft; documenting sources; writing theological footnotes well; preventing plagiarism; and preparing the completed paper.

Notes

1 Alister E. McGrath, *Christian Theology: An Introduction* (Oxford: Blackwell, 2001), 3.

2 Elizabeth A. Johnson, *Friends of God and Prophets: A Feminist Theological Reading of the Communion of Saints* (New York: Continuum, 1998), 1.

3 Bernard Lonergan, *Method in Theology* (New York: Herder and Herder, 1972; reprint, Toronto: University of Toronto Press, 1994), 127 (page references are to the reprint edition). Lonergan's original term for the subdisciplines of theology is "functional specialties."

4 The exemplary text is Wayne C. Booth, Gregory G. Colomb, and Joseph M. Williams, *The Craft of Research*, 3rd ed. (Chicago: University of Chicago Press, 2008), which offers a more comprehensive survey of the research process than is addressed here and can be used fruitfully in conjunction with this chapter.

5 I am indebted to Booth et al., *Craft of Research*, for their use of this term to describe the research process, though they do not elaborate on it in their own text.

6 Ibid., 10.

7 Carol Delaney, *The Seed and the Soil: Gender and Cosmology in Turkish Village Society* (Berkeley: University of California Press, 1991), 4.

8 William V. Harris, *Ancient Literacy* (Cambridge: Harvard University Press, 1989), 3.

9 Billy Collins, "I Chop Some Parsley While Listening to Art Blakey's Version of 'Three Blind Mice,'" in Collins, *Picnic Lightning* (Pittsburgh, PA: University of Pittsburgh Press, 1998), 10–11.

10 Hans-Georg Gadamer, *Truth and Method* (New York: Seabury Press, 1975), 328.

11 See William S. Baring-Gould and Ceil Baring-Gould, *The Annotated Mother Goose: Nursery Rhymes Old and New, Arranged and Explained* (New York: Clarkson N. Potter, 1962), 156, who cite an interpretation that identifies "the farmer's wife" with Queen Mary I of England, and the "three blind mice" as Anglican clergymen Thomas Ridley, Richard Latimer, and Thomas Cranmer, who were burned at the stake under the Roman Catholic Queen's brief reign (1553–1558).

12 See Billy Collins, "Questions About Angels," in *Questions About Angels: Poems* (Pittsburgh: University of Pittsburgh Press, 1999), 25–26.

13 Anselm of Canterbury, "Why God Become Man," in *A Scholastic Miscellany: Anselm to Ockham*, ed. and trans. Eugene R. Fairweather (Philadelphia, PA: Westminster, 1956), 100–83.

14 Thomas Aquinas, *Summa Theologiae*, Q.1, and A.4, in *Thomas Aquinas: Selected Writings*, ed. Ralph McInerny (London: Penguin, 1998), 489.

15 See Chapter 1, above, under "Writing Theology as a Scholastic Science with Thomas Aquinas."

16 See, e.g., Shubert Ogden, *Is There Only One True Religion or Are There Many?* (Dallas: Southern Methodist University Press, 1992); Hans Kung, *Infallible? An Unresolved Inquiry* (New York: Continuum: 1994); Robert L. Kinast, *What Are They Saying about Theological Reflection?* (Mahweh, NJ: Paulist, 2000); Rowan Williams, *Why Study the Past? The Quest for the Historical Church* (London: Dartman, Longman, & Todd, 2005).

17 Paul Tillich, *Systematic Theology*, 3 vols. (Chicago: University of Chicago Press, 1951–1963), 1:162; Elizabeth A. Johnson, *She Who Is: The Mystery of God in Feminist Theological Discourse* (New York: Crossroads, 1992), 3; Jon Sobrino, *Jesus the Liberator: A Historical-Theological View* (Maryknoll, NY: Orbis, 1998), 1.

18 See also the strategy for developing a research question in Booth et al., *Craft of Research*, 45–48.

19 Rudolf Bultmann, *Jesus Christ and Mythology* (New York: Charles Scribner's Sons, 1958), 49–50.

20 John Dominic Crossan, *The Birth of Christianity: Discovering What Happened Immediately After the Execution of Jesus* (New York: Harper Collins, 1998), 139.

21 See Sobrino, *Jesus the Liberator*, 6: "The purpose of this christology is to put forward the truth of Christ from the standpoint of liberation"; Paul Tillich, *Systematic Theology*, vol. I (Chicago: University of Chicago Press, 1951), 8: "The following system is an attempt to use the 'method of correlation' as a way of uniting message and situation. It tries to correlate the questions implied in the situation with the answers implied in the message"; Elizabeth A. Johnson, *She Who Is: The Mystery of God in Feminist Theological Discourse* (New York: Crossroad, 1995), 9: "Taking a cue from feminist methodologies in related fields, I ask whether, when read with a feminist hermeneutic, there is anything in the classical tradition that could serve a discourse about divine mystery that would further the emancipation of women."

22 Roger Haight, *Dynamics of Theology* (New York/Mahwah, NJ: Paulist Press, 1990; reprint, Maryknoll, NY: Orbis Books, 2001), 189.

23 Gale Yee, "The Author/Text/Reader and Power: Suggestions for a Critical Framework for Biblical Studies," in *Reading from This Place*, vol. 1: *Social Location and Biblical Interpretation in the United States*, ed. Fernando F. Segovia and Mary Ann Tolbert ((Minneapolis: Fortress, 1995), 116.

24 See McGrath, *Christian Theology*, 3.

25 For an excellent introduction to library research in both print and electronic contexts, see William Badke, *Research Strategies: Finding your Way Through the Information Fog*, 5th ed. (Bloomington, IN: iUniverse LLC, 2014).

26 See Chapter 4, above, under "What Is a Theological Essay and Why Do Theologians Write Them?"

27 Kenneth Burke, *The Philosophy of Literary Form: Studies in Symbolic Action*, 3rd ed. (Berkeley: University of California Press, 1973), 110–11. See also Chapter 14, under "Writing the Online Course Discussion Post Well: Concluding Reflections and Suggestions."

28 See Gerald Graff and Cathy Birkenstein, *They Say/I Say: The Moves That Matter in Academic Writing*, 2nd ed. (New York: W.W. Norton, 2010).

29 I am indebted here to conversations with Paul M. Smith, Retired Professor of Theological Bibliography and former Director of the Beardslee Library, Western Theological Seminary, Holland, MI, who introduced courses on Theological Bibliography with this question to engage his students more personally in the research process.

30 See Chapter 3 above, pp. 51–57.

31 Natalie Goldberg, *Writing Down the Bones: Freeing the Writer Within* (Boston: Shambala, 1986), 127.

32 Tillich, *Systematic Theology*, I:184.

33 Serene Jones, *Feminist Theory and Christian Theology: Cartographies of Grace* (Minneapolis, MN: Fortress, 2000), 61–63.

34 See J.M. Swales and H. Najjar, "The Writing of Research Article Introductions," *Written Communication* 4 (1987): 175–92, and John M. Swales and Christine B. Feak, *Academic Writing for Graduate Students: Essential Tasks and Skills*, 3rd ed. (Ann Arbor: University of Michigan press, 2012), 327–63.

35 Fredrica Harris Thompsett, Mary Wolfe Professor Emerita of Historical Theology, Episcopal Divinity School, assigns an "Application Paper" in her church history courses that follows this "research-in-place" pattern.

36 This organizational pattern was first noted in scientific writing by Swales and Najjar, "Writing of Research Article Introductions."

37 Swales and Feak, *Academic Writing for Graduate Students*, 174.

38 Roger Haight, "The Case for Spirit Christology," *Theological Studies* 53 (1992), 257.

39 I have italicized the "question language" in order to emphasize Johnson's use of it here.

40 Elizabeth A. Johnson, "Jesus, the Wisdom of God: A Biblical Basis for Non-Andocentric Christology," *Ephemerides Theologicae Lovanienses* 61 (1985): 263.

41 I have italicized the language of "creating a research space" in order to emphasize Schüssler Fiorenza's use of it here.

42 Elisabeth Schüssler-Fiorenza, *Jesus: Miriam's Child, Sophia's Prophet: Critical Issues in Feminist Christology* (New York: Continuum, 1995), 3.

43 Lucretia B. Yaghjian, "Ancient Reading," in *The Social Sciences and New Testament Interpretation*, ed. Richard L. Rohrbaugh (Peabody, MA: Hendrickson), 206.

44 As an example of that genre, my article "Ancient Reading" quoted above provides a "cross-disciplinary survey of relevant literature on ancient reading for the non-specialist reader" (ibid., 206).

45 Eunjoo Mary Kim, "Conversational Learning: A Feminist Pedagogy for Teaching Preaching," *Teaching Theology and Religion* 5/3 (2002), 168.

46 Haight, "Case for Spirit Christology," 257n.1.

47 Jerome H. Neyrey, S.J., "The 'Noble Shepherd' in John 10: Cultural and Rhetorical Background," *Journal of Biblical Literature* 120/2 (2001): 267.

48 See ibid., 268: "Our hypothesis is that the labeling of the shepherd as 'noble' [*kalos*] reflects the rhetorical topos of 'noble death' in the rhetoric of praise in the Hellenistic world. When John 10:11–18 is compared with this topos, we shall see that it is carefully structured according to the topos of noble death."

49 For a counter example of the order I have proposed here, see Albert Schweitzer's use of the "Create a Research Space" path, below.

50 Susan Brooks Thistlewaite and Mary Potter Engel, eds., *Lift Every Voice: Constructing Christian Theologies from the Underside* (San Francisco: HarperSanFrancisco, 1990), 2–3.

51 See Stanley Hauerwas, "Christian Ethics in America: A Promising Obituary," in *Introduction to Christian Theology*, ed. Roger A. Badham (Louisville, KY: Westminster John Knox, 1998), 103–20.

52 See Werner J. Jeanrond, "Correlational Theology and the Chicago School," in *Introduction to Christian Theology*, ed. Badham, 147–48.

53 We have already dealt with "Developing a Thesis/Claim/Answer" in Chapter 3, above, and the steps provided there can be used for making a research claim as well.

54 See above, "The Create-a-Research-Space Path."

55 Johnson, "Jesus the Wisdom of God," 263.

56 William Stafford, "A Course in Creative Writing," in *The Way It Is: New and Selected Poems* (St. Paul, MN: Graywolf Press, 1999), 195.

57 Haight, "Case for Spirit Christology," 259.

58 Francine Cardman, "The Praxis of Ecclesiology: Learning from the Donatist Controversy," *Catholic Theological Society of America Proceedings* 54 (1999): 25.

59 Anne Deneen, "The Field at Midnight: Living with Spirit as Communion in Action" (S.T.L. Thesis, Cambridge, MA: Weston Jesuit School of Theology, 2003), 1.

60 See, e.g., Kwok Pui Lan, "Jesus/the Native: Biblical Studies from a Postcolonial Perspective," in *Teaching the Bible: The Discourses and Politics of Biblical Pedagogy*, ed. Fernando F. Segovia and Mary Ann Tolbert (Maryknoll, NY: Orbis Books, 1998) 68–95.

61 Albert Schweitzer, *The Quest of the Historical Jesus: A Critical Study of Its Progress from Reimarus to Wrede* (1906; reprint, Baltimore: Johns Hopkins University Press, 1998). Quotations are from pp. 1, 2, 6, 4, 11–12.

62 See Chapter 6, under Documenting Print/Electronic Sources in Turabian/Chicago Style.

63 See Thomas A. Kane, *The Dancing Church: Video Impressions of the Church in Africa* (Mahweh, NJ: Paulist Press, 2010), DVD Video.

64 Notable exceptions are Carla De Sola, *The Spirit Moves: Handbook of Dance and Prayer* (Richmond, CA: The Sharing Company, 1977); Carolyn Denning, *The Liturgy*

as Dance and the Liturgical Dancer (New York: Crossroads, 1984); Thomas Kane and Robert VerEcke, *Introducing Dance in Christian Worship* (Washington, DC: Pastoral Press, 1984).

65 See Avery Dulles, *Models of the Church* (Garden City, NY: Doubleday Image Books, 1978).

66 See Thomas H. Groome, *Sharing Faith: A Comprehensive Approach to Religious Education* (San Francisco: Harper and Row, 1991).

67 This outline was originally presented by Janice S. Farnham, formerly Assistant Professor of Church History, Weston Jesuit School of Theology, Cambridge, Massachusetts, at a WRITE Program Faculty Conversation on November 1, 2002, and is used here with her permission.

6

Writing Theological Research Well (II): Rhetorics of Organization and Documentation

To impose a useful order on all [your] information, you need a principle of organization.

—WAYNE BOOTH et al., *The Craft of Research*

The footnote is bound up, in modern life, with the ideology and technical practices of a profession ... [and] ... learning to make footnotes forms part of this modern version of apprenticeship.

—ANTHONY GRAFTON, *The Footnote: A Curious History*

Starting points

"If you don't know where you are going," says the African proverb, "any road will take you there."[1] If you have completed the theological memos in the last chapter, you know where you are going and you are on the right road. You have chosen a theological research project and reviewed the literature. You have claimed a research niche and completed a research proposal that maps your project. Now what? Many theological writers arrive at this point but still struggle with the research skills of organization and documentation, which we explore in this chapter.

Organization is a rhetoric, or element of purposeful communication, inseparable from the material that it shapes. When you organize, you prioritize your research, weave it purposefully into your own narrative in an order that corroborates your argument, and proceed to write a first draft. Documentation, on the other hand, provides a return path between the theological research you have cited and its original source and ensures that credit is given to those who have preceded you on the journey. These dynamics are interactive: the rhetoric of organization keeps us focused on the completion of the project, while the rhetoric of documentation paves the way back to its original sources. We begin this chapter, then, with these questions: (1) What are the organizational dynamics of writing theological research well? (2) What are the organizational mechanics of integrating reading, writing, and research to write a first draft of a theological research essay? (3) What are the requirements for documenting sources and avoiding plagiarism in a theological research essay? Before we proceed to the first question, you are invited to reflect on your own method of organizing the theological writing and research process in the following theological memo:

> *THEOLOGICAL MEMO 1: Organization as an Organic Process: What is your own "organic" way of organizing the research process for a theological research project? Do you record information from your sources on note cards? On computer databases? In notebooks? By highlighting and classifying relevant quotes from your readings? Do you organize your research notes by author? By topic? By sub-headings from your outline? Do you actively write during the note-taking process, or do you merely record information? Please list the strengths and weaknesses of your organizational process, as reflected in writing your most recent research essay.*

What are the organizational dynamics of writing theological research well?

Writing a theological research project is a complex and multitasked undertaking that favors the organizationally competent. However, even the organizationally challenged can learn how to manage the writing and research process if they are able (1) to build on the strengths they already have; (2) to experiment with new strategies that will develop those strengths; and, informed by both of these exercises, (3) to draft a concrete but flexible organizational "map of completion" for a research project.[2]

Building on your strengths

The first step in developing an organizational plan for successful completion of a theological research project is to take an inventory of the organizational strategies you are already using effectively to complete writing tasks. For example, some of my students block out an afternoon a week that is written into their appointment book throughout the semester to work on a project in consecutive stages. Others devote concentrated blocks of time to research projects, in the order of their semester due date. Some students complete all their reading and research on a project before shaping it into a rough draft. Others prepare an outline early in their process and complete research and writing for one section of their outline at a time; still others more visually oriented create a "storyboard," or a wall chart of their outline as it develops.[3] When you review the organizational "strengths" that you listed in Theological Memo 1, which of them can you build on to manage more effectively the writing and researching process?

Do not be surprised, however, if some of your organizational strengths are hidden in what you have previously identified as "weaknesses." After castigating herself repeatedly for procrastinating before tackling writing assignments, one of my students came to the realization that procrastination was an effective strategy for managing her writing process. It kept her perfectionist tendencies at bay, provided her with a nonnegotiable writing deadline, and enabled her to hand in every writing assignment on time throughout her seminary program, even if it took a "crash program" in order to do so. Reviewing the organizational "weaknesses" that you listed in Theological Memo 1, which of them can you identify as assets, not deficits of your writing and research process?

Developing your strengths with new strategies

The second step in organizing yourself and your research project is to reflect on the organizational strengths that you would like to develop further and to identify one new strategy that you will use to complete your research project. For example, I have never been able to make a detailed outline of a research project at the beginning of the process, because even in a research essay, I must initially write to find out what I want to say. I do prepare a "Preliminary Map of Completion" similar to the one I describe in the next section. At times, however, pieces of the research puzzle get lost along the way as my writing takes me places that I did not expect to go! In writing this book, therefore, I have paused at the midpoint of each chapter to redraft a "Map of Completion" that tells me what sections I have completed, what sections must still be completed, and what loose threads must still be woven into the chapter at the appropriate places. This strategy allows me to begin with a more free-flowing outline of the chapter, which suits my organizational style, but it also lets me elucidate the outline in greater detail in the midst of the writing process and fill in missing links as I write. What new strategies might you try on for size to manage your writing and research process more strategically?

Drafting a preliminary map of completion

Having identified the strengths you wish to build on and the strategies you wish to "try on," the final step in managing a writing/research project is drafting a "Preliminary Map of Completion" for your research project. My "Preliminary Map" includes: (1) the writing and research task(s) to be completed, which I break into smaller chunks, or "bird by bird," as instructed by Anne Lamott;[4] (2) the available time I have for completion of the tasks; (3) a tentative timeline for completion of the various pieces of the project; and (4) a working schedule of completion which, as Annie Dillard reminds me, functions as "a net for catching days" and "defends from whim and chaos."[5] Because I am notorious for taking more time than I have allotted to complete a section, or an article, or a chapter, I have learned to under-commit myself and to cut myself some slack along the way by readjusting my schedule more realistically. I have also learned to accept the fact that I cannot impose arbitrary deadlines on a creative process, even if I must at times surrender the full course of that process to firm deadlines that I must meet. Either way, with apologies to Yogi Berra, "It's not written until it's written!"

There is no "one size fits all" strategy for writing and research management, nor is there a "magic bullet" that will transform the organizational process of writing theological research well into a proverbial "piece of cake." What works for me may not work for you, but finding out what does work for you is key to getting the job done. Whatever your preferred way of tackling a research project might be, its successful completion will require both a mastery of the organizational dynamics that are operative from the beginning to the end of the research process and a self-mastery that enables you to take charge of that process. If you take the time to complete them, the Inventory and Drafting Plans in Theological Memo 2, below, will help you, as writing consultant Joan Bolker advises, to "choose a work style [or organizational style] that suits you, not who you'd like to be."[6]

THEOLOGICAL MEMO 2: Writers' Organizational Style Inventory:

- *What is your ideal way of organizing a writing and/or research project?*
- *What is your actual way of organizing a writing and/or research project?*
- *What are the strengths of your present organizational style?*
- *What strengths would you like to develop further?*

Drafting a Preliminary Map of your Writing/Research Project:

- *What time do you have available for completion of your project (block it out)?*
- *Can you break your research/writing process into smaller, manageable units?*
- *Please revise the task list below to fit your own writing/research process, and then estimate roughly how much time each task will take:*
- *Engaging in initial reflection and research on a topic*
- *Doing a preliminary review of the literature*
- *Developing a thesis question*
- *Completing major research for project*
- *Solidifying the research claim*
- *Drafting a preliminary outline*
- *Writing a project proposal*
- *Organizing research into an outline/draft*
- *Preparing a preliminary map of completion*
- *Writing the first full draft*
- *Preparing a midpoint map of completion*
- *Writing the revised draft*
- *Completing the final draft*
- *Checking footnotes and bibliography*
- *Formatting and submission of project*
- *On the basis of the estimates you have made for completion of these tasks, prepare a timeline that works back from the due date of the project to the beginning of your writing and research process.*
- *Establish a (daily, weekly) working schedule for completion of the project and commit it to writing.*
- *Cut yourself some slack where necessary along the way.*
- *Remember, finally, "It's not written until it's written!"*

What are the organizational mechanics of integrating reading, writing, and research to write a theological research essay?

While these organizational dynamics will help you to manage the research-writing process, they are incomplete without the organizational mechanics of integrating reading, writing, and research to write a first draft of a theological research essay. By "integrating reading, writing and research," I do not mean writing the paper the night before it is due, with books scattered across your desk that you frantically rifle through, looking for the perfect quote that you thought was in that book but was not, and then, having found it, you add to the paper and hurriedly insert the last footnote as dawn breaks over your (almost) dead body. While the occasional research project written in that adrenalin-charged mode may keep the wolf (or at least your professor) from the door, I invite you to imagine reading, writing and research as integrated processes that begin to intertwine with your first day of research and do not slacken their collaboration until you complete the final draft of your paper. If this sounds more like a slight of hand trick than a skill achievable in your lifetime, please keep reading as we first look at the processes discretely and then proceed to the mechanics of integrating reading, writing, and research to write theological research well.

Reading, writing, as/and research: A methodical overview

The "Three R's" of every research project are **R**eading, (W)**R**iting, and **R**esearch. Yet, the reading and writing both arise from the research and are fundamental to the research. Whether your research question leads you to printed materials, electronic sources, or both, your research will require reading and inspire writing. "To do research," writes Joan Bolker, "is to inquire, to dig one's way into a problem, and writing is one of the best tools available for such work."[7] Social scientist Laurel Richardson explains further, "Writing is not just a mopping-up activity at the end of a research project [but] ... also ... a method of discovery and analysis."[8] Yet, that discovery and analysis most often begins with reading what others have written, so we will enter the research process by returning to the task of reading theology well.[9]

Organizing the reading for theological research

We have previously outlined the "Read Three Times" method in Chapter 3 of this book. Adapting this model to writing theological research,[10] you might want to read first for theological method, asking "What is this author doing?" Second, you might read for theological foundations, asking, "Where does he or she fit in 'the literature' "? Third, you will be invited to read "researchfully," as will be described below. But how will you decide where to begin and how to proceed?

Read important authors or texts first (primary theological authors rather than secondary sources about them), and the less important ones next. If you do not know yet who or what is more or less important, read what attracts you and decide for yourself. Read some authors analytically, with conceptual rigor. Read others more gently, to agree, disagree, qualify, or simply admire. Use the book's index as you read. It is time-consuming and often unnecessary to read from cover to cover. You are ready to stop reading when the reading becomes repetitious, when you are not learning anything anymore, when you are reading in order to avoid writing, and when you have run out of time!

"Researchful" reading

Even if you have been practicing the "Read Three Times" method introduced in Chapter 3, you may find reading for a research project a more complex task than reading for shorter critical papers. First of all, you must read more material. Second, you must read intentionally, in terms of your own research inquiry, not merely in response to your professor's question. In addition, you must pose your particular question to various texts and authors who will not always give you the answer on a silver platter, since it is your question and not theirs. Finally, you must put those authors and texts in conversation with each other in response to your question and draw the results of that conversation into your own critical synthesis. In short, you must master the art of "researchful reading," which requires that you "research" your question as you read, and approach reading as a proactive research tool, not merely a passive activity.

One of the most useful methods for this kind of "researchful reading," described by Mortimer Adler and Charles Van Doren in their classic *How to Read a Book*, outlines a "syntopical" strategy for organizing and "re-directing" reading according to particular research questions and concerns, based upon a set of questions that you as reader direct to the authors you are reading on a similar subject.[11] This method allows you to set the agenda for your reading, rather than reading passively with no substantive focus. Theological Memo 3 invites you to use this "syntopical" method in connection with your own research:

THEOLOGICAL MEMO 3: "Syntopical Reading":[12] *Using the "Syntopical Reading Worksheet" on the following page for your response,*

(1) *Identify a particular question or problem that has arisen in the course of your research. (It might be a straightforward question, such as, "Is the Apostle Peter the author of 1 and 2 Peter," or a subtler question that will not yield a "Yes" or "No" answer, such as "What resources does Luther's doctrine of grace provide for a feminist understanding of Lutheran theology?")*

(2) *From your initial bibliography on your topic, select three sources that would be most relevant to the question you are asking.*

(3) *Read (or reread) each of these sources in the light of your question, and mark those passages that most directly relate to your problem.*

(4) *Summarize in your own words what each text says, directly or by inference, in response to your question.*

(5) *If it is possible at this point, categorize the responses to your question in a way that helps you to analyze the data (e.g., by theological positions; methodological approaches; pro/con arguments).*

(6) *Write the "answer" to your question that you have derived from your reading/synthesis/analysis of the texts in a brief sentence or two. If no answer emerges, simply record the results of your inquiry, including (a) what you learned, (b) what questions remain, and (c) what you still need to know.*

Syntopical Reading worksheet

My Reading/Research Question
(Choose a question that has emerged from your own reading, reflection, and research that has relevance for your theological writing/research project, and write it here.)

Sources to be Interrogated
(Provide a bibliographical citation for each source/text you are using for this Syntopical Reading Assignment.)
(1)
(2)
(3)

Textual Responses
(Include relevant quotes/references from each source that provide information for answering your question.)
(1)
(2)
(3)

My Synthesis/Analysis of Textual Responses
(Summarize what each text says in answer to your question in your own words.)
(1)
(2)
(3)

My Concluding Response to the Question
(Write the "answer" to your question derived from your reading/synthesis/analysis of the texts in a brief sentence or two—or, if no answer emerged, simply record the results of your inquiry—what you learned, what questions remain, what you still need to know.)

From reading researchfully to taking notes in your own way

The fine art of taking research notes from your reading is a crucial but often underrated skill. Note taking is the first step in the process of assimilating another author's work into your own research project, and that process requires care and vigilance, lest it go awry and open the writer to unintentional acts of plagiarism. To prevent this cardinal sin of academe,[13] note-taking also can also provide a housekeeping system for article summaries, direct quotes, bibliographical citations, and other research materials. A research essay will be no better than the research notes supporting it.

There are many ways of taking notes for a research project, and the best way is "your own way." But for your own instruction and amusement, take a walk through your library's reading room the next time you are there, and look over the other readers' shoulders as unobtrusively as you can to see how they are taking notes. You will find some people still taking notes on index cards. You will find others scribbling diligently on yellow lined pads or spiral notebooks. You will find many others taking notes with notebook or tablet computers. Whatever your own preferred note-taking style, you will avoid the eleventh-hour scenario described earlier if you provide complete bibliographical information on each notation, including page numbers, and check quotations for accuracy before moving to the next note. When you paraphrase material, keep the original quote on the same page or opposite side of a notecard so that you can check your paraphrase against the original.

There are as many ways to organize your note-taking process as to take notes. You can write notes according to the particular *topics* on your outline. You can write notes in response to particular *articles* included in your research. If an article or book chapter is particularly crucial for your argument, it is a good idea to make an outline of the article, labeling subcategories of relevant topics and quotes in the left-hand column of your yellow pad, or according to your own notation on computer files. If you are taking notes on computer files, there are many ways to categorize your material. You can categorize files by the individual sources you have researched. You can categorize files by subtopics or ideas, or according to topics and subheadings of your outline. You can also create a computer database on your paper/topic to collect or generate footnotes, or you can use available software for that purpose.[14]

However you take notes, the moment will come when you must make the transition from "taking notes" to "writing research." The more "written" vs. "recorded" notes you have, the easier the transition to writing will be, and the more time that you take "writing research" in your own words, the less time "writing a first draft" will take. One way to jump-start the research writing process is to cross-reference your outline and your notes, and adjust the outline accordingly as you incorporate material from the notes into it. But, you will eventually need to quote and paraphrase some of your sources as you write. How, then, can you effectively weave your research into the narrative of your essay? First, you need a well-developed research argument to guide your presentation of supporting materials. Second, you need to develop the research-writing skills of quotation, paraphrase, and textual elucidation, as we shall see shortly. But, first we turn to mapping a research argument.

Mapping a research argument

Essential to the process of integrating reading, writing, and research is an outline of your research argument, which will serve as a road map for the integration of your notes, quotes, and other supporting material into your research narrative. A research argument follows the same protocols of argumentation introduced in Chapter 3, and those protocols are presupposed in the comments that follow.[15] A research argument is distinctive, however, in that it relies not merely on inductive or deductive logic to prove its claim, but upon the sources that support and document it. At the same time, the argument it advances is both autonomous and answerable to those sources.

A research argument is answerable to the sources that substantiate its claim, since the argument is dependent upon the evidence that the research provides for demonstration of its validity. However, a research argument is also autonomous in that it makes an original claim that is more than the sum of the evidence backing up the claim. However necessary they are for the substantiation of the argument, a string of sources does not an argument make. Nor, as we shall see shortly, can you expect your readers to assemble your argument painstakingly by themselves from an extended sequence of quotes. The argument must have its own narrative line, which the research relentlessly follows and substantiates, one citation at a time.

By a "narrative line," I mean that your research argument should be conceived as an unfolding mystery story with a problem to be solved and a case to be argued, not as a static deposition of facts and research data.[16] Whether that narrative line is rendered initially in a standard outline, a visual map,[17] or in the intuitive regions of your own composing process,[18] a well-delineated research argument will help you to manage the research process effectively. It should begin with a broad statement of your research claim (subject to further refinement as the project proceeds) and then provide an overview of the main points of your argument as you envision it from the beginning to the end of your essay. Before we proceed to the writing process of integrating reading, writing, and research to write theological research well, you are invited to draft the "narrative line" of your argument in Theological Memo 4:

THEOLOGICAL MEMO 4: Mapping Your Research Argument:

Please prepare a "map," outline, or diagram of your research argument by (1) *writing the research claim for the paper you are working on at the top of the page*; (2) *listing the main points of your argument as it will unfold from the beginning to the end of your essay; and (3) aligning your research sources—articles or books to be cited, direct quotes, paraphrased materials, and so on—with the appropriate "points" of your argument. While the order may (and probably will) change as you continue to write the essay, this "map" will help you to integrate your reading, writing and research into a coherent and sustained narrative.*

Integrating reading, writing, and research to write theological research well

The next step in integrating reading, writing, and research into a theological research essay is honing the research-writing skills of *quotation*, *paraphrase*, and *textual elucidation*. We have already seen that writing and research are not entirely separate stages in the process, although we often think of them that way. For experienced scholars, taking notes from research sources is not mere dictation, or slavish copying of other people's material. At its best, this process inspires an active, dialogical conversation with your sources, from the beginning to the completion of the project. Such a conversation can only begin, however, when we really understand what the sources are saying—when we do not merely repeat what they say, but rather read them attentively enough to put their statements into our own words. That is why the best research writing comes from writing as you do your research and read your sources, not by merely "writing up" your research after it has all been done. As we have seen, such writing includes taking notes from sources, making notes in response to sources, paraphrasing quoted material as you read it, providing complete bibliographical information as you go, and finally weaving this "research-in-writing" into a coherently written essay. We can follow the stages of such an active research/writing process and see its metamorphosis into a well-wrought theological narrative, exemplified by the selections below from Elizabeth Johnson's *She Who Is: The Mystery of God in Feminist Theological Discourse:*[19]

Summarizing your source/author

The first step in the conversation is summarizing your source/author. Building upon the summarizing skills that were introduced in Chapter 4,[20] your goal here is to answer the question, "What my author is saying is… .," accurately, succinctly, and clearly. See, for example, how Johnson summarizes the theological contribution of Yves Congar:

> In Europe Yves Congar has synthesized the learning of a lifetime in his trilogy on the Holy Spirit which gives an excellent comprehensive overview of the history of the doctrine of the Spirit and its ecumenical thorniness in relation to Orthodox churches. With a view toward contemporary concerns, he also adduces historical precedent for casting the Spirit in a feminine mold, calling the Spirit the feminine person in God, or again, God's femininity.[21]

Questioning your source/author

The next step in the conversation is questioning your source/author. What questions do you have about a particular statement? What do you need clarified? What does not ring true? What seems like a biased judgment? What do you not yet understand? What is in conflict with other sources/authors on this subject? See how Johnson (quoting Rosemary Ruether) questions Congar's view of the "feminine":

> As Rosemary Ruether astutely formulates the fundamental question: "Is it not the case that the very concept of the 'feminine' is a patriarchal invention, an ideal projected onto women by men and vigorously defended because it functions so well to keep men in positions of power and women in positions of service to them?"[22]

Talking back to your source/author

Talking back to your source/author might follow, after you have raised the questions above. Imagine that you are having a conversation with the author; note where you do not agree with her, and explain why; refer him to another source you have read; make a note of evidence not accounted for, or perhaps a need for more evidence on a particular point. Make your own rebuttal of the author's argument factual and fair-minded, as Johnson does in the rebuttal below:

> In a church rigorously structured by patriarchal hierarchy, a Dominican, a Franciscan, and a Jesuit have tried to alleviate the sexism of the central symbol for God by imagining the Holy Spirit as feminine. I for one appreciate their efforts even as I criticize their results.... Besides the very real question of whether nature or culture shapes [their] descriptions of feminine roles, their effect on the being and function of concrete, historical women is deleterious and restrictive.... When used to describe the Holy Spirit as the feminine dimension of God, the result is not a view of God that may liberate, empower, or develop women as imago Dei in all their complex female dimensions.[23]

Incorporating your source/author into your own research argument

The final objective of this process is incorporating your source/author into your own research argument. Evoking such metaphors as "spinning, weaving and quilting," Johnson models the process that she describes in her own scholarship "as it seeks to articulate new patterns from bits of contemporary experiences and ancient sources":

> Spinning, weaving, and quilting, all taken from women's domestic chores, provide an evocative description of scholarship as it seeks to articulate new patterns from bits of contemporary experiences and ancient sources. In the spirit of these metaphors, this exploration attempts to braid a footbridge between the ledges of classical and feminist Christian wisdom.[24]

Quoting directly

The first and most direct way of incorporating your research into your own narrative is to *quote directly*. However, experienced theological researchers quote with care. While direct quotes should be used sparingly, they are used appropriately to lend authority to an argument, to provide a necessary building block for your own argument, or to strengthen an argument with a quintessential statement that does not lend itself to paraphrase. In the selection below, Johnson quotes Roger Haight's more general description of "a focus for a theology" in order to identify and particularize her own:

> Making a fundamental option as such is not unique to feminist theology. Every theological reflection has a center of gravity that unifies, organizes and directs its attention. Roger Haight describes it well:
>
> A focus for a theology then is the dominant interest, passion and concern, the unifying theme that holds the whole of it together as a coherent vision.... Like the

> lens that draws rays of light to a center, but without blocking any of their light, so too a centering concern of theology should organize and unify theological data thematically, but without negating the legitimate concerns represented by other and lesser problems.[25]
>
> The lens of women's flourishing focuses faith's search for understanding in feminist theology.

Notice how Johnson has used Haight's quote adroitly to illuminate her own feminist theological "focus" without compromising his words, or wrenching them out of context for her own purposes. She has also enveloped it within her own narrative cohesively and seamlessly. Whenever you incorporate a direct quote in your narrative, the quote and your narrative should be grammatically congruent, and the quote should be connected with what precedes it and with what follows it by your own introductory and/or concluding commentary, however brief. The goal is to weave the quote into your own argument, not to showcase the quote for its own sake.

Paraphrasing and summarizing

The second way of incorporating your source/author into your own research focus is to *paraphrase* the text in your own words in order to *summarize* relevant material. As Johnson does consummately in the passage below dealing with Thomas Aquinas' *quaestio* concerning whether God can be addressed as "person," paraphrasing is especially useful when you are summarizing an argument or trying to explain a concept in simpler language:

> In one of those myriad interesting little discussions that Aquinas carries on in the formal framework of the *quaestio*, he deals luminously with the legitimacy of this spiritual development. The question at hand is whether it is proper to refer to God as "person." Some would object that this word is not used of God in the Scriptures, neither in the Old Testament nor in the New. But, goes his argument, what the word signifies such as intelligence is in fact frequently applied to God in Scripture, and so "person" can be used with confidence. Furthermore, he muses, if our speech about God were limited to the very terms of Scripture itself, then no one could speak about God except in the original languages of Hebrew and Greek![26]

Synthesizing

The third and most intellectually demanding way of incorporating your author's material into your own narrative is to *synthesize* your author's argument into your own research argument by categorizing, or classifying, different responses to the question being probed. To "synthesize" means to draw together a selected cache of materials into one cohesive and significant narrative. This strategy enables you to cast a wider net over a theological discussion, often in preparation for introducing your own argument. In the quote below, Johnson surveys six "ways of speaking about God" in contemporary theological discourse, prior to critiquing their patriarchal bias and introducing her own feminist proposal:

> In response to the insufficiencies of classical theism, a goodly number of theologians have been seeking other ways of speaking about God. These theological efforts are leading to discourse about, in Anne Carr's felicitous summary, the liberating God, the incarnational God, the relational God, the suffering God, the God who is future, and the unknown, hidden God of mystery.[27]

By using these writing/research strategies as you go, you will write as you do research, rather than being overwhelmed by the transition from "research" to "writing."[28] You will also be ready to proceed to the task of organizing your research to write a first draft, to which we turn next.

Organizing research to write a first draft

If the task of organizing your research to write the first draft of a project seems daunting, you are not alone. Many years after Albert Schweitzer wrote his *Quest for the Historical Jesus*, he described the difficulties he faced in shaping his research into a coherent narrative:

> After I had worked through the various lives of Jesus, I found it very difficult to organize them into chapters. After vain attempts to do this on paper, I piled all the "lives" in one big heap in the middle of my room, selected a place for each of the chapters in a corner or between the pieces of furniture, and then, after considerable thought, sorted the volumes into the piles to which they belonged. I pledged myself to find a place for every book in some pile, and then to leave each heap undisturbed in its place until the corresponding chapter in the manuscript was finished. I followed this plan to the very end. For many months people who visited me had to thread their way across the room along paths that ran between heaps of books.[29]

Nor, according to Annie Dillard, does the task become any easier when making revisions from a first draft to a second draft. In her luminous reflection *The Writing Life*, she confessed, "You can easily get so confused writing a thirty-page chapter that in order to make an outline for the second draft, you have to rent a hall."[30]

Organizing research by outlining

Whether or not your own prospect of shifting from research to writing a first draft appears as daunting as Schweitzer's or Dillard's, one way to do this is to draft a working outline for your project from the reading and research that you have completed thus far, from which you will subsequently write your first draft. If you do not have your own method, begin by:

- **Gathering** all your reading and research notes into one place (if they are on computer, print out hard copies for more convenient access);
- **Clearing a space** for the process of sorting, classifying and labeling your materials;

- **Sorting** your materials broadly according to topics, questions, or sections of your project;
- **Classifying** each broader section into sub-sections, organized in the order that you wish to present the material in the paper;
- **Labeling** each section and subsection with a title or brief phrase that identifies it;
- **Discarding** (or putting aside) any extraneous material that does not fit into your sections or subsections;
- **Outlining** your material, using your preferred outline mode.

Organizing research by drawing a first draft

A second strategy for moving from research to writing a first draft is to "draw a first draft." This method is designed for those whose writing and thinking styles are more "right-brained" and intuitive, but it often provides "left-brained" writers with new ways of looking at their material as well. Before you begin the actual writing of your first draft, review your research notes and put them into an order that makes sense to you. Take a few moments to discern the movement of your argument and the shape your project might take. When you are ready, take out a large piece of blank paper and something to draw with. Using pencil, pen, crayons, or paint, draw a picture, diagram, or "map" of what you want to say and in what order you want to say it.[31]

Do this in any way you wish and in any combination of words and diagrams. The process will be most helpful if you let the drawing take precedence over the words that describe it. When you have finished your picture, hang it up near your desk as a creative "icon" to keep you centered and focused on the writing task. When you complete your project, you might wish to compare the final shape and organization of the written paper with your exploratory "picture." If all else fails, you will have stimulated your brain by using a different creative medium. If you are more fortunate, you may find yourself sitting down to begin writing your first draft, inspired by the "map" you have just created.

Organizing research by writing

A final strategy for moving from research to writing a first draft is to start writing. If you have already begun to write in the course of your research and have organized your research according to an outline that you will follow as you write, this strategy invites you to begin with what Joan Bolker calls a "Zero Draft,"[32] which precedes a "first draft" but moves the writer purposefully toward it. Guided by your outline and research notes, begin where you need to begin, and end where you need to end (there is a strong precedent in Western Civilization to begin in *medias res* rather than at the beginning, and there is no reason why you should not follow suit). If footnotes are required along the way, insert them but do not interrupt your writing at this point to attend to them. When you are finished, let the writing sit overnight and then put a frame around it by responding to these questions:

- Has your writing forged a path to your first draft, or has it begun your first draft?
- If you wish to include it in your first draft, where does this writing belong in your essay (beginning? middle? end?)?
- What have you learned from the writing that you did not know before?
- What needs to be rewritten to include the new insight(s)?
- What research gaps need to be more fully written out?
- What other revisions are necessary for inclusion in a first draft?

Writing theological research three times: A draft by draft plan

Instructed by Jaroslav Pelikan, you are already familiar with the "Write Three Times" method introduced in Chapter 2 of this book. While writing a twenty-page theological research paper in *one* draft, let alone three, may not be a task for the fainthearted, the "write three times" method will reward those who adapt it to the requirements of writing theological research by preparing (1) a *research-driven* draft, (2) a *writer-driven* draft, and (3) an *audience-driven* draft. I am not suggesting that you write three separate drafts "from scratch," but rather that you build on each previous draft in the writing of the next one. Nor am I suggesting that you rigidly separate the acts of research and writing in this drafting process, but rather that you give each draft the precedence that it is due within that process.

The research-driven draft

In a theological essay, research is used to inform readers, to demonstrate the validity of a research claim, and to provide evidence for the argument advanced by the essay. If a completed theological research paper is like a starlit constellation in the night sky, the research on which it is based is like the individual stars that comprise the constellation. Just as stars in a particular configuration represent "Orion" or "The Big Dipper" to the initiated eye, so the points of your research should form a pattern of exposition or argument that is recognizable to your readers. The purpose of preparing a "research-driven" draft is to discern that pattern by placing your research in a logical and sequential order that develops your research claim and draws your argument forward through the evidence that you present.

In this draft, your research is the engine that drives the writing process, but you are behind the wheel of the car and can steer that process according to your own best working method. As suggested above, you might choose to organize your research into an outline of the paper. Alternately, you might choose to put all your notes and quoted material in the narrative order that will be followed in the paper. One of my colleagues organizes her book chapters by the quotations she will be citing or paraphrasing and inserts them in a sequence that forms the backbone of her argument for that chapter before writing any of her own narrative. Yet, it is the intuitive path that the researcher takes through the material that forms the pattern, and what is as yet unwritten is often guiding the process. "Facts are stupid things," Louis Agassiz taught his students, "until brought into connection with some general law."[33] If "general law" sounds too abstract for your theological project, consider the goal of a research-driven draft that of bringing the research you have done into a constellation of meaning that blazes with significance through the night sky, even before you have connected the dots with your writing.

The writer-driven draft

In writing theological research, the research must lead to the writing, but the writing must focus, clarify, and connect the pieces of research. At the same time that the research must ground the writing, the writing must guide the research into a coherent narrative. With the writer now in the driver's seat, her goal in this draft is twofold: (1) to funnel the research into the written flow of the narrative and (2) to order the narrative into a rhetorical framework that facilitates the flow. The writer steering the process does this (a) by "writing up" research notes into complete sentences and well-formed paragraphs; (b) by providing an introduction, analytical and interpretive commentary, appropriate narrative transitions, and conclusion that transmute the "raw" research into a cohesive written document; and (c) by dividing the narrative into smaller, appropriately titled sections that further enhance the written delivery of the essay.[34] At this point, she might choose to reread the draft and make any necessary revisions, or she might relegate all revisions to the following, "audience-driven" draft. Either way, the completed draft should now look as much like a research essay as Orion looks like Orion in the night sky. Before your professor examines every page with an exacting academic telescope, however, it is time to prepare an audience-driven draft, to which we turn next.

The audience-driven draft

To write an audience-centered draft, it is necessary to shift gears and put your audience, metaphorically if not literally, in the driver's seat. To do this takes imagination, for the first step is to reread your essay as if you were one of its readers, not its writer. This might require that you put yourself in your reader's shoes, asking, "Is this clear? Does it make sense? Have I provided enough commentary on that quotation? What would my professor say in response to this claim? What should I say to anticipate that response? Are there grammatical errors that break the flow of the reading? Have I been careless with mechanics (punctuation, spelling, and so on)?"

Yet, writing for an audience does not just mean filling in the gaps and cleaning up your grammar and punctuation. The goal of an audience-driven draft is to produce a research essay that someone else would read because they wanted to, not just because they had to. Admittedly, the primary audience of a theological research paper is usually the professor who has assigned it, and that professor does indeed "have to" read it. Nevertheless, the sheer delight that professors experience when they find themselves enjoying, rather than merely "evaluating" a student paper, is worth the work you might have to put in to achieve that level of reader response.

Writing, revising, and rewriting "between the drafts"

In an engaging and wise essay that challenges academic writers not to revise their own voices out of a research essay, Nancy Sommers muses, "Where does revision come from? ... What happens between the drafts? Something has to happen or else we are stuck doing mop and broom work, the janitorial work of polishing, cleaning and fixing what is and always has been. What happens between the drafts seems to be one of the great secrets of our profession."[35]

Before we conclude this three-draft research-writing process, I encourage you to think about what happens between your drafts that stimulates or stymies the revision process. For no matter how smoothly or fitfully your writing goes, there will always be revisions. Granted also that some routine "janitorial work" will be an inevitable part of the revision process, can you think of a time when an insight inserted itself mysteriously between draft 2 and draft 3, and "re-envisioned" the implications of your research? Can you think less happily of another time when the revisions you made on a paper suppressed your argument rather than enhancing it? If you can discern what made the difference between those two experiences, you will be well on your way to revising and rewriting more productively "between the drafts." While you are reflecting on these questions, I will make a few suggestions from my own experience of revising and rewriting theological research essays.

To begin with, the revision process in a theological research essay is admittedly more challenging than if one were revising a shorter paper. What you revise on page 15, for example, might affect what you have already said on page 3, so each revision needs to be made in the context of the whole document. Be especially vigilant to track changes in your original research claim that are reflected in your conclusion, but may necessitate a revised introduction. If you do not make the necessary revisions at the beginning of your essay, readers may form expectations that are not fulfilled in the denouement of the essay. Checking for the congruence of your introductory research claim and your concluding argument is like balancing the sides of an equation, and no less crucial an operation.

Second, reading your draft "paragraph by paragraph" to make sure that each paragraph (1) begins with something resembling a topic sentence, and (2) advances your narrative (and the research argument it is unfolding) appropriately is a useful way to begin the revision process. I say "*something resembling* a topic sentence" in order to encourage your own authorial creativity, but I retrieve the *topic sentence* from its current disfavor among some writing teachers because if you have one, your readers will know immediately what the paragraph is about, and you will too, when you reread the essay. If, in addition, you find a paragraph or paragraphs that do not seem connected to what precedes them or to what follows them, you can make the necessary adjustments by (a) moving them to the appropriate place in the narrative, (b) providing the transitional material to fit their present position in the narrative or (if upon rereading they appear to be extraneous or superfluous) by (c) cutting them from the draft altogether.

Finally, I urge you to read your draft, quotation by quotation, asking the same questions: (1) What is the "topic" of the quotation, and is it clear from the textual elucidation that accompanies it? (2) Does the quotation support and advance the research argument, and is that also clear from the textual elucidation that accompanies it? *By far the greatest temptation besetting writers of research essays is that of over-quoting their sources, and under-elucidating what has been quoted.* Those who fall prey to this temptation will often argue that their research argument requires the extensive quotation of sources that they have provided but provide their readers with little guidance in interpreting that material. Abstruse German theologians may be able to get away with this studied indifference toward their readers, but Karl Rahner did not try to do so in his *Foundations of Christian Faith*, and you are well advised to avoid this pitfall as well. You will do so if you exercise this revision process ruthlessly, cutting unnecessary quotations, paraphrasing where possible, and conversing critically with those voices that you retain. What is ultimately at stake is the suppression or expression of your own theological voice, no less as a researcher than as an interpreter of theological texts.[36]

Preparing and presenting the audience-driven draft

If you have successfully transformed your research-driven draft into a writer-centered research essay, you will be on your way to producing an "enjoyable" piece of writing. (Recall that Augustine affirmed its capacity to "give pleasure" as a worthy goal for any piece of writing.)[37] Assuming that you have reread your draft with your audience in mind and made the indicated revisions, you might still solicit a willing reader to read the draft and invite feedback. Remind your reader that you will not have time to radically rewrite the paper at this stage, but you would welcome feedback in particular areas of your choosing. Nonnative writers of English are especially encouraged to solicit peer or faculty feedback before handing in the final essay, at whatever level of writing support they require.[38] But all writers benefit from a reader over their shoulder, whether the reader is another student, a roommate, a partner or spouse, a writing coach provided by the school, or the professor for whom the paper is being written.

Once your reader has returned your paper to you and you have attended to their suggestions, you are ready to prepare the paper for final presentation or "delivery." Just as the delivery of a speech was the final arbiter of a speaker's performance, so the final presentation of a paper is crucial to its reception by readers, and especially the professorial readers who are evaluating your work. Failure to follow your professor's specifications for final submission of the paper will compromise its effective delivery. Failure to indent paragraphs, paginate your essay, run a spell check, or correct careless mechanical errors will further flaw your written performance, however brilliant the paper might be. Finally, and most importantly, failure to document your sources correctly, and in the documentation style required by your school, will not only weaken your credibility as a theological writer and researcher, but it will also predispose you to acts of intentional or unintentional plagiarism. Before your paper will be ready for the "Checklist for Final Preparation of a Theological Research Paper" that concludes this chapter, we must move from the rhetoric of organization to the rhetoric of documentation.

What are the requirements for documenting sources and avoiding plagiarism in a theological research essay?

Documentation of sources is not merely a requirement, it is a rhetoric, or element, of purposeful communication that confers credibility and authority upon your work. Because acts of plagiarism undermine both of these, we turn first to the question of plagiarism; then we consider how to write footnotes well; finally, we will provide a brief guide to documenting sources, according to Turabian/Chicago style.

Plagiarism preventions and interventions

Like the sin against the Holy Spirit that Jesus pronounces unforgivable in the gospels,[39] plagiarism is the unpardonable sin of writers and researchers in any academic discipline. Plagiarism is the unintentional or intentional act of incorporating the ideas or words of someone else into your own writing without properly acknowledging them. At its root, however, plagiarism is occasioned by a failure to trust our own words, before it becomes a moral failure occasioned by the theft of someone else's words. This lack of trust in our own words can become more pronounced in an academic environment that requires us to write from authoritative sources at the same time that we are urged to be original.[40] The best prevention against plagiarism is to learn to write theological research well enough to trust your own words. That being said, the most effective intervention lies in recognizing the reciprocal relationship between your words and those of your sources, and observing the rules of scholarly etiquette, or bibliographical citation, which govern that relationship.

"The word in language," writes Mikhail Bakhtin, "is half someone else's. It becomes 'one's own' only when the speaker [or writer] populates it with his own intention, his own accent, when he appropriates the word, adapting it to his own semantic and expressive intention."[41] While Bakhtin is describing the social and "multivocal" nature of all language, he aptly describes the process of writing theological research (or any kind of research).[42] The research process begins with reading and reflecting upon other people's words. When we write in conversation with those words, our words are "half someone else's," a phenomenon which literary scholars call "intertextuality." In the writing of theological research, we make these words our own by refocusing them through the lens of an original research claim. Nevertheless, we must acknowledge that "half" which is still "someone else's" by citing the author and informing readers where to find their words. If we do not, we have committed the act of plagiarism.

We have been looking at the research process as a conversation in which we build our own contributions upon the words and ideas of "someone else," just as others are building upon our words and ideas. Whether we quote another directly or reference her in a footnote, we are appropriating her words for the purposes of our own research. In our individualistic Western culture, however, an individual's words and ideas constitute "intellectual property,"[43] and plagiarism, as a failure to acknowledge one's sources properly, constitutes a violation of that conversation. In order to make someone else's word your own in the writing of theological research, you first have to give it back to them by acknowledging that they said or wrote it. If someone else wrote it, quote it, and/or footnote it!

Plagiarism, paraphrase, or summary?

Citing a direct quote in a paper is a straightforward process that requires only that you provide the citation information accurately and in the required format. Citing information that is paraphrased or summarized is more challenging, especially if you rely too heavily on the author's original language rather than rendering the text in your own words. *While paraphrase of a source without appropriate citation constitutes plagiarism, simply placing a footnote at the end of material that you have transcribed from your source without translating it into your own words also constitutes plagiarism.* The following theological memo invites you to select the paraphrase/summary of the source material least susceptible to this offense:

> *THEOLOGICAL MEMO 5: Plagiarism, Paraphrase or Summary? Please read the following quotation, and three students' attempts to paraphrase or summarize it in their own papers. Which paraphrase/summary most successfully avoids plagiarism? Which paraphrase/summary is guilty of plagiarism? Please write your own version of this summary/paraphrase and include the appropriate citation.*
>
> Lured by the Spirit, women now turn away from the disparagement of their embodied selves imbibed from the patriarchal tradition and turn toward a full embrace of their own blessed worth, cherishing themselves anew as religious subjects, created by God, redeemed by Christ, graced by the Spirit, called to responsibility in this world, and destined for life in glory. This becomes a baseline from which critical and creative thinking and action proceed. Amid incalculable personal, political, and spiritual suffering resulting from women's subordination in theory and practice, Christian feminism labors to bring the community, its symbols and practices, into a closer coherence with the reign of God's justice.[44]
>
> *(1) Women today turn away from letting the patriarchal tradition disparage their embodied selves and embrace their own blessed worth, amid untold suffering which results from their subordination in theory and practice.*
>
> *(2) According to Elizabeth Johnson, Christian feminists today reject the devaluation of their "embodied selves" by the Church's patriarchal tradition and work to bring the community into greater harmony with God's justice.*
>
> *(3) Instead of accepting the disparagement of themselves which is part of the patriarchal tradition, Christian women today are following the lure of the Spirit and cherishing themselves anew as persons created by God, redeemed by Jesus, graced by the Spirit, called to be responsible in this world, and destined for glory. In this they find a baseline for critical and creative thinking and action.*

A cross-cultural caveat

We will look more carefully at footnote conventions and scholarly etiquette in the next section, but the most common way to acknowledge another's words is by quoting directly and using quotation marks, or by treating a longer citation as a block quotation with a bibliographical footnote. Some non-Western cultures, however, have differing conventions concerning scholarly citation and acknowledgment. If you write something that I like, I am free to use it without acknowledging that you wrote it first. What you wrote simply becomes incorporated into what I am writing, with no quotation marks distinguishing what you wrote from what I am writing. Writing and research in these cultures are conceived as collective enterprises, not individual, creative acts.[45] That is not the case, however, in the theological schools where I teach, and I suspect it is not the case where you are learning to write theology well.

Preventing plagiarism as a theological task

In the schools where I teach, theological authorship, or "the assumption that the theologian is a creative agent whose talent is essential to the performance and the results of the theological task,"[46] is taken for granted. Thus, preventing plagiarism is not merely an academic requirement, but a crucial theological task. "Who steals my purse, steals trash," Shakespeare's Iago says to Othello, but who steals my words and ideas, steals my God-given creativity, and with it, my very soul. Thus, the failure to acknowledge my sources is not only a dishonorable act that violates those whose work I have plagiarized, but it also dishonors and violates the God from whom all creativity springs. Ultimately, however, my act of plagiarism dishonors and violates me, because I have not trusted my God-given agency to enflesh the words I write and create "a new thing" (Isaiah 43:19) through the research that I do. From a theological standpoint, plagiarism constitutes a refusal to cocreate with the God who invites and authorizes our theology, and a refusal to participate with God in the graced but grinding labor of incarnation, which in this context means writing theology well.

Shifting the theological metaphor slightly, plagiarism also constitutes a double-edged sin of omission and commission. We *commit* acts of plagiarism by virtue of what we *omit* from the writing and research process, whether deliberately or by default. Often the omissions are subtle, seemingly inconsequential, and unintentional. Nevertheless, to write theological research well, plagiarism in any form and for whatever reasons is unacceptable. A "Plagiarism Prevention and Intervention Checklist" that you can adapt to your own theological research writing follows.

Plagiarism prevention and intervention checklist

The following "omissions" make plagiarism a "sin of commission" as well:

- Have you omitted quotation marks when quoting a theological author directly?
- Have you omitted the name of the author in your text when quoting indirectly from that author?
- Have you omitted proper acknowledgment of the author in an appropriate bibliographical citation?
- Have you failed to paraphrase the author's writing in your own words and omitted quotation marks when "borrowing" from the original?

To avoid committing the act of plagiarism, do not omit:

- Learning the proper rules for quotation and documentation, according to the style manual (APA, Turabian/Chicago, MLA) required by your school;
- Providing full documentation for all sources, from the beginning of the note-taking process to the conclusion of your final essay draft;
- Citing quotations in your research notes accurately and in full, using quotation marks and/or parenthetical citations where necessary;
- Learning to paraphrase sources without plagiarizing them by writing them in your own words at best, and revising the language of your sources when all else fails;
- Writing theological footnotes well, which we turn to in the next section.

Writing theological footnotes well

Footnotes, placed at the bottom of the page on which they appear, or endnotes, placed at the conclusion of a completed text, provide documentation for sources cited in the text and authorial commentary to qualify, amplify, and elucidate the text.[47] While sources abound on how to document sources according to a particular academic style, almost nothing has been written on how to write footnotes well.[48] Yet, as Anthony Grafton explains in his "curious history" of this genre, "the footnote is bound up, in modern life, with the ideology and technical practices of a profession," and learning to write footnotes forms a part of the process of apprenticeship required for practice in that profession.[49]

The lack of attention to the actual writing of footnotes may be due to the fact that writing footnotes is a means of scholarly communication intended primarily for those already initiated into the discourse at hand—in other words, "insiders," who, by definition, already know how to reproduce this documentary apparatus. The scholar may write his book for a general audience, but she will invariably write footnotes/endnotes for other scholars; thus reading footnotes becomes a scholarly litmus test that separates the "sheep" from the "goats," or scholarly experts from the general reading audience. For this reason, womanist theorist bell hooks does not use footnotes when she wants her work to be accessible to a wider audience of black women than her own circle of scholars:

> When I wrote my first book, *Ain't I a Woman: Black Women and Feminism*, the issue of class and its relationship to who one's reading audience might be came up for me around my decision not to use footnotes....I told people that my concern was that footnotes set class boundaries for readers....Certainly I did feel that choosing to use simple language, absence of footnotes, etc. would mean I was jeopardizing the possibility of being taken seriously in academic circles but then this was a political matter and a political decision. It utterly delights me that this has proven not to be the case and that the book is read by many academics as well as by people who are not college educated.[50]

For different reasons, Roman Catholic theologian Karl Rahner declined to use footnotes in his *Foundations of Christian Faith*, explaining:

> In view of the origins of this book and its introductory character, the author considered it superfluous to add subsequently explanatory footnotes and references to literature. In the framework of this book that would seem in him to be a learned pretense to which he is not inclined.[51]

Jesus Historian John Meier, on the other hand, seeks to write for both general and scholarly audiences in his three-volume *The Marginal Jew: Rethinking the Historical Jesus*, by writing the text in "language intelligible to ... the general educated reader," and relegating "more technical questions and detailed discussions of literature ... to the notes, where doctoral students and scholars can pursue particular problems at greater length and find references for further reading."[52]

While hooks, Rahner, and Meier have chosen footnote conventions (or the lack of them) in deference to particular audiences, traditional scholarship depends upon a system of citation, references, and critical notes to locate the scholarly conversation within a particular discourse community, to establish parameters of authority and accountability for carrying on that conversation, and to establish scholarly credibility. Documenting a research project accurately and in appropriate form is an exact science that can be learned with the aid of a style manual, but providing clear, readable notes that interface critically with the text is an art that is best learned from other scholars.

For example, traditional instruction on research documentation for undergraduate research papers privileges the "general reader" and cautions against distracting readers with too many notes that detract from your main argument.[53] While this is appropriate advice for introductory researchers, more specialized researchers privilege the scholarly "experts" in the field, who will typically read the footnotes and bibliography first, to determine whether the book will be useful to their own research. Hence, as the authors cited above have shown us, the type of documentation used in a project will vary according to the writer/researcher's purpose and the audience for whom they are writing.

Traditional instruction on research documentation for undergraduate writers also tends to distinguish the "main body" of the project from the "notes," which are simply there for the purpose of documenting sources. For experienced scholar/researchers, however, there is a much more integral relation between the "body" of the discussion and the "critical notes" engendered by the discussion. In different drafts of a paper, for example, text can be transferred to footnotes and vice versa, depending upon the audience addressed and the space constraints.[54] However it is composed, it is always helpful to imagine a footnote as an organic counterpoint and commentary upon your argument, not merely a means of covering your tracks with the appropriate bibliographical citation.

For example, theological scholars can construct their own "symbolic world" of the literature that they are reviewing by introducing brief, suggestive citations in the text that direct readers actively to the notes, where each citation is elaborated more fully, without burdening the text and its readers with too many references within the narrative. Elizabeth Johnson uses this strategy in the introduction to *She Who Is* to gather those in whose company she too is "turning from the restrictive inheritance of exclusive God-talk" to seek a more adequate way to speak about God:

> For some, the journey involves a sojourn in the darkness and silence, traversing a desert of the spirit created by the loss of accustomed symbols. [6] For others, new language is born as women gather together creatively in solidarity and prayer, and as sister scholars uncover alternative ways of speaking about divine mystery that have long been hidden in Scripture and tradition. [7] In this matrix feminist theologians, engaging in the traditional theological task of reflecting on God and all things in the light of God, are shaping new speech about God that, in Rebecca Chopp's memorable phrase, are discourses of emancipatory transformation, pointing to new ways of living together with each other and the earth. [8][55]

While the text unfolds with a clarity and integrity that stands on its own, each numbered footnote functions like a computer icon, inviting the reader to "click," or proceed to the note, for a fuller display of information that readers can access at their own pace. If we were to turn to note [6], following Johnson's evocation of "a sojourn in the darkness and silence, traversing a desert of the spirit created by the loss of accustomed symbols," we would read:

> This experience has been perceptively analyzed by Constance Fitzgerald, "Impasse and Dark Night," in *Living with Apocalypse: Spiritual Resources for Social Compassion*, ed. Tilden Edwards (New York: Harper & Row, 1984) 95–116.[56]

Both the textual citation and the supporting footnote function together to introduce readers to the territory that *She Who Is* will traverse and reinforce each other rhetorically through the echoing language of text and footnote and the authoritative citation of its source. Thus, it is not enough to write a theological footnote well; it is also necessary to cite it correctly in the requisite documentation style, which we turn to now.

From writing to citing footnotes well

Finally, all footnotes must follow a consistent form of documentation or citation. While citation styles differ, the standard elements of a citation include author, title of publication, edition, place of publication, publisher, and date of publication. In the United States, the most common citation styles are APA (American Psychological Association), MLA (Modern Language Association), and Turabian/Chicago style. The *SBL Manual of Style* adapts Turabian/Chicago style for writers and scholars engaged in biblical research.[57] While the examples of footnotes that follow are in Turabian/Chicago style, you are advised to follow the style of citation required by your own school or professor.

Footnotes that cite research sources are called *reference notes*, and footnotes that qualify, amplify, or comment upon the text of the research essay are called *content notes*. Every footnoted source should also be cited in a *bibliography* at the end of the paper. When a reference is inserted parenthetically in the text of a document, it is called an "in-text citation" and is included in a corresponding *reference list* at the end of the paper. For theological writers, footnotes and bibliography are more commonly used for extended research essays, while in-text citations may be used for shorter, "research-in-place" papers. Guided by Kate Turabian, we look at footnotes/bibliography below.

First, we turn to a brief overview of writing the most commonly used *reference notes* in Turabian style. Second, we consider when "to footnote or not to footnote," followed by a representative sampling of footnotes that you will need to document a theological research project.[58] Some concluding guidelines for writing theological footnotes well will draw this section to a close.

Documenting print sources in Turabian/Chicago style: An overview

All of the references below have been prepared according to Kate L. Turabian, *A Manual for Writers of Term Papers, Theses and Dissertations: Chicago Style for Students and Researchers* 8th ed. (2013). See Chapter 17, 164–215, for more examples of footnote (**N**) and bibliographic (**B**) citation, or http://www.press.uchicago.edu/books/turabian/turabian_citationguide.html.

- **Book (One Author):**
  (**N**)
  Karl Rahner, *Foundations of Christian Faith: An Introduction to the Idea of Christianity* (New York: Seabury Press, 1978), 51–53.
  (**B**)
  Rahner, Karl. *Foundations of Christian Faith: An Introduction to the Idea of Christianity*. New York: Seabury Press, 1978.

- **Book (Editor or Compiler(s) as Author):**
  (**N**)
  Judith Plaskow and Carol P. Christ, eds., *Weaving the Visions: New Patterns in Feminist Spirituality* (SanFrancisco: Harper and Row, 1989).
  (**B**)
  Plaskow, Judith and Carol P. Christ, eds. *Weaving the Visions: New Patterns in Feminist Spirituality*. SanFrancisco: Harper and Row, 1989.

- **Parts of Edited Collections:**
  (**N**)
  Rebecca S. Chopp, "The Poetics of Testimony," in *Converging on Culture: Theologians in Dialogue with Cultural Analysis and Criticism*, ed. Delwin Brown, Sheila Greve Devaney, and Kathryn Tanner (Oxford: Oxford University Press, 2001), 56–70.

(B)
Chopp, Rebecca S. "The Poetics of Testimony." In *Converging on Culture: Theologians in Dialogue with Cultural Analysis and Criticism*, edited by Delwin Brown, Sheila, Greve Devaney, and Kathryn Tanner, 56–70. Oxford: Oxford University Press, 2001.

- **One Source Quoted in Another:**
  (N)
  Wilhelm Bousset, *The Antithesis between Jesus' Preaching and Judaism: a Religious-Historical Comparison* (Gottingen: Springer-Verlag, 1892), 30; quoted in Albert Schweitzer, *The Quest of the Historical Jesus: A Critical Study of its Progress from Reimarus to Wrede* (Baltimore: Johns Hopkins Press in association with The Albert Schweitzer Institute, 1998), 242.
  (B)
  Bousset, Wilhelm. *The Antithesis between Jesus' Preaching and Judaism: a Religious-Historical Comparison*. Gottingen: Springer-Verlag, 1892, 30. Quoted in Albert Schweitzer, *The Quest of the Historical Jesus: A Critical Study of its Progress from Reimarus to Wrede*. Baltimore: Johns Hopkins Press for The Albert Schweitzer Institute, 1998.

- **Article in a Theological Dictionary or Encyclopedia:**
  (N)
  Rosemary Radford Ruether, "Feminist Theology," in *The New Dictionary of Theology*, ed. Joseph A. Komonchak, Mary Collins, and Dermot A. Lane (Wilmington, DE: Michael Glazier, 1988), 391–96.
  (B)
  Ruether, Rosemary Radford. "Feminist Theology." In *The New Dictionary of Theology*, edited by Joseph A. Komonchak, Mary Collins, and Dermot A. Lane. Wilmington, DE: Michael Glazier, 1988: 391–96.

- **Journal Article (with volume and date):**
  (N)
  Dirkie Smit and Francois Wessels, "An Ethics of Writing? On Writing as a Social Activity," *Scriptura* 57 (1996): 125–38.
  (B)
  Smit, Dirkie and Francois Wessels. "An Ethics of Writing? On Writing as a Social Activity." *Scriptura* 57 (1996): 125–38.

- **Journal Article (with volume and issue number):**
  (N)
  Michael W. Harris, "African American Religious History in the 1980's: A Critical Review," *Religious Studies Review* 20, No. 4 (1994): 263–75.
  (B)
  Harris, Michael W. "African American Religious History in the 1980's: A Critical Review." *Religious Studies Review* 20, No. 4 (1994): 263–75.

- **Magazine Article:**
  (N)
  Luke Timothy Johnson, "After the Big Chill: Intellectual Freedom and Catholic Theologians," *Commonweal* 133, No. 2 (January 27, 2006): 10–14.
  (B)
  Johnson, Luke Timothy. "After the Big Chill: Intellectual Freedom and Catholic Theologians." *Commonweal* 133, No. 2 (January 27, 2006): 10–14.

- **Book Review in a Journal:**
  (N)
  Bjorn Krondorfer, Review of *The Sex Lives of Saints: An Erotic Hagiography*, by Virginia Burrus, *JAAR* 74 (2006): 259–62.
  (B)
  Krondorfer, Bjorn. Review of *The Sex Lives of Saints: An Erotic Hagiography*, by Virginia Burrus. *JAAR* 74 (2006): 259–62.

- **Thesis or Dissertation:**
  (N)
  Anne L. Deneen, "The Field at Midnight: Living with Spirit as Communion in Action" (S.T.L. Thesis, Weston Jesuit School of Theology, 2003), 1.
  (B)
  Deneen, Anne L. "The Field at Midnight: Living with Spirit as Communion in Action." S.T.L. Thesis, Weston Jesuit School of Theology," 2003.

Documenting electronic sources in Turabian/ Chicago style: An overview

All of the references below have been prepared according to Kate L. Turabian, *A Manual for Writers of Term Papers, Theses and Dissertations: Chicago Style for Students and Researchers* 8th ed. (2013). See Chapter 17, 164–215, for more examples of documenting electronic sources, or http://www.press.uchicago.edu/books/turabian/turabian_citationguide.html.[59]

Electronic Books:
(N)
Karl Rahner, *Grace in Freedom* (New York: Herder and Herder, 1969) section 2, accessed September 18, 2014, http://www.religion-online.org/showbook.asp?title=2079.
(B)
Rahner, Karl. *Grace in Freedom*. New York: Herder and Herder, 1969. Accessed September 18, 2014. http://www.religion-online.org/showbook.asp?title=2079.

Web Sites:
(N)
Miroslav Volf, "Miroslav Volf on Trends in American Religion & the Challenge of Exclusion and Embrace in Christian Practice," interview by Tracy Schier,

Resources for American Christianity, February 2, 2002, accessed September 18, 2014, http://www.resourcingchristianity.org/interview/miroslav-volf-on-trends-in-american-religion-the-challenge-of-exclusion-and-embrace-in-christian-practice.

(B)

Volf, Miroslav. "Miroslav Volf on Trends in American Religion & the Challenge of Exclusion and Embrace in Christian Practice." By Tracy Schier. *Resources for American Christianity*. February 21, 2002. Accessed September 18, 2014. http://www.resourcingchristianity.org/interview/miroslav-volf-on-trends-in-american-religion-the-challenge-of-exclusion-and-embrace-in-christian-practice.

Electronic Journals:

(N)

Hanna Stettler, "Sanctification in the Jesus Tradition," *Biblica* 85 (2004): 153–78, accessed September 18, 2014, http://www.bsw.org/biblica/vol-85-2004/sanctification-in-the-jesus-tradition/163/

(B)

Stettler, Hanna. "Sanctification in the Jesus Tradition," *Biblica* 85 (2004): 153–78. Accessed September 18, 2014. http://www.bsw.org/biblica/vol-85-2004/sanctification-in-the-jesus-tradition/163/

Online Newspapers and News Services:

(N)

John Thavis, "On Second Day of Meetings, Cardinals Turn Attention to Conclave," *Catholic News Service*, April 5, 2005, accessed September 18, 2014, http://www.catholicnews.com/data/stories/cns/0502047.htm.

(B)

Thavis, John. "On Second Day of Meetings, Cardinals Turn Attention to Conclave," *Catholic News Service*, April 5, 2005. Accessed September 18, 2014. http://www.catholicnews.com/data/stories/cns/0502047.htm.

Online Reference Works:

(N)

W. Ullman and G. Schwaiger, "Papacy," *New Catholic Encyclopedia*, 2nd ed. (Washington, DC: Catholic University of America, 2003), 829, accessed April 6, 2005, Gale Virtual Reference.

(B)

Ullman, W. and G. Schwaiger. "Papacy." *New Catholic Encyclopedia*, 2nd ed. Washington, DC: Catholic University of America, 2003. Accessed April 6, 2005. Gale Virtual Reference.

To footnote or not to footnote?

What is and is not footnoted in a research project depends to some degree on the audience for whom you are writing. In general, anything that can be assumed to be "common knowledge" to your readers need not be footnoted.[60] Second, when a broad swath of material has been synthesized from multiple sources to provide an introduction or overview, one footnote of acknowledgment listing all the sources consulted can be used in lieu of multiple footnotes sprinkled throughout the section.[61] Third, repeated quotes from one author or theologian in an essay analyzing their work can be cited with in-text citations rather than footnotes, to keep the documentation less cumbersome.[62] Finally, biblical quotes are usually cited within the text, following one introductory footnote identifying the edition of the Bible from which the quotes have been taken.[63] The goal is to cite the sources that are required to give credit where credit is due, without overburdening readers with unnecessary documentation. The guidelines that follow provide examples of when and what kind of footnotes are typically used to write theological research well:

- *The first, full reference* of every source needs a footnote:
  1
  Hermann Reimarus, "Concerning the Intention of Jesus and His Teaching," in *Fragments*, ed. Charles H. Talbert, trans. Ralph S. Fraser (Philadelphia: Fortress Press, 1970), 64.

- *Subsequent references* to a previously cited text need a footnote:
  2
  Ibid., 65. [Use "Ibid." to cite the work immediately preceding in the previous reference.]

  Or:

  2
  Reimarus, *Fragments*, 66.

- *Cross-references* to a cited text need a footnote:
  3
  See Mark Allen Powell, *Jesus as a Figure in History: How Modern Historians View the Man from Galilee* (Louisville, KY: Westminister John Knox Press, 1998), for a contemporary critical assessment of Reimarus' *Fragments*.

- *"Reviews of the Literature"* can be briefly surveyed in a footnote:
  4
  Some essays that may serve as an introduction to Spirit Christology are the following: James G.D. Dunn, *Jesus and the Spirit* (London: SCM, 1975); idem, *Christology in the Making* (Philadelphia: Westminster, 1980); Olaf Hansen, "Spirit Christology: A Way Out of Our Dilemma?" in *The Holy Spirit in the Life of the Church*, ed. P. Opsahl (Minneapolis: Augsburg, 1978), 172–203; and Norman Hook, "A Spirit Christology," *Theology* 75 (1972): 226–32 . . . .[64]

- *Definitions of textual terms* often require a footnote:
  5
  By a "transcendent dimension" I mean a dimension that goes beyond the particular words on a page toward a more universal consciousness reflected in the writing that some would call God; others, the good; still others, a shared human experience and destiny.

- *Citation of alternate views* to reinforce scholarly objectivity is often footnoted:
  6
  For pro and contra, see Leonie J. Archer, *Her Price Is Above Rubies: The Jewish Woman in Graeco-Roman Palestine* (Sheffield: Sheffield Academic Press, 2000), 154–184; Antoinette Clark Wire, "Gender Roles in a Scribal Community," in *Social History of the Matthean Community: Cross-Disciplinary Approaches*, ed. David Balch (Minneapolis: Fortress, 1991): 87–121.

- *Additional quoted material* that elucidates the text can be footnoted:
  7
  As Elisabeth Schüssler Fiorenza continues, "[The gospel writers] did not simply want to write down what Jesus said and did. Rather, they utilized the Jesus traditions that were shaped by Jesus' first followers, wo/men and men, for their own rhetorical interests and molded them in the light of the political-theological debates of their own day." See Schüssler Fiorenza, *Jesus and the Politics of Interpretation* (New York: Continuum, 2001), 246.

- *Authorial "glosses"* on the text of the paper may be footnoted:
  8
  To my knowledge, no one has published an etymology of the word "Christology" that traces it back to its Enlightenment origins. Yet the word is non-existent until the Enlightenment critique of the person and doctrine of Jesus Christ necessitated a more technical nomenclature.

- *Authorial "indebtedness"* is typically footnoted:
  9
  I am indebted to David Smith for sharing his dissertation-in-progress and alerting me to Burton Mack's portrait of Mark as "gospel writer," in "Can We Hear What They Heard? An Investigation into the Orality of Mark" (Ph.D. Diss. in progress), chapter 2, 27.

Keeping footnotes in their place

For most theological writer/researchers, the writing of footnotes is secondary to the primary task of researching and writing the paper. Footnotes are intended to support your argument, not to draw attention to themselves. When footnotes are well written and carefully cited, they give a paper authority, scholarly credibility, and rhetorical force. In sum, a well written footnote is one that is clear, concise, accurate, rendered in one's own academic voice, and formatted according to the convention of the style of citation required for the paper.

When a footnote is well written, readers find themselves reading the notes as avidly as the text of the paper. In the absence of formal instruction on how to write footnotes, most of us hone this craft by reading the footnotes of published theologians for style as well as substance and developing our own style of composing and recording footnotes in the light of those models. Some theologians compose footnotes as they write, in order to provide more continuity with the text as it unfolds. Others write their footnotes in full only after the text has been completed, recording only basic documentation data until they are ready to compose the notes in full.

However footnotes are written, they are not as innocuous or irrelevant as some students think. I know of one marriage that broke up because of one partner's refusal to go out to dinner with her spouse when she was putting footnotes in final form for her dissertation. (Not surprisingly, the scrupulous researcher in question is a biblical scholar of no small repute today.) Whether or not you share this scholarly obsessive-compulsive disorder, learning to write footnotes well will serve you well in all the theological writing you do and equip you as well for future writing and research projects in other disciplines.

Some concluding guidelines for writing theological footnotes well

- Follow one style of documentation for a research project and use it consistently throughout the project.
- Record all necessary bibliographical information in your chosen documentation style upon first consulting a source.
- Provide citation information in *reference notes* and *content notes* clearly, accurately, concisely, and consistently in your chosen style of documentation.
- If material would interrupt the flow of your argument but would still amplify or support the argument, insert it in a *content note*. If the argument would be incoherent without the material, retain the material in the text of the essay.
- Write *content notes* clearly and concisely in your own style. While there is much variation in footnote writing style, authorial notes are sometimes written in a more conversational tone than that used in the text, just as "asides" to the reader in novels are typically written in more informal diction than the author's narrative.
- In short, use footnotes judiciously but not slavishly when they are needed to document, explain, or otherwise support your text. Too many footnotes convey an obsequious deference to scholarship at best and an inability to distinguish "common knowledge" in a field from material requiring citation at worst.
- Even the most perfunctory footnote provides a return path for your reader between your theological research and its original source and paves a potential path toward new knowledge that you may not traverse yourself, but may bring others to research territories that you have not dreamed of.
- Even the most pedantic footnote may strike one of your readers as a "page-turner," if they are "on the same page" of your research.
- The next time you compose a footnote, imagine yourself writing to a lost love and to a new friend who will meet each other at the intersection of

your footnote and the source it documents. At what quotation or citation will their paths converge? You may never know, but you can do your best to quote accurately, document the reference scrupulously, and write your theological footnote well.

THEOLOGICAL MEMO 6: A Checklist for Final Preparation of a Theological Research Paper: This theological memo provides a checklist for you to use in preparing a final draft of a theological research essay for final submission to your professor. Block out adequate time for this process—do not try to do it an hour before the paper is due! Read through the "Checklist" first, and prioritize the items according to your own needs. Then, print out a clean copy of your draft, and perform the indicated "checks" on the paper, item by item, making the necessary corrections as you go. When you have completed the "Checklist," insert the corrections in the "delivery" draft of the paper, and read it one more time before submitting it to your professor. Finally, customize the checklist more specifically for the next time you must "write theological research well."

A checklist for final preparation of a theological research paper

- Read for a clearly articulated introduction, research claim, and "map of paper."
- Read for a consistent and coherent organizational structure.
- Read for accurate phrasing of headings and/or subheadings.
- Read for clarity and simplicity of style.
- Read for grammar and punctuation.
- Check pagination of paper, and insert page numbers if you have not yet done so.
- Use a spell-check.
- Prepare footnotes and bibliography according to your designated style of citation.
- Double-check all references for appropriate documentation style.
- Check all direct quotations against original sources for accuracy.
- Check all citations and page numbers against original sources for accuracy.
- Prepare a title page according to course or style sheet specifications.
- Spell your professor's name correctly—he or she will appreciate it!
- Print out the paper and read it one more time for last-minute corrections.
- Make final corrections and reprint (if necessary) before handing in the paper.
- **Hand in the paper and breathe a sigh of relief!**

Concluding reflections: Writing theological research well (II)

The conclusion to a theological research essay should (1) recapitulate the research argument in a brief summary that gathers the threads of the essay together; (2) reflect briefly on the implications of the research for the theological proposal being advanced; (3) acknowledge any loose ends that remain; and (4) invite readers to choose one or more of the threads to weave into their own theological research and reflection, or one or more of the loose ends to lead them to a new theological research project. The goal is to provide closure while inviting readers into an ongoing conversation in the light of their own theological contexts and commitments.

In this conclusion, I can hope to do no less. Flowing from the rhetorics of research and investigation introduced in Chapter 5, in this chapter, we have continued to unfold the process of "writing theological research well" through its rhetorics of organization and documentation. First, we probed the organizational dynamics of writing theological research well. Next, we outlined the organizational mechanics of integrating reading, writing, and research to write theological research well, and adapted the "write three times" method for writing a theological research essay. Finally, we turned to the rhetoric of documentation, including plagiarism preventions and interventions, an overview of documentation in Turabian style, writing theological footnotes well, and a concluding checklist for preparation of a research paper.

In this book, I have divided "writing theological research well" into two chapters that provide a linear and task-oriented progression through the writing and research process. The process will unfold differently for each person engaging it, and not always in the sequence described here. Moreover, space constraints have not allowed me to include detailed protocols for specific kinds of theological research papers in church history, ethics, or related subdisciplines. I rely for those upon the instructions your professors provide when assigning research papers in their own courses. I have left the discussion of online research skills and resources to Chapter 14 (below), which I encourage you to consult in tandem with this chapter.

I invite you in closing to choose one thread woven through this discussion that lures you to write theological research differently and follow it to the next paper that you must write. If that paper is engendered from your own questions, engages an answering conversation, carves your own research niche in the unraveling of that question, and moves diligently and with patience in your own way from a preliminary research claim to a coherent theological research essay, you cannot help but write theological research well. In the meantime, we press on to apply these skills to the task of biblical research and interpretation in Chapter 7, "Writing the Biblical Essay Well: Rhetorics of Exegesis and Interpretation."

Notes

1 Quoted in Edward Rodman, "A Lost Opportunity? An Open Letter to the Leadership of the Episcopal Church from Ed Rodman, Coordinator of the Episcopal Urban Caucus," in *"To Heal the Sin-Sick Soul": A Spirituality for the Struggle Against Racism*, ed. Emmet Jarrett (Boston: The Episcopal Urban Caucus, 1996), 76.

2 I am indebted to the following sources in this discussion of organizing the writing and research process: Joan Bolker, *Writing Your Dissertation in Fifteen Minutes a Day* (New York: Henry Holt, 1998); Wayne C. Booth, Gregory G. Colomb, and Joseph W. Williams, *The Craft of Research*, 3rd ed. (Chicago: University of Chicago Press, 2008); Annie Dillard, *The Writing Life* (New York: Harper & Row, 1989); and Anne Lamott, *Bird by Bird: Some Instructions on the Writing Life* (New York: Pantheon Books, 1994).

3 See the useful examples in Booth et al., *Craft of Research*, 130–31, 175–76.

4 See Lamott, *Bird by Bird*, 18–19.

5 Dillard, *Writing Life*, 32.

6 Bolker, *Writing Your Dissertation*, 54.

7 Ibid., xiv.

8 Laurel Richardson, "Writing: A Method of Inquiry," in *Handbook of Qualitative Research*, ed. Norman K. Denzin and Yvonne S. Lincoln (Thousand Oaks/London: Sage Publications, 1994), 516.

9 See Chapter 3 above under "Reading," 43–45, for the "Read Three Times" method.

10 This discussion is indebted to WRITE International Writers' Workshop presentation by Roger Haight, Weston Jesuit School of Theology, November 4, 1997.

11 See Mortimer J. Adler and Charles Van Doren, "Syntopical Reading," in Adler and VanDoren, *How to Read a Book* (New York: Simon & Schuster, 1972), 309–36.

12 This assignment is adapted from Adler and Van Doren, "Syntopical Reading," 335–36.

13 See "Plagiarism Preventions and Interventions" below.

14 Many college and seminary libraries subscribe to a bibliographic management system like "Endnote" or "RefWorks." If your school is one of them, it is worth the time and energy to attend a training session to learn how to use the tool in your writing of footnotes and bibliography. See also the electronic resources for doing theological research included in Chapter 14 below, under "A Digital Writer's Toolbox."

15 See Chapter 3 above, "Prerequisites of Writing Theological Argument in an Academic Voice," 47–51. See also Booth et al., *Craft of Research*, 3rd ed., "Making a Claim and Supporting It," 105–70, for a more detailed treatment of argumentation within the research process.

16 See, e.g., Marjorie Hope Nicholson, "The Professor and the Detective," in *The Art of the Mystery Story*, ed. Howard Haycroft (New York: Simon and Schuster, 1946); and Robin W. Winks, ed., *The Historian and the Detective: Essays on Evidence* (New York: Harper & Row, 1969).

17 See "Organizing *Research* to Write a First Draft" below for further suggestions.

18 See the example below, under "the research-driven draft," of my colleague, who inserts her quotes first and then weaves her narrative through the quotes. There is an exception to every rule!

19 Elizabeth A. Johnson, *She Who Is: The Mystery of God in Feminist Theological Discourse* (New York: Crossroad, 1995).

20 See Chapter 4 above under "Writing the Theological Summary Well," 65–66.

21 Johnson, *She Who Is*, 51.

22 Ibid., 49, 284n.

23 Ibid., 53–54.

24 Ibid., 12, 17–18.

25 Ibid., quoting Roger Haight, *An Alternative Vision: An Interpretation of Liberation Theology* (New York: Paulist, 1985), 53.

26 Johnson, *She Who Is*, 6.

27 Ibid., 21, 271n.

28 See also Booth et al., *Craft of Research*, "Engaging Sources," 84–100, for additional resources.

29 Albert Schweitzer, *Out of My Life and Thought: An Autobiography*, trans. A.B. Lemke (New York: Henry Holt, 1933; reprint, Baltimore: Johns Hopkins, 1998), 46 (reprint edition cited above).

30 Dillard, *Writing Life*, 46.

31 For a sampling of digital mind-mapping tools to facilitate this process, see Chapter 14 below under the heading, "A Digital Writer/Researcher's Toolbox."

32 See Bolker, *Writing Your Dissertation*, 49–63.

33 Samuel H. Scudder, "Take This Fish and Look at It," in *Readings for Writers*, 2nd ed., ed. Jo Ray McCuen and Anthony C. Winckler (New York: Harcourt Brace Jovanovich, 1997), 106.

34 "Whether written, oral, or visual/oral (electronic), each rhetorical act culminates in delivery," feminist rhetoricians Lisa Ede, Cheryl Glenn and Andrea Lunsford remind us ("Border Crossings: Intersections of Rhetoric and Feminism," *Rhetorica* 13 [1995]: 429).

35 Nancy Sommers, "Between the Drafts," in *Landmark Essays on Writing Process*, ed. Sondra Perl (Davis, CA: Hermagoras Press, 1994), 222.

36 See Chapter 10 below, "Rewriting Theology Well (I): Rhetorics of Style and Voice," for elaboration.

37 See Chapter 4 above, "Writing the Theological Essay Well," under "Concluding Reflections."

38 See Chapter 13, below, "Writing in a New Language: Rhetorics for International Student Writers and their Tutors," under the heading, "Writing with Tutors and Peer Writing Partners to Empower the Writing Process."

39 Mathew 12:31–32; Mark 3:28–30; Luke 12:10.

40 See OWL (Purdue University Online Writing Lab), "Avoiding Plagiarism," accessed September 23, 2014, https://owl.english.purdue.edu/owl/resource/589/01/ for a more detailed discussion of plagiarism and preventive strategies for academic writers. See also Stephen Weidenborner and Dominick Caruso, "Avoiding Plagiarism," in *Writing Research Papers: A Guide to the Process* (Boston: Bedford/St. Martin's, 2001), 145–49.

41 Mikhail M. Bakhtin, *The Dialogic Imagination*, ed. Michael Holquist, trans. Caryl Emerson and M. Holquist (Austin: University of Texas Press, 1981), 294.

42 See the helpful comparison of "multivocality" and intersubjectivity in the context of writing from sources in Thomas J. Farrell, "Writing, the Writer, and Lonergan:

Authenticity and Intersubjectivity," in *Communication and Lonergan: Common Ground for Forging the New Age* (Kansas City, MO: Sheed & Ward, 1993), 25–26.

43 For an excellent discussion of plagiarism and its relationship to the concept of intellectual property, see Ronald B. Standler, *Plagiarism in Colleges in the USA*, 2012 (accessed September 23, 2014) http://www.rbs2.com/plag.htm. Sandler includes a helpful list of links to other websites dealing with plagiarism. See also the International Center for Academic Integrity, which provides resources "to combat cheating, plagiarism, and academic dishonesty in higher education" and to cultivate "cultures of integrity" in academic communities around the world, accessed September 23, 2014, www.academicintegrity.org.

44 Elizabeth A. Johnson, *Friends of God and Prophets: A Feminist Theological Reading of the Communion of Saints* (New York: Continuum, 1998), 35.

45 See Helen Fox, *Listening to the World: Cultural Issues in Academic Writing* (Urbana, IL: NCTE Press, 1994), for an excellent discussion of these cross-cultural differences. Cross-cultural perspectives on plagiarism are also discussed in Nancy Jean Vyhmeister, *Your Indispensable Guide to Writing Quality Research Papers for Students of Religion and Theology* (Grand Rapids, MI: Zondervan, 2001), 45.

46 See John Thiel, *Imagination and Authority: Theological Authorship in the Modern Tradition* (Minneapolis, MN: Fortress, 1991), ix. Thiel ultimately critiques the Romantic paradigm of the individual author in favor of a more social and communal understanding of the contemporary theological author, who writes both with and on behalf of wider commitments and communities. He would thus understand what Bakhtin says about the word being "half someone else's."

47 I am treating footnotes and endnotes as interchangeable entities in this discussion. The 8th edition of Turabian (See Kate L. Turabian, *A Manual for Writers of Term Papers, Theses, and Dissertations: Chicago Style for Students and Researchers*, 8th ed., rev. Wayne C. Booth, Gergory G. Colomb, Joseph M. Williams, and the University of Chicago Press Editorial Staff [Chicago: University of Chicago Press, 2013]) recommends the use of footnotes for the convenience of readers but advises writers to weigh their options according to "their field, their readers, and the nature of their project" (16.3–3.1, 155). *The Chicago Manual of Style*, on which Turabian is based, acknowledges both the reader-friendliness of footnotes and book publishers' frequent preference for endnotes (*The Chicago Manual of Style*, 16th ed. [Chicago: University of Chicago Press, 2010], 16.19–24, 599–600). Readers of this book should follow the documentation styles specified by their schools and/or professors.

48 This discussion, however, is indebted to the following sources: Sylvester P. Carter, *Writing for Your Peers: The Primary Journal Paper* (New York: Praeger, 1987), 34–36; 106–15; bell hooks, *Talking Back: Thinking Feminist/Thinking Black* (Boston: Beacon Press, 1989); Susan M. Hubbuch, *Writing Research Papers Across the Curriculum*, 3rd ed. (Fort Worth, TX: Harcourt Brace, 1992), 224–40; Turabian, *Manual for Writers*, 8th ed., 155–6.

49 Anthony Grafton, *The Footnote: A Curious History* (Cambridge: Harvard University Press, 1997), 5.

50 hooks, *Talking Back*, 81.

51 Karl Rahner, *Foundations of Christian Faith: An Introduction to Christianity*, trans. William V. Dych (New York: Crossroad, 1984), xiv.

52 John P. Meier, *The Marginal Jew: Rethinking the Historical Jesus*, vol. 1, *The Roots of the Problem and the Person* (New York: Doubleday, 1991), 12–13.

53 Hubbuch, *Writing Research Papers Across the Curriculum*, 238.

54 If I have written a twenty-five-page paper that must be cut to ten pages for a conference presentation, I can relegate less essential material to the footnotes and reinsert that material in the text when preparing the paper for publication.

55 Johnson, *She Who Is*, 5.

56 Ibid., 276n6.

57 For further reference, see the *Publication Manual of the American Psychological Association*, 6th ed. (Washington: APA, 2009); Joseph Gibaldi, *MLA Handbook for Writers of Research Papers*, 7th ed. (New York: Modern Language Association, 2009); *The Chicago Manual of Style*, 16th ed. (Chicago: University of Chicago Press, 2010); Turabian, *Manual* 8th ed.; and *The SBL Manual of Style*, 2nd ed. (Atlanta, GA: SBL Press, 2014).

58 Although the 7th and 8th editions caution researchers against including too much "substantive material" in notes (Turabian, *Manual*, 8th ed., 158.), I follow Turabian's original distinction between reference notes and content notes (Turabian, *Manual*, 6th ed., 118). All of the examples of Turabian/Chicago style cited are my own unless footnoted, in which case I give credit where credit is due.

59 The electronic citations in this section were initially prepared and updated for the 2nd edition of this book by Aura Fluet, Senior Assistant Director, Library Services, Episcopal Divinity School, Cambridge, Massachusetts.

60 For example, in the previous section on "Plagiarism Preventions and Interventions," I did not footnote the quote from Shakespeare's *Othello*, "Who steals my purse steals trash," even though this text is addressed to theological students, not English majors. I have presumed my readers to be culturally literate enough to recognize this quote, since much of Shakespeare has become proverbial in English-speaking countries. If, however, I were writing primarily for an international audience, I would document the quote out of consideration for readers for whom Shakespeare's works are not part of common cultural parlance.

61 See. e.g., n. 45, above.

62 For standard styles of in-text citation, see *Turabian*, 8th ed., 161–63.

63 See Chapter 7 below, "Writing the Biblical Essay Well (I)," for a fuller discussion.

64 Roger Haight, "The Case for Spirit Christology," *Theological Studies* 53 (1992): 257n1. I have not reproduced the full footnote here, which includes ten sources in all.

7

Writing the Biblical Essay Well—I: Rhetorics of Exegesis and Interpretation

Exegesis is a normal activity in which all of us engage every day of our lives. Whenever we hear an oral statement or read a written one and seek to understand what has been said, we are engaging in exegesis.
—JOHN H. HAYES and CARL R. HOLLADAY, *Biblical Exegesis*

Exegesis ... is investigation, conversation, and art.
—MICHAEL GORMAN, *Elements of Biblical Exegesis*

[Philip] asked, "Do you understand what you are reading?" [The Ethiopian eunuch] replied, "How can I, unless someone guides me?"[1]
—Acts 8:30–31

Starting points

Even if Hayes and Holladay (above) describe exegesis as "a normal activity in which all of us engage every day of our lives,"[2] many students faced with writing their first biblical essay would disagree. On the one hand, the genre is a highly technical one, requiring adherence to a prescribed process of textual *exegesis*, or explication, which seems to leave no room for individual creativity. On the other hand, preparing a biblical essay presupposes competency with a wide array of biblical research tools, at the same time that students are advised not to use those tools until they have come up with their own "creative" *interpretation* of the text.

The resolution of this seeming paradox is at the heart of writing the biblical essay well, and Michael Gorman's definition of exegesis as both "investigation" and "art" provides one path toward reconciling these opposites.[3] But, whether exegesis is art, investigation, or an exchange of lively conversation among first-century or twenty-first-century exegetes, to write the biblical essay well, you must first be able to write biblical exegesis well. Yet, written biblical exegesis utilizes skills that you have already used to write theological research well, while the biblical essay directs those skills to an extended project of biblical interpretation.[4] We will therefore engage the process of "Writing the Biblical Essay Well" in two parts. This chapter introduces the writing of biblical exegesis, based on the critical historical method. Chapter 8 introduces the writing of an extended biblical essay, using various hermeneutical approaches. We begin by asking three preliminary questions about writing the biblical exegesis well.

Writing the biblical exegesis well: Preliminary questions

The goal of a biblical exegesis is to guide other readers through a biblical text, as Philip guided the Ethiopian eunuch in the passage excerpted above, so that they can "understand what they are reading" (Acts 8:30). However, no one can help others understand what he or she has not first understood and interpreted for herself or himself. In the conviction that one way in which we come to understanding is through writing about what we do not initially understand, this chapter will guide you in the process of writing the exegetical essay well by addressing the following questions: (1) What is biblical exegesis? (2) Why do biblical scholars write exegesis? (3) How does biblical exegesis differ from the theological genres that we have encountered far? (4) What is a biblical exegesis/essay, and how shall we write it?

What is biblical exegesis?

The word "exegesis," from the Greek *exegeisthai*, "to interpret," derives from *ex* and *hegeisthai*, "to guide or lead." The writer of an exegesis attempts to guide the reader through a passage of Scripture toward a critical appropriation of its meaning with a particular end in view, whether the goal is to lead a Bible study, to preach a sermon, or to write a scholarly essay. The biblical exegesis is not an autonomous genre, however, even in its most discrete form as an "exegesis paper." It is rather an indispensable tool of biblical investigation that falls within the wider area of biblical *hermeneutics*, by which I mean both the theory and practice of biblical interpretation as it seeks to understand "what the text meant" for its original audience and "what the text means" for us today.[5] Thus, while the biblical exegesis was once deployed as a relatively "fixed form" to establish the "original meaning" of a text, much contemporary biblical scholarship concurs with Sandra Schneiders that "exegesis [alone] cannot establish the meaning of texts, but it is almost always a necessary ingredient in construing the (or a) meaning of ancient texts."[6]

Why do biblical scholars write exegesis?

Whenever a biblical scholar seeks to recover the meaning of a biblical text in its original context, he or she employs the tools of biblical exegesis. Embracing the hermeneutical premise that the meaning of biblical texts is not transparent, but polyvalent and even problematic, they turn to exegesis to shed light upon the author's original intention in writing the document and its initial reception by its audience.[7] However, the biblical exegete does not do antiquarian research for its own sake but in order to help contemporary readers "understand" biblical texts. As one of my own biblical professors once confessed, "I spend my whole life looking for the meaning behind the text, or the original intention of its author."[8] Understood as a means of marking the historical distance between the biblical text that we read today and the world of its original writing, the exegetical task is described in graphic detail by an eighteenth-century German New Testament scholar who challenged his students to:

> Put yourself into the position of those to whom the apostle first gave these books. Transport yourself in spirit to the time and place where they were first read. As far as possible, strive to understand the apostles' practices, customs, habits, opinions, ideas, proverbs, imagery, and vernacular and the way in which they tried to persuade others or elicit belief in their own arguments.[9]

How does biblical exegesis differ from the theological genres that we have encountered so far?

To engage in biblical exegesis is not to engage in an interpretive or imaginative free-for-all, but requires that you interpret a biblical text critically and systematically, using a particular interpretive method or combination thereof (historical-critical method, narrative or rhetorical criticism, social science criticism, feminist criticism, and so on), and a particular set of tools (concordances, commentaries, Bible dictionaries, and so on). Moreover, the methods that comprise biblical exegesis also constitute a "rhetoric," in that they describe a recurring exegetical structure that is informed by the method of exegesis that is used.[10] We will return to these methods and tools in more detail presently, but it will be helpful at the outset to further clarify what *written* biblical exegesis *is* and what it *is not*, beginning with the latter.

What written biblical exegesis is NOT

A written exegesis is not (1) a theological reflection on a biblical passage or (2) a personal commentary on the passage. It is not (3) a sermon or (4) a "verse by verse" explication of a passage for its own sake. (5) It is not, finally, a review of the literature on a given passage, or (6) a pastiche of what you have learned "about" the passage from your research with no controlling thesis or hermeneutical method[11] driving the research.

What written biblical exegesis IS

(1) Exegesis is *an interactive process of biblical interpretation* between reader and text whose purpose is to lead the interpreter to the original context of the passage and its meaning for its original hearer/readers, in order to facilitate interpretation of the Bible in the life of the church and the world today.[12] This process presupposes a genuine engagement between the interpreter and the text being interpreted and begins with his or her own questions about the text. While many research sources may be consulted to answer those questions, the biblical exegesis is essentially an exercise in textual interpretation. Some exegesis assignments will ask you to deal only with the meaning of the text in its original context, while others will also

require a "contemporary pastoral application" in conclusion. To write exegesis well, you must respect both sides of this hermeneutical equation through your own process of discovery of what your text originally "meant" and what it might "mean" today.

(2) Exegesis is *a multidisciplinary method of biblical analysis* that embraces linguistic criticism, literary criticism, cultural/historical criticism, social science criticism, theological criticism, ideological criticism, and a host of other critical frameworks as conceptual lenses through which to understand and interpret the biblical documents. As we shall see in more detail shortly, the classical method of biblical scholarship is the *historical-critical method*, which, since the Enlightenment, has undertaken historical investigation of the Bible as a corrective to biblical interpretations that were the products of their own cultural and doctrinal environments. Since this method is "still the basis of many university and seminary courses in Bible,"[13] you will not get very far in the writing of an exegesis paper without it, even if your own hermeneutical preferences lie elsewhere. Yet, each of these methods comes with its own assumptions, presuppositions, and cultural conditioning; and each stands in need of critique.[14] To write exegesis well, therefore, it is necessary to become familiar with the available methods of biblical interpretation, beginning with the historical-critical method, and to employ them judiciously but not slavishly in your own exegetical work.[15]

(3) Exegesis is *a homiletical practice of biblical interrogation* that is taught in theological schools and seminaries as an integral component of students' pastoral apprenticeship for interpreting and preaching the Bible in a variety of ministerial contexts. Toward this end, the goal of doing and writing exegesis is your own internalization of an exegetical methodology that will serve you well as a public pastor, theologian, or ministerial professional. While you will probably not be writing exegesis papers all your life, you may be writing sermons every week, if you are preparing for ordained ministry.

"For those of you who will be preaching regularly," one biblical professor advises her students, "working with the text in its context using only concordances and Bible dictionaries (and a few select commentaries in your personal library) is something you can and SHOULD do week after week for sermon preparation."[16] The assumption behind this practice is that in order to break open a biblical text for contemporary reader/hearers, one must first return to the original meaning of the text, and not leave home without it, wherever your final journey with the text takes you. By developing your own exegetical path from the lectionary text in front of you, to the text as it was heard and read in its own cultural milieu, to the text that is being heard and read by your congregation (or other audience) today, you will avoid *eisegesis*, for example, reading your own meaning into the text, or the "I like to think" syndrome, a favorite expression of a minister in my youth who was regularly guilty of that fallacy.

In addition, when the goal of preaching is at the forefront of an exegetical assignment, the exegesis typically concludes with an "application" section that invites you to reflect upon its contemporary meaning in the light of a particular situation, audience, or ministerial context. Whether or not the assignment also requires you to develop the "application" into a full sermon, to write exegesis well in this context, you must not return home without drawing the text forward into your own understanding of its relevance for "today." But, what is this exegetical methodology in which you must first gain proficiency?

(4) Finally, exegesis is a *research-driven project of biblical investigation* that follows a specified form and a systematic, if at times circuitous, progression of inquiry. An exegesis paper is a biblical research project whose purpose is to solve the interpretive puzzle posed by the text that it investigates.[17] Yet, while exegesis, like any research project, also begins with research questions, it does not move as quickly toward the articulation of a "thesis statement" as a typical research essay does. Rather, exegetical research is a highly inductive process, moving from the particular features of a text, to its historical background and context, to an interpretation of that text for a particular audience. Just as one must begin with individual pieces in order to put a puzzle together, in an exegesis paper, the researcher must begin with particular textual problems and procedures of investigation in order to arrive at an interpretive synthesis that makes sense of the whole text. However, contemporary biblical interpretation employs a diversity of exegetical methodologies, driven by the kinds of questions being asked about a given text. In general, these methodologies can be classified under two types: *critical-historical* (the term used here and in Chapter 8 to describe biblical exegesis/essays employing the "historical-critical" method for writing the biblical essay well) and *critical-hermeneutical* (the term used here and in Chapter 8 to describe biblical essays employing various contemporary hermeneutical approaches for writing the biblical essay well).[18]

Critical-historical methods of exegesis place the recovery of the original "meaning" of the text as a priority, place the "historical-critical" method at the center of the exegetical process, and delineate a path that moves from a detailed literary analysis of the text to historical investigation of both text and context through a traditional progression of critical lenses (source criticism, form criticism, redaction criticism, tradition criticism, historical criticism, and so on, in order to get there). As Joanna Dewey describes,

> [It is] the method of interpreting a passage by trying to place oneself in the place of the composer and the original hearer/readers of the passage. It is aimed at discovering or recovering (insofar as possible) the precise meaning(s) of a given text in its first century context: What is the author... saying? What means does s/he use to say it? What did the passage convey to its original hearers?[19]

In its most relentless forms, this method has been critiqued as "exegesis as information."[20] Nonetheless, it continues to be used by exegetes not only to probe the biblical past, but to illuminate the present, as Daniel Harrington seeks to do when he asks, "What can we learn from the church in the New Testament?" and finds resources in the letters of Paul for dealing with pastoral problems in the Roman Catholic Church.[21]

Critical-hermeneutical methods of exegesis, on the other hand, while not leaving the original context of the documents behind, are also focused upon drawing the text forward for contemporary audiences.[22] Toward that end, the critical-hermeneutical exegete may bring many other methods of biblical interpretation into play as well (literary criticism, rhetorical criticism, social science criticism, feminist criticism, postmodern criticism, and so on), depending upon the purpose of the exegesis and the audience that is being addressed. As a critical-hermeneutical exegete who applies Paul Ricoeur's categories of the world behind the text (the text as historical "window"), the world of the text (the text as it exists in itself and "mirrors" the reader's experience of engaging it), and the world in front of the text (the world that the text projects and invites the reader to enter) to the exegetical enterprise,[23] Sandra Schneiders speaks for many "critical-hermeneutical" exegetes when she writes that her approach "rejects none of the advances of modern critical biblical sscholarship," but "on the contrary,... affirms the absolute necessity of solid, multidisciplinary, ideologically sophisticated exegesis as the basis for interpretation."[24] Thus, while *historical-critical* methods remain strategic to *critical-hermeneutical* exegesis, they are deployed as *one* method among many, or *one* stage in the exegetical process, rather than as *the* exclusive way of proceeding.

What method of exegesis, then, should you use for a particular exegetical assignment? While the questions you have about the text will predispose you to particular exegetical methods, your professor's instructions for the paper will provide crucial information at this point. If, for example, the goal of the assignment is historical reconstruction of the text in its original setting and its appropriation by its first-century audience, followed by a separate "application" section, your professor will probably provide you with a procedural outline that follows the critical-historical method.[25] If, on the other hand, your professor invites you to choose your own method of interpretation from a catalog of contemporary critical methods,[26] your completed essay will probably reflect the "critical-hermeneutical" model of exegesis. Very often, however, an assignment will incorporate both of these approaches, and it will be up to you to put the pieces together in a way that produces an integrated exegetical essay. Ultimately, as New Testament professor Christopher Matthews advises his students, "The particular relevance of the various methods and procedures of exegesis to any given text must be determined on a case by case basis by the interpreter."[27]

There are many excellent resources available to facilitate the task of biblical exegesis, and the particulars of the exegetical research process, many of which I have cited in the notes for this chapter. What is lacking are comparable resources for *writing* the exegesis or developing a biblical exegesis assignment into a more comprehensive biblical essay.[28] In response to that need, this chapter provides a "critical-historical" *writing path* through the exegetical research process that can be adapted to the particular requirements of the biblical exegesis paper that you are writing, and Chapter 8 provides a "critical-hermeneutical" *writing path* for the writing of the extended biblical essay, with specific writing tasks highlighted in ***boldface.***

What kinds of biblical papers are assigned in biblical studies courses, and how shall we write them?

There are as many variations on biblical exegesis essays as there are professors assigning them, but they typically fall into one of the following categories: (1) the *biblical exegesis paper*, in which the writer presents a straightforward exegesis of a particular biblical text in brief (5–7 pages) or elaborated (10–12 pages) form; (2) the *biblical exegesis essay*, which builds upon that exegetical work to develop a longer (15–20 pages) essay that applies or interprets the biblical research within a wider field of inquiry. Because most biblical professors will assign their students one or more *exegesis papers* as stepping-stones to writing the more extensive *biblical exegesis essay*, we will turn first to the writing of a straightforward biblical exegesis paper.

Writing biblical exegesis well: Preliminary strategies

The writing of an exegesis, like Julius Caesar's Gaul, is typically divided into three parts: (1) preparing to do the exegesis, (2) doing the exegetical research, and (3) writing the exegesis. We follow this natural progression here, since it provides a logical point of departure for the task. However, rather than saving the "real writing" until the final stages of the project, the method introduced here will encourage you to employ "writing" not merely in the "end zone," but as an ongoing means of inquiry that will form the backbone of the exegetical process from the beginning of your work to its conclusion.

Just as previous chapters have provided a series of Theological Memos appropriate to the theological genre covered in that chapter, in this chapter, you will find a series of twelve Exegetical Memos that are designed to provide a sequential, but not inflexible, process for writing the biblical exegesis well. These exegetical memos follow the *historical-critical path*, and their goal is to help you to interpret your biblical text as it would be heard, read, and understood in its original context. You should use these memos in conjunction with your professor's guidelines, however, not as a substitute for them. Because the memos are meant to be adapted to the requirements of the particular paper you are writing, you may find yourself responding to some of them and not to others, and in a different order than the one presented here. However, if you persevere in the "writing" of each memo, you should have a written "research draft" of your biblical exegesis completed at the conclusion of the process. In the pages below, a synopsis of each Exegetical Memo is followed by a more detailed exposition of the critical operations required in each of them.

Writing the critical-historical exegesis well in twelve exegetical memos

EXEGETICAL MEMO 1: Previewing the Assignment, Selecting a Text for Exegesis
Read the assignment carefully and rewrite it in your own words; select a biblical passage for exegesis; prepare a timeline for preparation and completion of the paper.

EXEGETICAL MEMO 2: Establishing the Text/Translation, Writing "Impressions" and "Questions"
(1) What Greek text underlies the translation? What decisions did the translators have to make in preparing the translation? What philosophy of translation underlies the text? (2) Write out your passage word for word, and read it attentively several times. Write three "impressions" and three "questions" about your text to begin your exegetical investigation.

EXEGETICAL MEMO 3: "Take This Text and Look at It"
What are the literary features of the text? Write a one-page literary analysis of your passage, concluding with a summary or paraphrase of the text in your own words.

EXEGETICAL MEMO 4: Integrative Literary-Exegetical Memo
Write a one-page memo that summarizes your literary-exegetical data and shows how they relate to your preliminary "impressions" and "questions" concerning your passage.

EXEGETICAL MEMO 5: Form/Tradition Criticism
What is the literary form, or genre, of the text? What was its original "setting in life" (*Sitz im Leben*)? Does its present form reflect earlier stages behind the text? In response to these questions, write a one-page summary of your text's form-critical and tradition history.

EXEGETICAL MEMO 6: Source Criticism
What biblical (or other) sources did my author use in this passage? Are there any tensions or disparities in the passage arising from the different sources used? Write a source analysis of your text in response to these questions.

EXEGETICAL MEMO 7: Historical Investigations
Identify your textual questions requiring historical investigation. Write them down, along with three or more research sources that you will consult in order to answer these questions. Finally, block out the time you will need to research and write a one-page memo in response to them.

EXEGETICAL MEMO 8: Contextual and Sociocultural Investigations
Make an inventory of the sociocultural questions and relevant sources you need to pursue in relation to your text. Summarize the results of your research into each of the questions you have asked, and synthesize these results in a concluding paragraph.

EXEGETICAL MEMO 9: Redaction Criticism
What theological elements in the text can be traced back to their "redactor," or "editor," and what editorial changes have been made? Do a one-page redactional study of Luke 4:1–13 (the temptation narrative) or of the text chosen for your own exegesis paper.

EXEGETICAL MEMO 10: Theological Words and Themes Revisited
Please identify one key word from your passage that reflects your author's theological outlook or agenda, and write a summary paragraph that assesses the theological significance of the word for your author and the text.

EXEGETICAL MEMO 11: Reconstructing What the Original Audience Heard/ Read
On the basis of your literary, historical, sociocultural and theological investigations, describe the original audience of your passage. If you can, place yourself among them, and ask one of the persons in the audience what the passage means. Write a "redaction" of your informant's response; conclude with a thesis statement and summary of the text's meaning for its original audience.

EXEGETICAL MEMO 12: Drafting a Preliminary Synthesis and/or Thesis Statement
(1) Reread each of the previous memos and highlight relevant material. (2) Look for common or recurring ideas, themes, or insights in that material. (3) Select the three most compelling of these to direct your writing. (4) Revisit the three themes to find the dominant interpretive thread. (5) When you have found a potential thesis arising from your synthesis, you will know; now write it.

Take this text and look at it

Exegetical memos 1–4, which focus on pre-exegetical preparation and literary analysis of the text, should be written without recourse to any outside sources beyond a concordance and Gospel Parallels (for Gospel texts).

***Exegetical Memo 1:** Previewing the Assignment, Selecting a Text for Exegesis*
You have been assigned a biblical exegesis paper on a biblical text of your choice that is due "x" days from today. The goal of this assignment is to discover the meaning of the passage that the author intended and the original audience heard and/or read.[29] Before you make your final choice of a Scripture text, however, pay careful attention to instructions like these given by Pheme Perkins to her students, and if you have any questions, clarify them with your professor:

> Select a passage ca. 6 to 10 verses. Make sure that you have chosen a section that is a *distinct unit* (i.e. a whole parable, but not its added sayings: Lk 16: 1–8a [=Unjust Steward]; what follows in vv.8b-13 are additional sayings added by Luke to interpret, apply the parable)....If you pick a text from the Lectionary... double check the divisions because they really chop things up.[30]

Equipped, then, with the specified text/translation of the Bible (e.g., Oxford Annotated Bible/NRSV) and a copy of the assignment, you are ready to (1) read the assignment carefully to determine what is required, and rewrite the assignment in your own words; (2) choose a biblical text to work with, based upon the guidelines of the assignment, and write a brief memo to yourself explaining what attracts you to this text; (3) prepare an initial timeline for preparation of the paper, working back from the due date, and commit it to writing in whatever way is most helpful to you.

Exegetical Memo 2: Establishing the Text/Translation, Writing "Impressions" and "Questions." This memo is divided into two parts: The first part requires you to translate the passage from the Hebrew/Greek and/or identify the English translation that you are using, and the second part directs you to begin your study of the passage by "writing it out, word for word."

(1) ***If you can translate your text from the original Greek/Hebrew, please prepare a written translation.*** (For beginning students who are not conversant in the biblical languages, it is sufficient to use an established version or translation, such as the NRSV; NAB; or other.)[31] *If you are working from a standard biblical translation, please indicate which one you are using and respond briefly in writing to the following questions: What Greek text underlies the translation? What decisions did the translators have to make in preparing the translation? In other words, what philosophy of translation is operative? For example, are the translators committed to preserving the original meaning of the text (as in the New Revised Standard Version) or to rendering a more contemporary, idiomatic translation (as in the Good News Bible)? Finally, if you are fluent in another language, you are encouraged to read your text in that language as well and note any variations in its translation.*

(2) ***Write out your passage word for word,*** not according to "verse" breaks, but according to the natural breaks in the text, as you experience them in your reading. Using your own "written" version, read the text aloud to yourself and silently several times, until you have begun to internalize the language, sound, and rhythm of the passage.

Stay as long as you can with the "text" as "text," without trying to decipher or interpret it. Then, when you are ready, but before you proceed to what the text "says" or "means," ***write three "impressions" (these can include previous readings that have influenced your present reading or immediate, "off the cuff" impressions) and three questions about your text (these should be your own questions about the text, however seemingly "stupid" or significant, that could potentially direct your own investigation of this passage. To the extent that your questions address the original context of the document, so much the better; but sooner or later one of them will necessarily lead you there, so do not be afraid to cast a wide net at this stage of the process).***

Exegetical Memo 3: "Take This Text and Look at It." With your impressions and questions close by, return to your own scrutiny of the text. Just as paleontologist Louis Agassiz's students were enjoined to "take this fish skeleton and look at it" in order to learn how to analyze and classify fossils, your task is to "take this text and look at it" with your own eyes to discern its literary structure and distinctive features.

What are the literary features of the text? Is it a historical narrative, parable, poetry, dialogue, and epistle? What structures provide clues to the beginning and the end of the passage? If you had to teach this passage in a Bible study, how would you outline and divide it into sections? How many parts are there? How do they relate to the whole piece? Is there progress in the flow of the narrative? Can you identify a climax? Are there any key words, recurring themes, and organizing metaphors? What does the passage show, prove, illustrate, and argue? When you read this text, what other biblical texts come to mind? If it contains references from other Old Testament or New Testament passages (the notes in a Study Bible, such as the Oxford Annotated Bible, will provide helpful cross-references), what are they? How does this wider textual frame of reference enrich your comprehension of your passage? ***Prompted by these questions and your own observations, please write a one-page literary analysis of your passage, concluding with a summary or paraphrase of the text in your own words.***

Exegetical Memo 4: *Integrative Literary-Exegetical Memo.* ***Write a one-page memo that summarizes your literary-exegetical data and shows how they relate to your preliminary "impressions" and "questions" concerning your passage.*** What have you learned from this literary investigation? What do you still need to learn to answer your questions? Historical background? The original setting (*Sitz im Leben*) of the passage? Etymology of a recurring Greek or Hebrew word? The role and function of (prophets, scribes, Pharisees, widows, children) in the original culture of the document? *What you still need to know will guide the rest of your inquiry, so it is important to formulate it carefully at this point in the process.*

Historical investigations

Exegetical Memos 5–8 will require biblical, historical, and "cultural world" research for their completion. See the notes for citation of primary sources, which should be supplemented by your own research.

Exegetical Memo 5: *Form/Tradition Criticism.* Having scrutinized your passage as a literary text to the best of your ability, it is time to cast a wider hermeneutical and historical net. Because form criticism "is both a literary and a historical operation,"[32] it provides a natural bridge from your initial analysis of the text as a literary structure in its own right to the historical aspects of exegetical research. Form criticism and tradition criticism, which Daniel Harrington conjoins in the "process of (1) discovering the original units of the tradition and (2) establishing the history of these units,"[33] can help you to answer such questions as, "What is the literary form, or genre, of my text? What was its original 'setting in life' (*Sitz im Leben*), or what purpose did it serve within its original community of listeners/readers? Is the form in which I am reading my text the original form of its transmission, or does it reflect earlier traditional units, or 'stages behind the text'?"[34]

While a skilled exegete can decipher much of a text's tradition history by analyzing the textual "units" within a passage, and their thematic continuity or discontinuity,[35] most exegetical novices rely on biblical commentaries to answer these questions, and to determine the form, or "genre" of their passage.[36] A commentary on your text will typically classify its form in terms of standard biblical genres.[37] ***Returning to your own passage in the light of these questions and those that follow, write a one-page summary of its form-critical and tradition history. What literary forms, or genres, are present? What social situation gave rise to this genre? (Many psalms, for example, were composed for liturgical worship; the gospels were not written as objective "biographies" of Jesus of Nazareth, but arose out of particular Christian communities reflecting upon the meaning of Jesus and his message for their own concrete situations.) What clues does your text provide concerning its original "setting in life"?***

Exegetical Memo 6: Source Criticism. **Even if you have determined the "form" and/or traditional units of your passage, an exegetical study of your text is not complete without an analysis of its sources.** To expedite this process, source criticism probes behind the text in its final written form to ascertain the original sources of the document. While form criticism asks the question, What is the text's original genre? and tradition criticism tracks the stages of oral and written tradition inherent in the text, source criticism asks, What sources did the author use in composing this text? For example, when the author of Luke's gospel portrays the Ethiopian eunuch reading from the book of Isaiah in his chariot, he is clearly using the Greek Septuagint as a source. Yet, scholars continue to sort out the sources referred to in the introduction to Luke's gospel (Luke 1:1),[38] just as students of the Synoptic Gospels pose source-critical questions in exegetical studies of passages with synoptic parallels.

What is the original source of the material (Mark? Q? the early Christian "tradition")? What is the relationship of my text to its sources? What is the relationship of my text's author to these sources? These questions are not only fundamental to a source-critical inquiry, but they also lead directly to redaction criticism, to be considered presently. But before we do, ***write a source analysis of your text that answers the following questions: What sources did my author use in this passage? Are there any tensions or disparities in the passage arising from the different sources used? How does your identification of a source-text for the text you are working with influence your own interpretation of this text?***

Exegetical Memo 7: Historical Investigations. Now that you have done a literary, form-critical, and source-critical investigation of your text, you are ready to address the historical questions that could not be answered without recourse to further research. Historical criticism can illuminate the literary background of your text (When was it written? By what author(s)? For what purpose?) and the subject matter of the text itself (What did it mean to be a "prophet" in the times of Elijah and Elisha recounted in I and II Kings [ninth century B.C.E]? Who were the tax collectors in the first-century C.E.? What clues do secular, non-biblical authors writing in the first century provide us about the historical Jesus of Nazareth?). Moreover, historical inquiry into your passage is the first step toward reconstructing the original context of your document and its author in order to "hear" your passage from the perspective of its original hearers and readers, which is the goal of the contextual and sociocultural investigations that follow in Exegetical Memo 8. First, however, you need to address the questions that have arisen in your study of the text thus far:

> ***Identify your own questions requiring historical investigation, and write them on a fresh notebook page or computer file, along with three or more sources that you will consult in order to answer these questions. Then, block out the time you will need to research these questions and to write a one-page memo in response to them.*** It is now time to select a standard commentary (or commentaries) on the biblical book in which your passage appears, using your professor's course bibliography as a guide.[39]

Exegetical Memo 8: Contextual and Sociocultural Investigations. Historical research on a biblical passage frequently leads to, or overlaps with, questions arising directly from the cultural context of the documents.[40] For example, if you were writing on Mark 2:23–28, in which Jesus' disciples pick grain on the Sabbath and provoke the censure of the Pharisees, you would need to know who the Pharisees were, and you would need information on the first-century C.E. cultural environment in which they exercised religious power. You would also need some historical background concerning Sabbath laws in first-century Judaism. Since a heated verbal exchange is going on between the Pharisees and Jesus that bears some similarities to other such exchanges in the Gospels, you might also ask what cultural situation (*Sitz im Leben*) inspired this and similar "controversy dialogues." Finally, since Jesus counters the Pharisees' censure of his disciples with the statement "Have you not read what David did...?" (Mark 2:25) and this "formula" phrase is repeated in parallel accounts of this story (Matt 12:3,5; Luke 6:3) it might also occur to you to ask what the word "reading" (*anaginosko*) meant in that first century context.

Returning to your own passage and the historical questions you have previously noted, make an inventory of the sociocultural questions you need to pursue, and the sources you will use in that process. If some questions overlap and/or subsume each other, revise your list accordingly. (If you can keep this process to no more than three "final questions," your work will be much more manageable.) Using the strategies for "researchful reading" and "taking notes in your own way" that were introduced in the previous chapter,[41] your next task is to answer the questions you have and/or shed light on them, not to answer every imaginable question about the text. At this point, you will need discipline to remain on the track of your own questions, rather than getting sidetracked by new investigations that are tangential to the original ones.

This research process may take an afternoon in the library or a week or two, depending upon your own schedule and preferred way of working.[42] Finally, when you are ready, summarize the results of your research into each of the questions you have asked, and synthesize these results into a concluding paragraph that locates your current position in regard to your passage, just as a global positioning instrument in your car tells you where you are en route to your destination. (Remember that the goal of this process is a coherent interpretation of the passage in its original context that will be reflected in an introductory "thesis statement," even if you are not there yet.)

Theological formulations

Exegetical Memos 9 and 10 invite you to apply your historical investigations of the text to an examination of your author's theological outlook, as it is reflected in redaction criticism and word/theme studies.

Exegetical Memo 9: *Redaction Criticism.* To "redact" is first of all "to put into writing," and secondarily, to edit what has been written.[43] When applied to redaction criticism, both senses of the word envisage the biblical writers as genuine authors, who wrote, selected, shaped, and edited their materials for particular audiences and for specific purposes.[44] That is why I have waited to introduce redaction criticism into the exegetical writing process until now. Although redaction criticism flows naturally from form criticism and source criticism and often follows them in a procedural outline of exegetical tasks, you must know something about the world of the author and their audience in order to understand their process of redaction, or more simply, why, how, and for whom they wrote what they wrote. Although redactional study should not be severed from its exegetical roots in source criticism and form criticism, it will yield more fruit for your own study after you have done some historical investigation of your text.

Before we proceed, however, it is worth delineating the connections between these operations more clearly. While source criticism is a text-directed tool that is deployed to discover the original sources of a biblical document, and form criticism is a genre-directed tool that is used to identify the original "setting-in-life" of those sources, redaction criticism is an author-directed tool that is concerned with how a particular biblical author has used those sources in his own writing, redacting, or editing of that document. First, however, there has to be some consensus on what the sources of a document are. That is why biblical scholars suggest that "source criticism is the necessary first step"[45] in redactional analysis of a document. There is, for example, major scholarly consensus that the authors of the synoptic gospels used common sources ("Q" and "Mark") and "special" authorial sources (e.g., Matthew's and Luke's respective nativity materials) in their gospel narratives.[46] The questions redaction criticism poses are, to what end were these sources strategically used, adapted, omitted, or edited by the author, and what do the author's redactions reveal about the theological agenda of the document? Not all biblical materials lend themselves to redactional analysis. However, it is applied fruitfully to texts bearing evidence of editorial stages of composition, and to the New Testament gospels in particular, as the exegetical memo below illustrates:

Imagine for a moment that you must write an exegesis of Luke 4:1–13 (the temptation of Jesus by Satan in the wilderness). After you have completed your literary-exegetical study of Luke's temptation narrative and are thoroughly familiar with it, compare and contrast Luke's account with the temptation narratives in Mark (1:12–13) and Matthew (4:1–11), using a gospel synopsis. Assuming that Mark's is the earliest version and that Matthew and Luke's version share the same source ("Q"), but also use their own (M and L) sources, please write a redactional analysis of Luke's version by answering the following questions: (1) What other sources (beside "Q") have been used in this narrative? (2) How does Luke's redaction of "Q" differ from Matthew's? (3) What additions, omissions and changes in vocabulary has Luke made? (4) How does the order of the narrative differ and what is the significance of Luke's order? (5) Does this author treat this topic elsewhere in his works? (6) Are there any parallels to this passage in the rest of the author's works? (7) Given the hypothesis that each gospel was written for a particular Christian community, or "early church," how might Luke's redactional changes reflect the theological interests and agenda of the Lukan community? (If you prefer to work with another gospel passage for a specific assignment in your writing of this memo, do not hesitate to do so.)

Exegetical Memo 10: *Theological Words and Themes Revisited.* A redactional study of a biblical passage often surfaces key words, themes, and ideas that the writer uses with some consistency to communicate a particular theological outlook. For example, you might have been struck by the use of "Spirit" language in each of the temptation narratives (Matt 4:1; Mark 1:12; Luke 4:1–2), while noting that Luke's description of Jesus as "full of the Holy Spirit" as he was "led by the Spirit" into the wilderness is distinctive by virtue of its emphasis. You might then ask, Where else in Luke do I find this "Spirit" language? While you will not have to go far to find Jesus returning to Galilee "in the power of the Spirit" (Luke 4:14), by consulting a concordance (an "analytical" concordance is most useful, since it will provide you with the original Greek terms that are translated differently in different biblical translations) and/or simply following the trail of "Spirit" language through your own rereading of the narrative, you will soon see why many have identified a "Spirit Christology" in Luke's gospel.[47] In this way, key words in an individual passage provide clues to your author's theological purpose, and enable you to place the passage within a wider interpretive framework.

Please identify one key word from your passage that reflects your author's theological outlook or agenda. Using an "analytical" concordance, and, if you are ambitious, Kittel's Theological Dictionary of the New Testament or Bromiley's one-volume abridgement of Kittel,[48] note the Greek word; define it briefly from the sources you have consulted; and make a list of its occurrences in the document from which your passage comes. Finally, write a summary paragraph that assesses the theological significance of the word for your author, and its particular significance for your biblical passage. What do you know now that you did not know before engaging in this word study? How has it affected your interpretation of the passage?

Arriving at a critical-historical interpretation

In Exegetical Memo 11, the goal is to interpret what the text meant in its original context. Your response should embrace both the meaning that the author intended and the interpretation of the audience for whom it was intended: in other words, what the audience would have heard, read, or understood when confronted by this text.

Exegetical Memo 11: *Reconstructing What the Original Audience Heard/Read.* You have now processed a great deal of information about the literary, historical, and theological dimensions of your text, and you have probed your author's context and purpose for writing the document. But, what do you know now about the original audience for whom your text was first written? Can you see them in your mind's eye? Can you hear the passage proclaimed as they would have heard it? Can you now interpret the passage as they would have understood it in their own context?

If your imagination needs to be primed for this exercise in sociohistorical reconstruction, you might pause for a moment to see how different biblical authors engaged in this very process. In Nehemiah 8, for example, the author provides a vibrant picture of an audience of returned exiles listening to the reading of the Law:

> When the seventh month came—the people of Israel being settled in their towns—all the people gathered together into the square before the Water Gate ... [where] the priest Ezra brought the law before the assembly ... [and] read from it facing the square before the Water Gate from early morning until midday, in the presence of the men and the women and those who could understand; and ... all the people wept when the heard the words of the law. [Neh 8:1–3a, 9b].

The full scenario is recorded in still more detail than I have included here, down to the raised wooden platform that Ezra stood upon and the Levites' rendering of the "sense" of the Hebrew inscribed on the scroll that Ezra was reading into the familiar Aramaic that the people "could understand." While it is not certain whether this passage forms part of Ezra's "Memoirs" or is a historical reconstruction of the event that the "Chronicler/editor" provided on the basis of his sources, its vivid portrait of the "original" audience is probably the product of both of these[49] and may well have inspired Luke's reconstruction of Jesus' reading from the scroll of Isaiah to a less hospitable audience in the synagogue at Nazareth (Luke 4:16–30).[50] After revisiting both of these biblical reconstructions of "original" audiences, how might you now proceed to reconstruct the original audience of your biblical text? This is the point at which disciplined historical imagination and culturally informed interpretation come into play, and some of the most significant biblical scholarship hinges on the exegete's ability to "hear voices in the distance coming closer."[51]

Hearing the Hebrew Scriptures loud and clear in Matthew's "formula quotations," for example, Krister Stendahl discerned a Matthean "school for teachers and church leaders" behind the composition of that gospel.[52] When he put his ear to the New Testament parable of the talents/pounds (Matt 25:14–30; Luke 19:12–27), Richard Rohrbaugh discovered a first-century agrarian peasant audience who heard the parable as "a warning not to those lacking adventurousness or industry, as frequently assumed in the West, but to those who mistreat the poor."[53] Hearing the footsteps of the women and children included in Matthew's two feeding narratives (Matt 14:21; 15:38) against their silence in the parallel narratives in Mark and Luke, Kathleen Corley recovered a more egalitarian Matthean audience in which women "are allowed a place at the table."[54] Finally, Antoinette Clark Wire employs the tools of classical and contemporary rhetoric to "reconstruct as accurate a picture as possible of the women prophets in the church of first-century Corinth."[55]

What enables a biblical scholar to hear those voices are not only the tools of historical research and cultural context but also the art of inference, which we have considered briefly in Chapter 6.[56] For historical reconstruction of any kind, inference builds upon what is known and historically verified to what might logically follow from those facts. Thus, historical reconstruction of an author, an audience, or the original context of either of these requires more courage and scholarly conviction than merely assembling facts about your passage and reshuffling them into an acceptable exegetical format.[57] The road from established fact to evidence-backed inference is fraught with obstacles, the most daunting of which is that you might be proved wrong. Nevertheless, resources abound for those willing to engage this exacting but creative task, the most important of which for this exercise will be your own exegetical imagination, disciplined by historical and sociocultural research:

Before you proceed, read through all of your previous Exegetical Memos, paying particular attention to information that will help you to construct a profile of your text's original audience. On the basis of your literary, historical, sociocultural and theological investigations into your text, describe the original audience of your passage in as much detail as you can. Who are they, and where do they fit in their society? Where are they as the document is heard or read? What is their relationship to the author of the document and/or to the person reciting/reading it? What concerns are being addressed specifically to them, and how are they responding to the material? If

your imagination cooperates, place yourself among them, and ask one of the persons in the audience who seems approachable what the passage means. Finally, write your own "redaction" of what your informant interpreted to you, concluding with a redaction of the text's meaning for its original audience that you will develop into a "preliminary synthesis/thesis statement" in Exegetical Memo 12 below.

From writing exegetical memos to writing the biblical exegesis well

Exegetical Memo 12, "Drafting a Preliminary Synthesis and/or Thesis Statement," provides a bridge to the writing of a full draft of the exegesis paper and is included in the next section. On our way there, let us assume that you have completed some or all of the Exegetical Memos above and are now ready to proceed with a complete draft of your exegesis paper. The most difficult step in writing a biblical exegesis is making the transition from collecting and recording data on your passage to synthesizing the data into a coherent interpretation of the passage. While your Exegetical Memos make up a preliminary "research draft" and may have helped you to synthesize your material as you write, you still are left with separate essays that "do not an exegesis paper make." What strategies will help you make the transition from your completed exegetical memos to a biblical exegesis paper?

First, I suggest that you look at the exegetical process that you have just completed and see if you can identify a rhetorical structure already inherent in your material. If you have followed the "critical-historical" method of exegesis, you will probably discover a fourfold structure of (1) *segmentation* (dividing the text into sections for linguistic and literary analysis), (2) *criticism* (applying individual historical-critical interventions to the text and/or its sections in a purposeful sequence), (3) *synthesis* (reassembling the text into a coherent syntactical structure), and (4) *reconstruction* (applying the historical-critical interventions to a reconstruction of the text's original intention, or meaning). We will return to this structure in our discussion of the rhetorics of the biblical essay in Chapter 8. In the meantime, it may help you to discern where you are and where you need to go to complete the writing of your exegesis. On the way, I invite you to build a rhetorical framework for your completed paper by "beading an exegetical necklace" that will (1) identify the thesis-thread upon which you will (2) string your exegetical "beads", (3) "bead the necklace" of your exegesis into a "text-first" or "context-first" track, and (4) clasp your exegetical "necklace" with a secure summary/conclusion.

Building a rhetorical framework by beading an exegetical necklace

Identifying the thread

Because the final goal of an exegesis paper is a credible and well-crafted interpretation of your passage, the first step in this process is to identify the main thread or thesis of your interpretation. Like the one thread that will unstitch a hem if you pull it the right way, the main thread of your exegesis may take time to identify. If that thread has not sufficiently revealed itself in the process of reconstructing the original audience and their interpretation of your passage, reread your Exegetical Memos and research notes until you find one word, theme, motif, character, or contextual clue that is woven through your research and invites you to unravel it. It might be a word that was translated or interpreted differently in its original context than it is today;[58] it might be a theological theme that is central to your passage;[59] it might be a narrative motif;[60] it might focus upon a character or characters from your passage,[61] or upon a concept from the cultural world of the text that illuminates its interpretation in its original context.[62] Finally, it might be a question that refuses to go away, however you try to reconcile it with the answers provided by your research.[63] Whatever thread you choose, it should be supple enough to follow the curve of your questions, but strong enough to support the string of evidence connecting those questions with your interpretation of the passage.

Without a connecting thread, you will not have an exegesis, but merely an unconnected catalog of information "about" your passage to which your professor might respond (as one of my biblical professors once did to just such a paper), "I understand the individual beads, but I do not quite see the necklace. Those who like beads will follow you well enough, but are you stringing them into a necklace?"[64] To string the beads of your exegesis into a necklace, you must first identify the interpretive thread that will provide the string and articulate it clearly in an introduction or thesis paragraph. We have already seen how biblical interpreters use their thesis paragraph to "claim a research space" in Chapter 5.[65] Just as in the theological research paper, the thesis paragraph of a biblical exegesis or longer essay can wind its *thread*[66] around an assertion to be defended:

> The contention of this paper is as follows: The ancient Israelite scribes were literate members of a primarily oral society, they undertook even their literate activity—that is, the copying of texts—with an oral mindset. When they copied their texts, the ancient Israelite scribes did not slavishly write the texts word by word, but preserved the texts' meaning for the ongoing life of their communities in much the same way that performers of oral epic re-present the ... tradition to their communities. In this sense, *the ancient Israelite scribes were not mere copyists but were also performers*. This contention is defended below, drawing from the text-critical study of the Hebrew Bible and the study of oral traditions.[67]

Alternatively, it can be proposed as a question to be investigated in the course of the exegesis/essay:

> The primary purpose of the following discussion is not to examine the question of the origin and the authenticity of this logion (Matthew 11:28–30)....Rather, *my purpose herein is to ascertain if Matthew's intent is to present Christ's promise of his rest as the fulfillment of the Messianic rest typified by the OT Sabbath.* Consideration will also be given to some cultic implications of the passage, including attention to the question of observance of the Sabbath day in the Matthean community.[68]

Whether you wind your own thread around an initial assertion (the deductive path) or question (the inductive path) will depend upon your subject, your audience, and your rhetorical preference. Moreover, while both of these authors employ the passive voice in deference to traditional academic conventions, those conventions are changing. I have cited these exemplary exegetical authors to demonstrate that the passive voice is still "active" in the literature of biblical studies. Nevertheless, I encourage you to use the first person and the active voice judiciously in your own scholarly writing, while noting that whether in the form of an assertion or a question, passively or actively voiced, the authors of the selections above have clearly displayed their "thread." Following their cue, Exegetical Memo 12 invites you to develop your "thread" into a preliminary thesis paragraph for your exegesis:

Exegetical Memo 12: *Drafting a Preliminary Synthesis and/or Thesis Statement.* This final exegetical memo invites you to write a preliminary synthesis and/or thesis statement for your exegesis paper by (1) rereading each of the memos you have written so far, and highlighting the material that strikes you, moves you, or generates questions that have yet to be pursued; (2) looking for common or recurring ideas, themes, or insights in the material you have highlighted; and (3) selecting the three most compelling of these and using them to direct your writing of a preliminary synthesis of your research on your passage. ***After letting this "synthesis statement" sit overnight, return to it when you have an hour to give to this process, and (4) revisit the three themes included in the synthesis, one by one, seeking the interpretive position or argument inherent in each of them, or in the connections that you have forged between all of them. (5) When you have found a potential thesis arising from your synthesis, you will know; now write it.*** Having done that, you will be ready to continue the process of preparing a first draft of your exegesis paper.

Stringing the beads

The second step of this exegetical writing process is stringing the beads in such a way that your readers will "see the necklace." This requires choosing an organizational structure that will display the beads of your interpretation in a logical and sequential manner. While your exegetical research process may well have been circuitous and recursive, like the journey "through the world's wilderness" of "long wandered man" in Milton's *Paradise Lost*,[69] your exegesis paper must unfold in a more straightforward way. If your professor has required that the written exegesis follow a specified format, then the exegetical beads of your necklace should be displayed in that format. If, on the other hand, your professor has invited you to organize your paper "in any order that seems to you to fit the material,"[70] there are two rhetorical tracks to guide your organizational process: (1) the "text first" track and (2) the "context first" track.

Beading the necklace: "Text first" or "context first"?

The brief introduction and/or thesis paragraph paves the way for both the "text first" and the "context first" tracks, but their respective starting points differ. The "text first" track begins with a detailed examination of the biblical text, utilizing the traditional order of the "critical-historical" method, and proceeds to matters of context and background that further elucidate the text and its interpretation.[71] The "context first" track, on the other hand, begins by probing the broader context of the passage, or a specific aspect of it, and proceeds to examine the text in the light of that context.[72]

If the interpretive "thread" that you have identified arises from textual or literary questions connected with your passage, the "text first" track may prove the most straightforward route for your exegesis. If, on the other hand, your "thread" arises from contextual data that must be elucidated before you can move to an interpretation of your passage, the "context first" track may be more suitable.[73] What is important is that your readers can "see the necklace," whether its beads begin with text or context. The outlines of each exegetical "track," below, are designed to help you do this:

Outlining the "text first" track:

- *Translation or transcription of passage:* If your assignment requires your own translation of the passage, include it on a separate sheet at the beginning of the exegesis. Otherwise, include the full text of your passage on a separate sheet, and identify the translation that you are using.[74]
- *Introduction and thesis/thread:* Provide a brief introduction to the passage, its textual context, and any questions or problems surrounding your own interpretation of the passage. Then reveal your own thesis/thread that you will pursue through the rest of the exegesis.
- *Textual explication by verse or thought unit:* Present a careful analysis of the text that identifies the genre of the passage, delineates its literary and rhetorical structure, and relates it to the passages that precede and follow it. You may find it helpful to present an initial outline of the sections of your passage before proceeding with a "verse by verse" or "thought unit by thought unit" explication of the text. As you proceed, present evidence for your conclusions and make your own judgments concerning the various exegetical options suggested by scholars, giving your own rationale for which interpretation is most adequate. Conclude this section with a brief summary of your textual analysis. What do you know if you know all this? What do you still need to know to complete your interpretation of the passage?
- *Discussion of the function of the passage in its own context:* What you do not yet know will lead you naturally to deal with the original context and background of your passage. In this section of the paper, your primary tasks are (1) to introduce contextual material that is relevant to your passage, remembering that not everything you have learned will be equally relevant; and (2) to integrate textual and contextual data to arrive at an interpretation of the passage in its own context. If your assignment includes an application of the passage for contemporary preaching, include it here. If problematic aspects of the passage for contemporary audiences remain, discuss them here. Before you complete this section, make sure that there are no loose "threads" or extraneous "beads" that you have not strung or saved for another necklace.

Outlining the "context first" track:

- *Translation or transcription of passage:* If your assignment requires your own translation of the passage, include it on a separate sheet at the beginning of the exegesis. Otherwise, include the full text of your passage on a separate sheet, and identify the translation that you are using.
- *Introduction and thesis/thread:* Provide a brief introduction to the passage that frames the text briefly in terms of its context and introduces any questions or problems surrounding your own interpretation of the passage. Since the "context first" track is a less traditional scheme for biblical exegesis than beginning with textual analysis, you might wish to explain that your text cannot be properly interpreted without reference to contextual material that will precede a more thorough study of the text.[75] Finally, reveal your own thesis/thread that you will pursue in the exegesis.
- *Contextual background (cultural, religious, social, political, biblical)*: What is the contextual material that a reader must know in order to interpret your passage correctly in its own context? Introduce background from the culture, or relevant cross-cultural models from the disciplines of cultural anthropology, ancient rhetoric and the social sciences that have helped you to hear and read your passage as its original audience would have heard/read it. Do not try to cover all areas, but choose the most relevant cultural information for the passage you are working on, and use it as a critical lens through which readers can better envisage the original context and audience of your text. If you can find an ancient source to further document your interpretation, do not hesitate to use it here. Conclude this section with a brief summary of your contextual analysis. What do you know if you know all this? What do you still need to know to complete your interpretation of the passage?
- *Explication of the text in the frame of its context:* Your primary task in this section is to interpret your text in the light of the contextual information you have presented in the previous section. You will still need to do a "verse by verse" or "thought unit by thought unit" explication of the text, preceded by a clarifying outline. However, the cultural information, insight, or model that you have presented in the first half of your paper will provide an interpretive frame for your textual analysis and should be woven tightly through your discussion of the text. This section should conclude with your interpretation of the passage in its original context, informed by the cultural information presented and the contextual lens through which you have viewed the text.

Clasping the necklace

If a necklace has no clasp to secure it, its beads will roll off their string. In the same way, if your exegesis paper has no summary or conclusion, its interpretation will appear fragmentary and incomplete. Moreover, if at this point you cannot summarize what you have said, that may indicate that you have "lost your thread" somewhere along the way and need to search for any missing "beads" that have disappeared with it. Even if all your beads are in place at this point, a good strategy for drafting a conclusion is as follows:

- First, reread your paper to see what you actually have said.
- Second, summarize the main points of your interpretation briefly.
- Third, acknowledge the questions or problems (if any) that still remain.
- Fourth, reiterate what you have accomplished in your exegesis in one final, suggestive sentence that provides adequate, if not irrevocable closure.
- Finally, check your exegesis paper against the "Biblical Writer's Checklist for an Exegesis Paper"[76] and check your footnotes and bibliography against "Documenting Sources in *SBL* Style"[77] below before proceeding to the next chapter to learn how to develop an extended biblical essay from an exegesis, and how to write the biblical essay well.

A biblical writer's checklist for an exegesis paper

A Close (Literary) Reading of the Passage:

- Comments on the structure of the passage: how it is framed; how words, phrases, or images are used in moving from the beginning to end of the passage; any problematic transitions.
- Comments on the location of the passage in the gospel. How it is tied to what comes before and/or after: How that context influences the expectations of meaning attached to the passage (or sets up expectations for what follows). Any explicit verbal links to the context?
- Provides an outline of the passage that enables the reader to see how it is put together; what the main and subordinate parts of the passage are; elements in its literary or rhetorical construction.

Reading in its Ancient Context: What It "Sounded Like" in Its Literary Environment:

- Comments on the literary genre of the passage; implies recognition of the basic features of the genre in antiquity. (A stronger answer shows these features in your text or notes its peculiarities.)
- Comparison of your passage, or some part of its imagery, language, etc., to Old Testament or Jewish antecedents. What stories, verses, images are being echoed?
- Where applicable: analysis of other variants of your passage within NT or other early Christian literature. What do the variants suggest about the history of tradition of this material?

Reading in Its Ancient Context: Recognizing the Social, Cultural, Religious Background:

- Notes points in text which require information about ancient culture, behavioral expectations, political situation, social structure, or religious customs; provides information from relevant sources (commentaries, dictionaries, etc.).

- Provides an actual example: quote, archaeological artifact or other first-century remains that illustrates the ancient context; compares details with what happens in the gospel story.
- Shows by applying insights from ancient cultural background how that information changes, clarifies, or makes more complex our understanding of the biblical text.

Reading as Explanation of the Details (verse by verse):

- Identifies, based on commentaries, major points that need explanation in each verse.
- Provides accurate information from commentaries to explain the points so identified.
- Recognizes ambiguities created by language as well as those due to lack of information.
- Identifies and highlights important theological or literary themes illustrated in the passage.
- Provides links to the work from which the passage is taken that illuminate what the author means by particular phrases, images, etc.
- Identifies disagreements in the scholarly literature about the meaning of the passage as a whole or particular details within it.
- Evaluates conflicting views, argues for one position as more probable than another.

Reading for Application: Significance for Pastoral Setting, Theological Reflection:

- Provides a clear explanation of the setting, audience, or issue to which the text is to be related. What the use of the text is: to provide reflection on an issue, to correct false perceptions, to enable individual or group transformation or interaction.
- Shows how the meaning(s) that emerge from the exegetical study of the text contribute to its application in contemporary context.
- Negotiates the problems of sociocultural differences between modern believers and the worldview of the biblical author.
- Has a clearly formulated "take-home" reading from the passage for the designated audience.

Academic Formalities in the Written Paper:

- Identifies translation used (where appropriate, reference to problematic issues of translation).
- Uses resources of a theological research library to obtain information regarding a biblical passage.

- Suitability of bibliography and use of scholarly resources to exegete the text in question.
- Suitable use of footnotes to identify sources of insights, information, interpretation (see "Documenting Sources in *SBL* Style," below).

Documenting sources in *SBL* style

"*The SBL Handbook of Style* has been created to help scholars, students, editors, and proofreaders of ancient Near Eastern studies, biblical studies, early Christianity, and rabbinic studies.... The handbook [supplements] *The Chicago Manual of Style (CMS)*, except in cases where the field very consciously and authoritatively adopts a different standard."

—*The SBL Handbook of Style*, 2nd ed., 1.[78]

Book:

(N)

Billie Jean Collins et al., eds., *The SBL Handbook of Style* (Atlanta, GA: SBL Press, 2014), 1.

(B)

Collins, Billie Jean, Bob Buller, and John F. Kutsko, eds. *The SBL Handbook of Style*. Atlanta, GA: SBL Press, 2014.

Journal Article:

(N)

Nancy R. Bowen, "The Daughters of Your People: Female Prophets in Ezekiel 17:23," *JBL* 118 (1999): 417–433.

(B)

Bowen, Nancy R. "The Daughters of Your People: Female Prophets in Ezekiel 13.17-23." *Journal of Biblical Literature* 118 (1999): 417–433.

An Article in an Encyclopedia or Dictionary:

(N)

Krister Stendahl, "Biblical Theology, Contemporary," *IDB* 1:418–32.

(B)

Stendahl, Krister. "Biblical Theology, Contemporary." Pages 418–32 in vol. 1 of *The Interpreter's Dictionary of the Bible*. Edited by G. Buttrick. 4 vols. Nashville: Abingdon, 1962.

An Article in a Lexicon or Theological Dictionary:

[For the discussion of a word or family of words, give entire title and page range]:

(N)

H. Beyer, "*diakoneo, diakonia,*" *TDNT* 1:223–224.

(B)

Kittel G. and G. Friedrich, eds. *Theological Dictionary of the New Testament.* Translated by G.W. Bromley. 10 Vols. Grand Rapids: Eerdmanns, 1964–76.

Bible Commentaries:
[*As the editors of The SBL Handbook of Style acknowledge:* "Properly citing bible commentaries can be complex, especially when the commentaries are (1) multivolume, or (2) in a series. Commentaries are normally cited just as any other book, with the commentary series name being the only significant addition. Since editors of commentary series usually acquire rather than edit, the names of general editors need not be included in bibliographic or note references." (7.3.9, p. 61).]

(N)

Morna Hooker, *The Gospel according to Saint Mark* (BNTC 2: Peabody, MA: Hendrickson, 1991), 223.

(B)

Hooker, Morna. *The Gospel according to Saint Mark.* Black's New Testament Commentaries 2. Peabody, MA: Hendrickson, 1991.

A Single Volume of a Multi-Volume Commentary in a Series:
Cited as a multi-volume work:

(N)

Mitchell Dahood, *Psalms: Introduction, Translation, and Notes* (3 vols: *AR* 16–17A: Garden City: Doubleday, 965–1970), 3:127.

(B)

Dahood, Mitchell. *Psalms. Introduction, Translation, and Notes.* 3 vols. Anchor Bible 16-17A. Garden City: Doubleday, 1965–71.

Using individual volumes as the basis for citation:

(N)

Mitchell Dahood, *Psalms 1, 1-50: Introduction, Translation, and Notes* (AB 16-17A: Garden City: Doubleday, 1966), 347.

(B)

Dahood, Mitchell. *Psalms: Introduction, Translation, and Notes.* 3 vols. Anchor Bible 16-17A. Garden City: Doubleday, 1965–71.

An Internet Publication with a Print Counterpart:

(N)

L. Juliana M. Classens, "Biblical Theology as Dialogue: Continuing the Conversation on Mikhail Bakhtin and Biblical Theology," *JBL* 122, no. 1 (2003): 127–144. Cited 25 September 2014. Online: http://www.metapress.com/content/G11812W226N042J7.

(B)

Classens, L. Juliana M. "Biblical Theology as Dialogue: Continuing the Conversation on Mikhail Bakhtin and Biblical Theology." *Journal of Biblical Literature* 122, no. 1 (2003): 127–144. Cited 25 September 2014. http://www.metapress.com/content/G11812W226N042J7.

An Internet Publication Without a Print Counterpart:

(N)

Thomas Talbott, "Heaven and Hell in Christian Thought," n.p. [cited 25 September 2014]. Online: http://plato.stanford.edu/archives/spr2014/entries/heaven-hell/.

(B)

Talbott, Thomas. "Heaven and Hell in Christian Thought." No pages. Cited 25 September 2014. Online: http://plato.stanford.edu/archives/spr2014/entries/heaven-hell/.

A sampling of online resources for biblical studies

Given the current explosion of online resources available for researching and writing a biblical exegesis, this chapter would not be complete without a brief sampling of those resources. While your own theological school or university will subscribe to more biblical research websites than are listed here, the links below are available to all users and provide an introduction to the rapidly growing collection of biblical research resources online.[79]

Portals

Bible Hub http://biblehub.com/

Bible Study Tools http://www.biblestudytools.com/

Bible Odyssey http://www.bibleodyssey.com/

Apocrypha and Pseudepigrapha – Online Versions

The Apocrypha http://www.sacred-texts.com/chr/apo/

Pseudepigrapha http://wesley.nnu.edu/sermons-essays-books/noncanonical-literature/noncanonical-literature-ot-pseudepigrapha/

Bible Parallels – Online

Parallel Bible http://www.biblestudytools.com/parallel-bible/

The Five Gospel Parallels http://www.utoronto.ca/religion/synopsis/

Parallel Texts in the Hebrew Bible http://proxy.eds.edu:2097/resource/parallel_hebrew_bible.xhtml

Parallel Texts Apocrypha http://proxy.eds.edu:2097/resource/parallel_apocrypha.xhtml

Parallel Texts in the New Testament http://proxy.eds.edu:2097/resource/parallel_new_testament.xhtml

Interlinear Testaments – Online
Hebrew Bible http://www.scripture4all.org/OnlineInterlinear/Hebrew_Index.htm
New Testament http://www.scripture4all.org/OnlineInterlinear/Greek_Index.htm

Online Reference Sources
Glossary http://www.bibleodyssey.com/tools/timeline-gallery.aspx
HarperCollins Bible Dictionary http://www.bibleodyssey.com/en/tools/harper-collins-dictionary.aspx
Image Gallery http://www.bibleodyssey.com/tools/image-gallery.aspx
Map Gallery http://www.bibleodyssey.com/tools/map-gallery.aspx
Time Line Gallery http://www.bibleodyssey.com/tools/timeline-gallery.aspx

Online Language Resources
New Testament Greek Lexicon http://www.biblestudytools.com/lexicons/greek/
Old Testament Hebrew Lexicon http://www.biblestudytools.com/lexicons/hebrew/
Hebrew Alphabet http://www.stanford.edu/class/hebrew/letters/index.html
Greek Alphabet http://www.greek-language.com/Alphabet.html

Concluding reflections: Writing the biblical exegesis well

"Do you understand what you are reading?" "How can I," the Ethiopian eunuch replied to Philip, "unless someone guides me" (Acts 8:30–31). The goal of every biblical exegesis is to help biblical readers understand what they are reading. However, in order to be guided by an exegesis paper, readers must first understand what you have written about the text they are reading. This chapter has provided an introduction and guide to writing the biblical exegesis well, first answering the questions, What is biblical exegesis and why do people write it? Second, we introduced the biblical exegesis paper and contrasted it with the critical-hermeneutical essay, to be discussed in Chapter 8. Third, we provided a process for writing the biblical exegesis in twelve "historical-critical" Exegetical Memos. Finally, we proposed two rhetorical frameworks for writing the final draft of a biblical exegesis paper: the "text first" track and the "context first" track.

To write a biblical exegesis well is no small achievement. If you have done so, take some time to reread what you have written and savor it before moving on to Chapter 8. If you are still struggling with your exegesis paper, be of good cheer. The biblical exegesis is ultimately written in order to disappear like alchemist's gold into other biblical genres. It disappears regularly into good preaching, leaving no traces of its labor behind but carrying with it the strength of solid biblical interpretation. It is frequently transformed into stimulating Bible studies that are well-grounded in the original context of the biblical text under scrutiny. It has become the inspiration for art and poetry and has even been known to enter surreptitiously into one's own spiritual life by providing fresh insights into scriptures worn thin by familiarity. Last but not least, it reappears frequently in "Part I" of an extended biblical essay that moves from reconstruction of "what the text meant" to contemporary reflection on "what the text means." It is in this guise that you will meet it in Chapter 8 and proceed to build upon your own completed biblical exegesis paper to "write the biblical (critical-hermeneutical) essay well."

Notes

1 All biblical quotations are taken from *The New Oxford Annotated Bible with the Apocrypha, New Revised Standard Version*, 4th ed., ed. Michael D. Coogan et al. (New York: Oxford University Press, 2010).

2 John H. Hayes and Carl R. Holladay, *Biblical Exegesis: A Beginner's Handbook*, 3rd ed. (Louisville: Westminster/John Knox Press, 2007), 1.

3 See Michael Gorman, *Elements of Biblical Exegesis: A Basic Guide for Students and Ministers*, Revised and Expanded Edition (Grand Rapids, MI: Baker Academic, 2010), 12.

4 See the elements of the critical theological essay in Chapter 3 above.

5 See the classic distinction of Krister Stendahl, "Biblical Theology, Contemporary," in *The Interpreter's Dictionary of the Bible*, ed. G. Buttrick (Nashville, TN: Abingdon Press, 1962), 1:418–32.

6 Sandra M. Schneiders, *The Revelatory Text: Interpreting the New Testament as Sacred Scripture* (Collegeville, MN: Liturgical Press [Michael Glazier], 1999), 124.

7 For a more comprehensive introduction to biblical exegesis, see the excellent article, "Exegesis," L.E. Keck and G.M. Tucker, in *The Interpreter's Dictionary of the Bible: Supplementary Volume* (Nashville, TN: Abingdon Press, 1976), 296–303.

8 Daniel J. Harrington, "Jesus and Hermeneutics," in response to a question posed in class discussion, Weston Jesuit School of Theology, Fall 1997, recalled here by co-professor Roger Haight.

9 J.J. Wettstein, "Uber die Auslegung des Neuen Testaments," *Novum Testamentum Graecum* (Amsterdam, 1751–52), 2:875; quoted in Werner Stenger, *Introduction to New Testament Exegesis*, trans. D.W. Stott (Grand Rapids, MI: Eerdmanns, 1993), 4.

10 This will be elaborated further in our discussion of the exegetical essay in Chapter 8 below, "Writing the Biblical Essay Well (II): A Critical-Hermeneutical Rhetoric."

11 For helpful "troubleshooting" guides for the preparation of exegesis papers, see Hayes and Holladay, "Integrating Exegetical Procedures," in *Biblical Exegesis*, 178–90; Gorman, "Exegesis and the Exegete: Errors to Avoid, Discoveries to Make," in *Elements of Biblical Exegesis*, 175–79.

12 See Frederick C. Tiffany and Sharon H. Ringe, *Biblical Interpretation: A Roadmap* (Nashville, TN: Abingdon Press, 1996), who describe this interaction in terms of "a dialogue of question and answer, hypothesis and test, suggestion and correction" that constitutes "close reading" of the biblical text (68).

13 Ibid., 29.

14 For a straightforward but contemporary exposition of the historical-critical method that acknowledges its inherent theological problems, see Stenger, *NT Exegesis*, esp. 5–7. See also Daniel J. Harrington, *Interpreting the New Testament: A Practical Guide*

(Wilmington, DL: Michael Glazier, 1985), which adapts the historical-critical method "fruitfully and effectively" to a literary-based approach (ix–x).

15 I make a preliminary distinction between "critical-historical" and "critical-hermeneutical" exegetical methods at the conclusion of this section. For a more comprehensive survey of contemporary exegetical approaches and methodologies, see Hayes and Holladay, *Biblical Exegesis*, Chapters 2–10, 34–166; Schneiders, *Revelatory Text*, 114–128. For a method of biblical interpretation that is committed to the diversity of textual communities and the interpretations they produce, see Tiffany and Ringe, *Roadmap*, 205–24.

16 Professor Joanna Dewey, *Guidelines for NT Exegesis* (Cambridge, MA: Episcopal Divinity School, 1997).

17 See Nancy Jean Vyhmeister, "Biblical Exegesis as Research," in *Your Indispensable Guide to Writing Quality Research Papers: For Students of Religion and Theology*, ed. N. Jean Vyhmeister (Grand Rapids, MI: Zondervan, 2001), 117–25.

18 As I use it here, the term "critical-historical" is analogous to "historical-critical." By transposing the compounds, I seek to emphasize the correlation between "critical-historical" and "critical-hermeneutical" approaches to the biblical essay, which should be read in tandem and written interactively in order to write the biblical essay well. "Critical-historical" methods are of course hermeneutical, in that they are oriented toward recovering the original meaning of a text. However, my terminology distinguishes between models of exegesis for whom the critical-historical method is normative vs. those that construe exegesis more broadly as the interpretive process by which one comes to understand a text, using a variety of hermeneutical approaches.

19 Dewey, *Guidelines for NT Exegesis*.

20 See Sandra M. Schneiders, *Written That You May Believe: Encountering Jesus in the Fourth Gospel* (New York: Crossroad, 1999), 18–20.

21 Daniel J. Harrington, S.J., "What Can We Learn From the Church in the New Testament?" in *The Catholic Church in the 21st Century: Finding Hope for Its Future in the Wisdom of Its Past*, ed. Michael J. Himes (Liguori, MO: Liguori Publications, 2004).

22 To determine your own operative biblical hermeneutic, see the "Self-Inventory on Biblical Hermeneutics" that Norman K. Gottwald and colleagues give to seminary students beginning their study of the Bible, in Norman K. Gottwald, "Framing Biblical Interpretation at New York Theological Seminary: A Student Self-Inventory on Biblical Hermeneutics," in *Reading from this Place: Social Location and Biblical Interpretation in the United States*, ed. Fernando F. Segovia and Mary Ann Tolbert (Minneapolis, MN: Fortress Press, 1995), 256–61.

23 Ricoeur's hermeneutical approach is elucidated in Schneiders, *The Revelatory Text*, 97–179. My brief summary here draws upon discussions in pp. 113–14, 151–52, and 167–68, respectively.

24 Schneiders, *Written That You Might Believe*, 21.

25 See, e.g., Vymeister's "Seven Steps for Exegetical Research," in *Quality Research Papers*, 117–25.

26 See, e.g., Catherine Murphy, "Exegesis," accessed September 22, 2014, http:// http:// www-relg-studies.scu.edu/facstaff/Murphy/courses/spir241/exegesis.htm

27 Christopher Matthews, "Developing an Exegetical Methodology," for a course taught at Harvard Divinity School, Cambridge, MA, Spring 1989.

28 A felicitous exception is Michael Gorman, "Practical Guidelines for Writing a Research Exegesis Paper" (241–46) along with "Three Sample Exegesis Papers" (247–75) in his revised edition of *Elements of Biblical Exegesis*. For the full citation, see note 3 above.

29 This assignment is adapted from Dewey, *Guidelines for NT Exegesis*.

30 Pheme Perkins, *NT Exegesis Paper Instructions* (Chestnut Hill, MA: Boston College, Spring 2002).

31 See the helpful discussion in Tiffany and Ringe, *Roadmap*, 72–74, regarding reading the passage initially in a number of translations and analyzing the elements of "interpretation" operative in each "translation." For help in weighing the strengths and weaknesses of various English translations, see "Choosing an English Translation for Use in Exegesis," in Gorman, *Elements of Biblical Exegesis*, 44–52.

32 Harrington, *Interpreting the New Testament*, 72.

33 Ibid.

34 For a more extended discussion of "tradition criticism" and its role in the exegetical process, see Hayes and Holladay, *Biblical Exegesis*, 115–26.

35 For an excellent discussion of this method and application to a form-critical analysis of Mark 2:13–17 and its gospel parallels (Matt 9:9–13; Luke 5:27–32), see Stenger, *New Testament Exegesis*, 44–49 and 61–72.

36 For some biblical scholars, the categories of "form criticism" and "genre criticism" are treated separately, even though "form criticism" has traditionally included the "setting in life" of a biblical document, which often determines the document's genre. See Stenger, *New Testament Exegesis*, 52–58.

37 For Gospel texts, see Rudolf Bultmann, *The History of the Synoptic Tradition*, rev. ed. (New York: Harper & Row, 1968); or Martin Dibelius, *From Tradition to Gospel* (New York: Charles Scribners' Sons, 1965); for Pauline texts, be alert to such Greek literary forms as epistolography, paraenesis, diatribal style, and other rhetorical modes. For Old Testament texts, see Klaus Koch, *The Growth of the Biblical Tradition* (New York: Charles Scribner's Sons, 1969), and Gene M. Tucker, *Form Criticism of the Old Testament* (Philadelphia, PA: Fortress, 1971). Look for hymns, case law, patriarchal narrative, prophetic call narrative, lament psalms, and so on.

38 See the helpful discussion in Harrington, *Interpreting the New Testament*, 57–58.

39 *You* could begin with a one-volume commentary such as *The New Interpreters Bible One Volume Commentary*, ed. Beverly Roberts Gaventa and David Peterson (Nashville, TN: Abingdon Press, 2010) or *The New Jerome Biblical Commentary*, ed. Raymond E. Brown, Joseph Fitzmyer, and Roland E. Murphy (Englewood Cliffs, NJ: Prentice Hall, 1990). You could then proceed to a more extensive volume-by-volume commentary directed toward a scholarly, seminary audience (*The Anchor Bible; Abingdon New Testament Commentaries; Hermeneia; Sacra Pagina)*, preferably one recommended on your course bibliography. For more current literature on your passage, you can use the ATLA Database (*Religion Index*) or consult *Old Testament Abstracts* and/or *New Testament Abstracts*, available now in print and electronic versions; if an earlier article is significant for your inquiry, a literature review in a more recent article will often blaze a trail to the article by citing it.

40 See Tiffany and Ringe, *Roadmap*, Chapter 4 ("Reading Contextually"), 89–109, for a more detailed discussion of contextual reading and research strategies. See also Chapter 12 ("Selected Resources for Biblical Studies"), 236–37, for bibliographical resources on "Social Worlds of the Bible," including materials from the fields of cultural anthropology, social history, and sociology of the ancient world.

41 See Chapter 6 above, 119–20.

42 See Chapter 6, above under "What Are the Organizational Dynamics of Writing Theological Research Well?"

43 *Merriam-Webster's Collegiate Dictionary*, 10th ed., s.v. "redact."

44 The term *redaction criticism* was coined by Willi Marxen in 1956 in a study of Mark's gospel. See Harrington, *Interpreting the New Testament*, 98.

45 Harrington, *Interpreting the New Testament*, 98. For some instructive examples of how redaction criticism is applied to Gospel texts and other New Testament texts, see "Examples of Redaction Criticism," 100–06 in the same chapter.

46 For exceptions to this "four document" consensus, see Howard C. Kee, "Synoptic Studies," in *The New Testament and its Modern Interpreters*, ed. E.J. Epp and G.W. Macrae (Philadelphia, PA: Fortress, 1989), 248–51.

47 A notable example is Roger Haight, *Jesus Symbol of God* (Maryknoll, NY: Orbis, 1999), 163–68, who cites the work of biblical scholars Joseph A. Fitzmeyer, *The Gospel According to Luke: Introduction, Translation and Notes* (Garden City, NY: Doubleday, 1981, 1985); and I. Howard Marshall, *The Gospel of Luke: A Commentary on the Greek Text* (Exeter: Paternoster Press, 1978).

48 See, e.g., John R. Kohlenberger, *The NSRV Concordance Unabridged* (Grand Rapids, MI: Zondervan, 1991); James Strong, *Strong's Exhaustive Concordance* (KJV; Gordonsville, TN: Dugan Publishers, Inc., n.d.); Gerhard Kittel, ed., *Theological Dictionary of the New Testament*, trans. and ed. Geoffrey W. Bromiley, Grand Rapids: Eerdmanns, 1964–76; Gerhard Kittel and Gerhard Friedrich, eds., *Theological Dictionary of the New Testament Abridged in One Volume*, trans. and abridged by Geoffrey W. Bromiley (Grand Rapids, MI: Eerdmanns, 1985).

49 See Bernhard W. Anderson, Steven Bishop, and Judith Newman, *Understanding the Old Testament*, 5th ed. (Englewod Cliffs, NJ: Prentice-Hall, 2006), 463–66. See also Anderson's Preface to the 5th edition, esp. "Reading the Bible in the 21st Century," xv–xvii. For a scholarly update concerning authorship and social context of Nehemiah 8:1–9, see David Janzen, "The 'Mission' of Ezra and the Persian-Period Temple Community," *Journal of Biblical Literature* 119 (2000): 619–43.

50 See Lucretia B. Yaghjian, "Ancient Reading," in *The Social Sciences and New Testament Interpretation*, ed. Richard Rohrbaugh (Peabody, MA: Hendrickson, 1996), 218–21.

51 This is how Antionette Clark Wire describes her task in *The Corinthian Women Prophets: A Reconstruction through Paul's Rhetoric* (Minneapolis, MA: Fortress, 1990), 196.

52 Krister Stendahl, *The School of St. Matthew, and its Use of the Old Testament* (Philadelphia, PA: Fortress Press, 1968; repr., Ramsey, N.J., Sigler Press, 1990), 35 (page reference is to the reprint edition).

53 See Richard L, Rohrbaugh, "A Peasant Reading of the Talents/Pounds: A Text of Terror?" *Biblical Theology Bulletin* 23 (1993): 32–39.

54 See Kathleen E. Corley, *Private Women: Public Meals: Social Conflict in the Synoptic Tradition* (Peabody, MA: Hendrickson, 1993), 144–45, 178–79.

55 Wire, *Corinthian Women Prophets*, 1.

56 See Chapter 5 above under "Carving a Research Niche, Crafting a Paper Topic."

57 See, for example, Marie Noonan Sabin, *Reopening the Word: Reading Mark as Theology in the Context of Early Judaism* (New York: Oxford University Press, 2002), as an example of this process of historical reconstruction.

58 See, e.g., Luke Timothy Johnson's analysis of *pistis Christou* in "Rom 3:21–26 and the Faith of Jesus," *Catholic Biblical Quarterly* 44 (1982): 77–90.

59 See, e.g., Bruce J. Malina, "Freedom: A Theological Inquiry into the Dimensions of a Symbol," *Biblical Theology Bulletin* 8 (1978): 62–75.

60 See, e.g., Howard M. Jackson's discussion of "the shed garment motif" in "Why the Youth Shed His Cloak and Fled Naked: the Meaning and Purpose of Mark 14:51–52," *Journal of Biblical Literature* 116 (1997): 273–89.

61 See, e.g., Claudia Seltzer, "Excellent Women: Female Witnesses to the Resurrection," *Journal of Biblical Literature* 116 (1997): 259–72.

62 See, e.g., Jerome H. Neyrey, "The Idea of Purity in Mark's Gospel," *Semeia* 35 (1986): 91–126.

63 See, e.g., Elizabeth E. Green, "Making Her Case and Reading it Too: Feminist Readings of The Story of the Woman Taken in Adultery," in *Ciphers in the Sand: Interpretations of the Woman Taken in Adultery [John 7:53–8:1]*, ed. L.J. Kreitzer and D.W. Rooke (Sheffield: Sheffield Academic Press, 2000), 240–67.

64 Jerome H. Neyrey, S.J., in a letter to the author, April 30, 1989.

65 See Chapter 5, above, 109, and 365 nn45, 46.

66 I render the "*thread*" of each thesis paragraph in *italics* for emphasis.

67 Raymond F. Person, Jr., "The Ancient Israelite Scribe as Performer," *Journal of Biblical Literature* 117 (1998): 602.

68 Samuele Bacchiocchi, "Matthew 11:28–30: Jesus' Rest and the Sabbath," *Andrews University Seminary Studies* 22 (1984): 289.

69 John Milton, *Paradise Lost, XII, 312–14*, ed. Merritt Y. Hughes (New York: Odyssey Press, 1962), 299.

70 Dewey, *Guidelines for NT Exegesis*, 4. In the same handout, Dewey also provides a "standard" outline that follows the "text first" track, which I have expanded here to more fully elaborate the exegetical writing process (below, 164–66).

71 This is the more typical order of biblical articles in standard exegetical journals as *Journal of Biblical Literature* and *Catholic Biblical Quarterly*. See, e.g., Gail O'Day, "John 7:53–8:11: A Study in Misreading," *Journal of Biblical Literature* 111 (1992): 631–40.

72 This order is more prevalent, though not exclusively so, in biblical journals committed to social and contextual interpretation, such as *Biblical Theology Bulletin*. See, e.g., Dennis Duling, "Egalitarian" Ideology, Leadership and Factional Conflict within the Matthean Group," *Biblical Theology Bulletin* 27 (1997): 124–37.

73 These tracks can be used interchangeably for presenting biblical papers to different audiences. For an audience for whom the original context of the biblical documents is of primary concern, the "context first" track is the preferred track. However, the same material can be presented to an audience more attuned to traditional "critical-historical" methods, using the "text first" track. See for example, Dennis C. Duling, "Matthew and Marginality," *SBL Seminar Papers* 32 (Atlanta, GA: Scholars Press, 1999), 642–71 (text-first track), and his subsequent "Matthew as Marginal Scribe in an Advanced Agrarian Society," *Hervormde Teologiese Studies* 58, no. 2 (2002): 520–75 (context-first track).

74 Even though you may exegete the text verse by verse, it is much easier to read and evaluate an exegesis paper that includes the full text of the passage one is reading about. Unless you are advised otherwise, your professor will appreciate your attention to this important detail.

75 See, e.g., Jerome H. Neyrey, “What’s Wrong with This Picture? John 4, Cultural Stereotypes of Women, and Public and Private Space,” *Biblical Theology Bulletin* 24 (1994): 77–91.

76 The “Biblical Writer’s Checklist for an Exegesis Paper” is adapted from Professor Pheme Perkins, Boston College, Chestnut Hill, Massachusetts, and is used with her permission.

77 Protocols for documenting biblical sources are based upon *The SBL Handbook of Style*, 2nd ed. (Atlanta, GA: SBL Press, 2014).

78 While the second edition of *The SBL Handbook of Style* continues to follow *The Chicago Manual of Style* in its basic documentation format, see “Rule Changes in the Second Edition,” Introduction to the 2nd ed., 1.

79 This “Sampling of Online Resources for Biblical Studies” was prepared by Aura A. Fluet, Senior Assistant Director, Library Services, Episcopal Divinity School. See also Gorman, *Biblical Exegesis*, “Selected Internet Resources for Biblical Studies,” 277–81; Hayes and Holladay, “Using Electronic Technologies in Exegesis,” 213–30.

8

Writing the Biblical Essay Well—II: A Critical-Hermeneutical Rhetoric

To interpret is to render near what is far.
—PAUL RICOEUR, *Hermeneutics and the Human Sciences*

Then beginning with Moses and all the prophets, he interpreted to them the things about himself in all the scriptures.
—LUKE 24:27

They said to each other, "Were not our hearts burning within us while he was talking to us on the road ... [and] opening the scriptures to us?"
—LUKE 24:32

Starting points

In this chapter, we turn from writing a biblical exegesis to writing a "critical-hermeneutical" biblical essay, which builds upon exegetical research to pursue a broader interpretive project. Beginning, for example, with an exegesis of Mark 5:24–34 (the hemorrhaging woman), a student writes a biblical essay concerning the ethical implications of that story for early Christian women and for Hispanic women with HIV/AIDS today. Beginning with an exegesis of Matthew's parable of the talents (Matt 25:14–30) within its own context, another student critiques contemporary pastoral interpretations of "stewardship." Beginning with an exegesis of Psalm 137 ("By the waters of Babylon"), an international student probes the exilic status of illegal immigrants from Rwanda, and the church's moral responsibility toward them. But, how do these writers get from "there" to "here"? They choose an interpretive method, or hermeneutic, that will enable them, as Paul Ricouer writes, to "render near what is far."[1] Because writing the biblical essay well not only entails interpreting texts well, but also requires selecting the appropriate hermeneutic from "there" to "here," this chapter is divided into two parts. The first part opens with a hermeneutical preface and presents a *reader's* interpretive "flow chart" that you will be invited to complete with your own hermeneutic of choice. The second part engages the *writing* of a biblical essay, using the method and structure of a critical-hermeneutical rhetoric.

A hermeneutical preface

Hermeneutics, defined simply, is the art and science of interpretation.[2] "To interpret," as we have seen, "is to render near what is far." Yet, in order to interpret something, whether far or near, one must also understand it. One way to gain this understanding is to go to the far country and immerse oneself in the culture, learning everything one can from the "natives" and other cultural informants. Equipped with this information, one might become a tourist guide who can "render near what is far" to an audience of armchair travelers, just as the writer of an exegesis provides his or her readers a "culturally correct" interpretation of the passage in its original context. That is the goal of critical-historical exegesis, which we correlate here and in Chapter 7 with the critical-historical biblical essay.

Another way to "render near what is far" is to build a bridge from the far to the near or draw it forward from there to here by interpreting it in the light of one's own hermeneutical questions and answers, as Luke's Jesus, "beginning with Moses and all the prophets,... interpreted to them the things about himself in all the scriptures" (Luke 24:27) on the way to Emmaus, and as we continue to do as we follow that "way" as contemporary interpreters of the scriptures. This is the goal of critical-hermeneutical interpretation and of the biblical essay that you will be invited to write, using the critical-hermeneutical path.[3]

But, there is "a more excellent way" that precludes neither of the other two, and that is simply to make the journey, step by step, from there to here, as the Emmaus travelers did, and allow it to transform us so that that we see, think, read, and live differently when we come home again. The disciples had probably heard the scriptures that were "interpreted to them" on the road so many times that they had stopped hearing them; but after they recognized Jesus "in the breaking of the bread" (Luke 24:30–31), they also recognized the risen Christ in the scriptures they had heard and hastened back to Jerusalem to witness to this transformed understanding of his mission and of their own discipleship. "Were not our hearts burning within us," they said, "while he was talking to us on the road... [and] opening the scriptures to us?" (Luke 24:32).

Hermeneutics as reading the word and reading the world

The Emmaus disciples had an advantage over us, however. They heard the Scriptures interpreted by the risen Christ, as he talked with them on the road. We read the same Scriptures from "lifeless letters"[4] on a page, and yet we still hope to "open the scriptures" to those who read our words. While not every biblical essay you write will ignite the hearts of your audience, a "conversion of heart" that begins with the exegete, preacher, or interpreter is the ultimate goal of all biblical interpretation, whether it bears fruit in preaching or writing. Yet, biblical preaching and writing are only as good as the reading that engenders them. "Really reading," writes Paulo Freire, "involves a kind of relationship with the text, which offers itself to me and to which I give myself and through the ... comprehension of which I undergo the process of becoming a subject,"[5] which for Freire means a person who can read "the word and the world,"[6] and can understand and articulate how they are reading both of these (text and context).

Friere's dialectic between "reading the word and reading the world" is hermeneutical, in that it recognizes that how one reads will influence what one writes. "What is written in the law? How do you read"? (Luke 10:26), Luke's Jesus asked the lawyer who wanted to know what he must do to gain eternal life. If someone were to ask you "how you read" what you read, what would you say? Do you read to discover the author's intended meaning? Do you read to understand the subject matter presented by the author? Do you read to develop your own interpretation of a text as a responsive reader? While you probably read for each of these purposes at various times, I invite you to reflect upon how you typically "read" biblical texts and to locate your own hermeneutical starting point as a biblical interpreter among the *author-centered* (represented by E.D. Hirsch), *subject-centered* (represented by Hans Georg Gadamer), and *reader-centered* (represented by Paul Ricoeur) positions represented on the "Flow Chart" below, which is elaborated in the next section.

From the *critical-historical* biblical essay to the *critical-hermeneutical* biblical essay: A hermeneutical flow chart

AUTHOR-CENTERED	*SUBJECT-CENTERED*	*READER-CENTERED*
E.D. Hirsch	Hans-Georg Gadamer	Paul Ricoeur
Validity in Interpretation	*Truth and Method*, 2ndRevEd	*Hermeneutics and the Human Sciences*
(New Haven: Yale Univ. Press, 1967)	(New York: Continuum, 1997)	(Cambridge: Cambridge Univ. Press, 1981)
WRITTEN TEXTS ARE SURROGATE SPEECH	*WRITTEN TEXTS ARE ALIENATED SPEECH*	*WRITTEN TEXTS ARE AUTONOMOUS*
"A written composition is not a mere locus of verbal possibilities, but a record ... of verbal actuality." [231]	*"All writing is a kind of alienated speech, and its signs need to be transformed back into speech and meaning."* [393]	*"Writing renders the text autonomous with respect to the intention of the author ..., the initial situation of discourse and the original addressee."* [139, 108]

MEANING IS DETERMINED BY THE AUTHOR'S INTENDED MEANING	*MEANING IS CO-DETERMINED BY THE INTERPRETER'S HISTORICAL SITUATION*	*MEANING IS CONSTRUED BY THE COMPLICIT READER*
"Textual meaning is the same as the author's meaning." [247]	*"The real meaning of a text as it speaks to an interpreter ... is always co-determined by the historical situation of the interpreter."* [296]	*"... the intended meaning of the text is not essentially the.. intention of the author ... but rather what the text means for whoever complies with its intention."* [161]
INTERPRETATION IS AUTHOR-CENTERED *"... the author's meaning, represented by his text, is un-changing and reproducible."* [217]	*INTERPRETATION IS SUBJECT-CENTERED* *"To understand ... is not really a relationship between ... the reader and the author, ... but about sharing in what the text shares with us."* [391]	*INTERPRETATION IS READER-CENTERED* *"To read ... is to conjoin a new discourse to the discourse of the text.... Reading is the .... act in which the destiny of the text is fulfilled."* [158, 164]
INTERPRETATION POSITS ONE HORIZON *"The interpreter's aim ... is to posit the author's ... horizon and exclude his own ... associations."* [222]	*INTERPRETATION FUSES HORIZONS* *"Understanding is always the fusion of horizons* [of author and interpreter] *supposedly existing by themselves."* [306]	*INTERPRETATION PROJECTS A HORIZON* *"What we ... appropriate for. ourselves, is not an alien experience ... but the horizon of a world ... ."* [178]
INTERPRETATION IS RECONSTRUCTION *"The interpreter's job is to reconstruct a determinate actual meaning, not a mere system of possibilities."* [231]	*INTERPRETATION IS CONVERSATION* *"To reach an understanding in a dialogue* [with a person or text] *is not merely a matter of ... asserting one's own point of view, but being transformed into a communion in which we do not remain what we were."* [379]	*INTERPRETATION IS APPROPRIATION* *"An interpretation is not authentic* unless *it culminates in some form of appropriation, ... the process by which the reader is broadened in his capacity to ... receive a new mode of being from the text itself."* [177, 193]

This hermeneutical flow chart[7] unfolds (1) an *author-centered* hermeneutic, represented by the literary theorist E.D. Hirsch,[8] which identifies textual meaning with the author's intended meaning and locates that meaning in the original horizon, or context, of the document; (2) a *subject-centered* hermeneutic, represented by Hans Georg Gadamer,[9] which correlates textual meaning with its subject matter and realizes that meaning through subject-centered conversation that brings about a fusion of horizons of the author and the interpreter; and (3) a *reader-centered* hermeneutic, represented by Paul Ricoeur,[10] which locates textual meaning in the interaction of the reader and the text, thereby projecting a new horizon. These positions also constitute successive "moments" in any process of biblical interpretation that moves exegetically from "what the text meant" to "what the text means" today. Because they also illuminate the task of writing in significant ways, we look below at the resources each of these hermeneutical positions provides for writing both the biblical exegesis and the critical-hermeneutical essay. In conclusion, you will be invited to draft a "hermeneutical flow chart" of your own that unfolds a *writer-centered* hermeneutic of your own choosing.

E.D. Hirsch's author-centered hermeneutic

E. D. Hirsch is a literary critic well known for his author-centered theory of textual interpretation, which he shares with traditional hermeneutical theologians such as Friedrich Schleiermacher and Wilhelm Dilthey.[11] Hirsch wrote initially in response to the "New Critics" who threw out the author with the bathwater, as it were,[12] but his hermeneutical position is consonant with the goals of historical-critical exegesis. A brief profile of his position is outlined on the hermeneutical flow chart.

Author-centered resources for writing the biblical exegesis/essay well

An *author-centered* hermeneutic provides resources not only for writing the critical-historical exegesis paper, but also for writing the critical-hermeneutical essay. First, it asserts that no scripture passage can be interpreted without reference to the author(s) who wrote it, the situation that engendered it, and the audience who first heard or read it. Thus, writing in this mode begins as a line of words that takes us back to its original horizon, before we follow it into other contexts.

Second, it follows that a critical-hermeneutical essay cannot build a bridge between there and here if the interpreter has not been there first to assess the lay of the land and the way of the original hearer/readers of the message. If an interpretation is to "fuse horizons," as Gadamer will instruct us to shortly, then there must be a clearly delineated "original" horizon with which to "fuse."

Finally, an author-centered hermeneutic empowers those "authoring" interpretations of scripture to trust their own construals of meaning and significance, while approaching the interpretive task with the appropriate humility of "probability," not the arrogance of certainty.[13] On this note of authorial circumspection, we turn to the *subject-based* hermeneutic of Hans-Georg Gadamer.

Hans-Georg Gadamer's subject-centered hermeneutic

Hans-Georg Gadamer is a German philosopher whose *Truth and Method* builds upon the "New Hermeneutical" theories of Bultmann and Heidegger[14] to adjudicate the truth claims of an authoritative tradition and the challenges facing contemporary interpreters, and in particular the post-Enlightenment disjunction between "truth" and "method."[15] With its emphasis upon the fusion of horizons of the author and the interpreter, Gadamer's hermeneutic is congenial to writing the critical-hermeneutical essay, or writing an "application" section of a biblical exegesis. A brief profile of his position is outlined on the hermeneutical flow chart.

Subject-centered resources for writing the biblical exegesis/essay well

A *subject-centered* and horizon-fused hermeneutic provides resources not only for writing the critical-hermeneutical essay, but also for writing the critical-historical exegesis paper. First, by instructing interpreters to center their writing in the subject matter of the text in order to build a bridge between the world "of the text" and what Paul Ricoeur will call the world "behind the text," Gadamer proscribes a purely "subjective" interpretation. However, he underscores the "productive" character of interpretation by his insistence that "understanding is always more than merely recreating someone else's meaning." From the writer's perspective, to fuse horizons is to pose one's own questions to the text and to think and write in response to them.[16]

Second, Gadamer provides a straightforward path to the "application" section that often concludes an exegesis paper. To provide a contemporary "application" of the exegesis involves moving from the "critical-historical exegesis" of the text within its own horizon to an explanation of the significance of the text for a specific audience today. To do this, you must write your way between these two audiences and their respective contexts by (1) clearly delineating the subject matter (or thesis) that connects them; and (2) providing readers with a map that details the connections you are making and the discontinuities that may remain.

Third, a critical-hermeneutical essay is to the genre of biblical interpretation what the constructive theological essay is to the genre of theological discourse. By imagining the dialogue between the critical-historical interpretation of the text and its contemporary interpreters as a conversation centered in the subject matter being addressed, the writer of a critical-hermeneutical essay can discover an essay structure unfolding in:

- an introduction that foregrounds the critical-historical (or exegetical) moment of interpretation;
- a dialogical section that raises contemporary questions in response;
- a proposal for a "fusion of horizons" that draws the text forward, employing either a "hermeneutic of generosity" or a "hermeneutic of suspicion;"[17]
- a concluding synthetic statement that recapitulates the interpretive proposal, reflects briefly on its implications, and invites further conversation.

Finally, Gadamer models a humility toward the "art" of writing at the same time that he stresses the importance of clear, unambiguous writing for the interpreter of written texts. "The art of writing," he acknowledges, "... is not an end in itself and therefore not the fundamental object of hermeneutical effort."[18] If writing is merely a vehicle for communicating subject matter rather than an object of meaning in its own right, then words are secondary to the meaning that they express. Nevertheless, Gadamer continues, "understanding is drawn on entirely by the subject matter,... [and] unclear thinking and 'bad' writing... undermine the basic presupposition of all hermeneutical success, namely the clear unambiguity of the intended meaning."[19] In other words, your writing should be like a scrupulously clean window through which the meaning of the subject matter can be clearly discerned by readers looking through its panes. This goal will become even more important as we turn now to Paul Ricoeur's *reader-centered* hermeneutic.

Paul Ricoeur's reader-centered hermeneutic

Paul Ricoeur is a French philosopher and interpreter of biblical and literary texts whose hermeneutical writings build upon Gadamer's ideas and draw out their implications in significant ways. They differ, however, in that Ricoeur understands writing as a fully autonomous mode of communication, not dependent upon speech but equal to it as a communicative medium.[20] Ricoeur therefore argues that exegesis "unfolds its procedures within the circumscription of a set of meanings that have broken their moorings to the psychology of the author."[21] As Ricoeur configures them, those procedures unfold in a continuum that enfolds what is "behind the text" (the world of the author), "of the text" (the world of the contemporary interpreter) and "before the text" (the world yet to be disclosed by the interpreter's engagement with the text).[22]

With its emphasis upon the *process* of "making one's own what was alien" in a text through the interpretive dynamic of reading, Ricoeur's hermeneutic provides a path from what he calls a "first naivete" toward a biblical text to a "second naivete" in which a new appropriation of the text is forged from the productive "struggle" between the traditional text and the contemporary reader.[23] Ricoeur's hermeneutic is most congenial for writing a critical-hermeneutical essay. A brief profile of his position is outlined on the hermeneutical flow chart.

Reader-centered resources for writing the biblical exegesis/essay well

Ricoeur's *reader-centered hermeneutic* provides many resources for the writing of the critical-hermeneutical essay. First, Ricoeur situates writing as an equal and integral partner in textual interpretation, not merely a stand-in for the real performers (author, subject, and readers). However, this semantic autonomy makes writing even more vulnerable to ambiguity and misunderstanding, as Plato pointed out long before Ricoeur.[24] It is therefore even more important that words say what they mean, and that writing conjoins the "sense" (the self-contained structure of the text) with its "reference" (what it means to say about the world beyond the text).

Second, Ricoeur invites readers and writers to project their writing "in front of the text" where the contemporary action is, not merely to reproduce other interpretations and contexts. This space in front of the text invites multiple critical and hermeneutical approaches to complete the hermeneutical circle of text, author, and interpretive community and embraces hermeneutics of generosity as well as hermeneutics of suspicion, as we shall see in our discussion of the writer-centered hermeneutic.

Finally, writing comes into its own in Ricoeur not merely as a window through which we see the subject matter, but as an interpretive world that is projected by the writer in the process of "appropriating what is alien" and making it one's own. It is not only the text being interpreted in some undifferentiated mental space that "projects a world," but the writer interpreting the text projects his or her "appropriation" of that world in writing for others to appropriate as well. In other words, in the writing of a biblical exegesis or essay, we not only encode thoughts, subject matter, and relevant research data, and arrange them in an orderly sequence, but in the process of interpretation, we also make our own what was initially alien, and invite others to follow us there, as Alice follows the white rabbit adventurously into "Wonderland" on the lure of a pocket watch protruding from his waistcoat pocket.

In this equally adventurous hermeneutical process, writing is not incidental, but integral to the lure of discovering, construing, and constructing meaning. Why else are you asked to write a biblical exegesis or a biblical essay if not to make the text and its interpretation your own? Thus, to write the biblical exegesis or critical-hermeneutical essay is not merely to follow the exegetical or rhetorical maps provided here, although these can be helpful. Just as writing theology well requires that you "work out a theology as you write," writing the biblical exegesis or essay well entails working out an interpretation as you write, in the constructive process of synthesizing the research you have done with your own construal of the text's meaning. When writing is the medium through which you interpret what the text projects, it has the capacity to project a world. The world that is projected, however, will depend upon the hermeneutic chosen by the writer, as we shall see as we proceed to the "writer-centered" hermeneutic, and finally, to the writing of the critical-hermeneutical essay.

The writer-centered hermeneutic

Each of the hermeneutical starting points that we have surveyed so far is a vehicle on the road to textual meaning, each driven by a different engine of the interpretive process. We have looked thus far at a hermeneutic driven by the original *author* of the text, by the *subject* of the text, and by the *reader* of the text. But, when an interpretation of a text is communicated in a written exegesis or essay, another contender enters the scene: the *writer*.

By "the writer," I mean any biblical interpreter who has chosen a particular hermeneutic, or pair of critical lenses, through which to read the text and write about it, and in particular those writing the biblical exegesis and/or essay in tandem with this book. By a *writer-centered hermeneutic*, I mean any interpretive method chosen by the writer for the purpose of explicating a biblical text in a particular way toward a particular end. For example, if I choose to apply Elisabeth Schüssler Fiorenza's feminist hermeneutic of "critical evaluation"[25] to the story of the woman taken in adultery (John 7:53–8:11) in order to critique it from a feminist perspective, I am exercising my prerogative as a "writer-centered" interpreter. If you choose to apply John Elliot's method of social scientific criticism[26] to the same text in order to illuminate its original context more effectively, you are similarly exercising your prerogative as a "writer-centered" interpreter. For example, the *Journal of Biblical Literature (JBL)* is currently utilizing such "writer-centered" methodologies as narrative, ideological and sociological approaches, along with more traditional "critical-historical exegesis," in its published articles.[27] Whatever interpretive method is chosen, the *writer-centered hermeneutic* places the writer of the exegesis or interpretive essay in the driver's seat with respect to the text being interpreted, both in terms of the hermeneutical method deployed and the style of writing employed.

This prerogative does not give writer-centered interpreters permission, like Lewis Carroll's Humpty Dumpty, to make the text mean "whatever they want it to mean," or to force the text to fit the hermeneutic or vice versa. Authorized by the semantic autonomy that Ricoeur has shown us to be inherent to written texts—that is, their emancipation from the original author, audience, and situation of composition—and limited by that same semantic autonomy, the writer's completed text will be subject to the same variables as the texts being interpreted. The "writer-centered hermeneutic," however, privileges the writer-interpreter's claims on the text rather than the text's claims on the writer-interpreter. While writers can and do "de-center" themselves in order to pursue specific interpretive goals (e.g., the critical-historical exegesis paper), a writer-centered hermeneutic empowers the writer to set the interpretive agenda (e.g., a feminist hermeneutic; a social science hermeneutic). It is in this sense that Terry Eagleton calls every act of interpretation a "re-writing" of the text being interpreted.[28]

For the conscientious writer-interpreter, there will also be constraints on the choice of a hermeneutic. To begin with, the *questions* you bring to the text will influence the critical method used to investigate those questions. Second, the *genre* of the text will determine the suitability (or unsuitability) of a particular critical method. Third, the *purpose* for which you are writing will render some interpretive options more appropriate than others. Finally, the *audience* for whom you are writing will affect your choice of a hermeneutic. Taking each of these factors into consideration as you proceed, I invite you now to get into the driver's seat, select a hermeneutic method for the text you will interpret,[29] and prepare to write the critical-hermeneutical essay well. Before we proceed, it is your turn to construct a hermeneutical flow chart:

CRITICAL-HERMENEUTICAL MEMO 1: Draft a hermeneutical flow chart that places your "default" hermeneutical position, or operative mode of biblical interpretation, at the center (one of those previously explored, or listed in Critical-Hermeneutical Memo 5 below, or one of your own choosing), with other methods that you employ for specific purposes (exegesis, preaching, prayer, biblical research essays) positioned in relation to it. Use the chart above as an example, but be creative in drafting your own. The purpose of this exercise is to help you identify your operative mode(s) of interpretation, and your "hermeneutical options" as a writer-interpreter of biblical texts.

The critical-hermeneutical path for writing the biblical essay well

While biblical essays written from "critical-historical" and "critical-hermeneutical" perspectives can both "render near what is far," we turn now to the "critical-hermeneutical" path, which invites you to interpret your exegesis text in the light of a contemporary issue and/or for a contemporary audience of your choice, without leaving the original context behind. To follow a path, however, it helps to have a map. Just as we wrote our way through the "critical-historical" path in twelve exegetical memos, we will shortly unfold a "critical-hermeneutical map" with four exegetical starting points, each of which includes a summarizing "critical-hermeneutical memo" to guide your writing process. First, however, we must define the biblical essay and describe its distinguishing features.

Introducing the biblical essay: Definitions and distinguishing features

What is a biblical essay? How does it differ from a biblical exegesis, on the one hand, and a theological essay, on the other hand? What is a critical-hermeneutical essay and how shall we write it? These questions recall those posed in Chapter 4, where we probed the essay as a literary and theological genre. This introduction to the biblical essay builds upon that generic profile;[30] but before we can distinguish the biblical essay as a subgenre in its own right, we must be able to define it.[31] As described in this chapter, the biblical essay is an extended exegetical project with a beginning, middle, and an end,[32] in which the initial exegesis provides a point of departure for a broader interpretive and/or research inquiry, rather than an end in itself. Thus, the biblical essay is distinguished from the biblical exegesis by its purpose.

Yet, the exegesis is to a biblical essay what a mathematical derivation is to a scientific essay, and how much of either process one rehearses in the respective essay will be determined by the audience for whom one is writing. In its simplest form, an exegesis paper that includes a "contemporary application" section as an integral conclusion to the paper, rather than as a separate section, constitutes an "exegesis-based" biblical essay. In its more sophisticated forms, a biblical essay in a scholarly journal might be comprised entirely of biblical interpretation[33] or historical research,[34] with only bare traces of the initial exegesis remaining. Most biblical essays that you will be asked to write will be situated between these two extremes.

While the biblical essay is distinguished from the biblical exegesis by its purpose, it is distinguished from the theological essay by its structure. To choose a methodical structure, as we have already seen, is to choose a rhetoric as well. Just as the theological method of "correlation" provides a rhetorical structure for a constructive theological essay,[35] the exegetical methodology of a biblical essay informs its structure correspondingly. For example, in Chapter 7, we identified the "text first" and "context first" tracks used to organize a "critical-historical" biblical exegesis paper. However, the historical-critical operations themselves (source criticism, form criticism, redaction criticism, and so on) constitute an exegetical method, or rhetoric: that is, a systematic procedure for working with the text that is reflected in its written structure. As we noted briefly,[36] that structure is characterized by:

- *segmentation* (dividing the text into sections for linguistic and literary analysis);
- *criticism* (applying individual historical-critical interventions to the text and/or its sections in a purposeful sequence);
- *synthesis* (reassembling the text into a coherent and meaningful syntactical structure);
- *reconstruction* (applying the historical-critical interventions to a reconstruction of the text's original intention, or meaning).[37]

What is a critical-hermeneutical essay and how shall we write it?

The critical-hermeneutical essay builds upon this exegetical rhetoric but develops it into an extended essay whose hermeneutical center of gravity rests upon what the text means today, without discounting its meaning in its original context.[38] Beginning from the presupposition that "the text mediates a meaning that is not behind it, hidden in the shroud of the past when the text was composed, but ahead of it in the possibilities of human and Christian existence that it projects to the reader,"[39] those on the critical-hermeneutical path direct their own contemporary questions to the text, and select a hermeneutical approach that responds most fruitfully to those questions.

To answer the question, "Was Luke's Jesus a feminist?" for example, it would be necessary to integrate a feminist hermeneutic with more traditional critical-historical methods. Similarly, the question, "Do the Genesis creation narratives support or suppress an ecological vision?" would require the interpreter to read the Genesis texts with biblical commentaries in one hand and contemporary ecological criticism in the other. While there is more than one way to structure a critical-hermeneutical essay, it unfolds here in four exegetical operations. They include: (1) literary-linguistic locations, (2) historical investigations, (3) theological formulations, and (4) hermeneutical destinations.[40] A "Critical-Hermeneutical Map" elaborates this fourfold process below:

The biblical essay: A critical-hermeneutical map

Literary-linguistic locations

The writings that make up the New Testament are first and foremost pieces of literature.
—DANIEL HARRINGTON, *Interpreting the New Testament: A Practical Guide*

Goal: Analyze the text to decode what it says and what makes it a "piece of literature."

Tools: The Oxford Annotated Bible (or Greek/Hebrew Bibles); Greek/Hebrew dictionaries (if working from your own translation); Greek/Hebrew Interlinear Bibles; other modern biblical translations for comparison/contrast; Analytical Concordance.

CRITICAL-HERMENEUTICAL MEMO 2: Write a one-page memo that addresses the questions below to describe what your passage says and how it says what it says.

- *Translation of Passage:* (Or) read your text in several biblical translations.
- *Textual Criticism*: What variant translations are cited in the textual notes?
- *Literary Structure:* Write out and outline the passage to discern its shape and logical or narrative progression.
- *Literary Genre*: Is it parable? Poetry? Epistle? Historical narrative? Or...?
- *Literary Context:* What comes before and after your passage? How does it fit into the whole document from which it comes?
- *Vocabulary/Key Words:* What words recur in the passage? What is distinctive about its language?
- *Narrative Criticism:* How does the narrative proceed? What are the operative dynamics of plot, character, and point of view? How is the narrative similar or different from other biblical narratives?
- *Rhetorical Criticism:* How does the passage communicate its purpose to readers? By logical argument? Preaching? Poetic images? Classical rhetorical modes?
- *Literary Devices:* Can you identify analogy? Metaphor? Symbolism? Irony? Foreshadowing? Inclusion? Chiasmus? Or...?
- *Stylistic Features:* Can you identify distinctive stylistic markers? Oral discourse modes? Parallelism? Use of typical literary conventions or formulas?

Historical investigations

Unfortunately I am not a debater, a storyteller, or a prophet. But I do hear voices in the distance coming closer.

—ANTOINETTE CLARK WIRE, *The Corinthian Women Prophets*

Goal: Locate the text in its historical context to determine its original meaning(s) in that context.

Tools: Bible Dictionaries and Encyclopedias; Introductions to the Hebrew Bible and New Testament; One-volume Commentaries; Commentary Series; *Old Testament Abstracts* and *New Testament Abstracts*; *The Religion Index* (print and/or ATLA online versions).

CRITICAL-HERMENEUTICAL MEMO 3: On the basis of your previous literary analysis and the following historical investigations, write a one-page memo describing what you think the text "meant" in its original context:

- *Source Criticism*: What is (are) the original source(s) of the document?
- *Form Criticism:* What is the "form" or genre of the document?
- *Situation/Environment:* What is the "*Sitz im Leben*" ("setting in life") of the passage?
- *Tradition Criticism:* What oral and written traditions inform the passage?
- *Historical Criticism*: What is the historical background and historicity of the passage?
- *Archaeological Criticism:* What light does archaeology shed upon the passage?
- *Social Science Criticism*: What are the sociocultural codes embedded in the text?

Theological formulations

The great contribution of redaction criticism... is that it called attention to the theological agenda of each of the evangelists and thus sensitized us to the... overwhelming importance of theology in the creation of and... understanding of the biblical texts.

—SANDRA SCHNEIDERS, *Written That You May Believe*

Goal: Analyze the text as a theological document to discover its theological "agenda."

Tools: Bible Dictionaries and Encyclopedias; Introductions to the Hebrew Bible and New Testament; One-volume Commentaries; Commentary Series; *Old Testament Abstracts* and *New Testament Abstracts*; *The Religion Index* (print and/or ATLA online versions); *Theological Dictionary of the New Testament; Theological Dictionary of the Old Testament.*

CRITICAL-HERMENEUTICAL MEMO 4: Using your previous literary/historical analysis and the questions below, write a one-page memo that explores the theological landscape of your passage and the theological "agenda" of its author and/or community.

- *Redaction Criticism:* What theological elements in the text can be traced back to their "redactor," or "editor," and what editorial changes have been made?
- *Key Words:* What clues do the "key words" identified in your literary analysis provide concerning the theology of the author/redactor?
- *Theological Orientations and Pastoral Situations*: What is the theological orientation of the text? Is it concerned with God, Jesus Christ, the Holy

Spirit, sin, grace, eschatology, or . . . . ? What can you discern about the author's theological perspective on these issues? Are there theological tensions, or does the text reflect a unified theological focus? If you are working with a New Testament text that is written to a particular community of believers, on the basis of what is written, what was going on in the church? To what pastoral, theological, or ecclesiological situation does this passage respond?

Hermeneutical destinations

To interpret is to render near what is far (temporally, geographically, culturally, spiritually).

—PAUL RICOEUR, *Hermeneutics and the Human Sciences*

Goal: Interpret what the text means today for a designated pastoral audience or community.

Tools: All of the previous literary, historical and theological investigations; Sandra M. Schneiders, "The World Before the Text," 157–79 in *The Revelatory Text: Interpreting the New Testament as Sacred Scripture*; Frederick C. Tiffany & Sharon H. Ringe, "Some Issues in Biblical Interpretation," in *Biblical Interpretation: A Roadmap*, 205–24.

CRITICAL-HERMENEUTICAL MEMO 5: Drawing upon all the exegetical resources that you have consulted thus far, the writing that you have done to synthesize them, and your own hermeneutical compass (from those suggested below or one of your own choosing) write a one-page memo in answer to the question, So what??? What does this text mean for ______(this person; this situation; this congregation; this ethnic, cultural, religious community) today, and why?

- *Canonical Criticism*: How is this text appropriated by believing communities?
- *Psychological Criticism:* What psychological dynamics illuminate the text?
- *Postmodern Criticism:* How does this text speak to a postmodern world?
- *Liberationist Criticism:* What word does this text speak to the oppressed?
- *African-American/Womanist Criticism:* To women and men of color?
- *Feminist Criticism:* To women who have been "written out" of the text?
- *Contextual Criticism:* To men and women in a diversity of cultural contexts?
- *Sexual Orientation Criticism:* To gay, lesbian, and transgendered persons?
- *Ecological Criticism:* To those using, abusing, and conserving God's creation?
- *Postcolonial Criticism*: To those oppressed by the legacy of Western colonialism?
- *Transformative Spirituality:* What does this text offer for an enhanced life of faith?

We will look at each of these critical-hermeneutical procedures briefly, each of which will be followed by a corresponding Critical-Hermeneutical Memo. Just as the twelve Exegetical Memos outlined in Chapter 7 provided a path for writing the biblical exegesis paper, the memos that follow will help us to plot the curves of a critical-hermeneutical essay on Mark 5: 25–34 (NRSV)—The Woman with a Flow of Blood.

> (25) Now there was a woman who had been suffering from hemorrhages for twelve years. (26) She had endured much under many physicians, was no better, but rather grew worse. (27) She had heard about Jesus, and came up behind him in the crowd and touched his cloak; (28) for she said, "If I but touch his clothes, I will be made well." (29) Immediately her hemorrhage stopped; and she felt in her body that she was healed of her disease. (30) Immediately aware that power had gone forth from him, Jesus turned about in the crowd and said, "Who touched me?" (31) And his disciples said to him, "You see the crowd pressing in on you; how can you say, 'Who touched me?' " (32) He looked all around to see who had done it. (33) But the woman, knowing what had happened to her, came in fear and trembling, fell down before him, and told him the whole truth. (34) He said to her, "Daughter, your faith has made you well; go in peace, and be healed of your disease."[41]

Literary-linguistic locations

The critical methodologies included here invite the interpreter to analyze and interpret the text to decode what it says and decide what makes it a "piece of literature." They include translation, textual criticism, literary structure, literary genre, literary context, vocabulary/key words, narrative criticism, rhetorical criticism, literary devices, and stylistic features. To synthesize this material, you are invited to write a one-page memo to describe what you think your passage "says" as a literary composition, and how it says what it says. For example:

> *CRITICAL-HERMENEUTICAL MEMO 6: Literary-Linguistic Locations.*
>
> The story of the woman with the flow of blood is a narrative within a narrative that begins with a woman's illness and ends with her public confession of healing, and with Jesus' public affirmation of her healing, not from touching his "cloak" but from trusting her own "faith" (Mark 5:34). While literary analysis of this story focuses upon its relationship to the "frame" story of the healing of Jairus' daughter (5:22–24, 35–4), it is a perfectly realized narrative that recounts not a merely a "private healing" but a "public proclamation" of the healing by the woman (v. 33) and by Jesus (v.34).
>
> In a "perfectly realized narrative," form and content conspire to weave the story's meaning into one seamless garment. The narrative unfolds in six parts: (1) The "suffering" woman identified (5:25) and her illness described (5:26); (2) The woman's "covert" action in response to her situation (5:27–28); (3) The "immediate" healing, and the woman's "private" recognition of it (5:29); (4) Jesus' "private" recognition of "power going forth" from him, inciting his

"public" appeal to the one who "touched him" (5:30); (5) the disciples' dismissal of his appeal, and Jesus' persistence in looking for the perpetrator (5:30–32); (6) The woman's public confession of healing (5:33) and Jesus' public affirmation of her faith and confirmation of her healing (5:34).

In sum, this story recounts a reciprocal and public proclamation of God's "power" (Greek *dynamis*), experienced not only by the "healed," but also by the "healer." The narrative moves from hiddenness [v. 27] to disclosure [v.33], and from private experience [v.30] to public witness [v.34]. Thus character, plot, conflict, and resolution collude to portray the healing as a two-way transaction in which both parties must actively engage before its fruits of "saving faith" [v.34)] can be realized.

Historical investigations

The critical methodologies included here invite the interpreter to locate the text in its historical context to determine its original meaning(s) in that context. They include source criticism, form criticism, tradition criticism, redaction criticism, historical criticism, archaeological criticism, and social science criticism. To synthesize this material, you are invited to write a one-page memo describing what you think the text "meant" in its original context. For example:

CRITICAL-HERMENEUTICAL MEMO 7: Historical Investigations.

To read this text in its original first-century context, we must: (1) read it through the lens of its religious and cultural context and (2) read it in its immediate literary context (the story of Jairus' daughter). In so doing, we discover "a tale of two daughters" healed and invited into a saving and liberating relationship with Jesus.

The text's original setting presents a woman physically ill, without apparent family, economically depleted (v. 25–26), ritually unclean (Lev 15:25–30), and thereby excluded from the covenant community. Because she knew that approaching Jesus directly would jeopardize his ritual purity, she "touched his cloak" from behind. Jesus, however, violated the purity system[42] by (1) asking, "Who touched me?" (2) searching for the person who had touched him; and (3) initiating a conversation with the woman that moved the healing from self-induced magic to an interpersonal encounter between a "patron" and a "client," reflecting God's relationship with his covenant community[43] and engendering fruits of healing and salvation. When the "woman" (5:25) is renamed "daughter" (5:34), she has been healed of her disease and of her illness and restored with the similarly healed daughter of Jairus as a "daughter" of the covenant community (5:34).

I agree with Ched Myers that "Mark shapes this story to intentionally juxtapose the two extremes of the Jewish social scale" and to reinforce kingdom values wherein all who "embrace the faith of the kingdom—a new social order with equal status for all" will be saved and "raised up."[44] Thus, this "tale of two daughters" provides a social leveling within its own context and a liberatory vision of the kingdom.

Theological formulations

The critical methodologies included here invite the interpreter to analyze the text as a theological document to discover its theological "agenda." They include redaction criticism, key words that reflect issues of theological concern to the author of the document, and questions arising from the *Sitz im Leben*, or situation and pastoral setting of the text. To synthesize this material, you are invited to write a one-page memo that explores the theological landscape of your passage and the theological "agenda" of its author and/or community. For example:

CRITICAL-HERMENEUTICAL MEMO 8: Theological Formulations.

All three redactions of this story of "the woman with the flow of blood" (Mark 5:25–34; Matt 9:20–23; Luke 8:43–48) emphasize the woman's faith, Jesus' power to "heal," or "save," and their intrinsic theological connection.

Faith (*pistis*) in the New Testament means trust or belief.[45] It refers here to faith in Jesus and his proclamation of God's reign. New Testament healing stories typically include a petitioner's request in "faith," the healer's response, and the conferral of healing. Jesus is portrayed with "power" (*dynamis*) from God "to heal" or "to save" (*sozo*). Greek *sozo* can mean both "to heal" and "to save," and both meanings inform the theological content of this story. The connection between them was reflected in first-century C.E. charismatic Judaism.[46] The cultural understanding of disease (an individual bodily malfunction) vs. illness (a public state of separation and cultural estrangement) strengthened this connection, so that one "healed" a "disease" but one was "saved" or "made whole" from an "illness."[47]

In its semantic conjunction of "to heal" and "to save" in the verb *sozo* and in the healing act of Jesus, this narrative discloses the full theological significance of the woman's healing. First, she experiences healing from her "disease," but her exchange with Jesus confirms that she is "saved" or "made whole" from her faith in God's power revealed in Jesus. For the early Christian community, this meant that in encountering Jesus, people encountered God, and God's power to heal, to save, and to make whole.

Hermeneutical destinations

The critical methodologies included here invite the interpreter to interpret what the text means today for a designated pastoral audience or community. They include canonical criticism, psychological criticism, postmodern criticism, liberationist criticism, African-American/womanist criticism, feminist criticism, contextual criticism, sexual orientation criticism, ecological criticism, post-colonial criticism, and transformative spirituality. To synthesize this material, you are invited to write a one-page memo in answer to the question, "So what? What does this text mean for (this person; this situation; this congregation; this ethnic, cultural, religious community) today, and why?" For example:

CRITICAL-HERMENEUTICAL MEMO 9: Hermeneutical Destinations.

"If I but touch his clothes I will be made well" (Mark 5:28). This conviction drove the woman of this story into a crowd who were pursuing Jesus on his way to a dying child. Driven by deteriorating health and dwindling economic resources, but aware of the purity taboos she would breach by direct contact, she touched Jesus' garment covertly and was healed secretly (or so she thought). What she underestimated then, and what women continue to underestimate today, is their own "power" (dynamis) to cross-cultural and cultic boundaries by faith in Jesus and the God he proclaimed.

"Who touched me?" Jesus asked? What was in that touch that would stop Jesus in the midst of a pressing crowd and cause him to risk cultic impurity? According to Mark, he was "immediately aware that power had gone out from him" (5:30), just as the woman was aware that her flow of blood was no longer "going out from her" (5:29). The power of touch connected them and drew the woman to Jesus, moved by her healing.

The woman's act had consequences. She made a claim on the power of Jesus that produced healing. But, Jesus responded with an answering claim that prompted her public acknowledgment of healing. Their encounter was the hinge upon which the doors of the kingdom of God opened, upon the woman's telling of the story, and Jesus' response, "Daughter, go in peace; your faith has saved you" (5:34).

Who is this woman? Where do we find her today? My biblical essay will focus on Hispanic women with AIDS and follow their journey from "disease" to "empowerment" using the cultural anthropology of Mary Douglas, the New Testament social science criticism of Bruce Malina and Jerome Neyrey, and the feminist biblical and ethical hermeneutics of Elisabeth Schüssler Fiorenza, Lisa Sowle Cahill, and selected cross-cultural feminist theorists.

From critical-hermeneutical memos to the critical-hermeneutical essay: Outlining a critical framework, building a hermeneutical bridge

The four exegetical-hermeneutical memos that you have just read follow the format of the one-page systematic reflection paper introduced in Chapter 3.[48] When used in the preparation of a biblical exegesis or essay, a one-page paper requires a concise, carefully researched synthesis of sources that presents suggestive evidence for a particular interpretation, to be further developed in the completed essay. The memos included here outline a fourfold critical framework that can be used to structure a biblical essay into literary-linguistic, historical, theological, and hermeneutical segments. They also provide the scaffolding upon which writers can build a hermeneutical bridge between the ancient biblical text and its contemporary contexts. If we revisit the memos from both of these perspectives, they will help us chart a rhetorical path toward a "critical-hermeneutical" biblical essay.

Outlining a critical framework

First, the literary-linguistic, historical, theological, and hermeneutical approaches employed in the memos above provide an outline and critical framework for the critical-hermeneutical essay. Not every biblical essay that you write will employ each of these methodologies equally, nor is the critical framework suggested here the only alternative for writing a critical-hermeneutical essay.[49] However, we use this critical framework as a starting point for writing a fully developed critical-hermeneutical essay, in confidence that you will adapt it to the requirements of your own biblical writing projects. Recalling the "beading an exegetical necklace" strategy that we used in Chapter 7 to move from the 12 "critical-historical" exegetical memos to a completed exegesis paper,[50] we will proceed by: (1) *identifying the recurring threads* that run through each of the "critical-hermeneutical" memos, (2) *choosing the rhetorical string* for the "beads" of the essay, (3) *stringing the beads* of each memo to move the argument forward most productively in a meaningful sequence, and (4) examining how successfully the four memos have provided the scaffolding for "building a hermeneutical bridge."

Identifying the recurring threads

Having completed each of the four critical-hermeneutical memos on Mark 5:25–34 (The Woman with a Flow of Blood), the writer's first task on the way to preparing a completed biblical essay is to identify the recurring thread (or threads) that are woven through each of the memos. Or to change the image, what is the principal "river" that "runs through" each of the memos, carrying with it the rich silt of the writer's research from its riverbanks?

First, what carries me in its wake from the first memo to the final one is the writer's assertion of the reciprocity of power exchanged between the hemorrhaging woman and Jesus. These memos suggest that the story is not merely about a sick woman reaching out to an indifferent source of "power" (*dynamis*) in order to be healed of her sickness, but also is about the woman's largely unacknowledged "power" to elicit a response from Jesus and engage him in her project, even at the risk of violating cultural codes (cultic purity laws).

Second, the merging currents of "saving faith" (*soza*) begin faintly in the literary-linguistic memo (187 above) and gather "historical" concreteness (188 above) and "theological" specificity (189 above) in those that follow to become a principal conduit of hermeneutical "empowerment" for contemporary women in the concluding memo (189–90, above). Finally, while it does not appear in the "literary-linguistic" memo, the stream of "cultic purity" that surfaces in the "historical" memo and in each of the memos that follows is indispensable to a full interpretation of the passage in its own context or in later contexts, as the concluding "hermeneutical" memo witnesses in its proposal to follow the woman's journey from "disease"' to "empowerment," using both contextual and contemporary hermeneutical resources.

Choosing the rhetorical string

Let us imagine that I am the writer of each of these critical-hermeneutical memos, and I have decided to apply a feminist hermeneutic to this passage, grounded in an explication of its original context. Having identified three recurring "threads" that connect my critical-hermeneutical memos, I must choose one dominant rhetorical string on which to hang the beads, or argument, of my essay. Or must I? If I cannot choose between them, I might decide to string three strands of beads that will be clasped by a hermeneutical "bridge" at the conclusion of the essay. If I have a highly synthetic mind, I might decide to braid each of the threads into one more comprehensive thesis. Finally, I might decide to choose one of them and recycle the others as literary, historical, or theological "beads" in support of my argument. After considering my options, I choose the first thread ("mutual empowerment and relationship") for my rhetorical string, because of its feminist hermeneutical potential.

Stringing the beads

Having chosen "mutual empowerment and relationship" as the rhetorical string for my critical-hermeneutical "necklace," I must now gather the beads from each of my memos that will support this thesis and move it forward into a credible argument. To do this, I first follow my thesis through each of the essays to see how and if it develops in the course of my exegetical writing process. I discover that the most cogent statement of the thesis appears in Critical-Hermeneutical Memo 2:

> In sum, this story recounts a reciprocal and public proclamation of God's power (Greek *dynamis*) experienced not only by the "healed," but also by the "healer."

While I have been fortunate in my first "literary-linguistic" memo to generate a working thesis that reverberates through subsequent memos, I must ask myself critically if I am "reading in" a contemporary feminist "egalitarian" agenda into Mark's text, rather than reading and/or hearing this story as Mark's original audience did. In short, my next task is to determine if this reading can be supported in its original context. To do this, I go through each of the memos in search of contextual clues. While the exegetical beads that I string will need further development and documentation in my completed essay, I first revisit the passage in relation to the story of the healing of Jairus's daughter, within which my pericope is intercalated, and then return to the threads of "saving faith" and "cultic purity" to reconstruct the meaning of the passage in its historical context. Focusing then on the "power" (*dynamis*) dynamics between Jesus and the woman, I turn to the *Theological Dictionary of the New Testament* for a fuller elaboration of *dynamis* in its New Testament context.

Finally, I find biblical resources for an interpretation of this passage that correlate the woman's power, which is dramatized but never explicitly acknowledged, with Jesus' unrelenting response to her overture, precipitated by his perception that "power had gone forth from him" (5:30). While the memos here blaze a trail but do not yet actualize the final paper in its entirety, my final hermeneutical memo draws this text forward by asking, asserting, and building a hermeneutical bridge from there to here:

> Who is this woman? Where do we find her today? My biblical essay will focus on Hispanic women with AIDS, and follow their journey from "disease" to "empowerment" using the cultural anthropology of Mary Douglas, the NT social science criticism of Bruce Malina and Jerome Neyrey, and the feminist biblical

and ethical hermeneutics of Elisabeth Schüssler Fiorenza, Lisa Sowle Cahill, and selected cross-cultural feminist theorists.

Building critical-hermeneutical bridges by writing the biblical essay well

There are bridges, bridges in the sky, and they are shining in the sun.
They are stone and steel and wood and wire, they can change two things to one.
They are languages and letters, they are poetry and all.
They are love and understanding, and they are better than a wall.[51]

Just as theologian Elizabeth Johnson sought to build a "hermeneutical span" to bridge the theological chasm between classical theology and Christian feminism,[52] many biblical scholars today seek to build bridges between the ancient biblical text and its contemporary environment. To build a bridge, however, implies that there are two separate entities that cannot be traversed without a means of conveyance from "there" to "here." For some biblical exegetes, to draw texts forward into the contemporary context results only in their decomposition and disintegration.[53] For others, bridge-building is a necessary and inevitable part of hermeneutics, or "the task of drawing out the significance of a biblical text into contemporary contexts."[54] Both of these perspectives have validity and need to be taken seriously. In order to write the critical-hermeneutical biblical essay well, however, you will need to learn how to build *rhetorical*, *contextual*, *hermeneutical*, and *dialogical* bridges. This chapter concludes with some bridge-building strategies for writers of the biblical essay.

Building rhetorical bridges with writing

Rhetoric is a bridge-building discipline, and well-wrought writing is one of its building materials. A critical-hermeneutical essay, like any essay, is only as good as the writing that inscribes it. By its very nature as a means of "written" communication in and through distance, writing builds bridges with words and writers are bridge-builders whose task is to connect those words meaningfully with the audience for whom they are written. Similarly, your writing should form a clear, coherent line of words that reaches out to your particular readers, transports them successfully from the beginning to the end of your essay, and bridges the gap effectively between exegetical and critical-hermeneutical sections. Toward these ends, Carmela D'Elia, the writer of the essay begun in the four previous memos, now walks her readers through a preliminary "map" of the paper in her introduction and weaves together both exegetical and critical-hermeneutical tasks in the process:

> In the cultural environment of the New Testament, gender defined the categories and boundaries with respect to "honor" and "shame." The state of pollution and the categories of "clean" and "unclean" also defined people's status. The story of the woman with the issue of blood (Mark 5:25–34) is exemplary of a village woman who was deemed "unclean." I recall this Scripture story not only to

> address this issue in its original New Testament context, but also for the light that it sheds upon women who continue to suffer from more subtle but no less harmful purity codes today.
>
> In this paper I will explore these issues first, depicting shame/pollution in the New Testament culture with respect to women more clearly. Secondly, I will do an exegesis of this text. Next, I will address the ethical dimensions, using Richard Hays' threefold structure of descriptive, synthetic and hermeneutic tasks. Within that framework, I will apply the work of Elisabeth Schüssler Fiorenza and Lisa Sowle Cahill to provide a contemporary understanding of purity/shame in the context of women/AIDS. Finally, I will engage the hermeneutic task through an ethical analysis that applies the tools of several feminist ethicists to Mark's text and its contemporary relevance to Hispanic women with AIDS.[55]

This introduction provides readers with a clear prospectus of the essay that follows and provides the writer with an outline that will keep her own writing on track. If you noticed that D'Elia has chosen a "context-first" pattern of organization for her project, you have read her outline well. We are also informed of the sociocultural, biblical and ethical theorists that the writer is using to build a feminist hermeneutical bridge that will conjoin Mark's first-century woman with a condition deemed "unclean" with twenty-first century Hispanic women suffering from the contemporary pollution of AIDS. How might you build your own rhetorical bridges well in your essay introduction, before proceeding to the exegetical and hermeneutical sections of your essay?

Building contextual bridges with sociocultural models

Out of the conviction that "cross-cultural reading of the Bible is not a matter of choice,"[56] biblical social science critics appeal to sociocultural models both to illuminate and bridge the gap between biblical and contemporary cultural understanding. As they are utilized in social-scientific criticism, "models are cognitive maps or lenses through which we perceive, filter and organize the mass of raw material available to our senses" into analyzable sociocultural patterns.[57] In the essay in progress here, cross-cultural models of honor/shame and purity/pollution are employed to interpret the hemorrhaging woman's story and to provide a context for understanding the "ancient Mediterranean" cultural dynamics of her interaction with Jesus and his with her. As we have seen, the writer grounds her contextual interpretation with Mary Douglas's anthropological model of purity, interpreted for New Testament studies by Jerome H. Neyrey,[58] and applies it to historical and contemporary women's experience. Using this model, she builds a cross-cultural bridge between honor and shame in first-century Mediterranean societies, eighteenth-century Hispanic cultures, and its more contemporary manifestations:

> The Mediterranean society is not the only society that imposes codes of behavior that undermine women and inflict oppression. Hispanic women are oppressed by a tradition of sexual attitudes and behavior beginning in the early 18th century in New Mexico. For instance, *shame* and *sexual purity* were reserved for women, while men increased their *honor* by conquering another man's woman.

> Traditionally, Hispanic women were expected to maintain the highest moral and spiritual standards of behavior, and a woman was considered shameful if she dishonored her husband or her father. This attitude has fostered a double standard in male and female behavior that has been perpetuated in Hispanic and Latin American society today. Finally, Hispanic women with AIDS today may have to bear the shame and stigma from the effect of men's double-standard.[59]

While not every biblical text lends itself to social-scientific criticism, sociocultural models can provide a cross-cultural bridge between contemporary and biblical culture, both in their articulation of cultural difference and in their identification of correlative cultural dynamics among particular ethnic groups today, as the writer of this essay demonstrates. What socio-cultural models might help you to elucidate the contemporary context of your passage?

Building hermeneutical bridges with cross-disciplinary conversations

In addition, cross-disciplinary conversations that link traditional biblical studies with other fields, such as Christian ethics, systematic theology, or pastoral studies, are providing bridges between biblical texts and other disciplinary contexts. The paper we have followed here, for example, was written for a "New Testament and Christian Ethics" course, which encouraged students to "build bridges between New Testament Studies and Moral Theology" in their course papers,[60] as the writer of our essay reads Mark's text through the lens of Lisa Sowle Cahill's feminist ethic:

> Lisa Sowle Cahill's notion of a Christian feminist biblical perspective on sex[61] centers on the values of community, solidarity, inclusiveness and compassion. Her ideas provide a lens for reading the text of the woman with the issue of blood because these are prophetic mandates in the early Christian communities that encouraged members to leave family behind and go on a mission to preach the Good News. It appears that the group that the woman went back to was mobilized by her new prophetic mandate: to be prophetic participants and not only followers. I believe that Cahill's positive Christian feminist ethic would want to lift the woman as an *exemplar* to the crowds and disciples. Finally, I believe that Cahill's call for solidarity in community suggests that the woman's exemplary faith, which leads her to proclaim the means of her cure, is a powerful indicator of an *exemplar character*.[62]

The cross-disciplinary biblical conversations that you will engage may be quite different from this conversation between Mark's gospel and feminist ethics. What extrabiblical courses and concerns might you draw into conversation with your biblical text, and in so doing, draw out its fuller implications?

Building dialogical bridges through a hermeneutics of diversity

Finally, many contemporary biblical interpreters, prompted by contemporary realities of cultural difference, opt for a hermeneutics of diversity in the reading of biblical texts that is realized through the exercise of a "dialogical imagination," as Kwok Pui

Lan exemplifies in *Discovering the Bible in the Non-Biblical World*.[63] The progenitor of this hermeneutics of diversity is Russian literary theorist Mikhail Bakhtin, who is not as interested in *interpretation* as in the *dialogue* between interpreters and the texts they interpret. At its best, this dialogue is informed by *intertextuality* (the interdependence of all written texts), *polyphony* (a multivocal chorus of cultural voices), and *heteroglossia* (intersecting social, cultural and ideological languages).[64] Bakhtin cautions both against "cultural immersion" into the alien context and against a hermeneutical "fusion of horizons" in cross-cultural dialogue, arguing that the integrity of each hermeneutical position must be maintained for the dialogue to be authentic and new meaning to emerge.[65]

While contemporary biblical interpreters have shown considerable interest in Bakhtin's work,[66] how might his "dialogical" perspective enrich your own writing of a critical-hermeneutical essay? With social science critics, he agrees that literature cannot be separated from its originating culture, or (accordingly), text from context.[67] With Gadamer and Ricouer, however, he insists that the meaning of a text transcends its own time, and only "ripens" to full flowering in "great time," that period of the ongoing "future" in which the text continues to be encountered by other readers, epochs, and cultures.[68] In distinction to Gadamer and Ricoeur, however, he conceives of textual meaning as "multivocal," or comprised of many voices and perspectives, all of which contribute to the reader's construction of meaning.[69] While Bakhtin first employed this approach in critical works on the novels of Dostoevsky,[70] it can be used as fruitfully with biblical texts, either by placing different but related texts in "dialogue" and letting the meaning emerge from that interaction,[71] or by listening to the different voices of a particular biblical text, and placing them in conversation with each other.[72]

In her own dialogue between the voices of the ancient biblical text and of cultural anthropologists, social science critics, feminist biblical scholars and ethicists, Hispanic women, and those who speak and write on their behalf, Carmela D'Elia has produced a "multivocal" and "dialogical" biblical essay. Her essay melds cultural voices and speaks in her own voice to conclude:

> In conclusion, our contemporary context of healing must continue to be nurtured by the goal of Mark's gospel to create a wholesome community in which people who have been excluded and need healing can now feel welcomed. The goal is for the renewal of our faith with the intention to be inclusive with our brothers and sisters who are suffering from the ravages of AIDS. Let us be proactive like the woman with the issue of blood who dared the crowds to initiate the healing and through her example initiate compassion with those who are in need, that the church may be an agent of healing by supporting people in all aspects of recovery.[73]

Concluding reflections: From building hermeneutical bridges to finding your own words

In this chapter, we looked first at three hermeneutical paths that biblical interpreters have followed in interpreting biblical texts. The first path was marked by a "cultural immersion" in the "alien" biblical world that initiated one as a "tourist guide" for other travelers. The second path was bridged by a "cultural fusion" between the horizons of the text and the contemporary interpreter through a process of conversation that left neither partner unchanged. The third path was defined simply by the journey, and its potential for transformation along the way. While the first path looked back to the writing of the critical-historical exegesis, and the second path provided a hermeneutical preface to writing the critical-hermeneutical essay, the third path invites you to return to your own biblical text and to draw it forward with your own words into the context where you are writing, teaching, preaching, or simply preparing a biblical essay.

According to Bakhtin, we speak and write from a linguistic storehouse that includes three kinds of words. First, there are impersonal words *belonging to nobody*, or dictionary-defined words that we use as we try to express what we want to say. Second, there are words that belong to *others*, or words that echo from the text you are interpreting, from the authors that you have read, and from the cultural context intersecting both of these. Last but never least, there are *your* own words, which are not independent of those that precede them, but have been internalized through your own cognitive process, and now speak with your own accent and expression.[74]

How can you find your own words to write after reading so many other words that have, as Bakhtin would say, "populated" you "with their intentions"?[75] First, take time to let the professor's lectures and your own research integrate with your own imagination. Second, do some exegetical "freewriting" without any texts in front of you, and see what emerges. Third, return to the biblical text and reread it. Finally, let your own words declare themselves during this distance from course lectures, research, and your own urgency "to get it written." Confident that you will indeed find the words to say what you want to say to write your own biblical essay well, the final memo invites you to write a *précis* for your own critical-hermeneutical essay, based upon the previous memos that you have completed in this chapter. In the next section of this book, we turn to "A Theological Style and Voice of One's Own" and lay the groundwork for that inquiry in Chapter 9, "Writing the Theological Imagination Well."

CRITICAL-HERMENEUTICAL MEMO 10: Writing a Précis for your Critical-Hermeneutical Essay. After you have completed the exegetical memos assigned in this chapter for a biblical project of your own, please reread them and prepare a précis, or one-page summary of the exegetical and hermeneutical argument of your proposed project. If written well, it might provide a cogent introduction to the essay.

Notes

1 Paul Ricoeur, *Hermeneutics and the Human Sciences*, ed. and trans. John B. Thompson (Cambridge: Cambridge University Press, 1994), 111.

2 "Hermeneutics," according to Paul Ricoeur, "is the theory of the operations of understanding in their relation to the interpretation of texts." Paul Ricoeur, "The Task of Hermeneutics," in *Hermeneutics and the Human Sciences*, 43.

3 Following Hans-Georg Gadamer's *Truth and Method* (New York: Continuum, 1997), 164–69, Herman Waetjen calls the first hermeneutical option "the hermeneutics of *reconstruction*" and the second option "the hermeneutics of *integration*." See Herman Waetjen, "Social Location and the Hermeneutical Mode of Integration," in *Reading from this Place: Social Location and Biblical Interpretation in the United States*, ed. Fernando F. Segovia and Mary Ann Tolbert (Minneapolis, MN: Fortress Press, 1995), 75–93.

4 See P.J.J. Botha, "Living Voice and Lifeless Letters: Reserve Towards Writing in the Graeco-Roman World," *Hervormde Teologiese Studies* 49 (1993): 742–59.

5 Paulo Friere, *Pedagogy of Freedom: Ethics, Democracy and Civic Courage*, trans. Patrick Clarke (Lanham, MD: Rowman & Littlefield, 1998), 34.

6 See Paulo Friere and Donald Macedo, *Reading the Word and Reading the World* (South Hadley, MA: Bergin and Garvey, 1987).

7 The Hermeneutical Flow Chart presented here is adapted and expanded from a class presentation by Daniel J. Harrington, Weston Jesuit School of Theology, October 1997.

8 E.D. Hirsch, *Validity in Interpretation* (New Haven, CT: Yale, 1967), 247, 217, 222.

9 Gadamer, *Truth and Method*, 296.

10 Ricoeur, *Hermeneutics and the Human Sciences*, 161, 158, 193.

11 For a summary of the contributions of each of these hermeneuticians, see Ricoeur, "The Task of Hermeneutics," in *Hermeneutics and the Human Sciences*, 45–53.

12 See Hirsch, "In Defense of the Author," in *Validity in Interpretation*, 1–23.

13 As Hirsch concludes, "Correctness is precisely the goal of interpretation and may in fact be achieved, even though it can never be known to be achieved. We can have the truth without being certain that we have it, and, in the absence of certainty, we can nevertheless have knowledge—knowledge of the probable" (*Validity of Interpretation*, 173).

14 See Hirsch, "Gadamer's Theory of Interpretation," in *Validity of Interpretation*, 246 and 246n2.

15 Sandra Schneiders distils Gadamer's position succinctly when she explains, "... when method controls thought and investigation the latter may lead to accurate data but it does not lead to truth" (*Revelatory Text*, 23).

16 Gadamer, *Truth and Method*, 375.

17 See Chapter 4 above under "What Are the Elements of the Critical Theological Essay?"

18 Gadamer, *Truth and Method*, 396.

19 Ibid.

20 Paul Ricoeur, "Speaking and Writing," in *Interpretation Theory: Discourse and the Surplus of Meaning*, ed. Paul Ricoeur (Fort Worth, TX: Texas Christian University Press, 1976), 25–44.

21 Ibid., 30.

22 Sandra Schneiders systematizes these movements in *The Revelatory Text*, 97–179.

23 Ricoeur, "Speaking and Writing," 44, 32.

24 See Plato, *Phaedrus*, trans. Walter Hamilton (London: Penguin, 1973), 97: "A writing cannot distinguish between suitable and unsuitable readers. And if it is ill-treated or unfairly abused it always needs its parent to come to its rescue; it is quite incapable of defending or helping itself."

25 Elisabeth Schüssler Fiorenza, *In Memory of Her: A Feminist Theological Reconstruction of Christian Origins* (New York: Crossroad, 1986).

26 See John H. Elliot, *What* Is *Social-Scientific Criticism* (Minneapolis, MN: Fortress, 1993). For further examples of social scientific criticism in this chapter, see 194–95 below.

27 See Susan E. Haddox, "*Journal of Biblical Literature* Today," Society of Biblical Literature Website/Forum Archive, accessed September 24, 2014, http://www.sbl-site.org/publications/article.aspx?ArticleId=270.

28 Terry Eagleton, *Literary Theory: An Introduction* (Minneapolis, MN: University of Minnesota Press, 1983).

29 See "The Biblical Essay: a 'Critical-Hermeneutical' Map" below, for a more complete list of hermeneutical methods. A brief summary of contemporary methods can be found in John H. Hayes and Carl R. Holladay, *Biblical Exegesis: A Beginner's Handbook* (Louisville, KY: Westminster/John Knox, 2007), 167–77 ("Exegesis with a Special Focus: Cultural, Economic, Ethnic, Gender, and Sexual Perspectives").

30 See Chapter 4, under "Concluding Reflections: Writing the Constructive Essay Well." These guidelines are equally applicable to "writing the biblical essay well."

31 While the term "essay" is used much more loosely in biblical studies than the term "exegesis," Professor R.J.D. Knauth's description of an "exegesis essay" as "closely analyzing a biblical text and then giving a contemporary or personal application" is representative of the sense in which I use the term in this book. See R.J.D. Knauth, "Syllabus for Old Testament Faith and History," Lycoming College, Fall 2014, accessed September 25, 2014, http://lycofs01.lycoming.edu/~knauth/REL113/113syllf14.htm. For a fuller description of Professor Knauth's protocols for researching and writing an exegesis essay, scroll down to **Exegesis Project Guidelines: Proposal and Self-Evaluation.** How does her process compare with that assigned by your professor?

32 Cf. Chapter 4, where the essay is defined as "a purposeful prose composition … with … an introduction, body, and conclusion, written … for a specific audience."

33 As, for example, Richard J. Clifford, "The Exodus in the Christian Bible: the Case for 'Figural' Reading," *Theological Studies* 63 (2002): 345–61.

34 As, for example, Walter Brueggemann, "On Scroll-Making in Ancient Jerusalem," *Biblical Theology Bulletin* 33 (2003): 5–11.

35 See Chapter 4 under "The Method of Correlation."

36 See Chapter 7 under "From Writing Exegetical Memos to Writing the Biblical Exegesis Well."

37 See Stenger, *New Testament Exegesis*, 24–27, for an elaboration of this structure in terms of "synchronic" (concerning the text as it is) and "diachronic" (concerning the text as it came to be) methods.

38 A critical-hermeneutical rhetoric, then, is one in which the hermeneutical method employed is the principal "rhetorical element of purposeful communication."

39 Sandra M. Schneiders, "The Approach Operative in this Book," in *Written That You May Believe: Encountering Jesus in the Fourth Gospel*, ed. Sandra M. Schneiders (New York: Crossroad, 1999), 162.

40 I have adapted this exegetical methodology from Sandra M. Schneiders, "The Approach Operative in this Book," in Schneiders, *Written That You Might Believe*, 20–22.

41 All biblical quotations are taken from *The New Oxford Annotated Bible with the Apocrypha, New Revised Standard Version*, 4th ed., ed. Michael D. Coogan et al. (New York: Oxford University Press, 2010).

42 Jerome H. Neyrey, "The Idea of Purity in Mark's Gospel," *Semeia* 35 (1996): 93.

43 Bruce J. Malina and Richard L. Rohrbaugh, *Social-Science Commentary on the Synoptic Gospels* (Minneapolis, MN: Fortress Press, 1992), 209.

44 Ched Myers, *Binding the Strong Man: A Political Reading of Mark's Story of Jesus* (Maryknoll, NY: Orbis Books, 1988), 202–3.

45 Rudolf Bultmann, "*pistis*," in Gerhard Kittel and Gerhard Friedrich, eds., *Theological Dictionary of the New Testament Abridged in One Volume*, trans. and abridged by Geoffrey W. Bromley (Grand Rapids, MI: Eerdmanns, 1985), 853.

46 Geza Vermes, *Jesus the Jew: A Historian's Readings of the Gospels* (Philadelphia, PA: Fortress Press, 1981), 372.

47 Malina and Rohrbaugh, *Social-Science Commentary on the Synoptic Gospels*, 209–10.

48 See Chapter 3 under "Writing the One-Page Systematic Reflection Paper: Was Jesus a Feminist?"

49 For cross-disciplinary essays integrating biblical texts with contemporary ethical reflection, for example, Richard Hays outlines a critical framework in three movements: (1) the *descriptive* task, which describes the moral visions implicit in particular New Testament texts; (2) the *synthetic* task, which synthesizes those visions in terms of suggestive biblical images (e.g., community, cross, and new creation); (3) the *hermeneutical* task, which offers hermeneutical proposals for applying biblical texts to contemporary ethical reflection. Daniel Harrington and James Keenan employed Hays's method, among others, in their collaborative courses at Weston Jesuit School of Theology, Cambridge, Massachusetts. See Richard B. Hays, *The Moral Vision of the New Testament: Community, Cross, New Creation: A Contemporary Introduction to New Testament Ethics* (San Francisco, CA: Harper San Francisco, 1996); Daniel Harrington and James Keenan, *Jesus and Virtue Ethics: Building Bridges Between New Testament Studies and Moral Theology* (Lanham, MD: Sheed and Ward, 2002), 21–22, 29.

50 See Chapter 7 under "From Writing Exegetical Memos to Writing the Biblical Exegesis Well."

51 The epigraph is quoted from the song "Bridges," words and music by Bill Staines, copyright Mineral River Music, 1985. Used by permission of the author.

52 Elizabeth A. Johnson, *She Who Is: The Mystery of God in Feminist Theological Discourse* (New York: Crossroad, 1992), 12.

53 So Paul Acheteimer, in "Ancient Document and Modern Culture: an Ecology of New Testament Interpretation," in an address to the New England Section of the Society of Biblical Literature, Episcopal Divinity School, Cambridge, Mass., April 26, 2004.

54 Harrington and Keenan, *Jesus and Virtue Ethics*, 19.

55 Carmela D'Elia, "The Woman with the Issue of Blood and the Ethical Implications for the Early Christians and Today," unpublished paper for *New Testament and Ethics*, Profs. Daniel J. Harrington, and James F. Keenan, Weston Jesuit School of Theology, May 2001, 1. This and subsequent excerpts from the paper are used with the author's permission.

56 Richard L. Rohrbaugh, ed., "Introduction," in *The Social Sciences and New Testament Interpretation*, ed. Richard L. Rohrbaugh (Peabody, MA: Hendrickson, 1996), 1.

57 Elliot, *What Is Social-Science Criticism?*, 42.

58 Mary Douglas, *Purity and Danger: An Analysis of the Concepts of Pollution and Taboo* (London: Routledge & Kegan Paul, 1966) and Neyrey, "Idea of Purity in Mark's Gospel."

59 D'Elia, "Woman with the Issue of Blood," 22.

60 As Daniel Harrington, and James Keenan. explain in their book, *Jesus and Virtue Ethics:* "This book is intended more as a heuristic probe, or a means toward encouraging further investigation and discovery, than a definitive statement .... The word *Bridges* in our subtitle indicates what we are trying to do. We are seeking to make links between two specialized theological disciplines that have seldom been joined together." (xv).

61 Lisa Sowle Cahill, "Sexual Ethics: A Feminist Biblical Perspective," *Interpretation* 49 (1995): 5–16.

62 D'Elia, "Woman with the Issue of Blood," 18–19.

63 See Kwok Pui Lan, *Discovering the Bible in the Non-Biblical World* (Maryknoll, NY: Orbis, 1995).

64 Mikhail M. Bakhtin, *Speech Genres and Other Late Essays*, trans. V.W. McGee (Austin, TX: University of Texas Press, 1986), 71–72, 112–13; M.M. Bakhtin, *The Dialogical Imagination*, trans. C. Emerson and M. Holquist (Austin, TX: University of Texas Press, 1986), 288–95.

65 See Bakhtin, *Speech Genres*, 7: "Such a dialogic encounter of two cultures does not result in merging or mixing. Each retains its own unity and open totality, but they are mutually enriched."

66 See, e.g., Barbara Green, *Mikhail Bakhtin and Biblical Scholarship: An Introduction*, Semeia Studies 38 (Atlanta, GA: Society of Biblical Literature, 2000), and most recently, L. Juliana M. Claassens, "Biblical Theology as Dialogue: Continuing the Conversation on Mikhail Bakhtin and Biblical Theology," *Journal of Biblical Literature* 122 (2003): 127–44.

67 Bakhtin, *Speech Genres*, 2–3.

68 Ibid., 4–5.

69 M.M. Bakhtin, "Discourse in the Novel," in *The Dialogic Imagination: Four Essays*, ed. Michael Holquist, trans. Caryl Emerson and Michael Holquist (Austin, TX: University of Texas Press, 1981), 278: "For the prose writer, the object is a focal point for heteroglot voices among which his own voice must also sound; these voices create the background necessary for his own voice ... without which they do not sound."

70 Mikhail M. Bakhtin, *Problems of Dostoevsky's Poetics*, ed. and trans. Caryl Emerson (Minneapolis, MN: University of Minnesota Press, 1984).

71 See L. Juliana M. Claassens and Paul Scott Wilson, *The God Who Provides: Biblical Images of Divine Nourishment* (Nashville, TN:Abingdon Press, 2004).

72 See, e.g., Ellen von Wolde, "Intertextuality: Ruth in Dialogue with Tamar," in *A Feminist Companion to Reading the Bible: Approaches, Methods and Strategies*, ed. Athâlya Brenner and Carole Fontaine (Sheffield: Sheffield Academic Press, 1997), 426–51.

73 D'Elia, "Woman with the Issue of Blood," 22.

74 Bakhtin, *Speech Genres*, 88.

75 Bakhtin, *Dialogical Imagination*, 293.

PART THREE

Toward a Theological Style and Voice of Your Own

9

Writing with Theological Imagination Well: Rhetorics of Analogy, Metaphor, and Symbol

Each of us understands each other through analogy or not at all.

—DAVID TRACY, *The Analogical Imagination*

Metaphor ... is the way we think.

—SALLIE MCFAGUE, *Metaphorical Theology*

Theology is a symbolic discipline; from beginning to end it deals with symbols.

—ROGER HAIGHT, *Dynamics of Theology*

Starting points

While much has been written about the theological imagination, little has been written about writing with theological imagination. Yet every time that you combine concrete images and conceptual language in a sentence to make a theological assertion, frame a theological reflection, or rewrite what you have written, you are exercising your theological imagination. But what enables theologians to join the concrete with the conceptual, the particular with the universal, the immanent with the transcendent in their writing? As David Tracy, Sallie McFague, and Roger Haight exemplify in the epigraphs above, theologians use the resources of analogy, metaphor, and symbol, which we explore in this chapter as rhetorics of the theological imagination.[1] We begin with the question, "What is the theological imagination and how shall we write with it?" Next we ask, "What are the rhetorics, or rhetorical elements of purposeful communication, inherent in the theological imagination?" Finally, we turn to sections on analogy, symbol, and metaphor, respectively, which we identify and elucidate as "writer-based" rhetorics for writing with theological imagination well. First, I invite you to exercise your own theological imagination in the following theological memo:

> *THEOLOGICAL MEMO 1: What is the theological imagination and how shall we write with it? What does the phrase "theological imagination" evoke for you? How would you define it? What are its elements? What theologians have engaged your own theological imagination? What theological writing assignments have*

challenged you to "write with theological imagination well"? Reflect on these questions, and write a definition of "theological imagination" to take with you as you read this chapter.

What is the theological imagination and how shall we write with it?

First, the theological imagination is a way of knowing that is mediated by the human mind. "Imagination," writes Suzanne Langer, "is the primary talent of the human mind, the activity in whose service language was evolved."[2] It is from this understanding of imagination as a synonym for the active mind making meaning in and through language that we have previously described the theological imagination as our active minds thinking, questioning, dreaming, creating, construing, constructing, critiquing, speaking, and writing in the concrete and conceptual language of theology.[3] As theological writers, we engage the theological imagination first as a way of knowing that is engendered by our own meaning-making imagination and embodied in the words we write. From this perspective Gordon Kaufman writes, "Theology is not merely a rehearsal and translation of tradition ... [but also] a creative activity of the human imagination seeking to provide more adequate orientation for human life."[4]

But if theology is "a creative activity of the human imagination," then those who engage it must still have something to imagine with. As Sallie McFague observes, "We never create—as the tradition says God did—out of nothing, but use what we have, seeing it in a new way."[5] For theological writers, that something includes both the resources of the biblical and theological traditions, and the reservoir of sense experience and personal, intellectual and contextual knowledge that each writer brings to the theological task. But what enables us to see in a new way? We must embrace the theological imagination not only as a way of knowing, but also as a way of seeing, which we turn to next.

Second, the theological imagination is a way of seeing grounded in acts of human perception that issue in physical and mental images—both the visual images produced by the retina and the mental images that we retrieve from memory or inventively create. We not only see with images; we think with images, and these two operations conjoin in the familiar response, "I see what you mean." As constitutive of the active imagination, an image is a verbal representation or mental picture of something that is not present. For example, "When the Sun rises," a companion asked poet William Blake, "do you not see a round disk of fire somewhat like a Guinea?" "O no, no," Blake replied. "I see an Innumerable company of the Heavenly Host crying 'Holy, Holy, Holy is the Lord God Almighty.' "[6] While both Blake and his companion saw the same sunrise, their mental images of it issued from different ways of seeing. Where one saw a common English coin emblazoned in the sunrise, the other beheld a theophany inspired by another writer—Isaiah—who heard the seraphim proclaiming God's holiness (6:1–3).

For Asian theologian Choan Seng Song, the difference between these perceptions lies in "the power of theological imaging," which derives ultimately from God "imaging God's own self in humankind," and giving us "the ability to image all created things in relation to God."[7] Like Song, one way that we exercise "the power of theological imaging" is through writing. Just as Blake's poetic image of the sunrise was informed both by his own apprehension of God's image in physical reality and by its "theological imaging" in Isaiah's writings, our own theological way of seeing must integrate our own perception and that bequeathed to us by our tradition. But even when we appeal to both of these, it can be difficult to separate the power of authentic theological imagination from the pull of our own illusions. To do so, we must embrace the theological imagination as a way of reflecting, which we turn to next.

Third, *the theological imagination is a way of reflecting* that filters images produced by the imagination and forms concepts in response to those images. The word *reflect* means literally "to bend or turn backwards," as light does when it "reflects" images in a mirror. If you picture yourself as you appear in your high school yearbook, and then see a very different image of yourself reflected in a mirror, you will involuntarily correct your mental image to match your "real" mirror image. A similar process of reflection allows us to corroborate or correct the theological images that we project in our writing. Just as for Song, God's self-imaging in creation provides a mirror for the theological imaging process, for H. Richard Niebuhr, Scripture reflects a "revelatory image" of God's self-disclosure in history by which we can distinguish theologically suspect images from theologically adequate images.[8]

Yet our theological imagination not only filters images; it also forms concepts in response to those images. A concept is a bundle of words that we use to think with, and we form concepts in the process of thinking with images. The process of theological reflection described by Killen and deBeer illustrates this interactive process. Reflecting on her volunteer work at a homeless shelter, Elaine wrote that it felt "like a steel rod across [her] shoulders." This image prompted her conceptualization, "Jesus does not ask us to be masochists, so I am going to quit this volunteer work." But that image was challenged by Jesus' "revelatory image," "Take my yoke upon you and learn from me... for my yoke is easy and my burden is light" (Matt 11:29), which invited Elaine to re-conceptualize her "steel rod" as a shared and thus more bearable burden.[9] Yet Elaine's theological imagination provided both *a way of reflecting* by filtering images and forming concepts, and *a way of connecting* them, which we turn to in conclusion.

Fourth, and finally, *the theological imagination is a way of connecting* concrete images and the concepts, abstractions, and generalizations that we derive from them into a unified theological reflection. "Imagination can be described as the basic process by which we draw together the concrete and the universal elements of our human experience,"[10] writes moral theologian Philip Keane. The understanding of "imagination" operative here is not synonymous with illusion or fantasy, but rather with the synthesizing intelligence of the creative mind, rooted in concrete reality but reflecting the transcendent, as plants photosynthesize the light that lures them toward new growth. Thus, theologian Kathleen Fischer describes imagination as an "inner rainbow," or "bridge," that "joins God and the earth, the sacred and the secular, bringing them into unity in our life"[11] and by extension, in our writing.

Every theological writing project invites its writer to engage the theological imagination as a way of connecting. When, for example, seminary student Denise Priestley wrote *Bringing Forth in Hope: Being Creative in a Nuclear Age*, she sought to connect her concrete experience of motherhood, a growing conviction that "the ultimate parenting issue is preventing nuclear war," and "a theology of hope that could provide the basis for the experience of motherhood" in a nuclear age. All of these elements coalesced for her in the biblical symbol of a woman giving birth in the shadow of a devouring dragon (Rev 12: 1–6), which Priestley used "to structure [her] examination of Christian hope" in her writing.[12] We will return to this symbol and its uses in "Writing with Symbol Well," below; but first we ask, "What are the rhetorics that empower the theological imagination?"

What are the rhetorics that empower the theological imagination?

As a way of knowing, seeing, reflecting, and connecting, writing with the theological imagination is a rhetorical process employing analogy, metaphor, and symbol as "rhetorics," or rhetorical elements of purposeful communication, to connect the concrete with the conceptual, the particular with the universal, and the immanent with the transcendent in our writing. Indeed, every act of purposeful communication is empowered by the imagination of the writer, speaker, or communicator. Thus, Ann Berthoff describes rhetoric as "a formulation of the laws of the imagination, the operation of mind by which experience becomes meaningful."[13]

In other words, rhetoric embraces not only *techne*, the skills that foster purposeful communication, but also *poesis*, the creative process that enables us to communicate in the first place. Central to that communicative process is using the resources of language, defined here as "rhetorics," to weave the images and concepts arising from our own theological imagination into seamless theological prose that "represent(s) different levels of being … in the same image, in the same and single act of perception,"[14] thus enabling us to connect our concrete experience with that which transcends it. Among these rhetorics are (1) analogy, which asserts that this is like (and unlike) that; (2) metaphor, which predicates that this is (or is not) that; and (3) symbol, which signifies that this means that, and makes what it means present. When used appropriately, each of these modes of figurative speech empowers us to write with theological imagination well, and we are ready to explore them in turn, beginning with analogy.

Writing with analogy well

Analogy: An introduction

"Analogy," Elizabeth Johnson observes, "shapes every category of words used to speak about God."[15] More fundamentally still, analogy shapes the very way in which we think and write about God. Whenever we assert that this is like (and unlike) that, and then draw out the implications of the comparison systematically, we are using the language of analogy. Whether we write concretely or conceptually, we draw upon what David Tracy calls an "analogical imagination" to write theology in creative conversation with our own experience of the world.[16] Yet the use of analogies to shape, order, and conceptualize experience is attested in the earliest written literature, from the Babylonian *Gilgamesh* to the Hebrew Bible to Homer's *Iliad* to the Hindu Upanishads. It has been argued that "analogy lies at the core of human cognition,"[17] spanning such disciplines as literature, philosophy, psychology, science, and religion in its systematic search for similitude.[18] Moreover, as we shall see as we proceed, both metaphor and symbol employ analogy in the very act of transcending it. But how does analogy help us to write the theological imagination well? To answer this question, we look first at two approaches to analogy that inform its definition in a theological context. Then we propose a "writer-based approach" to analogy that integrates these two approaches. Finally, we exemplify some specific ways for theological writers to use analogy as a rhetoric of the theological imagination.

Analogy: A preliminary definition

While *analogy* is defined differently in different disciplinary contexts, the word *analogy* has its roots in the Greek word *analogia*, or "proportion." Defined as a logical category, an analogy is a set of correspondences[19] or resemblances between certain attributes of two different entities that renders them "analogous," "proportionate," or similar to each other, notwithstanding their differences. Defined as a literary device, an analogy is an extended figure of speech that discovers, develops, and elaborates meaning through a systematic ordering of similarities that are conceptually and grammatically parallel. Since the writing of theology embraces both "logical" and "literary" categories, both of these definitions are comprehended in the theological understanding of analogy developed here, and we will return to them in a concluding section on "Writing Analogy Well." Construed theologically, however, analogy has been defined both as a philosophical-ontological concept, exemplified by the *classical* approach to analogy, and as a linguistic-rhetorical construct, exemplified by the *contemporary* approach to analogy. As we shall see, these approaches are not exclusive but interactive in writing the theological imagination well.

Analogy: Classical approaches

How does one speak of God, or write about God, when God is transcendent and infinite and the speaker or writer is human and finite? In response to this question, Thomas Aquinas posited a "principle of analogy" between God and God's creation, which we have called the *classical approach to analogy*.[20] Aquinas' principle of analogy is based upon a philosophical-ontological concept that predicates an "analogy of being" (*analogia entis*) between God and the world. Because God has expressed God's "Being" in every act of creation, all of created reality participates in "Being," even though the "being" of creature and Creator is not equivalent. Therefore attributes drawn from the realm of human experience can be predicated, or asserted, of God, neither univocally (in an identical way) nor equivocally (in a different way) but analogically (incorporating both identity and difference). Accordingly, we can say, or write, that the love of human parents for their children is analogous to the love of God the divine Parent for all of creation, even if the two "loves" are not identical. While our analogies will always "limp," Aquinas would say that without this analogical relation between God and creation, we could not speak or write about God at all.[21]

While the *classical approach to analogy* has been very vulnerable to theological imaginations that begin with the fact of sin, rather than grace, and contend that a God-initiated "analogy of faith" (*analogia fidei*) must precede any credible theological imaging,[22] its implicit theology of the creative process proves fruitful for theological writers. For example, when C.S. Song describes God as "imaging God's own self in humankind," and giving us "the ability to image all created things in relation to God,"[23] he is retrieving the resources of this classical approach to analogy to write the theological imagination well. When novelist Madeline L'Engle writes, "God is constantly creating in us, through us, with us, and to cooperate with God is our human calling,"[24] she is also making an analogy between God's creative activity and our own collaboration with it. Following her cue, every time that you draw upon the creative inspiration of God in writing a theological paper, you are invoking the classical principle of analogy.

Analogy: Contemporary approaches

If the *classical approach to analogy* begins with a philosophical-ontological concept, the *contemporary approach to analogy* begins as a linguistic-rhetorical construct. "Recent work on analogy," explains David Burrell, "concurs that it does not represent a theory nor a metaphysical contention, so much as a fact about language and the way we use language."[25] Linguistically, this approach engages analogy as a cognition-driven language practice through which we discern similarities and discover relationships between previously unrelated things in the process of making meaning. As Anne Berthoff describes, "Analogy is the principal means of articulating relationships and thus of forming concepts."[26] While Janet Soskice's definition of analogy differentiates it usefully from metaphor as a "linguistic device [that] deals with language that has been stretched to fit new applications, yet fits the new situation without generating for the native speaker any imaginative strain,"[27] analogy is on a linguistic continuum with metaphor and symbol,[28] and bleeds into them. Rhetorically, this contemporary approach embraces analogy as a communication-driven language practice used for specific theological purposes to address particular theological audiences, whether that purpose is to articulate an "analogical imagination" that characterizes the task of the systematic theologian,[29] to elucidate the theological use of analogy as a metaphorical extension of ordinary language,[30] or to retrieve analogical languages of affirmation and negation to critique exclusively androcentric God-talk.[31]

Your own linguistic-rhetorical uses of analogy may be more modest than those described above. Yet if you were to show me the most recent theological paper that you have written, I suspect that I could find more than one example of analogy embedded in its methodical structure, grammatical syntax, verbal imagery, and God language. If you have ever written a paper that asserts similarities between different theological methodologies or subject matter, you have begun to write analogy well.

If you have ever explained a difficult theological concept in a paragraph by making an analogy to something more common or less complex, you have begun to write analogy well. If you have ever developed a comparison of two theological or biblical themes using syntactically parallel sentences (e.g., "Just as…, so also…"), you have begun to write analogy well. If you have ever struggled to describe your own imagination of God in words that respect God's transcendence while reflecting your human experience, you have begun to write analogy well. To exemplify, we turn to a *writer-based approach to analogy* that invites us to join other theological writers in writing analogy well.

Writing with analogy well: A writer-based guide

We have looked briefly at the *classical* (philosophical-ontological) *approach* to analogy and the *contemporary* (linguistic-rhetorical) *approach* to analogy, both of which continue to inform the current theological landscape.[32] While I have distinguished these approaches for the purposes of this introduction, they are not so easily separated in practice, nor should they be. When we use language to speak and write about God, it will reflect our own understanding of language, human reality, and God. To use analogy well, then, you need not choose between these two approaches. Rather, by following the thread of your own theological imagination, you can weave them together into a *writer-based* approach to analogy employing (1) an analogical method, or rhetoric, to structure a theological paper; (2) analogical speech, or syntax, to shape theological subject matter into sentences and paragraphs; and (3) an analogical process of negation, to preserve the integrity of theological words pointing toward mystery, which will be exemplified in the theological memo that concludes this section.

Writing analogy well as analogical method, or rhetoric

First, theological writers use an analogical method, or rhetoric, to structure theological papers, as David Tracy does in *The Analogical Imagination*. By "analogical imagination," Tracy means the mind's innate capacity to say, "this is like that," in the midst of what is "different from that," and to draw out the implications of that similitude in an orderly manner that is reflected in the structure of the writing. By analogy, Tracy means a "*language* of ordered relationships articulating similarity-in-difference," in which "the order is developed by explicating the analogous relationships among various realities (self, others, world, God), by clarifying the relationship of each to the primary analogue, the meaning chosen as the primary focus for interpreting reality."[33] By "similarity-in-difference," Tracy means that things must be different to begin with in order for analogy to be fruitful. It takes no imagination to see the similarity between peas in a pod, but "to spot the similar in the dissimilar," writes Aristotle, "is a mark of poetic genius."[34] It is with such "similarity-in-difference" that the "analogical imagination" is concerned. Finally, this exercise of the analogical imagination has a hermeneutical goal—to draw classic doctrines of the Christian faith into contemporary reinterpretation in a theologically plural context, without compromising their essential meaning. Thus,

Christian systematic theology at its best exemplifies this "analogical imagination" as it unfolds creatively but systematically from its original analogue, "the event of Jesus Christ."[35]

Yet Tracy not only describes the analogical imagination as a systematic theological method; in so doing, he also unfolds a rhetorical structure for writing a theological essay that takes analogy, or "similarity-in-difference," as its starting point. Tracy employs this structure to discover the "similarity-in-difference" between theologies of "manifestation" (sacrament-based), "proclamation" (Word-based), and "prophetic action" (praxis-based), respectively, and finds a common denominator in their appeal to "grace," disclosed in Jesus Christ, as "the central clue to the nature of all reality."[36] Yet this same structure can be used for more modest theological projects. If, for example, you must analyze the positions of two or more theologians on particular doctrines or theologies, and conclude with your own creative appropriation of the doctrine for contemporary Christians, this "analogical" rhetoric can provide a suggestive template. Proceeding methodologically from the rhetoric of correlation that we examined in writing the constructive theological essay,[37] that structure includes: (1) identifying the classic and corresponding analogues, or analogical elements; (2) ordering the corresponding analogues; (3) explicating the similarities-in-difference; and (4) reimagining the classic analogue for contemporary audiences.[38]

Identifying the classic and corresponding analogues

Let us imagine that you have been assigned a systematic reflection paper requiring you to draw together the theologies of Augustine, Aquinas, and Luther, choosing one classic doctrine that each deals with distinctively. The first step is identifying and briefly introducing the classic analogue, or doctrine, that you will be writing about, and the corresponding analogues that you will be placing in relation to it. Following Tracy's cue, let us imagine that you choose "grace" (G) as your classic analogue, and Augustine's (G1), Aquinas' (G2), and Luther's (G3) understandings of grace as corresponding analogues. The first section of your paper should provide a brief introduction to the concept of grace that will serve as the classic analogue to which each corresponding construal of grace will be related. Your introduction should include a basic definition of the term and a concise overview of its biblical and theological significance, guided by the particular focus of your own paper.

Ordering the corresponding analogues

The second step is *ordering the corresponding analogues* (G1, G2, and G3) according to your own theological rationale. When in doubt, choose chronological order, as I have here, for it will provide its own logic and momentum as you proceed. On the other hand, you might choose other ordering principles that flow from your own theological priorities, such as beginning with the theologian closest to your own tradition, and concluding with the theologian most distant from it. The order you choose is an integral element in writing analogy well, and should provide a supple but steady ladder upon which your analogical imagination can move strategically from similarity to difference and back again.

Explicating the similarities-in-difference

The third step is *explicating the similarities-in-difference* between G1, G2, and G3, keeping in mind that difference is the soil in which seeds of analogy sprout. Sometimes the similarities between analogues will strike you more profoundly than the differences. At other times, you will struggle to find similarities within difference. If the differences prevail, you may need to write a different paper altogether; but if a common thread presents itself, you should proceed by (a) summarizing briefly each theologian's concept of grace; (b) describing and drawing out the implications of their differences, while keeping your writing hand on the pulse of the similarities you have discovered; and (c) identifying one or more common threads that run through the differences in a cogent, summarizing statement.

Reimagining the analogue

The fourth step is *reimagining the analogue* by offering your own appropriation of the concept of grace, flowing from the common river that you found running through the "graced" landscapes of Augustine, Aquinas, and Luther, filtered through the reservoir of your own analogical imagination. For example, in the study that inspired our hypothetical essay above, Roger Haight rediscovers grace as the experience of liberation upon which contemporary theologies of liberation are based.[39] David Tracy pursues grace across the diverse terrains of theologies of manifestation, proclamation, and prophetic action to find "the Love who is God" at the end of his journey.[40] Charting her own imagination of grace from the intersections of feminist theory and Calvinist tradition, Serene Jones reenvisions the local church as "*graced* community."[41] The theological memo that concludes this section will invite you to exercise your analogical imagination on a writing project of your own choosing. First, however, we look at writing analogy well with analogical paragraphs, sentences and words, respectively.

Writing analogy well with analogical speech and syntax

Analogy not only provides an analogical rhetoric to structure theological papers. It also inspires extended analogies by which theological writers shape theological subject matter into analogical paragraphs and sentences. For example, theologians frequently develop analogies from contemporary culture in order to answer a theological question or elaborate an *argument*, as John Hick does in the paragraph below. Drawing an analogy between the principle of complementarity in modern physics and the complementary ways in which human beings experience "the divine Reality," he writes:

> [C]an the divine Reality … be authentically experienced by millions of people as a personal God, and also by millions of others as the impersonal Brahman or Tao or Sunyata? Perhaps there is a helpful analogy in the principle of complementarity in modern physics. Electromagnetic radiation, including light, is sometimes found to behave like waves and sometimes like particles. If we experiment upon it in one way we discover a wave-like radiation, whilst if we experiment upon it

> in another way we discover a procession of particles. The two observations have both had to be accepted as valid and hence as complementary.... Analogously, it seems the case that when humans "experiment" with the Real in one kind of way—the way of theistic thought and worship—they find the Real to be personal, and when other humans approach the Real in a different kind of way—the way for example of Buddhist or Hindu thought and meditation—they find the real to be non-personal. This being so, we may well emulate the scientist in their realistic acceptance of the two sets of reports concerning the real as complementary truths.[42]

Writing analogical paragraphs well

If you look carefully, you will see that Hick's extended analogy follows a similar pattern as the structure for an "analogical" paper.[43] However, like most extended analogies, it does not dwell upon "difference," but builds rather upon the similarities of the analogues that are elucidated in the paragraph. After pressing the question that prompts the comparison, Hick (1) identifies the primary analogue (the principle of complementarity); (2) elaborates it in a few carefully crafted sentences that describe the dual (wave and particle) perspectives of electromagnetic radiation; (3) explicates the corresponding analogue, that is, the theistic and non-theistic ways of construing the "divine Reality"; and (4) argues in conclusion for theologians to be instructed by the scientific analogy, and to "reimagine" their own theological perspectives accordingly.

Writing analogical sentences well

This use of extended analogy operates analogically on the level of the sentence as well. See, for example, the consistency of David Tracy's syntactic parallelism in the extended analogy that he draws between Christian systematic theology and the English Language (the syntactic parallels are highlighted in italics):

> *We find ourselves in* Christianity *as we find ourselves in* the English language: an incredibly dense forest of syntax, grammar, history; a forest which grew not in the manner of the gardens of Versailles—the manner of theory—but in the manner of history itself into ever-changing, ever-stable possibilities of meaningful communication.... *Fortunately, however*, for reading and writing English... *there is a syntax and a grammar* which have remained relatively stable in this history-laden forest of a language—a forest which is in truth our primary home for whatever meaning we may grasp.... *There also exists, again fortunately, a basic grammar* for Christian systematic theology....[44]

Through this analogy that imagines both the English language and Christian systematic theology as dense, impenetrable forests, Tracy asserts that Christianity is a language, just as English is a language, and that systematic theology provides a grammar for the language of Christianity, just as the English language possesses a conventional grammar that regulates its use. At the same time that he makes this conceptual analogy, the syntactic structures of his own writing (e.g., "*we find ourselves in* Christianity *as we find ourselves in* the English language") exemplify and reinforce the analogy. We will look further at the uses of syntactic sentence structures to compare and contrast theological subject matter in Chapter 11. When these syntactic structures are used to form extended analogies, they are operating analogically as well. For example, the sentence, "Just as Christology is the theology of Jesus of Nazareth, so too ecclesiology is the theology of the Christian community in history," introduces an extended analogy linking Christology and ecclesiology.[45] Yet at the deepest level, analogy inheres in the basic building block of language—the word. In order to probe these depths, we turn in conclusion to analogical words, and the theological writer's struggle to articulate the mystery to which they point.

Writing analogical words well

If, as Elizabeth Johnson writes at the beginning of this section, "[a]nalogy shapes every category of words used to speak about God,"[46] then we can expect to find an analogical imagination both informing and critiquing the words we choose to write theology well. As Aquinas first proposed, "Words are used of God and creatures according to an analogy, that is a certain proportion, between them,"[47] and this correlation, however contested, continues to inform theological writing. Yet Aquinas also cautioned that analogical words point to God's mystery; they do not possess it univocally. Given the ever-present tendency to interpret the language of analogy as literal information about God, this caveat continues to chasten theological writers. As an antidote, Elizabeth Johnson retrieves the analogical process of "affirmation, negation, and eminence" developed by early Christian theologians to speak about God in words derived from experience but destined to transcendence:

> A word whose meaning is known and prized from human experience is first affirmed of God. The same word is then critically negated to remove any association with creaturely modes of being. Finally, the word is predicated of God in a supereminent way that transcends all cognitive capabilities. For example, when we say that God is good, the movement of meaning carried in the reference to God also indicates that God is not good the way creatures are good, but God is good in an excellent way as source of all that is good. At this point we can no longer conceive the meaning of the word good, although it continues to point in the direction of holy mystery.[48]

If this classical trajectory of affirmation, negation and transcendence strikes you as an arcane theological exercise in verbal hairsplitting, I invite you to compare its conceptual movements with your own struggle to find words that fit the meanings you wish to convey in a typical theological paper. If you are a writer who weighs every word carefully and waits patiently for the right word to break through your incoherence, you are no stranger to this analogous process of articulating words hopefully, retracting them fitfully, and finally returning to the word that will best bear your meaning, however imperfectly. In the same way, classical and contemporary theologians seek to correct their analogical imaginations through the purifying process of negation, lest their analogies become perfunctory and their imaginations of God illusory. Before we move on to writing metaphor well, the theological memo below invites you to apply your own "analogical imagination" to the process of "affirmation, negation and eminence" described above, and/or to write a theological essay employing David Tracy's "analogical rhetoric":

THEOLOGICAL MEMO 2: This theological memo unfolds in two parts:

(A) Following Elizabeth Johnson's example above, (1) please complete the affirmation "God is__________________" with a word that is rooted in your own experience and context (e.g., loving, wise, powerful, compassionate). (2) Follow this affirmation with a statement of negation that circumscribes and redefines the word in its God-directed context by "removing any association with creaturely modes of being." (3) Finally, re-affirm the word attributed to God "supereminently," or without any human qualification, in a statement that points your reader "in the direction of holy mystery."

(B) When you have completed this process, please prepare a hypothetical outline for a theological paper that uses David Tracy's "analogical rhetoric" to develop the previous exercise into a more substantial project that places your reformulated "God-word" in relation with analogous or different imaginations of that word.

Writing with metaphor well

Metaphor: An introduction

If analogy asserts that something is *like* something else in corresponding ways but different in others, metaphor states that something *is* something else, which, literally speaking, it is not. This general definition of metaphor and its relation to analogy will be refined as we proceed. However, even before we can define them perfectly, Walter Brueggemann reminds us, "Our life is fed and shaped by our metaphors."[49] Thus, recognizing metaphor in the biblical and theological writing that you read and using metaphorical language effectively in your own writing are critical skills for theological writers. "The most important thing is to be good at metaphor," Aristotle advised his students, "for making good metaphors depends on perceiving the likenesses in things."[50] But how, then, does the language of metaphor differ from the language of analogy?

While Roman Catholic theologian Elizabeth Johnson conceives all theological words, including metaphors, as "shaped" by analogy, Protestant theologian Sallie McFague distinguishes between the "analogical" and "metaphorical" languages of theology, contending that the language of analogy begins with *similarity*, while the language of metaphor begins with *dissimilarity*.[51] Taken at face value, this assertion may oversimplify a more nuanced conversation between theologians for whom an "analogical imagination" responds effectively to the challenges of writing theology in the twenty-first century, and those for whom the language of metaphor more adequately addresses that task.[52] Nevertheless, these two starting points direct us to two broader interdisciplinary approaches to metaphor that lead to different ways of construing it, which will enable us to answer the question, How can an understanding of metaphor and the words comprising them help us to write the theological imagination well?

Metaphor: The word-based approach

According to contemporary theorists, there are two ways of approaching metaphor that inform its definition in particular contexts. The first, and more traditional approach, is *word-based*: with Aristotle and a long line of literary critics after him, it defines "metaphor" as a particular kind of *word* that is compared with another word to produce a "figure of speech" that re-names the first word.[53] From this perspective, the word "metaphor" is defined as an implicit comparison[54] between two dissimilar things ("My love *is* a rose"), in which the "*similarity* within dissimilarity" is emphasized; it functions broadly as a noun, or name-word and is interpreted as a surface feature of language, or as an element of literary or rhetorical "style."[55]

When metaphor is construed on the level of the word as a rhetorical embellishment rather than a constitutive element of language itself, it is relegated to the realm of "mere" word choices and stylistic effects, and related to "what I write" rather than to "how I think." For example, I might decide that my love was more like a "sunflower" than a rose, and revise the metaphor accordingly, but the substitution of "sunflower" for "rose" would not radically alter the basic meaning of my assertion that my love was like a "flower." Thus, say its contemporary critics, a mastery of this *word-based* use of metaphor may enhance writing style rhetorically, but its use of language is incidental, not instrumental.[56]

Metaphor: The sentence-based approach

The second, more contemporary approach to metaphor is *sentence-based:* it defines metaphor in the context of the full sentence in which it appears and locates it in the deep structures of language because it understands metaphor as constitutive of the way that we use language to think and communicate. As I.A. Richards and Paul Ricoeur would explain, without the complete sentence, "My love is a sunflower," I do not have a metaphor; I simply have the word "love"—the *tenor* of the metaphor; and the word "sunflower"—the *vehicle* of the metaphor.[57] Moreover, without the verb "is" linking *tenor* ("love") and *vehicle* ("sunflower"), there would be no metaphor. Thus, metaphors do not merely name what we already know by another name; they predicate something new that could not be known without them. In this sense, they are not merely "pretty words"; they are "propositions that, if taken literally, would be absurd."[58]

Nevertheless, they are propositions of a particularly critical kind for theological writers, in that this construal of metaphor is characterized by its capacity to hold in tension two dissimilar, or opposing things in which the writer has, as Aristotle wrote, "perceived similarities," and in so doing, as Paul Ricoeur writes, to "tell us something new about reality."[59] Building upon this understanding, but bending it back toward the level of the word in spite of herself, McFague defines metaphor as "a word or phrase" that is used, not appropriately, but "inappropriately."[60] For McFague, the "impropriety" of the word interrupts our habitual response to it, thus opening us to a deeper and more profound comprehension of the similitude it images.

For example, if the minister of your very traditional congregation were to lead the congregation in the Lord's Prayer using the words, "Our Mother, who art in heaven," parishioners accustomed to addressing God as "Father" might be shocked. Following their initial shock, they might complain to the minister that the word *mother* was used inappropriately in the Lord's Prayer. Yet for some, the common human experience of mothering or being mothered might temper their shock and open their imaginations to the "similarity in difference" implicit in the image. Those parishioners who return to church the next week might begin to hear the word *mother* metaphorically, and find their God language enriched accordingly. If the metaphor has sufficient "staying power" to become a "model,"[61] the similarities will be perceived more readily than the differences, and they may be expressed "analogically," as Julian of Norwich anticipates in her well-known meditation on God as Mother in Jesus, the second person of the Trinity:

> As truly as God is our Father, so truly is God our Mother, and he revealed that in everything…I am he, the power and goodness of fatherhood; I am he, the wisdom and the lovingness of motherhood… [and]….From this it follows, that as truly as God is our Father, so truly is God our Mother….And so Jesus is our true Mother in nature by our first creation, and he is our true Mother in grace by his taking our created nature. All the lovely works and all the sweet loving offices of beloved motherhood are appropriated to the second person, in whom we have this goodly will, whole and safe forever, both in nature and in grace….[62]

For McFague, if not for all Christian congregations, the metaphor, "God is Mother" has achieved the status of a "model." Yet she continues to teach us that an effective theological vocabulary must begin with discontinuity, dissimilarity, and the ever-present tension of "and it is not."[63] In so doing, she also moves adroitly between metaphorical "words" and the metaphorical models informing them,[64] just as Julian of Norwich does in the passage above. At their best, these metaphors stretch our theological imaginations without abandoning the tradition that engenders them, just as many biblical metaphors of God, like "the Lord is my shepherd," were initially subversive but have now become "traditional."[65]

Yet what is conventionally "analogical" for me may be an unsettling "metaphor" to you, and if the metaphor is too unsettling, you may not be able to follow my use of the word or image. For example, while Kwok Pui Lan surveys contemporary christological metaphors of Jesus as "Corn Mother," "The Feminine Shakti" and "The Theological Transvestite" in an article addressed to a culturally diverse audience of religious scholars,[66] she might present the same images in a more pastoral way if she were inviting white middle-class American women at her local parish with little background in feminist theology to expand their metaphorical imaginations of Jesus. Conversely, what is metaphorically "shocking" to you may be "business as usual" to me. Thus metaphors and the metaphorical words that express them are only as effective as the theological writers who choose them and the audiences that receive them, and even then, their acceptance may be fraught with tension and struggle. While McFague defines metaphor as a word or phrase used "inappropriately," her final criterion for adequate God-metaphors for women is "whether they are *appropriate* ones in which to suggest dimensions of the new divine-human relationship intrinsic to the [Christian] tradition."[67]

Toward a writer-based approach to metaphor

We have looked here at two approaches to metaphor—*word-based* and *sentence-based*—that form part of the contemporary theological conversation. To use metaphor well, you need not choose between these two approaches, but rather to "hold them in tension" as you forge your own *writer-based* approach to the use of metaphor in theological writing. As we have seen, Aristotle himself described the metaphor-making process as "*perceiving* similarities" in disparate things, not merely as replacing one word for another; but he recognized with all writers of literature that metaphors are comprised of words, even if not all words are metaphors. Moreover, theologian Sallie McFague's metaphorical method invites us to move freely but deliberately between metaphor at the level of the word (and the phrase) to that of the sentence, and to the more systematic structure of metaphorical models, without sacrificing one for the other.

At the same time, the sentence-based approach to metaphor correctly asserts that a complete metaphor is syntactically enclosed in a sentence; it does not signify as a metaphor without a tenor, a vehicle, and a predicating verb. The sentence-based approach also invites us to relate the metaphorical language that we employ to the metaphorical models informing it. From either starting point, metaphor is a way of getting from where we are to where we are not, and words are the vehicles that get us there. To do that, you will at times need to use metaphorical language that asserts similarity, or "stock" metaphors, by which I mean metaphors that are already available to you from the Christian tradition. At other times you will need to use "shock" metaphors, some of which also come from the Christian tradition,[68] but by which I mean "live" metaphors that emerge from your own theological reflection, and which, as Paul Ricouer explains, may not be found in any dictionary.[69] In sum, we need words *and* sentences, similarity *and* dissimilarity, "stock" metaphors *and* "shock" metaphors to write theology well, as we shall see in the following guide to writing with metaphors.

Writing with metaphor well: A writer-based guide

Every time that you write a theological paper, you think in metaphors and write with metaphors. Moreover, behind the metaphors that you write with are metaphorical concepts that reflect your view of reality.[70] For example, when Roger Haight asks, "How does one *arrive at* a theological *position*?"[71] the metaphorical concept, "a (theological) position is a journey" is embedded in the verb "arrive at." However, if Haight had written, "How does one *take* a theological position?" he would have consciously or unconsciously invoked the metaphorical concept, "a (theological) position is war."[72] The metaphorical constructs that I cite here from the work of linguist George Lakoff and philosopher Mark Johnson may be caricatures, but they reiterate the point made earlier that metaphorical language is integral to the meaning that we wish to convey.

Thus, our focus here is on the language that you choose to express metaphorical concepts in the process of writing theology well. When the poet Robert Burns first wrote, "My love is a red, red rose," that rose sent deep roots down into the soil of his poetry, so that we continue today to speak of roses as communicating the language of love. In the same way, the metaphorical language that you use—whether consciously or unconsciously—should be rooted organically in your own conceptual process of writing theology well. That being said, metaphors and the metaphorical words that comprise them serve strategic purposes in theological writing, on the level of the word, the sentence, and the larger structure of the work.

First, theological writers use metaphors to describe their writing process and methodological plan, as Serene Jones deftly describes her process of "Mapping Feminist Theory and Theology" in *Feminist Theory and Christian Theology: Cartographies of Grace*:

> Taking up the role of cartographer in the pages ahead I lay feminist theory over the terrain or landscape of Christian doctrine to see how the lines of theory might map the contours of theology. I like the image of remapping because it captures well the fact that feminist theory's principal contribution to theology lies in analyzing and reorienting the conceptual markers that Christians use to describe the terrain of their faith. The cartographical metaphor makes clear feminist theory is concerned not so much to reconstruct the terrain of faith as to provide markers for traveling through the terrain in new ways.[73]

While the metaphor of "mapping" is rapidly becoming a "stock" metaphor rather than a "shock" metaphor, Jones applies her "cartographic metaphor" creatively and with precision to the theological task of defining the relationship between feminist theory and feminist theology. What other metaphors might aptly and accurately describe the writing process and methodological plan of your next theological essay?

Second, theological writers use metaphors to name and describe transcendent subject matter. If, for example, you are reading or writing christology, you will not get very far without encountering metaphor. However domesticated it has become in the contemporary language of faith, Peter's christological confession, and "You are the Christ, the Son of the living God" (Matt 16:15) is a metaphor that challenged many of its original hearers. Similarly, Roger Haight identifies "And the Word became flesh" (John 1:14), or "incarnation," as "the foundational metaphor for understanding Jesus Christ that underlies Logos Christology."[74] Similarly, when Jon Sobrino writes of the "unprotected masses" murdered in El Salvador that "[t]hey are the Suffering Servant and they are the crucified Christ today," he is using language that is simultaneously metaphorical and christological.[75] If you were asked to write a christology paper in answer to the question, "Who do you say that I am?" what metaphorical language might you employ to articulate your own christology?

Third, theological writers employ metaphor to name and frame their theologies, as Sallie McFague unfolds a Christian nature spirituality through the lens of a metaphorical theology in her narrative exegesis of the metaphor (and book title) *Super, Natural Christians*,[76] or as Kevin Burke employs Ignacio Ellacuria's metaphor of "the ground beneath the cross" as the title and organizing metaphor of his book,

The Ground Beneath the Cross: The Theology of Ignacio Ellacuria. Finally, Elizabeth Johnson borrows Pope Paul VI's felicitous metaphor of Mary as "truly our sister" to provide a title and root metaphor for her book, *Truly our Sister: A Theology of Mary in the Communion of Saints*. What suggestive metaphors from your own reading might you combine with a designated topic to provide a title and a structure for your next theological essay?

Fourth, metaphors are used to make theological assertions, using both the logic of predication and the lure of the image. For example, David Tracy calls the Johannine assertion that "God is love" (I John 4:6b) "the central Christian metaphor," adding that "if one has never been scandalized by this central Christian metaphor—and the ancients were right to be scandalized—one has never understood its radicality and its oddness."[77] Yet theological metaphors do not merely assert that "God is love." They also describe the shape, texture, and contours of that mystery through images drawn from human experience. As Roger Haight explains, "Religious language always has a metaphorical structure, because the referent God is always conceived implicitly 'like' what is conveyed by ordinary language about this-worldly objects."[78] According to Rebecca Chopp, who likens the practice of feminist theology to a communal piecing together of "the warming quilt of God," the "metaphor of quilting ... names the reality of how women begin to describe the work and task of theology":

> Theology no longer uncovers unchangeable foundations or hands down the cognitive truths of tradition or discloses the classics or even figures out the rules of faith, as suggested by modern and contemporary metaphors of doing the work of theology. Rather, quilting, weaving and constructing become the focus of theological work as a communal process of bringing "scraps" of materials used elsewhere and joining them in new ways.[79]

How might metaphors drawn from your own experience render your own theological assertions more lucid and credible?

Fifth, metaphors can organize and unify a sentence, paragraph, or longer text, just as John's Jesus declares, "I am the vine, you are the branches" (John 15:6) and proceeds to elaborate the metaphor describing the organic relationship between his disciples (the *branches*) and himself (the *vine*) to produce a unified discourse (John 15). In order to sustain textual coherence, however, the writer must use metaphorical language carefully and consistently. For example, if the author of John's gospel had written, "I am the vine, and you are the fishes," the "mixed" metaphors would interrupt the unity of the text. Yet for many people, "I am the vine, you are the branches" has become a dead metaphor, or a metaphor that has been deadened either by hearing it too often or by hearing it literally rather than figuratively.[80] Thus, one of the tasks of the theological writer is to make the "dry bones" of familiar biblical metaphors live. Biblical theologian Walter Brueggemann argues further that "the pulpit ... is the place for imaginative speech" that is formed at the intersection of "the text and the tradition that give us material for new metaphors" and "the present reality ... which energizes and illuminates the metaphors."[81] How well did you do this in your last biblical exegesis paper or sermon?

Sixth, theological writers employ metaphor in order to conjoin literal and figurative language in their theological articulations. While Sandra Schneiders asserts correctly that metaphors make statements that would be "absurd if taken literally," metaphorical language weaves both literal and figurative senses into a new fabrication of reality. Choosing the metaphorical concept of "discovery" to describe her task in *More Than Chains and Toil: A Christian Work Ethic of Enslaved Women*, womanist theo-ethicist Joan Martin names that task "both literal and figurative": "finding blackwomen's historical experience of work ... internal perspectives of blackwomen themselves, and ... their external perspectives on colonialism, enslavement and oppression."[82] In other words, Martin approached the enslaved black women whose stories were included in her book both literally—as historical persons whose stories she recounted as "sacred texts"—and figuratively, as the collective "voices of enslaved Christian women" whose moral agency forged a work ethic that was "more than chains and toil."[83] How effectively have you conjoined literal and metaphorical language in your last theological paper?

Finally, and most importantly, theological writers use metaphors appropriately, and that "propriety" is determined by the theological writing task that they are engaging. As Sallie McFague explains, "Theologians ... are poets insofar as they must be sensitive to the metaphors and models that are at once consonant with the Christian faith and appropriate for expressing that faith in their own time, and they are philosophers insofar as they must elucidate in a coherent, comprehensive, and systematic way the implications of these metaphors and models."[84] To be sure, some of the theological papers that you write will require the systematic language of the philosopher. Others will give you the license to write as the poet you were born to be, especially when your task is that of re-invigorating traditional metaphors that have lost their force by looking at them through contemporary lenses. Most of the papers that you write will fall somewhere between both of these, in the continuing tradition of a "middle style" that integrates the poet's language of metaphor with the theologian's conceptual clarity. Before we move on to the language of symbol, I invite you with Karl Barth to reflect metaphorically on the discipline of theology as poet, philosopher, or a felicitous combination of both, in the following Theological Memo:

> *THEOLOGICAL MEMO 3: Aristotle tells his students that the metaphors they employ should arise from their own experience, and at the same time connect with the experience of their readers. Drawing from his European context, Karl Barth described the discipline of theology as "a landscape, like the landscape of Umbria or Tuscany, in which distant perspectives are always clear," and continued, "Theology is a masterpiece, as well-planned and yet as bizarre as the cathedrals of Cologne and Milan."[85] Following the example of Barth's metaphors, write a brief reflection that completes the assertion "Theology is ..." with a metaphor or metaphors from your own experience and exercise of theological imagination.*

Building a bridge from metaphor to symbol: An interlude

What is the relationship between metaphor and symbol, and why is it important? If metaphor asserts that something *is* something else, which, literally speaking, it is not (A *is/not* B), symbol is that "something else" bearing significance in and of itself and pointing beyond itself (A⇒ *or* B⇒).[86] For example, when you send your love roses with a card that says, "You are the most beautiful rose in my garden," your metaphor limits the signification of the roses. But if your card simply says, "Love," the roses will signify your love for her, but the symbol will not be limited by the terms of the initial metaphor. Like the shawl of Jean Diego that was unwrapped to reveal miraculous roses that left an imprint of the Virgin's apparition on the cloth, your roses might also bear the imprint of transcendence, and move your love to praise the God who created them.

When this wider range of signification evokes the transcendent, Paul Tillich contends, "symbolic language alone is able to express the ultimate" because "it opens up levels of reality that are otherwise closed to us."[87] Yet for Paul Ricoeur, "symbols have roots" that bind them to the cosmos while metaphor, with its origin in language and the poetic imagination, possesses a freedom to reinvent reality that is not available to the symbol.[88] Similarly, for Sallie McFague, symbol tends to become tied to traditional theological language and is therefore less malleable than metaphor in the process of theological construction. While acknowledging that "symbols need metaphors, for without them they are dumb," and "metaphors need symbols, for without them they lose their rootedness in life," she finds that metaphors redescribe reality, while symbols are more likely to reinscribe it.[89] Roger Haight, on the other hand, employs symbol as the primary mode of his own theological imagination, and describes metaphor as a precise kind of conceptual symbol; but he nonetheless suggests that "descriptions of how the metaphor functions resemble the dynamics of symbols." He thus sees the languages of symbol and metaphor as equally functional for bridging the gap between similarity and difference in doing theology.[90] Finally, Elizabeth Johnson commends analogy, metaphor and symbol to her readers as comparable elements of the theological imagination when she writes, "Speech about God is always indirect, having a metaphorical, analogical, or symbolic character."[91]

In the end, both metaphor and symbol and the dynamics informing them enable theological writers to negotiate the clash between literal and non-literal levels of meaning common to religious language and religious texts. Both metaphor and symbol enable writers, and in particular, theological writers, to respect the dialectical nature of "words about God," in the knowledge that the metaphor or symbol both "is and is not" what is symbolized. Consequently, both metaphor and symbol allow writers, and in particular, theological writers, to transcend literal language at the same time that they are using it to make clear, focused, and credible theological assertions. Both metaphor and symbol require writers, and especially theological writers, to balance the concrete and conceptual elements of their theological statements. Finally, both metaphor and symbol invite writers, and in particular, theological writers, to participate in the metaphoric and symbolic processes that they are probing through the very act of writing, or "working out a theology as they go." But how do theological writers employ symbol specifically as a rhetoric, or purposeful element in writing the theological imagination well? To answer this question, we go to the final section of this chapter, "Writing with Symbol Well."

Writing with symbol well

Symbol: An introduction

If recognizing, using, and writing metaphor well is critical to the writing of theology, recognizing, using, and writing with symbol is equally crucial. Human beings, writes Kenneth Burke, are "symbol-using, symbol-making and symbol-misusing" animals.[92] We use a system of commonly shared symbols called "language" to communicate with other people. These symbol systems are human creations, borne of our capacity to abstract, generalize, and agree upon the meaning of symbols through that process of abstraction and generalization. Thus, human beings are symbol-makers as well as symbol-users, and symbols provide a common language for those who embrace them. Yet symbols can unite and divide, liberate and manipulate, enlighten and deceive, invite love, or incite hatred. In short, symbols can be misused, but according to Burke, "the use of language as a symbolic means of inducing cooperation in beings that by nature respond to symbols"[93] also provides the antidote: "writing with symbol well."

It is the theologian's nature, no less than the rhetorician's, to respond to symbols. As Roger Haight suggests, "Theology is a symbolic discipline.... From beginning to end it deals with symbols."[94] Yet theological writers are not immune from the misuse of symbol, and must learn to read, write, and interpret the language of symbol in order to use it effectively. But in order to use symbol well, it is first necessary to define it. Thus, Paul Tillich advises theological writers, and "every writer who uses the term 'symbol'... [to] explain his [or her] understanding of it."[95] We begin, then, with four starting points for defining symbol that provide a composite, writer-based definition of symbol. Finally, we suggest specific ways for theological writers to write with symbol well.

Definitions of symbol: Four starting points

While the use of symbol is common to many disciplines, a common definition of symbol is hard to find.[96] As described here, symbols are literal objects, entities, artifacts, persons, events, texts, or concepts that have a meaning beyond their literal signification which must be interpreted. But in order to be interpreted, symbols must first be identified as symbols, and how we identify and interpret a symbol will depend upon how we define the word "symbol." Even within the discipline of theology, the word "symbol" is construed differently, depending upon the starting point from which it is defined. Therefore, we look below at four starting points for defining symbol as theological readers and writers: (1) the *sign-based* definition of symbol; (2) the *meaning-based* definition of symbol; (3) the *mediation-based* definition of symbol; and (4) the *text-based* definition of symbol.

Sign-based definition of symbol

From this starting point, a symbol is something that (a) points to what it signifies but (b) does not "participate in that to which it points."[97] When, for example, God "set a bow in the clouds" to symbolize his covenant with Noah (Gen 9:12–17), the rainbow was a "sign" of the covenant but not synonymous with it. According to this definition, a "symbol" is virtually identical with a "sign." For Kenneth Burke, for example, words function symbolically as "signs" that point to the things that they signify but remain separate from them, whether their referents are concrete objects (like a "tree") or conceptual realities (such as "grace").[98] Similarly, the mathematical symbol "r" in the formula "πr^2" signifies the radius of the circle but is not identical with it. Embracing a semiotic continuum, then, that extends from simple traffic signs to traditional symbols like the hawk and the dove, the *sign-based* definition of symbol is common to the disciplines of linguistics, philosophy, science, and mathematics.

However, this *sign-based* conception of symbol also informs the understanding of religious writers and theologians for whom symbols represent the realities they signify but remain to some degree distinct from them. For example, John Calvin uses "sign" and "symbol" interchangeably to refer to the eucharistic elements of bread and wine, which "represent the invisible food which we receive from the holy body and blood of Christ."[99] While he cautions on the one hand against dissevering the *signs* "from their meanings to which they are in some degree annexed," he acknowledges on the other hand "that the breaking of the bread is a *symbol*, not the reality."[100]

Similarly, the *Book of Common Prayer* uses the words "symbol" and "sign" interchangeably in the Celebration and Blessing of a Marriage. When the celebrant asks God's blessing on the couple's wedding rings, he or she prays, "Bless, O Lord, this ring to be a *sign* of the vows by which this man and this woman have bound themselves to each other," and when the couple exchange rings, they say to each other, "I give you this ring as a *symbol* of my vow . . . ."[101] The operative definition of symbol is that of sign; the wedding ring is a sign of the wedding vows but it does not participate integrally in them, as the couple pronouncing them do. Finally, when writer Mary McCarthy called the Roman Catholic sacrament of the Eucharist a good "symbol," and Flannery O'Connor retorted, "If it's a symbol, the hell with it," O'Connor was equating McCarthy's use of the word "symbol" with sign, and thereby distinguishing the sacrament of Christ's "real presence" from a symbol that merely "pointed to" that reality.[102]

However the term is construed, every symbol begins as a sign that points us beyond itself. Perhaps every *sign-based symbol* is like a rainbow that transfixes us with its brilliance while pointing us beyond it to the pot of gold, or to Oz, or—for theological writers—to the God of the covenant who created it. Thus, when you encounter a *sign-based* approach to symbol in a theologian's work, first ask yourself, "How does the writer define *sign* and *symbol*?" Then ask yourself, "What does the symbol point to?" Finally, ask yourself, "What does the symbol mean?" That question will lead you to the *meaning-based* definition of symbol that we turn to next.

Meaning-based definition of symbol

If the first defining moment of a symbol is its capacity to point to what it signifies, the second defining moment is its meaning-making and meaning-bearing potency. From this starting point, a symbol is a concrete object or entity—a stone, a rainbow, a loaf of bread, a tree —which is set apart because of the meaning that it embodies and evokes. The meaning can come from the cosmos, from culture, from religious experience of the sacred, or from deep within the human psyche.[103] It can be inherent in the object, or it can be attributed to the object by the beholder. Marked by this meaning, stone, rainbow, bread, and tree become *more than* they were before, while remaining what they are.[104]

For example, when Jacob awoke from his dream of the angelic ladder and its climactic theophany, the stone that served as his pillow became *more than* just any stone; it became a sacred object and simultaneously a symbol of God's dwelling that he marked "as a memorial stone" (Gen 28:16–18). Similarly, when contemporary poet Conrad Aiken writes, "Music I heard with you was more than music, And bread I broke with you was more than bread," the "more than" saturates the symbols through the communion of the lovers.[105] Yet the *meaning-based symbol* also functions as a *sign*, and John Calvin conflates them in his interpretation of Adam's tree of life and Noah's rainbow as "signs" placed by God "in natural objects" and inscribed with new meaning through the Word: "the tree was previously a tree, and the bow is a bow: but when they were inscribed with the word of God ... they began to be what they previously were not."[106]

Yet *meaning-based* symbols are "more than" signs: they do not just point to the reality they signify; they are bearers of meaning in their own right, and produce what Paul Ricoeur describes as a "surplus of meaning" in the process of being interpreted.[107] However, *meaning-based* symbols eschew abstraction; they depend upon a dynamic interaction with meaning-bearing objects for their efficacy. Their meaning may proliferate but remain rooted in immanent reality, as does the rose that inspired Gertrude Stein's "a rose is a rose is a rose."[108] Conversely, it may open the door to transcendence, like the rose that exfoliated for Dante into a symbol of beatification with God.[109] When a *meaning-based* symbol bears the presence of the transcendent, it becomes analogous to a "concrete" religious symbol, which embraces "things, places, events, or persons, which mediate a presence and consciousness of another reality."[110] In correlation, then, with the meaning-bearing entities that elicit them, *meaning-based* construals of symbol are common to psychoanalysis, anthropology, sociology, literature, and theology, in which they are central to the practice of theological reflection, the interpretation of Christian doctrine, and the celebration of liturgy.[111]

Perhaps every *meaning-based symbol* is like a ladder that we climb between sleep and waking to move between what a symbol points to and what it means. Thus, when you encounter a *meaning-based* approach to symbol in these contexts, first ask yourself, "What is the *meaning-bearing object* that activates the symbol?" Then ask yourself, "What is the *meaning* conveyed by the symbol?" Finally, ask yourself, "How is that *meaning* communicated, or *mediated*, by the symbol?" That question will lead you to the *mediation-based* definition of symbol, which we turn to next.

Mediation-based definition of symbol

If the first defining moment of a symbol is its capacity to point to what it signifies, and the second defining moment is its meaning-making and meaning-bearing potency, the third defining moment of symbol is its mediation of a meaning or reality that transcends the symbol itself. In the sense that we are using it here, "mediation" refers to the act of symbolic communication whereby a symbol not only "points" and "means," but also "mediates" a meaning or reality that could not be known without the symbol. While every symbol points to a meaning beyond itself and proliferates meaning that is "more than" itself, a *mediation-based symbol* also "participates" in that to which it points and means, and invites participation in that reality, which we identify here as the transcendent reality of God.[112] However, *mediation-based* symbols not only reveal and make present the transcendent God; they also mediate a personal relationship between human beings and God.[113]

For example, when Moses beheld the flaming bush in the shadow of Mount Horeb that "burned but was not consumed," it functioned first as a *sign-based symbol* that *pointed* him toward the transcendent God, by prompting him to "turn aside and look at this great sight...." But it was not enough for Moses to see the flames rising from the middle of the bush. He also wanted to know what they *meant*. When Moses began to ponder "why the bush [was] not burned up" (Exod 3:3), it functioned, secondly, as a *meaning-based symbol* that might well have led him to interpret the fire as a sign of God's presence (see Gen 15:17; Exod 19:18; Ps 104:3–4; Ezek 1:27). But it is one thing to identify the meaning of a symbol, and quite another thing to encounter God in the symbol. When God addresses Moses from the bush that continues to burn but is not consumed (Exod 3:4), it functions, finally, as a *mediation-based* symbol that not only participates in the theophany that the divine fire and voice mediate, but also invites Moses to participate in a personal relationship with the God of his ancestors by planting his bare feet upon the holy ground staked out by the symbol.

Yet Moses' fiery encounter with the God of his ancestors was more than a means of personal revelation. It was a mode of symbolic communication, conveyed by the symbol of the burning bush and the voice that it mediated. We have already defined "mediation" as a form of symbolic communication. How, then, does a *mediation-based symbol* communicate? Three characteristics of this process are critical for reading, interpreting, and writing with symbol.[114]

First, *mediation-based symbols* are driven by a theory of symbolic realism, which affirms that symbols are not mere signs, but truly participate in the realities that they signify. This assertion is grounded in the conviction that symbols really are what they say they are, and really do what they say that they do. In other words, the burning bush really was a burning bush, and it really did communicate God's reality and make the God of his ancestors present to Moses.

Second, *mediation-based symbols* operate dialectically,[115] which means that they both are and are not what they literally signify. For Moses, the God of his ancestors was truly present in the burning bush, disclosed as a divine voice speaking from the tongues of flame. At the same time, the burning bush was "not" God; it remained an ordinary desert bush, irradiated by a brush fire, or by the setting sun, or by Moses' visionary experience. Just as we saw the "is and is not" of metaphor constantly in play in the language of classical and contemporary theology, the "dialectical" quality of symbol functions analogously as a vehicle of symbolic communication.

Finally, *mediation-based symbols* elicit the engaged participation of the one interpreting the symbol. Not every shepherd herding flocks in the shadow of Mount Horeb noticed the burning bush, but Moses did. Not everyone walking on a beach "sees a world in a grain of sand," but the poet William Blake did.[116] However, without the responsive participation of prophet, poet, or theological writer from the depths of their own faith and imagination, there would be no symbolic communication.

The mediation-based symbol and the religious symbol

Mediation-based symbols are also known as "religious symbols" in the writing of contemporary theologians. Like any *mediation-based symbol*, a *religious symbol* both points to something beyond it and participates in the reality to which it points. As we have already seen, religious symbols point to, participate in, and make present the transcendent reality of God.[117] Yet Stephen Happel reminds us that "religious value is not added to the symbol as though propositional doctrines were aggregated to an already established clear statement. Rather religious symbols, working the way metaphors do, awaken in participants an encounter with an ultimate Other at the limits of human existence."[118] From this perspective, Roman Catholic theologian Walter Kasper identifies the covenant of marriage as "a religious symbol that points to God's faithfulness," and its expression in the "marital faithfulness" of the couple as "both a symbol that points to a reality beyond itself and a participation in the faithfulness of God."[119] Similarly, Paul Tillich identifies the Christian cross as a symbol that invites participation in the Christian mystery that it symbolizes; Karl Rahner identifies the human body as a symbol; and Roger Haight identifies Jesus as "symbol of God."[120]

Perhaps every *mediation-based symbol* is like a burning bush that is not consumed: it beckons to us from whatever flocks we are tending at the time and ignites in us a desire for an encounter with transcendence. In that spirit, when you encounter a *mediation-based* approach to symbol, first ask yourself, "What is being mediated by the symbol?" Then ask yourself, "How is that symbolic communication effected?" But the only way that the symbol can ultimately communicate to a wider audience is if it is committed to writing, as was the story of the burning bush in Exodus. Thus, Moses, who is remembered as the original "writer" of the Pentateuch, leads us and lures us to *the text-based definition of symbol*, which we turn to in conclusion.

Text-based definition of symbol

For theological writers, the fourth and culminating moment of symbol is its committal to writing as a *text-based symbol*. If a *sign-based symbol* points to what it signifies, a *meaning-based symbol* produces a "surplus of meaning" that transcends its original signification, and the *mediation-based* symbol not only "points" and "means," but also "mediates" a reality that could not be known without the symbol, a *text-based symbol* is a written symbol defined by the author of a text that can be classified as a sign-based, meaning-based or mediation-based symbol within that text, but which may or may not serve as any one of these symbols outside of the text. For example, white whales are not universal symbols of evil outside of *Moby Dick*, but Melville's white whale is a *text-based* symbol that functions for Captain Ahab as a *mediation-based symbol* of malevolence. The *text-based symbol*, then, is analogous to a "literary symbol." Yet symbols encountered in theological texts are not exclusively "literary," so for our purposes, "text-based" symbol is more inclusive.[121]

The *text-based* definition of symbol is common to the fields of literature, history, theology, biblical studies, and all text-based disciplines. When Flannery O'Connor identifies the water stain on the ceiling of a sick room as "the Holy Ghost" in her story "The Enduring Chill," she is employing a *text-based symbol.*[122] When Albert Outler symbolizes "the predicament of the church historian" through the untimely fall of Theodosius' horse that sent the emperor to his death, he is using a *text-based symbol.*[123] When Jesus speaks to the Samaritan woman at the well about "living water," the writer of John's gospel is using a *text-based* symbol. To be sure, text-based symbols do not cease signifying, making meaning, and mediating the realities that they inscribe. What they do, however, is to communicate those realities through a written text. But how do their authors use *text-based symbols* to write theology well? In the examples below, we can identify (1) constructed symbols; (2) interpreted symbols; and (3) appropriated symbols.

Constructed symbols

Some *text-based symbols*, like O'Connor's water stains, are *constructed* by the author, and their meaning is bound to the particular text in which they appear. For example, water stains do not routinely represent the Holy Spirit, but in "The Enduring Chill," O'Connor makes that symbolic identification prescient for the reader as the stains converge for the ailing Asbury into the image of "a fierce bird with spread wings" that ultimately descends at the story's end, "emblazoned in ice instead of fire":

> ...he lay for some time staring at the water stains on the grey walls. Descending from the top molding, long icicle shapes had been etched by leaks and, directly over his bed on the ceiling, another leak has made a fierce bird with spread wings. It had an icicle crosswise in its beak and there were smaller icicles depending from its wings and tail. It had been there since his childhood and had always irritated him and sometimes had frightened him. He had often had the illusion that it was in motion and about to descend mysteriously and set the icicle on his head.[124]

While the image of the descending dove is a traditional symbol of the Holy Spirit, O'Connor's representation of it as an icicle-clad water stain is her own imaginative construction, or more properly, that of her protagonist. The *constructed* symbol, then, invites writers to exercise their own symbolic imaginations within the parameters of the particular text that they are writing, or reading, as our next writer exemplifies.

Interpreted symbols

Other *text-based symbols*, like that of Theodosius' horse, are *interpreted* by the author from the reading of another text, and carry symbolic weight by virtue of that interpretation. What for some readers of history would be a regrettable but almost overlooked accident of history—that of the Emperor Theodosius II falling from his horse and ultimately to his death on July 25, 450 C.E.—became for church historian Albert Outler both a historical fact with profound ecclesiological consequences and a symbol of God's "real presence in every crisis of human decision—where history's meanings are born or aborted."[125] In calling our attention to "the role of Theodosius' horse in the story" through his *interpreted* symbol, Outler invites alertness to potential symbols in our own reading that might reward further reflection and interpretation.

Appropriated symbols

Finally, other *text-based symbols* are *appropriated* by the author from the traditional repertoire of symbols, which have a more universal range of meaning and transcend the reference of the immediate text in which they appear. For example, the "living water" that Jesus promises the Samaritan woman draws its symbolic significance from a well much deeper than the one where the woman was drawing water. When Johann Baptist Metz poses the questions, "What does man live on? What bread does he eat? Which food nourishes his life?"[126] he is not only drawing upon *text-based* symbols from Scripture; he is also appealing to a more universal symbolism correlating bread with spiritual nourishment. Yet even these *writer-appropriated* symbols must be "appropriate," or specific to the text in which they are used, and Metz grounds his own symbolism in the "eucharistic 'bread of life,'" which "nourishes us toward love," but for his mystical-political vision, becomes "the food of revolutionary conversion."[127] The "bread" broken by Metz for his readers successfully integrates the universal and contextual elements of the symbols, and invites us to a similar imagination of symbol in our own writing.

You might at this point be tempted to ask, "Isn't every theological use of symbol *text-based*, in that the symbol is encountered within a written biblical or theological text?" Even if it has its origin as a *sign-based symbol*, Noah's "bow in the cloud" comes to us as a *text-based symbol*; even if Jacob's memorial stone is a *meaning-based symbol*, it communicates to readers today through the medium of a written text. "The symbol... only gives rise to thought if it first gives rise to speech," writes Paul Ricoeur,[128] and symbolic speech is only drawn forward through history when it is committed to writing. Yet symbolic religious communication is not limited to speech, and is typically precipitated by an experience that is only subsequently given written expression. The stone had to manifest itself as a symbol to Jacob before it could be fixed in writing as a sacred text. The water stain adumbrating the Holy Spirit in O'Connor's story had to be communicated in a text before it could resonate symbolically with other readers.

For theological writers, this committal of symbol to writing is both a gift and a burden. It is a gift because we would not know of Noah's "bow in the cloud" or Jacob's stone without the *text-based symbol*, but it is a burden because when symbols become fixed in writing they can lose their original potency. But as the antidote to the misuse of symbol is also its cure—that is to say, "using language as a symbolic means of cooperation among those who by nature respond to symbols"—so the antidote to the fixation of symbols in writing is also writing, as writers like you discover, develop, reconstruct, and rewrite symbols in writing theology well. To do this we must now move to a *writer-based* definition of symbol.

Writing with symbol well: A writer-based guide

It is very difficult to write theology well without writing with symbol well. This is because writing with symbol well is not like sprinkling your writing with symbols, as you might sprinkle blueberries on the top of a bowl of cereal. It is more like baking a blueberry buckle, in which the blueberries and their topping coalesce to form one scrumptious dessert. Similarly, when you write with symbol well, symbolic language and subject matter are inherent in the deep structures—not just in the outer surfaces—of your writing. For example, when Karl Barth writes, "The angels will laugh when they read my theology,"[129] I suspect that he literally meant what he said. Yet his literal assertion is inseparable from the symbolic language through which he imagines those ineffable messengers of the transcendent shaking their heads at his feeble attempts to write about their realm. In other words, Barth's angels "laugh" at his theology both as literal beings and as symbols of the transcendent order that they mediate. Similarly, when you write with symbol well, the literal and symbolic levels of your writing will cohere in language and content. "For the one who participates in the symbolic signification," Paul Ricoeur explains, "…there are really not two significations, one literal and the other symbolic, but rather a single movement, which transfers him from one level to the other and which assimilates him to the second signification by means of…the literal one."[130] Keeping this "double intentionality"[131] of symbolic communication firmly in mind as we proceed, we focus in this section on the ways that theological writers (1) discover, (2) develop, (3) dialogue with, (4) deconstruct, and (5) reconstruct symbols in their writing. We then conclude with some final reflections on writing with symbol well.

Discovering the symbol

If "the symbol gives rise to thought,"[132] as Paul Ricouer suggests, and thought gives rise to writing, then the first thing that theological writers must do to write with symbol well is to "discover" the symbol or symbols that trigger their reflection, and subsequently their writing. This does not necessarily mean finding a new symbol that no one has discovered before. More often, it means identifying a symbol that engenders a theological question that you wish to investigate, illuminates your investigation of the question, and engages your participation in the reality of the symbol. The symbol may come from your own experience, from a biblical or theological text, from your contemporary cultural context, or from a felicitous conjunction of all of the above, filtered through the sieve of your own theological imagination. Just as we previously observed Denise Priestley crafting her experience of motherhood, the global threat of nuclear war, and the biblical symbol of the woman giving birth in the shadow of the dragon (Rev 12: 1–6) into a contemporary theology of hope,[133] she describes here the discovery of the biblical symbol that triggered this symbolic confluence:

> In starting out to write this book, I discovered a passage from Scripture which engaged my mind, my heart, my imagination—which spoke to me of the struggle going on between hopelessness and hope….It is the symbol from Chapter 5 of the Book of Revelation: a woman gives birth while a dragon stands before her ready to devour her child. This symbol will serve to structure my examination of Christian hope.[134]

Following Priestley's cue, what biblical or theological symbols have leapt from the page into your own theological imagination, in conjunction with your experience or contemporary issues arising from it? How might you reflect on what you have discovered and connect it to your own experience and context to write with symbol well in your next theological paper?

Developing the symbol

If, as Paul Ricoeur also suggests, symbols have a "surplus of meaning" that can never be completely contained in our conceptualization of them,[135] then it also follows naturally that the second thing that writers must do to write with symbol well is to develop the range of meaning and interpretation of the symbol that they have discovered by (1) situating the symbol in its original context; (2) tracing the development of the symbol from its original signification to its contemporary construals; and (3) relating the symbol to analogous symbols or symbolic texts that both corroborate and clarify its interpretation. Thus, after introducing the symbolic text in Revelation 12 of the woman with child threatened by the dragon, Priestley engages first in historical exegesis, identifying the woman with "the people of God," the dragon with "all that is ... opposed to Yahweh," and the child with "Jesus Christ, God incarnate ... the grounds for all hope."[136] While space does not permit Priestley to follow this symbol through successive stages of interpretation,[137] she moves swiftly to our contemporary struggle with the threat of nuclear destruction, using "the symbol of the dragon ... to personify the evil at work in our own historical situation" and the symbol of childbirth as a "countersign of hope." Finally, she "examine(s) other [biblical] texts which use the symbol of childbirth analogously to John's use of it in Revelation ... as a symbol for hope."[138] Given this suggestive but flexible trajectory, how might you develop a biblical or theological symbol by tracing its path from its original context through other moments of interpretation to your own appropriation of it in the paper that you are writing?

Dialoguing with the symbol

If Ricoeur is likewise correct that symbols are always "bound to the cosmos," or analogously, to the "sacred universe" that engenders them,[139] then the third thing that writers must do to write with symbol well is to dialogue with the symbol on the basis of their own experience. When there is no dialogue with the doctrinal symbols that have arisen from Christian faith, they lose their symbolic efficacy and cease to be elements of purposeful communication in the transmission of that faith. When, on the other hand, theological writers engage in active dialogue with the symbols that they are interpreting, they contribute to that "surplus of meaning" which continues to bear those symbols meaningfully into our own time and place. Thus, after establishing through her exegetical analysis that the woman in Revelation 12 is appropriately interpreted as a symbol of hope in our own context, Priestley proceeds to dialogue with this symbol in the light of her own experience of motherhood. In that process, she discovers a "symbolic gap" within our contemporary theological imagination of the nuclear "apocalypse" that must be bridged if she, other mothers, and all the people of God are "to bring forth in hope."[140] Priestly acknowledges that her own dialogue with the symbol must "facilitate the reader's own experience with the woman," for "it is only as the reader's own experience is illumined by the woman's story that the reader can come to recognize that he or she is also being called to bring forth in hope."[141] In the same way, your own dialogue with the symbols that you bring to your writing should engage your readers in the symbolic identification that you are proposing. How, then, might you dialogue with the symbol that you are interpreting in your paper? What experiences shed particular light upon your understanding of it? How might you build a bridge from your own appropriation of the symbol to that of your readers?

Deconstructing the symbol

If Ricouer also asserts correctly that symbols, in being bound to cosmos and sacred universe, "plunge us into the shadowy experience of power,"[142] then dialogue with symbols will sometimes require deconstructing them, in order to critically assess the power that they wield, who benefits from that power, and who is excluded from it. As Belden Lane cautions, "We can never assume, in some naively pious way, that the operation of symbols... is simply a reflection of theological categories. They are inextricably bound up with specific social and historical contexts, even with questions of contest and exchanges of power... ."[143] Sometimes symbols stop working because they are used to reinforce existing religious or cultural power bases rather than to empower new imaginations of the transcendent.

For example, Priestley must deconstruct the hermeneutical notion of a simplistic "one-to-one correspondence with every single number and symbol in the Book of Revelation" before she can witness to the power of symbolic identification resonant in the story of the woman. At the same time, she must deconstruct existing cultural symbols of "nuclearism"—our contemporary dragon—that replace the power of God with the power of the bomb. Finally, she must deconstruct Christian symbolizations of hope that are inadequate to the task of "grounding ourselves in the hopes of our God in salvation history, in the call to give birth, to choose life, to confront and conquer death" in the face of the "death-dealing arms race."[144] Following her clues, what needs deconstructing in your discovery, development, and dialogue with your symbols before you can proceed to a concluding, constructive interpretation of them in your paper?

Reconstructing the symbol

If, finally, "the symbol gives rise to thought,"[145] and thought gives rise to writing, as we said at the beginning of this section, then the most important thing that theological writers must do to write with symbol well is to reconstruct the symbol or symbols engendering their reflection for particular audiences and contexts through their writing. Just as deconstructing is a process of taking things apart to analyze and repair them, reconstructing is a process of reassembling them with whatever new parts are necessary to keep them moving forward from their original context to the one in which you are interpreting them. As we have already seen, the writer reconstructs the symbol by reinterpreting it in its contemporary context and inviting the reader's symbolic identification with it. The writer, however, has no other way to effect that reconstruction except through language.

For example, Priestley first asks herself and her readers, "Can we identify with this woman today? Is this story of Revelation 12 also our story?" In response, she asserts,

"We are called as a people to give birth in the face of the dragon. Such birthing is an act of hope." In this sentence, our story becomes the woman's story, and the symbol our reality. As she continues to reconstruct the symbol, it attracts other symbolic resonances as she writes, "The symbol of the woman in Revelation 12 is ... a symbol of the cross, and thus a symbol of hope. It is important with this symbol not to move too quickly to the birth of new life, but rather to stay with the woman's travail, experiencing what it requires of her to give birth in the face of the dragon." By identifying with the woman's travail, Priestley's readers are transported to the desert, where they "are called as Church, the place between the dragon's rule of the world and the birthing of God's reign."[146] Prompted by this transformative reading, how might you reconstruct the symbol that you are unfolding so that your readers might follow you into contemporary crossroads of God's reign?

THEOLOGICAL MEMO 4: Writing with Symbol Well in Five Easy Pieces: In the previous section, we observed Denise Priestley write with symbol well in an essay that was originally written as her Master of Divinity thesis while she was a student at the Jesuit School of Theology in Berkeley, California. Along the way, you were also invited to discover, develop, dialogue with, deconstruct and reconstruct the symbolic subject matter in a theological paper of your own. This theological memo invites you to put those pieces together in a coherent essay.

Perhaps you must write a paper introducing the doctrine of the Trinity to an eighth grade confirmation class, or trace the symbol of Sophia/wisdom from biblical sources into contemporary feminist theology to write a ritual for a women's liturgy at your church. Perhaps you are critiquing the symbol of church "unity" in your denomination because it seems to suppress the diversity of God's people, or describing an object with symbolic significance for you to reflect upon your own faith development in a reflection paper. Perhaps your task is similar to one of these, but deals with different symbols, symbolic subject matter, purposes and audiences.

Complete this theological memo in concert with a paper that you are writing by (1) indicating the topic of your paper and the symbols or symbolic subject matter that you are dealing with; (2) identifying the audience for whom you are writing (not just your professor, but a wider ecclesial "public"); (3) reviewing any writing that you have done previously for the paper; (4) organizing your writing or notes according to the proposed order of: (a) discovering; (b) developing; (c) dialoguing with; (d) deconstructing; and (e) reconstructing the symbol(s) or symbolic subject matter you are working with; (5) writing a completed draft of your paper that is based upon this model, or upon one of your own that enables you to write with symbol well.

Concluding reflections: Writing the theological imagination well

In this chapter we have explored "Writing the Theological Imagination Well" through the rhetorics of analogy, metaphor and symbol. We first introduced the theological imagination as a way of *knowing, seeing, reflecting and connecting* in the process of writing theology well. We then identified the rhetorics of analogy, metaphor and symbol as elements of purposeful communication in that fourfold process. Finally, we offered writer-based guides for writing with analogy, metaphor and symbol, respectively.

In the end, the theological imagination far exceeds our ability to capture it in a chapter about how to write it. As theological writers in a culturally diverse postmodern context, we must with Kwok Pui Lan acknowledge "the cracks, the fissures, and the openings, which refuse to be shaped into any [imaginative] framework."[147] As theological writers in a world fractured by sin, we must with Flannery O'Connor let our theological imaginations "reflect our broken condition and the face of the devil we are possessed by" no less than "the image at the heart of things" that we seek in our writing or in our lives.[148] Finally, with Bernard Shaw's Joan of Arc, we must trust our own theological imaginations, for "that is how messages of God come to us."[149]

When you are writing with theological imagination well out of the perfect conjunction of your own wisdom, passion, intellect and theological vision, you will not need this book to tell you how to do it. When that does not happen, however, you may find it helpful to reflect on how analogy, metaphor and symbol contribute to writing the theological imagination well. We concluded the section on metaphor with Sallie McFague's observation that theologians—and by extension, theological writers—must be both philosophers and poets. Since the language of analogy is rooted in the scholastic tradition of classical medieval theology, we might think of it as the language of the philosopher. Since contemporary theologians have retrieved the language of metaphor to do justice to the poetic and parabolic nature of the theological task, we might think of it as the language of the poet. Since the language of symbol embraces both of these without erasing either of them, we might name symbol the language of the theologian. But the goal of this chapter is to claim all three of these as theological languages par excellence; for together, all of these elements conspire to help us write the theological imagination well. Equipped with these gifts—for gifts they are—we turn now to "Rewriting Theology Well (I): Rhetorics of Style and Voice."

Notes

1 David Tracy, *The Analogical Imagination: Christian Theology and the Culture of Pluralism* (New York: Crossroad, 1981), 447; Sallie McFague, *Metaphorical Theology: Models of God in Religious Language* (Philadelphia: Fortress, 1982), 15; Roger Haight, *Dynamics of Theology* (Mahweh, NJ: Paulist Press, 1990; Reprint: Maryknoll: Orbis Books, 2001), 142 (page reference is to the reprint edition).

2 Suzanne K. Langer, "On Cassirer's Theory of Language and Myth," in *Reclaiming the Imagination: Philosophical Perspectives for Writers and Teachers of Writing*, ed. Anne E. Berthoff (Portsmouth, NH: Heinemann/Boynton/Cook Publishers, 1984), 152.

3 See Chapter 2, above under "What is Theological Reflection and Why Do Theologians Write It?"

4 Gordon D. Kaufman, *Theology for a Nuclear Age* (Philadelphia: Westminster Press, 1985), 20.

5 McFague, *Metaphorical Theology*, 35.

6 William Blake, [A Vision of the Last Judgment] From the Notebook (1810), in *William Blake: Complete Writings*, ed. Geoffrey Keynes (Oxford: Oxford University Press, 1966), 617.

7 Choan Seng Song, *Theology from the Womb of Asia* (Maryknoll, NY: Orbis Books, 1986), 63.

8 H. Richard Niebuhr, *The Meaning of Revelation* (New York: MacMillan, 1941; reprint New York: Collier Books, 1960), 69, 89. (Page references are to the reprint edition.) Niebuhr calls these "evil imaginations of the heart," and "adequate images of an observing mind," respectively.

9 Patricia O'Connell Killen and John deBeer, *The Art of Theological Reflection* (New York: Crossroad, 1994), 37–38.

10 Philip S. Keane, *Christian Ethics and Imagination: A Theological Inquiry* (New York/ Ramsey NJ: Paulist Press, 1984), 81.

11 Kathleen R. Fischer, *The Inner Rainbow: The Imagination in Christian Life* (New York/ Ramsey, NJ: Paulist Press, 1983), 7.

12 Denise Priestley, *Bringing Forth in Hope: Being Creative in a Nuclear Age* (New York/ Ramsey, NJ: Paulist Press, 1983), 4–5. The book was originally written as the final project of her program for the degree of Masters of Divinity at the Jesuit School of Theology at Berkeley, California.

13 Ann E. Berthoff, "From Problem-Solving to a Theory of Imagination," in *Rhetoric and Composition: A Sourcebook for Teachers*, ed. Richard L. Graves (Rochelle Park, NJ: Hayden Book Co, 1976), 290.

14 William Lynch, "Theology and the Imagination," *Thought* 29 (1954): 66.

15 Elizabeth A. Johnson, *She Who Is: The Mystery of God in Feminist Theological Discourse* (New York: Crossroad, 1995), 114.

16 Tracy, *Analogical Imagination*, 405–44.

17 Douglas R. Hofstadter, "Analogy as the Core of Cognition," in *The Analogical Mind: Perspectives From Cognitive Science*, eds. Dedre Gentner, J. Holyoak, and Boicho N. Kokinov (Cambridge, MA: Massachusetts Institute of Technology Press, 2001), 499–537.

18 For literature, see R.W. Gibbs, Jr., *The Poetics of Mind: Figurative Thought, Knowledge and Understanding* (New York: Cambridge University Press, 1994). For philosophy, see David Burrell, *Analogy and Philosophical Language* (New Haven: Yale University Press, 1973). For psychology, see Gentner et al., *The Analogical Mind*. For science, see Mary Hesse, *Models and Analogies in Science* (Notre Dame, IN: Notre Dame University Press, 1966). For religion, see Tracy, *Analogical Imagination*, 445–56.

19 Metaphors (defined in the next section) are a sub-class of analogies if "set of correspondences" is defined as one or more correspondences. Metaphors are in a class separate from analogies if "set of correspondences" is defined as two or more correspondences. For the purposes of this book, either definition suffices.

20 Thomas Aquinas, *Summa Theologica: Complete English Edition in Five Volumes* (Westminster, MD: Christian Classics, 1961), 1.4.3. Recent commentators on Aquinas insist that his principle of analogy was distinctively linguistic, or rhetorical, as well, and should not be confused with his student and interpreter Cajetan's ontological approach to analogy. See, e.g., David Burrell, *Aquinas: God and Action* (Notre Dame: University of Notre Dame Press, 1979).

21 This summary of the classical approach to analogy has drawn from Paul Avis, *God and the Creative Imagination: Metaphor, Symbol and Myth in Religion and Theology* (London: Routledge, 1999), 70; Johnson, *She Who Is*, 113–15; and Dan R. Stiver, *The Philosophy of Religious Language: Sign, Symbol and Story* (Oxford: Blackwell, 1996), 23–29.

22 The classic argument is from Karl Barth, *Church Dogmatics*, ed. and trans. G.W. Bromily et al. (London: T.T. Clark International, 2004), 2/1:237–43.

23 Song, *Theology from the Womb of Asia*, 63.

24 Madeleine L'Engle, *Walking on Water: Reflections on Faith and Art* (Wheaton, IL: Harold Shaw, 1980; reprint New York: Farrar, Strauss & Giroux/North Point Press, 1995), 81 (in reprint edition).

25 David Burrell, "Analogy," in *The New Dictionary of Theology*, eds J.A. Komonchak, M. Collins, & D.A. Lane (Wilmington, DL: Michael Glazier, 1988), 14.

26 Ann E. Berthoff, *Forming/Thinking/Writing: The Composing Imagination* (Rochelle Park, NJ: Hayden Book Company), 138.

27 Janet Soskice, *Metaphor and Religious Language* (Oxford: Clarendon Press, 1985), 64.

28 See Avis, *God and the Creative Imagination*, 76–77.

29 Tracy, *Analogical Imagination*, 421–38.

30 Burrell, *Analogy and Philosophical Language.*

31 Johnson, *She Who Is*, 236–37.

32 As we shall see in the next section on metaphor, analogy has proved more congenial to Roman Catholic than to Protestant theological imaginations. As John Thiel ("The Analogy of Tradition: Method and Theological Judgment," *Theological Studies* 66 [2005]) acknowledges, "As much as analogy in a traditional key has been rendered theologically questionable, it is yet interesting to note how analogy has persisted as a theme in Catholic thought" (366). A succinct but pointed summary of contemporary Roman Catholic reflection on analogy and its Reformation critique can be found in Johnson, *She Who Is*, 116–17.

33 Tracy, *Analogical Imagination*, 408.

34 The quotation from Aristotle's *Poetics* is cited by Tracy, *Analogical Imagination*, 410. See note 50 below for the full citation.

35 Tracy, *Analogical Imagination*, 408.

36 Ibid., 420.

37 See Chapter 4, 74–79.

38 See Tracy, *Analogical Imagination*, 408–11, and 429–38, for a model essay based upon this process which is subsequently identified as a "basic structure" for writing a systematic theology (444n41). I have simplified and adapted the rhetorical process implicit in his explication for theological student writers.

39 Roger Haight, *The Experience and Language of Grace* (New York/Mahwah, NJ: Paulist, 1979), 143–60.

40 Tracy, *Analogical Imagination*, 438.

41 Serene Jones, *Feminist Theory and Christian Theology: Cartographies of Grace* (Minneapolis: Fortress Press, 2000), 153–76.

42 John Hick, *The Second Christianity* (London: SCM Press, 1983), 86–87.

43 See above, under "Writing Analogy Well: A Writer-Based Guide": (1) identifying the classic and corresponding analogues, or analogical elements; (2) ordering the

corresponding analogues; (3) explicating the similarities-in-difference; (4) re-imagining the classic analogue for contemporary audiences.

44 Tracy, *Analogical Imagination*, 373.

45 See chapter 10 below, and Roger Haight, *Christian Community in History*, I (New York: Continuum, 2004; repr. London and new York: Bloomsbury/T.T. Clark, 2014), 1:ix (page references are to the first edition).

46 Johnson, *She Who Is*, 114.

47 Aquinas, *Summa Theologica*, Ia q.2, aa.2-3.

48 Johnson, *She Who Is*, 113.

49 Walter Brueggemann, *Hopeful Imagination: Poetic Voices in Exile* (Philadelphia: Fortress Press, 1986), 38.

50 Aristotle, *The Poetics*, trans. Gerald F. Else (Ann Arbor: University of Michigan Press, 1967), Chapter 22, 60.

51 Sallie T. McFague, *Metaphorical Theology: Models of God in Religious Language* (Philadelphia: Fortress Press, 1982), 198n16. Connecting the "metaphorical sensibility" with contemporary Protestant theology, she explains: "The Protestant tradition is, I would suggest, 'metaphorical'; the Catholic, 'symbolical,' (or 'analogical' for contemporary Catholicism) .... The Protestant sensibility tends to see dissimilarity, distinction, tension and hence to be skeptical and secular, stressing the transcendence of God and the finitude of creation. The Catholic sensibility tends to see similarity, connection, harmony, and hence, to be believing and religious, stressing the continuity between God and creation" (13).

52 For a helpful review of the conversation, see McFague, *Metaphorical Theology*, ix–xi and 198n16.

53 Aristotle, *Poetics*, chapter 22, 60.

54 In contrast, of course, to a *simile*, a word denoting an explicit comparison between two things ("My love *is like* a rose").

55 See Aristotle, *On Rhetoric: A Theory of Civic Discourse*, ed. and trans. George A. Kennedy (New York and Oxford: Oxford University Press, 1991), 2, 1405a, where "word choice" and "metaphors" are discussed in tandem.

56 For a well-formulated summary of this position, see Sandra Schneiders, *The Revelatory Text: Interpreting the New Testament as Sacred Scripture*, 2nd ed. (Collegeville, MN: Liturgical Press/Michael Glazier, 1999), 29–33.

57 I.A. Richards, *The Philosophy of Rhetoric* (New York: Oxford University Press, 1965; reprint 1979), 89–138 page references are to the reprint edition); Paul Ricoeur, *Interpretation Theory: Discourse and the Surplus of Meaning* (Fort Worth: Texas Christian University Press, 1976), 45–69.

58 Schneiders, *Revelatory Text*, 30–31.

59 Aristotle, *Poetics*, Chapter 22, 60; and Ricoeur, *Interpretation Theory*, 53.

60 Sallie McFague, *Models of God: Theology for an Ecological, Nuclear Age* (Philadelphia: Fortress Press, 1987), 33.

61 Cf. McFague, *Metaphorical Theology*, 23: "... a model is a dominant metaphor, a metaphor with staying power."

62 Julian of Norwich, *Showings*, ed. and trans. Edmund Colledge and James Walsh (New York: Paulist Press, 1978), Chapter 59, 295–97.

63 McFague, *Metaphorical Theology*, 13.

64 Ibid., 108–11. See also Ricoeur, *Interpretation Theory*, 64.

65 In the biblical context, "shepherds" were dirty, lower class peasants, and "far from being regarded as either gentle or noble, in Jesus' time, shepherds were often considered as dishonest, outside the law." See Raymond E. Brown, *The Birth of the Messiah: A Commentary on the Infancy Narratives in Matthew and Luke* (Garden City, NY: Doubleday/Image Books, 1979), 420.

66 Kwok Pui Lan, "Engendering Christ: Who Do You Say That I Am?" in *The Postcolonial Imagination and Feminist Theology* (Louisville, KY: Westminster John Knox Press, 2005), 176–78.

67 McFague, *Metaphorical Theology*, 167.

68 In *Hear Then the Parable: A Commentary on the Parables of Jesus* (Minneapolis: Fortress, 1989), Bernard Brandon Scott calls "stock metaphors" *epiphoric* and "shock metaphors" *diaphoric*, explaining that "[m]ost common metaphors are epiphoric: the associations are bearers of the implied meaning. But in the Jesus tradition, the relation is frequently diaphoric: Jesus' discourse changes or challenges the implied structural network of associations" (61).

69 Ricoeur, *Interpretation Theory*, 52. "Live metaphors are metaphors of invention within which the response to the discordance of the sentence is a new extension of meaning.... There are no live metaphors in a dictionary."

70 George Lakoff and Mark Johnson, *Metaphors We Live By* (Chicago: University of Chicago Press, 1980), 3–6.

71 Haight, *Dynamics of Theology*, 1.

72 Ibid., 46.

73 Jones, *Feminist Theory*, 19.

74 Roger Haight, *Jesus Symbol of God* (Maryknoll, NY: Orbis Books, 1999), 438.

75 Jon Sobrino, *Jesus the Liberator: A Historical-Theological Reading of Jesus of Nazareth*, trans. Paul Burns and Francis McDonagh (Maryknoll, NY: Orbis Books, 1998), 271.

76 Sallie McFague, *Super, Natural Christians: How We Should Love Nature* (Minneapolis: Fortress Press, 1997); Kevin F. Burke, *The Ground beneath the Cross: The Theology of Ignacio Ellacuria* (Georgetown: Georgetown University Press, 2004); and Pope Paul VI, "Marialus Cultus," (56) quoted in Elizabeth Johnson, *Truly our Sister: A Theology of Mary in the Communion of Saints* (New York: Continuum, 2004), 134.

77 David Tracy, "God is Love: The Central Christian Metaphor," accessed September 26, 2014, John Mark Ministries, http://www.jmm.org.au/articles/14077.htm.

78 Haight, *Jesus Symbol of God*, 470.

79 Rebecca S. Chopp, *Saving Work: Feminist Practices of Education* (Louisville, KY: Westminster John Knox Press), 73.

80 See Thomas S. Kane's helpful distinction between a "cliché" and a "dead metaphor" in *The New Oxford Guide to Writing* (New York: Oxford University Press, 1988): "a cliché attempts to be original and perceptive but fails. A dead metaphor, on the other hand, makes no pretense to newness; it has dried and hardened into a useful expression for a common idea (e.g., 'the heart of the matter': 'the mouth of the river'; 'the key to the problem')." Using the term in its more pejorative sense, poet Donald Hall provides his own cautionary list of "dead metaphors" to be avoided by poets and writers of serious prose in "Hall's Index," in Donald Hall, *Breakfast Served Anytime All Day: Essays on Poetry New and Selected* (Ann Arbor: University of Michigan Press, 2003), 180–86.

81 Breuggemann, *Hopeful Imagination*, 99.

82 Joan Martin, *More Than Chains and Toil: A Christian Work Ethic of Enslaved Women* (Louisville, KY: Westminster John Knox Press, 2000), 2.

83 Ibid., 152.

84 McFague, *Models of God*, 32–34.

85 Karl Barth, "Theology," in *God in Action*, trans. E.G. Homrighausen and Karl J. Ernst (Edinburgh: T. and T. Clark, 1936), 39–57; quoted in Alister E. McGrath, ed., *The Christian Theology Reader*, 4th ed. (Oxford: Wiley-Blackwell, 2011), 36.

86 While biblical critic Robert Funk in *Language, Hermeneutics and the Word of God* (New York: Harper & Row, 1966), identifies the second term, or "B" term of a metaphor exclusively with the "symbol" (137), this is not typically the case with poetic metaphors, as X.J. Kennedy points out: in Emily Dickinson's poem, "The Lightning is a Yellow Fork," "the symbol is the lightning, not the fork." See X.J. Kennedy and Dana Giola, *An Introduction to Poetry*, 9th ed. (New York: Longman, 1998), 255.

87 Paul Tillich, *Dynamics of Faith* (New York: Harper & Row, 1957), 41–42.

88 Ricoeur, *Interpretation Theory*, 69.

89 McFague, *Metaphorical Theology*, 121.

90 Haight, *Jesus Symbol of God*, 13.

91 Johnson, *She Who Is*, 201.

92 While Burke uses the terminology of "symbol" rather than "language" in order to encompass a wider range of human activity than the linguistic, he uses the category of language to exemplify his definition, and I follow his precedent here. See Kenneth Burke, *Language as Symbolic Action: Essays on Life, Literature and Method* (Berkeley: University of California Press, 1966).

93 This is, of course, Burke's classic definition of rhetoric. See Kenneth Burke, *A Rhetoric of Motives* (Berkeley: University of California Press, 1969), 43.

94 Haight, *Dynamics of Theology*, 142.

95 Tillich, *Dynamics of Faith*, 41.

96 Paul Ricoeur distinguishes the usage of "symbol" in psychoanalysis, poetics, and history of religions, concluding, "the problem of symbols is dispersed among many fields of research and so divided among them that it tends to become lost in their proliferation." See Ricoeur, *Interpretation Theory*, 53.

97 See Tillich, *Dynamics of Faith*, 42, for whom a symbol both points to and participates in what it signifies.

98 See Burke, *Rhetoric of Religion*, 18, 7–8.

99 John Calvin, *Institutes of the Christian Religion*, trans. H. Beveridge (Grand Rapids, MI: Eerdmans, 1957), 2:557–58 (book 4, ch. 17).

100 Calvin, *Institutes*, 2:560, 564 (book 4, ch. 5, 10, 17). Notwithstanding the richness and nuance of Calvin's theology of the spiritual presence of Christ in the eucharist, his use of "sign" and "symbol" gravitates more toward the symbol as "sign."

101 *The Book of Common Prayer According to the Use of the Episcopal Church* (New York: Seabury, 1977), 427.

102 See *The Habit of Being: Letters of Flannery O'Connor*, ed. Sally Fitzgerald (New York: Farrar, Strauss and Giroux, 1979), Letter to "A," dated December 16, 1955, 125. For Flannery O'Connor's view of literary and religious symbol, see Lucretia B.

Yaghjian, "Flannery O'Connor's Use of Symbol, Roger Haight's Christology, and the Religious Writer," *Theological Studies* 63 (2002): 268–301.

103 Ricoeur argues that religious symbols have their pre-linguistic roots in the cosmos and are bound to the cosmos, in that "the symbols only come to language to the extent that the elements of the world themselves become apparent" (*Interpretation Theory*, 61). For culture, see Clifford Geertz, *The Interpretation of Cultures* (New York: Basic Books, 1973), who defines culture as "an historically transmitted pattern of meanings embodied in symbols ...." (89). For religious experience of the sacred, see Mircea Eliade, *The Sacred and the Profane: The Nature of Religion*, trans. Willard R. Trask (New York: Harper Torchbooks, 1961): "... for those who have a religious experience all nature is capable of revealing itself as cosmic sacrality" (12). For the human psyche, see Violet S. deLaszlo, ed., *Psyche and Symbol: A Selection from the Writings of C.G. Jung* (Garden City, NY: Doubleday Anchor Books, 1958): For Jung, the "living symbol expresses an essential unconscious factor," and "the more widely this factor operates, the more ... valid is the symbol" (xxi).

104 Eliade, *Sacred and the Profane*, 11–12.

105 Conrad Aiken, "Discordants," in *Conrad Aiken: Selected Poems*, with a new foreword by Harold Bloom (Oxford: Oxford University Press, 2002), 271.

106 Calvin, *Institutes*, 2:504 (book 4, ch. 14, 18).

107 Ricoeur, *Interpretation Theory*, 54–57.

108 Gertrude Stein, *Lectures in America* (New York: Random House, 1935).

109 Dante Alighieri, *Paradise*, trans. A. Esolen (New York: Modern Library, 2004), Canto XXX, pp. 325–26.

110 See Haight, *Jesus Symbol of God*, 196–202.

111 For psychoanalysis, see, e.g., Ana-Maria Rizzuto, *The Birth of the Living God: A Psychoanalytic Study* (Chicago: University of Chicago Press, 1979). For anthropology, see, e.g. Clifford E. Geertz, "Deep Play: Notes on the Balinese Cockfight," in *The Interpretation of Cultures: Selected Essays* (New York: Basic Books, 1973), 412–53. For sociology, see, e.g., Ann Swidler, "Culture in Action: Symbols and Strategies," *American Sociological Review* 51 (1986): 273–86. For literature, see, e.g., William Tyndall, *The Literary Symbol* (New York: Columbia University Press, 1955); and Northrop Frye, *Anatomy of Criticism* (New York: Atheneum, 1966), 71ff. For theological reflection, see, e.g., Killen and deBeer, *The Art of Theological Reflection*, 37–40. For the interpretation of Christian doctrine, see Haight, *Dynamics of Theology*, 163–66 (1990); and Avis, *God and the Creative Imagination*, 139. For the celebration of liturgy, see Peter E. Fink, "Theoretical Structures for Liturgical Symbols," *Liturgical Ministry* 2 (1993): 125–37.

112 My definition of the "*mediation-based*" symbol is indebted to Roger Haight's construal of the religious symbol in Haight, *Dynamics of Theology*, 132–42, and *Jesus Symbol of God*, 196–202, and to Paul Avis' discussion of symbol and religious imagination in Avis, *God and the Creative Imagination*, 103–13. As I construe them here, the *mediation-based symbol* and the *religious symbol* are analogous.

113 See Fink, "Liturgical Symbols," 135, who draws fruitfully upon the work of John MacMurray to explore the relational dynamics of liturgical and religious symbols.

114 For a more comprehensive discussion of symbolic communication and its relationship to the doing and writing of theology, see Haight, "Symbolic Religious Communication," in *Dynamics of Theology*, 146–66.

115 Haight, *Jesus Symbol of God*, 201–02. Paul Ricoeur similarly calls attention to the "tensive" nature of symbol, by which they exist in creative tension between their literal signification and "surplus of meaning" (*Interpretation Theory*, 55–57).

116 William Blake, "Auguries of Innocence," in *Blake: Complete Writings*, ed. Keynes, 431.

117 Haight, *Jesus Symbol of God*, 199.

118 Stephen Happel, "Symbol," in *The New Dictionary of Theology*, ed. J.A. Komanchak et al. (Wilmington, DE: Michael Glazier, 1987), 998.

119 Walter Kasper, *Theology of Christian Marriage* (New York: Crossroad, 1984), 34, 23.

120 Tillich, *Dynamics of Faith*, 125; Karl Rahner, "The Theology of the Symbol," in *Theological Investigations*, vol. 4, trans. K. Smith (Baltimore: Helicon Press, 1966), 221–52; Haight, *Jesus Symbol of God*, 12–15.

121 *Text-based* symbols are also analogous to conceptual religious symbols, or "words, notions, concepts, ideas, sayings, or texts that mediate a deeper consciousness of a level of reality that goes beyond their overt meaning." See Haight, *Jesus Symbol of God*, 13.

122 O'Connor writes to Caroline Gordon Tate, "I'm busy with the Holy Ghost. He is going to be a waterstain—very obvious but the only thing possible." See O'Connor, *Habit of Being*, 257.

123 Albert Outler, "Theodosius' Horse: Reflections on the Predicament of the Church Historian," *Church History* 57(1965): 251–61.

124 Flannery O'Connor, "The Enduring Chill," in The *Complete Stories of Flannery O'Connor* (New York: Farrar, Strauss and Giroux, 1979), 365–66, 382.

125 Outler, "Theodosius' Horse," 260.

126 Johannes Baptist Metz, *The Emergent Church: The Future of Christianity in a Postbourgeois World* (New York: Crossroad, 1981), 34, 41.

127 Ibid., 41.

128 Ricoeur, *Interpretation Theory*, 55.

129 Quoted in Tracy, *Analogical Imagination*, 421.

130 Ricouer, *Interpretation Theory*, 55.

131 The term is Paul Ricoeur's. See Paul Ricouer, "The Hermeneutics of Symbols and Philosophical Reflections: I," trans. David Savage, in *The Conflict of Interpretations*, ed. Don Ihde (Evanston, Ill.: Northwestern University Press, 1974), 289–90.

132 Ricoeur, *Interpretation Theory*, 55.

133 See note 12, above.

134 Priestley, *Bringing Forth in Hope*, 5.

135 Ricoeur, *Interpretation Theory*, 56–57. Another way that Ricouer expresses this is, "Symbols give rise to an endless exegesis" (57).

136 Priestley, *Bringing Forth in Hope*, 15–18.

137 For an exemplary model of the genetic development of a concrete symbol (Jesus) from biblical sources to classical doctrines to contemporary construals, culminating in that of "Jesus Symbol of God," see Haight, *Jesus Symbol of God*, 28–40.

138 Ibid., 25,37, 5–6.

139 Ricoeur, *Interpretation Theory*, 61–62.

140 Priestley, *Bringing Forth in Hope*, 18, 27ff.

141 Ibid., 18.

142 Ricoeur, *Interpretation Theory*, 69.

143 Belden C. Lane, "Spider as Metaphor: Attending to the Symbol-Making Process in the Academic Discipline of Spirituality," in Elizabeth A. Dreyer and Mark Burrows, *Minding the Spirit: the Study of Christian Spirituality* (Baltimore: Johns Hopkins University Press, 2005), 113.

144 Priestley, *Bringing Forth in Hope*, 23, 33, 66–67.

145 Ricoeur, *Interpretation Theory*, 55.

146 Priestley, *Bringing Forth in Hope*, 21, 24, 57, 69.

147 Kwok, *Postcolonial Imagination and Feminist Theology*, 30.

148 Flannery O'Connor, "Novelist and Believer," in *Mystery and Manners: Occasional Prose*, ed. Sally Fitzgerald (New York: Farrar, Straus & Giroux, 1969), 168.

149 George Bernard Shaw, *St. Joan* (New York: Brentano's, 1924), 16.

10

Rewriting Theology Well (I): Rhetorics of Style and Voice

It is depressing that those who serve God and love [God] sometimes write so badly, when those who do not ... take pains to write so well.

—THOMAS MERTON, *The Sign of Jonas*

*You come to your **style** by learning what to leave out ... [and] ... in the process of simplifying oneself, one often discovers the thing called **voice**.*

—BILLY COLLINS, in BEN YAGODA, *The Sound on the Page*

Starting points

The preceding chapters of this book have provided a guide to some commonly encountered theological genres and how to write them. Yet knowing how to write a particular theological genre is not synonymous with writing it "well." While the theologically gifted who write without revising will always be with us,[1] what separates writing theology from "writing theology well" for the rest of us is the process of rewriting. However, the act of rewriting, driven by each writer's rhetoric, or procedural method of revision, requires (1) some internal criteria, or intuitive sense of "style," for evaluating what you have written; (2) some external standard, or normative model of "style," to guide the rewriting; and (3) an active integration of both of these with your own "voice," or the persona that your writing projects.

To rewrite theology well, therefore, we must know what constitutes *style* and *voice* in writing before writing theological words, sentences and paragraphs well (Chapter 11), or developing a rhetoric of revision (Chapter 12). Toward those ends, this chapter asks (1) What is *style*, and how do writers define it? (2) What is *theological style*, and how do theological writers define it? (3) What is *voice*, and what is the relationship between *style* and *voice* in theological writing? (4) How does one identify, develop and refine *a theological voice and style of one's own*? First, the following theological memo invites you to reflect on your own understanding of writing "style":

> *THEOLOGICAL MEMO 1: What do you mean when you use the word "style" to describe writing? What do you mean when you use the word "style" to describe your own writing? Respond to these questions briefly before reading this chapter.*

What is "style," and how do writers define it?

When applied to writing, your "style" is simply a synonym for "how you write." We will come back to this linguistic definition, but first we need to cast a wider net. "Style is a word everybody uses, but almost no one can explain what it means," Francis-Noel Thomas and Mark Turner write.[2] This ambiguity is rooted in the history of classical rhetoric, where "style" (*lexis* in Greek and *elocutio* in Latin) was variously defined: (1) *linguistically*, in terms of word choice, figurative language, or length of sentences;[3] (2) *generically*, as a "kind" of style arising from these linguistic features, or from the written genre that the style informs;[4] (3) *epistemologically*, as a way of thinking, or "conceptual stance" inherent in the chosen style;[5] (4) *pluralistically*, in terms of the diverse "styles" available to the speaker or writer, as over against one definitive "style," incorporating of all of the above; and (5) *rhetorically*, or in relationship to the audience addressed.[6]

For example, Aristotle typifies a Greek rhetorical model of style that subordinates the *lexis*, or "linguistic style" of an oration to its *logos*, or "subject matter." Although he was initially apologetic about including a chapter on "style" in his *Rhetoric*, Aristotle justified this inclusion on the grounds that "it is not enough to have a supply of things to say, but it is also necessary to say it in the right way" in order to communicate to particular audiences. On the same grounds, he pronounced "a different *style*... appropriate for each genre," thereby connecting style with genre and acknowledging stylistic pluralism. Aristotle's ideal prose style combined "clarity, sweetness, and strangeness," and prized argumentative skill above stylistic embellishment.[7] Thus, the speaker's goal was a disciplined but distinctive style that did not distract from the subject matter but disappeared artfully into it.[8]

The pseudo-Ciceronian author of the *Rhetorica ad Herennium* (90 B.C.E.), on the other hand, typifies a Roman rhetorical model of style [*elocutio*], or "the adaptation of suitable words and sentences to the matter invented."[9] As one of the five canons of Roman rhetoric, "style" inhered in the relationship between form and content, even when these elements were considered separately.[10] Moreover, the shifting relationships between form, content and audience were epitomized in three rhetorical styles: (1) the "high," or grandiloquent style, (2) the "middle," or moderate style, and (3) the "low," or plain style.[11] Reflecting Cicero's vision of rhetoric as a wide-ranging pedagogical apprenticeship for public life, the Roman rhetorical model of style was informed by a political stance in which style, together with "wisdom," were tantamount in moving audiences to responsible action.[12] Thus, the speaker's goal was not a style that "disappeared" into the subject matter but one that employed dignity, decorum, and appropriate embellishment to enhance its delivery to the intended audience.[13]

An understanding of style is no less instrumental to the contemporary writer's craft than it was to the classical orator's eloquence.[14] The English word "style" derives from the Latin *stylus*, or writing instrument, and has come to epitomize "good writing." Contemporary writers also construe style (1) *linguistically*, on the basis of its surface features, as Strunk and White exhort readers to "use the active voice" and "omit needless words";[15] (2) *generically*, as Walker Gibson describes "tough," "sweet," and "stuffy" styles of American writing;[16] (3) *epistemologically*, as Thomas and Turner define style in respect to its "conceptual stand";[17] (4) *pluralistically*, as T.S. Eliot acknowledges "a wide scope for legitimate divergences of style; no one age, and certainly no one writer, can establish a norm;"[18] and (5) *rhetorically*, in relationship to the writer's audience, as Richard Coe advises, "An inappropriate style can ... offend readers, sometimes even cause them to stop reading."[19]

Contemporary writers add one more prerequisite to this profile, without which our own approach to style would be incomplete. They also construe style (6) *individually*, as "the writer's fingerprint."[20] Ben Yagoda explains, "Style in its deepest sense is not a set of techniques that just happen to be associated with a particular person, but a presentation or representation of something essential about him or her—something that ... cannot be disguised, no matter how much the writer may try."[21] If one's individual style cannot be disguised, however, it can be camouflaged by poor writing that obscures it. Out of this conviction, William Zinsser writes, "Since style is who you are, you only need to be true to yourself to find it gradually emerging from under the accumulated clutter and debris, growing more distinctive every day."[22] Because "you come to your style by learning what to leave out," poet Billy Collins corroborates, "style is usually clarified and intensified in the process of revision."[23] Whether your prime example of individual style is Hemingway's staccato sentences or Virginia Woolf's more lyrical prose rhythms, style for contemporary writers is never mere self-expression. Like dough that is re-kneaded once, twice, or three times before its final rising and baking, a writer's style comes to its fullness in the process of revision and rewriting.

This brief survey of style in classical rhetoric and contemporary writing suggests that how we define "style" will depend on our point of departure. Starting with students who begin the task of writing theology with the writing style that they have while seeking to develop the theological style that they need, we can define "style" functionally as *how you write what you write, when you write in a given genre, from a particular stance, for a specific audience*. Let us look at each of these elements in turn, exemplified by theological writers whose diverse styles will prompt the next question, What is theological style and how shall we define it?

Style is "how you write"

Style is first of all "how *you* write." Style embraces the words you choose, the diction you use, the syntax of your sentences and the punctuation that connects them, as well as the technical terms, connecting words, colloquial and figurative language that you draw upon. In short, style reflects all of the linguistic choices you make on the level of words, sentences, and paragraphs. Yet style is never merely individual. Style is always filtered through a legacy of language and culture, whether at our mother's knee, at the feet of a teacher, through the pages of our favorite authors, in conversation with theological mentors, or in conformity with a particular "house style." But however your style is filtered through this rich rhetorical legacy, the irreducible essence of "how *you* write" will remain. Notice, for example, how Elizabeth Johnson's compelling portrait of the biblical Sophia in her essay, "Jesus the

Wisdom of God," resonates with the vibrancy of her own metaphoric language at the same time that it follows the biblical style of her material and conforms to the "house style" of an academic essay:

> After appearing briefly and elusively in the Book of Job at a preliminary stage of personification (ch. 28), Sophia strides into the Book of Proverbs with a noisy public appearance (1.20–33). She is a street preacher, a prophet who cries aloud in the market and at the city gates a message of reproach, punishment and promise.... In Sophia's last appearance in Proverbs, the street preacher, life-giver, agent of just governance, architect of creation and God's darling becomes a compelling hostess (9.6). Having built a house and set her table, she sends her maidservants out to the public crossroads... to be proclaimers of the invitation: "Come, eat of my bread and drink of the wine I have mixed (v.5)."[24]

Style is "how you write what you write"

While the style of every writer is distinctive, all of the linguistic choices that constitute your written "style" will be tempered by "what you write," or the subject matter of your writing. Moreover, the relationship between "what you write" and "how you write" is fundamental to an understanding of "theological" style. Roger Haight presupposes this relationship when he writes, "Respecting the transcendent character of faith and revelation, theology communicates no immediate information about God. This negative axiom invites a critical attentiveness to theological prose: how is the author dealing with transcendent subject matter?"[25] Haight's question is addressed to the theological reader, but it challenges every theological writer who must decide how to write about "transcendent subject matter," and in what style. Catholic theologian Karl Rahner advises those writing theology to "respect the symbolic nature of its discourse."[26] Anglican theologian and former Archbishop of Canterbury Rowan Williams adds that writing about God should "decline the attempt to take God's point of view (i.e., a 'total' perspective)."[27] In a more popular vein, syndicated columnist Dave Barry cautions, "There is a lot of what I call 'God writing' in the newspaper. We're taught to sound authoritative and professional, and often to sound boring."[28] While your own theological writing may sometimes sound "authoritative and professional," it need not sound boring. See how theologian Belden Lane prepares to write theological prose by hiding playfully in the shadows of Rublev's icon of the Holy Trinity:

> Contemplating the icon, I will... [trace] a path down to the... base of a table around which the three persons of the Trinity are seated. Like a child playing in kindergarten, I will imagine myself sneaking up to the small drawer in the side of that table, crawling into it and pulling it shut behind me. The members of the Trinity will pretend not to notice, going along with the game. They will ignore me, as I lie there in the darkness, surrounded by Father, Son and Holy Spirit speaking together in lively conversation. In that place I will try to write out of the sublime forgetfulness of what I hear.[29]

Style is "how you write what you write, when you write in a given genre"

The style of your writing will also be informed by the genre in which you are writing. When South African feminist theologian Denise Ackerman decided to write a book "for the general reader, for people in the churches" rather than for "the academy," she recognized that if she were to move out of her habitual academic style of writing, she would have to shift writing genres as well. Embracing the genre of the personal letter as "a vehicle to keep me from academic excesses," she decided to "write letters to people who matter to me, about the themes that have been at the core of my search for healing and freedom."[30] Thus, changing the genre of her theological writing necessitated a corresponding change in writing style—from an impersonal academic style to a personal, more vulnerable style that would not allow her to "hide behind the tricks that govern academic writing."[31] Yet every writing style comes equipped with its own bag of tricks, and it is more often necessary for students writing theology to shift from non-academic to academic writing styles. This too can be a constructive choice, as Lisa Ede, Cheryl Glenn, and Andrea Lunsford describe in their article, "Rhetoric and Feminism":

> In order to claim authority and agency, to function as subjects in the discursive arena and thus further feminism's emancipatory goals, some feminists choose (as we choose in this essay) to adhere to the stylistic conventions of traditional western discourse—conventions that sharply dichotomize the public and the private, that devalue personal experience in favor of "objective" facts, "rational" logic, and established "authorities."[32]

Style is "how you write what you write when you write from a stance"

The style of your writing will also be informed by the conceptual stance from which you write. Construing style not merely as "the garment of thought" but as its embodiment, the first century C.E. literary critic Longinus asserted, "A great style is the natural outcome of important thoughts."[33] I call this stance "epistemological" because it reflects the writer's way of thinking and of knowing. The word *epistemology* means literally, "to cause to stand" (Greek *epi+ histemi*). Thomas and Turner explain, "In any given style, positions will be assigned to truth, language, the writer and the reader," and "different stands on [these] elements of style" produce different prose styles. If, for example, I think that truth is universally apprehensible but independent of my own apprehension of it, my primary task as a writer will be to apprehend that truth, to formulate its premises in a logical and coherent fashion, and to communicate it in writing that is "clear but not commonplace."[34] Variations of this "classic" style abound in academic discourse, but its precision of language, its logical patterns of argumentation, and its use of analogy and parallelism to universalize the argument are characteristic. See, for example, the style in which Roman Catholic theologian Bernard Lonergan describes the theological task:

> Now theology, and especially the empirical theology of today, is reflection on conversion. But conversion is fundamental to religion. It follows that reflection on conversion can supply theology with its foundation and, indeed, with a foundation that is concrete, dynamic, personal, communal, and historical. Just as reflection on the operations of the scientist brings to light the real foundation of the science, reflection on the ongoing process of conversion may bring to light the real foundation of a renewed theology.[35]

If, on the other hand, I think that truth is plural, often elusive, and integral to the form or context in which it manifests itself, dwelling neither exclusively apart from me nor within my own grasp but discovered interactively in the process of thinking, writing, and living, that perspective will influence my choice of a writing style. While I may still choose to write in the "classic" theological style of Lonergan for an academic audience, I may also experiment with other writing "styles," depending upon the context in which that truth is engaged, and the audience for whom it makes a difference.[36] Writing from a feminist, contextual stance in answer to her mother's question, "What is theology?" Denise Ackerman chooses a personal, epistolary style that is tentative, still in process, characterized by figurative language and concrete images, addressed both to her mother and to the wider audience whom she represents:

> I owe you a more thoughtful explanation about what I mean by theology. I need to tell you how I stumbled into theology and how, as a woman, I found my own voice as a theologian. I must admit that I am still sorting this out for myself. To find my way, I am sketching a landscape on which my faith journey is marked with all its vicissitudes. Picturing you sitting in your wing-backed chair listening to me helps me to mark the connections between theology, feminism, ideology, the bible, the church, and the way we speak about God.[37]

Style is "how you write what you write when you write for an audience"

In sum, the style of your writing must be geared to the audience for whom you are writing. All of the constituents of writing style that we have described above—language, subject matter, genre, conceptual stance, and the stylistic range of individuality and pluralism implicit in all of these—finally play into the audience's hand, because "the act of writing... has its end in its audience."[38] Prompted by David Tracy, we have previously identified three theological audiences, or "publics": (1) the academy, (2) the church, and (3) the wider society.[39] While each "public" must be addressed in its own vernacular, theologians must also establish authority, credibility, and good will with whatever audience they are addressing. One of the ways this is done is by choosing an appropriate style of writing for that audience.

For example, in the introduction to his "Letter from a Birmingham Jail," written to a critical audience of "fellow clergymen" in 1963, Martin Luther King Jr. employs a respectful but rhetorically strategic style that seeks to bridge the gap between himself and his detractors by identifying with them as a "fellow clergyman," responding graciously to their criticisms, and addressing them as "men of genuine good will":

> My Dear Fellow Clergymen.... While confined here in the Birmingham city jail, I came across your recent statement calling my present activities "unwise and untimely." Seldom do I pause to answer criticism of my work and ideas. If I sought to answer all the criticisms that cross my desk, my secretaries would have little time for anything other than such correspondence... and I would have no time for constructive work. But since I feel that you are men of genuine good will and that your criticisms are sincerely set forth, I want to try to answer your statement in what I hope will be patient and reasonable terms.[40]

Yet before the Montgomery, Alabama bus boycott in 1955 that initiated King's movement of non-violent resistance, King addressed his own Holt Street Baptist Church congregation in a more colloquial, pastoral and prophetic style that stressed his solidarity with them and sought to mobilize them "for what lies ahead" by writing them into history books that then excluded them:

> And as we stand and sit here this evening, and as we prepare ourselves for what lies ahead, let us go out with a grim and bold determination that we are going to stick together. Right here in Montgomery when the history books are written in the future, somebody will have to say "there lived a race of people, black people, fleecy locks and black complexion, of people who had the moral courage to stand up for their rights." And thereby they injected a new meaning into the veins of history and of civilization. And we're gonna do that. God grant that we will do it before it's too late.[41]

Language, subject matter, genre, conceptual stance, stylistic individuality and pluralism, audience—all of these elements conspire to produce the distinctive but elusive quality of writing that we call "style." But what, you may be asking, has any of this to do with "rewriting theology well"? At the beginning of this chapter I suggested that to revise your own writing you must develop an intuitive sense of "style" to evaluate what you have already written and a normative model of "style" to guide the rewriting. Because a "normative" writing style never exists independently of its subject matter or genre, theological writers must find a normative style to guide their rewriting within the discipline of theology. Yet the strikingly different examples of "theological style" in the selections above give no evidence of a normative theological style to guide our rewriting. This leads us to the question, "What is theological style, and how do theological writers define it?" To answer it, we will look both at theological style narrowly conceived and at theological style broadly conceived. First, you are invited to respond to this question from your own experience as a theological writer in the following theological memo:

> *THEOLOGICAL MEMO 2: What is theological style, and how do you define it? Reread the previous section on "style" and the selections of the theological authors whose writings exemplified it. After you have done so, please write a one-page reflection to answer the question, "What is theological style, and how do you define it?"*

What is theological style, narrowly conceived, and how do theological writers define it?

To describe "style" as "theological" is to define it generically, in terms of the genre of theology. Thus, theological style, narrowly conceived, is determined by its genre, and the written conventions of that genre. Three theological genres that we have explored in this book are the pastoral reflection paper, the systematic reflection paper, and the constructive theological essay, each with its own conventional style of writing. Yet every contemporary theological genre and the style that exemplifies it are indebted to its historical predecessors. Thus, to answer the question, "What is theological style, and how do theological writers define it," we begin with three classic theological writers, St. Augustine, St. Thomas Aquinas, and Julian of Norwich, who exemplify pastoral, systematic, and constructive styles, respectively. In the Theological Memo following this section, you will be invited to identify three theologians of your choosing whose writings exemplify these styles in our contemporary context.

Saint Augustine

The fourth chapter of Augustine's *On Christian Doctrine* (427 C.E.) is an early Christian manual of pastoral style in which, as we noted in Chapter 1, Augustine applied the category of "style" bequeathed to him by Cicero and Roman rhetoric to early Christian discourse.[42] For Augustine, there was no contradiction between *elocutio* ("style") and *evangelium* (the Christian gospel); on the contrary, *elocutio* was integral to communicating the Christian message. He adapted its "plain," "moderate," and "grand" styles for the pastoral purposes of teaching, preaching,[43] and persuasion,[44] and identified these styles in the writings of Cyprian, Ambrose, and biblical authors, who exemplify: (1) choosing a style commensurate with subject matter, purpose, and audience; (2) mixing styles for rhetorical effect in preaching and writing;[45] and (3) using rhetorical means of persuasion in the service of the Christian message and the God who inspired it, and not merely to please an audience.[46] Augustine's synthesis of rhetoric and theology challenges us to ask with him, "While the faculty of eloquence, which is of great value in urging either evil or justice, is in itself indifferent, why should it not be obtained for the uses of the good in the service of truth?"[47] Whenever you write a pastoral reflection paper that flows rhetorically from your passion for faith, justice, and truth, you are writing in Augustine's shadow.

Thomas Aquinas

If Augustine provided an early Christian template for "pastoral style" in *On Christian Doctrine*, Thomas Aquinas patented the Scholastic template for "systematic style" in the *Summa Theologica* (1273).[48] The "faculty of eloquence" (*eloquentia*) celebrated by Augustine appears only four times in his *Summa Theologica.*[49] Yet the first words that Aquinas spoke in his "Inaugural Sermon" (1256) as a newly minted Master of Theology were from Augustine's *On Christian Doctrine.*[50] However, while Augustine synthesized rhetorical and theological styles, Aquinas and the Scholastics ultimately separated them. This rhetorical–theological divide was implicit in the Aristotelian distinction between rhetoric (the art of persuasion) and dialectic (the art of reasoning) that became explicit when theology was declared a "science" and elevated beyond the liberal arts of the *trivium* and *quadrivium*, including literature.[51] On the one hand, the Renaissance rhetorician Peter Ramus reinforced this rupture by disjoining rhetorical "style" from dialectic, or "True Reason,"[52] the province of philosophers and Scholastic theologians. On the other hand, both Erasmus and Luther denounced the Scholastic "style" of academic theology in favor of an emerging style of Reformation theology based not on Scholastic syllogisms but on the biblical sources.[53] Yet whenever you ask a theological question, develop a thesis statement, or write a systematic reflection paper, you are standing on the shoulders of Aquinas and his Scholastic colleagues.

Julian of Norwich

In December 1273, in Naples, Italy, three months before he died, Thomas Aquinas had a vision of such intensity that he stopped writing. In 1373, in Norwich, England, Julian of Norwich had a series of "deathbed" visions so compelling that when she recovered she started writing her *Showings*, or *Revelations of Divine Love*. Before its completion in 1413, she would write both a "first" and a "final" draft of this work, which is not only the earliest extant writing in English by a woman, but also a shining medieval example of "constructive" theological style.

A "constructive" theological style integrates both "pastoral" and "systematic" styles in its "rhetoric of correlation," thereby allowing the writer more freedom of expression.[54] During a time when theology was written in Latin by learned men for learned men in a prescribed "systematic" style, Julian wrote in the English vernacular, in the first person, for her "fellow Christians," and embraced a "proto-feminist" theology that claimed her own role in the church—and that of all women—on the authority of the God who bid her to write: "But because I am a woman, ought I therefore to believe that I should not tell you of the goodness of God, when I saw… that it is his will that it be known?"[55] Far from being a "mere" woman mystic, she constructed an incipient metaphorical theology in which "God is our Mother as truly as God is our Father," weaving both pastoral and systematic reflection through her metaphorical and discursive language to communicate her message. Similarly, whenever you weave pastoral and systematic styles into a vibrant constructive theological essay, you are following Julian's stylistic precedent.

THEOLOGICAL MEMO 3: Pastoral, Systematic and Constructive Styles and the Contemporary Theological Writer: Reflect on the theological authors that you have recently read for your courses in respect to their exemplification of pastoral, systematic, and/or constructive theological styles. Please choose one contemporary author to represent each of these respective styles, just as the discussion above identified Augustine, Aquinas and Julian of Norwich with a particular theological style. Finally, write a one-page reflection that explains why you chose the particular authors you did to represent the respective styles that you have attributed to them.

What is theological style, broadly conceived, and how do theological writers define it?

In the previous examples, we have defined "theological style" generically, in relation to the genres of "pastoral reflection," "systematic reflection," and "constructive theological essay." But what if we once again cast a wider net? Theological style is also characterized by its language, subject matter, conceptual stance, diversity, and audience. For example, contemporary theological writers have defined theological style (1) *linguistically*, as Thomas Merton enjoins those writing about God to do so "in sentences that are [not] half-dead";[56] (2) *generically*, as Rowan Williams identifies celebratory, communicative, and critical *styles* of theology;[57] (3) *epistemologically*, as Paul Tillich asserts, "Every style points to a self-interpretation of man";[58] (4) *pluralistically*, as Rowan Williams enjoins readers to "affirm theologically the propriety of different [theological] styles";[59] and (5) *rhetorically*, as David Tracy correlates the *style* of a theological "classic" with its "publicness," or effective communication to audiences.[60]

As we shall see in more detail shortly, many feminist theologians re-envision "style" through the metaphor of "voice," adding the category of (6) *theological voice* to this profile, as, for example, Elisabeth Schüssler Fiorenza encourages her students to "*find their theological voices* by developing discourses of critique, empowerment and possibility."[61] We will follow this movement from theological "style" to "voice" more pointedly after considering the question, What is theological style, broadly conceived, and how shall we define it?

What is theological style, broadly conceived, and how shall we define it?

If "style" is defined as how you write what you write, when you write in a given genre, from a particular stance, for a specific audience, then "theological style," broadly conceived, is *how you write theology when you write in a given theological genre, from a particular theological stance, for a specific theological audience, using your own words, your own sentences, your own paragraphs, your own images, your own arguments, your own metaphors, and your own voice*. Three important points follow from this definition.

First, there is not one "theological style," but a diversity of "theological styles" constitutive of the stylistic conventions of the written genre (pastoral reflection, systematic reflection, constructive theological essay, and so on) and the writer's individual style and voice (the "personal voice," the "academic voice," and various combinations of both of these). As Rowan Williams cautions, "One of the temptations of theology has been—at least in the modern era—to suppose not so much that there is a normative content for theological utterance, but that there is a normative *style*."[62]

Second, this diversity of theological styles does not imply that theological writing can be done "free style," since each "theological style" is driven by the conventions of its genre and the expectations of its audience. It thus behooves you to familiarize yourself with both of these when beginning a theological writing assignment. "When I assign a biblical essay," one of my professors told the class not merely in jest, "I do not want a literary critique of the contemporary Nigerian novel."

Third, your mastery of theological style will only be as good as the words, sentences and paragraphs that you write, for as we will see in the next chapter, they are the rhetorics, or purposeful elements of theological style. Before we do, we must explore a final element of theological style that is rapidly becoming an alternative expression of it: *voice*. What, then, is *voice*, and what is the relationship between *style* and *voice* in theological writing?

What is *voice* and the relationship between *style* and *voice* in theological writing?

To answer the question, "What is voice," we must first discern the relationship between style and voice in theological writing. A writer's style can be syntactically clear and grammatically correct but lack that extra "something" that is needed to write theology well. In the epigraph that introduces this chapter, Thomas Merton laments the poor writing of many who "love God and serve [Him]," and explains further, "I am not talking about grammar and syntax, but about having something to say and saying it in sentences that are not half dead."[63]

We have all written more than our share of "half-dead" sentences. You may think that theological writing for the "academy" encourages this kind of writing in the interests of scholarly objectivity and "theological correctness."[64] If, for example, in a paper on Mary of Nazareth, you write, *The following theological methodology was utilized to interrogate prevailing traditions pursuant to a theology of Mary*, I might be tempted to ask, "Is anybody home?" From my reader's perspective, you have deadened your style by suppressing your "live" voice and using the passive voice. You have hammered another nail in the coffin by relying on abstract terminology ["theological methodology"] rather than active description of the methodology [e.g., "feminist"; "liberationist"; "historical-critical"] to communicate your precise meaning. Finally, you have allowed rigor mortis to set in by exchanging an engaged authorial presence for an artificial academic persona. You may have done all of the above in order to emulate the "academic" voice that you thought your professor wanted. Yet an academic voice does not have to be enunciated in "half-dead" sentences.[65]

But what, you might ask, will make the dry bones of these sentences live? What makes the "dry bones" of a sentence live is the "voice" of the person who writes it. As author Mary McCarthy observes, "If one means by style the voice, the irreducible and always recognizable and alive thing, then... style is really everything."[66] But "if one means by *style* the *voice*," as McCarthy says, then it is equally true that "voice is really everything." What, then, is voice?

What is *voice*?

If style is the flesh of writing, voice is its breath. "The best writing," Peter Elbow observes, "has *voice*: the life and rhythms of speech."[67] For author Eudora Welty, "voice" is "the sound that falls on the page" as one writes and reads what one has written.[68] Yet when applied to writing, "voice" is a metaphor whose roots reach deep into the soil of orality. For Greek and Roman students of rhetoric whose goal was eloquence in public speaking, "style" itself was "voiced" (recall that the Latin word for style is *elocutio*, from which our word "elocution" comes). For contemporary writers, however, "voice" is more broadly conceived as "a composite of all the rhetorical and stylistic techniques a writer chooses, consciously or unconsciously, to use to present his or her self to an audience."[69] More specifically, Peter Elbow distinguishes "five senses of 'voice' as it is applied to writing: (1) audible voice (the sounds in a text); (2) dramatic voice (the character or implied author in a text); (3) recognizable or distinctive voice; (4) voice with authority; (5) resonant voice or presence."[70] All of these senses relate and resonate in that finely tuned instrument that we call the writer's "voice." For the moment, however, we can define *voice* simply as what readers hear when they read your writing.

What is the relationship between *style* and *voice* in theological writing?

Just as our definition of "style" was dependent upon the point of departure, "voice" in writing is defined differently from different vantage points, two of which we shall track shortly. And just as the continuum of style moves from conventional formats to individual expressions of a writer's style, so the trajectory of voice in writing embraces both the "personal voice" and the "academic voice" that we have used for writing "pastoral reflection papers" and "systematic reflection papers," respectively.

However, while contemporary rhetoric tries to distinguish style and voice, the boundaries between them are not fixed, but fluid. As we have seen, Mary McCarthy first distinguishes style and voice, then defines style as voice, but finally concludes, "'style' is everything." Lest you are tempted to attribute McCarthy's ambiguity to the effects of her "Catholic Girlhood" or to the fact that she is a novelist and not a theologian, Rowan Williams' distinction between "theological style" and "theological voice" is similarly blurred. In a "typology of theological activity" that prefaces a collection of his theological essays, Williams uses "styles of theology" and "theological voices" interchangeably and defers to the diversity of theological "style or mode or 'voice' " without trying to disentangle them.[71] Moreover, because the category of "theological style" reflects a patriarchal tradition that has regulated "normative" theological styles of discourse, many feminist theologians have claimed the metaphor of "voice" as a more liberating rhetorical synonym. Yet even when writing in "a different voice,"[72] feminist theologians write with distinctive "styles" that we have already admired in this book. What shall we make of this linguistic confusion?

Distinguishing the terms *style* and *voice* is a bit like trying to separate egg yolks and egg whites. If you want to make an angel food cake from scratch, you will have to break the eggs, one by one and gently gather the whites into one bowl, while reserving the yolks for another purpose. In the same way, we can—and I have—differentiated *style* from *voice* on the basis of what readers "hear" in your writing. But if you want to make an omelet, you will need to use "whole" eggs, and the yolks and the whites will be inseparable once you have folded them into the omelet. In the same way, it should be ultimately impossible to separate "style" and "voice" when you have completed a good theological essay. We are separating them here in order to more clearly distinguish the elements that both of them bring to writing theology well.

Voice, then, is style's soundtrack. It is that residual organ of orality invigorating the text that refuses to be suppressed by the silence of "lifeless letters,"[73] just as a "*son et lumiere*" presentation at Versailles brings its ancient history to life against the darkness of the night sky. Similarly, voice is style's megaphone, through which the writer enunciates the writing on the page into the mind, heart, and ear of the reader. Voice, finally, is what enables readers not only to read the words of your writing, but also to hear the voice of the writer and converse with you as they read. I invite you to consider what readers "hear" when they read your writing in the next theological memo:

> *THEOLOGICAL MEMO 4: What do readers hear when they read your writing? This theological memo invites you to become more familiar with your writing voice, in collaboration with a writing partner/listener. Choose a recently completed theological essay that represents your best work, and read the first page silently to yourself. Then read the same page aloud to a classmate or other writing partner, who will then describe both the sound of your language (e.g., "rhythmic"; "dissonant"; "clear as a bell"; "a clanging symbol") and its emotional tone (e.g., "strident"; "subdued"; "confident"; "hesitant"). After you have briefly recorded your partner's feedback, repeat the exercise as a listener and respondent for your partner. After s/he has had an opportunity to record your feedback, compare the descriptions of what each of you heard. Were there noticeable similarities or differences in your writing voices? Reflect briefly on what you learned about your writing voice from your classmate's feedback and the comparison of your writing voices.*

Toward a theological voice of one's own

If you have completed the theological memo above (and even if you haven't), you may still be hesitant to define *voice* merely in terms of "what readers hear when they listen to your writing." On the one hand, you may be struggling to find a strong and confident writing voice to negotiate conventions of theological writing which seem to silence that voice before it can be "heard into speech"[74] (or writing). On the other hand, you may have lost a once strong and confident writing voice to a cacophony of voices that you are choosing variously to use in order to write for different theological audiences. Implicit in both of these struggles is the desire to identify, develop and refine "a theological voice of one's own." By "a theological voice of one's own" I do not mean a privatized and idiosyncratic theological voice, nor a self-aggrandizing authorial persona, but a voice that confidently speaks and writes the "hope that is in that is in you" (I Peter 3:15) in conversation with other voices in a way that is faithful, credible, critical, and heartfelt. Thus, a voice of one's own is a voice that one "owns," whether it is "personal," "academic" or a combination of both of these. Can readers hear that voice when they listen to the sound of your writing on the page?

Underlying each of these struggles and their confessed goal of a resonant theological voice are competing conceptions of voice that are constantly in play as we write, however we dichotomize them or try to reconcile them: (1) the "Find Your Voice" path; and (2) the "Choose Your Voice" path.[75] Writers embarking upon the "Find Your Voice" path learn from the literary tradition of poets and creative authors that they must first "find" their own "authentic" voice before the dry bones of their sentences will live. Thus, "voice" is construed as an elusive, mysterious expression of the individual, creative self that transcends both stylistic conventions and audience expectations but is ultimately vindicated by both of these. For theological writers on this path, *finding* a theological voice of one's own is antecedent to *having* one.

Writers embarking upon the "Choose Your Voice" path, on the other hand, learn from social constructionists like Mikhail Bakhtin that that there is no individual "voice of one's own" to find, since language itself is "multivocal," and all conceptions of voice are socially constructed.[76] Thus, the dry bones of their sentences must be invigorated with voices other than their own in order to "live," and the "voice" that their writing projects is more like a "persona" that the writer adopts for a particular purpose than an individual "voiceprint" of the writer's soul. For theological writers on this path, *having* a theological voice at all is contingent upon other voices that have entered into dialogical relation with our own. As you read the descriptions of these two conceptions of "voice," you are probably identifying with one more than with the other. However, when we define voice simply as what readers hear when they read your writing, both paths converge, at least long enough for us make some connections between them on the way toward identifying, developing and refining "a theological voice of your own."

How does one identify, develop, and refine a theological voice of one's own?

Just as there is no such thing as a normative "theological style," there is no univocal "theological voice" but rather a polyphonic register of theological voices through which the breath of God resonates in response to particular contexts, concerns, callings, and communities. Among these theological voices is, of course, your own. How can you identify, develop and refine it?

First, in order to develop a "theological voice of your own," you must have "a writing voice of your own." But you already *have* a writing "voice," as the previous theological memo has demonstrated. You do not need to "find your voice" before you can write "with voice," or "choose a voice" in which to write. At times you may need to gain confidence in the "voice" you have in order to let it resonate more clearly. At other times you may need to let go of that voice in order to give other voices in your writing precedence.

Second, you will learn to find that voice in conversation with other voices, at the same time that you will recognize the echo of those voices in the sound that your own words make on the page. Third, as our previous distinction between "personal" and "academic" voices corroborates, the voice that readers hear in your writing will differ according to the audience for whom you are writing, just as your speaking voice may vary in different conversational contexts. Some of the most poignant theological writing today chooses to be "a voice for the voiceless" by employing a more inclusive theological style, as we shall see in the next chapter.[77] Finally, I suspect that the "personal" and "academic" voices of theological discourse are not as opposed as we sometimes make them, and that those who have developed "a theological voice of their own" have also learned how to integrate them in a way that makes the dry bones of their sentences live.[78]

With all this in mind, let us see if we can reinvigorate the sentence about Mary of Nazareth by rewriting that first sentence, "*The following theological methodology was utilized to interrogate prevailing traditions pursuant to a theology of Mary,*" with an ear more attuned to what readers hear when they read your writing. From that starting point, you might, like Elizabeth Johnson, introduce your methodology with this sentence:

> My point of departure is the global chorus of women's voices today, which, heard in all fullness, offers both critical and creative theological interpretations of the marian tradition.[79]

In so doing, Elizabeth Johnson has written in her own "active" voice and from her own "point of departure." She has also introduced her methodology through concrete, choral metaphors ("the global chorus of women's voices today") that invigorate the more abstract "critical and creative interpretations" of which they sing. Moreover, she has emulated the voices of her intended readers ("heard in all their fullness") through her vividly auditory use of language, rather than silencing them with a detached academic monotone. Finally, she has done all of this in language that is clear, communicative, stylistically distinctive, and evocative of her own voice.

Elizabeth Johnson did not write the first, "half-dead" sentence that we started with. I did. If it sounded to you like a bad parody of writing in an academic voice, you are already beginning to develop an "ear" for theological style and voice. Just as Eudora Welty listened to "the sound of the page" to rewrite her short stories, listening to the sound that your writing makes on the page will help you to rewrite theology well. As Billy Collins corroborates, "In the process of simplifying... one often discovers the thing called voice.... Eventually, I was confident enough to write a simple sentence, and then I began to recognize the sound of my own writing."[80] Yet you do not have to be a poet to recognize that however pronounced the sound, or *voice*, of your writing, it is *style*, understood simply as the words that you write with and combine into sentences and paragraphs, which gives your writing its distinctive voice. Thus, style and voice collude to create the sound and sense that your words make on the page, and we come full circle to explore those elements of theological style in the next chapter.

Before we do, one more question must be addressed. While we have looked at three "generic" or "normative" models of theological style in this chapter that provide an "external standard" for your writing and rewriting, we have not yet identified any "internal criteria" constitutive of "an intuitive sense of style" for evaluating what you have written. I have saved this task for the end, because it is properly your job, not mine. I can identify my own internal sense of "right" writing style, but I cannot presume to identify yours. Since style and voice are so intertwined in writing, the previous discussion of "a theological voice of your own" should help you to recognize your internal stylistic criteria and give them "voice." You will find additional tools for sharpening your felt sense of style and voice through the process of revision in Chapter 12, "Rewriting Theology Well." However, I conclude this chapter with a profile of "theological plain style," adapted from Strunk and White's *Elements of Style*, which my students have found helpful in identifying, analyzing, and refining their own writing styles. The final theological memo below will invite you to analyze your own writing style in accord with that profile.

Theological plain style: A profile for theological writers

While not all theological writing is "plain," contemporary "plain" style, characterized by clarity, conciseness, and correctness, provides a common denominator for evaluating and revising theological writing. We can question the conceptual stance inherent in this style, as many have.[81] Nonetheless, for theological writers, a mastery of "plain style" is foundational, in that all writing must be clear, precise and accessible to its audience in order to communicate "God-language." You may not always choose "plain style" as your predominant mode of writing, but it will provide sound criteria for "rewriting theology well." Here are some characteristics of "theological plain style," followed by guidelines for use of inclusive language (one of its characteristics),[82] and a "Heuristic for Analyzing Writing Styles":

Characteristics of theological plain style for theological writers

- Plain style articulates a structure that readers can follow.
- Plain style begins paragraphs with "topic sentences" or "transitional sentences."
- Plain style invites the writer to "write naturally," but to stay out of the way.
- Plain style prefers the active to the passive voice.
- Plain style favors specific, concrete language over abstract, generalized language.
- Plain style uses nouns and verbs before adjectives, adverbs, and "fancy words."
- Plain style "omits unnecessary words."
- Plain style prefers positive assertions to indefinite negative statements.
- Plain style avoids overstatements, qualifiers, and figures of speech.
- Plain style expresses similar ideas in similar grammatical form.
- Plain style keeps modifiers close to the words that they modify.
- Plain style keeps verb tenses consistent within a piece of writing.
- Plain style places the emphatic words of a sentence at the end or beginning.
- Plain style is not "drab" but "elegant."
- Plain style requires rewriting and revision to get it right.
- Plain style encourages the use of inclusive language as appropriate.

Inclusive language style sheet for theological writers

Avoid gender-exclusive language for God whenever possible. Use gender-inclusive, gender-varied, non-gender specific, or non-personal language.

Examples	Alternatives
Our Father who art in heaven …	Our Father and Mother in heaven …
The Lord	Sovereign One
Kingdom of God	Reign of God

Avoid male pronouns for God. Repeat the word "God" or use analogous language, such as "the divine," "Godself," "God's own self":

Examples	Alternatives
God is in his heaven; all's right with the world.	God is in heaven; all's right with the world.
God hears the prayers of His people.	God hears the prayers of God's people.
God revealed himself in Jesus Christ.	God revealed God's own self in Jesus Christ.

Avoid the generic use of man and other words with masculine markers whenever possible.

Examples	Alternatives
Mankind	humankind, human beings, people
Man's dreams	our dreams
The common man	the average person, common humanity

Avoid using man/woman in terms describing occupations that include both women and men.

Examples	Alternatives
chairman	chair, moderator, head
fireman, mailman	firefighter, mail carrier
policeman/policewoman	police officer

Avoid generic use of the male pronoun as an inclusive third-person singular personal pronoun.

Recast into the plural:

Example	Alternative
Each ordination candidate must write his bishop.	Ordination candidates must write their bishops.

Rewrite in gender-considerate language:

Example	Alternative
The typical seminarian worries about his writing.	The typical seminarian worries about writing.

Replace masculine pronouns with one, you, or "he or she":

Example	Alternative
If a student is ill, he will be excused.	If a student is ill, he or she will be excused.

Alternate male and female pronouns:

Example	Alternative
How can a student learn to write effectively? What does he need? How should he begin?	How can a student learn to write effectively? What does she need? How should he begin?

Avoid using the masculine pronoun to refer to an indefinite pronoun (everybody, everyone, anybody, anyone); instead, use the plural pronoun as an inclusive substitute.

Example	Alternative
Everyone in the class should bring his lunch.	Everyone in the class should bring their lunch.

THEOLOGICAL MEMO 5: A Theological Writer's Heuristic for Analyzing Writing Styles:[83] *Use the "Theological Writer's Heuristic" below to analyze your own writing style in a recently written theological or biblical paper:*

I. Words, vocabulary, diction:

Is the vocabulary: General or specific?
Abstract or concrete?
Formal or informal?
Latinate (using polysyllabic words)?
Anglo-Saxon (using monosyllabic words)?

What is the average proportion of: Nouns?
Verbs?
Adjectives?
Adverbs?
Technical (pastoral/theological) terms?
Figures of speech?
Clichés?
Jargon?

Is the diction: descriptive, expository, argumentative, polemic, poetic, pastoral?

II. Sentences: *What is the average number of words in each sentence?*

Are the sentences *simple* (subject/verb/object)? *Compound* (independent clauses connected by *and*, *or*, *nor*, *but*)? *Complex* (composed of both dependent or subordinate and independent or insubordinate clauses)?

What is your typical sentence word order (subject/verb/object? inverted order? introductory subordinate clause? Or??)

III. Paragraphs:
What is the average number of sentences in a paragraph?
How many topic sentences and transitional sentences can you identify in your paragraphs? What transitional phrases and logical connectors (for, therefore, since, because, now, in sum...) are most common in the paragraphs? How often do you use them?

Concluding reflections: Rewriting theology well: Rhetorics of style and voice

In this chapter, we have asked (1) What is *style*, and how do writers define it? (2) What is *theological style*, narrowly and broadly conceived, and how do theological writers define it? (3) What is *voice*, and what is the relationship between *style* and *voice* in theological writing? (4) How does one identify, develop, and refine a theological voice and style of one's own?

First, we surveyed classical and contemporary rhetorical perspectives on style and observed that different stylistic starting points, such as language, subject, genre, stance, and audience generate different theological "styles." Second, we identified pastoral, systematic, and constructive styles as "normative" theological styles. Third, we explored "voice" in writing as a synonym for "style" and found it integral to identifying, developing, and refining a theological voice of one's own. Finally, we proposed a "theological plain style" as a template for identifying, developing, and refining a theological style of one's own. What will bind all of these elements into a mature theological voice/style, is you, the writer, and your distinctive way of using words, sentences, and paragraphs to write theology well, which we probe in the next chapter.

Notes

1 Teresa of Avila, Hans Urs Von Balthasar, and Mother Theresa are among those who have confessed never to revise their original writings.

2 Francis-Noel Thomas and Francis Turner, *Clear and Simple as the Truth: Writing Classic Prose* (Princeton: Princeton University Press, 1996), 9.

3 Aristotle, *On Rhetoric*, ed. and trans. George A. Kennedy (New York and Oxford: Oxford University Press, 1991), 3.2–12, pp. 220–57.

4 *Rhetorica ad Herennium*, 4.1–12 in James L. Murphy and Richard A. Katula et al., *A Synoptic History of Classical Rhetoric*, 2nd ed. (Davis, CA: Hermagoras Press, 1994), 119ff; Cicero, *De Oratore*, 3, in Murphy and Katula, *Synoptic History*, 153–57; and Demetrius, *On Style*, in *Ancient Literary Criticism: the Principal Texts in New Translations*, ed. D.A. Russell and M. Winterbottom (Oxford and New York: Oxford University Press, 1988), 173–215.

5 See Longinus, *On the Sublime*, 9, trans. W. Hamilton Fyfe, in *Aristotle* (Cambridge: Harvard University Press [Loeb], 1932), 419: "A great style is the natural outcome of important thoughts." Quoted in Thomas and Turner, *Clear and Simple*, 76, to whom I am indebted for their connection of "style" with a "conceptual stand" [4–6].

6 "The function of speech is to influence the soul," says Socrates, and different souls are influenced by different styles of speeches. Plato, *Phaedrus and Letters VII and VIII*, 271, trans. W. Hamilton (London: Penguin Books, 1983), 91.

7 Aristotle, *On Rhetoric*, 3.1.1; 3.12.1; 3.2.8 (pp. 217, 255, 222).

8 For Aristotle's philosophical "stance" toward rhetoric, see Kennedy's introduction in *On Rhetoric*, 8–13. Thomas and Turner concur that "there is nothing new in the idea that a style is effectively a stand on a small number of central issues," pointing out that "classical rhetoricians analyzed contrasting styles from this perspective, and routinely demonstrated that what was good or appropriate to one style might [not] ... be for another." *Clear and Simple*, 72–73.

9 *Rhetorica ad Herennium*, 1.2 (p. 117).

10 See Cicero, *De Oratore*, 3.20, in Murphy and Katula, *Synoptic History*, 153: "No matter the subject or goal of any oration, it must consist of matter and form, and although neither can be separated except in the abstract, I will give my views on style, the form which language should take."

11 The Greek rhetorician Demetrius had included a fourth, "forcible" style in the first century B.C.E./C.E. *On Style*, but the "high," "middle," and "low" styles became standard for Roman rhetoric. See Edward P.J. Corbett, *Classical Rhetoric for the Modern Student*, 2nd ed. (New York: Oxford University Press, 1971), 600.

12 See Cicero, *De Inventione*, 1.1, in Murphy and Katula, *Synoptic History*, 137: "I believe that oratory has been helpful to mankind, but wisdom must accompany eloquence."

13 Cicero, *De Oratore*, 3.20.90 (pp. 154–55). For an excellent discussion of the political stance of Roman rhetoric and its stylistic ramifications, see Don H. Compier, *What Is Rhetorical Theology? Textual Practice and Public Discourse* (Harrisburg, PA: Trinity Press International, 1999), 3–9.

14 See, most recently, Steven Pinker, *The Sense of Style: The Thinking Person's Guide to Writing in the 21st Century* (New York: Viking/Penguin Group, 2014).

15 See William Strunk Jr. and E.B. White, *The Elements of Style*, 4th ed. (Needham Heights, MA: Longman/Allyn & Bacon, 2000), 18, 23. William Strunk provides the catalogue of correct usage; E.B. White appends "An Approach to Style."

16 See Walker Gibson, *Tough, Sweet and Stuffy: An Essay on Modern American Prose Styles* (Bloomington and London: Indiana University Press, 1966).

17 Thomas and Turner, *Clear and Simple*, 4.

18 T.S. Eliot, *What is a Classic?" An Address Delivered before the Virgil Society on the 16th of October 1944* (London: Faber and Faber, 1945), 25–27; reprinted in T.S. Eliot, *On Poets and Poetry* (London: Faber and Faber, 1957), 66, quoted in Thomas and Turner, *Clear and Simple*, 16.

19 Richard M. Coe, *Form and Substance: An Advanced Rhetoric* (New York: John Wiley & Sons, 1981), 157.

20 Consciousness of individual style in classical rhetoric was subservient to the other elements of style. Cicero, for example, encouraged orators to develop an individual style, but always in keeping with the generic style in which the speech was composed. See Cicero, *De Oratore*, 3.7 (p. 154).

21 Ben Yagoda, *The Sound on the Page: Style and Voice in Writing* (New York: Harper Collins, 2004), xvii.

22 William Zinsser, *On Writing Well: The Classic Guide to Writing Nonfiction*, 30th Anniversary Edition (New York: HarperCollins, 2006), 25.

23 Billy Collins, quoted in Yagoda, *The Sound on the Page*, 123, 138.

24 Elizabeth A. Johnson, "Jesus, the Wisdom of God: A Biblical Basis for Non-Andocentric Christology," *Ephemerides Theologicae Lovanienses* 61 (1985): 264–65.

25 Roger Haight, *Jesus Symbol of God* (Maryknoll, NY: Orbis Books, 1999), 9.

26 Karl Rahner, "The Future of the Religious Book," in *Theological Investigations*, vol. 8, trans. David Bourke (New York: Herder & Herder, 1979), 255–56.

27 Rowan Williams, *On Christian Theology* (Oxford: Blackwell, 2000), 6.

28 Dave Barry, quoted in Yagoda, *The Sound on the Page*, 132.

29 Belden Lane, "Saints and Writers: On Doing One's Work in Hiding," *Theology Today* 59 (2003): 616.

30 See Denise M. Ackerman, *After the Locusts: Letters from a Landscape of Faith* (Grand Rapids, MI: William B. Eerdmanns, 2003), xii.

31 Ibid., xvi.

32 Lisa Ede, Cheryl Glenn, and Andrea Lunsford, "Border Crossings: Intersections of Rhetoric and Feminism," *Rhetorica* 13 (1995): 423.

33 Longinus, *On the Sublime*, 9, quoted in Thomas and Turner, *Clear and Simple*, 76.

34 Thomas and Turner, *Clear and Simple*, 22, 27, 74.

35 Bernard Lonergan, "Theology in Its New Context," in *A Second Collection*, ed. William F. Ryan and Bernard J. Tyrrell (Philadelphia: Westminster, 1983), 67.

36 For example, the philosopher Beryl Lang identifies two contemporary styles of philosophical writing, each of which issue from different conceptual stands: (1) the *neutralist*, or classical style, "in which the philosophical writer draws on an independent and supposedly style-less body of prepositional assertions that the philosopher first discovers and then arranges or reformulates," and (2) an *interactionist*, or postmodernist style, wherein "the writer, in choosing a form or structure for philosophical discourse, is, in that act, also shaping the substances or content which the form ... will be 'of.'" See Beryl Lang, *The Anatomy of Philosophical Style* (London: Blackwell, 1990), 14–15.

37 Ackerman, *After the Locusts*, 24.

38 Flannery O'Connor, *The Habit of Being: Letters of Flannery O'Connor*, ed. Sally Fitzgerald (New York: Farrar, Strauss and Giroux, 1979), 458.

39 Chapter 1, above, under "Writing Theology in Our Own Context and Its Audiences."

40 Martin Luther King, Jr., "Letter from a Birmingham Jail," in *I Have a Dream: Writings and Speeches that Changed the World*, ed. James Melvin Washington (San Francisco: HarperSanFrancisco, 1992), 84.

41 Martin Luther King, Jr., "Speech at Holt Street Baptist Church (1955)," in *The Eyes on the Prize Civil Rights Reader: Documents, Speeches and First-Hand Accounts from the Black Freedom Struggle 1954–1990*, ed. Clayborne Carlson et al., (New York: Penguin Books, 1991), 51.

42 See Chapter 1, under "Writing Theology as a Rhetorical Art with Augustine of Hippo." The writings of many patristic theologians—Tertullian, St. John Chrysostum, and

Gregory of Nazianzus, among others—are steeped in the classical rhetorical tradition, but Augustine's articulation of a "theory" of Christian rhetoric based upon classical models is distinctive. See George A. Kennedy, *Classical Rhetoric and Its Christian and Secular Tradition from Ancient to Modern Times* (Chapel Hill: University of North Carolina Press, 1980), 149–60; and David Cunningham, *Faithful Persuasion: In Aid of a Rhetoric of Christian Theology* (Notre Dame: University of Notre Dame Press, 1991), 33–34.

43 Literally, "praising and blaming," or what Aristotle calls *epideictic* rhetoric. For example, Cyprian and Ambrose use the *moderate style* for treatises praising virginity and explaining how those who have taken vows of "virginity" should act (St. Augustine, *On Christian Doctrine*, trans. D.W. Robertson, Jr. (Indianapolis: Bobbs-Merrill [Liberal Arts Press], 1958), 4, 21, 47–48).

44 See Augustine, *On Christian Doctrine*, 4, 21, 46. To choose a level of style, in other words, was also to predispose oneself to a kind of language in conformity with the style: hence "St. Ambrose also, when he is urging a very important matter concerning the Holy Spirit, so that he may show it to be equal with the Father and the Son, … uses the subdued style of speaking. For the thing discussed does not need verbal ornaments, nor motions of the affections to persuade, but evidence as proof."

45 Ibid., 4.22.51: "For when one style is maintained too long, it loses the listener."

46 Ibid., 4.25.55: "Thus we use the ornaments of the moderate style not ostentatiously, but prudently."

47 Ibid., 4.2.

48 For a fuller treatment of the *summa*, the *quaestio*, and the *article*, see Chapter 1, above under "Writing Theology as a Scholastic Science with Thomas Aquinas."

49 See, e.g., Thomas Aquinas, *Summa Theologica: Complete English Edition in Five Volumes* (Westminster, MD: Christian Classics, 1961), 2. Q. 175; 2. Q. 183.

50 "According to Augustine in *On Christian Doctrine* 4.12, one skilled in speech should so speak as to teach, to delight, and to change; that is, to teach the ignorant, to delight the bored and to change the lazy. The speech of Sacred Scripture does these three things in the fullest manner." See Thomas Aquinas, "The Inaugural Sermons," in *Thomas Aquinas: Selected Writings*, ed. and trans. Ralph McInerny (London and New York: Penguin Books, 1998), 5.

51 See Ernst Robert Curtius, *European Literature and the Latin Middle Ages* (New York: Harper and Row, 1963), 53–56.

52 See Cunningham, *Faithful Persuasion*, 21. For a more substantial treatment of Ramus, see S.J. Walter J. Ong, *Ramus, Method and the Decay of Dialogue* (Cambridge, MA: Harvard University Press, 1958), 5.

53 See John W. O'Malley, *Four Cultures of the West* (Cambridge, MA: Harvard University Press, 2004), 106, 158–61.

54 See Chapter 4, above under "Charting the Rhetorics of the Constructive Theological Essay: Identification, Correlation, Suspicion, Construction."

55 Julian of Norwich, *Showings*, ed. and trans., E. Colledge and J. Walsh (New York/ Ramsey: Paulist Press, 1978), vi, 135. For an excellent rhetorical study of Julian of Norwich, see Cheryl Glenn, "Julian of Norwich and Her Rhetoric of Theology," in *Rhetoric Retold: Regendering the Tradition from Antiquity through the Renaissance* (Carbondale, IL: Southern Illinois University Press, 1997), 93–103.

56 Thomas Merton, *The Sign of Jonas* (New York: Doubleday Image Books, 1956), 66.

57 See Williams, *On Christian Theology*. For celebratory, see xiii-xiv: "... typically the language of hymnody and preaching," but embracing the more poetic theologies of Von Balthasar and Eastern Orthodoxy, among other examples. For communicative, see xiv: "Theology [that] seeks to persuade or commend, to witness to the gospel's capacity for being at home in more than one cultural environment," including Clement, Origen, liberation theology, and feminist theology. For critical, see xv: "This nagging at fundamental meanings is what constitutes a critical theology," including negative theology, Western philosophical theology, and postmodern theology.

58 Paul Tillich, *Theology of Culture*, ed. Richard C. Kimball (New York and London: Oxford University Press, 1959), 70.

59 Williams, *On Christian Theology*, 9.

60 David Tracy, *The Analogical Imagination: Christian Theology and the Culture of Pluralism* (New York: Crossroad, 1987), 109, 129–30. Tracy defines a "classic" as those "expressions of the human spirit [which] so disclose a compelling truth about our lives that we cannot deny them some kind of normative status .... We name these ... classics."

61 Elizabeth Schüssler Fiorenza, *But She Said: Feminist Practices of Biblical Interpretation* (Boston: Beacon Press, 1992), 188.

62 Williams, *On Christian Theology*, 9.

63 Merton, *Sign of Jonas*, 66.

64 See, on the contrary, Helen Sword, *Stylish Academic Writing* (Cambridge, MA: Harvard University Press, 2012), who argues that "even within the constraints of disciplinary norms, most academics enjoy a far wider range of stylistic choices than they realize" and surveys "the work of academic writers from across the disciplines who stretch and break disciplinary codes—and get away with it" (vii).

65 *An* "academic voice" *is a* formal scholarly voice used in theological writing for the academy (see Chapter 2 above under "Writing Theological Reflection papers: Purpose, Style, Voice"). While the passive voice and the suppression of the authorial "I" remains conventional in scientific and technical academic writing, scholars in the humanities—including theology and biblical studies—favor the active voice, and with it, the judicious use of the authorial first person (*I*, *my*, and so on).

66 Mary McCarthy, quoted in Yagoda, *The Sound on the Page*, 23.

67 Peter Elbow, "The Shifting Relationships Between Speech and Writing," in *Everyone Can Write: Essays Toward a Hopeful Theory of Writing and Teaching Writing* (New York: Oxford University Press, 2000), 159. See also Peter Elbow, *Vernacular Eloquence: What Speech Can Bring to Writing* (New York: Oxford University Press, 2012).

68 Eudora Welty, quoted in Yagoda, *The Sound on the Page*, 35. See also Karyn L. Wiseman, "Writing for the Ear," in Eric D. Barretto, ed., *Writing Theologically: Foundations for Learning* (Minneapolis, Fortress Press, 2015), 33–43.

69 Margaret K. Woodworth, "Teaching Voice," in *Voices on Voice: Perspectives, Definitions, Inquiry*, ed. Kathleen Blake Yancey (Urbana, IL: NCTE Press, 1994), 145–46.

70 See Peter Elbow, "What Do We Mean When We Talk About Voice in Texts?" in *Voices on Voice*, ed. Yancey, 2.

71 See Williams, *On Christian Theology*, xvi.

72 See Carol Gilligan, *In a Different Voice: Psychological Theory and Women's Development* (Cambridge, MA: Harvard University Press, 1982).

73 See P.T. Botha, "From Living Voice to Lifeless Letters: Reserve Towards Writing in the Graeco-Roman World," *Hervormde Teologiese Studies* 49 (1993): 742–59.

74 Nelle Morton, *The Journey is Home* (Boston: Beacon Press, 1985), 55. In this pioneering feminist theological reflection, Morton encouraged the process of "hearing ourselves into speech."

75 I am indebted to Paula Gillespie, "Classroom Voices," in *Voices on Voice*, ed. Yancey, 159–71, for this categorization, which she identifies as "Romantic" and "social constructionist" approaches to voice.

76 As Mikhail Bakhtin writes, "... the internally persuasive word is half-ours and half someone else's. Its creativity and productiveness consists precisely in the fact that such a word awakens new and independent words ... and does not remain in an isolated and static condition." See Mikhail M. Bakhtin, *The Dialogic Imagination*, trans. C. Emerson and M. Holquist (Austin: University of Texas Press, 1986), 345–46. See also the discussion of Bakhtin's multivocality in Chapter 6, above, under "Plagiarism Preventions and Interventions," and Chapter 8 above, under "Building Dialogical Bridges with a Hermeneutics of Diversity" and "Concluding Reflections."

77 See, for example, the writing of Latin American theologians Elsa Tamez and Jon Sobrino in Chapter 11, below, "Rewriting Theology Well (II): Rhetorics of Words, Sentences, and Paragraphs," under "Writing Theological Paragraphs Well with Elsa Tamez and Jon Sobrino."

78 For more on integrating "personal" and "academic" voices in the writing of a constructive theological essay, see Lucretia B. Yaghjian, "Teaching Theological Reflection Well, Reflecting on Writing as a Theological Practice," *Teaching Theology and Religion* 7/2 (2004): 83–94.

79 Elizabeth A. Johnson, *Truly Our Sister: A Theology of Mary in the Communion of Saints* (New York: Continuum, 2003), xv.

80 Interview with Billy Collins, quoted in Yagoda, *The Sound on the Page*, 123.

81 See, for example, Arthur Plotnik, *Spunk and Bite: A Writer's Guide to Punchier, More Engaging Language and Style* (New York: Random House Reference, 2005). See also Pinker, *Sense of Style*, who advocates the "classic style" described in Thomas and Turner as a more congenial style than Strunk and White's "plain" or "practical" style for twenty-first century, postmodernist writers seeking to provide readers with "a window onto the world" (26–56).

82 The characteristics are adapted from Strunk and White's *The Elements of Style*, 15–33. The guidelines are adapted from Thomas H. Groome, *Language for a "Catholic" Church: A Program of Study*, rev. ed. (Kansas City, MO: Sheed & Ward, 1995).

83 Adapted from Corbett, *Classical Rhetoric for the Modern Student*, 450–58.

11

Rewriting Theology Well (II): Rhetorics of Words, Sentences, and Paragraphs

Theological doctrine is a body of spoken or written words.

—KENNETH BURKE, *The Rhetoric of Religion*

A clear sentence is no accident. Very few sentences come out right the first time, or the third. Keep thinking and rewriting until you say what you want to say.

—WILLIAM ZINSSER, *On Writing Well*

A sentence should contain no unnecessary words, a paragraph no unnecessary sentences, for the same reason that a drawing should have no unnecessary lines and a machine no unnecessary parts.

-WILLIAM STRUNK, JR., *The Elements of Style*

Starting points

Theological style is crafted from words, sentences, and paragraphs, which we explore in this chapter as rhetorics, or elements of purposeful composition and communication in writing theology well.[1] While sections on "words," "sentences," and "paragraphs" are standard features of writing and rhetoric textbooks,[2] we approach these rhetorics as rubrics of a theological grammar, and ask, How do theological writers use words, sentences and paragraphs to write theology well? To answer this question, we look respectively at what words, sentences, and paragraphs do in theological writing.

Do not feel obliged to read this chapter in one sitting. Turn to it when you need to hone your word choice, sharpen your sentences, or write a statement of your theology in one paragraph.[3] Use it as a resource for your own writing, rewriting, and refining of theological style, and in conjunction with the chapters preceding and following it. In the meantime, we proceed to our first question: What do theological words do?

What do theological words do? Finding, choosing and using words well to write theology well

Finding the right words to write theology well is a sacred no less than a stylistic task. "If God's self-manifestation is called 'the word,'" Paul Tillich asserts, "this...emphasizes the holiness of all words as an expression of the spirit."[4] In the light of these challenges, what kinds of words do we find, choose, and use to write theology well, and what do those words do? First, we turn to the "parts of speech" that theologians have traditionally prioritized in speaking and writing theologically—*nouns* and *verbs*.

The parts of speech and their place in theological prose

According to Thomas Aquinas, nouns and verbs combine to form the logical statements that ground theological discourse; hence with his mentor, Aristotle, he considered the ability to use nouns and verbs deftly and with precision fundamental to theological articulation.[5] While contemporary theologians cast a wider net in their discussion of theological language,[6] Strunk and White concur with Aristotle and Aquinas, saying "Write with nouns and verbs."[7] But how do nouns and verbs help us specifically to write theology well?

Nouns

Nouns, or "name-words" (Latin *nomen*, "name"), name persons, places, things, actions, qualities, and concepts, including the concept of God. From its inception, theology has had an obsession for "naming": naming God; naming Jesus Christ; naming Christian experience in its individual and communal dimensions; naming the world, culture, or context engendering that experience; and finally, naming the theological enterprise itself, and the various theologies emerging from it. In short, says Elisabeth Schüssler Fiorenza, "Theology is best understood as the activity and practice of naming the Divine."[8] But because God language is not literal but analogical, Aquinas explains, "we see the necessity of giving to God many names."[9] To be sure, theologians have inherited many names from the Christian tradition, such as "Jesus Christ," "trinity," "grace," and "salvation." Yet theologians continue to use new nouns to clarify, redefine and rename traditional theological subjects.

To name theological subjects effectively, nouns must be (1) *accurate*, (2) *apt*, and (3) *articulate*. To select nouns that fit these specifications is a labor of love no less than writing. Nouns that are *accurate* "call a spade a spade": they name the person, concept or thing clearly and correctly. Just as my freshman English professor told me not to use the noun "utensil" when "fork" or "knife" would be more accurate, theological ethicist Joan Martin explains why she uses the composite noun *blackwomen* "as a more accurate social construction of identity than *black* [women] as a mere adjective" in her book, *More Than Chains and Toil: A Christian Work Ethic of Enslaved Women.*[10]

Nouns that are *apt* are appropriate and intelligible to the context of what is named. Thus David Tracy names the various constituencies addressed by theologians as "publics" in the context of his claim that "all theology is public discourse."[11] Nouns that are *accurate* and *apt* will be *articulate*: they will name their subjects with verisimilitude. When a name has verisimilitude, it is linguistically correct, theologically credible and culturally resonant. When those elements converge, the noun—or name—becomes paradigmatic for those who use it. Thus contemporary theologian Elizabeth Johnson explores "the mystery of God in feminist theological discourse" and asserts that "SHE WHO IS can be spoken as a robust, appropriate name for God."[12] Yet this (pro)noun/name for God is also a verb (She who IS), which brings us to the next section.

Verbs

Verbs (Latin *verbum*, "word,") are words that express *being*, *action*, and *process* in the active or passive voice. "Verbs," writer Natalie Goldberg tells her students, "are the action and energy of a sentence." If this is true of writing in general, it is no less true of theological writing. When Buckminster Fuller says that "God is a verb, not a proper or improper noun," he imagines God as a dynamic, evolving process rather than as a static, unchanging persona. When Jurgen Moltmann says, "God suffers," he implies with process theologians that God not only acts, but can be acted upon. When Elizabeth Johnson constructs the God-term "SHE WHO IS," she moves with other feminist theologians toward an intuition of God not only as a verb, but as a being verb.[13] Yet you do not have to be a process theologian, a feminist theologian or an architect to understand how integral verbs are for writing theology well.

Being Verbs

Being verbs ground theological statements about God and God's creation. Although the verb "is" has been called "the weakest verb in the language,"[14] *being verbs* bristle with potency when they are predicated of God. When the Psalmist declares, "The Lord *is* my shepherd" (Psalm 23:1), the verb "is" resonates with strength, not weakness. In Hebrew, the divine name YHWH is connected with the verb *hayah*, "to be," and when Moses asks God whom he should say has sent him to free his people, God replies, "...you shall say to the Israelites, I AM has sent me to you" (Ex 3:14).[15] Deliberately echoing this declaration, the Jesus of John's gospel asserts, "...before Abraham was, I am" (John 8:58), and the rest of that Gospel continues to unfold "I am" statements that are boldly calculated to tell readers who Jesus *is* (e.g., the gate [10:9], the way [14:6], the vine [15:5], the resurrection and the life [11:25]).

Being verbs not only evoke the divine mystery and its disclosure in Jesus Christ. They also signify human "being" and its relationship to the transcendent. When God called to Abraham on his terrible mission to sacrifice his son Isaac, Abraham responded, "Here I am" (Gen 22:11). In response to the startling announcement of her maternity "by the Holy Spirit," Mary of Nazareth first asked, "How can this *be*?" and then replied, "*Here am I*, the servant of the Lord; *let it be*...according to your word" (Luke 1: 34,38). When Simon Peter was asked by the high priest's servants on the night of Jesus' arrest if he was a disciple of Jesus, Peter said, "*I am not*" (John 18:17, 25). Thus *being verbs* carry the weight of our finitude and our transcendence as creatures of God "in whom we live and move and have our being" (Acts 17:28), just as they image God's being. For those seeking to write theology well, *being verbs* should be used respectfully, and not merely as weak substitutes for the more precise *active verb* that eludes us.

Active Verbs

Active verbs describe the theological task. "Active verbs express meaning more emphatically and vigorously than their weaker counterparts—forms of the verb *be* or verbs in the passive voice," Diana Hacker advises.[16] This should come as no surprise to theological writers, since theologians "do" theology, and have done so from the beginning. Anselm defines theology as "faith *seeking* understanding." Contemporary theologian Dorothee Soelle redefines it as "faith *struggling* for the clarity of its cause."[17] For Krister Standahl, the theological task entails "*worrying* about what God *worries* about when God gets up in the morning," while South African theologian Denise Ackerman calls it "sustained reflection about what we *worry about*, what we *believe* and what we *do* about what we *believe*."[18] Rowan Williams literally "verbalizes" theology when he writes, "The meanings of the word God are to be discovered by *watching* what this community *does*—not only when it is consciously *reflecting* in conceptual ways, but when it is *acting*, *educating* or *'inducting,' imagining* and *worshiping*."[19]

Process Verbs

Process verbs motivate theological reflection in its narrative and analytical forms. Process verbs are verbs that unfold actions that proceed intentionally or implicitly toward completion—like *walk, talk, tell, see, think, analyze, argue, write*, *reflect*, and so on. We have already identified theological reflection as a "dynamic *process* of reflection" and described the four movements of that process in Chapter 2.[20] What else but active verbs can render a process dynamic? Recall the strong use of *process verbs* in the pastoral reflection paper in which the writer reflected on why she followed Jesus:

> How do I *follow* Jesus? Although the verb "*to follow*" *made* radical claims on Jesus' original disciples, the verb "*to accompany*" *provides* me with a more radical image of discipleship today. This image *empowered* me during my first CPE experience, when the chaplain *supervising* me *noticed* me *following* timidly at her heels into the oncology ward. With one *compelling*, *beckoning* gesture, she *invited* me *to walk* with her, not behind her, *to meet* the patients confidently as a co-chaplain in ministry.[21]

Process verbs also motivate the theological writing task posed by a particular assignment. If readers are to follow the process of your paper smoothly, it is essential to choose verbs that describe the operations of the paper with precision. For example, if the first step of your paper is *to outline* the criteria for an adequate christology, the second step is to *compare* and *contrast* a christology from above and a christology from below, and the final step is to *construct* an adequate contemporary christology, you will do well to use these precise verbs to describe your process.

Verbs that combine precision with metaphorical potency will enliven your writing. For example, Elizabeth Johnson previews the final section of *Truly Our Sister: A Theology of Mary in the Communion of Saints* for her readers using the metaphor of a mosaic to describe her process. In this passage Johnson's vigorous and varied use of verbs forms the backbone of her narrative and draws readers actively into her project. Notice that nouns and verbs (italics mine) work together to delineate Johnson's "mosaic" design, since every main verb links a noun/subject and direct object or predicate. Note as well that the ratio of *active verbs* to *being verbs* is 13 to 1:

> ... Part 5 ... *engages* in a close reading of thirteen scripture passages in which Mary *appears*. These stories *encode* the theological memory of the early church, which *wrote* her into the faith event of salvation *coming* from God in Jesus through the power of the Spirit. Every story *is* like a tile of colored stone. *Assembled* together *they form* a mosaic of this Spirit-filled woman, who, in company with other significant gospel persons, *partnered* the redemptive work of God. *Stepping back* and *viewing* the mosaic as a whole, the last chapter *situates* Mary in the whole cloud of witnesses who *accompany* the church on its following of Jesus, *ending* with her own revolutionary prayer, the Magnificat.[22]

Passive Verbs

We have previously noted misuses and abuses of the passive voice in academic writing in Chapter 10.[23] While George Orwell vehemently exhorts writers, "Never use the passive when you can use the active,"[24] theological authors do sometimes use passive verbs in juxtaposition with active verbs when introducing their theses and outlining their arguments. For example, in "The Case for a Spirit Christology," Roger Haight writes, "In what follows *I shall outline* a number of general premises of theology that come to bear on Christology. The number of the premises that *are selected is not meant to be* exhaustive."[25] In the first sentence, Haight chooses the first-person/active voice to describe his own authorial task ("I shall outline a number of general premises ... ."). In the second sentence, Haight's emphasis is upon the "premises" to be outlined, which he foregrounds by using the passive voice. Wayne Booth suggests that author-researchers use the first person/active voice when describing their own thesis, research process and conclusions in an article, and the passive voice when referring to the subject of their research, or to research procedures common not merely to the author but to the academic community addressed in the paper.[26] Following Booth's precedent, I encourage you to use passive verbs purposefully but sparingly to write theology well.

In summary, nouns and verbs work together in theological writing (1) to name theological subject matter, including "the Divine"; (2) to ground statements about God and human beings; (3) to define the theological task; (4) to motivate theological reflection; and (5) to delineate the writer's expository process. The theological memo below invites you to review and refine your use of nouns and verbs:

> *THEOLOGICAL MEMO 1: Using Nouns and Verbs to Write Theology Well: Select a paper you are currently working on, and count the number of words in the draft. Using different colored markers, highlight each noun and each verb in the paper, and count them. What is the ratio of verbs/nouns in your paper? What*

is the ratio of being verbs/active verbs/passive verbs in your paper? Compare the number of nouns and verbs with the total number of words in your paper. What percentage of your words are nouns? What percentage are verbs? Please reflect on your use of nouns and verbs as exemplified in this analysis, and revise your draft accordingly.

Choosing theological words well—a selective sampling

If you have concluded from this theological introduction to the parts of speech that both nouns and verbs are needed for writing theology well, you are correct. Yet you may still be asking, What about adjectives and adverbs? How can we assert that "God is *good*," or dare to "sin boldly," without them? While linguists, logicians and theologians frequently distinguish between *substantive* (nouns or pronouns) words and *modifiers*, or descriptive words (adjectives and adverbs), all language predicated of God is descriptive. How can we call God "Father" or "Mother" without simultaneously naming God substantively and describing God adjectivally?[27] We will return to the specific use of "modifiers" when we turn to sentences, but at the moment we will imagine all theological language as descriptive, and consider the kinds of words that we most often reach for when engaging in this descriptive task. The next section selectively categorizes words that theological writers frequently use to imagine God, to engage in theological reflection, to construct theological positions, and to expand their theological imaginations: *concrete* words, *conceptual* words, *critical* words, *constructed* words, and *figurative* words.

Concrete words

First, we use *concrete* words, those physically and experientially tangible words that ground our theologizing, to provide ballast, clarity and balance between the necessary flights of abstraction to which theological writing is prone. Yet "concrete" and "abstract" words are not diametrically opposed but dialectically engaged with each other as a theology unfolds. "Theoretical knowledge," writes Roger Haight, "is always tied to concrete images," since "even our most abstract ideas and propositions always carry along, or imply, or create some concrete imaginative proposal."[28] While Karl Rahner might have been prone to theological abstraction, he advised theological writers to begin with "concrete" abstractions, such as "work, love, death, and all the well-worn and familiar matters with which human life is filled."[29]

Concrete words are not limited to the vocabulary of contemporary life, however. The Bible is a lexicon of concrete language par excellence, and Fredrica Harris Thompsett uses the biblically resonant words, "*created, chosen, pursued, sent*, and *trusted*" to paint an ecclesiological portrait of "the people of God" for Episcopalian laity. While Thompsett uses each of these words as touchstones introducing a more detailed depiction of a biblical ecclesiology, their derivative verbs similarly depict the God who "creates" a people, "chooses" them, "pursues" them, "sends" them forth, and "trusts" them to continue God's work in the world. See how simply but seamlessly Thompsett elaborates on the word "created" in a style that resonates with concrete language:

> The church as God's people is first of all *created*, called into life. This accords with the Greek word for church, ekklesia, meaning called forth, summoned,

> empowered, lifted up. The biblical creation story is neither detached nor impartial. It communicates God's nature, or anthropology, as well as our own . . . . In Genesis God calls us to join in working toward the further realization of creation. By describing the church as God's *created people* from the beginning we acknowledge God's work and ours.[30]

> *THEOLOGICAL MEMO 2: How "concrete" was the vocabulary of your last theological paper? Reread a paper that you have recently completed, and circle or highlight each concrete noun, verb and adjective that you find. Does concrete language balance your more abstract language? Do any words weave a structural or narrative pattern through the paper (such as the words "created," "chosen," pursued," "sent," and "trusted," above)? What strategies would help you to write more concretely?*

Conceptual words

Second, we use *conceptual* words, or thought-bearing words, to think and reflect theologically. Conceptual words are used both to name theological concepts (e.g., "eschatology;" "soteriology"; "grace") and to engage in theological reflection. Since the discipline of theology is concerned by definition with "thinking about God," the words we choose will reflect that conceptual bias. However, conceptual language does not have to be obfuscating language. It is as important to render concepts clearly as it is to describe physical things concretely, and the same process of definition and explanation obtains for both. See how Roger Haight balances the concrete and the conceptual through a precise but penetrating style that invites the reader into the very experiences of grace that are described:

> Grace is operative in the experience of infinite longings, of radical optimism, of unquenchable discontent, of the torment of the insufficiency of everything attainable, of the radical protest against death, the experience of being confronted with an absolute love precisely where it is lethally incomprehensible and seems to be silent and aloof, the experience of a radical guilt and of a still-abiding hope . . . . These elements are in fact tributary to that divine force which impels the created spirit—by grace—to an absolute fulfillment . . . .[31]

While much of the conceptual language of theology is directed primarily to other theologians, many contemporary theologians are casting a wider net for their writing, and are adjusting their styles accordingly. Confessing that "the technical language of theology can be . . . off-putting and inaccessible," Serene Jones describes "Christian theology" conceptually and then concretely at the beginning of her book *Feminist Theory and Christian Theology*:

> I situate this project within the work of a long line of theologians who have shared in the critical task of helping the church reflect on its present-day witness and practice and to see if it continues to be faithful to the revelation of God manifest in Scripture, tradition and the ongoing life of the Christian community . . . . This means I have to ask: Would what I'm saying make sense to people who sit in church pews on Sunday morning? Does it make a difference

in their lives? Does it help us to pray? Does it assist the church in serving God's purpose of liberation?[32]

THEOLOGICAL MEMO 3: How well did your "concepts" grow in your last theological paper? Please reread a paper you have recently completed in which you define and develop a theological concept, and circle or highlight the conceptual words/phrases used in the paper. Are all "concepts" clearly defined? Is conceptual language effectively balanced by concrete language? If conceptual words are difficult for you to define or develop in your writing, what strategies would help you to write with conceptual clarity and balance?

Critical words

Third, we use *critical* words to analyze, evaluate and mount theological critiques, as discussed previously in writing the critical theological essay.[33] For Gordon Kaufman, "the task of theology is to *assess* and *criticize* received ideas of God in terms of their adequacy in expressing God's absoluteness and God's humaneness, and to reconstruct the image/concept of God" for our contemporary situation in the light of that assessment and criticism.[34] Critical words are also addressed to entire theologies and theological methods, as for some of its critics, "Twentieth-century theology begins with a resounding 'No!' proclaimed in 1918 by Karl Barth in his book ... *The Epistle to the Romans*."[35] Critical words also include "dialectical words" that hold theological realities in tension (e.g., "*negative contrast* experiences"; "hermeneutics of *suspicion*;" oppression), and motivate theologies of liberation, proposals for religious pluralism, and critiques of modernity mounted by postmodern theologies. Finally, critical words embrace the language of negative theology. Mark Taylor, for example, has coined the word "A/theology" to describe his theological position.[36]

Critical words are "critical" to writing theology well. However, when critical words are used unreflectively they become jargon rather than words judiciously chosen. See, for example, how carefully Elisabeth Schüssler Fiorenza employs "critical" words in her feminist critical hermeneutic, and specifies the content of her criticism (italics mine):

> A feminist hermeneutics *cannot trust* or accept Bible and tradition simply as divine revelation. Rather it must *critically evaluate* them as patriarchal articulations .... This *critical insight* of a feminist hermeneutics has ramifications not only for historical scholarship but also for our contemporary political situation *because the Bible still functions today as a religious justification and ideological legitimization of patriarchy*.[37]

THEOLOGICAL MEMO 4: How carefully are you using "critical" words in your own theological writing? Reread a critical theological essay that you have recently completed, and circle or highlight all critical terms (e.g., "analyze," "critique", "evaluate") used in the essay. Is your use of these terms clear from the context of your work? Do they accurately reflect what you are doing in the paper? What would help you to use critical language more effectively?

Constructed words

Theologians not only choose words from those already in the lexicon, but also coin, or "construct" words and phrases that more adequately capture their theological imagination. At times, theologians coin new words to express the ultimately inexpressible: as Augustine remarked of Trinitarian language, "The formula three persons has been coined, not in order to give a complete explanation by means of it, but in order that we might not be obliged to keep silent."[38] As we noted in Chapter 7, Willi Marxsen coined the term "redaction criticism" to describe the authorial processes of the gospel writers.[39] However, most theologically "coined" words do not appear *ex nihilo*, but in creative tension with traditional theological vocabulary. For example, Elizabeth Johnson's coinage of "SHE WHO IS" is indebted to Aquinas' prior designation of "HE WHO IS" to identify divine essence with existence,[40] and Mark Taylor's "A/theology" is incomprehensible without the word "theology" that it negates.[41] In *Gyn/Ecology: The MetaEthics of Radical Feminism*, Mary Daly creates "New Words" to encapsulate her "radical feminist" revisioning, but acknowledges, "Often the New Words arose as a result of chases through the dictionary, which involved the uncovering of etymologies, definitions, and synonyms, which in turn led to further word-hunts and Dis-coverings."[42]

You do not have to be a renowned theologian or a radical feminist philosopher to construct words and phrases that best express your theological meaning. Finding and forming "God-words" is a natural part of the theological process. Students writing theology from other cultural contexts regularly construct "new" theological words by introducing them into their own writing from those contexts. In order to contextualize the feminist theology that she was constructing for her South Indian context, my student named it "Crab Theology" from a local proverb comparing women disparagingly to "crabs."[43] In his desire to move his Tanzanian Anglican diocese from an ecclesial model of monarch/chief to a "servant model" of ministry, another student constructed a *mhudumu* model of episcopacy, using the traditional word for "minister" in the local Tanzanian language.[44] Do not be afraid to tap the resources of your own context for words that capture your theological imagination for your readers.

THEOLOGICAL MEMO 5: Reviewing course reading for "constructed words": Whenever you do your course reading, keep a notebook to record any words that the authors have "coined," along with their rationale for doing so. If you find no "coined" words in your reading, please reflect upon why the author has not employed them. If you find "coined" words, please choose one, and, in a brief reflection, evaluate its continuity with the "tradition" and with your own experience as a theological reader and writer.

Figurative words

Finally, figurative words form such common figures of speech as simile, analogy, metaphor and symbol, which we have already used to "write with theological imagination well" in Chapter 9. Thus figurative words are words used imaginatively, not literally, to bridge the concrete and the conceptual in theological writing. While there is no real consensus on the meaning of the word, "literal,"[45] the literal meaning presumed here is that of a word's dictionary definition. When Megan Beverly names the feminist practice of preaching "the warming quilt of God," and Rebecca Chopp extends the metaphor to embrace the feminist practice of theology,[46] both writers are using those words figuratively, not literally. If Elizabeth Johnson writes correctly that theological affirmations about God cannot be taken as "direct transcripts of reality,"[47] then the conscientious use of figurative words to intimate the divine is crucial for those desiring to write theology well.

What, in conclusion, do theological words do? They name God (*theos logos*) and our relation to God and God's creation. They ground our theologizing in physical reality and sense experience; they enable us to think and reflect theologically; they "coin" new theological construals; they motivate and mount critique; and they bridge the concrete and conceptual in theological writing through images, similes, analogy, metaphor, and symbol. All of these words, when combined, form sentences that make theological statements, which we turn to next. Before we do, here is a concluding checklist for choosing and using words in theological writing:

Choosing and using words: A theological writer's checklist

- Choose words that mean what you want to say, and search until you find them.
- When in doubt about the meaning of a word, consult the dictionary.
- If the "right" word will not come, write the word that most closely approximates it and check your thesaurus for cognates and synonyms.
- Begin and end an essay with your own words, and do not abandon them in the middle.
- Quote the words of others "word for word" and cite them properly (see Chapter 6).
- Repeat words for emphasis or syntactical clarity, but not indiscriminately.
- Use technical theological terms accurately, and define any unfamiliar or ambiguous terms.
- Balance conceptual with concrete words, literal with figurative words, and complex with simple words for clarity, balance and beauty of theological style.
- When you use figurative language, keep images and metaphors consistent.
- Use "God-words" humbly, reverently and sparingly.
- Do not use clichés without a very good reason for doing so.

What do theological sentences do? Writing sentences well to write theological sentences well

Words without sentences are like bricks without mortar. Although individual words *have* meaning, they do not by themselves *make* meaning. To make meaning, words must form sentences. By traditional definition, a sentence is a group of words expressing a "complete thought." But just as individual bricks do not make a wall without a bricklayer, isolated words do not form sentences without writers and speakers ordering words into meaningful grammatical patterns that reflect their own style.

If words spell out an initial alphabet of style, sentences inscribe its signature. Recorded by the priestly writer of Genesis, God's first words in the Bible were spoken in a complete sentence: "Let there be light" (Gen 1:3).[48] Moreover, the syntax of that sentence, repeated eight times in the narrative (1:3, 6, 9, 11, 14, 20, 24, 26), signals the creative action of God, and the "style" of the sentence echoes the "voice" of its speaker. When you struggle to write a good sentence you may not aspire to these divine prerogatives. Yet all sentences signal the styles of their creators through that convergence of sound and syntax that Eudora Welty calls "the sound of what falls on the page,"[49] which we have identified previously with the writer's "voice." In this chapter, we will review "writing sentences well" and then consider what theological sentences do in the hands of skilled theological stylists.

At its syntactical level, a sentence consists of a *subject* (noun) and a *predicate* (verb) that communicate *what who or what is doing* (or "being") and constitute an *independent clause*: for example, *God created*; *God is*. When we add an *object* (following a "doing" verb) or ***complement*** (following a "being" verb) to the sentence, it tells us *who is doing what to whom or what:*[50] *God created the heavens and the earth*; ***God is good.*** When we join *two subjects* and *two predicates* (or *independent clauses*) with a coordinating conjunction (such as "and"), we create a *compound sentence* (*God called the light day*, ***and*** *the darkness he called night*). When we join a subject and a predicate (or *independent clause*) with a dependent clause (or ***subordinate clause***) introduced by a subordinating conjunction (such as "because"), we construct a *complex* sentence (e.g., *So God blessed the seventh day and hallowed it*, ***because on it God rested from all the work that he had done in creation.***)[51]

This brief review of the elements of the English sentence is provided to refresh your memory of basic sentence structure and to provide a common grammatical vocabulary that we will build upon as we proceed.[52] Yet "a sentence is more than its subject, verb and object" and the clauses that bring it to logical and grammatical completion. As Joseph Williams explains, "It is a system of systems whose parts we can fit together in very delicate ways to achieve very delicate ends—if we know how."[53] In this section, then, we will first consider "how to write sentences well" before proceeding to a more pointed discussion of "writing theological sentences well." To begin with, I invite you to answer the question, Do you like sentences? in the Theological Memo below:

> *THEOLOGICAL MEMO 6: "Do you like sentences?" Choose a recently completed theological paper that you were pleased with when you handed it in to the professor, and reread it, sentence by sentence. Underline (or highlight) five sentences that you like and five sentences that you do not like as well. What do the sentences in each category have in common (e.g., careful or careless word choice; clarity or awkwardness of syntax; correct or faulty use of sentence parallelism or subordination; rhythm and texture of sentences; grammatical errors, and so on)? Respond to this question as specifically as you can, and summarize what you have learned from this critique of your own sentence-writing style.*

Do you like sentences?

"A well-known writer got collared by a university student who asked, 'Do you think I could be a writer?' 'Well,' the writer said, 'I don't know....do you like sentences?' "[54] In order to like a sentence, I must be able to understand it, and in order to be understood, the sentence must be written clearly. Yet what makes us like (or dislike) a sentence is its style—or the shape that its words take on the page—and its voice—or the sound of that its words make on the page. Writers who like sentences are more likely to look at their shape on the page, to listen to their sound on the page, to "feel" the "rightness" or the "wrongness" of the sentence in their bones, and to write or revise it according to that "felt sense."[55] For that reason, writers who like sentences are more likely to write clear and understandable sentences.

Even if you do not like sentences, there is no escaping them if you wish to write theology well. A sentence is the road that the reader travels to get from one statement to the next in a longer piece of writing, and the path of a sentence can proceed no further than the thoughts engendering it. If your thinking is clear, the sentence will be clear. If your thinking is unclear, your sentence will be unclear. As William Zinsser acknowledges in one of the epigraphs that begin this chapter, "A clear sentence is no accident....Keep thinking and rewriting until you say what you want to say."[56] In order to rewrite sentences that reflect our thinking more effectively, however, we must first review "how to write sentences well":

How to write sentences well: A brief review

In order to write sentences well: (1) you must learn to recognize a sentence when you see one; (2) you must learn to write sentences that others will recognize as sentences when they read them; and (3) you must learn to write sentences that are not only *recognizable*, but also *readable*, or clear, coherent and fluent. If you are confident of your ability to write a recognizable and readable sentence, please feel free to proceed to the next section on "What Do Theological Sentences Do"? If you would find a brief review of sentence construction and correction useful for "rewriting theology well," I invite you to read on.

Capitalizing and punctuating sentences correctly

Without correct capitalization and punctuation, sentences are difficult to recognize. The following summary of these sentence mechanics will help you to write recognizable sentences: (1) *Capitalize* the first word of every sentence. (2) Use a *period* (.) to end a declarative sentence. (3) Use a *question mark* (?) to conclude a question. (4) Use a *comma* (,) followed by a coordinating conjunction [e.g., and, but] to join independent clauses, to join independent and dependent clauses, and to give the reader a breathing space between thoughts. (5) Use a *semi-colon* (;) to conjoin two complete sentences (independent clauses). (6) Use a *colon* (:) to set off a series of items, precede an emphatic concluding sentence, or introduce a block quotation. (7) Use *dashes* (– –) with discretion to set off parenthetical material in a sentence.

(8) Use an *exclamation mark* (!) infrequently; let the sentence you write convey the intended emphasis. By capitalizing and punctuating your sentences correctly, you will take the first step toward writing sentences well.

Ordering sentences clearly and coherently

Sentences that follow the basic word order of *subject/verb/object/complement* are recognizable and readable. If you wish to write coherent sentences, select this pattern as your "default" sentence order, inverting the order occasionally for greater sentence variety. If you wish to express your meaning clearly, choose the right *noun* to "name" your *subject, object,* and/or *predicate*. Do not use *pronouns* carelessly, but match each one with its *antecedent*. Avoid the undifferentiated use of "it," "this," "that," or "which." Use *active verbs* whenever possible, and do not use *nouns* or *noun phrases* to do the work of *verbs*. Do not overuse the *verb "to be,"* but do not hesitate to use it when you need to. Limit the number of *modifiers (adjectives and adverbs)* in a sentence. Use them to clarify the meaning of the word being modified, not merely to embellish your writing. By ordering sentences clearly and coherently, and choosing words accordingly, you will take another step toward writing sentences well.

Combining sentence elements skillfully

In recognizable and readable sentences, sentence "sense" is mirrored by sentence "structure." Writers do this is by combining sentence elements correctly through *coordination* and *subordination*.[57] *Coordination* links equal ideas with coordinating conjunctions *and, but, nor, for, or, so,* and *yet*. *Subordination* distinguishes between them with subordinating conjunctions or relative pronouns *although, since, whenever, which, because, in order that,* and so on. To give equal weight to ideas in each phrase or clause of a sentence, use *coordination*. To distinguish between main ideas and subordinate ideas, establish logical relationships between them, or provide supporting information, use *subordination*. By combining sentence elements skillfully to correlate sentence "sense" with "structure," you will take another step toward writing sentences well.

Correcting sentence errors effectively

You must recognize the errors that you make in order to correct them effectively. The three most common sentence-level errors are (1) *run-on sentences* (or *comma-splice* sentences) that have commas between independent clauses where periods, semi-colons or conjunctions should be; (2) *incomplete sentences* (or *sentence fragments*) that are punctuated like complete sentences but lack a subject, verb, or object in the main clause; and (3) non-agreement of subject and verb. Many of these errors can be avoided if you "listen" to your sentences as you write them, and write as you would speak them. We tend to be more simple and straightforward when we speak than when we write, and less prone to awkward and ungrammatical sentence syntax. For example, if I *write* the sentence,

> The *Summa Theologica* by Thomas Aquinas was condemned in 1278 [,] the condemnation was revoked in 1325, four years after Aquinas was canonized,

I have committed a "comma splice" error resulting in a "run-on sentence." If I were to "speak" the same sentence in class, I would pause naturally to take a breath between the first and second sentence, perhaps correcting the sentence to read:

> Thomas Aquinas' *Summa Theologica* was condemned in 1278, *but* the condemnation was revoked in 1325, four years after Aquinas was canonized.

In the same way, if I *write* the sentences,

> Liberation theology is done on behalf of the "crucified people." *Which Latin American theologian Jon Sobrino writes about in his most recent book ....*,

I might overlook the sentence fragment subordinated by the relative pronoun "which." If I stop to read it out loud, however, I am more likely to "hear" the suspicious use of "which" that renders the second "sentence" incomplete, and revise the sentence to read:

> Liberation theology is done on behalf of the "crucified people" whom Latin American theologian Jon Sobrino writes about in his most recent book....

Finally, if I *write* the sentence,

> In the cultural context of the biblical documents, shame and sexual purity was relegated to women,

I might not notice the lack of agreement between subject (plural) and verb (singular). Reading it aloud, however, I will "hear" the incorrect use of a singular verb with a plural subject, and correct it to read,

> In the cultural context of the biblical documents, shame and sexual purity were relegated to women.

If you find yourself getting tangled up in a sentence construction that "sounds wrong" on paper, it probably is wrong. By speaking the sentence out loud to yourself and writing out what you say, you will cultivate another strategy essential to writing sentences well.

Constructing sentences fluently

To write sentences well, you must make them readable as well as recognizable. Readable sentences must be clear, coherent, and fluent. To be fluent, a sentence must follow naturally from what precedes it and flow seamlessly into what comes after it. Whatever its length, a fluent sentence has a musical quality; the words fall off the pen and onto the page with the natural rhythms of speech. Moreover, just as half notes and whole notes in music create different rhythms, long and short sentences create different sentence rhythms. Too many short sentences in succession give the reader a choppy, staccato ride. Too many long sentences leave the reader too exhausted to continue the journey. Sentence fluency modulates these rhythms through the interaction of sound, sense and subject matter.

Longer sentences often provide essential description or explanation, while shorter sentences enunciate thesis statements and summarize previous information. Longer sentences are more easily comprehended when they are preceded or followed by short ones. Whether long or short, what you want readers to remember should be at the end of a sentence; what they need to get there should be at the beginning. If you stumble on any word along the way, it should be reconsidered, and if necessary, replaced by one that "sounds right." As we have already noted in the previous section on "voice," by listening to the sound that your sentences make as they strike the page and correcting them accordingly, you will increase your sentence fluency and take yet another step toward writing sentences well. Following the theological memo below on "Writing and Rewriting Your Own Sentences Well," we turn to "Writing Theological Sentences Well."

THEOLOGICAL MEMO 7: Writing and Rewriting Your Own Sentences Well: This introduction to "Writing Sentences Well" has reviewed: (1) capitalizing and punctuating sentences correctly; (2) ordering sentences clearly and coherently; (3) combining sentence elements correctly; (4) correcting sentence errors effectively; and (5) constructing sentences fluently. Return to the theological paper that you critiqued for the last theological memo, and copy the sentences that you didn't like on a fresh page or computer file. Referring to the guidelines elaborated above, correct each of your sentences by (1) identifying the sentence problem (e.g., fragment; run-on, word order); (2) indicating necessary corrections; (3) revising your sentences accordingly.

Writing theological sentences well: A historical introduction

The basic linguistic unit of doing and writing theology is the *sentence*. Medieval theologian Peter Lombard introduced this term into theological discourse in 1150 with his *Quattuor Libri Sententiarum*, or *Four Books of Sentences* (literally, "opinions" or "sentiments" expressed in brief, declarative statements), a textbook of citations from scripture and the patristic writers that addressed theological and doctrinal questions. While Lombard's "Sentences" referred initially to theological "statements" of the authorities, the term came to embrace the compiler's "sentences" about the "sentences," and later to describe the grammatical unit of language used to speak or write them.[58]

While one contemporary theologian calls *The Sentences* "one of the most boring books that was ever written,"[59] writing a commentary on *The Sentences* was the equivalent for medieval theological students of writing a graduate theological thesis today. Long before nailing his 95 Theses to the church door at Wittenberg, Martin Luther delivered a course of lectures on *The Sentences*.[60] Thus studying *The Sentences* and responding to it taught generations of theologians how to write good theological sentences themselves, and its methodical progression from questions to assertions to arrive at a concluding theological synthesis persists in microcosm in the writing of all theological sentences. To observe this pattern more closely in the contemporary writing of theology, we must ask, "What do theological sentences do?"

What do theological sentences do?

When I think theologically, I think in sentences. For example, as I am writing this sentence, I am thinking, "What do theological sentences do?" The shape of the question—which is an interrogative sentence—prompts my answers, which form themselves in simple declarative sentences: (1) They ask questions. (2) They make assertions. (3) They define terms. (4) They compare and contrast positions. (5) They summarize. (6) They draw conclusions. In other words, when I struggle to "work out a theology as I write," I work it out on the level of the sentence, and I compose different kinds of sentences for different theological tasks. In the examples that follow, we shall see how skilled theological writers answer the question, "What do theological sentences do?"

They ask questions

We have already noted in Chapter 5 the importance of questions for theological research.[61] Our goal here is to look more carefully at how theologians "write" their questions. Look, for example, at this interrogative sentence:

> *The important questions to be asked by theology are .... Who should do theology and where, in whose interests and for whom?*[62]

In twelve words, Johann-Baptist Metz articulates four theological questions that not only define the parameters of the immediate discussion, but also encapsulate his political theology in a nutshell. Stylistically, the four questions unfold in a logical and balanced progression from the beginning of the sentence to the end. Just as Metz's question has become a standard point of departure for theological reflection in the the intervening years years since he first posed it, its written expression remains exemplary for those who seek to write theological questions well.

They make assertions

If the *sentence* is the basic linguistic unit of writing theology, then the theological *assertion* forms the basic theological sentence. By "theological assertion" I mean a one-sentence statement that articulates a theological thesis, claim, premise or position.[63] For example, "A theologian's job is to help Christians think about God, other people—and nature—so that we can, will act differently toward them,"[64] is a theological assertion. When a theological assertion introduces a longer essay that argues or explicates it in a systematic way, it is called a "thesis statement."[65] In a well written theological assertion, the grammatical structure of the sentence is congruent with its theological content, and the logic of the sentence flows from that content. Sally McFague introduces *Super, Natural Christians* with this assertion:

> *The thesis of this book can be stated simply: Christian practice, loving God and neighbor as subjects, as worthy of our love in and for themselves, should be extended to nature.*[66]

Stating her thesis "simply," McFague uses the structure of a complex sentence to unfold its theological elements, metaphorically conjoin them, and hold them in balance:

Christian practice,......................................should be extended to nature.
loving God and neighbor
as subjects,
as worthy of our love
in and for themselves,

While the subject, "Christian practice," and its predicate, "should be extended to nature," define the parameters of the thesis and the sentence, each word of this assertion is essential to its theological content. Since "Christian practice" is an all-embracing term, "loving God and neighbor as subjects" is added to define that practice more concretely. Since not all of her audience may be familiar with this technical but, for her argument, crucial use of the word *subject*,[67] she appends a final adverbial phrase to describe how "subjects" are to be loved: "as worthy of our love in and for themselves." Following a deductive path, McFague renders each modifier more specific than what it modifies, while all are embedded within the more general assertion that they particularize.

Two stylistic suggestions flow from McFague's theological prose. First, do not underestimate the value of cumulative sentence structure, in which modifiers are added on, like box cars on freight trains, behind or before the main elements of the sentence, not as excess baggage, but as essential carriers of meaning. Secondly, do not believe everyone who tells you that nouns and verbs are more important to writing good sentences than the words that modify them.[68] McFague has used the structure of the cumulative sentence and its modifiers adeptly to qualify, particularize and enrich her theological thesis. Moreover, when she asserts, "Christian practice" (defined and refined as we have seen above) "should be extended to nature," she extends her "metaphorical theology" and "ecological theology" developed in previous books to fit the contours of a new project—a "Christian nature spirituality."[69] In so doing, she links grammatically ("Christian practice"..."nature") what she will conjoin metaphorically in the writing of the book. It will take her the rest of the book to finish the work, but the theological assertion that impels it has been constructed in one carefully honed sentence, as you too will do when you master the art of writing theological assertions well.

They define terms

Theological sentences are also used to define theological terms. We have already considered the importance of defining premises and vocabulary when developing a theological argument.[70] Our focus here is on writing a definition in a coherent, well-crafted sentence. Consider again the definition cited in Chapter 3:

> *Christology is a subdiscipline of theology; it is the study and discussion of Jesus Christ, or Jesus as the Christ.*[71]

In order to situate the discipline of Christology in its wider disciplinary context, Roger Haight uses a compound sentence. The first part of the sentence broadly defines Christology as a "subdiscipline of theology"; the second part of the sentence defines the term specifically in terms of its "christological" subject matter. The language used is simple and straightforward, but Haight does not hesitate to add modifying phrases in the interests of theological clarity. For example, he qualifies the title "Jesus Christ" with the clarifying phrase, "or Jesus as the Christ." But what if one is dealing with a term that is not so easily defined, even in a compound or complex sentence? We return briefly to Sallie McFague, who must now define "nature" in order to more fully elaborate a "Christian spirituality of nature."

When you are dealing with a term that is difficult to define, the first thing to do is to tell readers so, as McFague confesses to her readers in a diffuse but coherent sentence:

> *In a sense, nature is everything, including ourselves; hence, trying to define it is like a fish attempting to define the ocean.*[72]

First, McFague expresses the horns of her dilemma in a carefully qualified ("In a sense") propositional statement ("nature is everything") and then in figurative language ("Trying to define it is like a fish attempting to define the ocean") that draws upon the imagery of the very "nature" that she is trying to define. In so doing, she adroitly balances "abstract" and "concrete" language, with the concrete image of the "fish attempting to define the ocean" having the last word. Not wishing to abandon the enterprise, however, McFague dives into that ocean and turns to the definitions of other theologians, one of which she embellishes in a grammatically and thematically integrated sentence:

> *Nature is "the totality of processes and powers that make up the universe," which of course includes human beings, but also black holes, electromagnetic fields, dirt, DNA, gravity, death, time and space, apples, quarks, trees, birth, microbes and mountains.*[73]

While McFague incorporates the definition into a complete sentence, she elaborates its contents in her own words. In so doing, she exerts control over her writing process, rather than relying on the grammar of the quoted material to provide sentence coherence. She declines to define "nature" in one sentence (if you want to know why, you must read her book). However, she does provide this summary statement before proceeding to a definition that will take more than a sentence to unfold:

> *In summary, nature has many meanings and none of them is "natural" or absolute.*[74]

Whether you begin with a standard definition of a theological concept, or redefine the concept for the purposes of your own project as McFague does here, you will need to learn how to write theological sentences well.

They compare and contrast theological subject matter

Theologians also use sentences to compare and contrast theological subject matter. When their goal is to compare or contrast one element of the subject matter equally with its coordinate, sentence coordination and/or parallelism provide balance and symmetry. However, when the goal is to subordinate one of the contrasted elements to the other in order of their importance, sentence subordination signals the disparity between the elements:

Sentence coordination

Theologians use sentence coordination (introduced by coordinating conjunctions such as *and, but, for, nor, so, yet*) to link equally important ideas or information. More precisely, theologians use parallel construction within a sentence to indicate an analogous relationship between the parts of the sentence and their subject matter.[75] For example, if you have been asked to compare the task of Christology with that of ecclesiology, you might begin with these sentences:

> Christology is the theology of Jesus of Nazareth.
> Ecclesiology is the theology of the Christian church.
> Christology demands a renewed imagination of Jesus of Nazareth in whom God was incarnate.
> Ecclesiology demands a consideration of the historical institution of the church in which God acts as grace.

You have made some significant comparisons between these two disciplines here, but your sentences remain discrete and structurally unrelated. See how Roger Haight weaves these assertions into grammatically parallel sentences in which form and function conspire fruitfully to compare the tasks of Christology and ecclesiology:

> Just as Christology is the theology of Jesus of Nazareth, so too ecclesiology is the theology of the Christian community in history.... Just as Christology demands a restoration of Jesus of Nazareth to the imagination as he in whom God was incarnate, so too ecclesiology demands a consideration of the concrete, social, and historical community and institution of the church as that in which God acts as grace.[76]

In this brief excerpt from an extended "parallel" paragraph, the author's goal is to link his previous book on christology with his current book on "historical ecclesiology," and to assert the logical continuity between the two projects. By using parallel construction both within and between sentences, Haight coordinates christology and ecclesiology on both grammatical and theological levels. First, the coordinating terms (*Just as ...., so too ....*) introduce and connect the clauses of the sentence. Next, the parallel subjects ("christology ... ecclesiology") share a main verb ("christology *is* .... ecclesiology *is*") that is repeated in both clauses of the sentence. Third, an identical sentence structure informs each part of the sentence:

> ***Just as****/Christology/****is/the theology of*** */Jesus of Nazareth,*
> ***so too*** *ecclesiology/****is/the theology of*** */ the Christian community in history.*

Finally, the parallel structure extends beyond the individual sentence to inform the structure of the developing paragraph (If you want to see how it ends, you must read the book). Parallel sentence structure tends toward stylistic formality, but when used judiciously, it adds a rhythm and elegance to theological prose that helps readers to follow the thrust of your ideas and the structure of the sentences that voice them.

Sentence subordination

While sentence parallelism is based upon coordination of sentence elements, sentence subordination is based upon the contrast between them. Theologians use sentence subordination (introduced by subordinating conjunctions and relative pronouns *after, although, as, because, if, since, that, which*, among others) to distinguish more important from less important points, to indicate logical relationships between them, and to place them in contrast. See, for example, how deftly contextual theologian Aylward Shorter employs both coordination and subordination in the following sentence:

> *Although* inculturation is one of the theological catchwords of the third world countries,... and *although* most African theologians are actually engaged in a conscious process of inculturation, very few have elaborated a theory of inculturation itself....[77]

First, Shorter introduces both his sentence and "the state of the question" with two "parallel" subordinate clauses that anticipate the main clause but are less in order of importance:

> *Although* inculturation is one of the theological catchwords of the third world countries.. and *although* most African theologians are actually engaged in a conscious process of inculturation....

While the first two clauses are grammatically and thematically parallel, they are "subordinate" in both respects to the main clause of the sentence:

> ...*very few have elaborated a theory of inculturation.*

The meaning of the sentence—that African theologians have tended to use the language and method of inculturation without an adequate theory of inculturation to inform their practice—is dependent upon both the main clause and the subordinate clauses for its full expression and comprehension. However, if we compare Shorter's sentence to a well-sharpened pencil, its main clause provides the "point," while the subordinate elements are "blunted" by its firm strokes.

Second, there is a logical pattern and coherence in Shorter's use of subordination, which moves (1) from the more general "inculturation as a catchword in third world countries"; (2) to the more specific country of "Africa"; (3) to "the African theologians" who are actually engaged in it; and finally, (4) to the "few" who have elaborated their own theology of enculturation (among whom Shorter will take his rightful place in due course). We have traveled a vast distance in this sentence, but the logical path has been so seamlessly incorporated into its structure and style that we hardly know that we have left home.

Finally, Shorter uses sentence subordination to place sentence elements and their respective subject matter in sharp rhetorical contrast. For example, in the main clause, the "few" who have "elaborated a theory of inculturation" are contrasted in the second subordinate clause to "most African theologians" who have not. Had the sentence read, *Inculturation is one of the theological catchwords of the third world countries*, ***and*** *most African theologians are actually engaged in a conscious process of inculturation*, we would compare rather than contrast the two clauses. Thus the mastery of sentence parallelism and subordination, and the knowledge of when to use each of them is essential if you wish to write theological sentences well.

They summarize and synthesize

Finally, theologians use sentences to summarize and synthesize theological materials.[78] We focus here on the "one-sentence summary" which does the work of a longer summary in one concise, synthetic sentence. While the goal of a longer summary is to condense and simplify the material that it summarizes, a one-sentence summary often synthesizes a broader swath of material in an epitomizing sentence. Summary sentences are typically introduced by the words, "in summary," "in sum," "to sum up," or "in other words." At their best, one-summary sentences provide a cogent, concise and carefully worded distillation of their authors' theological research and reflection. They may be aphoristically terse, like Sallie McFague's one-sentence summary below:

> In sum, a Christian nature spirituality is Christian praxis extended to nature.[79]

Yet one-sentence summaries can also stretch the boundaries of the sentence in order to recapitulate previous material, as in this summary sentence by Elizabeth Johnson:

> To sum up: separated and idealized, given a life story in which she is submissive, desexualized, and fixated on motherhood, and then sent back as a model for women subordinate to men, the traditional image of Mary emerges from critical feminist analysis as a male-designed creation that functions to define and control women.[80]

The sentence may also function as the proverbial "topic sentence" of a paragraph, inviting further explication at the same time that it draws previous threads to a conclusion, as does McFague's summary sentence that "deconstructs" previous definitions of nature:

> In summary, nature has many meanings and none of them is "natural" or absolute.[81]

On the other hand, it may conclude the paragraph, as this one-sentence summary that concludes a discussion of "Roads Not Taken" in Johnson's *Truly Our Sister* does:

> For the renewal of the doctrine of God liberated from the restrictions of patriarchy, for empowering women to claim their own dignity made in her image and likeness, and for the transformation of the church into a community of the discipleship of equals, this female imagery needs to disperse beyond Mary back to its source.[82]

Wherever it occurs, a one-sentence summary provides a reprise and a respite for writer and reader before proceeding to the next paragraph, page, section, or chapter. In summary, then, theological sentences (1) ask questions; (2) make assertions; (3) define terms; (4) compare and contrast; and (5) summarize and synthesize theological subject matter. Yet sentences must combine with other sentences to form paragraphs to create a theological essay. We turn next, then, to "Writing Theological Paragraphs Well," following this final checklist for "Writing Sentences Well":

Writing sentences well: A theological writer's checklist

- Use *subject/verb/object/complement* word order for basic sentence structure.
- Vary word order and structure to introduce complexity without sacrificing clarity.
- Choose coordinate clauses for comparison, and subordinate clauses for contrast.
- Use parallel structure to signal comparisons and balance sentence components.
- Punctuate sentences with care to avoid run-on sentences and fragments.
- Make every word in a sentence count.
- Listen to the sound of your sentence; then ask, does it make sense?
- If you stumble over a word or phrase, delete it.
- Follow the trail of a sentence, but cut the leash when it reaches a dead end.
- Keep rewriting until the sentence rings true and says what you want it to.

What do theological paragraphs do? Writing paragraphs well to write a theological paper well

If words and sentences spell out a writer's style, paragraphs broadcast that style through sentence-level repetition of key words, images and syntactical structures and paragraph-level patterns of organization within a particular piece of writing. The word "paragraph" is derived from a Greek word (*para*=alongside + *graphein*=to write) meaning "to add a clause to a legal contract." It came to mean a written mark in the margin of a Greek manuscript that helped readers to find their place and gave them a breathing space, and that mark would ultimately become the standard paragraph symbol, the pilcrow [¶] used by proofreaders today to indicate paragraph indentation. While paragraph indentation continues to help modern readers find their place in a theological essay and to provide a breathing space, paragraphs are more than their indentation. At their best, paragraphs are coherent textual units that "add a clause" to the contract that the writer has made with the reader to assert, define, explain or unfold a theological topic. Thus the paragraph is not merely a structural marker; it is also a strategic means of organizing and unifying an essay.

Nonetheless, different writers describe paragraphs differently. For some, a paragraph is like a funnel; it begins with a broad general statement that the writer narrows with each subsequent sentence to produce a pointed and specific thesis statement.[83] For others, a paragraph is like a hand that gathers, using its opposing thumb to categorize what has been gathered into a coherent topic sentence.[84] Others describe a paragraph as a dance in which "the topic sentence draws a circle, and the rest of the paragraph is a pirouette around that circle."[85] How would you describe a paragraph? From your own experience of reading and writing paragraphs, what would you compare it to? To introduce our discussion of writing paragraphs well, I invite you to answer the question, What is a paragraph like? in the Theological Memo below:

> *THEOLOGICAL MEMO 8: What is a paragraph like? You have written paragraphs all your life, but have you ever tried to describe one? Choosing a short theological paper that you have recently completed, examine the paragraphs that comprise the paper and number them in the order in which they appear. Then select three paragraphs that represent your best writing, and compare them. What characteristics of good writing do they share? What is distinctive about them as paragraphs? From your examination of these paragraphs, please identify three characteristics that all (not just your own) well-written paragraphs share. Finally, giving your left brain a rest and engaging the creativity of your right brain, write a brief paragraph in answer to the question, What are my paragraphs like?*

Every paragraph that I have ever read fits novelist Elizabeth George's definition of "a collection of sentences unified by one prevailing topic that's either stated or implied."[86] If a sentence is a group of words expressing a complete thought, a paragraph is a group of sentences following a train of thought to its next destination. In order to comprise a paragraph, however, sentences cannot be thrown at random at the reader. Each sentence in the paragraph must follow from the previous one and lead logically into the one that follows it, just as the order of the locomotive, freight cars, and caboose in a moving train follows from their different functions in respect to the train. Similarly, the placement of *introductory paragraphs*, *expository paragraphs*, *evidential paragraphs*, *transitional paragraphs*, and *concluding paragraphs* in a piece of writing brings the writing to completion, just as a train proceeds smoothly between stations to its final destination. While these generic paragraph forms provide templates for negotiating basic essay structure for all modes of writing, we will look at them more pointedly in relation to the question, What do theological paragraphs do?

First, however, I invite you to return to your own reflection on what a paragraph is like, and revisit the three characteristics of well-written paragraphs that you identified. If you identified *unity*, *coherence* and *emphasis* as the "trinity" of paragraph writing, or some similar characteristics, you and I just might have had the same high school English teacher.[87] When they are used judiciously, these three rhetorical signposts provide writers of paragraphs with criteria by which they can edit and revise their own paragraphs and evaluate those of others.

Unity

To have unity, a paragraph must focus on one idea, stated or implied, and every sentence in the paragraph should sharpen that focus, not dilute it. A paragraph that does not have unity is like a broken traffic signal that points in all directions at once, rather than providing the correct turn signal at the intersection. Similarly, in a paragraph that lacks unity, individual sentences point in all directions rather than following the lead of the topic sentence, or main idea of the paragraph. A paragraph with unity is like a carefully wrapped package in which the wrappings are integral to the gift enclosed. How carefully have you attended to the unity of your paragraphs?

Coherence

Coherence is the glue that produces a unified paragraph, and it operates on the level of words, phrases and sentences. When a paragraph has coherence, its sentences function as contributing parts of an integrated whole. The glue that makes the parts cohere includes (1) repetition of key words and phrases; (2) logical (e.g., *if, therefore, because*) and chronological (e.g., *when, after that, until*) markers; and (3) transitional connectors (e.g., *Having examined this, we move now to that*). A paragraph without coherence will seem to disintegrate as you read it, because the writer has not provided enough connectives to make the sentences adhere. A paragraph with coherence is like a symphony orchestra that plays as one finely tuned instrument. How does your paragraph play when you reread it by ear, sentence by sentence?

Emphasis

A paragraph has emphasis if it brings its controlling idea to full expression and closure in the words needed for the task—neither more nor less. Lengthy paragraphs tend to obscure emphasis, just as short, choppy paragraphs interrupt it. While not all paragraphs in an essay may require the same level of emphasis, a paragraph with emphasis motivates readers with its energy and economy of language. Readers overlook paragraphs without appropriate emphasis in their impatience to get to the next one. A paragraph with emphasis is like a mantra in which every word contributes to the culminating force of the prayer. How well have you motivated your paragraphs with emphasis?

The long and the short of it

As William Strunk instructs us in his chapter epigraph, a paragraph should be as long as it needs to be and no longer. There is no "standard" paragraph length that fits all sizes and situations. A quick survey of paragraphs in your local newspaper, your church newsletter, your favorite magazine, and the theological article that you are reading for tomorrow's assignment will reveal a striking diversity of paragraph lengths, each governed by its own context and conventions. For example, paragraphs in academic theological journals and books tend to be longer than paragraphs in *The National Catholic Reporter* or *Christianity Today*. Similarly, paragraphs in a one-page theological reflection paper that you write will be shorter than paragraphs in a 25-page theological research paper.

Three paragraphing suggestions flow from my own reading of student papers. First, indent every paragraph intended to be one. If paragraphs are not properly indented, your professor will find it more difficult to follow the progression of your argument, and may give up in despair. Second, keep paragraph length for short papers between 50 and 100 words per paragraph (3–5 paragraphs per page), and for long papers, 100–150 words per paragraph (2–3 paragraphs per page). If you must write the occasional paragraph that extends for a full page, make sure that it provides a followable path for readers from the first to the last sentence. Nothing is more dispiriting than a never-ending paragraph that requires readers to blaze their own trail through its fine print. Finally, be aware of your own "default" paragraph style, and build on it. If you are addicted to long paragraphs, compose them with clarity and elegance and vary them with shorter, more succinct ones. If your paragraphs are more like soundbites than solidly developed sections of an essay, keep the force and focus of your brevity, but provide further explanation, examples or supporting detail in succeeding sentences to complete your paragraph. If you do this with unity, coherence and emphasis, the length of the paragraph will take care of itself.

When you write theological paragraphs well, this trinity of unity, coherence and emphasis will brood silently over your own creative powers of composition in the process of writing. You will not ordinarily say to yourself, "I must write a paragraph that has unity, coherence and emphasis," but rather, "I must write a paragraph that says what I want to say." Employed as criteria for writing paragraphs well, however, these categories will help you to critique a paragraph after you have written it and to revise your work accordingly. The next theological memo invites you to use the heuristic below as a revision tool:

Writing paragraphs with unity, coherence, and emphasis: A revision heuristic

UNITY: Does my paragraph have unity, or does something not fit?
Does every sentence belong where I have placed it?
Is any sentence redundant or irrelevant?

COHERENCE: Have I repeated keywords effectively without being redundant?
Have I provided enough logical and/or chronological connectors?
Have I provided enough transitional phrases?

EMPHASIS	Is the length of the paragraph consistent with its level of emphasis? Is the paragraph fully developed? Does it "stop" or "end?" Does the paragraph conclude appropriately within the essay?

THEOLOGICAL MEMO 9: Revising Paragraphs Well: Most writers cannot think about writing a good paragraph and write it at the same time. Consequently, well-written paragraphs have usually been revised by their authors. To test this hypothesis for yourself, choose a short theological paper that you have been assigned (a one-page paper is ideal for this exercise), and prepare a first draft of the paper. Using the "Unity, Coherence, and Emphasis" heuristic for writing paragraphs well provided above, please critique each paragraph of your draft in the light of these criteria, and revise your paragraphs accordingly. Of the three criteria, which were you already observing in your paragraph-writing process? Which were most helpful in your revising process?

Final considerations

"O Lord," prays one of John Updike's characters, "bless these poor paragraphs, that would do in their vile ignorance your work of resurrection."[88] However important they are to rewriting theology well, the criteria of unity, coherence and emphasis for writing and revising effective paragraphs are not the final arbiters of well-written paragraphs, especially for those who wish to write theology well. A paragraph is characterized not only by the qualities it has, but also by the work that it does. Have you ever considered that when writing theological paragraphs well you are participating in the work of resurrection that all writing aspires to?

At their best, unity, coherence and emphasis are woven seamlessly into paragraphs that do many different things. Each of the paragraphs below also witnesses to "generations yet to come" and hence to resurrection. As we look below at the different things Latin American theologians Elsa Tamez and Jon Sobrino do with their paragraphs, I invite you to keep all of these criteria actively in play, including Updike's. At the same time, I invite you to think about the one thing that the paragraphs that you write should do.

However diverse their purposes, all well-written paragraphs *develop a controlling idea, using particular rhetorical or organizational patterns*. Rhetorical patterns of development are as old as the classical topoi from which they are derived—Aristotle, Cicero, and Quintilian all provided their readers with patterns for organizing a speech, tailored to its particular genre. Similarly, if you leaf through any contemporary writer's handbook, you will invariably find a section devoted to "patterns of paragraph development,"[89] including such standard patterns as Narrative, Description, Definition, Example, Classification and Division, Cause and Effect, Comparison and Contrast, Logical Progression, Question/Answer, Problem/Solution, and so on. Most of the time, we do not run to a writing textbook to choose a pattern of paragraph development; the pattern chooses us in the very process of composing the paragraph, and arises from the function of the paragraph within the essay framework.[90] Therefore, rather than examining all of these patterns of development here, we will identify those used most consistently in theological writing as we ask the more pointed question, What do theological paragraphs do?

What do theological paragraphs do? Writing theological paragraphs well with Elsa Tamez and Jon Sobrino

Like sentences, paragraphs also ask questions, make assertions, define terms, compare and contrast positions, summarize, synthesize and draw conclusions. On the level of the paragraph, however, these operations become developmental patterns that arise from their rhetorical function. What then, do theological paragraphs do? They *introduce* a theological question or assertion; they *exposit*, or expound upon those questions and assertions by defining, classifying, comparing and contrasting, and providing examples; they *cite evidence* relevant to the theological argument, and analyze and evaluate that evidence; they *make transitions* between subject matter and respective essay sections; and they *conclude* by summarizing, synthesizing and bringing to closure. Identifying the developmental pattern of the paragraph and its rhetorical function, we look below at what Latin American theologians Elsa Tamez and Jon Sobrino do with (1) introductory paragraphs; (2) expository paragraphs; (3) evidential paragraphs; (4) transitional paragraphs; and (5) concluding paragraphs.[91]

Introductory paragraphs

Introductory paragraphs invite readers into the writer's topic and provide a bird's eye view of the book, chapter, essay, or section to follow in a style that combines conceptual clarity with well-crafted rhetoric. Some introductory paragraphs begin with a question to which the paragraph provides the answer; others begin with an assertive "topic sentence" that becomes more focused and pointed as the paragraph proceeds. Introductory paragraphs must provide the lure that hooks readers and induces them to read on.

In the first paragraph below, Elsa Tamez introduces the topic of justification by faith in her Latin American context, using a question-answer pattern of development, and her answer to the opening question in the first sentence provides the topic sentence in the second. In subsequent sentences she expands upon the importance of the question and suggests the criteria for an adequate theological response. In the second paragraph, Jon Sobrino introduces *Jesus the Liberator* in a straightforward topic sentence, which is illuminated by a comparison-contrast pattern of development in subsequent sentences: "Jesus Christ Crucified" is juxtaposed with "Jesus the Liberator"; "history" is countered by "faith"; and in the concluding sentence, the ongoing struggle of "crucifixion" and "liberation" defines the very context in which the book is being written. Which paragraph provides the stronger lure for you? What bait does each writer provide?

> 1. Is the question of justification by faith relevant today in Latin America? The validity or relevance of the theological question of justification is accountable to the life experience and practice of Christians, churches and poor people in general. From that beginning point, this Christian doctrine must be examined in

light of the Word as it is known in Scripture and in history, and as it has been and continues to be appealed to in the life of many Christians of Latin America who seek to be faithful to God. Moreover, often when the presence of the crucified and risen Word is lived intensely (as in acute cases of oppression and repression), those situations themselves carry the voice of God that makes its appeal to all of us, to every theology, and to every doctrine. (p. 19)

2. This book seeks to present the Christ who is Jesus of Nazareth, and so I have called it "Jesus the liberator." This choice of title was not easy, however, since writing from Latin America and specifically from El Salvador, we tend to speak of "Jesus Christ crucified." Faith points ineluctably to the first title; history forcefully reminds us of the second. Nevertheless it is a fact that the return to Jesus of Nazareth has been the means of retrieving, historically too, a new image of Christ and that this has developed a fruitful faith for believers, for the church and for the processes of liberation. Therefore, this book is written in the midst of crucifixion, but definitely in the hope of liberation. (p. 1)

Expository paragraphs

Expository paragraphs convey information and explain ideas and concepts. Some expository paragraphs begin with a "topic sentence" that they develop, elaborate and unfold within the parameters of the paragraph. Others move more deliberately toward the topic sentence in a pattern of increasing specification. While each expository paragraph is a distinct textual unit, it should flow from the paragraph that proceeds it and lead into the paragraph that follows it; thus each expository paragraph should further develop the "train of thought" linking the whole composition. While expository paragraphs can take many forms, they typically (1) articulate the topic at the beginning of the paragraph; (2) restrict, narrow or qualify the topic in succeeding sentences; and (3) exemplify or illustrate it in the final section of the paragraph. The concluding sentence of an expository paragraph often provides a mini-summary of the paragraph and/or provides a transition to the next paragraph.

In the first expository paragraph below, Tamez employs the pattern of definition—or more properly, redefinition—to interrogate the opening biblical assertion that "all human beings are sinners." Sentence by sentence, she argues gently but firmly for defining sin as social injustice as opposed to a "spiritualization of sin," which, she contends in a concluding topic sentence, "has often made it difficult to identify in concrete realities—an identification that is the precondition for fighting against sin." In the second paragraph, Sobrino uses the pattern of logical progression to provide a rationale for his "liberatory" christological project, which culminates in his claim that in a context where Jesus is "used" by all sides of the struggle, "it is the responsibility of christology to show his true face, so that he may be used well,... at the service of the *mysterium liberationis* and against the *mysterium iniquitatis*." Which paragraph seems stronger, more sequentially structured, and more coherent? What stylistic effects did the writer of your preferred paragraph use to write the paragraph well?

1. Clearly, as the Bible asserts, all human beings are sinners. In practice, however, there is a paradox: The poor, whose sins cannot be compared to those of the powerful, are those who more consistently recognize their faults. Injustice

becomes obvious when it is committed against those who, with greater frequency, remember that they are sinners. We know that sin cannot be reduced to social injustice, but in the present moment in Latin America, it is vital to make people see that any dehumanizing situation is an offense to God, and for that reason it is a manifestation of sin. The spiritualization of sin has often made it difficult to identify in concrete realities—an identification that is the precondition for fighting against sin. (p. 21)

2. Of all the contextual reasons [for this christology], the first is ethical in nature. In Latin America, Jesus is still an important reality; he is present in the masses, unlike in Africa and Asia, and he is still actively present, unlike in Europe and the first world in general. This presence is differentiated, naturally, but whether it is as a reality of faith or as a historical personage or as a socio-cultural symbol, it is there. And not only is it there, but it is used, in various ways, to defend one type or another of human, social and political venture. All this to different degrees, of course, but it still seems to me accurate to state that in a still culturally and socially Christian continent all are concerned to have Jesus Christ on their side, or at least not to seem to have him against them. In this situation, given that Jesus Christ is in fact used, it is the responsibility of christology to show his true face, so that he may be used well, so that Jesus Christ may be at the service of the **mysterium liberationis** and against the **mysterium iniquitatis**. (pp. 4–5)

Evidential paragraphs

Evidential paragraphs introduce or include textual evidence to support, corroborate and exemplify the writer's assertions. The textual material can be woven through the text of the paragraph, and set off by quotation marks, or it can be separated from the paragraphs with block quotations. The choice of either method will be determined by (1) the length of the quotation, and (2) the emphasis that the writer seeks to place upon the quotation. In both cases, the evidential material must be grammatically consonant with the rest of the paragraph, and the writer should interpret, illuminate or dialogue with the quoted material in the course of the paragraph.

In the first "evidential" paragraph below, Tamez uses a pattern of "Example" in citing evidence, and a pattern of "division and classification" in choosing her sources according to (1) "the need to reinterpret the doctrine of justification by faith"; and (2) "to propose important elements by which to reread it." In the second, Sobrino employs "narrative" and "example" to provide historical evidence of the original presence of a "liberation" theology among "oppressed Indians." Which paragraph seems more successful in showcasing the evidence and integrating it into the writer's narrative? What stylistic conventions did the writer of your preferred paragraph use to cite authorities effectively?

1. The many examples in Latin America of the rediscovery of relevant dimensions of the bible and tradition include various articles by authors from different confessional backgrounds. Examining these articles through the lenses of current meanings of the doctrine and current challenges of our reality allows one to see the need to reinterpret the doctrine of justification by faith, and to propose important elements by which to reread it. For example, from the

Lutheran perspective, Walter Altmann proposes the following rereading of the doctrine:... (pp. 25–26, n25)

In Luther's time, the juridical terminology of justification became important; the problem of guilt and condemnation worried not only Luther but a whole people and a whole era. But we would be deceiving ourselves if we thought that the doctrine of justification, as Luther formulated it, could retain the same relevance for all eras and situations. Such a perennial theology does not exist. (25)

2. In Latin America, faith in Christ succeeded in surviving through the centuries without special christological discussions, and it could be said that there was no specifically Latin American Christology. It is true that at its beginnings there was very powerful meditation on the presence of Christ in the oppressed Indians, which objectively pointed towards a Christology of the "body of Christ." Guaman Poma, for example, said, "By faith we know clearly that where there is a poor person there is Jesus Christ himself," and Bartolome de las Casas declared, "In the Indies I leave Jesus Christ, our God, being whipped and afflicted, and buffeted and crucified, not once but thousands of times, as often as the Spaniards assault and destroy those people." But this original christological insight did not thrive, and what became the tradition was a christology based on the dogmatic formulas, in which—however well they were known and understood—what was stressed was the divinity of Christ rather than his real and lived humanity. (p.11)

Transitional paragraphs

Transitional paragraphs provide a bridge from one section of an essay to the next section. While transitions can be signaled with concluding or opening sentences of a paragraph, a transitional paragraph allows reader and writer a respite before proceeding to the next task, just as a frog might alight on a lily pad long enough to sight the school of minnows that he hopes to feast on for breakfast. Because their purpose is to provide just such a "rest stop" for readers, transitional paragraphs are usually brief, providing just enough information to induce the reader to press on to the next section.

In the first paragraph, Tamez employs a pattern of classification and division to provide a transition from what has gone before to a summary of its implications, motivated by "three concerns" that she enumerates before moving to her next section. In the second paragraph, Sobrino employs chronological development to move adroitly "from what has been said in the last section" to analyzing "the most novel features of this image, those which it would be most useful for theoretical christology to consider." Which transitional paragraph best combines succinctness with sufficient information for a reader to move confidently to the next section?

1. A reading of these contributions to the discussion of justification by faith shows us that there is in Latin America an impetus toward contextualizing justification by faith beginning with the reality of poverty and struggle, leading people to recover or rediscover in it dimensions relevant for the reality, and thereby to enrich Latin American theological thought....Three concerns emerge in these discussions. The first and most prominent is the task of relating justification to

> the justice of God. The second important concern, although it has received less attention, is the affirmation of human dignity by the event of justification. Finally, in some of these articles one can see an interest in underlining the sense of free grace in the practice of justice and in a utilitarian society. (p. 27)

> 2. What was said in the last section should be enough to secure acceptance of the new image of Christ, but it has also been sanctioned, in its essential features, by the Latin American church and now forms part of "our church tradition," constituted by Medellin and Puebla. I now want to analyze the most novel features of this image, those which it would be most useful for theoretical christology to consider. (p. 17)

Concluding paragraphs

Concluding paragraphs provide closure for writer and reader by (1) reiterating the main points that have been presented; (2) restating the thesis in the light of its substantiation and exemplification; (3) reflecting on the journey that has led to this concluding moment; and (4) acknowledging directions for further research and reflection. Tamez concludes her first chapter in a clear, precise, academic voice:

> In this chapter I have tried to stress the importance of the setting in which Christology is done and define it as adequately as possible. For Latin American Christology, this place is the situation of the poor, which is ultimately an option whose justification is to be found only within the hermeneutical circle: from the standpoint of the poor we think we come to know Christ better, and it is this better-known Christ, we think, who points us to where the poor are....
>
> In the next chapter I shall analyze the precise significance of the historical Jesus in Latin American christology, but let me repeat that the ultimate reason for this—and what distinguishes it from other christologies' reasons for going back to Jesus is the ecclesial and social setting of this Christology: in the world of poverty the poor and Jesus of Nazareth converge and point to each other. (p. 35)

However, concluding paragraphs can also combine academic and more reflective styles, as the conclusions to their authors' introductions do below. In the first paragraph, Tamez returns to the pattern of definition, asserting that "in Latin America the word 'liberation' best encompasses the various emphases or approaches to the rereading of justification by faith presented here," and weaves the threads of "justification," "oppression" and "liberation" into a concluding statement. In the second paragraph, Sobrino meditates on the process of writing his book in the midst of "the situation in El Salvador," which "[provided] a powerful hermeneutical backdrop for understanding Christ and give the gospel the taste of reality." Which is the stronger conclusion? Why?

> 1. In Latin America the word "liberation" best encompasses the various emphases or approaches to the rereading of justification by faith presented here. Certainly justification includes being liberated by God "from sin, the law, and death"— in all of their concrete manifestations—in order to engage oneself without fear in the practice of justice that our people need so greatly. The new dimension of this rereading of the doctrine is not in the well-known formulation "freed

> from ..., for ...," which already involves a big step if it is taken seriously. What is novel for us is the consideration of justification and liberation from a historical perspective of oppression, poverty, and struggle. In the present moment, the doctrine of justification is being confronted radically by the reality of injustice, whose products are the deaths of thousands of innocent people, and the loss of humanity for thousands more. Those products of injustice constitute the principal challenges of the Latin American reality to a rereading of the doctrine of justification by faith. (p. 36)

> 2. To close this long introduction, I should say that the process of writing this book has been a slow one, owing to the situation in El Salvador. To put it simply, there has not been much time to read and research all that I should have liked and should have done. This book has been written in the middle of war, of threats, of conflict and persecution, producing innumerable emergencies requiring an immediate response, and therefore innumerable interruptions to the work schedule. The murder-martyrdom of my brother Jesuits, of Julia Elba and Celina Ramos, left my heart frozen and virtually empty. But this is not the whole, or even the major significance of this book being written in El Salvador. The reality of this country has made me think a lot, and has also helped me to think about Jesus Christ. This is why I began this introduction by asking about the most appropriate title: Jesus liberator or crucified. In any case, so much tragedy and so much hope, so much sin and so much grace provide a powerful hermeneutical backdrop for understanding Christ and give the gospel the taste of reality. (pp. 7–8)

What, in sum, do theological paragraphs do? As we have seen in this section, they introduce theological questions and assertions; they develop those questions and assertions through exposition and elaboration; they cite and evaluate evidence; they signal transitions between subjects or sections; they provide closure and conspire to produce a completed essay, article or book. To do all of these things, they employ patterns of development that arise from the function of the paragraph, just as the patterns of development that you choose to write theological paragraphs well will arise from the function of the paragraph that you are writing. They exhibit unity, coherence, and emphasis, just as the theological paragraphs that you write will embody these qualities as you continue to cultivate them.

But, as Elsa Tamez and Jon Sobrino witness, theological paragraphs can do more than that. "Standing alongside" the theological writers who compose them, paragraphs can mark our passage through the writing we do and the theological journey that engenders it. They can witness to oppression and liberation, and forge a path from one to the other. They can interrogate the tradition that they expound, probe the history that they narrate, and reinterpret both of these in the light of contemporary theological situations and contexts. Finally, they can reflect the relationships between writing the paragraph and living in the world "alongside" which the paragraph is written. Just as Jon Sobrino kept writing *Jesus the Liberator* "in the middle of war, of threats, of conflict and persecution," we are challenged to write our next theological paragraph well in the midst of the injustice that it decries. Just as Elsa Tamez kept writing *The Amnesty of Grace* empowered by "the voice of God that makes its appeal to all of us," we are invited to listen for that voice as we write our next theological paragraph well. In that spirit, the concluding theological memo invites you to "write your theology in one paragraph":

> *THEOLOGICAL MEMO 10: Writing Your Theology in One Paragraph: What is the operative theology out of which you live, reflect, work, play, worship, engage in theological study, and do ministry? What is the operative theology that shapes your relationship to God, your neighbor, the stranger, the earth, and yourself? Using these questions as touchstones, and the guidelines for writing theological words, sentences and paragraphs well in this chapter as needed, please write a one-paragraph statement of your operative theology for an audience of your choice (yourself; your congregation; your professor). You may wish to check your completed paragraph against the "Theological Writer's Checklist for Writing Paragraphs Well" that follows.*

Writing paragraphs well: A theological writer's checklist

- Have you indented each block of text intended as a paragraph?
- Does your paragraph have a main point that is stated or implied?
- Does your paragraph have a topic sentence that identifies the main point?
- Does your paragraph have an identifiable beginning, middle and end?
- Does your paragraph have an identifiable pattern of development?
- Does each sentence in the paragraph contribute to its development?
- Does each sentence in the paragraph contribute to the unity of the paragraph?
- Does each sentence in the paragraph cohere through repetition of words, use of parallel constructions, and logical/chronological connectors?
- Do paragraphs provide necessary transitions to what precedes or follows them?
- Is the length of the paragraph appropriate for its purpose and level of emphasis?

Concluding reflections: Writing theological words, sentences, and paragraphs well

In this chapter we have provided a theological writer's grammar for writing words, sentences and paragraphs well by asking the question, "What do theological words, sentences and paragraphs do?" Words enable us to name God, to "do" theology, and to describe the theological imagination that flows from both of these. Sentences enable us to ask theological questions, make theological claims, and define, synthesize and summarize them. Paragraphs enable us to develop those claims into a coherent theological essay. Finally, learning to write words, sentences and paragraphs well is integral to developing an internal sense of theological style, and prepares us for the concluding chapter of Part III, "Rewriting Theology Well: A Rhetoric of Revision."

Notes

1 They are elements of composition in that we use them to compose theological prose; they are elements of communication because they constitute both the medium and the message conveyed to readers by that writing.

2 See, for example, Donald Davidson, *American Composition and Rhetoric*, 5th ed. (New York: Charles Scribner's Sons, 1968); Diana Hacker and Nancy Sommers, *A Writer's Reference*, 7th ed. (Boston, MA: Bedford/St. Martin's, 2011).

3 Theological Memo 10 at the end of this chapter will invite you to do so.

4 Tillich, *Systematic Theology*, 3 vols. (Chicago: University of Chicago Press, 1951–63), 1:241.

5 Out of that conviction, and following Aristotle's earlier exposition, Aquinas devoted a substantial section of his *Commentary on Aristotle's On Interpretation* to defining each of these parts of speech and situating them within the grammar of theological assertion. The application of this logical exposition to "writing theology well" is my own. Thomas Aquinas, *Commentary on Aristotle's On Interpretation* 1–5, in *Thomas Aquinas: Selected Writings*, ed. Ralph McInerny (London: Penguin, 1998), 456–81.

6 For example, Abraham Herschel argues that "we have … no nouns by which to describe the divine essence; we have only adverbs by which to indicate the ways in which God approaches us." See Elizabeth A. Johnson, *She Who Is: The Mystery of God in Feminist Theological Discourse* (New York: Crossroad, 1995), 240, citing Abraham Heschel, *God in Search of Man* (New York: Harper and Row, 1965), 121.

7 William Strunk, Jr. and E. B. White, *The Elements of Style*, 4th ed. (New York: Allyn & Bacon, 2000), 71.

8 Elisabeth Schüssler Fiorenza, "Introduction: Feminist Liberation Theology as Critical Sophiaology," in *The Power of Naming: A Concilium Reader in Feminist Liberation Theology*, ed. E. Schüssler Fiorenza, (Orbis: Maryknoll, 1996), xxxiii.

9 Thomas Aquinas, *Summa Contra Gentiles*, Vol. 1 (Garden City, NY: Doubleday, 1957), 31:4, quoted in Johnson, *She Who Is*, 117.

10 Joan M. Martin, *More Than Chains and Toil: A Christian Work Ethic of Enslaved Women* (Louisville, KY: Westminster John Knox Press, 2000), 153n1.

11 David Tracy, *The Analogical Imagination: Christian Theology and the Culture of Pluralism* (New York: Crossroad, 1981), 3ff.

12 Johnson, *She Who Is*, 13, 242.

13 Natalie Goldberg, *Writing Down the Bones: Freeing the Writer Within* (Boston, MA: Shambala, 1986), 87; R. Buckminster Fuller, *No More Secondhand God and Other Writings* (Carbondale: Southern Illinois University Press, 1963); Jurgen Moltmann, *The Crucified God: The Cross of Christ as the Foundation and Criticism of Christian Theology*, trans. R.A. Wilson and J. Bowden (New York: Harper and Row, 1973), 269. See Johnson's discussion of Mary Daly and Catherine LaCugna in *She Who Is*, 238–39.

14 Richard A. Lanham, *Revising Prose*, 2nd ed. (New York: Charles Scribner's Sons, 1979; New York, Macmillan, 1987, 1 (page references are to the Macmillan edition). A 5th edition of the book is now in print as well (New York: Longman, 2006).

15 See Elizabeth Johnson's analysis of the Exodus passage and its relation to ontological language in *She Who Is*, 241.

16 Diana Hacker and Nancy Sommers, *A Writer's Reference*, 7th ed. (Boston, MA: Bedford/St. Martin's, 2011), 156.

17 See Chapter 3, "What is Theological Argument and Why Do Theologians Write It?".

18 The quotation is attributed to Stendahl by Letty Russell and cited in Denise M. Ackerman, *After the Locusts: Letters from a Landscape of Faith* (Grand Rapids: Eerdmanns, 2003), 27.

19 Rowan Williams, *On Christian Theology* (Oxford: Blackwell, 2000), xii.

20 See Chapter 2 above under "A Rhetoric of Process."

21 See Chapter 2 above under, "Why Do I Follow Jesus?"

22 Elizabeth A. Johnson, *Truly Our Sister: A Theology of Mary in the Communion of Saints* (New York: Continuum, 2004), xvi.

23 See Chapter 10 above under "What is ... the Relationship between Style and Voice in Theological Writing?"

24 George Orwell, "Politics and the English Language," in *George Orwell: A Collection of Essays* (Garden City, NY: Doubleday Anchor Books, 1954), 176.

25 Roger Haight, "The Case for a Spirit Christology," *Theological Studies* 53 (1992): 259–60.

26 Wayne C. Booth, Gregory G. Colomb, and Joseph M. Williams, *The Craft of Research*, 3nd ed. (Chicago: University of Chicago Press, 2008), 262–64. See also Steven Pinker, *The Sense of Style: The Thinking Person's Guide to Writing in the 21st Century* (New York: Viking/Penguin, 2014), who corroborates Booth's argument and extends it to any rhetorical situation in which "a writer needs to steer the reader's attention away from the agent of an action" (55–56; and see also 135–37, which approves the passive voice when needed for syntactical clarity).

27 See also Roger Haight's illuminating discussion of the word "grace" as both "substantive" and "adjectival" in traditional Christian usage, and the proliferation of "secondary meanings" from the "core" meaning of the word that results from that overlapping usage: Roger Haight, *The Experience and Language of Grace* (New York: Paulist Press, 1979), 6–9.

28 Roger Haight, *Jesus Symbol of God* (Maryknoll, NY: Orbis Books, 1999), 191.

29 Karl Rahner, "The Future of the Religious Book," in *Theological Investigations*, vol. 8, trans. David Bourke (New York: Herder & Herder, 1979), 252–53. The reflections on "concrete words" recapitulate a previous discussion in Lucretia B. Yaghjian, "Flannery O'Connor's Use of Symbol, Roger Haight's Christology, and the Religious Writer," *Theological Studies* 63 (2002), 298–301.

30 Fredrica Harris Thompsett, *We Are Theologians* (Cambridge: Cowley Publications, 1989; repr. New York: Church Publishing, 2004), 13 (page numbers cited are from the reprint edition).

31 Haight, *Experience and Language of Grace*, 128.

32 Serene Jones, *Feminist Theory and Christian Theology: Cartographies of Grace* (Minneapolis, MN: Fortress Press, 2000), 11–12.

33 See Chapter 4 above under "Writing the Critical Theological Essay."

34 Gordon Kaufman, *God–Mystery–Diversity: Christian Theology in a Pluralistic World* (Minneapolis, MN: Fortress Press, 1996), 49.

35 Mark C. Taylor, "The Ends of Theology," in *Introduction to Christian Theology: Contemporary North American Perspectives*, ed. Roger A. Badham (Louisville, KY: Westminster John Knox, 1998), 258.

36 Ibid., 263.

37 Elisabeth Schüssler Fiorenza, *Bread Not Stone: The Challenge of Feminist Biblical Interpretation* (Boston, MA: Beacon Press, 1984), x.

38 Augustine, *The Trinity*, 5.9.10, trans. Stephen McKenna, *The Fathers of the Church*, vol. 45 (Washington, DC: Catholic University of America Press, 1963), quoted in Dan R. Stiver, *The Philosophy of Religious Language: Sign, Symbol and Story* (Cambridge, MA: Blackwell, 1996), 1.

39 See Chapter 7 above, under "Theological Formulations."

40 Johnson, *She Who Is*, 13, 242.

41 See n. 35 above.

42 Mary Daly, *Gyn/Ecology: The MetaEthics of Radical Feminism, With a New Intergalactic Introduction by the Author* (New York: Beacon Press, 1990; orig. 1978), xix, 24.

43 Lalrinawmi Ralte, "Crab Theology: A Critique of Patriarchy – Cultural Degradation and Empowerment of Mizo Women," D.Min. Thesis, Episcopal Divinity School, Cambridge, MA, April, 1993.

44 Simon E. Chiwanga, "Beyond the Monarch/Chief: Reconsidering the Episcopacy in Africa," in *Beyond Colonial Anglicanism: The Anglican Communion in the Twenty-First Century*, ed. Ian T. Douglas and Kwok Pui Lan (New York: Church Publishing, 2001), 297–317.

45 See, e.g., Giles Fauconnier and Mark Turner, *The Way We Think: Conceptual Blending and the Mind's Hidden Complexities* (New York: Basic Books, 2002), 69. For a brief but informative discussion, see "Literal and figurative language," Wikipedia: the free encyclopedia, accessed October 1, 2014. http://en.wikipedia.org/wiki/Literal_and_figurative_language.

46 Megan Beverly, "Preaching from a Feminist Perspective: a 'Crazy Quilt'," 2–3; in Rebecca S. Chopp, *Saving Work: Feminist Practices of Theological Education* (Louisville, KY: Westminster John Knox Press, 1995), 73.

47 Johnson, *She Who Is*, 113.

48 Literally in Hebrew, "Let light be."

49 Eudora Welty, quoted in Ben Yagoda, *The Sound on the Page: Style and Voice in Writing* (New York: HarperCollins, 2004), 35.

50 To write clear and concise sentences, Richard Lanham advises, "Look for the action. Ask yourself, who's kicking who?" As an English Professor Emeritus at UCLA who knows better, he adds parenthetically, "Yes, I know, it should be *whom*, but doesn't it sound stilted?" (See Richard Lanham, *Revising Prose* [New York: Charles Scribner's Sons, 1979]). Whether or not one approves of his grammatical choices, Lanham has taken his own advice in subsequent editions of his book by cutting two chapters from the original edition (see "Preface to the Second Edition," vii), and revising even more stringently in the 5th edition (New York: Pearson/Longman, 2007), while adding a chapter on revising "Electronic Prose" (111–23).

51 All biblical citations (Genesis 1:1b; 3; 5; 2:3) are taken from *The New Oxford Annotated Bible with the Apocrypha, New Revised Standard Version*, 4th ed., ed. Michael D. Coogan et al.(New York: Oxford University Press, 2010).

52 I have made use of the following sources in this review of sentence structure and in the section to follow on "Writing Sentences Well": Donald Davidson, *American Composition and Rhetoric*, 5th ed. (New York: Charles Scribner's Sons, 1968; Diana

Hacker and Nancy Sommers, *A Writer's Reference*, 7th ed. (New York: Bedford/St. Martin's, 2011); Thomas Kane, *The New Oxford Guide to Writing* (New York: Oxford University Press, 1988); Andrea A. Lunsford, *The Everyday Writer*, 5th rev. ed. (Boston, MA: Bedford/St. Martin's, 2012).

53 Joseph M. Williams, *Style: Ten Lessons in Clarity and Grace*, 3rd ed. (New York: HarperCollins, 1989), 78–79. An 11th ed. is now available: Joseph M. Williams and Joseph Bizup, *Style: Lessons in Clarity and Grace*, 11th ed. (Boston, Pearson, 2012).

54 Annie Dillard, *The Writing Life* (New York: Harper & Row, 1989), 70.

55 Writers have borrowed this concept from Eugene Ghendlin, *Focusing* (New York: Bantam Books, 1981). See, e.g., Peter Elbow, "Wrongness and Felt Sense," in Elbow, *Everyone Can Write: Essays Toward a Hopeful theory of Writing and Teaching Writing* (New York: Oxford University Press, 2000), 137–41; Sondra Perl, "Understanding Composing," *College Composition and Communication* 31, no. 4 (1980): 363–69.

56 Zinsser, *On Writing Well*, 13.

57 See below, "What Do Theological Sentences Do?"

58 *Oxford English Dictionary (Compact Edition)*, 1971 ed., s.v. "Sentence."

59 Alister E. McGrath, *Christian Theology: An Introduction* (Oxford: Blackwell, 2001), 34.

60 See Peter Lombard, Vol. I, ed. Marcia L. Colish (Leiden: E.J. Brill, 1994).

61 See Chapter 5 above under "The Form of the Question."

62 Johann-Baptist Metz, *Faith and History in Society*, trans. David Smith (New York: Seabury Press, 1980), 58–59.

63 For a fuller description of the nature of theological assertions, see Roger Haight, *Dynamics of Theology* (Mahweh: Paulist Press, 1990; repr. Maryknoll, NY: Orbis, Books, 2001), 44–48 (Page references are to the reprint edition).

64 Sallie McFague, *Super, Natural Christians: How We Should Love Nature* (Minneapolis, MN: Fortress Press, 1997), 2.

65 We have already proposed a method for generating a thesis statement (see Chapter 3 above under "Developing a Theological Thesis Statement). We focus here upon writing it in a grammatically and theologically precise sentence.

66 McFague, *Super, Natural Christians*, 1.

67 McFague (*Super, Natural Christians*, 2) proceeds to argue that "a Christian spirituality should be based on a subject-subjects model of being, knowing and doing in place of the subject-object model of Western culture."

68 See Richard A. Coe, *Form and Substance: An Advanced Rhetoric* (New York: John Wiley, 1981), 184–87, for a spirited defense of the cumulative sentence.

69 See Sallie McFague, *Metaphorical Theology: Models of God in Religious Language* (Philadelphia, PA: Fortress Press, 1982); *Models of God: Theology for an Ecological, Nuclear Age* (Philadelphia, PA: Fortress Press, 1987); *The Body of God: An Ecological Theology* (Minneapolis, MN: Fortress Press, 1993).

70 See Chapter 3 above under "Stating Premises and Defining Vocabulary."

71 Haight, *Jesus Symbol of God*, 15.

72 McFague, *Super, Natural Christians*, 16.

73 Ibid., 180n19. The definition quoted is from Gordon Kaufman, *The Theological Imagination: Constructing the Concept of God* (Philadelphia, PA: Westminster, 1981), 213.

74 McFague, *Super, Natural Christians*, 20.

75 Strunk and White, for example, advise writers to "express coordinate ideas in similar form." See *Elements of Style*, 26.

76 Roger Haight, S.J., *Christian Community in History: Historical Ecclesiology* (New York: Continuum, 2004; repr. London and New York: Bloomsbury/T.T. Clark, 2014), 1:ix (page references are to the first edition).

77 Aylward Shorter, *Toward a Theology of Inculturation* (Maryknoll, NY: Orbis Books, 1988), 77–78. I am indebted to the late Victor Okumu, OSB, for drawing my attention to this quote in Pontiano Vistor Okumu, "Where the Mind Meets the Heart: Interpreting African Christian Theology" (STD thesis proposal, Weston Jesuit School of Theology, February 2005).

78 To summarize is to digest or condense a longer text using one's own words. For a fuller discussion of "Writing the Theological Summary," see Chapter 4 above. To synthesize is "to draw together a selected cache of materials into one cohesive and significant narrative." See Chapter 6 above under "Synthesizing."

79 McFague, *Super Natural Christians*, 24.

80 Johnson, *Truly Our Sister*, 36.

81 McFague, *Super Natural Christians*, 24.

82 Johnson, *Truly Our Sister*, 92.

83 See Sheridan Baker, *The Complete Stylist and Handbook* (New York: Thomas Y. Crowell, 1976), 51–53.

84 Ann E. Berthoff, *Forming/Thinking/Writing: The Composing Imagination* (Rochelle Park, NJ: Hayden, 1978, 158–59.

85 Francis Christensen, "A Generative Rhetoric of the Paragraph," *College Composition and Communication* 16 (October 1965): 144–56, quoted in Coe, *Form and Substance*, 134.

86 Elizabeth George, *Write Away: One Novelist's Approach to Writing and the Writing Life* (London: Hodder and Stoughton, 2004), 177.

87 The nineteenth-century rhetorician Alexander Bain introduced these criteria in his *English Composition and Rhetoric* (1866). For a contemporary assessment of his contribution, see Erika Lindemann, *A Rhetoric for Writing Teachers*, 3rd ed. (New York: Oxford University Press, 1995), 142–43.

88 John Updike, "The Blessed Man of Boston, My Grandmother's Thimble, and Fanning Island," in *The Early Stories, 1953–1975* (New York: Alfred A. Knopf, 2003), 92.

89 See, e.g., Hacker and Sommers, *Writer's Reference*, 34–39; Lunsford, *Everyday Writer*, 51–57.

90 See Richard A. Meade and W. G. Ellis, "Paragraph Development in the Modern Age of Rhetoric," *English Journal* 59 (1970), 222.

91 We cite from Elsa Tamez, *The Amnesty of Grace: Justification by Faith from a Latin American Perspective*, trans. Sharon H. Ringe (Nashville, TN: Abingdon Press, 1993); and Jon Sobrino, *Jesus the Liberator: A Historical-Theological View*, trans. Paul Burns and Francis McDonough (Maryknoll, NY: Orbis Books, 1993). Page numbers are provided in parentheses in the text.

12
Rewriting Theology Well (III): A Rhetoric of Revision

Revision is all there is.

—NANCY SOMMERS, "Between the Drafts"

Starting points

In his conclusion to Strunk and White's *The Elements of Style*, E.B. White cautions us that there is "no infallible guide to good writing, no assurance that a person who thinks clearly will be able to write clearly..., no inflexible rule by which writers may shape their course. Writers will often find themselves steering by stars that are disturbingly in motion."[1] Undaunted nonetheless by this lack of fixed stars in the writer's night sky, White appended his own rhetoric of writing and revision to the second and subsequent editions of Strunk's original handbook of style.[2]

By what stars, fixed or otherwise, do you chart your course as a theological writer? If Nancy Sommers is right that "revision is all there is,"[3] then those guiding stars will not take you far without a rhetoric of revision. Therefore, in this chapter I invite you to identify your own rhetoric, protocols, or purposeful elements of revision, guided by the lodestar of "revision" and the lodestar of "style." We have already tracked the lodestar of "style" in "Rewriting Theology Well (I): Rhetorics of Style and Voice," and in "Rewriting Theology Well (II): Rhetorics of Words, Sentences, and Paragraphs." Imagine with me, then, that the "revision star" is presently rising, while the clouds of white paper that you have crumpled up in your struggle to write theology well obscure the "style star" beyond all recognition. In the faith that the ability to rewrite theology well will surface where the paths of both of these stars converge, this chapter invites you to develop a theological style of your own through an individualized rhetoric of revision that integrates rewriting, revision, and becoming your own best editor.

Rewriting, revision, and becoming your own best editor

While the processes of *revision* and *rewriting* are often considered more strategic to good writing than that of *editing*, each of these processes are integrally connected. The process of *rewriting* engages writers in a process of *revision*, but in order to revise writing effectively, writers need to become "their own best *editors*," as writing guru Donald Murray explains.[4] The word *editus* means "to bring forth; to put forth; to bring to birth." Understood in this way, editing is an integral part of the creative process. While we often think of an editor as a professional wordsmith who is paid to edit the writing of others, everyone who writes is an editor. In the process of writing that last sentence, for example, I have edited it several times already and revised the sentence accordingly. To do that, however, I had to "train [myself] to step back from [my] work," as Murray writes, "and see it with a reader's eye."[5] However, when you step back to see your writing "with a reader's eye," you initiate the process of *revision*, which literally means "to see again." That process in turn elicits *editing*, and *editing* requires *rewriting* of what is edited. We will keep these three interrelated processes in play as we prepare to rewrite theology well by engaging in a focused but flexible rhetoric of revision that unfolds as an editing process which you will revise to fit your own your own theological writing style and context.[6]

THEOLOGICAL MEMO 1: What editing skills do you have, and what editing skills do you need? Do a ten-minute freewriting exercise describing your present process of editing/revising theological papers. If you don't have an articulated process, think about the last paper you wrote and answer the following questions: (1) How many drafts did you write? (2) Did you make any revisions before handing in the final draft? (3) What criteria of good writing, or "style," guided your revisions? (4) How much writing time did you devote to writing the first draft and subsequent drafts? (5) What works well for you and what needs work in your revision process? (6) What editing/revision strategies would help you to rewrite theology well?

Editing draft I: The chopping block

Aim for the chopping block. If you aim for the wood, you will have nothing. Aim past the wood, aim through the wood; aim for the chopping block.

—ANNIE DILLARD, *The Writing Life*

As Annie Dillard implies in the above epigraph, in editing a first draft, most writers chip away at their writing rather than cutting through it clearly by "aiming for the chopping block."[7] Consequently, even when writing assignments specify a page limit, it is not always easy to observe those limits. In the early writing stages, this is inevitable. If we do write everything three times,[8] overwriting is appropriate in the early stages of a project. In order to find out what we really want to say, we may require the luxury of throwing much of it away. But what if we are easily lured by the sound of our own words, and the way they look on a page? In later drafts, we should cut (a) content no longer necessary to the development of our thesis; (b) excessive quoted material that can be paraphrased or summarized; (c) words and phrases that do not carry their weight in the communication process.

THEOLOGICAL MEMO 2: The Chopping Block. Choose a theological paper for which you have a working draft that needs revision.

(1) Read it once for content: Does it (a) say what you want to say, or (b) are you still finding out what you want to say? If (a) you are ready to proceed to the chopping block; if (b) make some notations of what is still needed to complete the draft, and then proceed as if it were ready for the chopping block.

(2) Content on the "chopping block": What blocks of content can be cut from your manuscript (paragraphs? sentences? footnotes?)? Look for: (a) material no longer relevant to your thesis or focus; (b) introductory paragraphs that repeat themselves; (c) digressions that do not advance your argument/narrative; (d) unsupported generalizations (rewrite them or remove them); (e) repetitious "metadiscourse," or writing about your writing and research process that does not advance the progress of your argument.[9] *When you are ready, delete this material, keeping a copy of all deletions, in case you should need to reinsert them at a later date.*

(3) Language on the "Chopping Block": What words, phrases, and sentences can be chopped? (a) Look for extraneous language that hides the noun, verb, and object of a sentence. As Richard Lanham suggests, ask, "Who's kicking who?" when your subjects and verbs become lost in cumbersome sentence structure.[10] *(b) Look for passive constructions that should be rewritten in the active voice, and eschew the "institutional passive," which often passes as "academic style."*[11] *(c) Look for "long words" used "when short ones will do."*[12] *(d) Look for endangered metaphors; clichés; theological jargon (vs. appropriate "technical" theological language). (e) Look for overlong sentences that will lose readers before they reach their conclusion. (f) Look for anything that "just doesn't sound right."*[13] *When you are ready, delete this material.*

(4) Your "first editing" draft: What remains is your "first editing" draft. If you have time, rewrite or put it into a new file. If you don't, re-read it and make any final corrections or deletions before proceeding to "Editing Draft II."

Editing draft II: The writing patch

You can easily get so confused writing a thirty page chapter that in order to make an outline for the second draft, you have to rent a hall. I have often "written" with the mechanical aid of a twenty-foot conference table. You lay the pages along the table's edge and pace out the work. You walk along the rows; you weed bits, move bits, and dig out bits, bent over the rows with full hands like a gardener.

—ANNIE DILLARD, *The Writing Life*

Editing is not only cutting and pruning; it is also waiting, watering, fertilizing, adding, transplanting, and—in whatever way appropriate to your work in progress—creating the conditions that make your writing grow and flourish.

Waiting

You will be a better editor of your drafts if you wait at least twenty four hours before re-reading them. Let them rest, like dough; punch them down, if necessary; then go and do other things. If what has risen surprises you, you have waited long enough!

Watering

In order to become your own best editor, it is necessary to recognize good writing when you see it. Begin with the theological reading you have been assigned. When an article is written well, ask yourself what makes the writing good. When an article is written poorly, ask yourself what makes the writing poor. Do this with every article you read, and create your own criteria for "good" theological writing.

Fertilizing

To nourish your own theological style, read the short fiction of Anton Chekov, Ernest Hemingway, Eudora Welty, and Flannery O'Connor, all of whom write with clarity and concision. Read the poetry of Emily Dickinson, Robert Frost, Mary Oliver and Billy Collins, all of whom are exacting wordsmiths. Read the essays of Annie Dillard, John McPhee, Richard Selzer, and Lewis Thomas, each of whom combines a distinctive voice with a disciplined prose style. Inspired by these exemplars and others of your own choosing, return to the theological authors that you are reading and make a list of "theological writing mentors" whose work you wish to emulate. What qualities attract you to their writing? What challenges do they pose as you return to your own?

Grafting

While some writers overwrite their first drafts, others underwrite them. If you have been told that your writing is "thin"; if comments like, "what do you mean?" "please develop further"; and "please give an example" reappear like rubber stamps in the margins of your papers; if you typically have difficulty filling the number of pages prescribed for the paper, you may need to graft new material onto the sparsely growing sections of your paper. If you ask yourself the above questions while editing your draft, and revise your text in response to them, you will take those words out of your professor's mouth, and pleasantly surprise him or her with a more complete paper.

Creating the conditions

Effective editing can make the difference between an excellent paper and an acceptable one. What conditions do you need in order to edit theology well? Do you need a quiet writing space? Do you need better time management skills? Do you need a "reader over your shoulder"? Do you need a "revision heuristic"?[14]

> *THEOLOGICAL MEMO 3: Transplanting or Rearranging. How free are you to move your writing around, once you have written it? Do your sentences get stuck between the furrows of your first draft before you have found what you really want to say? This editing draft invites you to walk "row by row" through your writing patch, and see how your garden grows:*
>
> *(1) Using your unedited draft, read it through for general organization, and outline it. Is it (a) logical? (b) sequential? (c) marked by smooth transitions?*

(d) unified and coherent (possessing a beginning, middle, and end)? Are there any (a) gaps? (b) non-sequiturs? (c) transitions omitted?

(2) Even if your draft reads well as you have written it, try (a) putting your conclusion at the beginning; (b) changing the order of your supporting points; (c) beginning your draft with the second paragraph. Like the Japanese art of feng shui, moving your writing around will release new energy and suggest new connections, even if you decide that its original structure is the best one.

(3) Whether you are dealing with a room, a painting, or a piece of writing, rearranging the elements of an artistic whole is integral to the process of "re-visioning" it. When, for example, the concluding sentence of an essay is recognized as the real thesis of the paper, a "re-visioning" of the paper will entail rearranging its parts as well. What further "re-visions" have suggested themselves from this exercise? Prepare a "second editing draft" that includes these revisions.

Editing draft III: Back to the drawing board

> *After Michelangelo died, someone found in his studio a piece of paper on which he had written a note to his apprentice, in the handwriting of his old age: "Draw, Antonio, draw, Antonio, draw and do not waste time."*
>
> —ANNIE DILLARD, *The Writing Life*

Sometimes the editing process sends us back to the drawing board. As we work with our material, we see that we need to rethink our thesis, gather more information, redirect the writing focus, or even start again from scratch. Some of the finest sermons are written after the writer has thrown the first, unsatisfying draft away. Some of the best papers you will write will emerge only after you have let go of a thesis statement that didn't say what you wanted to say, or after you have deleted a section of the paper that distracted readers from your argument rather than directing them to it. Do not be afraid of this development. Be willing to go back to the drawing board, and pay attention. It is your own best editor speaking to you!

THEOLOGICAL MEMO 4: Back to the Drawing Board. If the need to rethink, re-gather, or redirect your writing focus should occur as you are working on one of these revision exercises, leave it for 10 minutes and go back to the drawing board! Do a 10-minute freewriting that answers the questions, What do I know and what do I need to know? What new center of gravity is emerging here? What is my next step (e.g., revise my thesis; do additional research to support a weak link in my argument; narrow my focus; talk to the professor; find a sympathetic reader)? When you have completed the freewriting, go back to your editing task with a clear conscience; you can return to the drawing board at your own discretion.

Editing draft IV: A theological style and voice of your own

> *You were made and set here to give voice to this, your own astonishment.*
>
> —ANNIE DILLARD, *The Writing Life*

Becoming your own best editor not only requires a mastery of common stylistic conventions; it also presupposes the acquisition of a theological style and voice of your own. We have already defined theological style as *how you write theology when you write in a given theological genre, from a particular theological stance, for a specific theological audience, using your own language and your own voice.*[15] Described in terms of genre, stance and audience, style refers to the public form of written discourse appropriate to the writer's subject or discipline, purpose, audience, or disciplinary community. Just as Clifford Geertz argues that anthropologists have particular styles that shape their observations, methods and theories in a creative, interactive way,[16] there is an interactive relationship between what a theologian writes ("content") and how he or she writes it ("style"). Described in terms of language and voice, style is what distinguishes one author's writing from that of another. Those distinguishing features are expressed in the writer's choice of language and its "sound on the page," which reveal the spirit of its author,[17] just as God's creation reveals the Creator for those able with Einstein to see God "in the details." But how do all of these conspire to produce a theological style and voice of one's own? We can only answer this question by looking at some examples.

> *THEOLOGICAL MEMO 5: Becoming Your Best Theological Editor. As we have seen throughout these chapters on "Rewriting Theology Well," developing a theological style and voice of your own does not happen in a vacuum. This Theological Memo invites you to "become your best theological editor" by reading the selections from the theological writers below, and analyzing their theological "style" and "voice." Begin by evaluating them in the light of George Orwell's revision heuristic, adapted for theological writers:*
>
> (1) *Never use a long word when a short one will do.*
> (2) *Never use a passive verb when an active verb will do.*
> (3) *Never use a metaphor or cliché you are used to seeing in print.*
> (4) *Never use a foreign word when an ordinary English equivalent is available.*
> (5) *Never use jargon, but use your thinking cap to find the word that fits your thought and says what you want to say.*
> (6) *Break any of these rules before writing something that doesn't sound right when you reread it.*[18]

Becoming your best theological editor: Analyzing styles and voices

(1) The Christian faith is the apprehension of the divine love and power which bears the whole human pilgrimage, shines through its enigmas and antinomies and is finally and definitively revealed in a drama in which suffering love gains triumph over sin and death. This revelation does not resolve all perplexities; but it does triumph over despair, and leads to the renewal of life from self-love to love. [Reinhold Niebuhr][19]

(2) How does one determine when a law is just or unjust? A just law is a man-made code that squares with the moral law or the law of God. An unjust law is a code that is out of harmony with the moral law. To put it in the terms of Saint Thomas Aquinas, an unjust law is a human law that is not rooted in eternal and natural law. Any law that uplifts human personality is just. Any law that degrades human personality is unjust. All segregation statutes are unjust because segregation distorts the soul and damages the personality. It gives the segregator a false sense of superiority, and the segregated a false sense of inferiority. [Martin Luther King, Jr.][20]

(3) For me the central question is: How is it possible for the formerly colonized, oppressed, subjugated subaltern to transform the symbol of Christ—a symbol that has been used to justify colonization and domination—into a symbol that affirms life, dignity, and freedom? Can the subaltern speak about Christ, and if so, under what conditions? What language shall we borrow? What are the dangers of doing so? Alternatively, if we need to ground our reflections in the culture and religiosity of our people, how can we avoid the pitfalls of cultural essentialism, nativism, and nationalistic ideologies? What makes it possible to say something new about Jesus/Christ? [Kwok Pui-Lan][21]

(4) Just as christology is the theology of Jesus of Nazareth, so too ecclesiology is the theology of the Christian community in history. And just as the category of symbol is descriptive of how Jesus is mediator of God, so too is the church often described as the community that continues to represent Jesus Christ in history, thus making it as a community a kind of primal social sacrament. The dialectical tension that obtains in christology finds its correlate in ecclesiology. Just as christology demands a restoration of Jesus of Nazareth to the imagination as he in whom God was incarnate, so too ecclesiology demands a consideration of the concrete, social, and historical community and institution of the church as that in which God acts as grace. [Roger Haight][22]

(5) A feminist hermeneutics cannot trust or accept Bible and tradition simply as divine revelation. Rather it must critically evaluate them as patriarchal articulations .... This critical insight of a feminist hermeneutics has ramifications not only for historical scholarship but also for our contemporary political situation because the Bible still functions today as a religious justification and ideological legitimization of patriarchy. [Elisabeth Schüssler Fiorenza][23]

(6) As I see it we have just one job to do. To change society and to have bread that day: for all time. For every day. Once and for all. That's what I find. If we're always going to be begging for a little bit of bread, today for today, and tomorrow and the day after tomorrow ... that way we'll always be in need. No: we'll just do the job once and afterwards we'll always have enough to eat and enough to wear and all the rest. That's what I meant when I said that Jesus wasn't really talking about a single day .... [Ernesto Cardenal][24]

(7) In this article, I shall argue that the Gospel of Mark does not have a single structure made up of discrete sequential units but rather is an interwoven tapestry or fugue made up of multiple overlapping structures and sequences, forecasts of what is to come and echoes of what has already been said. I shall then suggest that such a nonlinear recursive compositional style is characteristic of aural narrative, and suggest a few implications. [Joanna Dewey][25]

(8) The poet in exile sings his people to homecoming. And that is a theme to which the exiled church in America is now summoned. The gospel is that we may go home. Home is not here in the consumer militarism of a dominant value system. Home also is not in heaven, as though we might escape. Home, rather, is God's kingdom of love and justice and peace and freedom that waits for us. The news is we are invited home (cf. Luke 15:17). The whole church may yet sing: "Precious Saviour take my hand. Lead me home!" [Walter Brueggemann][26]

(9) Diversity is not something to be afraid of. But for many theologians, particularly in the West, diversity is unsettling. All defenses go up, as though the intermingling of the gospel with different cultures is a weakening of faith and a destruction of its purity. But the Spirit breaks forth in the midst of color, contrasts and plurality; and it is there that the gospel is made known as the transforming power of God brings the new into being. The words of Lamin Sanneh, the Yale missiologist, are strikingly relevant at this juncture. He says, "For all of us pluralism can be a rock of stumbling, but for God it is the cornerstone of the universal design." [Christopher Duraisingh][27]

(10) The perfection of charity is eschatological, but its practice is deeply historical and profoundly communal. It always tends toward that perfect love that casts out fear (I John 4:18). Charity is the ecclesiastical virtue because it is the bridge that joins history and hope. It is also the theological virtue for, in the end, as Paul, Augustine and Thomas Aquinas all knew, it is only charity that endures. We will still live in charity when faith has been transformed into the vision of God and hope is fulfilled by God's presence. What better reason for living in charity now—especially in the church? [Francine Cardman][28]

THEOLOGICAL MEMO 6: Analyzing Theological Styles and Voices.

(1) The theological styles and voices represented above are deliberately various. Indeed, they may seem to defy categorization; but do they? On the basis of these random samples, can you suggest three "common" characteristics of theological style?

(2) Now consider the voice in each of these excerpts. Which ones are written in a personal voice? Which ones are written in a public, or academic voice? In which passages do you hear the voice the most loudly? In which is the voice subordinate to the style? Does your answer to this question give you some clues for integrating "theological style" and personal "voice"?

(3) Choose one of the excerpts above, do a brief stylistic analysis of it using George Orwell's revision heuristic (see below), and then rewrite it in your own voice and language, condensing, expanding, paraphrasing or editing as appropriate:

(a) Active or passive verbs?
(b) "Long" or "short" words (and sentences)?
(c) Cliches? Dead metaphors?
(d) Foreign words?
(e) Jargon (vs. accepted theological language)?
(f) "Broken" rules that work or don't work?

(4) Now return to your own paper draft and reread it for style and voice. Keeping in mind that writing for the traditional theological academy typically requires a more public voice than writing on the theological margins, make any further revisions appropriate to the theological context for which you are writing.

Editing draft V: The peer editing heuristic

Nothing is so powerful as a chance to see your words through the eyes of others.

—PETER ELBOW, *Writing with Power*

Becoming your own best editor does not only mean learning how to edit your own work; it also means knowing when you need, with Peter Elbow, "to see your words through the eyes of others."[29] For some of us, this is most helpful early in the process; for others, feedback on early drafts can confuse or even stifle our own voice and vision. For international and multilingual students, tutorial feedback and proofreading assistance can be invaluable; for all students, a final proofreading by other eyes than the author's can make the difference between an excellent paper and a "pretty good" or "passable" performance.

THEOLOGICAL MEMO 7: Personal Salvation or Peer Editing Model?

The theological writing life is often based upon a "personal salvation" model of writing. I write "in secret" for my professor. I quietly rue or relish the grade I am given, and then begin the process again. Published theologians, on the other hand, employ a "peer editing" model of rewriting. They write a paper and ask for their colleagues' feedback. They submit the paper to a conference, and receive more feedback. One or two years later, the article is published. Five years later, the article engenders a book that has been read in various stages of completion by more readers, and revised accordingly.

To be our own best editors, we need peers to edit us, just as they need us to edit them. Using the Peer Editing Heuristic that follows, please exchange drafts with a writing partner, edit your partner's draft, and share editorial feedback with each other, remembering that the goal is to encourage revision, not to rewrite the paper.

Editing for your peers: A working heuristic

The outline below provides a step-by-step process for peer editing that you may adapt for particular theological genres into a peer review heuristic of your own:

CONCEPTUAL READING: A BROAD OVERVIEW
Read the paper first for a broad overview, by asking:

A. What is the author's purpose?
B. What is the author's main idea, or thesis?
C. How well is the subject conceptualized?
D. Who is the theological audience addressed?
E. What theological genre is it (pastoral/systematic reflection, exegesis)?
F. What logic of organization is used? (inductive? deductive?)
G. What questions do you have after this first reading?

SPEED READING, or WORD-SKIMMING
Read the paper again, but this time read only the necessary words:

A. How much can you skim without losing the sense of the essay? (English is at least 50% redundant; only about half the words an author writes are essential to understanding the ideas.)
B. What words make you stop or stumble? Why?

CRITICAL READING: WHAT RESONATES? WHAT NEEDS REVISION?
Now read the paper carefully as a friendly critic evaluating the paper:

A. What resonates? What did you like about the paper! Cite examples.
B. Your suggestions should respect the author's purpose, not your expectations.
C. What needs revision? Why:
    1. Thesis too broad, too narrow, or undeveloped?
    2. Introductory "map" of paper misleading or lacking?
    3. Supporting ideas not adequately developed?
    4. Too many quotes or not enough documentation?
    5. A structural or organizational fault (please identify)?
    6. No conclusion to tell us what we now know?
    7. The paper doesn't deliver what the introduction promises?
D. Make an outline of the paper that indicates where the "structural fault" is.
E. Make a list of key terms and identify those requiring clearer definition.

PROOFREADING

The proof of a completed paper is in the quality of this final reading:

A. General stylistics (revisit Orwell's revision heuristic or White's "Reminders")
B. Sentences (awkward? overlong? subjects and verbs free and clear?)
C. Transitions between paragraphs (smooth? terse? non-existent?)
D. Grammar and punctuation (use your eyes, your ears, and a good style manual, where needed)
E. Manuscript formatting (outline? headings? subheadings? footnotes? bibliography?)
F. Final comments? (The last word should energize, not paralyze the writer!)

Editing draft VI: Editing for grammatical grace

THEOLOGICAL MEMO 8: Editing For Grammatical Grace. When your paper is ready for final editing, use this checklist as needed to check for grammatical errors. (It was originally written for international student writers, but if you are a grammatically challenged native speaker/writer of English, you may find it helpful too.) You may wish to customize this checklist for your own editorial needs by adding your own typical grammatical errors:[30]

1. Do subjects and verbs agree in person and number (He don't/doesn't like to write)?
2. Does every noun that needs an article (a/an/the) have one?
3. Are sentences written in the correct word order (subject/verb/object/complement) for standard written English?
4. Do verb tenses agree (I could if I would)?
5. Have you used an infinitive (to study) where you need a gerund (studying)?
6. Do pronouns agree with their antecedents in gender, number, and case (The boy broke his leg; the girl brought her boyfriend with her)?
7. Have you ended every complete sentence with a period (.)?
8. Does a semi-colon join two independent clauses; if it does, it will look like this!
9. Have you used commas to join independent and dependent clauses? (If you have, it will look like this!)
10. When you use a colon, does it: introduce a clause, phrase, or series of elements that expand or elucidate the meaning of what preceded it?
11. Is your writing free of double negatives (It won't do her any good)?
12. Have you checked your paper for your most typical mistakes (keep a record of these and add them below):
13.
14.
15.

A revision heuristic of your own

One of the best-kept writing secrets around is that the more you revise, the clearer, more fluid, and more natural your writing will be.

—JOAN BOLKER, *Writing Your Dissertation in Fifteen Minutes a Day*

In this chapter we have explored some techniques for "rewriting theology well" through an interactive rhetoric of editing and revision. You were first invited to describe your present process of revising written work, and to assess the strengths and weaknesses of that process. We then introduced a sequence of editing and revising strategies for you to negotiate in a series of editing "drafts." "Editing Draft I," "The Chopping Block," focused on revision as a process of deleting unnecessary words, sentences and paragraphs. "Editing Draft II," "The Writing Patch," focused on revision as a process of grafting onto, transplanting, or rearranging what you have already written. "Editing Draft III" took you "Back to the Drawing Board" to refocus or "re-envision" your writing draft. "Editing Draft IV" prompted you to identify "a Theological Style of Your Own" by "becoming Your Best Theological Editor" and editing the writing of published theological authors. "Editing Draft V" invited your participation in a "Peer Editing Heuristic" of writing and revision. Finally, "Editing Draft VI" provided a grammatical checklist for final proofreading.

You will not use all of these editing strategies every time that you write a paper. Yet if Joan Bolker is correct when she says, "The more you revise, the clearer, more fluid, and more natural your writing will be,"[31] then the more skillfully you can revise your own writing, the more surely you will write theology well. Thus the goal of this chapter is to help you develop an effective revision heuristic, or set of paper-editing protocols that reflect your own style of writing and revision. For example, some people write a first draft of a paper before revising it. Other people revise their writing as they write. Some people elicit feedback on early drafts of their work, while others prefer to receive feedback on penultimate drafts.

However you choose to revise, edit and rewrite, a revision heuristic is simply a set of questions and/or procedures to guide you through your revision/editing process. Before preparing it, you will need to return to your reflections on your revision process in "Theological Memo 1"[32] and the issues that you identified as needing work, for these are the areas where you will need the prompting of a revision heuristic. If you routinely fail to provide a well-rounded conclusion to your essay, your revision heuristic should provide a task-specific question or prompt to remind you to do so. If you forget to spell check your essay in your haste to print out a copy thirty minutes before the paper is due, your revision heuristic should remind you to do so.

Your revision heuristic should also provide a coherent procedure for undertaking the revision process that you will be able to internalize as you continue to write and rewrite theology well.[33] For example, you might begin by checking for the main parts of the paper (thesis, supporting arguments, transitions, and conclusion) and proceed to the close reading issues (style, language and punctuation). Here is a sample revision heuristic created by one of my students for writing a one-page systematic reflection paper:

One-page systematic reflection paper revision heuristic[34]

Answering the question:

- Have I answered the question in a one-sentence thesis/claim?

Developing the thesis/claim: Have I developed the thesis/claim by

- Qualifying it?
- Defining necessary terms?
- Stating my focus or perspective (if appropriate)?
- Identifying the warrants of the argument?

Substantiating the argument: Have I substantiated the thesis statement by

- Providing relevant evidence from assigned readings?
- Unfolding the evidence in a logical, linear manner?
- Covering all the sub-points implicit in the thesis statement?
- Drawing the implications of the evidence credibly and coherently?

Concluding the paper: Have I provided a concise summary/conclusion that

- Concludes in terms of the thesis statement?
- Summarizes (in brief) the evidence I have presented?
- Employs assertive (not merely descriptive) language?
- Provides a strong finale in its final sentence?

Editing the paper: Have I spell checked and edited the paper for

- Awkward phrasing (remember subject/verb/object word order)?
- Wordy sentences (cut unnecessary words, don't overuse commas)?
- Correct in-text documentation and spelling of authors' names?
- Proper one-page format (final cut for word count, adjust margins)?

Concluding reflections: Rewriting theology well

"Revision," Nancy Sommers remarked at the beginning of this chapter, "is all there is." Even as I read the proofs for the second edition of this book, I am still revising it, and the only thing that will stop this process is its committal to print. Yet whether we are writing a one-page paper or a 450 page book, a time comes when we must say, "It is finished," and trust that the words we wrote will be sufficient to the task for which we have written them.

In that spirit, we return, finally, to the question with which we began. What stars, fixed or otherwise, help you to chart your course as a theological writer? To answer that question, I have invited you to create a revision heuristic that you can use as a tool for rewriting theology well. You can make it general enough to fit most of your theological assignments, or specific enough to fit a particular kind of theological paper, as the writer did in the "Systematic Reflection Paper Revision Heuristic" on the previous page. Just as a particular process of theological reflection is first engaged in deliberately and then internalized, so a revision heuristic invites you first to articulate your revision process and then to internalize it as you use it consistently to edit, revise and rewrite your papers. One day, you may throw the script away and proceed with your revisions confidently, just as you don't need a map of the night sky when you can locate the North Star from the bowl of the Big Dipper and then identify many more of the constellations in the night sky. But both novice and seasoned sailors need to know the location of the North Star and the major constellations, and writers need to identify the rhetorical elements that guide them, even if their paper trail marks an uncharted course. In the meantime, I invite you to persevere on this journey as we proceed in Part IV to write theology well in new contexts, beginning with "Writing Theology Well in a New Language," addressed to international students and their tutors, and concluding with "Writing Theology Well in a Digital Environment," addressed to all students writing theology in that environment.

THEOLOGICAL MEMO 9: A Revision Heuristic, and "List of Good Writing Reminders" of Your Own. Read E.B. White's "An Approach to Style (With a List of Reminders") in Strunk and White, The Elements of Style, *66-85. You might also wish to review the "Elements of Theological Plain Style" at the conclusion of* Chapter 10 *in conjunction with this memo. Since it is necessary to have a style, or standard of good writing, in order to develop a heuristic for revising writing, make a list of five "Good Writing Reminders" in the spirit of those that E.B. White appended to Strunk and White's* The Elements of Style. *Then, using the "Systematic Reflection Paper Revision Heuristic" above as a suggestive template, develop a "revision heuristic" for the next paper that you must write, or for a draft of a paper that you have already written. After you have used your revision heuristic to revise one of your papers, reflect on the strengths and weaknesses of your heuristic, and edit, revise and rewrite it accordingly.*

Notes

1 E.B. White, "An Approach to Style (With a List of Reminders)," in *The Elements of Style*, ed. William Strunk, Jr. and E.B. White, 4th ed. (Needham Heights, MA: Allyn & Bacon/New York: Longman, 2000), 66.

2 Ibid., 70–85.

3 Nancy Sommers, "Between the Drafts," in *Landmark Essays on Writing Process*, ed. Sandra Perl (Davis, CA: Hermagoras Press, 1994), 217–24.

4 Donald Murray, "The Editor's Craft," in *Writing for Your Readers: Notes on the Writer's Craft from the Boston Globe*, 2nd ed. (Boston: Globe/Pequot Press, 1992), 147.

5 Ibid.

6 The rhetoric of revision that I develop here is indebted to the following sources: Theodore A. R. Cheney, *Getting the Words Right: How to Rewrite, Edit and Revise* (Cincinnati, OH: Writers Digest Books, 1983); Richard Coe, *Form and Substance: An Advanced Rhetoric* (New York: John Wiley, 1980), 74–106; Peter Elbow, *Writing with Power: Techniques for Mastering the Writing Process* (Oxford: Oxford University Press, 1981), 121–72; Richard A. Lanham, *Revising Prose*, 5th ed. (New York: Pearson/Longman, 2007); Murray, "The Editor's Craft," 147–54; George Orwell, "Politics and the English Language," in *A Collection of Essays* (Garden City, NY: Doubleday Anchor Books, 1954), 162–77; Strunk and White, *Elements of Style*, 70–85.

7 Annie Dillard, *The Writing Life* (New York: HarperCollins, 1989), 59.

8 See the "Writing Three Times" process outlined in Chapter 2 above under "Writing the One Page Pastoral Reflection Paper."

9 As Joseph M. Williams clarifies, "Metadiscourse is the language we use when we describe what we are doing as we think and write about the content of our own primary ideas, or what we want our readers to be doing as they read" (*Style: Ten Lessons in Clarity and Grace*, 3rd ed. [New York: HarperCollins 1989], 27–29). When a paper begins with an organizational map that tells readers how the argument will proceed, the author is using "metadiscourse" appropriately. If, however, the metadiscourse takes on a life of its own that distracts the reader from the main argument of the paper, the writer should consider saving that material for a "process" paper and deleting it from the work at hand.

10 Lanham, *Revising Prose*, 5th ed, 14–20.

11 See Williams, *Style*, 26–27.

12 See Orwell, "Politics and the English Language," 162–77, esp. 176. Orwell's 1946 essay is a classic critique of the abuses of language and their consequences for public discourse that warrants careful rereading today.

13 Sociology professor Howard Becker advises the students in his writing seminar, "We can't write ... or even rewrite by treating whatever rules we might decide on as algorithms .... We do it by ear," by which he means, "We use what 'sounds good' or 'looks good' to us." See Howard S. Becker, *Writing for Social Scientists: How to Start and finish Your Thesis, Book or Article*, with a chapter by Pamela Richards (Chicago: University of Chicago Press, 1986), 68–89.

14 A revision heuristic is simply a set of questions that you ask yourself at the completion of a draft to guide the revision process. See the "One-Page Systematic Reflection Paper Revision Heuristic" at the end of this chapter.

15 See Chapter 10, "What is Voice, and the Relationship between Style and Voice in Theological Writing?"

16 See Clifford Geertz, *Works and Lives: The Anthropologist as Author* (Palo Alto, CA: Stanford University Press, 1988).

17 As E. B. White concurs, "All writers, by the way they use language, reveal something of their spirits, their habits, their capacities, and their biases" ("Approach to Style," 67).

18 This revision heuristic is adapted from Orwell, "Politics and the English Language," 176.

19 Reinhold Niebuhr, *Faith and History* (New York: Charles Scribner's Sons, 1951), 233–34.

20 Martin Luther King, Jr., "Letter from a Birmingham Jail," in *I Have a Dream: Letters and Speeches That Changed the World*, ed. James Melvin Washington (San Francisco, CA: Harper San Francisco, 1992), 89.

21 Kwok Pui-Lan, "Engendering Christ: Who Do You Say that I Am?" in *Postcolonial Imagination & Feminist Theology*, ed. Kwok (Louisville, KY: Westminster/John Knox Press, 2005), 168–69.

22 Roger Haight, *Christian Community in History: Historical Ecclesiology*, Vol. 1 (New York: Continuum, 2004; repr. London and New York: Bloomsbury/T.T. Clark, 2014); page references are to the first edition.

23 Elisabeth Schüssler Fiorenza, *Bread Not Stone: The Challenge of Feminist Biblical Interpretation* (Boston, MA: Beacon Press, 1984), x–xi.

24 "Julio," in Ernesto Cardenal, *The Gospel in Solentiname*, 4 vols. (Maryknoll, NY: Orbis Books, 1978), 1:213.

25 Joanna Dewey, "Mark as Interwoven Tapestry: Forecasts and Echoes for a Listening Audience," *Catholic Biblical Quarterly* 53 (1991): 221–36.

26 Walter Brueggemann, *Hopeful Imagination: Prophetic Voices in Exile* (Philadelphia, PA: Fortress Press, 1986), 130.

27 Christopher Duraisingh, "Toward a Postcolonial Re-Visioning of the Church's Faith, Witness and Communion," in *Beyond Colonial Anglicanism: The Anglican Community in the Twenty-First Century*, ed. Ian T. Douglas and Kwok Pui Lan (New York, NY: Church Publishing, Inc., 2001), 350–51.

28 Francine Cardman, "The Praxis of Ecclesiology: Learning From the Donatist Controversy," *CTSA Proceedings* 54 (1999), 37.

29 Elbow, *Writing with Power*, 145.

30 For a concise, reader-friendly style manual to use in tandem with this editing checklist, see Andrea A. Lunsford, *Easy Writer*, 5th ed. (Boston, MA: Bedford/St.Martin's, 2014), which includes access to accompanying online resources at https://bedfordstmartins.com/easy.

31 Joan Bolker, *Writing Your Dissertation in Fifteen Minutes a Day: A Guide to Starting, Revising and Finishing Your Doctoral Thesis* (New York: Henry Holt, 1998), 116.

32 See above, under "Rewriting, Revision, and Becoming your Best Editor."

33 I am indebted to Richard Coe (*Form and Substance*, 99–102) for introducing me to the revision heuristic as a pedagogical tool that I have adapted for use with theological student writers.

34 This revision heuristic was used for writing the paper, "Was Jesus a Feminist," introduced in Chapter 3.

PART FOUR

Writing Theology Well in New Contexts

13

Writing Theology Well in a New Language: Rhetorics for International Student Writers and Their Tutors

At first, when I learned to write the theological paper in English, I was confused about whether I was studying theology or learning English.

—OH DONG KYUN, M.A.T.S., Episcopal Divinity School, 1996

It is more difficult to write in one's own language; for there one knows precisely what the words mean. In a foreign language one doesn't know it quite so well, and so one can let the words mean just what one wants them to mean.

—NEILS BOHR[1]

Starting points

A South Korean theology student writes in a reflection paper, "At first, when I learned to write the theological paper in English, I was confused about whether I was studying theology or learning English." As an international student seeking to write theology well in a North American academic context, have you experienced this confusion between studying theology and learning how to write it well in English? Or, like the Danish scientist Neils Bohr, can you write more freely in a foreign language than in your native language by giving yourself permission to be a novice rather than an expert in the new language?

Wherever you find yourself on this linguistic continuum, this chapter is for all international student writers desiring to write theology well in English, and for tutors seeking resources for tutoring in a theological context. While many international students whom I teach claim English as a "second language" (ESL), just as many fall more accurately into the pedagogical context of the teaching of English for Speakers (and writers) of Other Languages (ESOL),[2] and the majority speak more than two languages, and are more accurately addressed as "multilingual writers."[3] Whether English is a second or twenty-second language, however, "writing theology well" in a North American academic context poses linguistic and cultural challenges.[4]

Toward that end, this chapter introduces rhetorics of communication, enculturation, and empowerment for "writing theology in a new language."

Please read this chapter along with the previous chapters in this book. It is intended to supplement, not repeat them. Four pedagogical premises informing current research in the teaching of ESOL ground my pedagogy. First, I presuppose a strengths-based pedagogy that defines linguistic difference as an asset, not a deficit (as in the terminology, "*non-native* English speaker," which I use in this chapter as a descriptive, not an evaluative term) in acquiring English language literacy,[5] and I invite my readers to do the same. Second, I acknowledge the growing diversity of ESOL and multilingual writers who will be reading this chapter,[6] and ask for my readers' patience as I seek to address that diversity responsibly while seeking common pedagogical ground in the language learning and enculturation issues explored here. Third, I affirm a shift from an exclusively pragmatic writing pedagogy to a critical writing pedagogy that invites students not only to learn language skills but also to critique the language and culture presupposed by them.[7] Finally, my pedagogical approach grounds English language learning and writing within the discipline-driven context of theology,[8] and invites readers to focus not only on learning English as a "non-native language,"[9] but also on naming and claiming theology as a common language.

It is easier to learn a new language when you share a common language that motivates the learning. In whatever language you first discovered reading, writing, and doing theology, you already belong to a common theological community. If you take the common language of theology as a starting point, your language learning will proceed more strategically, and empower you academically, pastorally, and personally during your theological study. The "theological memo" below invites you to reflect upon your personal and vocational goals for learning to write theology in a new language:

> *THEOLOGICAL MEMO 1: Reflect upon the path that has brought you to study theology as an international student, by writing in response to these questions:*
>
> - *When did theology first become more than a word to you?*
> - *How did that insight or experience lead you to study theology in your native country and as an international student?*
> - *What (or who) is empowering you to read and write theology well in a new language? What difference will your mastery of spoken and written English make for you, for the people you serve, and for your future ministry?*
> - *In the light of your personal, vocational, and ministerial goals, what are your objectives for improving your proficiency in spoken and written English?*

Rhetorics of communication, enculturation, and empowerment

In this chapter we explore (1) "Rhetorics of Communication," or basic principles undergirding the process of language learning; (2) "Rhetorics of Enculturation," or the contextual dimensions of language that engage learners in cultural immersion, with particular emphasis upon North American and cross-cultural writing cultures; and (3) "Rhetorics of Empowerment," or practical strategies for facilitating students' progress in reading and writing theology in a new language. Some international students reading this chapter may find it too elementary and others not elementary enough. Either way, I invite you to follow me to the next section on "Rhetorics of Communication," where we begin with two basic paths of language learning, one of which may be your own.

Rhetorics of communication

Learning to read and write in a new language: Immersion and instruction paths

There are two main paths of language learning: (1) the *immersion* path, in which one learns a language through everyday interaction with other speakers and with the culture in which the language is spoken; and (2) the *instruction* path, in which one learns a language through systematic instruction in its grammar, or linguistic "rules."[10] Language-learning proceeds most effectively when both of these paths reinforce each other through practice. The following "rhetorics of communication" will guide our discussion of "learning to write (theology) in a new language":

1. Language-learning is a skill that can be improved through *immersion*, *instruction*, and *practice* in speaking, reading, and writing the new language.
2. The goal of language learning is *to equip speakers/writers to communicate effectively, not just "correctly,"* within a particular language community.
3. To communicate effectively in a new language community, *speakers/writers must be willing to risk enculturation* into its academic and societal context.
4. A corollary goal of language learning is *to empower speakers/writers to enter into critical dialogue with the new culture*, not merely to reproduce it.
5. A primary means of this empowerment is *reading and writing in the new language*, since these are mutually reinforcing skills.
6. In order to learn to write theology in a new language, *you must make writing in the new language your practice.*

Language-learning is a skill that can be improved through immersion, instruction, and practice in speaking, reading, and writing the new language. Three pedagogical premises flow from this principle. First, language-learning is a *skill* that can be *learned* by those who apply themselves to the language-learning process. Second, this *skill* can be *improved* through various methods of teaching and learning (*immersion, instruction*, and *practice*). Finally, the *skill* of language learning is comprised of "*sub-skills*" (e.g., speaking, reading, and writing) that can be *improved* with *practice*, one "*sub-skill*" at a time.

Drawing these pedagogical premises together, I invite you to read this chapter from the presupposition that *writing* theology in a new language is a particular *skill* that can be *learned* and *improved* through *immersion* in the writing process, *instruction* in the syntax, structure and style of "standard written English," and *practice* in both of these through the writing, editing, and revising of the theological papers assigned for your courses, one paper at a time. The most important of these words is *practice.*

The goal of language learning is to equip speakers/writers to communicate effectively, not just "correctly," within a particular language community. Effective communication in any language entails more than correctness. It requires a desire to communicate, a purpose that drives one to do so, and an understanding of the context in which the communication takes place. For those learning to speak or write in a new language, an obsession with "*correctness*" for its own sake can pose a serious obstacle to effective *communication.* That is why language learners who are willing to make mistakes along the way often communicate more effectively in a foreign country than those who become tongue-tied in their efforts to speak the language correctly.

You will learn how to write theology well in a new language more effectively by writing with the fluency that you have than by moving too quickly toward the editing, or "correcting" process. Admittedly, papers submitted to professors should be written as correctly as possible. Toward that end, assistance from professors or writing tutors can be invaluable in preparing papers for final submission. However, improvement in your English writing skills will not ultimately come from tutors' corrections or comments, but from your conscientious writing, revision, and rewriting of your papers in the light of them, one paper at a time.

To communicate effectively in a new language community, speakers/writers must be willing to risk enculturation into its academic and societal context. To learn a new language requires enculturation into the context of that language. On a biological level, the very structure of our brains changes to accommodate the data retrieval required for communicating in more than one language. On a cultural level, our image of the world must undergo a Copernican shift that relinquishes our own language and culture as the center of the universe. Language learning opens the learner to new worlds, but it also has the potential to change the learner's world. For most multilingual writers, learning to *write* in a new language demands the most profound change and inspires the most resistance, because it requires learning a new way of thinking as well.[11] How does the five-stage process of enculturation below compare and contrast with your own experience of enculturation?[12]

- *Culture Shock* is engendered by speakers'/writers' experiences of cultural alienation, disorientation, and vulnerability in attempting to communicate in the new language.
- *Culture Block* is characterized by resistance to conventions of the new language and culture that conflict with speakers'/writers' cultures of origin.
- *Culture Shift* is marked by speakers'/writers' initial process of accommodation to the new language and its context, driven more by cultural necessity than by choice.
- *Culture Drift* is distinguished by an extended period of internal acculturation during which speaker/writers accommodate more actively to the new linguistic culture.

- *Culture Dance* is identified by a fluency in the new language commensurate with speakers'/writers' fluency in their own language, and by their ability to "shuttle between" these linguistic cultures[13] as gracefully as dancers change partners.

THEOLOGICAL MEMO 2: Please reflect upon your own experience(s) of enculturation in the course of your English language study. Do the five stages of "Culture Shock"; (2) "Culture Block"; (3) "Culture Shift"; (4) "Culture Drift"; and (5) "Culture Dance" correlate with your own experience? If they do, what stage of the process are you currently experiencing? How would you describe that stage from your own perspective? If the categories described above do not fit your experience, please name and describe the stages of your own enculturation process.

A corollary goal of language learning is to empower speakers/writers to enter into critical dialogue with the new culture, not merely to reproduce it. While anyone who undertakes the task of learning a new language must risk enculturation in the midst of that process, being enculturated into a new linguistic culture does not mean that one should uncritically accept all the norms and values of that culture. At its best, enculturation provides a starting point for cultural contrast, comparison, and critical dialogue with the new culture, especially in relation to one's own culture.[14]

To enter into critical dialogue with a new culture, Paulo Freire and Donald Macedo invite you to learn to "read the word and the world"[15] of that culture, which constitute what Freire calls the skills of critical literacy, as diligently as you learn the grammar and syntax of the new language. If you are reading and writing theology in a new language, you will engage in this kind of critique as a matter of course. If you are well read in the theology of your own cultural context, it will provide a crucial vantage point for cultural critique. But before one can "read the word and the world" of the new culture so as to enter into critical dialogue with it, one must be able to read and write fluently in the new language, which brings us to the last two principles.

A primary means of this empowerment is reading and writing in the new language, since these are mutually reinforcing skills. Reading and writing are interdependent, or "mutually reinforcing" skills. We learn to write by reading what others have written, and we become more skillful readers by writing about what we have read. Reading can help you to write more fluently in the new language if you (1) record new vocabulary words (and their definitions) encountered in your reading; (2) notice the typical sentence structure (e.g., subject/verb/object) used by authors, and the logical and sequential composition of paragraphs; (3) outline the organizational structure of the article (introduction, thesis statement, development of arguments, and conclusion); (4) identify the level of diction used ("standard written English"); and (5) write reading notes or comments in English in a "reading journal" as you read.

In order to learn to write theology in a new language, you must make writing in the new language your practice. If you want to learn to write theology well in a new language, you must write theology in the new language. You will probably not become a fluent writer overnight. You may be frustrated and dissatisfied with your papers more often than you are satisfied with them—at least at the beginning. But keep writing theology in the new language—make it, as writer Natalie Goldberg says, "your practice"[16]—and approach every paper you are assigned as an opportunity to engage in that practice. "But how should I begin?" you might ask. The next theological memo invites you to reflect on your typical way of beginning the writing process, after which we will turn our attention to "Rhetorics of Enculturation" in preparation for writing a theological paper in a North American academic context.

THEOLOGICAL MEMO 3: "How Should I Begin?" When you are writing a paper in your native language, what is your typical writing process? How do you begin? How do you organize your material? Do you write to find out what you want to say or do you write from an outline that tells you what you want to say? What are the hardest and the easiest parts of the writing process for you when you are writing in your native language? Has this process changed in any way when you write in English? If so, how? Please reflect on the similarities and/or differences between writing in each language.

From instruction, immersion, and practice to rhetorics of enculturation

Writing your first, or twenty-first, theological paper in "Standard Academic English" can be challenging. Whether you have studied English in your native country for ten years, or have just completed a three-month intensive English course, writing theology in a non-native language requires more than language *instruction*. As we have seen, it also requires a cultural *immersion* in the language community for whom you are writing, and *practice* in integrating linguistic and cultural aspects of the writing task with the theological subject matter. What is also needed, therefore, is a cross-cultural orientation to the academic contexts in which you are learning to read and write theology in a new language, which we turn to now in "Rhetorics of Enculturation."

Rhetorics of enculturation for writing theology well in a North American context

I introduced this chapter with the reflection of Reverend Oh Dong Kyun, an Anglican priest from Seoul, Korea, who wrote, "When I first learned to write the theological paper in English, I was confused about whether I was studying theology or learning English."[17] When Dong studied English in Korea, his program of English language instruction was completely separate from his Korean theological education, and he had read very little theology in English. When he began to study theology in English, he found the English language inadequate to express such seminal Korean theological concepts as *han*, for which the typical English translation, "suffering of the people," does not communicate the deeper significance of its meaning in Korean. However, because a contextual definition of this concept was crucial to an understanding of

Korean spirituality, he decided to write his first theological reflection paper on the meaning of *han* in the Korean context.

When his professor returned his first paper to him, Dong became more confused. The academic but rhetorically indirect style of writing that he had learned in Korea differed from the reflective but rhetorically direct style of writing that the professor expected for a theological reflection paper. "You have explored the concept of *han* very well from your reading of other theologians," he wrote, "but what does *han* mean for you—for your own theological perspective? You don't summarize what you have learned and you don't come to any firm conclusions. I also recommend that you seek tutorial help to strengthen your English writing skills."[18]

After reading his professor's comments, Dong found a writing tutor who helped him with his English writing skills, one paper at a time. He attended a writing workshop for international student writers that helped him to navigate the differences between his Korean style of academic writing and the North American academic writing culture, in order to write a theological paper that met his professor's expectations. Dong is now teaching theology in Korea and evaluating his own students' papers from a Korean perspective. Before he returned to Seoul, however, he wrote an honors M.A. thesis in English on "Interreligious Spiritual Dialogue in Korea."[19] In two years, he became theologically, linguistically, and culturally fluent in English, as you will, if you persevere in your own program of study and avail yourself of the resources you need to empower you in that process. We will return to these linguistic resources in due course, but we look now at writing a theological paper in a North American academic context.

Writing theology, writing culture in a non-native language

"Learning to write in an American style, it is much more than learning a new technique," writes Carla, a Latina graduate student at the University of Michigan. "It is the way this culture 'normalizes' you to the system, shaping on you new values and new ways of looking at the world."[20] For Carla, as for Dong, "learning to write in an American style" meant learning to write an essay that was direct, concise, and to the point, with a thesis, or argument to be defended, a logical progression of supporting points and evidence to support the argument, and a straightforward conclusion that reiterated and reinforced the argument. But why did writing a paper in this way seem to require an indoctrination into American values for Carla, and a relinquishing of her own cultural values?

According to Helen Fox, Carla's writing tutor, North American academic style, with its emphasis upon critical thinking, analytical writing, and a concise, expository style, is not merely a style of writing. It is also a way of thinking, and hence of understanding how the world works,[21] based largely upon the Western, Aristotelian rhetoric and pedagogy presented in Chapter 3 of this text, "Writing Theological Argument Well."[22] There is nothing inherently wrong with this way of thinking and writing. However, it does not constitute the only way to "write the word and the world." Out of the convictions that "a culture's rhetoric constitutes an interface where the prescriptions of the language meet the practices of the culture,"[23] and that we can describe that interface more precisely as a "writing culture,"[24] the discipline of "contrastive rhetoric" provides a helpful starting point for identifying writing cultures and distinguishing between them.

For example, in a typology of different cultural writing patterns identified from compositions of his multilingual students, Robert Kaplan identified four basic organizational paths in the diagram below: (1) a straight line represents the North American (English) writing culture as linear, concise, direct, and to the point; (2) a series of parallel zig-zag lines identify Semitic writing cultures that present material in parallel segments rather than hierarchical progression; (3) a spiraling circle describes Oriental writing cultures that approach their subject in an oblique, indirect, and non-assertive way; and (4) a series of zig-zag lines diverting from the "straight and narrow" indicate Romance Language, Russian, and German writing cultures with a digressive, expansive style:[25]

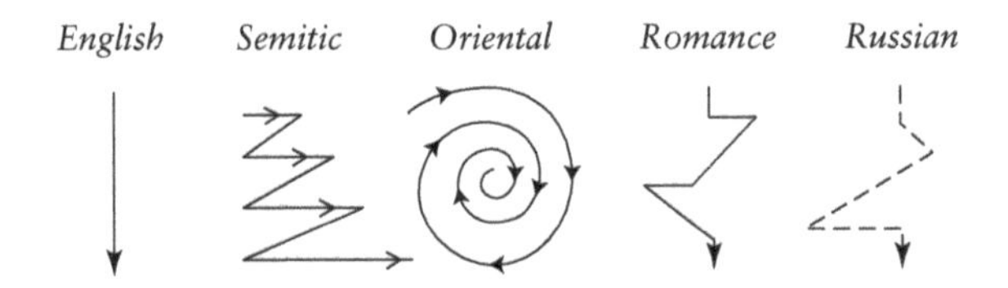

Kaplan envisioned this early model of "contrastive rhetoric" as a descriptive typology of cultural writing patterns, not as a prescriptive endorsement of one cultural style over against another. However, language teachers have sometimes used this typology in a way that Kaplan never intended, to privilege the North American academic writing style as the superior rhetoric and to render the others inferior to it. Moreover, in recent years this model has been critiqued for its tendency toward cultural caricature and its consequent failure to reflect the broader multiculturalism and linguistic diversity that multilingual students draw upon when they write in a new language.[26] Yet most of my students continue to find these models useful for illuminating rhetorical differences between writing cultures and for developing their own cultural writing models when Kaplan's categories do not fit their own contexts.[27] I invite you to reflect upon your own writing culture of origin in the light of Kaplan's models, in the theological memo below:

> *THEOLOGICAL MEMO 4: A Model for Writing Theology in Your Culture: Please reread the summary of Robert Kaplan's "Cultural Thought Patterns in Intercultural Education" above, and write briefly in response to the following questions: (1) Which of Kaplan's cross-cultural writing models most adequately describes the thought patterns of writing in your own writing culture of origin? (2) If none of the models adequately captures your own writing culture, please construct a model, diagram, or written description that would help someone from another culture to understand how to write a paper at a graduate school or seminary in your native country (For example, one of my African students proposed a "hiding in the bush" model as typical of the keenly observant but reticent African multilingual writer).*[28]

Writing theology, writing culture in a North American academic context

The rhetorical profiles below contrast North American academic culture with "cross-cultural writing cultures," represented by the non-native, and particularly non-Western, students whom I teach.[29] Which profile below best describes your own writing culture?

North American Writing Culture	**Cross-Cultural Writing Cultures**
Low-context communication style (Information is spelled out by the writer for a diverse audience.)	*High-context communication style* (Information is encoded in the context shared by writer/audience.)
Direct, assertive rhetoric (State thesis directly, defend argument clearly, end assertively.)	*Indirect, respectful rhetoric* (Introduce thesis indirectly, unfold argument gently, end respectfully.)
Digressions denote poor writing (Preference for stylistic brevity.)	*Digressions develop good writing* (Preference for narrative elaboration.)
Individualistic writing voice (I write as an individual for whom writing is "intellectual property," and plagiarism is a cardinal sin.)	*Collectivist writing voice* (I write as part of a culture in which "it takes a village to write a paper" and plagiarism is a foreign concept.)
Emphasis on "original" writing (I must write in my own words and "acknowledge" sources.)	*Emphasis on "traditional" writing* (I must write traditional words "acknowledged" by the culture.)
Emphasis on "critical" writing (Good writing critiques authorities.)	*Emphasis on "authoritative" writing* (Good writing "copies" authorities.)
Academic writing a gateway (Academic writing proficiency is a gateway to academic achievement.)	*Academic writing an obstacle* (Academic writing is an obstacle en route to academic achievement.)

North American and cross-cultural academic writing cultures in profile

If you have found these rhetorical profiles somewhat simplistic and schematic, you are not alone. As anthropologist and ethnographer James Clifford acknowledges, "Cultures do not hold still for their portraits,"[30] and even if they did, the attempt to schematize them can be counterproductive. For example, if you are a multilingual writer from a Western country, you may have identified more with the "North American Writing Culture" Profile than with the "Cross-Cultural Writing Cultures" Profile. If, on the other hand, you are a multilingual writer educated in a Third World, post-colonialist country, you may bring a more complex story of literacy to this conversation that defies easy categorization. Therefore, before we proceed to consider the implications of these profiles for your own writing, the next theological memo invites you to write your own Literacy Autobiography:

> *THEOLOGICAL MEMO 5: Writing a Literacy Autobiography: A literacy autobiography*[31] *recounts the history of your important literacy experiences throughout your life: learning to read and write, and particular memories of that process; people who were part of that learning process (parents, teachers, other significant mentors along the way); pieces of writing that you remember happily or unhappily; goals that you set for yourself in reading and writing in your native language, and in mastering other languages as a multilingual writer. Please write a one-page reflection on your journey from literacy in your native language (LI) to a second language (L2), and consider what was similar and different in each of these journeys. When you have completed this Theological Memo, please proceed to the expanded profile of North American and Cross-Cultural writing cultures below, and critique it through the cultural lens of your own Literacy Autobiography.*

North American academic writing culture

North American academic writing is characterized by a "low context" style of communication, in which everything must be "spelled out" rather than inferred from a shared context.[32] Thus, North American academic writers are taught: (1) to tell their readers exactly what they are going to do at the beginning of their essay; (2) to do it (i.e., write it) in the "body" of the essay; and (3) to tell readers what they have done at the conclusion of their essay—just in case a reader missed something along the way. The standard writing pattern is direct and "to the point," characterized by Kaplan's straight arrow,[33] and any digression from this pattern is considered poor writing. Writers speak as individual and original scholars, and their writing must reflect their own ideas, properly acknowledge the writing of others, and show evidence of critical thinking through scholarly critique of authoritative sources. What they write is their own "intellectual property," and any violation of that "property" constitutes plagiarism. The goal for this culture is proficiency in academic writing, which provides a gateway to academic achievement.

Cross-cultural writing cultures

Cross-cultural academic writing is characterized by a "high-context" style of communication, in which much information is left for readers to supply from their own contexts. Thus, cross-cultural academic writers do not feel constrained to "tell" readers everything they are going to do in an essay, since to do so would imply that the readers were not intelligent enough to follow the argument for themselves.[34] In contrast to the direct rhetorical style of North American academic writing, cross-cultural writing cultures prefer to begin an essay with indirection and discretion, to develop an argument more deliberately, and to conclude more respectfully than assertively. Within this more deliberate style, digressions contribute sophistication to essay development and exemplify good writing. For many cross-cultural writers, the academic voice is a collective voice, not the voice of an individual scholar, and there is a concomitant respect of "classic," traditional, and authoritative writing, which the good writer follows, emulates, and reproduces, often in an honorific gesture to the original author. Writing is viewed more as a collective cultural project than an individual performance, and plagiarism can therefore be a difficult concept to understand. This writing culture perceives academic writing as an obstacle on the way to academic achievement, especially insofar as the mastery of this North American Academic style threatens cross-cultural writers' loyalty to their own writing culture.

Implications for writing theology well in a new language

To write theology well in a new language, then, it is not enough to learn the grammar and vocabulary of the language. It is also necessary to negotiate the thinking patterns, or rhetorical paths, of the new language, without leaving your own behind. Immersion in a new culture need not and should not entail abandonment of one's own culture, or one's own voice.[35] Moreover, the challenges of academic socialization are not limited to multilingual students. They are also experienced by domestic students for whom academia and/or theological education is an "alien culture." To feminist students attempting to reconcile the requirements of an academic, "patriarchal" writing style and their own feminist interpretation of the Bible, Elisabeth Schüssler Fiorenza explains, "[T]o become a member of the community of scholars, students have to internalize the entire constellation of beliefs, values, techniques, shared worldviews, and systems of knowledge as maps or guidelines for thinking and speaking [*and writing!*] in a scholarly way."[36] In order to address this audience, she urges students to "strive for intellectual bilingualism which speaks with a foreign accent."[37]

Similarly, writing in a North American academic style can also be understood as writing for a specific audience. As we have previously discussed in Chapter 1, the audiences for whom theologians write are not only plural, but radically diverse.[38] If such a variety of audiences exist within the discipline of theology itself, it should come as no surprise that different theological contexts and cultures will have different audiences as well. To learn to write for a North American theological audience should not preclude your continuing to write for audiences closer to home; it will simply extend your fluency as a theological writer. How else can one "go into all the world and proclaim the gospel to all of creation" (Mark 16:15) today? If, in the process, you become a cross-cultural pastor or teacher or theologian, your words will build bridges for others to traverse between contexts and cultures as well in a world that desperately needs those words.

Nonetheless, however open you are to this process of enculturation, the differing pedagogical styles in your new context and your original academic culture may be disconcerting. "Professors talk much too fast, and I can't write my lecture notes fast enough," a student from the Ukraine confesses. "The American students question the professors in a way that is not respectful, and the professors want us to participate in class discussion," a student from Taiwan adds. "How can they expect us to find words fast enough in English to match the American students?" "And the reading is impossible," a Columbian student admits despairingly. "It takes me half a day or more to read one article only, and then to write the paper each week—I am always in a terrible struggle." "And then," adds a Japanese student who has taught English literature to Japanese high school students, "I can't find out the way of writing here—I work so hard on my paper, and when the professor returns it, I am told I have not answered the assignment."

Are these scenarios familiar to you? Although issues of linguistic comprehension may seem overwhelming at first, they will improve as you become more familiar with the "North American English" accent and its variations. Similarly, different classroom styles, including the more "democratic" discussion format described above, will become more comfortable as you continue to attend classes, day by day. However, "cultural problems" that are misunderstood by students or their professors as "writing problems" are not so easily resolved until it is clear whether "writing" or "culture" is the root of the problem. Consider, for example, the writing issues and the cultural issues that interface in the following questions.

What does the assignment require?

You may not initially understand what is required in a paper assignment, for academic writing conventions are sometimes assumed to be common knowledge, when in fact they are not common to all educational (or theological) contexts. Suppose that you are asked to write an "Application Paper" for your church history class, and you don't know what an "Application Paper" is. Many students may have the same problem, but may hesitate to ask a question, for fear of sounding foolish. However, asking questions of professors in a North American academic context is appropriate and encouraged. If the instructions for the assignment are not clear to you, do not hesitate to ask the professor, another student, or your writing tutor to explain more clearly what the assignment involves.

Why doesn't the professor understand?

If you are unfamiliar with writing in the "North American academic style" described here, your professors may have difficulty understanding the argument of your paper. If you feel that your professor has not understood what you were trying to say (or write!) in your paper, make an appointment to discuss the paper. If you feel that your paper has been misunderstood or evaluated without appropriate sensitivity to your own cultural context and way of writing, be prepared to discuss these concerns with your professor. You will not be considered impertinent for initiating this conversation with your professor. You will be commended, like the steward in Luke's gospel, for your academic prudence (Luke 16:1–9).

Is it a "writing problem" or a "cultural problem"?

Even if you do make that appointment, your professor may still confuse "writing problems" (e.g., failure to begin with a clearly stated "thesis"; too much dependence upon quoted sources and not enough of one's own "critical" or "original thinking") with differing cultural perceptions of what constitutes "good" academic writing. Most professors will evaluate your paper primarily on the basis of its theological content, not on its grammatical correctness. They will understand the theological content more clearly, however, if you present it in a North American academic style. Before we proceed to our final section, "Rhetorics of Empowerment for Writing Theology Well in a New Language," here is a "Multilingual Writer's Checklist for Writing in a (North) American Academic/Analytic Style":

Writing in a North American academic/analytic style: A writer's checklist

"Analytical writing," explains Helen Fox,... is at once a writing style, a method of investigation, and a world view that [is] part of western cultural heritage."[39] Here is a summary of its stylistic characteristics:

It is *linear:* the writing unfolds in a clear, step-by-step, logical progression of facts, ideas, or arguments.

It is *deductive:* each paragraph or section begins with a general, analytic statement, followed by specific examples that lead the reader toward a summary/conclusion.

It is *methodical:* it is governed by a purposeful order that is logically coherent and appropriate to the nature of the analysis.

It is *critical:* it examines those facts, ideas, and arguments methodically in order to evaluate their intellectual credibility.

It is *rational:* it makes judgments and recommendations concerning those facts, ideas, and arguments on the basis of specific "reasoned" conclusions.

It is *original:* it offers an original interpretation of those facts, ideas, and arguments that expresses the writer's own point of view, not merely summarizing other positions.

It uses *literal language* to define terms and state premises and conclusions precisely.

It uses a *direct style*, without embellishments, "asides" to the reader, or digressions.

It uses *research* to substantiate the writer's own argument, and synthesizes material from different sources into a coherent pattern that readers can follow.

It uses *documentation* to attribute accurately to other authors the ideas and information that their work has contributed to the writer's analysis.

THEOLOGICAL MEMO 6: What would you add to or subtract from this checklist to make it more useful for writing and editing your own papers? Please prepare your own "Multilingual Writer's Checklist for Writing in a North American Analytic/Academic Style."

Rhetorics of empowerment for writing theology well in a new language

In the previous section, we have explored rhetorics of enculturation for writing theology in a new language. Yet an understanding of the protocols of a new writing culture, or critiquing them in the light of your own culture, will not make issues of writing proficiency in the new language go away. At one of the first writing workshops that I facilitated for international students, Takako, a Japanese biblical studies student, approached me and explained, "I have a simple purpose for coming to this workshop. I want to be able to write my papers in correct English. The cultural and critical issues you have addressed are not my main concern. Can you help me learn to write English correctly or not?"

Twenty years after facilitating that workshop, I am writing this chapter out of the conviction that providing practical writing support for my ESOL students and inviting them to embrace a culturally critical writing pedagogy are not mutually exclusive endeavors.[40] At the time, however, I simply confessed to Takako, as I would in speaking to any of you reading this chapter, that it would not be possible in a one-day workshop to help her with all the issues involved in "learning to write English correctly," but that I could look at the paper that she brought with her that day, and edit it with her according to written academic English. Dealing with one paper at a time, we continued to work together for the duration of her seminary studies. When she completed her doctorate in biblical studies five years later, Takako had confidence in her own English writing proficiency. Yet her conversation with me initiated that process by (1) identifying clearly what she needed to empower her writing process; and (2) asking directly for the specific help she needed. Following the Theological Memo below that asks you to identify what specific help you need right now to write theology in a new language, this section surveys resources, skills, and strategies for reading, writing, correcting, and rewriting that will help you to gain proficiency in written academic English.[41]

THEOLOGICAL MEMO 7: What Help Do You Need to Write the Next Theological Paper? (1) Identify specific needs (e.g., stronger computer skills; more information from the professor; tutoring in grammar and stylistic issues); (2) Explain how you will go about getting the help you need, using the resources available at your school or seminary (e.g., a writing and/or academic support center) and resource persons (e.g., computer training assistants; professors; writing tutors; classmates).

Reading theology skillfully and strategically in a new language

The most persistent struggle for most of my students is the formidable amount of reading assigned for their classes. While the heavy volume of reading is daunting to American students as well, it poses an even more difficult challenge to students reading theology in a non-native language. What is needed, therefore, is a reading strategy that encourages selectivity without sacrificing comprehension of content.

"Speed reading" or "smart reading"?

"Speed-reading courses" require an advanced level of reading comprehension and are only recommended for international students with advanced English reading and writing skills. A more practical strategy for students with average English comprehension skills is "smart reading," which involves (1) prioritizing reading assignments according to their importance for each class session rather than attempting to read everything in sight; (2) "skimming the surface" of books or articles to gain an overview of the work; (3) selecting relevant parts of the text for more substantive reading; and (4) recording reading notes in a journal or on computer, filed according to the course for which the readings are assigned.[42]

The following "smart-reading" strategy, adapted from American scientists' descriptions of how they read research articles,[43] can streamline your own reading of theological articles. These "expert" academic readers choose to read selectively and "against the grain" of the linear style in which they themselves write scientific articles. As one scientist explains, "I think if you go right into an article, and you read it word for word from the beginning, what happens is that you'll be pulled along by the author and you're not going to be critical .... As opposed to, if you have an overview, then you can keep your critical facility alive."[44] This "smart-reading" method is equally useful for multilingual students who seek to read more strategically.

THEOLOGICAL MEMO 8: Smart Reading for Reading Theology Well: Choose a reading assignment from one of your courses that must be completed for the next class meeting. Select one of the assigned readings to complete in connection with this Theological Memo. Reading at your own pace and from simpler to more complex material, you are invited to:

- *Read the table of contents, introduction, and/or thesis paragraph*
- *Read the conclusion, summary, or final chapter of the article/book*
- *Scan section/chapter headings of the article/book for an overview*
- *Read relevant sections in more detail, as required for the assignment*
- *Evaluate the author's claims in the light of the evidence presented*
- *Write a summary/response to the reading while it is fresh in your mind*

Reading focus groups

Another way to deal with the demands of course reading is to form "Reading Focus Groups," in which classmates meet regularly in small groups to discuss class readings. Each student is responsible for preparing one of the readings, which he or she then summarizes for the group. After each participant has presented their own reading report for that session, a brief group discussion follows that tries to relate the readings to the course topic and/or to evaluate each author's particular contribution to the conversation. Some professors build these study groups into the class structure, but even if you must form your own, participation in a Reading Focus Group will help you manage your workload and read theology well, while building a supportive classroom community at the same time.

Writing-focused reading

A final strategy to facilitate course reading is "writing-focused reading," or reading selectively the specific materials that you need to complete a particular assignment. This strategy works well for courses that include weekly reflection papers for which a variety of readings are assigned, of which you choose to read only those relevant to your paper topic. But once you have read the selected material, you must still write the paper. We proceed, then, to skills and strategies for empowering your writing of theology in a new language.

Writing theology skillfully and strategically in a new language

One principle guiding this chapter is that in order to learn to write theology well in a new language, you must make writing in the new language your practice. All of the tools, skills, and strategies that we will explore below presuppose that you are engaging in that "practice" by writing for your courses. However, when a paper is due tomorrow or soon after, you may need a more concrete plan of action, not merely a "practice session," to empower your writing process. I invite you to return to the question introduced in Theological Memo 7, which I shall rephrase here in a slightly different way: "What do you need to empower your writing process and make it more effective?"

Writing "tools" and/or writing "tutors"?

When my students answer this question, some students name writing "tools" of various kinds, from developing stronger computer skills to improving English vocabulary or grammar, while others seek writing tutors to correct their papers for idiomatic usage and grammatical accuracy. In my experience, students who use both writing "tools" and writing "tutors" to facilitate their writing process make the most progress, while those who rely exclusively on tutors to "correct" their papers do not develop their own English writing proficiency as effectively. What follows are some suggestions for assembling a toolbox for writing theology in a new language, and some guidelines for working with a writing tutor.

Tools to empower the writing process: A multilingual writer's toolbox

These *writing tools* will help you become a more effective multilingual writer:

- Computer access and proficiency in writing with computers
- A working knowledge of your school library and its resources

- An assignment calendar to manage time and paper due dates
- A good English language dictionary published in the USA
- A good English grammar handbook and "hands on" approach to learning grammar as you write
- The "academic style manual" required by your school
- Familiarity with your school's "Academic Integrity" policy

Computer access and proficiency in writing with computers. As the next chapter will explore more fully,[45] no writing tool has streamlined the process of putting words on paper as significantly as the computer. If computer literacy and your own computer are already in your writer's tool kit, you are most fortunate. However, the lack of these need not stop you from gaining computer access at your school and acquiring digital writing skills. Most schools and seminaries have computer facilities that are available for student use, and most libraries have "technology librarians" or student assistants who provide computer tutorials or other individualized instruction. If you are taking online courses, your school will also have a technical support staff to help you set up your computer for online access to these courses.[46] If you take the time to acquire proficiency in computer skills early on, you will have claimed a powerful writing tool for your tool kit, and, more importantly, for all the subsequent writing you will do as a multilingual student.[47]

A working knowledge of your school library and its resources. A working knowledge of your school library and its resources is essential for writing theological research in a new language. Library orientation sessions provide a user-friendly overview of the layout of the library, staff librarians available to assist you, and procedures for using the online catalogue, checking out reserve books and circulating materials, and scanning or making Xerox copies of documents. As I am writing this chapter, new electronic research tools are being introduced daily in theological school and university libraries, along with tutorials designed to help students use them. Knowing your library and its resources well will enable you to write theology well by giving you the tools to access the materials you need when you need them.[48]

An assignment calendar to manage time and paper due dates. What is your typical process for managing your academic schedule? If you were educated in a "Lecture/Examination" system that had a final examination at the end of the course, preparing for that final examination required time management that was relentless but forgiving; if you got behind, there was still time to "catch up." How will your strategy change when written assignments are due more regularly throughout the semester?

In North American academic cultures, a course syllabus distributed to students on the first day of class provides both a schedule of assignments and the due dates for completion of the assignments. If you record all of your paper due dates from course syllabi on your own appointment calendar or smart phone at the beginning of the semester, you will learn how much time you can give to a particular assignment before the next one is due, and plan your time accordingly. You can also work back from the due date of a project to estimate the time that you will need to complete the work. Always give yourself extra time to complete the project, and write it into your calendar. Finally, take time to rest, as the creating God did on the seventh day, even if you have not finished the task. Good schedules empower writers; they do not imprison them.

An English language dictionary published in the USA. If you have come from a non-English-speaking country, you probably have a good dual-language dictionary. This should be supplemented with an English language dictionary published in the USA, which will provide both standard and idiomatic definitions of words. The standard authority for accurate spelling of American English words is *Webster's Third New International Dictionary* or its abridged version, *Merriam-Webster's Collegiate Dictionary*, 11th ed.[49] Since words are the backbone of any language, and since your own acquisition of English vocabulary will expand your ability to communicate effectively, a dictionary of American English idioms will also be helpful.[50] For students with intermediate to advanced English writing skills, a good Thesaurus will provide a wide range of synonyms for the words of your choice.[51] Yet words need to be used in the appropriate context, so take care in using the resources of a thesaurus judiciously, checking idiomatic usage before using the word in your paper.[52]

An American English grammar handbook and a "hands-on" approach to learning grammar as you write. If you are using an English grammar handbook from your initial study of English as a non-native Language, you should supplement it with an up-to-date handbook published in the USA that includes a section devoted to "multilingual writers."[53] Regular use of a grammar handbook can help you to identify your most typical errors and provide corrective examples for making the necessary revisions. Reading an English grammar handbook from cover to cover and memorizing its contents will not transform your English writing skills overnight, however. What is also needed is a "hands-on" approach to learning grammar as you write, which one International Student Writing Center director calls "grammaring," by which she means learning grammar in the context of writing, not according to an inflexible rulebook.[54] In other words, grammatical proficiency is an empowering tool when it flows from your desire to communicate effectively in writing, not when you are trying to follow a list of rules that inhibit writing for fear of committing a grammatical "error."[55] Whether working on your own or with a tutor to achieve this goal, a grammatically correct and carefully proofread paper will distinguish the writer who prepared it from others who have not taken the time to do so. The following theological memo invites you to prepare a "Personal Editing Checklist" of your common writing problems and grammar mistakes, along with "grammaring" guidelines for finding and fixing those problems.[56]

> *THEOLOGICAL MEMO 9: Preparing a Personal Editing Checklist for Writing Theology in a New Language: (1) Identify your most challenging writing problem, e.g., writing good thesis statements, writing topic sentences, using commas correctly, making good transitions, using correct word order, using articles correctly, choosing specific words, being concise, or any other writing topic involving grammar, punctuation, or other concerns. (2) Research this problem and how to solve it using this textbook, your preferred writing/grammar handbook, and/or online websites, such as the online writing lab, https://owl.english.purdue.edu/.*[57] *(3) On the basis of your research, please develop a* ***Personal Editing Checklist*** *of your most common writing issues and grammar mistakes and* ***rules*** *for* ***finding*** *and* ***fixing*** *the problems on your checklist.*

The "academic style manual" required by your school. The theological research paper is a standard genre of the theological curriculum, and proper citation and documentation of research sources is mandatory. If you have previously written research papers or a thesis to complete a theological degree, you have already mastered a system of academic citation. If you have not written papers requiring documentation of sources, you may not be familiar with this academic practice. The sooner you identify the academic style required at your school and familiarize yourself with its conventions, the easier writing a theological research paper will be when you are required to do so.

At the school where I teach, "Chicago Style" is preferred, and the two manuals used are *The Chicago Manual of Style*, 16th ed., and its condensed version, Kate L. Turabian, *A Manual for Writers of Term Papers, Theses and Dissertations* (8th ed.).[58] Other common citation styles are MLA (Modern Language Association)[59] and APA (American Psychological Association).[60] Some professors ask only that you choose a style of documentation and use it consistently. If you are writing a thesis, you should expect more standardized requirements. By learning the system of academic citation used at your school, you will not only empower your writing process; you will expedite your research process as well.

Familiarity with your school's Academic Integrity policy. Plagiarism, or the failure to properly acknowledge one's research sources, remains the "unforgivable sin" of North American academic cultures, as I have explained previously in Chapter 6.[61] Your school will probably have its own policy on "Academic Integrity," or the accepted practices of honest and responsible scholarship. A school's policy statement is a binding legal document that is usually included in your academic handbook and/or on the school's website. Avoiding plagiarism does not require relinquishing tutorial help or writing support. It simply requires that the paper you have written is your own work and that the sources cited are properly acknowledged and documented, whether you are using print or online sources. If you have any questions about your school's policy, do not hesitate to ask your professor or dean for clarification. Because there is nothing more empowering to multilingual writers than completing a well-written paper that integrates linguistic proficiency and theological imagination, we move on to strategies for empowering the writing process by writing with tutors and peer writing partners.

Writing with tutors and peer writing partners to empower the writing process

Writing is often portrayed as a solitary and lonely process, but writers rarely write alone. Published authors rely on their editors for feedback before submitting a manuscript in its final form. Writers of scholarly articles submit their work to a prior process of peer review and make recommended revisions pending final acceptance of the article. Most writers are indebted to mentors, colleagues, family, or friends willing to support them by reading drafts-in-progress, offering suggestions for revision, or simply encouraging them to keep writing and rewriting.

Writing in a "non-native language" puts additional demands on the writer, however, and often requires writing support equal to those demands. In preparing to write this chapter, I asked several international student graduates what their most important source of writing support was during their theological study in the United States. Despite their linguistic and cultural diversity, they all responded that working with a writing tutor on a regular basis was their primary source of support. Some of them sought out a writing tutor for editorial help with standard written English. Others needed a cultural informant to help them write theology in a North American academic style. Still others required sustained tutorial assistance with a thesis project, necessitating coaching in editorial, rhetorical and research documentation skills. As each of these students struggled to "write theology well in a new language" they were driven by a common desire to bring their linguistic proficiency up to the level of their theological competency, and writing tutors helped them to bridge that gap.

If you share this desire to enhance your theological literacy with greater fluency in standard written English, a writing tutor can help you to realize that goal. Writing tutors support students by "teaching" from the papers-in-progress that students bring to them for consultation and feedback. Most theological schools provide (1) *"Professional" writing tutors*, skilled in tutoring writing and in the writing of theology, (2) *"Peer" (fellow student) writing tutors*, who possess strong academic writing and tutoring skills along with willingness to work with students requiring their assistance, and (3) *"Peer" writing partners*, who provide mutual writing support to each other in their quest to write theology well. Here are some things to keep in mind in selecting a tutor and some guidelines for empowering the writer–tutor relationship.

Choosing a writing tutor: Mending a paper or mentoring writing practices?

As a multilingual writer, you probably have expectations of what the tutorial process should provide you, arising from your specific needs for writing support. The tutorial models described below form a continuum that begins with "mending" papers and culminates in "mentoring" writing practices:[62] (1) the *paper-mending* model; (2) the *process-mentoring* model; (3) the *project-mentoring* model; and (4) the *practice-mentoring* model.

The paper-mending model. The "paper-mending" model limits the tutor's role to editing the paper to render it error-free. The exclusive use of this model is discouraged in most academic writing centers, since it places too much emphasis on "fixing the writing" rather than on facilitating the writer's development of skills needed to review written work and revise accordingly. Although peer or professional "paper-mending" tutors may focus on both the syntactical clarity and the grammatical accuracy of a paper, the model presupposes a firm distinction between the form of a paper and its content, and conceives of the tutor primarily as the student's proofreader, or "personal editor,"[63] with minimal emphasis placed upon tutorial critique of the student's draft or upon students' authorial responsibility for their own writing.

Multilingual students need help in correcting their papers in a timely and effective way, and will often opt for this tutorial model as the shortest distance between their uncorrected paper and the assignment due date. However, when this model is isolated from other parts of the tutorial process, it is not educative but addictive.

It fosters a tutorial co-dependency that is disempowering for both writer and tutor. By surrendering all of their writing to a tutor for correction, students forfeit the chance to learn from their mistakes, and reinforce their own dependency upon an outside tutorial prompter, without whose off-stage intervention they will forget their "lines." Similarly, by complying with students' requests for a "quick fix" of their papers instead of inviting students to re-envision the paper in the full integrity of its form and content, tutors reinforce their own indispensability at the same time that they surrender their power as effective educators and mentors. However, when the "paper-mending" model becomes a "mentoring" process in which students work with tutors to correct their papers, it approximates a "process-mentoring" model, which we turn to next.

The process-mentoring model. The "process-mentoring" model focuses on the writer's process of producing writing, and on the mentoring relationship between writer and tutor that ensues from that process. Whether "process-mentoring" tutors are professional writing consultants or peer tutors, their role is not merely to correct the student's paper but also to accompany the writer as he or she writes, and to mentor the process from the resources of their own writing experience and expertise. Just as the spiritual director companions persons in their prayer at times by focusing intently on that prayer and at other times by staying out of the way of God's deeper writing on the heart, those tutoring out of this model place the writer's work at the center of the conversation, but decline the role of "playing God" and defer to the writer's own authorial and editorial process.[64] Yet they work "with" writers on whatever stages of the writing process require attention, as long as the process remains collaborative, and the pen stays firmly in the writer's hand.

The gift of this model is its conviction that patiently mentoring the writer's process is an empowering means of supporting a writer's progress, whether students are dealing with language issues, composing strategies, or confidence in their own writing. Ideally, this mentoring provides a strong source of writing support that is both relational and focused upon concrete issues emerging from students' own writing-in-progress. What is difficult to negotiate in this model is the tension that can arise between students' expectations of leaving the session with a finished "product" and the tutor's commitment to a messier, more open-ended, but ultimately more "productive" writing process. Yet for students writing theology in a new language, this process is also constrained by the theological subject matter and the particular genres of writing common to the discipline. Keeping the gifts of the "process-mentoring" model securely in our pockets as we proceed, we move on to the "project-mentoring" model of tutoring writing.

The project-mentoring model. While the "process-mentoring" model is centered in the writer's process and the tutor's expertise in mentoring that process, the "project-mentoring" model takes the subject, or discipline, of the writing as its starting point, and approaches the tutorial task from that perspective. The goal of the "project-mentoring" model is to provide discipline-specific writing support, without leaving the writing process behind. Thus, project-mentoring tutors are typically faculty thesis advisors, faculty assistants enrolled in doctoral programs, professors conferring with students about written course work, and professional or peer writing tutors trained in the academic discipline (e.g., theology) of the writing that students bring to them. Writing tutors who help multilingual students to write in a North American academic context are also drawing from the project-mentoring model.

The gift of this model is its discipline-driven focus and integration of what one writes with how one writes. It is far easier, for example, for tutors to help a student construct and correct a biblical exegesis paper if they are familiar with that biblical genre and have written exegesis papers themselves. Thus, the project-centered model of tutoring can provide students with strategic disciplinary coaching that a non-specialist writing tutor cannot provide. The temptation of this model is to construe its own disciplinary discourse as a rhetorical norm and to take for granted that students will be able to master it, when in fact it may be as "new" a language as any that multilingual students are dealing with. Finally, while writing tutors and thesis directors may choose to separate their respective roles of mentoring the "writing" and mentoring the "subject matter,"[65] this model can prompt students to relegate their "writing" to a lower position than the theological subject matter informing it. Yet the goal of this model is clear, transparent writing that disappears into the subject that it is elucidating as invisibly as dewdrops on the grass evaporate in the morning sunlight, while remaining integral to the atmosphere. Because only practice can help a writer to achieve this goal, we move on to the "practice-mentoring" model of tutoring, which gathers up each of the previous models but also goes beyond them.

The practice-mentoring model. The practice-mentoring model of tutoring conceives of writing as a bundle of interconnected skills, or practices that can be taught, tutored, mentored, and learned.[66] While the previous mentoring-based models were committed to mentoring the writer's process and the writer's disciplinary projects, respectively, this model construes the tutor as orchestrating linguistic, rhetorical, and theological practices into one well-tuned tutorial session in the "process" of working with student "papers" and "projects." Out of the conviction that the practice of writing incorporates linguistic skills, composing processes, discipline-driven protocols, and the operations of editing and revision that distil all of these into a completed writing project, it incorporates each of the previous tutorial models into an integrated web of "practices" that converge whenever a tutor fully engages a student paper. This does not mean that the tutor will deal with every aspect of a student's paper at every session, or that such a practice would even be desirable. It means that the paper will not be dissected as a complex of isolated "problems" nor compartmentalized in terms of its form and content. Rather, it will be envisioned as a unified piece of writing that writer and tutor collaborate to bring to completion.

The gift of this model is its comprehensive view of the practice of writing and its practical integration of all of the tutorial tasks represented by the previous models. For students striving to write theology well in any language, the practice-mentoring model offers the most integrated approach. The drawback of this model is its tendency toward tutorial overload for the student and for the tutor. Moreover, this model of tutoring requires tutors conversant both in the subject matter of the discipline informing the writing and in the tutorial skills practiced in the previous models. Needless to say, it also presupposes students willing to invest time and energy on their own writing. However, the benefits of the "practice-mentoring" model of tutoring far outweigh its disadvantages, as a concluding story about Takako, with whom we began this section, will illustrate.

The practice-mentoring model in practice. When Takako asked me if I would help her correct her biblical studies paper, her model of the perfect tutor was that of a "personal editor" who would "mend" the grammatical and syntactical errors in her paper. When we began to work together, I "mended" her paper while encouraging a "process-mentoring" model of tutoring. We looked at her essay organization as well as at grammar and syntax, but the more we worked together, the less we chased after errant commas or debated what articles were needed with "count" and "non-count" nouns.

What drew us deeper into her own writing process were her biblical subject matter and methodologies, coupled with the tasks of structuring the paper rhetorically and presenting her argument in syntactically clear and cogent prose. Thus, before we knew it, we had moved to "project-mentoring" concerns, but without leaving her writing process behind. At the same time, Takako was developing her own consciousness of writing in English as an integrated set of practices in which she was slowly but surely gaining competency. Over the course of a semester, we moved from "paper-mending" to "process-mentoring" to "project mentoring" to "practice mentoring," and thus toward a more productive model of the tutorial process.

Depending upon your own needs for writing support, you have probably been more attracted to one of these models than another. Yet whatever your needs, a writing tutor can provide you not only with someone who can "mend" your paper, but also with a competent and caring writing "mentor" who will work with you to become a more skilled multilingual writer as you strive to write theology well in a new language. Toward that end, we move, finally, to some guidelines for working with a writing tutor.

Preliminary guidelines for working with a writing tutor

Working with a writing tutor begins with a "relationship" between two persons that has a specific purpose—to help the writer to communicate more effectively in "standard written English" as tutor and writer engage in the tutorial process. Intrinsic to that relationship for both tutor and writer is a respect for the other person and the boundaries that each person has established to facilitate their work together. Second, there must be a willingness to engage in the challenging process of intercultural communication intrinsic to such tutorial relationships. Finally, the tutorial relationship flourishes when it is practiced as a form of faithfulness to the work of "writing theology well in a new language," to the writer and tutor committed to that work, and to the God who calls each to the work. But what is the work of tutoring writing, and how do the tutor and the writer practice it? The best way for you to answer this question is to work with a tutor, or better yet, *write* with a tutor. The theological memo that concludes this section will invite you to do just that, after we have introduced a tutorial writing plan that guides you through the process. Finally, with the pen firmly in your hand, you will be invited to write a "contextual" theological reflection paper at the close of this chapter.

Writing with a tutor: a tutorial writing plan

Writing with a tutor unfolds as a process that can be correlated with the "write three times" method, which we have used previously to write a pastoral reflection paper.[67] Just as in the first stage of the writing process, the writer writes to find out what s/he wants to write, in the first stage of the tutorial process, the tutor is engaged in (1) *finding out what the writer wants to write by identifying the writing issues presented.* Just as "writing that and only that" constitutes the second stage of the "write three times" process, the second stage of the tutorial process involves (2) *helping the writer to write that and only that through a collaborative process of linguistic correction and structural revision.* Just as "writing so that others would want to read it" is the final stage of the "write three times" process, the final stage of the tutorial process is (3) *returning the writing to the author for a final rewriting for intended readers.* We will look at each of these stages in turn.

Finding out what the writer wants to say and identifying the writing issues. Your writing tutor will begin by carefully reading your paper, in whatever stage of completion it is when you bring it to the tutorial session. He or she will then ask you to explain or clarify anything in the paper that he or she does not understand. Most of the time, you will know what your paper needs before your tutor does, and you may begin the session by informing your tutor of the particular issues that you need help with during the session. That is, after all, why you are seeking tutorial help.

After you and your tutor have clarified any remaining questions about your paper, your tutor will address the writing issues that you have requested help with, and/or those that s/he has identified in your paper. Because most tutorial sessions have clearly defined time limits, you and your tutor may need to prioritize those issues in the order of their importance. Sometimes words you have already written may need grammatical or syntactical correction. Sometimes ideas lurking just beneath the surface that you are not sure how to express will need to be put into words. Sometimes the structure of your paper will need a clearer thesis statement, or a more linear style of argument. While your priorities and your tutor's priorities may not always be the same, writing tutors do recognize their responsibility to help you produce a coherent, theologically crafted and corrected paper. Thus, the next tutorial task involves helping the writer to revise the writing by a collaborative process of revision.

"Writing that and only that" in a collaborative process of linguistic correction and structural revision. For all writers, revising writing is a process of "writing that and only that" which the writer wants to say in the best possible way. For multilingual student writers, preparing a carefully edited final draft can be more challenging, and tutors may collaborate in the revision process in different ways. Some writing tutors work electronically via email, and invite students to send writing in progress, which the tutor comments upon electronically and returns to the student in an answering email. Others limit their services to what can be done in a tutorial session. Still others ask students to submit papers for them to read, comment upon and/or correct prior to the tutorial session. Most tutors envision this stage of the tutorial process as a collaborative practice. As one of those writing tutors, I ask students to sit with me as we work through the structural revisions and the linguistic corrections that I have suggested, and encourage them to make the final corrections and revisions in their own handwriting. If I, in turn, have misread students' language and have edited a sentence inappropriately, they correct my English and we revise it accordingly. This process prepares them for the final, but most critical stage of a tutorial session: returning the writing to its author for final rewriting for its intended readers.

Returning the writing to its author for a final rewriting for intended readers. According to an old English proverb, the proof of the pudding is not in the cooking but in the tasting. Similarly, the success of a writing tutorial is not in the tutor's instruction, but in the author's final rewriting of the paper for intended readers. As I have already suggested, the most important thing that a writing tutor can do *for you* is to collaborate *with you* in your own writing process—not merely by mending your paper, or even by mentoring your writer's progress, but by laboring with you like a midwife as you labor to write theology well in a new language. You are the rightful author of all that you write, and the tutorial process should support your authorship, not usurp it. Hence the final presentation of your paper will be in your hands. If you have made all the revisions and corrections and have proofread the paper one final time to catch any typographical errors, your paper is now ready for the next reader—your professor. The next Theological Memo invites you to reflect on your experience of "writing with a tutor":

> *THEOLOGICAL MEMO 10: This theological memo invites you to reflect on your experience of "writing with a tutor" as follows: (1) What writing issues did you ask the tutor for help with? What writing issues did the tutor identify as needing attention? Were there any similarities between both of these? (2) What suggestions for your paper were most useful to you? What did you learn about your writing from the session with the tutor? (3) How did you go about preparing the final draft of the paper? Please describe your process as specifically as you can (For example, did you merely make the indicated corrections, or did you make structural revisions in the paper?). (4) Did "writing with a tutor" help you to write a better paper? If so, how so? If not, what would have made the process more helpful to you?*

Concluding reflections: Writing theology well in a new language

We began with the common language of theology as a starting point for writing theology in a new language, and we return to this common language at the end. While your experience of writing with a tutor is still fresh in your mind, I invite you to focus on a theological conversation that came about as you worked together on your writing. Conversation about "theological writing" can add a transcendent dimension to the tutorial process that can help you to break the language barrier, and perhaps already has.

The "transcendent dimension" that I refer to here is neither an "other-worldly," "out-of-body" experience nor an abstract theological realm into which only the "initiated" may enter. It is the experience of linguistic communion with another person that equals more than the sum of each partner's words but discloses through those words a deeper word that embraces both of them, yet could not have been articulated without the conversation. Whether conferring with a professor over a theological paper topic, discussing the paper with a tutor, or sharing drafts-in-progress with your peers, have you ever had the experience of being drawn into a communion that re-orients the conversation and culminates in a common insight? You thought that you were talking about focusing your thesis paragraph and correcting its language, but suddenly rhetoric and grammar give way, or lead the way, to what you really want to say about the challenge of reconciliation in Rwanda, or the concept of grace in Latin American liberation theology. When you put what you want to say in the words that you have to say it, your conversation partner is silent for a few seconds and then simply says, "Yes"—because the new word has embraced both of you, and any other words would be superfluous.

At this moment, you are speaking in the common language of theology, without erasing its local expressions, just as on the day of Pentecost, "devout Jews from every nation" heard the apostles "speaking about God's deeds of power... in their own languages" (Acts 2:5,11). Neither writer, professor, tutor nor writing partner can make this communion happen, but when it does, you will know that you sit and speak on holy ground that will continue to support your writing when the conversation is over and your paper is fully written. But the only way to create the conditions for this "Pentecost" is to keep writing and conversing and correcting and rewriting, one paper at a time.

Yet writing out of the common language of theology emerges not only from the communion of Pentecost, but also from the confusion of Babel, without which there would be no recognition of linguistic difference or translation from one language to another. While you are writing the next theological paper, try to imagine that process as a continuous act of translation in which the resources of your own linguistic heritage are distilled into the English words on the page. Sometimes students ask, "Should I compose papers in English or in my own language?" Yet you never really leave your own language behind in using the new one, any more than a bumper crop of squash or corn leaves the soil that it grows in and the nutrients it has absorbed from the sun and the rain behind. Similarly, the theology that you write in any language will be informed by your context and language of origin. If you continue to draw deeply from the wells of your own theological context while learning to write theology well in a new language, then you may one day provide streams of living water to an audience wider than you can now imagine.

My goal in this chapter has been to provide you with some writer's tools to keep in your pocket as you continue to write theology in a new language. The most important of them will be the pen in your own hand and the words you write with it. To reinforce this point, I conclude with a story. Roberto Rodriguez, a nationally syndicated Latino-American newspaper columnist and cultural critic, was driving home to Albuquerque after a book tour in Los Angeles, California and Tucson, Arizona, when U.S. border patrol agents detained him outside of Los Cruces, New Mexico.[68] Although Rodriquez informed them that he was an American citizen and produced a valid passport to prove it, the border police ordered him out of his car, checked his passport, searched his vehicle with police dogs, and submitted him to extensive questioning. Finally, when asked if he was carrying any weapons, he replied, "I carry pens."[69]

Having convinced the U.S. border patrol that he was neither an illegal alien nor a drug smuggler, but a writer, Rodriguez returned home without further interception. This chapter will not be complete, however, until the pen is in your hand, and you have made writing theology well in the new language as a cultural critic your practice.[70] In the confidence that you also have a pen in your pocket that marked your own passage across the border and will bring you home again as a confident multilingual writer, I invite you below to write a theological reflection from your own context that engages in critical dialogue with the context in which you are presently studying theology.[71]

THEOLOGICAL MEMO 11: Writing a Contextual-Dialogical Theological Reflection: Choose a theological concept that is formative for your own theology (creation, sin, grace, salvation, God, Jesus Christ, Trinity, or?), and write a critical-dialogical theological reflection, using the questions below as a guide:

(1) *Define this concept traditionally according to your own faith tradition;*
(2) *Describe this concept contextually within your own cultural/theological context;*
(3) *Place the "traditional" and "contextual" profiles in critical dialogue with each other. What are the gifts and limitations of each model?*
(4) *Assess the adequacy of the traditional model as opposed to your proposed "enculturation" of this concept for your own cultural, theological, or pastoral context, and provide a concluding critical evaluation from your current theological perspective.*

In this chapter we introduced rhetorics of communication, enculturation, and empowerment for "writing theology well in a new language." Beginning with the common language of theology shared by all multilingual students desiring to write theology well, we proceeded to "Rhetorics of Communication" and reviewed some basic principles of the language-learning process. Second, we turned to "Rhetorics of Enculturation," which provided a cross-cultural orientation to the academic contexts in which students learn to read and write theology in a new language. Finally, we explored "Rhetorics of Empowerment" for facilitating students' writing progress, from writing tools to writing tutors to engaging in critical dialogue while continuing to write theology well in a new language. Now the coast is clear, the border crossing is free of obstacles, and the pen is in your hand. Godspeed and good writing!

Notes

1 Quoted in Abraham Pais, *Niels Bohr's Times, In Physics, Philosophy, and Polity* (Oxford: Clarendon Press, 1991).

2 A. Suresh Canagarajah, *Critical Academic Writing and Multilingual Students* (Ann Arbor, MI: University of Michigan Press, 2002), 8–11, argues convincingly for the use of ESOL terminology, since it is inclusive of ESL (English as a Second Language), EFL (English as a Foreign Language), and NNES (Non-native English Speakers).

3 I follow Canagarajah's (*Critical Academic Writing*, 8–16) and Andrea A. Lunsford's use of this term in Lunsford, *The Everyday Writer*, 3rd ed. (Boston, MA: Bedford/St. Martin's, 2005), 491–518.

4 In this chapter I will use "international student" as a geographically descriptive term referring to students enrolled in theological schools or universities outside of their own

countries of origin; I will use "multilingual writer" as a linguistically descriptive term identifying the student as a speaker/writer of two or more languages, with varying degrees of fluency in those languages; and I will identify the context in which I teach and write as "North American."

5 A. Suresh Canagarajah, "Toward a Writing Pedagogy of Shuttling between Languages: Learning from Multilingual Writers," *College English* 68 (2006): 589–604; Bobbi Olson, "Rethinking Our Work with Multilingual Writers: the Ethics and Responsibility of Language Teaching in the Writing Center," accessed April 9, 2014, https://praxis.uwc.utexas.edu/index.php/praxis/article/view/103/html

6 Canagarajah, *Critical Academic Writing*, 8–9.

7 Christine Pearson Casanave, *Controversies in Second Language Writing: Dilemmas and Decisions in Research and Instruction* (Ann Arbor, MI: University of Michigan Press, 2004), 199–204.

8 See Gabrielle Kelly O.P., *English for Theology: A Resource for Teachers and Students* (Hindmarsh SA: ATF Press, 2004); Cheri L. Pierson, Lonna J. Dickerson, and Florence R. Scott, *Exploring Theological English: Reading, Vocabulary, and Grammar for ESL/EFL* (Carlisle: Piquant Editions, 2010); and Cheri Pierson and Will Bankston, "English for Bible and Theology: Communicating Theology Across Cultural and Linguistic Borders," *Teaching Theology and Religion* 16 (2013): 33–49.

9 While I concur with current ESOL writing pedagogy that this definition is deficit-based, I will use it descriptively but selectively in this chapter, when other terminology is less precise or more cumbersome.

10 See, e.g., W. Ross Winterowd, *The Culture and Politics of Literacy* (New York: Oxford University Press, 1989), 52–58; and Ilona Leki, *Understanding ESL Writers: A Guide for Teachers* (Portsmouth, NH: Heinemann/Boynton-Cook, 1992), 10–23.

11 See Helen Fox, *Listening to the World: Cultural Issues in Academic Writing* (Urbana, IL: NCTE Press, 1994), 71. See also William B. Badke, *Beyond the Answer Sheet: Academic Success for International Students* (New York/Shanghai: iUniverse, 2003).

12 While the stages of cultural adjustment have been variously documented in the ESL literature, the trajectory here correlates with that literature but is based upon conversations with international students in the WRITE Program at Episcopal Divinity School, Weston Jesuit School of Theology, and the Boston College School of Theology and Ministry. See also D.A. Larson and W.A. Smalley, *Becoming Bilingual* (New Canaan, CT: Practical Anthropology, 1972); T. J. Lewis and R. Jungman, eds., *On Being Foreign: Culture Shock in Short Fiction* (Yarmouth, ME: Intercultural Press, 1986); Leki, *Understanding ESL Writers*, 44–46.

13 See Canagarajah, "Toward a Writing Pedagogy of Shuttling Between Languages," 589–604.

14 See Canagarajah, *Critical Academic Writing*, who stresses the importance of developing this "critical" perspective as a multilingual student writer.

15 For Freire, "reading the word and the world" describes the skills of critical literacy. See Paulo Freire, *Education for Critical Consciousness* (New York: Continuum, 1982); Paulo Freire and Donald Macedo, *Reading the Word and Reading the World* (South Hadley, MA: Bergin and Garvey, 1987).

16 Natalie Goldberg, *Writing Down the Bones: Freeing the Writer Within* (Boston, MA: Shambala, 1986), 11–13.

17 Oh Dong Kyun, Reflection Paper for WRITE Program course, M. A. T.S., Episcopal Divinity School, 1996.

18 Ibid.

19 Oh Dong Kyun, "Interreligious Spiritual Dialogue in Korea," M.A.T.S. thesis, Episcopal Divinity School, 1996.

20 Quoted in Fox, *Listening to the World*, 77.

21 Fox, *Listening to the World*, xviii–xxii; 125–26.

22 See Chapter 3, "What Is the Genre of Argument and Why Do People Write It?"

23 Carolyn Matalene, "Contrastive Rhetoric: An American Writing Teacher in China," *College English* 47 (1985): 790.

24 For an expanded definition of a "writing culture" as I use the term here, see Lucretia B. Yaghjian, "Writing Cultures, Enculturating Writing at Two Theological Schools: Mapping Rhetorics of Correlation and Liberation," *Teaching Theology and Religion* 5 (2002): 129.

25 See Robert Kaplan, "Cultural Thought Patterns in Intercultural Education," *Language Learning* 16 (1966): 1–20, from which the figure is taken. Leo Loveday, *The Sociolinguistics of Learning and Using a Non-Native Language* (Oxford: Pergamon Press, 1982), 75–76, extends the pattern to German discourse.

26 See the helpful discussion of "Contrastive Rhetoric" in Casanave, *Controversies in Second Language Writing*, 26–62; see also Canagarajah, *Critical Academic Writing*, 63–68; Fox, *Listening to the World*, xix; and Matalene, "Contrastive Rhetoric," 790.

27 For example, Kaplan's models do not deal with cultures in which post-colonial "hybridity" renders a "monolingual" writing model too simplistic, or with African and other cultures for whom writing remains in the cultural shadow of orality.

28 I am indebted to the late Victor Okumu for this model, which he had hoped to elaborate further in an article.

29 My rhetorical profiles are indebted to Helen Fox's "thick description" of the rhetoric of "world majority" students (see Fox, *Listening to the World*, 107–26), corroborated by my own classroom experience. Needless to say, not all of these rhetorical contrasts apply to all students.

30 James Clifford and George E. Marcus, eds., *Writing Culture: the Poetics and Politics of Ethnography* (Berkeley, CA: University of California Press, 1986), 10.

31 For more on the content and context of the "Literacy Autobiography," see Casanave, *Controversies in Second Language Writing*, 10–11.

32 For a fuller definition of "Low Context" and "High Context" cultures, see Edward T. Hall, *Beyond Culture* (New York: Anchor/Doubleday, 1976; reprint, Anchor/Doubleday, 1989), 91 (page reference is to the reprint edition).

33 See Robert Kaplan's diagram, above.

34 This is not only true of Asian academic writing cultures, but also of many European academic writing cultures. German scholars, for example, are not expected to write "down" to the level of their audiences; on the contrary, the burden of comprehension is upon the audiences who read them. See L. Loveday, *The Sociolinguistics of Learning and Using a Non-Native Language* (Oxford: Pergamum Press, 1982).

35 See Rosemary Viete and Phan Le Ha, "The growth of voice: Expanding possibilities for representing self in research writing," *English Teaching: Practice and Critique* 6, no. 2 (2007): 39–57, accessed November 7, 2014, http://education.waikato.ac.nz/research/files/etpc/2007v6n2art3.pdf

36 Elisabeth Schüssler Fiorenza, *But She Said: Feminist Practices of Theological Education* (Boston, MA: Beacon Press, 1992), 181.

37 Ibid., 183.

38 See Chapter 1, "Writing Theology in Our Own Context and Its Audiences."

39 Fox, *Listening to the World*, 125.

40 Lucretia B. Yaghjian, "Pedagogical Challenges in Teaching ESOL/Multilingual Writers in Theology and Religion," American Academy of Religion presentation, San Diego, California, November 22, 2014.

41 This term is used interchangeably with 'standard written English." I use it here because it more aptly describes the collaborative process of writing engaged by multilingual writers and tutors.

42 See also the "Reading Three Times" method outlined in Chapter 3.

43 See D. Charney, "A Study in Rhetorical Reading: How Evolutionists Read 'The Spandrels of San Marco,'" in J. Selzer, ed., *Understanding Scientific Prose* (Madison,WI: University of Wisconsin Press, 1993), 203–31, quoted in Cheryl Geisler, *Academic Literacy and the Nature of Expertise: Reading, Writing and Knowing in Academic Philosophy* (Hillsdale, NJ: Lawrence Erlbaum, 1994), 21.

44 Ibid.

45 See Chapter 14, "Writing Theology Well in a Digital Environment: Rhetorics for Online Writers and Researchers."

46 For brief introductions to writing with computers, see Andrea A. Lunsford, "Writing with Computers: The Basics," in *The Everyday Writer*, 3rd ed. (Boston, MA: Bedford/St. Martin's, 2005), 101–08.

47 See, for example, Chapter 14, under "A Digital Literacy Checklist for Online Writers and Researchers," for a step-by-step guide through this process.

48 I have taught students who failed to do course reading for a full semester because they never located the reserve desk, or were too timid to ask where required research materials were shelved. The best way to learn your way around your school library is to work as a student assistant, as many international students I have taught have done. In the meantime, do not hesitate to ask for library research assistance when needed!

49 I follow this recommendation from Kate L. Turabian, *A Manual for Writers of Research Papers, Theses, and Dissertations*, 8th ed., ed., rev. Wayne C. Booth, Gregory G. Colomb, Joseph M. Williams, and the University of Chicago Press Editorial Staff (Chicago: University of Chicago Press,), 2013. For American English dictionaries for ESOL students, see *Oxford Advanced Learner's Dictionary*, 8th ed. (International Student's Edition), accessed April 15, 2014, http://www.amazon.com/Oxford-Advanced-Learners-Dictionary-International/dp/0194799123/ref=sr_1_1?ie=UTF8&qid=1394051925&sr=8-1&keywords=9780194799126; *Cambridge Advanced Learner's Dictionary with CD-ROM*, accessed April 15, 2014, http://www.amazon.com/Cambridge-Advanced-Learners-Dictionary-CD-ROM/dp/1107619505/ref=sr_1_1?ie=UTF8&qid=1394053671&sr=8-1&keywords=Cambridge+Advanced+Learner%27s+Dictionary+%28Book+%26+CD+ROM%29.

50 See, for example, *Cambridge Dictionary of American Idioms* by Paul Heacock (Cambridge: Cambridge University Press, 2003); *From the Horse's Mouth: Oxford Dictionary of English Idioms*, 3rd ed., ed. John Ayto (Oxford: Oxford University Press, 2003); *Webster's New World American Idioms Handbook* by Gail Brenner (Indianapolis, IN: John Wiley Publishers, 2003). For online sources, see *The Free Dictionary*, accessed April 15, 2014, https://idioms.freedictionary.com; *Using English. Com, accessed* April 15, 2014, http://www.usingenglish.com/reference/idioms/.

51 I recommend *The Original Roget's International Thesaurus*, 6th Rev. ed., ed. B.A. Kipfer (New York: Harper Collins, 2001), which remains the finest English language thesaurus. For a more reader-friendly format, see *Merriam Webster's Collegiate Thesaurus* (Springfield, MA: Merriam-Webster Inc., 1988). For online sources, see http://thesaurus.com, accessed April 15, 2014; https://education.yahoo.com/reference/**thesaurus**/; Macmillan Dictionary/Thesaurus, accessed April 15, 2014, http://www.macmillandictionary.com/us/about_thesaurus.html

52 Many ESOL writing teachers and tutors discourage their students from using a thesaurus when writing papers, and encourage them to use the vocabulary that they have, however limited, before consulting other resources. Students should give precedence to instructions of their teacher/tutors, whatever this book says!

53 See, e.g., Diana Hacker and Nancy Sommers, *A Writer's Reference*, 7th ed. (New York: Bedford/St. Martin's Press, 2011); Andrea A. Lunsford, *Easy Writer*, 5th ed. (New York: Bedford/St. Martin's Press, 2013); and Lunsford, *Everyday Writer* (see note 1 above). These texts are available in Print and E-Book editions, with links to web-based supplementary resources for those purchasing the texts.

54 See Diane Larsen-Freeman, "Transfer of Learning Transferred," *Language Learning* 63 supp. 1 (2013): 107–29.

55 In the initial stages of the writing process, English professor Peter Elbow's advice to his students applies to multilingual writers as well: "For most people, nothing helps their writing so much as learning to ignore grammar as they write." See Peter Elbow, *Writing With Power* (New York: Oxford University Press, 1981), 168.

56 This Theological Memo is adapted from a class handout by Jennifer Mawhorter, Writing Center Director, Claremont School of Theology, California, and is used with her permission.

57 Many universities have developed online writing labs (OWLs) that provide an online alternative to the standard grammar handbooks. The OWL at Purdue University is the longest running, the most comprehensive, and also the most user-friendly: see the Purdue Online Writing Lab, accessed November 8, 2014, https://owl.english.purdue.edu. For an online website devoted more specifically to theological writing, see The Duke Divinity School Center for Theological Writing, accessed November 8, 2014, https://divinity.duke.edu/initiatives-centers/center-theological-writing/writing-resources.

58 *The Chicago Manual of Style*, 16th ed. (Chicago: University of Chicago Press, 2010); Kate L. Turabian, *A Manual for Writers of Research Papers, Theses, and Dissertations: Chicago Style for Students and Researchers*, Rev. Wayne C. Booth, Gregory G. Colomb, Joseph M. Williams, and the University of Chicago Press Editorial Staff (Chicago: University of Chicago Press, 2013).

59 Joseph Gibaldi, *MLA Handbook for Writers of Research Papers*, 7th ed. (New York: Modern Language Association), 2009.

60 *Publication Manual of the American Psychological Association*, 6th ed. (Washington, DC: American Psychological Association, 2009).

61 See Chapter 6, above, "Plagiarism Preventions and Interventions."

62 The four tutorial models that follow are distilled from my own experience of tutoring writing in a theological context. The following tutorial resources have confirmed, corrected, and helped me to refine the models: Donald A. McAndrew & Thomas J. Reigstad, *Tutoring Writing: A Practical Guide for Conferences* (Portsmouth, NH: Heinemann/Boynton/Cook, 2001); Emily Meyer and Louise Z. Smith, *The Practical* Tutor (New York: Oxford University Press, 1987). Ben Rafoth, ed., *A Tutor's Guide:*

Helping Writers One-to-One (Portsmouth, NH: Heinemann/Boynton/Cook, 2001); Shanti Bruce and Ben Rafoth, *ESL Writers: A Guide for Writing Center Tutors*, 2nd ed. (Portsmouth, NH: Heinemann/Boynton/Cook, 2009).

63 See Muriel Harris and Tony Silva, "Tutoring ESL Students: Issues and Options," *College Composition and Communication* 44, no. 4 (1993): 525–37.

64 See Lucretia B. Yaghjian, "Hidden Treasures in Theological Education: The Writing Tutor, the Spiritual Director, and Practices of Academic and Spiritual Mentoring," *Teaching Theology and Religion* 16 (2013): 221–45.

65 I work frequently with faculty thesis advisors who ask students to submit chapters to their writing tutors first for general editing and "process-mentoring," prior to submitting the chapter for theological critique. This practice allows advisors to focus on content issues in their own reading of the material.

66 For a fuller discussion of "practices" in relation to theological writing, see Lucretia Bailey Yaghjian, "Writing Practice and Pedagogy across the Theological Curriculum: Teaching Writing in a Theological Context," *Theological Education* 33 (1997): 50–53, 66n40.

67 See Chapter 2, "Writing the Pastoral Reflection Paper."

68 See Roberto Rodriguez, *Codex Temuanchan: On Becoming Human* (Bloomington, IN: Indiana University Press, 1998), in which he explores issues of Chicano (Mexican) identity.

69 For a full account of the story, see Demetria Martinez, "When a Clean Car Makes You Suspect," *National Catholic Reporter*, January 15, 1999.

70 For this appropriation of Friere's notion of "critical literacy," see Winterowd, *The Culture and Politics of Literacy*, 176–205.

71 This theological memo assignment can be expanded to form the basis of a theological research paper or thesis project, according to the requirements of your own program. See also Stephen Bevans, *Models of Contextual Theology*, rev. ed. (Maryknoll, NY: Orbis, 2002).

14

Writing Theology Well in a Digital Environment: Rhetorics for Online Writers and Researchers

A fundamental characteristic of the very historicity of human experience … is communication in and through distance.

—PAUL RICOUER, *Hermeneutics and the Human Sciences*

Computers are not "just tools" for writing. Networked computers create a new kind of writing space that changes the writing process and the basic rhetorical dynamic between writers and readers.

—*The WIDE Research Center Collective, "Why Teach Digital Writing?"*

Starting points

Since the publication of the first edition of *Writing Theology Well* (2006), theological students have been "writing theology well" in ever widening contexts, including online learning environments. When the theological seminary where I teach introduced an online "distributed learning"[1] program ten years ago, I was asked to take my class online. A digital immigrant myself with limited technological literacy or expertise, I was not unlike other theological colleagues who had to learn with their students how to navigate this new learning environment.

While my "Writing Theology Well" course and others like it are now routinely offered online, few resources are available to assist theological students with the challenges of writing theology well "from a distance." Toward that end, this chapter provides an introduction to writing theology well in a digital environment, focusing first on writing digital genres and then, more briefly, on digital resources for theological researchers. It is addressed to online students and to all students using computer-mediated communication to bridge the gap between writer and audience. But is this purpose so different than that from which writing first developed?

Not only is writing a technology, as Walter Ong reminds us, "calling for the use of tools and other equipment: styli or brushes or pens, carefully prepared surfaces such as paper, animal skins, strips of wood, as well as inks or paints, and much more."[2] Writing was also the original distance learning technology, and has been used throughout history to communicate with people beyond one's immediate range of oral communication. However disparate they are in time and place, both Paul's letters to the early Christian churches and Martin Luther King's "Letter from a Birmingham Jail" were written in order to reach an audience too far away to be addressed "face to face." Similarly, every time that you begin to write, you project a line of words beyond the page that has the potential to bridge the distance between you and your audience, whether that audience is your mother living across the country, your professor who has requested you to submit a paper via email, a professional colleague requesting your response to a project proposal, or your parishioners, with whom you communicate weekly through a parish newsletter or blog. What has changed is not the use of writing as a distance learning technology, but the multiple contexts in which we use it.

Writing in a digital environment: Preliminary questions

In this chapter I will invite you to do consciously and reflectively in an online environment what you have been doing all your life when you write "in and through distance," in tandem with your theological and biblical studies, and in conjunction with your ministerial vocation—where you will use writing to preach, to teach, to offer public prayer, and to communicate with parishioners online and offline.[3] I will ask you shortly how your own writing process has been influenced by the digital environment. We begin, however, with three questions: (1) What is "digital writing"? (2) What are "digital writing skills" and how do they differ from traditional writing skills? (3) What digital writing skills do you have and need for writing theology well in a digital environment?

What is digital writing?

Digital writing refers to any writing that is produced on the computer and distributed through digital environments and tools (e.g., the Internet, the World Wide Web, Facebook, Twitter, your Email provider, or I-phone).[4] Emails, blogging, texting, Facebook Pages, Twitter feeds, electronic journals, and websites—all of these provide different platforms for digital writing. In addition, digital writing encompasses a wide range of multi-media communications, including audio texts, video texts, and social media.[5] But what about the writing that you and I do on our computers at work, at school, and in between?

The fact that I am composing this chapter on my notebook computer does not make my writing digital, nor does the first draft of a paper you are writing on your Tablet while drinking a Latte at Starbucks constitute digital writing. At that stage of the process, you and I are simply using the computer as a writing tool, rather than a pen or a pencil. However, when I send this chapter to my editor via an email attachment, and she returns the draft to me with her comments in an answering email, or when you post a draft of your paper on your course website for others to read and respond to, we and our writing have entered a digital environment. Thus, what makes writing "digital" is the connectivity which allows an enhanced mode of communication between author (you and me) and audience (your classmates; my editor), and invites both synchronous (at the same time, as in text messaging) and asynchronous (at different times, as in email or discussion board postings) interaction. Considered in that light, how much digital writing have you done today? (Emailing? Texting? Instant Messaging?) What digital tools have you used? (Desktop, Notebook, or Laptop Computer? Centralized "cloud" computers? Tablet? Smart Phone?) What digital writing skills have you exercised in the process? To answer that question, it may be helpful to ask another one. What are "digital writing skills" and how do they differ from traditional writing skills?

What are digital writing skills? How do they differ from traditional writing skills?

Whether you are an online student communicating with your professor or a residential student composing a course blog, writing for a digital environment requires the same skills required for writing theology well that we have previously explored in this book. To begin with, we ask, "Who writes what to whom and for what purpose?"[6] Just as in print settings, so also in online settings, we need to write to a specific audience with clarity, conciseness, and a purpose for writing to that audience, in the appropriate style and genre.[7] However, when writing for an online course, the challenges of "writing in and through distance"[8] become more pronounced.

First of all, consider the difference between meeting with your professor after class to discuss a grade on a paper and emailing him with the same questions and concerns. In a face-to-face interaction, physical gestures and voice intonation can facilitate your communication—a welcoming smile (☺), a question posed clearly but politely, a respectful pause between your professor's explanation of her evaluation of your paper and your response. However, in an email communication there is no face-to-face contact facilitating the interaction, and the efficacy of your message rests entirely on what you write and how you write it. If you do not observe the accepted conventions of email "netiquette,"[9] your professor may be offended. If you are angry about a grade you think was unfair, the tone of your message may reflect your anger, and further alienate your professor. As Plato's Socrates observed when comparing speech to writing, without the presence of its author, "... writing cannot distinguish between suitable and unsuitable readers. And if it is ill-treated or unfairly abused it always needs its parent to come to its rescue; it is quite incapable of defending or helping itself."[10]

Second, writing in digital spaces rewards brevity and directness, as the *Yahoo! Style Guide* asserts unequivocally in language that adapts Strunk and White's *The Elements of Style* to an online environment: "Get to the point.... Keep it short.... Keep it simple."[11] Yet, in digital spaces, this brevity often happens at the expense of traditional style and syntax, notwithstanding Yahoo's separate guidelines for writing on mobile devices.[12] In the current texting vernacular, for example, the most overtly theological affirmation is OMG; a long-standing friendship is BFF; a shared joke is LOL. If you are a Facebook user, you probably have written many one sentence Facebook posts accompanying a picture (worth 1,000 words). If you have a Twitter account, you have learned how to communicate what is on your mind in 140 character "tweets," and your followers have responded accordingly.

While this abbreviated style is accepted for Facebook posts, Twitter tweets, texting, and instant messaging, "OMG" style can undermine academic theological style, which requires complete sentences in which subject matter and reflection upon it are developed deliberately and in more detail. At the same time, if you are a Twitter user or follower, one biblical professor challenges you to write thesis statements for a biblical paper on Twitter in 140 characters, and then to develop the stated thesis into a fully researched biblical paper. Can you do it? I encourage you to follow him![13]

Third, writing in digital spaces is not only alphabetic but also graphic, utilizing a variety of media as part of the written communication. The integration of print and graphic elements requires not only rhetorical skills but also technical expertise in what Troy Hicks calls "crafting digital writing."[14] For example, in the digital writing environment, you may be invited not only to write a traditional research paper, but also to prepare a PowerPoint (or other presentation software) presentation that integrates text, audio, and video components to advance your research argument. How would you proceed with this multimodal research project? How would it change your typical approach to writing a research paper?

While Troy Hicks argues convincingly that "student writers in the twenty-first century are doing much more than alphabetic print on paper; they are increasingly exploring images, videos, slideshows, wikis, podcasts, digital stories, and other kinds of digital writing that allow them to share their work beyond their classroom walls,"[15] the technology of writing integrated a variety of alphabetic, visual, and artistic media from its inception.[16] Consider Egyptian hieroglyphics, which were pictographic rather than syllabic. Consider the Rosetta Stone, which seemed to be an indecipherable series of miniscule line drawings until they were recognized as parallel linguistic translations of the same text. Consider the dedicated "writing" of religious icons, which are "read" as visual embodiments of the Word.[17] Consider medieval illuminated manuscripts, in which "the words themselves became a decorative element."[18] Thus, the integration of print, audio, and visual media in the digital environment adds technological capability and expertise to what has been a mixed media enterprise from the genesis of the written word. If you are writing on Facebook or tweeting on Twitter and posting photographs along with your messages, you are already "crafting digital writing" in your own writing spaces. If you have prepared PowerPoint presentations using different type fonts to enhance your presentation and graphics to illustrate your text, you are following the ancient precedent of medieval illuminators to integrate the printed word with decorative arts and illustrations.

Finally, and most importantly, writing digitally presupposes technology and its accompaniments: computer access, provided, ideally, by your own computer of choice, with appropriate virus protection software;[19] a reliable Internet connection;[20] and sufficient expertise with the basics of computer technology to utilize these digital tools successfully online. For example, if your internet service is not a high-speed provider, you may encounter difficulties in connecting to online course web conferences, or in accessing the course website. If you are unable to navigate the course management software used by your school to deliver online assignments, discussion boards, and weekly announcements, you will not be able to participate in the course. If you don't know how to access blogger.com or wordpress.com, you will be hard pressed to create your own blog for the first assignment, however competent a writer you are.[21] While the acquisition of digital writing skills necessarily begins with the writing skills you already have, it may also require learning new skills in response to the technological challenges of a digital environment.

Many readers of this chapter have successfully transitioned from writing without computers to writing with computers and have become proficient users of digital technologies. If you are among these, you belong to a growing population of "digital immigrants" who are "rapidly learning, of necessity or by desire, to live in the digital culture" of the twenty-first century.[22] Others may not remember a time that they didn't write with computers and utilize digital media in their writing and research. If this group describes you, then you belong to the growing population of "digital natives," "born into an online world at the end of the 20th century."[23] Yet all of us, whether digital immigrants, digital natives, online, or residential students, share the challenge of writing theology well in this environment.

What writing skills do you have and need for writing theology well in a digital environment?

The rest of this chapter addresses that challenge by exploring the ways in which writing in a digital environment has informed and transformed the landscape of "writing theology well" by (1) embedding digital writing genres in a theological context and (2) digitizing processes of theological research, documentation, and plagiarism preventions and interventions. We focus first on three digital writing genres encountered in writing theology well for online courses—email, course discussion posts, and blogs—and provide rhetorics, or generic guidelines for writing each of these genres that can be adapted to students' course requirements. Second, we provide a brief overview of digital tools for writing theological research well, along with protocols for preventing plagiarism in an online environment. Before we proceed, I invite you to consider the digital writing skills you have and need to write theology well in a digital environment in the Theological Memo below:

> *THEOLOGICAL MEMO 1: What does the phrase, "digital writing skills," mean to you? Please describe it in your own words and give two or three examples of these skills. In the light of what you have written, what digital writing skills do you have and need to write theology well? In other words, what digital writing skills have you used in writing your last theological paper? What digital writing skills did you wish you had when writing the paper? How have your writing process, research process, and delivery of written work changed as a consequence of using digital writing tools and technologies? What writing and research practices have remained the same? On the basis of your reflection, please identify one gift and one challenge for you in writing theology well in a digital environment.*

Writing the theological genres in a digital environment: Online rhetorics for writing emails, discussion posts, and blogs

How has writing in a digital environment informed and transformed the landscape of "writing theology well?" To answer this question, we must first acknowledge the interdependence of emerging technologies of writing and the social and cultural forces fostering their development. As Clay Shirky explains, "Technologies that make writing abundant always require new social structures to accompany them."[24] For example, while the invention of Gutenberg's printing press in 1450 provided the technology for the mass production of the Gutenberg Bible (1456) and other printed books, the Protestant Reformation, which began officially in 1517 with an act of writing engendered by its author Martin Luther's own reading of the Bible,[25] provided the audience essential to the profitable production of those books. But the relationship between new technologies of writing and the social structures supporting them is reciprocal. Just as the revolutionary technology of the printing press fostered the Protestant Reformation through the printing and dissemination of the Bible and writings of Reformation theologians like Luther, the Protestant Reformation fostered the technology of writing by greatly increasing the demand for copies of the Bible and other printed books.

In the same way, theologian Benjamin Myers' explorations of the intersections between twenty-first century web technologies and the production and delivery of theological discourse[26] invite us to follow the migration of traditional theological genres into digital environments, creating new, digital genres, and rhetorical guidelines for writing them. Instructed by Myers, we will soon look more specifically at the ways that the digital genre of blogging has informed and transformed the theological landscape, and provide rhetorics for "writing theology well by creating a blog."[27] But the emergence of the "Web Log," or "blog," is indebted to earlier online genres: electronic mail (email), which pioneered networked communication on the Web, providing a precedent for "writing in and through distance" to designated recipients; websites, providing bloggers with a web location accessible to their readers through a domain name; and web pages populating the website, providing bloggers with a platform for their blog "posts."

But what does this brief overview of online modes of communication have to do with writing theology well? Whether you are an online or an on-site student, you will be using email to communicate with course professors and administrative staff, and you will be posting regularly on course discussion boards to engage with course material in conversation with your fellow students. Because facility and fluency in writing these online genres well will also prepare you for writing theology well by creating a blog, we turn next to writing online genres of email and web page-based course discussion posts in a theological context.

Writing emails well in a digital environment: Online rhetorics and rubrics

Whether you are an online or an on-site theological student, you most likely have an email account at the school where you are studying, and you have most likely written and received a variety of email communications to and from school administrators, faculty, and fellow students in the course of your studies. If you are enrolled in a distance learning or distributed learning program, the use of email is even more essential for keeping in contact with professors when procedural questions arise, course content needs clarification, or you need to communicate information outside of a public forum, such as requests for extensions due to illness or other personal circumstances. Yet more often than not, we approach email as an inferior mode of writing, using it merely as an expedient means of soliciting and sharing information.

Every time that you send an email message or reply to a message that you have received, you are communicating through writing, and the quality of that email communication will only be as good as the quality of your writing. What, then, do you need to know to write emails well to professors, administrative staff, and fellow students in an online learning environment? First, you need to identify what kind of writing, or genre, an email message is, in order to write effectively in that genre. Second, you need to consider the audience to whom you are writing, in order to write your message appropriately for that audience. Third, you need to clarify the purpose of the email message, in order to make it clear to your audience. Finally, you need to write your email message well, according to conventions of email etiquette, or "netiquette."[28] We will consider each of these tasks in turn.

What kind of writing, or genre, is an email message?

As a kind of writing, email is difficult to classify, because it is a flexible form of electronic communication encompassing brief business memorandums and more formal letters as well as newsletters, advertisements, and attachments of written documents, photographs, and audio and video downloads, to name only a few of the materials regularly appearing in our inboxes. But as we have learned previously, all writing emerges from a context, and the written genre of email arose as an information and communication networking tool in the digital context of the late twentieth century, predating the inception of the Internet but developing in tandem with it.[29]

Yet email is not merely a means of conveying information; it is also a rhetorical act of purposeful communication.[30] As an electronic writing genre, email incorporates the written memorandum, the letter, and spoken conversation into its rhetorical profile. As David Tuffley explains, "Remnants of the Memo can be seen in the header where the To: Cc: and Subject: fields closely emulate that of the traditional Memo."[31] Kathleen Yancey describes basic email as "like writing a letter; it is signaled by greetings, emoticons, closings ... combining elements one would expect in letters, on the phone, or in face-to-face conversation."[32] For theological and biblical writers, however, the Christian epistle provides a precursor to this genre, and its originator, Paul the Apostle, has been called "the most influential letter writer of antiquity."[33] As Stanley Sowers reflects, "Something about the nature of early Christianity made it a movement of letter writers," perhaps because "the letter is adaptable to a wide range of circumstances and purposes but always has the characteristic of being a 'communication' between people who are separated."[34] In the same way that Paul's letter writing has also prompted one Biblical professor to call him "a prototypical distance educator,"[35] email might be considered a prototypical distance genre enabling online theological students and their professors to communicate "in and through distance." Moreover, just as the Apostle Paul adapted the Greco-Roman genre of letter writing to his own purposes in writing to the churches of the early Christian movement, so twenty-first century email has been described as "a genre-in-the-making"[36] that you and I are contributing to with every email that we write. If that is indeed the case, it behooves us to reflect on how we are presently writing and responding to email messages. Toward that end, I invite you to respond to the following Theological Memo before we proceed:

> *THEOLOGICAL MEMO 2: How many email messages have you received today? How many email messages have you written? Please identify an email conversation with a professor or fellow student arising from your theological course work that you have recently initiated and/or replied to. How would you describe the stylistic features of the original message and of the reply to the message? Can you identify specific elements of the message and reply that are* ***typical*** *of email correspondence? Can you also identify* ***individual*** *stylistic features characteristic of your own email compositions? In what way are you contributing to the ongoing "genre-in-the-making" of email? In what way are you following conventions already in place? Does it make any difference if and when you are writing email messages in a theological context (to professors or parishioners or fellow students)?*

Who is the audience to whom your email message is addressed?

Just as the audience for whom we write theology well has the potential "to determine what kind of theology we write and how we write it,"[37] the audience, or individual recipient of an email message, should likewise influence what we write and how we write it. Sometimes we spend more time thinking about the more abstract audiences for whom we write academic papers than we do the individual recipients to whom we write email messages. Yet they too constitute audiences worthy of consideration! Writing Professor Peter Elbow identifies three different audiences for whom students write that are applicable to email audiences: (1) audiences with authority—such as professors; (2) audiences of peers—such as fellow students; and (3) audiences of allies—such as friends and/or mentors with whom you have developed a more personal relationship.[38] In this discussion, we will focus on writing emails to the first two audiences.

When you email a classmate to inquire about the online class session that you missed, you might write, *Hey Mark, How goes it, dude? Were you online at the web conference yesterday? Can you believe I forgot all about it? Did I miss anything?* Let's assume that the informal tone of your message is well received by Mark, who readily responds with the information that you need. Let's also assume that in emailing a fellow student rather than your professor for the information, you made the right call. If, however, you had emailed your professor, *Hey Prof! How goes it, dude? Sorry I didn't make it to the web conference yesterday. Did I miss anything?* chances are that your message would not be well received by your professor. But if he were a professor and a poet with a wry sense of humor like Tom Wayman, he might respond:

> Nothing. When we realized you weren't here
> We sat with our hands folded on our desks
> In silence, for the full two hours
> Everything. I gave an exam worth
> 40 percent of the grade for this term
> and assigned some reading due today
> on which I'm about to hand out a quiz
> worth 50 percent. . . .[39]

If you wish to read this poem in its entirety or hear it read, you can Google "Did I Miss Anything?" and download one of many YouTube versions of the poem available.[40] If you do, I suspect that you will never again ask a professor that question!

However, most of your professors will not be poets with a wry sense of humor, but beleaguered academics receiving hundreds of emails a day from other students and colleagues, while trying to safeguard their own professorial space in the midst of the demands of cyberspace. How, then, should you write emails to a professorial audience? The first step is to acknowledge that you are writing to an audience with academic authority over you, and to write appropriately. Hierarchical relations have been embedded in rhetorical theory and practice from Greco-Roman times, and Christian rhetors were likewise trained to speak and write according to the rubrics of those relations.[41] But there is a better reason to write emails well to your professors. They are your primary audience for writing theology well, and they want to support you in that process. If you can write an email to them well, they will begin to recognize the writer @ the address and respond to you accordingly. But what you write and how you write will also be determined by your purpose for writing the email message. The next step is to clarify the purpose of your email message in order to make it clear to your audience.

What is the purpose of your email message?

However various our purposes for sending an email message, in all email communications the sender writes the recipient with a purpose. If you are the sender and the intended recipient is your professor, the purpose of your message will probably have to do (1) with requesting information from the professor (e.g., "I'm not clear about this requirement on the Syllabus") or (2) conveying information to the professor (e.g., "I will not be able to attend next week's web conference because I will be having surgery"). But have you stated the purpose of your email in a way that is clear to your professor?

All of us have written and received two kinds of emails: "first contact" messages and "follow-up" messages. To initiate an email communication you write a "first contact" email, which explains the purpose of the message and then makes a request of the recipient or conveys particular information. If that initial email achieves its purpose and the recipient responds with the information requested, you have written the email well. However, if their response does not satisfactorily reply to the original email message, this may be due to your failure to state clearly the purpose of your email, or to provide all of the information needed to respond appropriately.

Since writing clearly has to do with crafting the email message carefully and choosing the right words to communicate what you want to say, recipients will be more likely to understand your message the first time around if you reread your message draft to make sure that you have stated your purpose for writing clearly and provided all the necessary information before sending it. If your message does not receive the specific response that you expected, remember that yours is not the only message competing for attention in your professor's inbox. In that case, do not hesitate to send a "follow-up" email that clarifies the purpose of your earlier email message, and politely restates the request you made and the response that you desire.[42] For example:

Writing an email message well to professors and colleagues: First contact and reply

THEOLOGICAL MEMO 3: Writing an Email Message Well to Professors and Colleagues:

Please read and review the "First Contact" email message and the "Reply" from the professor below. Keeping our previous discussion of "genre," "audience," and "purpose" in mind, how would you revise the student's initial email in such a way that a "follow-up" email would not have been required? If you were the student seeking the recommendation, how would you write the "follow-up" email requested by the professor in a more considerate manner?

First contact email and reply

TO: lyaghjian@eds.edu

SUBJECT: Graduate School Recommendation—Urgent!

Dear Professor Yaghjian:
I need a recommendation from you to support my Ph.D. application to the Boston College School of Theology and Ministry 'Theology and Education' degree program." The deadline for all application materials is December 15, 2015.

I apologize for the short notice but I sincerely hope that you will be able to support my application with a letter of recommendation. Please let me know asap,

Sincerely,
Joe Student

TO: jstudent@eds.edu

SUBJECT: Graduate School Recommendation—Urgent!

Dear Joe:
Thank you for your email message. Do I remember correctly that you were a student in my fall 2013 "Writing Theology Well" class? Before I can agree to write a letter of recommendation for your application to the BCSTM Ph.D. program, I need more information about your program goals, your proposed areas of specialization, and your specific reasons for applying to the program. I also need to know if the recommendation is to be submitted online, and to what address if so. Thank you for providing me with this information at your earliest convenience. After I have reviewed it, I will get back to you regarding the recommendation.

Sincerely,
Lucretia Yaghjian

Writing the email message well: A netiquette for theological and biblical writers

Email is an electronic mode of written communication requiring well-honed writing skills, an ability to apply those skills to an electronic context, and a knowledge of email etiquette, or more broadly, "netiquette," which Virginia Shea defines as "a set of rules for behaving [and writing] properly online."[43] Like the personal or business letter that it emulates, email is both a rhetorical and a relational genre. As a rhetorical genre, it is driven simply by purposeful communication, or the sender's reason for writing the recipient. As a relational genre, however, it is rooted more profoundly in communication between human persons "who cannot not communicate," and should reflect the communicative relationship that the sender and the recipient share.[44]

In the confidence that you are already communicating effectively on email and other social networks with fellow students, friends, and other familiars with whom you share personal relationships, we focus here on writing an email message well to professors, with whom your relationship will be professional and deferential. Many professors do encourage egalitarian relationships with their students and respond graciously to email messages in whatever form they are received. Speaking, however, as one of those professors, when a student writes me an email that is not only clearly written but is also courteous and respectful of our academic relationship, I respond more enthusiastically than I do to an email message that addresses me as an indentured servant. Wouldn't you? Let's go back to the email message introduced in "Theological Memo #3" to exemplify writing an email message well to your professor. Toward that end, we first enumerate ten steppingstones in this process:

- STATE THE SUBJECT OF YOUR MESSAGE IN A NUTSHELL on the subject line of the message, providing any identifying information necessary for the professor to authenticate your email, along with the specific purpose of your message:

  SUBJECT: Request for Recommendation from Joe Student/WTW 101/Fall 2013

- CHECK THE PROFESSOR'S EMAIL ADDRESS AND ADDRESS THE PROFESSOR with his or her surname and academic title, unless your relationship is more informal:

  TO: lyaghjian@eds.edu

  Dear Professor Yaghjian:

- OPEN WITH A GREETING TO THE PROFESSOR, taking a cue from the tradition of early Christian letter writing. An opening greeting is like a handshake that extends hospitality to the recipient, and gives the sender an opportunity to establish his or her relationship with the message recipient, if needed:
  I hope you are well. I was a student in your Writing Theology Well 101 class in fall 2013. It got my writing off to a great start during my first year in seminary.

- STATE PURPOSE OF EMAIL IN A CLEAR, CONCISE, SPECIFIC SENTENCE:
  I am writing to ask if you would be willing to write a recommendation to support my Ph.D. application to the Boston College School of Theology and Ministry 'Theology and Education' degree program.

- ADD EXPLANATORY SENTENCE(S) to provide more detailed information:
  In Professor Thomas Groome's course, 'Sharing Faith,' I became interested in Communicative Theology's potential for faith formation in parish religious education, and I wish to do doctoral study in this field. If you are willing to write a recommendation for me, it can be submitted online. The deadline for all application materials is December 15, 2015.

- INDICATE WHAT RESPONSE YOU DESIRE from the professor. Protocols regarding responding to emails vary widely, but if you ask courteously for a response by a specific date, you are likely to receive one:

  Thank you for letting me know if you are able to support my application with a letter of recommendation, if possible by the end of this week. Please let me know also if you need any additional information in order to write the letter, and I will be happy to provide it.

- INCLUDE A THANK YOU TO THE PROFESSOR prior to or as a part of the closing:
  I greatly appreciate your willingness to consider writing a recommendation for me, and look forward to hearing from you soon.

- CLOSE YOUR MESSAGE APPROPRIATELY for a professional communication, providing your full name and an email signature that provides the recipient with the necessary contact information for a timely response:

  Sincerely (Yours truly, Best regards),
  Joe Student

  Joe A. Student
  M.Div. 2016
  Episcopal Divinity School
  Cambridge MA 02138
  Cell phone: 617-123-4567
  Email: joestudent@eds.edu

- REREAD AND PROOFREAD the full email message for grammar, spelling, punctuation, and tone of the communication before clicking on SEND:

TO: SUBJECT: Request for Recommendation from Joe Student/WTW 101/Fall 2013

Dear Professor Yaghjian:
I hope you are well. I was a student in your Writing Theology Well 101 class in fall 2013. It got my writing off to a great start during my first year in seminary.

I am writing to ask if you would be willing to write a recommendation to support my Ph.D. application to the Boston College School of Theology and Ministry "Theology and Education" degree program. In a course with Professor Thomas Groome on "Sharing Faith," I became interested in Communicative Theology's potential for faith formation in parish religious education, and I wish to do doctoral study in this field. If you are willing to write a recommendation for me, it can be submitted online. The deadline for all application materials is December 15, 2015.

Thank you for letting me know if you are able to support my application with a letter of recommendation, if possible by the end of this week. If you need any additional information in order to write the letter, I will be happy to provide it. I greatly appreciate your willingness to consider writing a recommendation for me, and look forward to hearing from you.

Sincerely (Yours truly, Best regards),
Joe Student

Joe A. Student
M.Div. 2016
Episcopal Divinity School
Cambridge MA 02138
Cell phone: 617-123-4567
Email: joestudent@eds.edu

Writing the email message well: Concluding reflections

We have suggested previously that email is a digital genre in the making, and that we as writers and recipients of email messages are contributing to this progression with every email message we write and reply to. As David Tuffley concedes in his e-book, *Email Etiquette*, "There are no 'official' rules governing electronic communication," but this has not stopped him or numerous others from offering their own guidelines for writing email messages well.[45] Given this opportunity to form and to be formed by your own negotiation of the genre, what rhetorical model are you providing for other email writers? As with every digital writing genre, the challenge is to integrate your own "e-writing" voice with evolving conventions of netiquette. However you put those pieces together, you are what you email. Whether your message is clear, readable, and respectful of its recipient, or sloppy, indecipherable, and inconsiderate of the recipient, you will be perceived accordingly. Moreover, with one click of the "Send" button, the message is "out there" for all to read. It behooves us, therefore, to write emails well, not only for the benefit of those receiving our messages but also in the interests of developing best practices for all users of this digital genre. But now we move on to another digital genre that you must also write well as an online or on-site student—the course discussion board post.

Writing course discussion board posts well: Online conversation through writing

The online course discussion board post has become a standard curricular component of "writing theology well" in on-site and online courses. For on-site courses, it provides an expanded classroom space that adds asynchronous conversation to synchronous class meetings, and provides a place for posting assignments to be read and reviewed before the next class session. For online courses, the discussion board post offers a virtual alternative to traditional class discussions, inviting students to engage asynchronously in "course talk" through writing.[46] As we have seen previously in our explorations of writing "voice," this rhetorical fluidity between "talk" and writing is rooted in the history of rhetoric itself, which began as instruction in "eloquentia" (eloquence) for speakers in the public forums of classical Greece and Rome, and was applied only secondarily to writing.[47]

If email is a digital genre "in the making," then the online course discussion board might be considered a digital platform "for the taking," since it is not genre-specific but provides a virtual learning space that professors can adapt to particular course requirements. What is common to most discussion board assignments is a weekly prompt, or question that students are required to respond to, and also to reply to other students' postings. For example, you might be required to post an initial response to the discussion board prompt early in the week, and to post a second response in reply to other students' postings later in the week. The goal here is not simply to showcase your own post, but to contribute to a constructive and multi-layered conversation in which all participants are teachers and learners. Does this happen regularly? In my experience, it does not, because our prevailing model of writing assignments is individual and singular, like an email message, not shared and collaborative, as the online discussion board encourages.

If it takes only take one student and one professor to write and reply to an email message well, it takes a village—or a full online or on-site class—to write discussion board posts well. While email messages facilitate electronic one-to-one communication, discussion board posts provide a digital platform for group conversation in the public forum of the class. At its best, the discussion board fosters a collaborative learning environment in which students write to learn and learn through writing and responding to each other's writing. But in order to participate successfully in discussion board groups and complete the course posting assignments, it is necessary to write discussion board posts well. Toward that end, we ask again: (1) What kind of writing, or genre, is the discussion board post? (2) Who is the audience of your discussion board post? (3) What is the purpose of your discussion post? Before we proceed, I invite you to revisit a recent discussion board posting that you have contributed to one of your courses, and your professor's instructions for writing and submitting the post, in the following Theological Memo:

THEOLOGICAL MEMO 4: Writing the Primary Online Discussion Board Post Well: Choose a recent "posting" assignment for one of your theological courses, and describe (1) the specific "prompt" for the assignment (e.g., the question that you are asked to respond to); (2) the professor's instructions for writing the post (e.g., word count; length specifications; stylistic requirements, such as writing in complete sentences and paragraphs; directives for incorporating quoted material or other research in the post); (3) requirements for submitting the post (e.g., the timeline for posting the response, and any other specific instructions regarding submission of the post). Following these instructions, please create a list of bullet points to assist you in writing discussion board posts for this course.

What kind of writing, or genre, is an online discussion board post?

If you have already written discussion board posts for online or on-site classes, you know that their theological genre can vary widely, according to the course protocols and the professor's prerogative. You have also probably written two kinds of discussion board posts: (1) the *primary* post, in which you respond directly to the discussion board "prompt" and (2) the *secondary* post, in which you respond to other students' posts as part of the threaded discussion.[48] The common rhetorical template for both of these postings is the "mini-essay," adapted to the purposes of each post. In response to the initiating "prompt," the *primary* post provides a brief, "on point" response to the presenting question that makes a concise but cogent assertion in one or two sentences; supports the assertion with references to course readings as appropriate; reiterates your main point in conclusion, or raises questions inviting response. We might call this template a "mini-deductive essay." In response to a previous posting, on the other hand, our template for the *secondary* post might be called a "mini-inductive essay." It may begin with a question, a disagreement with the previous post, a request for clarification, or a reflection that builds on the previous post, and then proceeds to provide whatever additional information is necessary to move the conversation forward. In order do that, however, you need to know whom you are writing. Thus, we turn next to discussion board audiences.

Who is the audience for your discussion post?

In a discussion board post, your audience includes both your professor and your fellow classmates, who are also required to contribute their own posts and to respond to those of other classmates. Writing for this more complex audience will provide you with good practice for writing a blog for a still more diverse audience, but it can be challenging to find a writing style and voice that works well both for your peers and for your professor. If the discussion board assignments constitute part of your grade, you might be tempted to write primarily for your professor—as if the posting were a mini-version of a course paper. Admittedly, some professors use the discussion board page more as a bulletin board for completed assignments than as a forum for online discussion, and if your professor is one of them, you must follow his or her directions. However, most of my faculty colleagues encourage the dialogue arising from class discussion board posts, and seek to facilitate, not dominate it. In that spirit, English professor Scott Warnock encourages his students to adopt a "semi-formal" style when posting that integrates elements of formal academic writing with a more conversational voice, appropriate to the ongoing dialogue of the postings. But before we look more specifically at how to write the discussion board post well, we need to look briefly at the purpose of the discussion board as an online writing and learning tool.

What is the purpose of the discussion board post?

"The word in living conversation is directly ... oriented toward a future answer-word: it provokes an answer, anticipates it and structures itself in the answer's direction."[49] Mikhail Bakhtin's depiction of the way that dialogue works in the novel describes well the purpose of the discussion board post, which is to engage online students in in a course-driven, "living conversation" through writing, analogous to an on-site class discussion in which students contribute verbally to the conversation. In a typical class discussion, the professor makes a statement or poses a question arising from the assigned readings, and waits for a student to respond. With luck, a student responds with a comment that elicits a further response from another student, at which point the professor might interject an observation or a clarification, which in turn provokes another student to join the discussion. In the same way, the goal of the online discussion board is to engender and facilitate this kind of ongoing conversation in a virtual learning environment, in which, as Bakhtin describes, "Understanding and response are dialectically merged and mutually condition each other,"[50] one discussion board post at a time. The advantage of the online discussion board is that you can take the time you need to read, reflect, and write in response to the opening prompt before joining the conversation and you don't have to wait your turn to contribute! Moreover, since many professors, myself included, employ discussion boards not only to initiate online class conversations but also to continue on-site class conversations, online discussion boards can also provide on-site students with opportunities to expand upon comments made in class or to share in writing what they could not formulate verbally in time to join the conversation.

Whether yours is an on-site or online class, the professor's prompt for the discussion board is typically an initial question or reflection to get the ball rolling, not an examination question that must be answered perfectly in order to pass the course. For example, here is an excerpt from an online discussion board conversation that took place in one of my theological writing courses:

Subject: Reflections on Writing Theological Reflection Well

Posted by: Lucretia Yaghjian

Date: Friday, September 27, 2013

To continue the conversation in class today (9/17/13) on "Writing Theological Reflection Well," please post your own definitions of "theological reflection" and your own process of writing theological reflection—based upon what you wrote in response to those prompts at the beginning of class. What did you learn about doing and writing theological reflection? What questions do you still have?

Subject: Reflections on Writing Theological Reflection Well

Posted by: Sandi A.

Date: Sunday, September 29, 2013

I see theological reflection as a comparison or contrast of my own experiences, beliefs and touchstones to a reading, biblical passage, or situation. It is a process of experiencing those readings from my own place and then trying to relate that experience to the reader. It really seems like God is meeting me where I am and asking me to draw closer to another source of information or opinion in which to examine our relationship.

This Friday's class ... was a workshop in the true sense of the word. I came away with a much clearer sense of the purpose of and spirit in which theological reflection is undertaken. Katie's description of "leading out" and Michael's relating reflection to CPE were eye-opening. My primary learning style is experiential, visual and auditory in nature. I relate to my world in a very affective way. It helps me to be able to see, touch, and discuss a concept.

Subject: Reflections on Writing Theological Reflection Well

Posted by: Katie H.

Date: Thursday, October 3, 2013

Sandi, I second your post! I really enjoy your description of a theological reflection. I am also really glad that our sharing was very helpful to one another. As school goes on I am finding that this is a survival technique I need to utilize more. While I may not directly copy someone's process, gathering ideas about how others approach writing assignments has been very helpful to me thus far. I hope that I can continue to try and be open to exploring and changing the way that I accomplish writing and other tasks.

In regards to writing in any theological style I am still focusing on the idea of leading out. I know that the combination of my past experiences and my theological understandings and interpretations will help me to grow small bits of information into well written papers.... I have just finished my first five papers of grad school and am excited to get them back and see what I need to work on.

Subject: Reflections on Writing Theological Reflection Well

Posted by: Noble S.

Date: Thursday, October 3, 2013

I still have a dual understanding of "writing theologically" and "writing academically." There are constant calls for "critical analysis" from our professors, and the danger for me, is applying MY OWN REFLECTION. Interestingly, biblical passages are also translations from a historical period and context, applied to modern thought. But, this is an academic institution, as I need to keep reminding myself.

My understanding of theological writing has been fueled by examples and approaches introduced at the beginning of the class, yet I find myself reflecting in my regular sermon preparation with theological (writing) in relation to the hermeneutical approach. Am I supposed to bridge the gap, and if so, will I be speaking the language my hearers would understand? As Sandi has indicated, our learning could be embraced as experiential, but I believe it should also be an evolving process of literary standards of intellect. The *theos logos* even applied to writing should therefore be an imperative.

Subject: Reflections on Writing Theological Reflection Well

Posted by: Lucretia Yaghjian

Date: Friday, October 4, 2013

Noble, you make a pointed distinction between "writing theologically" and "writing academically," and that distinction resides in the differing functions of 'critical analysis" and "YOUR OWN REFLECTION." I would like to know more about why it is dangerous to apply "your own reflection" in a course paper.... If theological reflection begins with (one's own) experience, as Sandi suggested and you noted from her post, shouldn't there be a way of bridging the gap between personal theological reflection and critical analysis? Let's continue to talk about this in class and online.

Writing the online course discussion post well: Concluding reflections and suggestions

We are leaving this online discussion board conversation "in medias res" (in the midst of the conversation),[51] but you will shortly have an opportunity to put your own oar in, as the rhetorician Kenneth Burke would say. Do you know his wonderful metaphor of the Parlor as a depiction of academic conversation?

> Imagine that you enter a parlor. You come late. When you arrive, others have long preceded you, and they are engaged in a heated discussion, a discussion too heated for them to pause and tell you exactly what it is about. In fact, the discussion had already begun long before any of them got there, so that no one present is qualified to retrace for you all the steps that had gone before. You listen for a while, until you decide that you have caught the tenor of the argument; then you put in your oar. Someone answers; you answer him; another comes to your defense; another aligns himself against you, to either the embarrassment or gratification of your opponent, depending upon the quality of your ally's assistance. However, the discussion is interminable. The hour grows late, you must depart. And you do depart, with the discussion still vigorously in progress.[52]

There are three acts in the drama of Burke's parlor metaphor: first, we enter the parlor to a conversation already in progress; then we listen attentively until the right moment comes to actively engage the conversation; finally, we leave the parlor because the hour is late and we must depart—with the ongoing conversation still ringing in our ears. Before we leave the online discussion post room in the Parlor, I invite you to reflect on the last question posed in the online discussion board above,[53] and respond with your own post in the Theological Memo below:

> *THEOLOGICAL MEMO 5: Writing the Secondary Online Discussion Post Well: The last discussion board post distinguishes between "writing theologically" and "writing academically," or between "critical analysis" and "YOUR OWN REFLECTION." If theological reflection begins with (one's own) experience, shouldn't there be a way of bridging the gap between personal theological reflection and critical analysis? Please imagine that you are one of the students posting on this discussion board, and write a discussion board post to continue, or complete, this conversation by "putting your oar in."*

Here are some concluding suggestions for writing the online discussion board post well:

- READ THE OPENING PROMPT WITH CARE and identify particular points requiring an answer. The first step in writing an effective discussion board post is reading the assigned prompt accurately in order to ascertain what is being asked and how to respond accordingly.

- RESPOND IN A BRIEF MINI-ESSAY NO MORE THAN ONE COMPUTER SCREEN IN LENGTH. Write your response in complete sentences and clearly defined paragraphs that can be easily read within the frame of one computer screen. Craft it as a mini-essay that responds to the initial prompt with an answering assertion, develops the assertion with brief but pointed reference to textual readings as appropriate, and concludes by reiterating the assertion or raising further questions that invite others into the conversation.
- PROVIDE TEXTUAL EVIDENCE OR PERSONAL EXAMPLES TO SUPPPORT YOUR POST AS APPROPROPRIATE. If the discussion board prompt refers to assigned readings, your post should show that you have read the material and can relate it to the presenting question. If the topic is experiential, personal reflection and examples are appropriate.
- READ OTHER POSTINGS WITH CARE AND RESPOND SUBSTANTIVELY, NOT SUPERFICIALLY. To respond appropriately to other students' posts, it is important to read them carefully, to respond with substantive, not superficial comments, and to be considerate of the other person's point of view, even if (and especially when) it challenges your own.
- DON'T FORGET TO RE-READ AND PROOFREAD YOUR POSTS BEFORE POSTING!

Writing theology well by creating a blog

If you can write an email message and a discussion board post well, you are well on your way to writing a blog. But why, you might ask, would one want to? As one who is better at encouraging others (usually my students) to become bloggers than at writing an ongoing blog of my own, I am sympathetic to all forms of resistance to the practice of blogging. Like Henry David Thoreau, who wrote about technological advances in mid-nineteenth-century America, "We are in great haste to construct a magnetic telegraph from Maine to Texas; but Maine and Texas ... may ... have nothing important to communicate,"[54]—I am not convinced that all of the millions of bloggers currently populating the blogosphere with their postings[55] have something to say to me, nor I to them. Nonetheless, I am convinced that blogging is an emerging theological genre that is reinforcing what theologians do best—engaging in *theos logos*, or "talk about God" with each other and with wider audiences—via the Web.[56] In the process, argues theologian Ben Myers, blogging is also re-shaping the ways that we read, write, and do theology,[57] and may be re-shaping the world as well, one blog post at a time. "With blogging, everyone can write to change the world," writes theologian Kwok Pui Lan. "Maybe you should start one too."[58] I will shortly invite you to do just that, but first we need to ask again: (1) What kind of writing, or genre, is the blog, or weblog? (2) Who is the audience of a (or your) blog? (3) What is the purpose of a (or your) blog? (4) How should you write it?

What kind of writing, or genre, is the blog?

Do you remember the first time you heard the word, "blog," or found yourself reading one? The word is an abbreviation of "weblog," which computer programmer Jorn Barger coined in 1997 when he needed a name for the "log" of interesting web items he posted daily on his website, "Robot Wisdom WebLog." Barger considered "the syllable 'blog'... hideous" and reputedly capitalized the "Log" in "WebLog" as a safeguard against the inevitable.[59] Nevertheless, programmer Peter Merholz transcribed the word as "We Blog" on his own blog in 1999, and a small tech company called Pyra Labs created the website Blogger shortly thereafter (purchased by Google in 2003), which provided free web hosting and user-friendly templates for blogging.[60] Today "blog" is both a noun (my blog) and a verb (to blog), there are over 181 million bloggers (a blogger is one who blogs) on the internet,[61] a new blog is created somewhere in the world every half a second,[62] and the blog has become a standard digital genre. But has it become a new theological genre as well? To answer this question, we must ask three further questions: (1) What is a "genre"? (2) What is a "theological genre?" (3) What is the relationship between written genres, their sociorhetorical contexts, and the technologies by which they are communicated?

"Genre" traditionally denotes a specific type of writing that is used and categorized according to a recognized system of classification within a particular culture, society, or discourse community. When we classify something, we give it a name that then becomes synonymous with the thing named. For example, fiction, poetry, and drama are names of genres universally recognized within Western culture as denoting particular types of literature. Similarly, by "theological genres" I mean those recognized forms of written discourse that are written read, and taught within particular theological communities, including the one where you are learning to write theology well. For example, I did not invent the theological genres identified in this book (theological reflection, theological argument, and biblical exegesis); I followed accepted nomenclature used to describe the various sub-disciplines of theological study, and the modes of writing generic to each of them. Knowing what genre something is helps one to read it intelligently and to write it according to the conventions of that genre. But there is more to recognizing genres and writing them well than knowing their names. Physicist Richard Feynman recalls his father teaching him "the difference between knowing the name of something and knowing something":

> "See that bird?" he says. "It's a Spencer's Warbler.... Well, in Italian it's a *Chutto Lapittida*. In Portuguese it's *Bom de Peida*. In Chinese, it's a *Chung-long-tah*, and in Japanese, it's a *Katano Ketada*. You can know the name of the bird in all the languages of the world, but when you're finished, you'll know absolutely nothing about the bird.... So let's look at the bird and see what it's doing—that's what counts."[63]

Likewise, what counts in contemporary discussions of genre is seeing what genres do and what rhetorical purposes they serve within particular discourse communities. What blogs do on a functional level is twofold: they provide information in the form of links to other Internet sources, updated daily, and/or they invite self-expression and reflection in frequently updated postings that invite responses in turn from those following the blog. Contemporary theologians are writing both kinds of blogs, but for the purposes of writing theology well we focus on the second kind of blog here. But does a "theological blog" constitute a genre of its own?

Deciding whether or not theological blogs can be considered a theological genre requires that we reflect on the relationship between the written genre, its sociorhetorical context, and the medium through which it is communicated. While some argue that the blog is not a new writing genre but simply a new mode of delivery for whatever writing is being communicated across the e-waves,[64] blogging as a form of written discourse arose from a digital context, and continues to be embedded in that context. Whatever its audience, purpose, or subject matter, blogging is not blogging unless it is produced and delivered digitally. Indeed, blogging would never have become a writing genre without the digital platforms provided by Blogger.com, and the digital progression from email messages to web pages to discussion boards and online forums that preceded it. As theologian Ben Myers corroborates, "Blogging is not merely a medium ... through which information is communicated. It is fundamentally a *practice*, a *technique* ... that cultivates particular forms of being and particular forms of sociality," all of which have theological implications.[65]

What is the difference between "working out a theology as [we] write," as Thomas Merton described, and "working out a theology as we blog?" First, the digital environment of blogging invites a more immediate relationship between authors and audiences, fostering a more informal theological style and voice. Just as the online professor is no longer the sage on the stage, but the guide on the side, the theological blogger is no longer the sage of the printed page, but an equal participant in an open-ended theological conversation. Second, the online practice of blogging expands both the scope of theological reflection and participation in theological conversation, as theological bloggers claim the online world as their province, like the pre-digital Sir Walter Raleigh in the sixteenth century, and invite a wider range of readers into their territory. Third, blogging in a theological context has gone a long way toward integrating theological imagination with pastoral reflection, linking the local pastor and the academic theologian more integrally in their efforts to work out a theology as they blog.[66]

Finally, blogs are rapidly becoming incorporated into theological education as platforms for re-envisioning traditional academic assignments and creating new ones.[67] When engaged as a theological practice by students, teachers, and writers of theology, blogging constitutes a theological genre.[68] If the medium, the message, and the theological practice of blogging are no less interwoven than the weeds and the wheat in Matthew's parable, far be it from us to separate them. Before we proceed, please use the following theological memo as an introduction to blogging in a theological context and to "working out your own theology as you blog":

> *THEOLOGICAL MEMO 6: Working Out a Theology as You Blog: Go to the "Top 100 Theology Blogs" website* [http://www.christiancolleges.com/blog/2009/top-100-theology-blogs/] *and browse through the blogs featured there. Choose three blogs that interest you, and compare and contrast them in terms of their audience, purpose, and blogging (writing) styles. On the basis of your comparison,*

contrast, and critique of the blogs you have chosen, prepare your own bullet points for "working out a theology as you blog."

Assuming, then, that blogging is an authentic digital writing genre,[69] I invite you to embrace blogging also as a theological genre empowering theological writers to write theology well by creating a blog. I suggested earlier that what theologians do best is to engage in "God-talk" with each other and with wider audiences—not merely to hear themselves talk, but to invite others to join the conversation. When theologians become bloggers, they are writing in a digital context and expanding the blogging genre to encompass the audiences, purposes, and ongoing discourse of theology. In so doing, they are contributing faithfully to the formation of online theological communities and widening the scope of participation in those communities.[70] In creating your own theological blog, you will extend the *theos logos* still further by inviting your own audience into the conversation. Because a blog's audience and purpose is determined by its author, I first invite you to complete the following Theological Memo, which asks what audiences and purposes might inspire you to create a blog.

THEOLOGICAL MEMO 7: Creating a Blueprint for a Blog: Imagine that you have been asked to create a blog as an assignment for one of your theological courses. Within the theological focus of the course, you are free to choose the topic of the blog, the target audience, and the purpose for writing it. What topic would you choose? Who would your target audience most likely be? What underlying purpose (beyond the course assignment) would inspire you to create the blog? Just as a child might build a sand castle at the beach with no worries about the tide sweeping it away, create a written blueprint of your imagined blog, including its topic, audience, and purpose, and keep it with you as we move on to consider audience, purpose, in preparation for writing a theological blog of your own.

Who is the audience for your blog?

When someone decides to create a blog, what comes first: the purpose for writing it or the audience to whom it is directed? Like the audience that Paul Ricoeur imagines for any piece of writing, a blog is potentially accessible to anyone on the Web who wishes to read it, but blogs attract audiences who have been attracted in turn by the author's invitation to join a particular conversation that each has in common. That said, blogging is a public genre that presupposes an audience, even if bloggers choose to make their blog "private," or accessible only by permission of the author. Whatever the purpose of the blog, it will not achieve that purpose without an audience of readers and responders.

In the first chapter of this book, I invited you to draw a diagram encompassing the theological audiences for whom you write, extending in concentric circles from professors and students in your immediate theological school community, to your church community, to your wider societal or cultural context.[71] We have already revisited some of those audiences in this chapter. We first considered how to write email messages well to a professorial audience of one. We proceeded to writing online discussion board posts well for a more diverse audience of students and professors. If each of these online audiences also represents widening concentric circles of writing in and through distance, then blogging audiences extend the circles still further, even if we begin by blogging in response to a course assignment closer to home. If, for example, you are assigned to write a blog for one of your courses, you will begin with an audience of classmates and professor, just as with the online discussion board posts. If, on the other hand, you blog to a wider audience beyond the borders of the online or on site classroom as well, you will be more likely to keep blogging after the class is completed.

For example, one of my students created a blog for her parish that explored Lenten disciplines through the ecological lens of a parish community garden. Another student and Anglican priest from Zimbabwe created a blog of daily Scriptural reflections from the Lectionary to connect with his parishioners "in and through distance." A third student created a blog to practice writing for her Episcopal Church General Ordination Examinations and concluded the blog when she successfully passed them. Each of these students had an audience in mind as they created their blogs, and that audience helped them to define the purpose of the blog, to continue blogging in response to audience comments and feedback, and to persevere with blogging over the long haul. A blog addressed only to your classmates and professor will provide you with a captive audience for a semester. A blog addressed to a wider audience of your own may inspire you to blog for a lifetime, or at least as long as you have a reason to do so. What audiences in the widening contexts of your academic, pastoral, professional, or personal life might be waiting for you to create a blog? Before you do, it is time to ask, "What is the purpose of your blog?"

What is the purpose of your blog?

"Blogs," writes Mary Cross in *Bloggerati, Twitterati: How Blogs and Twitter Are Transforming Popular Culture*, "satisfy a basic human need for self-expression and ... the basic human desire to be heard, to have an audience."[72] For Ben Myers, blogging is "a practice of self-formation—a new way of working on the self, of forming community and identity."[73] Finally, Carolyn Miller and Dawn Shepherd suggest that blogs fulfill a "widely shared, recurrent need for cultivation and validation of the self."[74] Leaving the desire for an audience where we have already addressed it in the last section, is the need for self-expression, self-formation, or self-validation enough to motivate you to create a blog? Why not take up finger painting or interpretative dance, or simply write in your own private journal?

Writing a blog, on the other hand, is hard work! Not only must you write fluently and update frequently with new posts and responses to your readers' comments, but you also must have enough digital savvy to navigate your blogging platform of choice successfully when adding photos, links, or other attachments to your posts. Most people do not start blogs without a purpose that supersedes self-expression, or for that matter, self-formation or self-validation, although any combination of these might be part of their motivation. They write a blog, first of all, because they have something to say and a purpose for saying it that is best served by the digital environment of blogging. Second, they choose to blog because it is the consummate digital genre for writing "in and through distance," thereby achieving not only self-expression but also self-transcendence, which is the goal of all writing generally, but more specifically of writing theology well.

I suggest that all writing seeks not only self-expression, but self-transcendence, in its desire to communicate beyond the self with a wider audience, whose alpha and omega is the communicating God.[75] While some would argue that digital writing lacks the permanence of print, what is posted on the Web possesses its own perpetuity and shares the transcendent properties of all writing that enlarges the community of discourse to embrace both contemporary audiences, "generations yet to come" (Psalms 102:10), and the God incarnate in all of them. As the Roman Catholic Archbishop of New York's blog proclaims, "God Is Everywhere, Even on the Blog."[76] Still, there must be a more immediate purpose for writing a blog "on the ground"—a blogology from below—whether one is writing a cooking blog with "Julie and Julia,"[77] a "Happiness Project" blog with Gretchen Rubin,[78] a "Faith and Theology" blog with Ben Myers,[79] or a blog on "Postcolonialism, Theology, and everything she cares about" with Kwok Pui Lan. Explaining the purpose for creating her blog, she wrote:

> My aim was rather simple. I would ask students in the Spirituality of the Contemporary World class to create a blog and post their journals there. I wanted to see how this worked. I created this blog and posted regularly .... Many students in the course did not continue blogging after the course was over. But I carried on and had fun writing it. In the year 2011, I posted 66 blogs. The number of blogs amounted almost to that of half a book.[80]

If you, like Kwok Pui Lan's students, are invited to write a blog for one of your theological courses, the initial assignment will provide you with a purpose for entering the blogosphere. But what will it take for you to keep blogging after the course is over? I think that it will take inviting conversation about your own theological imagination "and everything you care about" in the hope and faith that others will care about what you are writing "in and through distance." This is not so different from what the prophet Habakkuk was enjoined to do when God invited him to "Write the vision; make it plain on tablets," so even one running (or hastily surfing the Web?) could read it (Hab 2:2). In the confidence that you are ready now to create a theological blog of your own, we look more specifically now at how to write it well.

Writing the theological blog well by reading and writing theology well

Let's assume that you have been assigned to start a blog for one of your courses that invites you to post reflections as you read and write theology well. It might read like this:[81]

> THEOLOGICAL MEMO 8: *Reading and Writing Theology Well to Create a Blog: Create a blog that will provide a platform for your theological and/or*

biblical reflections on course readings in a style and voice that will engage both your course participants and a wider audience of your own choosing. Limit individual posts to 300 words. As you reflect on the readings, you might consider the reading in relation to its historical or theoretical context; you might write about something in the reading that you don't understand; you might ask an insightful question about the reading and then answer your own questions, or you might decide to read the text through the lens of your own contemporary experience. Finally, and most importantly, you are invited to write this blog in your own theological voice.

How would you begin to write this blog? You are invited to write in a digital genre that favors simplicity, brevity, and postings to an audience that begins in your online or on-site classroom but transcends it. You are responding to an academic assignment that requires critical response to course readings, along with the expectation of writing theology well. How will you satisfy all of these expectations, let alone the different audiences represented here?

You have two choices. You can fulfill the assignment by writing offline, as you would for any theological reflection on course readings. Given this scenario, you reflect on the readings, write in response to them, edit and revise as appropriate, and copy it to your blog. Who would ever know that your online blog was composed offline? Even if they did, what would it matter if you completed the assignment successfully and were graded accordingly? But what if you were to engage the blogging exercise not only as a course assignment but also as a creative rendezvous with a new digital and theological genre?

Given that scenario, the first step is to create your blog at a blogging website, such as Blogger, WordPress, or TypePad.[82] The second step is to write your first blog post online, in the confidence that it will not be accessible to readers until you click on "publish" to authorize its public posting. There are many print and Web resources that provide protocols for writing blogs well. All of them emphasize (1) writing simply and clearly, (2) posting and updating frequently, and (3) inviting and responding to comments regularly.[83] According to Kwok Pui Lan, blogging requires "thinking on the fly" and "writing fast," using "simple sentences and simple words."[84] Ben Myers describes his blog writing process this way:

> Writing for my own blog is not generally planned and considered in advance. I don't take a ponderous walk to decide what to say, nor do I draft a text and then carefully comb over it with successive stages of revision and refinement. In blogging, the goal is not to produce a polished text, but to initiate discussion . . . . A blog post isn't generally the expression of a preexisting idea; it is itself the instantaneous production of thought.[85]

The experienced blogger's ability to write fast, on the fly, in readable and engaging prose that "is itself the instantaneous production of thought" does not, however, give novice bloggers permission to write hasty, sloppy posts, especially if their goal is to write theology well! Blogging is both a digital genre and a writing genre. Even *Blogging for Dummies* prioritizes "writing well" as paramount for creating a successful blog.[86] Be assured that all theologians writing blogs proofread and spell-check them before making their posts public.

Moreover, when blogging becomes a part of the theological curriculum, the genre may have to shift to accommodate course requirements and expectations, and—for those desiring to write theology well—may require a slower and more deliberate style of blogging. Indeed, even a cursory survey of theological blogs on the Web uncovers a wide range of blogging styles, from brief bullet point posts to more measured prose reflections.[87] Given the importance of "reflection" in a theological context, can theological blogging not accommodate that slow lane of theological thinking and writing for those who need time, space, and opportunity to reflect in tranquility, like poets, saints, and the rest of us?

It is time to return to your theological blogging assignment. How will you fulfill your course requirements when creating a theological blog, addressed to a wider audience of your own choosing? By imagining one person in that audience as a representative reader, writing the blog in your own theological voice and in a style appropriate to the person you have chosen, while still attending to the particulars of the blogging assignment. Toward that end, you may find it helpful to review the templates for the one-page "Pastoral Reflection" and "Systematic Reflection" Papers provided in Chapters 2 and 3.[88] You may also want to try "free writing" your blog in order to gain fluency and free your theological voice.[89] Here is one student's response to the blogging assignment given in Theological Memo 7, for a "Theological Themes in Church History" course:

Here I blog: I can do no other! A religious education director's reflections

If Martin Luther were posting his 95 Theses today, he would have posted them on the Wittenberg Church website, or on his own blog. As digital editor of The Economist *Tom Standish writes in* The Writing on the Wall, *in his own time Martin Luther was "a particularly adept user of social media systems, with consequences that reverberate to this day."*[90] *When Luther posted his document on the church door in October 1517 to denounce the sale of indulgences and initiate an open academic debate regarding their theological legitimacy, did he suspect that it would "go viral"? As both pastor and theologian, Luther used the medium of the community noticeboard to communicate his message, long before blogging, Facebook, or Twitter, and his cooperative social networks did the rest.*

It seems that Luther's followers "liked" what he wrote and circulated copies of the document (in Latin) within academic circles; a German printer produced, printed, and distributed a readable German translation; and one "follower" wrote, "Hardly fourteen days had passed when these propositions were known throughout Germany and within four weeks almost all of Christendom was familiar with them" (53).

Leaving Luther, Facebook, and Twitter aside, how effectively are pastors and theologians using blogging today? In "Blogging as Theological Discourse," Ben Myers sees blogging fostering a more informal theological style and voice; expanding participation in theological conversation; and integrating theological imagination and pastoral reflection (54–55). I don't expect this blog to go viral any time soon, but as a Parish Religious Education Director, I wish to incorporate these touchstones into my blog posts on course readings, so that my middle school bloggers, who are also my wider audience, can join the conversation. Let the blogging begin! [300 words]

Writing your theological blog well: Concluding reflections and suggestions

Now it is your turn to create a blog of your own. Will blogging become your writing genre of choice as you continue your theological study? Will one of your blog posts "go viral" and reach interested readers half a world away? Or, after keeping a course blog for a semester, will you decide that blogging isn't for you? I can't answer these questions for you, but I encourage you to keep your creative rendezvous with this new genre long enough to let it inspire you to write theology well in a digital environment, and in so doing, to write your vision of the love of God and neighbor so that those on the Web can read and respond to you. I also encourage you to check out the *Writing Theology Well* website at Bloomsbury.com for updates to this chapter.[91]

Here are some concluding suggestions for writing your theological blog well:

- READ THE BLOGGING ASSIGNMENT with an active theological imagination.
- CHOOSE A TOPIC AND WORKING TITLE for your blog post.
- IMAGINE ONE PERSON FROM YOUR AUDIENCE reading what you write.
- PREPARE TO WRITE IN A STYLE AND VOICE appropriate to that person.
- BEGIN YOUR BLOG WITH INFORMATIVE AND CATCHY SENTENCES,
- OR ... WITH A PROVOCATIVE OR ENGAGING QUESTION.
- CONNECT YOUR INTRODUCTION to the specific blogging assignment.
- DEVELOP YOUR MAIN POINT(S) from the reading(s) with references as needed.
- DRAW YOUR REFLECTIONS TO A CONCLUSION within the stated word count.
- INVITE COMMENTS FROM YOUR AUDIENCE, if appropriate.
- RE-READ YOUR POST, SPELL-CHECK, AND REVISE AS NEEDED.
- RE-READ ONE MORE TIME BEFORE POSTING, and offer a prayer of thanksgiving to God who is everywhere, even on the Blog!
- CLICK ON "PUBLISH."
- CHECK TO SEE THAT YOUR POST IS ONLINE.
- BREATHE A SIGH OF RELIEF that you have "blogged theology well"!

Writing theological research well: A digital appendix

This chapter has provided an introduction to writing theology well in a digital environment, focusing on writing digital genres in a theological context. We conclude with an overview of writing theological research well in a digital environment, focusing on the way that digital research tools have enriched and challenged the research process. This section should be read as a "Digital Appendix" to Chapters 5 and 6, which review the traditional skills that a theological writer/researcher needs to cultivate.[92] It includes an introduction to writing theological research in a digital environment, a Digital Literacy Checklist for Online Writers and Researchers, a Digital Writer/Researcher's Toolbox of research tools, organized according to the steps of the writing/research process, and concludes with a reflection on evaluating Internet sources and preventing plagiarism in a digital environment.

Writing theological research in a digital environment: Preliminary questions

Once again, we begin with three questions: (1) What are "digital research tools" and how have they influenced the research process? (2) What are "digital research skills" and how do they differ from traditional research skills? (3) What digital skills and tools do you have and need for writing theological research well?

What are digital research tools and how have they influenced the research process?

A tool is an instrument or device that is designed to help you get a particular job done. "In order to do a job right," my carpenter father-in-law always said, "you need the right tools." This is no less true for carpenters than for digital researchers, who have a rapidly expanding arsenal of digital tools at their disposal for navigating every aspect of the research writing process. As an introduction to this dazzling array of digital tools, I invite you to visit DIRT,[93] a Digital Research Tools website that provides a regularly updated registry of digital tools for scholarly use. You will also find a Digital Writer/Researcher's Toolbox, organized by the sequential steps of the research and writing process, at the end of this section.[94]

How have these tools influenced the research process? This all depends upon whether researchers have the skills to use the tools. For those who do, digital research tools help users to navigate the research process more efficiently and creatively, offering interfaces between print, audio, and video platforms, and providing applications designed to facilitate every stage of the writing and research process. However, to reap the benefits of these research tools, users must master the skills to use them effectively, which brings us to our next question.

What are digital research skills and how do they differ from traditional research skills?

Digital research skills are the skills that researchers need to use the digital tools available for research in a networked environment, from search engines and data bases to tools for brainstorming, note-taking, organizing, and citing research sources. If you have ever "Googled" someone or something, you have used a digital tool. If your search provided you with the results that you needed, or if you refined it by substituting a more precise keyword or employing one of Google's more specialized search services, such as Google Scholar, you have exercised your own digital research skills. But not all digital research tools are as user-friendly as Google.[95] Just as you must learn the necessary skills for operating a power drill before you can use the tool effectively in your workshop, so you must develop the digital skills necessary for using a bibliographical management tool like RefWorks for organizing and documenting your research sources.[96] Familiarity with digital research tools and the acquisition of digital research skills combine to produce digital literacy, which in turn enables twenty-first-century researchers to engage in research, construct new knowledge, and communicate it in a networked environment.

If you are a "digital native," you have acquired this digital literacy by osmosis, and are already using these tools proficiently and productively. If you are a "digital immigrant" who wrote your first research papers using library card catalogues, searching for resources in the library stacks, and writing bibliographical entries and research notes on three by five cards, working with digital research resources may require a steeper learning curve. Wherever you are on this continuum, the acquisition of digital literacy is an ongoing process, not a once-for-all accomplishment. Nor are we recommending that you throw out the proverbial baby with the bathwater, exchanging all of the traditional academic research and writing skills that you have cultivated for the latest version of Scrivener.[97] No digital tool can replace the curiosity that generates a research question, even with the digital tools to help you pursue it. Similarly, no digital tool can write your research paper for you, however skillfully you use it. Keeping that in mind, in the Theological Memo below, I invite you to answer the third question posed at the beginning of this section for yourself: "What digital tools and skills do you have and need for writing theological research well?"

> THEOLOGICAL MEMO 9: *What digital tools and skills do you have and need for writing theological research well? What digital tools are you presently using to search, find, organize, and cite the resources for your theological research projects? What more traditional research and writing practices do you continue to find helpful? Please reflect on the digital research skills that you have and need for successfully navigating your next theological research project. Then place a plus sign (+) next to the skills you have and a minus sign (-) next to those you need on the "Digital Literacy Checklist" below:*

A digital literacy checklist for online writers and researchers[98]

Be familiar with:

- identifying your computer operating system and software versions
- keyboard shortcuts for frequently used functions: save, cut, copy, paste, undo, select all
- minimizing, maximizing, and manually resizing windows
- maneuvering (viewing, cut, copy, and paste) between multiple open windows or applications
- creating and sharing screenshots
- using more than one internet browser:
    - recognizing and using links,
    - right click (or option + click) menus,
    - using search engines,
    - using multiple tabs or windows,
    - using bookmarks/favorites,
    - page refresh,
    - download settings (default download save location),
    - enabling/disabling popup blocker,
    - enabling/disabling menu bars,
    - access and modify security settings,
    - clearing cache and/or history and temporary files,
    - zooming in/out (how this impacts layout on some web pages)
- PDF files; reading, downloading from websites, and creating PDF files from Word (or other text-based document) files
- using zipped, or compressed, files—creating and unpacking
- your computer's default settings regarding: which programs open specific file formats, folder settings, save location, download location, monitor resolution settings (including changing when necessary)
- connecting to wireless networks, and updating the password for saved wireless network profiles
- popular file extensions and appropriate software/apps for opening each, including common audio, video, and image files:.doc, .docx, .ppt, .xlsx., .wav, .mov, .jpg, .mp3, .png, etc. manual and automatic installation of updates for your Operating System, office productivity software, browsers, and specifically: Adobe Reader, QuickTime, Adobe Flash Player, Java

Also important:

1. Develop a digital filing system that works for you so you can easily find your files and saved content.
2. Develop a backup plan for your files. There are lots of options for making sure you always have a backup copy of your files; external drive, disc, USB flash drive, online service, etc. Many of these come with software that allows you to schedule automatic backups so you don't have to remember to do it manually.
3. Practice your manual dexterity for controlling the mouse or trackpad:
   a. Can you execute click + drag maneuvers with just a track pad? single-handed?
   b. Distinguishing among and clicking the desired buttons/links when they may be very close together in proximity on the screen.
   c. Get familiar with the tools that are available to help you with this.

Locate your local tech support resources for computer problems and/or training needs.

Word processing software—whatever you use, Google Docs, MS Word, MS Office web apps (Office 365), Open Office, etc.—be comfortable with the following tasks: (in no particular order)

- footnotes and endnotes
- page numbers
- saving files to a specific location—which you can remember how to locate later
- paragraph settings; especially indent tools, and line spacing
- Review mode: viewing comments (from other editors or as faculty feedback)
- using bulleted and numbered lists, and outline formatting
- understand what spell-check will, and won't, do for you
- inserting images in files
- modify font, size, color, and style
- adjusting page margins and layout

Bonus items: (things that will save you time)

- modify default (normal.dot) template for new documents
- be able to navigate using the tab, directional arrows, and enter keys
- find out what every key on your laptop/keyboard does; including function keys
- edit screenshots before sending/sharing
- adjusting application (word processing) automated correction settings to your preferences
- When you need more information than is provided here, search the Internet!

A digital writer/researcher's toolbox

The chart that follows provides an inventory of digital tools and websites devoted to specific phases of the writing and research process, from choosing a topic and generating a research question to preparing a literature review, determining research methods and methodology, collecting and cataloguing data, writing, editing, and bibliographic citation, and presentation, or delivery of a research project. You will find URL's for each of the tools listed at the end of the chart. While many of these digital research tools are also listed in the DIRT Directory, this inventory uses the traditional steps of the writing-research process as a filter for your exploration of these websites, which Theological Memo 10 invites you to begin below:

> *THEOLOGICAL MEMO 10: What is your "digital literacy quotient," estimated from the difference between your plusses (+) and minuses (-) on the Digital Literacy Checklist above? However you do the math, I suspect that the more plus signs you have, the higher your digital literacy quotient will be, but every minus sign you have will lower it accordingly. One way to raise it is to experiment with digital tools that you haven't used before, and choose one or two of them to engage more actively. I invite you to choose one step of the research process from the Digital Writer/Researcher's Toolbox that you are currently engaging in your own research, and browse among the digital tools available. Choose one tool that looks helpful, proceed online to its website, and sign in as a user. Beginning with its tutorial for new users, work with the tool to see if you can use it fruitfully for your own project. Does it provide the resources you need? Is it user-friendly? If not, what did you need that was not provided? Write a brief reflection on how this digital tool might help you (or not) write theological research well.*

Research-writing steps	**Aspects of the process**	**Digital research tools**
Topic and Research Question	• Concept mapping • Brainstorming • Forming a working thesis	• Lucidchart • Freemind • Coggle • Mindjet • Wordle • Text 2 Mind Map • CMAP • bubbl.us
Literature Review	Annotated bibliography • Summarizing • Paraphrasing • Direct quote	• Noodle Tools • iAnnotate • Sente 6 (iPad, Mac)

(*Continued*)

Research-writing steps	Aspects of the process	Digital research tools
Methodology and Methods	Identify the methodology: Why? • Creating a research space • Applying a Filter • Research is not value-free Methods: How? • Questionnaires • Surveys • Case studies • Ethnographic research • Research paper	• SurveyMonkey • Poll Everywhere • All Our Ideas
Data Collection	• Reading for Research • Note taking • Organizing research • Citation Tools	• Readsy • Evernote • Instapaper • Onenote • Trello • Pocket • Dropbox • Zotero • RefWorks • EndNote • Diigo
Writing, Editing, and Bibliographic Citation	• Zero draft • Final draft • Referencing	• Scalar • Wordpress • Scrivener • Anthologize
Delivery	• Collaboration • Presentation	• Canva • Prezi • Haiku Deck • Slideshare • WebSlides • Academia • Mendeley • Participad

URLs

Lucidchart	https://www.lucidchart.com/
Coggle	https://coggle.it/
Wordle	http://www.wordle.net/
CMAP	http://cmap.ihmc.us/
Freemind	http://freemind.sourceforge.net/wiki/index.php/Main_Page
Mindjet	http://www.mindjet.com/mindmanager////
Text 2 Mind Map	https://www.text2mindmap.com/
bubbl.us	https://bubbl.us/

Noodle Tools	http://www.noodletools.com/
iAnnotate	http://www.branchfire.com/iannotate/#makepaperjealous
Sente 6 (iPad, Mac)	http://www.thirdstreetsoftware.com/site/Sente.html

SurveyMonkey	https://www.surveymonkey.com/
Poll Everywhere	http://www.polleverywhere.com/
All Our Ideas	http://www.allourideas.org/

Readsy	http://www.readsy.co/
Evernote	https://evernote.com/
Instapaper	https://www.instapaper.com/
Onenote	http://www.onenote.com/
Trello	https://trello.com/
Pocket	https://getpocket.com/
Dropbox	https://www.dropbox.com/
Zotero	http://www.zotero.org/
RefWorks	http://www.refworks.com/
EndNote	http://endnote.com/
Diigo	http://www.diigo.com/

QDA Miner	http://provalisresearch.com/products/qualitative-data-analysis-software/

Scalar	http://scalar.usc.edu/scalar/
Wordpress	http://wordpress.org/
Scrivener	http://www.literatureandlatte.com/scrivener.php
Anthologize	http://anthologize.org/

Canva	https://www.canva.com/
Prezi	http://prezi.com/
Haiku Deck	https://www.haikudeck.com/
Slideshare	http://www.slideshare.net/
WebSlides	http://slides.diigo.com/
Academia	http://www.academia.edu/
Mendeley	http://www.mendeley.com/
Participad	http://participad.org/

Concluding reflections: Evaluating internet sources and preventing plagiarism in a digital environment

> *The kingdom of heaven is like a net that was thrown into the sea and caught fish of every kind; when it was full, they drew it ashore, sat down, and put the good into baskets and threw out the bad. So it will be at the end of the age....*
>
> —*Matthew 13:47–49*

When Jesus spoke this parable and those remembering it wrote it down, it is unlikely that their imagination of "the end of the age" included the creation of the Internet and the World Wide Web. Yet we who live in these latter days of networked communication in a digital environment might think that this parable was all about us. Doing research on the Internet and preventing plagiarism in that environment require us to do three things. First, we must learn how to search intentionally for different kinds of digital resources—from standard online databases to "Invisible Web" resources.[99] Second, we must cast a wide net in our digital searching and develop criteria to help us separate relevant resources from those less relevant or reliable. Finally, we must use Internet resources responsibly, cite them accurately, and authenticate our own writing by distinguishing it clearly from that of our sources.

You have already learned how to search for print and online sources on computer, even if you were weaned on card catalogues but have become de facto digital natives. As long as your search remains within library premises, on site or online, you have a trustworthy filter for the resources that you find. You might compare searching within library resources and data bases to fishing in a local pond that has been stocked with healthy, farm-raised fish. In that controlled environment, you will not need to worry about evaluating your resources.

But when you cast a wider net, like the fishermen in Matthew's gospel, the resources you retrieve are less trustworthy. Anyone can publish anything on the Web, and many do. Moreover, websites do not have the permanence of print books. How, then, do you separate the good resources from the bad? You need to develop criteria for what you keep and what you throw away, rooted in your own research priorities. But what if you are a novice and not an expert in the field that you are researching? The same critical skills that you use when reading theological articles can be applied to evaluating a website, which the Harvard University Writing Program website distils into three criteria: authorship, objectivity, and currency.[100] You can also refine your search strategies and skip this step altogether, prompted by Stephan Spencer's Google Power-Searching video.[101] Finally, you need to separate the fish you have caught (your own writing) from what has been imported from other ponds (your Web sources) while integrating your catch (the research) into your narrative to authenticate your own writing.

Authenticating one's own writing has been an author's prerogative from the beginning of written communication, even though the twenty-first-century preoccupation with academic integrity is distinctive to Western academic culture. The Apostle Paul concluded his Second Letter to the Thessalonians with this imprimatur: "I, Paul, write this greeting with my own hand. This is the mark in every letter of mine. This is the way I write" (II Thess 3:17). In so doing, he authorized proclamation and publication of his letter by spoken and written word. Paul probably dictated his epistle to a scribe, and appended his own signature to authenticate it, as was the custom of the time. But his practice of writing "in his own hand" at the end of the document is not so far removed from our own need as twenty-first-century theological writers and researchers to authenticate our work. What is the mark in everything you write that authenticates its academic integrity?

Those writing theological research well in a digital environment have a more challenging task in practicing academic integrity, since the Web has made it very easy to copy, cut, paste, forward, post, and retweet what one has read without attribution.[102] Moreover, protocols for defining plagiarism on the Web have not been regularized. Yet the same guidelines for giving credit to your print sources apply also to research on the Web. Unauthorized use of Internet materials, even if inadvertent, constitutes plagiarism. If, like Paul, you write "in your own hand" and with your own mark of authenticity, all will be well.[103]

In this chapter we have explored writing theology well in a digital environment, focusing on online writers and researchers. First, we provided an introduction to digital writing and the skills that digital writers need to cultivate in an online environment. Next, we provided online rhetorics for writing the digital genres of Emails, Discussion Posts, and Blogs for online or on-site courses. We concluded with a Digital Appendix to writing theological research well. I hope that readers will actively contribute to updating this chapter on our Writing Theology Well website,[104] and I invite you to keep writing theology well online, whether on-site or from a distance, for the love of God and neighbor and "for generations yet to come" (Psalm 102:18).

Notes

1 As the American Association of Theological Schools defines these terms, "distance learning" programs are programs in which degrees can be completed online, while "distributed learning" programs provide a hybrid of online and face-to-face components. See Russell Haitch, "All Learning is Distance Learning," in Steve Delmater et al., "Technology, Pedagogy, and Transformation in Theological Education: Five Case Studies," *Teaching Theology and Religion* 10 (2007): 72–75.

2 Walter J. Ong, *Orality and Literacy: The Technologizing of the Word* (1982; repr. London: Routledge, 1988), 81.

3 See Julie Anne Lytle, *Faith Formation 4.0: Introducing an Ecology of Faith in a Digital Age* (New York: Morehouse Publishing, 2013), for an excellent pastoral and pedagogical resource integrating digital technology with evangelization and faith formation. See also Adam J. Copeland, "Writing Digitally," in Eric D. Barreto, ed., *Writing Theologically: Foundations for Learning* (Minneapolis: Fortress Press, 2015, published in time for me to cite it in this chapter, but not in time to use it in my own research.

4 This definition of digital writing follows that of The WIDE Research Center Collective, Michigan State University, "How Technology Changes Writing Practices," in *Why Teach Digital Writing?*, accessed July 15, 2013, http://www.technorhetoric.net/10.1/coverweb/wide/kairos2.html. See also Danielle Nicole DeVoss, Elyse Eldman-Aadahl, and Troy Hicks, *Because Digital Writing Matters: Improving Student Writing in Online and Multimedia Environments*/National Writing Project; with Danielle Nicole DeVoss,

Elyse Eldman-Aadahl, and Troy Hicks (San Francisco, CA: Jossey-Bass, 2010); Andrea Baer, "Keeping up with ... DIGITAL WRITING," Association of College and Research Libraries, accessed April 28, 2014, www.arl.org.

5 Troy Hicks, *Crafting Digital Writing: Composing Texts Across Media and Genres* (Portsmouth, NH: Heinemann, 2013), 5–6.

6 See Chapter 1, "The Sociorhetorical Context of Writing Theology."

7 See Chapter 10, "What Is 'Style,' and How do Writers Define It?"

8 Paul Ricoeur, "The Hermeneutical Function of Distanciation," in Ricouer, *Hermeneutics and the Human Sciences*, ed., trans. John B. Thompson (Cambridge: Cambridge University Press, 1981), 131.

9 See below, under "Writing the Email Message Well: A Netiquette for Theological and Biblical Writers."

10 Plato, *Phaedrus*, ed., trans. Walter Hamilton (New York: Penguin Books, 1973), 275, p. 97; and Hicks, *Crafting Digital Writing*, 11–27.

11 Chris Barr and Senior Editors of Yahoo!, *The Yahoo! Style Guide: The Ultimate Sourcebook for Writing, Editing, and Creating Content for the Digital World* (New York: St. Martin's Griffin, 2010), 5–7.

12 Ibid., 189–96.

13 See Robert Williamson, Jr., "Using Twitter to Teach Reader-Oriented Biblical Interpretation: 'Tweading' the Gospel of Mark," *Teaching Theology and Religion* 16 (2013): 274–86.

14 Hicks, *Crafting Digital Writing*, 11–27.

15 Ibid., 2.

16 See Ewan Clayton, *The Golden Thread: The Story of Writing* (orig. UK: Atlantic Books, 2013; Counterpoint: Berkeley, CA: 2014).

17 "It is said that icons are not painted, they are written (that they are written has its origin in the similarity of icon painting process to the writing and copying of old manuscripts—the painter painted the 'original' again and again and was also considered to be more a craftsman than an artist)." See "Icons—Windows to Another World," accessed June 18, 2014, www.prayerofheart.com/icons/html.

18 Ibid., 53.

19 As Neil J. Rubenking writes in his *PC Magazine* blog (April 23, 2014), "Going without antivirus protection isn't an option." For more information on choosing appropriate antivirus software for your own computer, see Rubenking's ratings of the best antivirus programs for 2014: Neil J. Rubenking, "The Best Antivirus for 2014," April 21, 2014, accessed June 18, 2014, www.pc.mag.com/article2/0,2817,2372364,00.asp; "The Best Free Antivirus for 2014," April 23, 2014, accessed June 18, 2014, www.pcmag.com/article2/0,2817,2388652,00.asp

20 While the choice of an internet service provider will vary according to availability in your own area, a high speed connection is optimal for students taking online courses. Please consult the following websites for basic information about choosing an internet provider: GCF Learnfree.org, "Internet 101: How to Choose an Internet Service Provider," accessed June 18, 2014, www.gcflearnfree.org/internet101/how-to-choose-an-internet-service-provider; USA.gov., "Choose an Internet Service Provider," accessed June 18, 2014, www.usa.gov/topics/science/communications/internet/service-provider.shtml

21 See below, under "Writing Theology Well by Creating a Blog."

22 Mary Cross, *Bloggerati, Twitterati: How Blogs and Twitter Are Transforming Popular Culture* (Santa Barbara, CA: Praeger, 2011), 35.

23 Ibid., 12. As Cross observes, Marc Prensky coined the terms "digital natives" and "digital immigrants" in an online essay in October 2001, accessed December 3, 2014, http://www.marcprensky.com/writing/Prensky%20-%20Digital%20Natives,%20 Digital%20Immigrants%20-%20Part1.pdf

24 Clay Shirky, "Why Abundance Should Breed Optimisim: A Second Reply to Nick Carr," Encyclopedia Britannica Blog, July 21, 2008, accessed August 1, 2013, www.britannica.com/blogs/2008/07/why-abundance-should-breed-optimism-a-second-reply-to-nick-carr

25 Martin Luther's "Disputation on the Power and Efficacy of Indulgences Commonly Known as The 95 Theses" was posted on the Castle Church door in Wittenberg, Germany, on October 31, 1517. For the full text, see *Martin Luther: Selections from His Writings*, ed. John Dillenberger (New York: Doubleday Anchor Books, 1961), 489–500. The document can be accessed online at the Internet Christian Library, accessed July 1, 2014, http://www.iclnet.org/pub/resources/text/wittenberg/luther/web/ninetyfive.html

26 Benjamin Myers, "Theology 2.0: Blogging as Theological Discourse," *Cultural Encounters* 6, no. 1 (2010): 47.

27 See below, under "Writing Theology Well by Creating a Blog."

28 See David Tuffley, *Email Etiquette: Netiquette for the Information Age* (Queensland: Altiora Publications, 2014), Kindle.

29 See "Email," *Wikipedia*, accessed July 2, 2014, http://en.wikipedia.org/wiki/Email.

30 See Chapter 1, "The Sociorhetorical Context of Writing Theology".

31 Tuffley, "Why You Should Read This Book," Kindle.

32 Michael Spooner and Kathleen Yancey, "Postings on a Genre of Email," *College Composition and Communication* 47 (1996): 254.

33 Tom Standage, *Writing on the Wall: Social Media: the First 2,000 Years* (New York: Bloomsbury, 2013), 47.

34 Stanley K. Stowers, *Letter Writing in Greco-Roman Antiquity* (Philadelphia, PA: The Westminster Press, 1986), 15–23.

35 Haitch, in Delmater et al., 74.

36 Ibid., 268.

37 See Chapter 1, "To Whom and for Whom is Contemporary Theology Being Written?"

38 Peter Elbow, "A Map of Writing in Terms of Audience and Response," in Elbow, *Everyone Can Write: Essays Toward a Hopeful Theory of Writing and Teaching Writing* (Oxford: Oxford University Press, 2000), 28–29.

39 Tom Wayman, "Did I Miss Anything," from *Did I Miss Anything*? Selected Poems 1973–1993 (Madeira Park: Harbour Publishing, 1993, www.harbourpublishing.com).

40 See, e.g., Tom Wayman, "Did I Miss Anything," Uploaded by Candace Brandt, September 24, 2012, accessed July 11, 2014, www.youtube.com/watch?v=eOjfbaA7rBs,

41 Stanley K. Stowers identifies three sets of relationships "in the social contexts of letter writing in the Greco-Roman world," including (1) hierarchical relations, epitomized by the patron-client relationship; (2) relationships between equals, epitomized by Greek and Roman institutions of friendship; (3) household relationships, which combine both hierarchical and egalitarian relationships. See Stowers, *Letter Writing in Greco-Roman Antiquity*, 27.

42 See the well-crafted lesson plan for a high school curriculum unit on Email, "Connect," accessed July 11, 2014, nvoc.careerforward.org/mvu/overview/cfwd_Connect.pdf

43 Virginia Shea, Introduction to *Netiquette*, accessed July 15, 2014, www.albion.com/netiquette/introduction.html

44 "The human *person* 'cannot not communicate'" is the first "metacommunicative axiom" of communication researcher and psychotherapist Paul Watzlawick, in Paul Watzlawick, Janet H. Beavin, and Don D. Jackson, *Pragmatics of Human Communication: A Study of Interactional Patterns, Pathologies, and Paradoxes* (New York: W.W. Norton, 1967), 54, quoted in Matthias Scharer and Bernd Jochen Hilberath, *The Practice of Communicative Theology: An Introduction to a New Theological Culture* (New York: Crossroad, 2008), 28–29.

45 Tuffley adds that while "there have been attempts to establish one standard or another as the default, there is no common agreement. As a general rule, though, netiquette involves the same principles of plain old etiquette—basic courtesy, respect, and ethics." See David Tuffley, *Email Etiquette*, Kindle.

46 See Scott Warnock, "Conversation: Online, Course 'Talk' Can Become Writing," in Scott Warnock, *Teaching Writing Online: How & Why* (Urbana, IL: NCTE Press, 2009), 68–93.

47 See Chapter 10, "What Is *Voice* and the Relationship Between *Style* and *Voice* in Theological Writing?"

48 I am indebted to Scott Warnock for this helpful rhetorical distinction between primary and secondary posts: see *Teaching Writing Online*, 81–82.

49 M.M. Bakhtin, "Discourse in the Novel," in Bakhtin, *The Dialogic Imagination: Four Essays*, ed. Michael Holquist, trans. Caryl Emerson and Michael Holquist (Austin, TX: University of Texas Press, 1981), 280.

50 Ibid.

51 I am grateful to Sandra Albom, Katie Holickey, and Rev. Noble Scheepers for their permission to include their class discussion board posts in the excerpt above.

52 Kenneth Burke, *The Philosophy of Literary Form: Studies in Symbolic Action*, 3rd ed. (Berkeley, CA: University of California Press, 1941), 110–11.

53 See above, 28.

54 Henry David Thoreau, *Walden*, Variorum Edition (New York: Washington Square Press, 1969), 38.

55 See Cross, *Bloggerati, Twitterati*, 39.

56 See David Tracy's trajectory of theological audiences, summarized in Chapter 1, "To Whom and for Whom is Contemporary Theology Being Written?"

57 See Myers, "Blogging as Theological Discourse," 53–60; and Myers' blog, "Faith and Theology," accessed July 24, 2014, www.faith-theology.com

58 Kwok Pui Lan, "Blogging to Change the World," accessed July 25, 2014, http://kwokpuilan.blogspot.com/2011/02/blogging-to-change-world

59 Cross, *Bloggerati, Twitterati*, 47.

60 Standage, *Writing on the Wall*, 225. See also *Wikipedia*, accessed August 1, 2014, http://en.wikipedia.org/wki/Blog

61 See "Buzz in the Blogosphere: Millions More Bloggers and Blog Readers," Nielson Newswire Online, August 3, 2012, accessed August 1, 2014, http://www.nielson.com/us/en/insights/news/2012/buzz-in-the-blogosphere-millions-more-bloggers-and-blog-readers

62 These figures were posted November 20, 2013 by Brendan Gaille, in Stats, WPVirtuouso, accessed August 1, 2014, http://www.wpvirtuouso.com/how-many-blogs-are-on-the-internet

63 Richard P. Feynmann, "The Making of a Scientist," in "*What Do You Care What Other People Think?" Further Adventures of a Curious Character* as told to Ralph Leighton (New York: W.W. Norton, 2001 [orig. 1988]), 11–19. See also Richard Feynmann, "The Difference between Knowing the Name of Something and Knowing Something," accessed August 2, 2014, https://www.youtube.com/watch?v=05WS0WN7zMQ.

64 This is Michael Spooner's position in Spooner and Yancey, "Postings on a Genre of Email," 262.

65 Myers, "Blogging as Theological Discourse," 53.

66 Ibid., 54–55.

67 See Roger Nam, "Blogs and Effective Teaching: Reimagining Our Physical and Symbolic Classrooms," PowerPoint Presentation for Wabash Center for the Teaching and Learning of Theology and Religion Workshop, American Academy of Religion, Baltimore, Maryland, November 21, 2013, accessed August 11, 2014, http://t.co/pFEahvRry7#wabsm2013-11-22.

68 I argue similarly for writing as a theological practice in Lucretia Bailey Yaghjian, "Writing Practice and Pedagogy across the Theological Curriculum: Teaching Writing in a Theological Context," *Theological Education* 33 (1997): 39–68.

69 Carolyn R. Miller and Dawn Shepherd, "Blogging as Social Action: A Genre Analysis of the Weblog," *Into the Blogosphere*, University of Minnesota, 2004, accessed July 29, 2014, http://newmediagenres.org/2013/11/blogging-as-a-social-action-a-genre-analysis-of-the-weblog-by-carolyn-r-miller-and-dawn-shepherd-summary-by-group-1/

70 Myers, "Blogging as Theological Discourse," 58.

71 See Chapter 1, "Theological Memo 4."

72 Cross, *Bloggerati, Twiterati*, 50.

73 Myers, "Blogging as Theological Discourse," 48.

74 Miller and Shepherd, "Blogging as Social Action," 8.

75 Scharer and Hilberath, *The Practice of Communicative Theology*, 64–66.

76 See Cross, *Bloggerati and Twiterrati*, 41.

77 The blog is now a published book: see Julie Powell, *Julie and Julia: 365 Days, 524 Recipes, One Tiny Apartment Kitchen: How One Girl Risked Her Marriage, Her Job, and Her Sanity to Master the Art of Living* (New York: Little Brown and Co., 2005).

78 Gretchen Rubin describes her purpose for "launching a blog" in Rubin, *The Happiness Project* (New York: Harper Collins, 2009), 74–79. Her companion blog site is The Happiness Project Tool Box, accessed August 1, 2014, www.happinessprojecttoolbox.com.

79 See above, Note 53, for the blog address.

80 Kwok Pui Lan, "Kwok Pui Lan: On postcolonialism, theology, and everything she cares about," accessed July 31, 2014, http://kwokpuilan.blogspot.com/2012/01/how-blogging-has-changed-my-thinking-and-writing

81 I am grateful to Roger Dam, Assistant Professor of Biblical Studies, George Fox Evangelical Seminary, Portland, Oregon, for inspiring this blogging assignment, which I have adapted for my own students and included in this chapter accordingly.

82 See www.blogger.com; www.wordpress.com; www.typepad.com. The first two offer free web hosting; TypePad charges a small monthly fee, but allows you to create static content pages as well. You can use the tutorials provided to help you create a blog on the site of your choice. You will be asked to designate your blog as "public" (with unrestricted access) or "private" (with access restricted to those you permit).

83 See, e.g., *The Yahoo! Style Guide*, (5–7), "Writing a Good Blog—For Dummies," accessed August 1, 2014, http://www.dummies.com/how-to/content/writing-a-good-blog.html, "The 12 Do's and Don'ts of Writing a Blog," http://www.writersdigest.com/online-editor/the-12-dos-and-donts-of-writing-a-blog.

84 Kwok, "How Blogging Has Changed My Thinking and My Writing" (see Note 78, above).

85 Myers, "Blogging as Theological Discourse," 54.

86 Amy Lupold Bair and Susannah Gardner, *Blogging for Dummies*, 5th ed. (Hoboken, NJ: John Wiley, 2014), 23–24.

87 For a representative sample of active Theological Blogs, see the ChristianColleges.Com "Top 100 theology Blogs" cited in Theological Memo 6, above.

88 See Chapter 2, "Writing the Pastoral Reflection Paper"; Chapter 3, "Writing the One-Page Systematic Reflection Paper."

89 See Chapter 2, "Freewriting or Outlining Draft #1: Finding Out What You Want to Say."

90 Standage, *Writing on the Wall*, 5.

91 For more information please go to http://www.bloomsbury.com/uk/writing-theology-well-2nd-edition-9780567499172/ and select the 'Online Resources' tab.

92 See Chapters 5 and 6.

93 See DIRT, accessed August 25, 2014, http://dirtdirectory.org.

94 I am indebted to Aura Fluet, M.T.S., MLIS, M.Ed., Sr. Assistant Director, Library Services, Episcopal Divinity School, Cambridge, Massachusetts, for preparing the Digital Writer/Researcher's Toolbox below and for her generous contribution to and consultation on this section on digital resources for writing theological research well.

95 My colleague Aura Fluet reminds me that "Google Searching has become somewhat of an art form," and recommends the O'Reilly Media Video by Stephan Spencer, "Become an Expert Google Searcher in an Hour," accessed September 1, 2014, http://youtube/368NSlwhBU, based upon Stephan Spencer, *Google Power Search: The Essential Guide to Finding Anything Online with Google* (Sebastapol, CA: O'Reilly Media, 2011).

96 See RefWorks, accessed September 1, 2014, https://www.refworks.com.

97 Scrivener is a content-generating and organizing tool for writers of long documents, including research papers, which provides applications for note-taking, cataloguing research, outlining, editing, and managing the writing process. "Scrivener won't tell you how to write—it just makes all the tools you have scattered around your desk available in one application." See Scrivener, accessed September 1, 2014, http://www.literatureandlatte.com/scrivener/php

98 This Digital Literacy Checklist was prepared by Christina Carr, Director of Technology Services at Episcopal Divinity School, Cambridge, Massachusetts. I gratefully acknowledge her permission to include it in this chapter.

99 "Invisible Web' is the term used to describe all of the information available on the World Wide Web that cannot be found by using general-purpose search engines" *or* "because of searchers' limited research skills." See Jane Devine and Francine Egger-Sider, *Going Beyond Google: The Invisible Web in Learning and Teaching* (New York: Neal Schuman, 2009); Devine and Egger-Sider, *Going Beyond Google Again: Strategies for using and Teaching the Invisible Web* (New York: Neal Schuman, 2013). See also "Invisible or Deep Web: What it is, How to Find It, and Its Inherent Ambiguity," accessed September 3, 2014, http://www.lib.berkeley.edu/TeachingLib/Guides/Internet/InvisibleWeb.html

100 See, for example, Harvard University Writing Program, accessed September 1, 2014, http://sites.harvard.edu/icb/icb.do?keyword=k70487&pageid+icb.page346375; Cornell University Library website, accessed August 25, 2014, http://olinuris.library.cornell.edu/ref/research/webcrit/html; University of California, Berkeley, website, accessed August 31, 2014, http://www.lib.berkeley.edu/TeachingLib/Guides/Internet/Evaluate/html

101 See note 95, above.

102 See Yale College Writing Center, "How to Copy and Paste without Plagiarizing," accessed September 3, 2014, http://writing.yalecollege.yale.edu/advice-students/using-sources/citing-internet-sources-copying-text-without-plagiarizing."

103 See above, Chapter 6, "Plagiarism Preventions and Interventions".

104 See note 91, above.

Epilogue: Writing Theology Well in Your Next Context: From Writing for Professors to Writing with a Professional Voice

Why don't you make writing your practice? If you go deep enough in writing, it will take you everyplace.

—NATALIE GOLDBERG, Writing Down the Bones

In this book, we have focused on writing theology well in an academic context, providing guidelines for writing such typical theological genres as theological reflection, theological argument, theological research, and biblical exegesis. In so doing, we have also focused on elements that inform all good writing: engaging in the processes of prewriting, freewriting, composing, and revising; writing for a particular audience in a style appropriate for that audience; integrating the freedom of imagination with the constraints of effective communication; organizing your time and your life to get the reflection paper written, the research project completed. By engaging writing as a theological practice, then, you have also had the opportunity to experience writing as a practice that encompasses ever-widening horizons, including your own personal and professional contexts that extend beyond the pages of this book.

As Natalie Goldberg discovered, and as I hope you have discovered in the process of writing theology well, if you make writing your practice, "it will take you everyplace." Your practice of writing theology well may lead you to further academic study. It may follow you to your first ministerial position as you write sermons, church newsletters, or a weekly column for the local paper. It may find you writing a curriculum, a grant, a letter to your bishop, or a resolution for your denominational convention. It may lure you to keep a journal during your first year as a pastor, religious education teacher, or supervisor of a homeless shelter. Or, it may lie dormant until you have time and inclination to pick up a pen again. I do not know where the practice of writing will take you, or in what context you will pick up that pen, but I do know that in order to get there, you will have to make the transition from writing for professors to writing with a professional voice.

To write with a professional voice is to write with the authorization of your chosen profession, whether that of ordained ministry, teaching, social work, community organization, or some other professional affiliation. The word "profession" (from the Latin *profiteor*) originally denoted a public acknowledgment of one's name, property, or business; it came to connote the public avowal of a religious vocation, as well. By analogy, to profess any vocation is to be "called," and to be called is to be given a mandate to speak, and hence a professional *voice*. Consider the differences, then, between writing for professors and writing with a professional voice.

When you write for professors, you write for a private audience whose members are paid to read what you write. When you write with a professional voice, you are paid to write for a public audience who will read what you write because of your professional status. When you write for professors, they know more than you do, but you must write as if you know what they know. When you write with a professional voice, you will write both for knowledgeable peers and ordinary readers, and you must write according to what each audience does or does not know. When you write for professors, they have the power to "grade" your writing and the responsibility to exercise that power judiciously. When you write with a professional voice, you have the power to "write with authority," and the responsibility to use that power prudently.

Yet, if you can write for professors, you can write with a professional voice. If you have learned to write theology well, you have already mastered the elements of a professional discourse in which the elements of writing well in any context are embedded, and you have written for different audiences. If you can write a reflection paper or a biblical exegesis paper, you have expertise in two homiletical genres that will conspire fruitfully in every sermon you write. If you can write theological argument, you can write a position statement on the environment for your denominational convention, or a grant to fund an environmental initiative within your own congregation. Even if all you can write is a one-page theological memo, you can write a cogent memo to your supervisor or a complete doctoral dissertation, depending upon the context.

You may not be called to be a theologian or a professional minister. Yet, the contexts for writing theology well are proliferating and will provide you with new contexts for communication not yet imagined. While many of my students are writing their Sunday sermons as I complete this book, other students have written books on spirituality, gender issues, and children's literature as a source of liberation or suppression of women. Still others have written for religious periodicals, newsweeklies, and religious television and radio programming. Others have written on behalf of minority job applicants and prevailed in getting them a position; created new religious websites, integrating text and hypertext; and successfully completed doctoral dissertations, theological memo by theological memo, as described above. What will you add to this list when you begin to write theology well in your next context?

"If you make writing your practice," Natalie Goldberg wrote, "it will take you everyplace." If someone had told me when I was teaching my first freshman English course that I would someday write a book called *Writing Theology Well*, I would have laughed like Sarah in response to the prophecy of her unexpected guests. If you find yourself laughing at someone who has encouraged you to keep writing theology well in your next context, do not be surprised to find yourself writing something that you have not yet imagined for an audience that is waiting for what you will write. When you do, I look forward to reading it. Until then, here are some final suggestions for writing with a professional voice:

- Know your professional audience, and adapt your writing to that audience.
- Acknowledge the power dynamics between you and your audience, and do not abuse them.
- Respect the writing conventions of your profession, and observe them.
- Identify the writing formats employed in your profession, and use them.
- Read exemplary writers within your profession, and learn from them.
- Write clearly and purposefully with your mind, heart, and imagination.
- Write prayerfully for the love of God and neighbor in whatever context you are writing.
- Write for yourself in order to do all of the above more effectively.
- Write for publication as the opportunity presents itself.
- Whatever you write, write well!

INDEX